Handbook of Research on Strategy and Foresight

Edited by

Laura Anna Costanzo

Lecturer in Strategic Management, School of Management, University of Surrey, UK

Robert Bradley MacKay

Senior Lecturer in Strategy, Business School, University of Edinburgh, UK

Edward Elgar
Cheltenham, UK • Northampton, MA, USA

Published by
Edward Elgar Publishing Limited
The Lypiatts
15 Lansdown Road
Cheltenham
Glos GL50 2JA
UK

Edward Elgar Publishing, Inc.
William Pratt House
9 Dewey Court
Northampton
Massachusetts 01060
USA

Paperback edition 2010

A catalogue record for this book
is available from the British Library

Library of Congress Control Number: 2008943824

Mixed Sources
Product group from well-managed
forests and other controlled sources
www.fsc.org Cert no. SA-COC-1565
© 1996 Forest Stewardship Council

FSC

ISBN 978 1 84542 963 8 (cased)
ISBN 978 1 84980 488 2 (paperback)

Printed and bound by MPG Books Group, UK

Contents

List of contributors   viii

Introduction   1
Robert Bradley MacKay and Laura A. Costanzo

PART I   PROBING THE FUTURE: CULTIVATING STRATEGIC FORESIGHT

1   Redefining strategic foresight: 'fast' and 'far' sight via complexity science   15
    Bill McKelvey and Max Boisot

2   Anticipating critique and occasional reason: modes of reasoning in the face
    of a radically open future   48
    David Seidl and Dominik van Aaken

3   Strategic foresight   66
    Ajit Nayak

4   The symbolism of foresight processes in organizations   82
    Jan Oliver Schwarz

5   Strategic foresight: counterfactual and prospective sensemaking in enacted
    environments   90
    Robert Bradley MacKay

6   Modal narratives, possible worlds and strategic foresight   113
    *Charles Booth, Peter Clark, Agnès Delahaye-Dado, Stephen Procter and
    Michael Rowlinson*

7   Scenarios as knowledge transformed into strategic 're-presentations': the
    use of foresight studies to help shape and implement strategy   128
    Thomas Durand

8   Researching the organization–environment relationship   144
    George Burt

PART II   FORESIGHT AND ORGANIZATIONAL BECOMING: STRATEGY PROCESS, PRACTICE AND CHANGE

9   Strategizing as practising: strategic learning as a source of connection   169
    Elena P. Antonacopoulou

10 Improvisational bricolage: a practice-based approach to strategy and
    foresight   182
    Miguel Pina e Cunha, João Vieira Da Cunha and Stewart R. Clegg

11 Micro-political strategies and strategizing in multinational corporations:
    the case of subsidiary mandate change   200
    Christoph Dörrenbächer and Mike Geppert

12 How organizational DNA works   219
    David Weir, Craig Marsh and Wilf Greenwood

13 Making sense of organizational becoming: the need for essential stabilities
    in organizational change   234
    Ian Colville

14 Agency in management of change: bringing in relationality, situatedness
    and foresight   249
    Ahu Tatli and Mustafa F. Özbilgin

15 The role of resources in institutional entrepreneurship: insights for an
    approach to strategic management that combines agency and institution   260
    Julie Battilana and Bernard Leca

PART III   SHAPING THE FUTURE: STRATEGIZING AND
           INNOVATION

16 The role of middle managers in enabling foresight   277
    Laura A. Costanzo and Vicky Tzoumpa

17 Hollow at the top: (re)claiming the responsibilities of leadership in
    strategizing   297
    C. Marlene Fiol and Edward J. O'Connor

18 Visions and innovation strategy   309
    Jonathan Sapsed

19 Innovation through ambidexterity: how to achieve the ambidextrous
    organization   324
    Constantinos Markides and Wenyi Chu

20 Fast cycle capability: a conceptual integration   343
    V.K. Narayanan

21 Interactions with customers for innovation   362
    C. Annique Un and Alvaro Cuervo-Cazurra

22 Organizational innovation of the Toyota Group   380
    Faith Hatani

PART IV   RESPONDING TO THE FUTURE: INTUITION, INERTIA
          AND STRATEGIC FLEXIBILITY

23 The role of intuition in strategic decision making   393
    Marta Sinclair, Eugene Sadler-Smith and Gerard P. Hodgkinson

24 (Un) great expectations: effects of underestimations and self-perception on performance   418
    Rodolphe Durand

25 Strategic foresight and the role of organizational memory within a punctuated equilibrium framework   435
    Stelios C. Zyglidopoulos and Stephanie W.J.C. Schreven

26 Adaptation, inertia and the flexible organization: a study of the determinants of organizational flexibility in an emerging economy   453
    Andrés Hatum and Andrew M. Pettigrew

27 Addressing path dependency in the capabilities approach: historicism and foresight meet on the 'road less travelled'   485
    Swapnesh K. Masrani and Peter McKiernan

28 Dynamic knowledge creation   505
    Taman H. Powell and Howard Thomas

29 Foreseeing the problem of conformity in strategy teaching, research and practice   518
    Gregory B. Vit

Index   529

Contributors

Dominik van Aaken is Assistant Professor of Strategy and Organization at the Center for Organizational Research at the University of Munich, Germany. He studied business administration and philosophy in Ingolstadt and Budapest. He earned his PhD at the University of Munich in 2007. Current research focuses on organization theory, ethics and the philosophy of science. Recent publications include two books: *Pluralismus als Ethik* (Pluralism as Ethics) (Metropolis, 2007) and *Betriebswirtschaftliche Forschung* (Research Methods in Management Studies) (Schäffer-Poeschel, 2007).

Elena P. Antonacopoulou is Professor of Organizational Behaviour at the University of Liverpool Management School, UK where she leads GNOSIS – a research initiative advancing Practice Relevant Management Scholarship. Her principal research interests include change and learning practices in organizations and the development of new methodologies for studying social complexity. She is currently undertaking a series of research projects in organizational learning, social practice and dynamic capabilities, working collaboratively with leading researchers internationally and with practitioners and policy makers in co-creating knowledge for action. She writes on all of the above areas and her work is published in international journals such as *Organization Studies*, the *Journal of Management Studies* and the *Academy of Management Review*. She is currently Associate Editor of the *British Journal of Management* and Subject Editor for Organizational Learning and Knowledge for the *Emergence: Complexity and Organizational Journal*. She was previously joint Editor-in-chief of the international journal *Management Learning*. She serves on the editorial boards of *Organization Science*, *Group and Organization Management*, *Society, Business and Organization Journal* and the *Irish Journal of Management*. She has recently completed a four-year prestigious Senior Research Fellowship as part of the Advanced Institute of Management (AIM) Research. She has held several leadership roles (at board, council and executive levels) in international professional bodies in her field including the Academy of Management (USA), the European Group for Organizational Studies, the British Academy of Management and the Society for the Advancement of Management Studies.

Julie Battilana is an Assistant Professor of Business Administration in the Organizational Behavior unit at Harvard Business School, Cambridge, MA, USA. A native of France, Professor Battilana earned a joint PhD in organizational behavior from INSEAD and in management and economics from Ecole Normale Supérieure de Cachan. Her research focuses on institutional change. She is particularly interested in analyzing the micro-foundations of institutional change. Her work aims to highlight the actors who are more likely to initiate changes that radically depart from the existing institutions in a field of activity. Her most recent projects focused on the influence of individuals' social position on their likelihood to initiate different types of radical changes in the healthcare sector in the United Kingdom. Professor Battilana's research received an honorable mention for best paper out of a dissertation from the OMT division of the Academy of Management in 2007. She has published or has articles forthcoming in *Strategic*

Organization, Organization, Leadership Quarterly, Research in Organizational Behavior, and the *Academy of Management Annals* as well as in handbooks of organizational behavior and strategy.

Max Boisot is Professor of Strategic Management at the Birmingham Business School, University of Birmingham, UK; Senior Research Fellow at the Snider Center for Entrepreneurial Research, The Wharton School, University of Pennsylvania; and Associate Fellow at the Said Business School, Oxford University. Between 1984 and 1989 he was dean and director of the China–Europe Management Program in Beijing. This has since evolved into the China–Europe International Business School (CEIBS) in Shanghai. He has published on China in the *Administrative Science Quarterly* and in *Organization Science*. His most recent book, *Knowledge Assets: Securing Competitive Advantage in the Information Economy* (Oxford University Press, 1998) was awarded the Ansoff Prize for the best book on strategy in 2000.

Charles Booth is Reader in Strategy and Organization at the Bristol Business School, University of the West of England, Bristol. He was one of the founding editors of the journal *Management & Organizational History*, and has served as the chair of the Management History Division of the Academy of Management. His current interests concern: (i) the use of counterfactuals and other forms of modal narrative in history, popular culture and organization studies; and (ii) aspects of social and collective memory in organizations, and in society.

George Burt is a Senior Lecturer in Strategic Management at the Department of Management, University of Strathclyde Business School, Scotland, where he was awarded his PhD in 2002. He is co-founder and track chair of the Strategic Foresight Special Interest Group at the British Academy of Management; and co-founder of the Centre for Scenario Planning and Future Studies at the University of Strathclyde. His research interests are in the organization–contextual environment relationship and he writes about the process of change and becoming in organizations. He has extensive consultancy experience, specializing in the application of the scenario methodology as a basis of organizational learning. He is co-author of the book *The Sixth Sense: Accelerating Organisational Learning with Scenarios*.

Wenyi Chu received her PhD degree in the field of strategy and international management from the London Business School, University of London, UK. She is currently an Associate Professor at the Department of Business Administration in National Taiwan University. Her main research areas include corporate strategy, international management, business groups, and strategy issues in emerging market economics, with papers published in many international journals such as *Small Business Economics, Expert Systems with Applications, Service Industries Journal*, the *Asia Pacific Journal of Management*, and *Global Economic Review*.

Peter Clark, PhD Loughborough, is Professorial Research Fellow in Organization Theory at Queen Mary's School of Business and Management, University of London, UK. His expertise is in such diverse areas as organizational theories of emergence and the 'history turn', critical realism, processual time frames, strategic time reckoning and structural assembly, revisionist organizational and management histories of America and transatlantic diffusion of innovations. His current research focuses on corporate uses of history in the UK–USA. He is currently writing a monograph on *American Repertoires of Control: Consumer Polity and Colonising Corporations*. His focuses are on organizational processes of becoming and not becoming within multilevel national contexts and problems of counterfactuals and impossible outcomes (superfactuals). His previous books include: *Organisational Design: Theory and Practice* (1972); *Action Research and Organisation Change* (1972); *Innovation and the Auto Industry*, with Richard Whipp (1986); *Anglo-American Innovation* (1987); *Organisation Transitions and Innovation Design*, with Ken Starkey (1988); *Innovation in Technology and Organisation*, with Neil Staunton (1989); and *Organisations in Action: Competition Between Contexts* (2000).

Stewart R. Clegg is Professor in the School of Management, University of Technology, Sydney, Australia and Director of ICAN Research (www.ican.uts.edu.au); a Visiting Professor of Organizational Change Management, Maastricht University Faculty of Business, as well as the Vrije University of Amsterdam, where he is Visiting Professor and International Fellow in Discourse and Management Theory, Centre of Comparative Social Studies, and also at the Copenhagen Business School. He is a prolific publisher in the leading academic journals in management and organization theory as well as the author of many books, among the more recent of which are *Managing and Organizations: An Introduction to Theory and Practice* (with Martin Kornberger and Tyrone Pitsis), *The International Encyclopaedia of Organization Studies* (co-edited with James Bailey), and *Power and Organizations* (with David Courpasson and Nelson Phillips). He has also published in many of the leading journals, including *Organization*, *Organization Studies*, the *Journal of Management Inquiry* and *Administrative Science Quarterly*. He has been an elected Fellow of the Academy of the Social Sciences in Australia since 1988, and a Distinguished Fellow of the Australian and New Zealand Academy of Management since 1998.

Ian Colville is Senior Lecturer in Organizational Change at the School of Management, University of Bath, UK. He has a first degree in psychology from Cardiff University, and an MPhil and PhD in management, from Bath University. He is director of the Change Management Forum at the University of Bath which aims to provide a place where thinking practitioners and academics interested in doing practice can meet to exchange perspectives on change and leadership. This way they hope to improve rigour and relevance in the academic arena. To this end, Colville has published with Karl Weick and Bob Waterman in the journal *Organization*, and most of his work is located within a sensemaking perspective. Other publications have appeared in such journals as *Public Administration*, *Organization*, *Long Range Planning* and *Accounting Organization and Society* along with a number of book chapters.

Laura A. Costanzo is a Lecturer in Strategic Management at the School of Management, University of Surrey, Guildford, UK, and a Scholar of the Advanced Institute of Management (AIM), UK. She holds a PhD from Leeds University Business School. Prior to joining the School of Management at the University of Surrey, she was a research fellow at the International Institute of Banking and Financial Services, University of Leeds. Her current research interests are in the areas of innovation management, learning processes within teams, strategic foresight and the role of intuition in top management teams' decision making. Her paper 'Avoiding the myopia of adaptive learning' (Costanzo, L.A.) was nominated in the category of the top 10 SMS/McKinsey Best Papers at the 23rd Annual International Conference of the Strategic Management Society, San Francisco. Her paper, co-authored with J.K. Ashton (2006) 'Product innovation and consumer choice in the UK financial services industry', *Journal of Financial Regulation and Compliance*, was awarded the Emerald Literati Network Awards for Excellence 2007. She co-chaired the track on 'Foresight and Organizational Becoming' at the British Academy of Management Conference (2004), St Andrews University and the track on 'Organizational Relationships' at the annual conference of the European Academy of Management in 2004 and 2006.

Alvaro Cuervo-Cazurra (PhD Universidad de Salamanca; PhD MIT) analyzes how firms become internationally competitive and how they become multinationals. He also studies governance issues, corruption in particular. Recently he has started a long-term research project analyzing developing-country multinationals. He is Assistant Professor in International Business at the Moore School of Business, University of South Carolina, Columbia, SC, USA.

Miguel Pina e Cunha (PhD, Tilburg University) is an associate professor at Faculdade de Economia, Universidade Nova de Lisboa, Lisbon, Portugal. He is conducting research in the area of emergent change and positive organizing. His publications have appeared in journals such as the *Academy of Management Review*, *Organization*, *Organization Studies*, the *Journal of Management Studies*, and *Human Relations*.

João Vieira Da Cunha is an assistant professor at the School of Management and Economics at Universidade Nova de Lisboa, Lisbon, Portugal. He holds a PhD in Management from MIT Sloan. His research focuses on the unprescribed and informal uses of information technology in organizations. Ethnography is his method of choice – he has spent considerable time with workers resisting change online and with salespeople improvising on management information systems in unexpected ways. His work has been published in the *Academy of Management Review*, *Human Relations* and the *Journal of Management Studies*.

Agnès Delahaye-Dado is a visiting research fellow at the Queen Mary School of Business and Management, University of London, UK. Research interests include American colonial and contemporary history, corporate history and studies of imperialism; forms and functions of the narratives; corporate history, narrative and business knowledge.

Christoph Dörrenbächer is Assistant Professor in International Business and Management, Faculty of Economics and Business in the University of Groningen, the Netherlands. He has worked as a consultant and research fellow at various organizations in Germany, including the Technical University Berlin and the Social Science Research Centre, Berlin. Visiting appointments were with the Manchester Metropolitan University, the Central European University (Budapest) and the United Nations Centre on Transnational Corporations (New York). He holds a PhD from the Faculty of Social Sciences of the Free University, Berlin. His current research focus is on knowledge transfer, subsidiary role development, social relationships and careers in multinational corporations.

Rodolphe Durand is Professor at HEC Paris, France, where he is in charge of the MBA specialization in strategy, and Visiting Professor at Cass Business School (City University, London). He studied at HEC (PhD) and at La Sorbonne (MPhil). He has participated in many Executive Education programs for companies including Renault-Nissan (in France), Suez (Europe and USA), Gaz de France among others and Trium Executive Education program. His primary research interests concern the analysis of firm perform-ance from a dynamic perspective using philosophical and sociological approaches. His works have been published in journals including the *Academy of Management Review*, the *American Journal of Sociology*, and the *Strategic Management Journal*. He received the Best Young French Researcher Award (AIMS, 1999), the R. Scott Award 2005 (American Sociological Association, 2005), and the HEC Foundation Best Paper of the Year (2006). Among others, he is an associate editor for the *European Management Review*, and an editorial board member for the *Strategic Management Journal*, *Strategic Organization*, and the *Journal of Management Studies*. He is also a prolific author of books, including the recent *Organizational Evolution and Strategic Management* (2006).

Thomas Durand is Professor of Business Strategy at École Centrale, Paris, France. His research interests focus on strategic management, the management of technology and innovation, organizational knowledge and competence. He is the author or co-author of books, including *Strategic Networks* (Blackwell, 2007) and *The Future of Business Schools* (Palgrave Macmillan, 2008). He is the current president of Société Française de Management. He also heads CM International, a management consultancy with 40 staff in France, Ireland, Spain and the UK.

C. Marlene Fiol received her MBA and a PhD in strategic management from the University of Illinois at Urbana-Champaign. She is currently Professor of Strategic Management and Health Administration at the University of Colorado at Denver, CO, USA. Her research interests include managerial and organizational cognition, organiza-tional learning, and organizational identity.

Mike Geppert holds a Chair in Comparative International Management and Organization Studies at the School of Management, University of Surrey, Guildford, UK. His general research interests are in the areas of international management and organization theory. His most recent research is focused on socio-political issues in multinational companies, cross-national comparisons of management and organizations, and transnational insti-tution building. His work is largely multidisciplinary, and has been published widely in quality academic journals such as *Human Relations*, the *Journal of Management Studies* and *Organization Studies*, and in books.

Wilf Greenwood is a strategist with parallel academic and business consultancy back-grounds founded on an early career in project management – most notably in the energy sector – and later in Internet network-computing and knowledge management. He is an ex-Affiliate Professor of Business on Masters' courses at CERAM (Grand-École), France and Visiting Professor at the International University of Monaco. He is also Visiting Professor at Virginia Commonwealth University in Richmond, Virginia, USA and Guest Speaker at the London School of Economics ('Organisational Social Psychology' group). See www.strategychain.com for further information.

Faith Hatani (PhD, University of Cambridge) is Lecturer in International Business at Manchester Business School, the University of Manchester and an Associate Fellow of the Advanced Institute of Management (AIM) Research, London, UK. Prior to beginning her academic career, she worked in the global logistics sector for more than eight years, based in Japan and Singapore. Her research focuses on inter-firm networks and clusters, the power structure in global value chains and the strategies of large global firms for emerging markets.

Andrés Hatum is Associate Professor of Human Resource Management at IAE Business and Management School at Austral University (Argentina). He received his PhD in management and organization from Warwick Business School at the University of Warwick in 2002. His research interests include flexibility in organizations and management across cultures in Latin-American countries. His research has been published in such journals as the *British Journal of Management* and in his new book *Adaptation or Expiration in Family Firms: Organizational Flexibility in Emerging Economies*.

Gerard P. Hodgkinson is Professor of Organizational Behaviour and Strategic Management, a Senior Fellow of the UK ESRC/EPSRC Advanced Institute of Management (AIM) Research, and Director of the Centre for Organizational Strategy, Learning and Change at the University of Leeds, UK. The (co-)author of three books and over 60 articles and chapters in scholarly journals and edited volumes, he is an Academician of the Academy of Social Sciences (AcSS) and a Fellow of both the British Psychological Society and the British Academy of Management. His research focuses on the analysis of cognition in organizations and applied psychometrics, including the development and psychometric evaluation of methods for eliciting and representing organizational actors' mental representations and instruments for the assessment of individual differences in the workplace. He was the Editor-in-Chief of the *British Journal of Management* (1999–2006) and currently co-edits the *International Review of Industrial and Organizational Psychology* and serves on several editorial boards including the *Academy of Management Review* and *Organization Science*. With William H. Starbuck he has recently co-edited *The Oxford Handbook of Organizational Decision Making*.

Bernard Leca is an associate professor in the Strategy Department at ESC Rouen, France. His research interests focus on institutional entrepreneurship, institutional work and power relations between organizations. His current research includes corporate social responsibility and cultural industries. His works have appeared in the *Journal of Management Inquiry*, *Human Relations*, *Organization* and the *Revue Française de Gestion*.

Robert Bradley MacKay is a Senior Lecturer in Strategy in the Business School at the University of Edinburgh. His research, teaching and consultancy interests include strategic foresight, competitive strategy and strategic futures planning. He has published in a range of scholarly journals including *Human Relations*, *ISMO*, the *European Management Review*, *Futures* and *Management and Organization History*. His research is interdisciplinary in nature, importing sensibilities from economics, history, sociology and psychology for the purpose of better understanding strategic phenomena. He is also a co-founder of both the Strategic Foresight Special Interest Group (SIG) of the British Academy of Management, of which he served as its Chairperson between 2003 and 2007, and the strategic foresight caucus of the Academy of Management.

Constantinos Markides is Professor of Strategic and International Management and holds the Robert P. Bauman Chair of Strategic Leadership at the London Business School, UK. He is also the Chairman of the Strategic and International Management (SIM) Department at LBS. A native of Cyprus, he received his MBA and DBA from the Harvard Business School. He is on the Editorial Board of the *Strategic Management Journal*, the *European Management Journal*, the *Academy of Management Journal*, the *Journal of Management and Governance* and *Sloan Management Review*. He has done research and published on the topics of strategic innovation, corporate restructuring, refocusing and international acquisitions. His last book (with Paul Geroski), entitled *Fast Second: How Smart Companies Bypass Radical Innovation to Enter and Dominate New Markets* was published in January 2005 and was on the Short List of the Financial Times–Goldman Sachs Management Book of the Year in 2005. He has just completed his new book entitled: *Game-Changing Strategies: How to Create New Market Space in Established Industries by Breaking the Rules*. This was published by Jossey-Bass in May 2008.

Craig Marsh is currently Research Associate at the Centre for Performance-Led human relations (HR), Lancaster University Management School, UK. He has nearly 20 years of experience of HR in industry, consulting, and academia. The early part of his career comprised senior HR roles in industry; at BP Exploration, where he specialized in organizational development, and at GEC–Marconi, where he was a site HR manager. This was followed by 5 years working in the field of HR executive education in the UK and France. Most recently, he was Associate Professor of HR at EDHEC, a French Grande École, and director of their full-time MBA programme. He has maintained a strong involvement in HR strategy and practice through his consulting work in Europe. His current research interests centre on the impact of HR performance management systems on middle and first-line management. He has recently completed a large-scale study of the impact of performance management in the Police Service. He has a first degree in classics from Oxford University and a PhD in management learning from Lancaster University.

Swapnesh K. Masrani holds a PhD from the University of St Andrews, Scotland, and is working as a Research Fellow in the School of Management, University of St Andrews. He is interested in cross-fertilization of research involving strategy, business history and history. Currently, he is studying the British industrial 'decline' between 1880 and the 1960s to re-examine the Chandlerian (and entrepreneurial failure) thesis and find alternative explanations in the textile industry using insights from strategic management and history. In particular, he is looking at the strategic response (both individual and collective) and problems faced by firms in implementing them in the Dundee jute industry and comparing it with the Lancashire cotton industry. His medium- to long-term research aim is to examine the evolution of business systems in India. His research has been published in *Futures*. Masrani is one of the co-founders of the Strategic Foresight Strategic Interest Group (SIG) of the British Academy of Management (BAM) and has held positions in both the British Academy of Management (BAM) and the European Academy of Management (EURAM).

Bill McKelvey is Professor of Strategic Organizing and Complexity Science at the UCLA Anderson School of Management, Los Angeles, CA, USA. Current writing focuses on philosophy of science, organization science, complexity science, agent-based computational modeling, and complexity leadership. His book, *Organizational Systematics* (1982) remains the definitive treatment of organizational taxonomy and evolutionary theory. He chaired the building committee that produced the $110,000,000 Anderson Complex at UCLA – opened in 1994; directed over 170 field study teams on 6-month projects concerned with strategic and organizational improvements to client firms; and initiated the founding of UCLA's Center for Human Complex Systems and Computational Social Science. Selected recent publications have appeared in: *Academy of Management Review*, *Strategic Organization*, *Journal of International Business Studies*, *Leadership Quarterly*, *Advances in Strategic Management*, *Journal of Business Venturing*, *Proceedings of the National Academy of Sciences*, *Organization Science*, and *International Journal of Innovation Management*.

Peter McKiernan is Professor of Management and Dean of the School of Management at the University of St Andrews, Scotland. Previously, he was Convenor of the Strategy and Marketing Group, Director of the Full Time MBA and Professor of Strategic Management at Warwick Business School. He has served as Chairman, President and is, currently, Dean of the Fellows College of the British Academy of Management. In addition, he has been Vice President and is, currently, President of the European Academy of Management. He sits on the Editorial Board of several international journals. McKiernan has published widely in strategic management, including two volumes on the historical development of the discipline and the best-selling book on transformational change, *Sharpbenders*. His scholarship has won prizes from the BAM, IBM, the British Diabetes Association and Scottish Enterprise. He has worked extensively with 'strategy in practice', where his work on strategic foresight has taken him into over a 100 global consultancy interventions.

V.K. Narayanan is the Associate Dean for Research, Director of the Center for Research Excellence and the Stubbs Professor of Strategy and Entrepreneurship at LeBow College of Business, Drexel University, Philadelphia, PA, USA. Narayanan holds a PhD in business from the Graduate School of Business at the University of Pittsburgh, Pennsylvania. He has won several awards, including the Corporate Leadership (2003) and Dupont MBA best teacher (2002) at Drexel University, and Distinguished Service (1998) and Doctoral Student Mentor (1999 and 2002) awards at the University of Kansas. In 2001, he was the recipient of one of the five Fulbright Alumni Awards, and in 1998, the Fulbright–FLAD award for teaching in Portugal. Narayanan has published four books and monographs. His most recent book, *Managing Technology and Innovation for Competitive Advantage* (2001), is a synthesis of his work over the last decade. In addition, he has published numerous articles and book chapters. His articles have appeared in leading professional journals such as the *Academy of Management Journal,* the *Academy of Management Review*, *Accounting Organizations and Society*, *Industrial Relations*, the *Journal of Applied Behavioral Science*, the *Journal of Applied Corporate Finance*, the *Journal of Applied Psychology*, the *Journal of Management*, the *Journal of Management Studies, Management Information Systems Quarterly*, *R&D Management* and the *Strategic Management Journal*.

Ajit Nayak is a Lecturer in Strategy at the School of Management, University of Bath, UK. His research interests are creativity, innovation and strategy, ontological and epistemological issues in management and issues of managerial identity. He is currently working on three projects: (i) Indian business elites, (ii) Entrepreneurship in a media culture: Evidence from the Dragons' Den, and (iii) Innovation, technology and consumption. Nayak has published in *Organization Studies*, *Long Range Planning* and *Organization*.

Edward J. O'Connor received his PhD in industrial/organizational psychology from the University of Akron. He is currently a Professor of Management and Health Administration at the University of Colorado at Denver, CO, USA. His research interests include physician–administration collaboration, leadership, organizational cognition, and entrepreneurship.

Mustafa F. Özbilgin is Professor of Human Resource Management at the Norwich Business School, University of East Anglia, Norwich, UK and director of DECERe (Diversity and Equality in Careers and Employment Research). His research focuses on equality, diversity and inclusion at work from interdisciplinary, international, and comparative perspectives. Drawing on empirical work in this field, he has published papers in journals, such as the *International Journal of Human Resource Management*, the *Journal of Vocational Behavior* and *Gender Work and Organization*, and seven research monographs, including *Global Diversity Management* (Palgrave, 2008). He is the editor of the journal, *Equal Opportunities International* (Emerald Press). He has previously worked at the University of Hertfordshire, University of Surrey, Queen Mary (University of London) and held visiting posts at CEPS-INSTEAD (Luxembourg), Cornell University (USA), and the Japan Institute of Labor and Policy.

Andrew M. Pettigrew is Professor of Strategy and Organization at Saïd Business School, University of Oxford, UK. Professor Pettigrew received his training in sociology and anthropology and conducted his first research among the Sebeii people in Uganda. He received his PhD from Manchester Business School in 1970, and has held academic appointments at Yale, Harvard, the London Business School and Warwick Business School. Pettigrew's research has pursued big intellectual and policy themes on the change, performance, strategy and governance of organizations in the private and public sectors in the UK and beyond. In his extensive body of work, he has advanced the understanding of the complex processes involved in the formulation of strategies in organizations and has systematically examined the linkages between external factors, internal processes, and outcomes. His long-term research interests have been in the study of decision making, power, strategy development, change, performance and corporate governance in private and public sector organizations in the UK and beyond. He has written, coauthored, or edited 16 books, and has published in most of the top management journals in the US and Europe. His current research interests include studies of the boards and directors of the UK's top 500 companies, and new forms of organizing and company performance in major corporations in Europe, Japan, and the US.

Taman H. Powell is an ESRC Post Doctoral Fellow in Strategy and Organisation at Warwick Business School, University of Warwick, Coventry, UK. His research is focused on the evolution of explicit processes to manage organizational knowledge and the impact that these processes have on knowledge-related practices. The broader aim of his research is to understand how managers can guide the evolution of organizations.

He holds a PhD from Warwick Business School, and an MBA (with distinction) from INSEAD. Prior to commencing his academic career, he worked for 10 years in management, starting in brand marketing with Procter & Gamble then moving to management consulting with Accenture (formerly Andersen Consulting).

Stephen Procter is Alcan Professor of Management and Director of Research at Newcastle University Business School, UK. His chief areas of research interest are new patterns of work in the public sector and the relationship between business history and organization studies. He has recently completed an ESRC-funded study on the use of corporate history as business knowledge and is currently involved in projects looking at new working patterns in the mental health services workforce and multi-agency working in public services. He is an elected member of the Council of the British Academy of Management, Chair of the Editorial Advisory Board of *Personnel Review* and Chair of the British Academy of Management Special Interest Group on HRM.

Michael Rowlinson is Professor of Organization Studies at the School of Business and Management, Queen Mary University of London. He has published a series of articles on the tensions between history and organization theory in journals such as *Business History*, *Organization Studies* and *Organization*. He has analysed the genre of corporate history in an article for the *Journal of Organizational Change Management*, and examined how organizations come to terms with the dark side of their history in an article for *Critical Perspective on Accounting*. He is the editor of *Management & Organizational History*.

Eugene Sadler-Smith is Professor of Management Development and Organizational Behaviour in the School of Management, University of Surrey, Guildford, UK. After a successful career in the gas industry, during which time he completed his PhD under the supervision of Richard J. Riding, at the University of Birmingham, 1988–1992 (part-time) on the subject of cognitive styles, he became a university lecturer in 1994. His research interests at the moment are centred upon the role of intuitive judgement in management decision making and management development. His research has been published widely in peer-reviewed journals such as the *Academy of Management Executive*, the *Academy of Management Learning and Education*, the *British Journal of Psychology*, the *Journal of Occupational and Organizational Psychology*, the *Journal of Organizational Behavior*, *Management Learning* and *Organization Studies*. He is the author of *Learning and Development for Managers: Perspectives from Research and Practice*, *Learning in Organisations* (with Peter J. Smith, Routledge, 2006) and *Inside Intuition* (Routledge, 2008). His work on intuition, as well as appearing in a number of scholarly journals, has appeared in professional magazines, *The Times* (including the Editorial of August 13, 2007), and on BBC Radio 4.

Jonathan Sapsed is an Innovation Fellow of the UK's Advanced Institute of Management Research (AIM) and a Principal Research Fellow of CENTRIM, University of Brighton, UK. His current research focuses on innovation in creative business, particularly the management of digital content creation, such as videogames and advertising. He is a Visiting Fellow at Imperial College Business School, and is an Associate Fellow of the Sawyer Business School, Suffolk University, Boston. He has been a researcher at SPRU, University of Sussex (where he studied for his doctorate), the London School of Economics, and Cranfield University. He was also a Visiting Scholar at the University of

California at Berkeley. He is Book Reviews Editor of *Technovation* and is on the editorial board of the *International Journal of Innovation Management* (IJIM). His work is published in *Research Policy*, *Organization Studies* and *International Journal of Management Reviews*.

Stephanie W.J.C. Schreven is a PhD student at the Maxwell Graduate School of Citizenship and Public Affairs, Syracuse University, Syracuse, NY, USA. Her dissertation examines ownership in culture, the conditions and ideologies that enable the current proliferation of property rights in culture as well as the tensions, contestations and alternatives that develop in response.

Jan Oliver Schwarz is a researcher in the field of strategic foresight and business wargaming. He currently is a PhD candidate at the Berlin University of the Arts, Germany. He previously earned an MA in general management from the University of Witten/Herdecke, Germany and an MPhil in futures studies from the University of Stellenbosch, South Africa. He has been a visiting scholar at the School of Management, University of St Andrews, Scotland and is the author of several articles on Strategic Foresight and co-author of the book *Business Wargaming: Securing Corporate Value* (2008).

David Seidl is Professor of Organization and Management at the University of Zurich, Switzerland. He studied management and sociology in Munich, London, Witten/Herdecke and Cambridge. He earned his PhD at the University of Cambridge in 2001. Current research focuses on corporate governance, organizational change and strategy. He has published in the *Journal of Management Studies*, *Organization*, *Organization Studies* and *Human Relations* and has (co-) produced several books, including most recently *Niklas Luhmann and Organization Studies* and *Organizational Identity and Self-Transformation: An Autopoietic Perspective*. He is co-editor of the forthcoming *Cambridge Handbook of Strategy as Practice*.

Marta Sinclair is currently a Lecturer of Comparative and Cross-cultural Management and the Acting Director of Bachelor and Master of International Business programs in Griffith Business School at Griffith University, Brisbane, Australia. She received her BA (linguistics) from Charles University (1975), her MA (education and human development) from George Washington University (1986) and her PhD (organizational behavior) from the University of Queensland (2003). She has extensive management experience in software localization, intercultural training, broadcasting, leisure and hospitality, real estate, and translation services from the USA and Europe. Her research focuses on the use of intuition and emotions in managerial decision making and problem solving. At present, she explores how these aspects affect knowledge transfer and team creativity.

Ahu Tatli is Lecturer in International Human Resource Management in the School of Business and Management at Queen Mary, University of London, UK. Her research interests are in the field of equality and diversity in organizations with a particular focus on multilevel exploration of agentic power and strategies of the key actors in the field. Her research work has investigated the equality and diversity agenda in public and private sector organizations in different industries including recruitment, manufacturing and creative and cultural industries. She completed her doctoral study at Queen Mary

University of London with a thesis that investigates the agency of diversity managers. She holds a BSc degree in sociology from Middle East Technical University, Ankara, Turkey, and a Masters degree in political science with a thesis titled 'Islamist Women in the Post 1980s Turkey: Ambivalent Resistance'. Prior to joining Queen Mary, she participated in various research projects on gender, equality and religion in Turkey.

Howard Thomas has been Dean of the Warwick Business School, University of Warwick, Coventry, UK since September 2000. He holds a PhD and DSc from the University of Edinburgh, Scotland and is internationally recognized as a leading expert in the field of strategic management. He is also a past President of the Strategic Management Society (SMS)(1997–2000), and in October 2005 he was elected as an Inaugural Fellow. He is an Honorary Life Member of the European Foundation for Management Development (EFMD) and is a current board member at the State Farm Bank in the USA. He is a Fellow of the Academy of Management (AoM) in the USA and also of the British Academy of Management (BAM), where he has been elected onto its Council. He is the current Chair of ABS (the Association of Business Schools in the UK), Chair of GFME (the Global Foundation for Management Education) and Chair Elect of AACSB (the Association to Advance Collegiate Schools of Business, International). He is editor, author or co-author of acclaimed management books including: *Strategy: Analysis and Practice, The Anatomy of Decisions, Risk Analysis, Decision Theory and the Manager, Managing Ambiguity and Change, Handbook of Strategy and Management, Building the Strategically-Responsive Organization, Strategic Integration, Strategy, Structure and Style, Strategic Renaissance and Business Transformation, Strategic Discovery: Competing in New Arenas, Strategic Flexibility: Managing in a Turbulent Environment, Strategic Groups, Strategic Moves and Performance, Entrepreneurship: Perspectives on Theory Building, Dynamics of Competence-Based Competition*, and *Drugs to Market.* He has also published a wide range of articles in areas which include competitive strategy, risk analysis, strategic change, international management and decision theory.

Vicky Tzoumpa is a PhD researcher in the School of Management at the University of Surrey, Guildford, UK. She graduated with an MSc (Hons) in international business management from the University of Surrey and she has a BSc (Hons) in business administration from the American College of Greece with a specialization in international business and European affairs. Her current research lies in the field of knowledge management and particularly she is investigating the role of middle managers in the process of knowledge transfer within cross-functional project teams.

C. Annique Un is Assistant Professor in International Business at the University of South Carolina's Moore School of Business, Columbia, SC, USA. Her research focuses on the management of knowledge and innovation in large multinational corporations (MNCs), international expansion and competition of developed country MNCs in developing countries, and transnational and comparative management of technological innovation strategies. Her research won the 2002 INFORMS Best Doctoral Dissertation Award. Some of her research can be found in *Research Policy*, the *Journal of Technology Management and Innovation, Research Technology Management, Advances in Strategic Management*, the *British Journal of Management*, the *Academy of Management Best Papers Proceedings, Global Firms and Emerging Markets in an Age of Anxiety* by Prasad and Ghauri (eds), *Creating Value through Global Strategy* by Arino, Ghemawat and Ricart (eds), and *A New Generation in International Strategic Management* by Tallman (ed.). She serves on the editorial board of *Organization Studies*.

Gregory B. Vit is Professor of Practice in Management in the Organization and Strategy Group at the Desautels Faculty of Management, McGill University, Canada. He is also the Director of the Dobson Centre for Entrepreneurial Studies at McGill University. Professor Vit's current research interests include organizational conformity and contrarianism, and the interplay between institutional forces, organizational forms, financial markets, and innovation. His paper, 'The multiple logics of conformity and contrarianism: the problem with investment banks and bankers' received the Breaking the Frame Award for best paper in the *Journal of Management Inquiry* in 2007.

David Weir is Professor of Intercultural Management at Liverpool Hope University and Affiliate Professor at ESC Rennes, Visiting Professor in Management Development at Lancaster University School of Management and at Bristol Business School in the UK. He was previously at CERAM Sophia Antipolis in France from 2001 to 2007. He was formerly Professor of Organisational Behaviour at Glasgow University, Professor of Management and Director of the Bradford University School of Management and Dean and Director of the Newcastle Business School. He has a special research, consulting and teaching expertise in intercultural management, especially in relation to the Middle East, operational middle management and risk and crisis management. He has researched and consulted in several Middle Eastern countries and with Craig Marsh and Wilf Greenwood undertook research for the Sergeants Central Committee of the Police Federation. He is the author of several books and many research articles.

Stelios C. Zyglidopoulos holds a PhD from McGill University and he is currently a Lecturer in Strategy at the Judge School of Business, Cambridge University, UK. He has previously held academic positions at Erasmus University, the Netherlands and the Rochester Institute of Technology (RIT), New York. His research interests include the management of corporate reputation, corporate social responsibility and performance; organizational imprinting and evolution; internationalization of high-tech clusters and strategic foresight.

Introduction
Robert Bradley MacKay and Laura A. Costanzo

Foresight is a unique and highly valued human capacity that is widely recognized as a major source of wisdom, competitive advantage and cultural renewal within nations and corporations.

(Chia 2004: 21)

Strategy has traditionally been described as being concerned with the long-term development of the organization (for example, Chandler 1962, p. 13; Andrews 1971, p. 29). This suggests that strategy making is, in essence, a future-oriented process. Many scholars of strategic management seem to concur. In his seminal book on competitive strategy, for instance, Porter offers a set of analytical techniques for predicting the industry's future evolution (1980, p. xxii). Similarly, in his articulation of a resource-based view of corporate strategy, Barney also identifies the future as an important determinant in building a competitive advantage. For Barney, firms that wish to generate above-normal returns for the implementation of product market strategies must have more accurate expectations about the future value of acquiring resources from factor markets, which are needed for strategy implementation (1986, p. 1239). Hamel and Prahalad also argue that successful, industry-leading companies compete for the future by identifying tomorrow's opportunities in the present and developing capabilities to exploit them (1994a, 1994b). If strategy is concerned fundamentally with the future, then it stands to reason that strategic foresight is an essential managerial competency. Indeed, Ahuja et al. argue that all major theories of competitive advantage assume that managers must have some degree of foresight. If they didn't, the argument follows, differences in firm performance could not be distinguished from luck (2005, p. 795).

The notion of strategic foresight is not novel. It has been long recognized as an important attribute of managing. As early as 1916, Henri Fayol, one of the earliest proponents of management theory, argued that: 'The Maxim, "Managing means looking ahead," gives some idea of the importance attached to planning in the business world, and it is true that if foresight is not the whole of management at least it is an essential part of it' (1916/1949, p. 43). Barnard, in his classic treatise on the functions of the executive, also suggests that the ends of an organization always refer to the future, 'and implies foresight in terms of some standard or norm of desirability' (1938, pp. 200–201). The philosopher Alfred North Whitehead, in a lecture at Harvard University in 1931, also drew attention to the importance of foresight to commerce. He proffered that the business mind of the future would require a further endowment beyond the practical routines of business praxis; it would require a philosophical power of understanding the complexities of society (Whitehead 1933, p. 123).

While strategic foresight is assumed to be a valued managerial competence, it appears that it continues to be an enigma to many strategic managers and scholars. Questions remain about what it is, whether it matters and what practices and processes lead to its cultivation. For example, tensions continue to exist over whether the *raison d'etre* of strategic foresight is prediction, preparation or both. The aim of this introduction is to initiate what we believe is an important conversation about strategy and foresight that continues on for 29 engaging and insightful chapters and, we hope, beyond.

What is strategic foresight?

Foresight is defined by the *Oxford English Dictionary* as 'the ability to predict and prepare for future events and needs' (Soanes and Hawker 2005, p. 393). For many management scholars, predicting the future is a desirable objective of strategic planning practice (Wiltbank et al. 2006). This is also reflected in companies where a predictivist perspective on foresight manifests itself in the form of their forecasting competence (Makadoc and Walker 2000, p. 854). Forecasting has been identified as one of the essential aspects of an economic organization's strategic planning processes (Makridakis and Wheelwright 1989). It is indispensable for predicting consumer demand characteristics, the future value of firm resources, establishing new operations and making substantial and often irreversible investments (Barney 1986; Makadok and Walker 2000). Forecasting normally consists of extrapolating data from past patterns and projecting it into the future using sophisticated statistical and econometric models. In the short term, forecasting techniques and the estimation of uncertainty are fairly reliable (Makridakis 1990, p. 60). But forecasting has an Achilles' heel that manifests itself in two significant limitations that can impair foresight. First, the consistent accuracy of forecasts can create a false sense of security. When there are sudden shifts in the business environment, forecasts can fail, making whole strategies obsolete; and, as a former strategic planner for Royal Dutch/Shell points out, it is at these times that they are needed most (Wack 1985a, p. 73). Second, while relatively accurate in the short term, in the medium to long term as political, economic, social, technological, natural and legal trends interact in unpredictable and novel ways, forecasting accuracy begins to diminish as environmental complexity and uncertainty increase. Endogenous and exogenous factors having deleterious influences on forecasting accuracy can stem from illusions of control (Durand 2003), changing patterns over time, the actions of people influencing future events, a new technological innovation or the failure of an existing one, sudden global financial fluctuations, changing elasticity of demand, barriers to entry becoming diminished or natural disasters (Makridakis 1990). The consequence, as Watkins and Bazerman (2003) suggest, is that some of the best-run companies with thoughtful managers and robust planning processes get caught unprepared by disastrous and unanticipated events. Uncertainty, they argue, can result in high probability – read predictable – events sometimes not occurring, and low probability events coming to pass.

Perhaps it was for reasons such as these that led Drucker to quip: 'Prediction is not a worthwhile managerial activity' (Drucker 1992, p. 98). Some scholars have gone so far as to argue that a move towards non-predictive strategy may be necessary (Wiltbank et al. 2006). Prediction, however, has its place in strategic planning. But it doesn't necessarily constitute strategic foresight in itself, because the forecasting and statistical techniques that it relies on cannot always account for seemingly random asymmetries or discontinuous change. The second element comprising strategic foresight, preparation, thus demands the difficult-to-quantify, dynamic properties of any given set of complex circumstances, particularly where social systems and markets are concerned, to be understood. This often necessitates a qualitative, soft systems approach.

To reinforce forecasting techniques and increase preparedness, many companies have turned to scenario planning. In Bain's annual survey of management tools, for instance, they found that since their survey began in 1993, corporate usage of strategic planning increased from 83 per cent in 1993 to 88 per cent in 2006 and scenario and contingency planning increased from 38 per cent in 1993 to 69 per cent in 2006 (Rigby and Bilodeau 2007). Unlike forecasting, scenario planning is designed to analyse how uncertainties might play out in the medium to long-term future. They help organizations to prepare for a range of possibilities in the future.

Scenarios are alternative stories about how the world could evolve. They do not try to predict the future, but to understand the complexity and unpredictability of future organizational environments. They find their roots in the work of Herman Kahn and the militarily-oriented RAND Institute in the 1940s, and their commercialization in companies such as Royal Dutch/Shell, IBM, Corning and General Electric can be traced to the 1960s. Unlike forecasts, they are focused 'less on figures and more on insight' (Wack 1985a, p. 84). While scenario planning has had numerous successes, most notably Royal Dutch/Shell's anticipation of the 1973 oil crisis, scenarios are not a panacea for failures in organizational foresight. Scenarios can be vulnerable to a range of information processing limitations and cognitive biases (MacKay and McKiernan 2004a, 2004b).

Indeed, in preliminary research into futures studies undertaken by the Hart–Rudman Commission into the National Security of the United States in the 21st century, the Commission found that 70 per cent of the 20 futures studies they looked at were either directly or indirectly modelled on the Royal Dutch/Shell 'intuitive logics' approach (see Wack 1985a, 1985b). In their review of the 20 futures studies, the Commission argues that several flaws limit the perspicacity of the planning approach. First, present challenges and concerns relevant to the 1990s tended to be focused on, such as challenges to national sovereignty, failed states, the uncertain impact of technological development and the information revolution rather than possible asymmetries arising in the future (1999, p. 20). Second, possibilities that could produce 'startling emergent behaviour' are overlooked by an emphasis on present concerns. The inability to pick up 'weak signals' (see Ansoff 1975, p. 21), the Commission suggests, may stem from the static caused by group behaviour. Furthermore, relying on experts, as with the Delphi technique, they propose, can diminish rather than augment weak signal reception (p. 19). They thus conclude that when dealing with the future, interrelated trends must be considered, human error in judgement must be acknowledged and uncertainty has to be accepted (p. 20).

The Royal Dutch/Shell account of their scenario planning successes, Mintzberg suggests, may well be more attributable to a talented group of planners and receptive managers being at their best in practice, rather than the planning approach itself (1994, pp. 249–50). Moreover, he argues that overly-formalized, rational strategic planning rooted in analysis does not necessarily connote synthesis (p. 13). This notion is not unique to strategic planning, but can be found at the centre of many philosophical debates in science. Toulmin, in *Foresight and Understanding*, for instance, argues helpfully that there is nothing wrong with prediction and its surrogates such as the calculus of corroboration and statistical significance tests, but what is predicted must be made sense of. In this endeavour, he advocates conceptual innovations, logical perspicuity, mathematical command, scrupulous honesty, speculative imagination, experimental inventiveness and ingenuity all as legitimate forms of scientific enquiry (1961, pp. 112–15).

In sum, strategic foresight requires a broad church. In this pantheon, ends such as prediction and preparation, as well as means such as forecasting and scenarios have their place. By integrating these different perspectives, 'deep understanding' (Tsoukas and Sheppard, 2004, p.2), which is predicated on a capacity to 're-educate attention' (Chia 2004, 21) towards the nuances of a complex world can be cultivated. But does strategic foresight really matter?

Does strategic foresight matter?
Planning procedures, Loasby argued some 40 years ago, should be designed to illuminate the existence and implications of uncertainty rather than obscuring it (1967, p. 308). This may well require a philosophical disposition conducive to the cultivation of foresight and deep understanding of past patterns, present circumstances and the possibility of a radically different future. One of the lessons elicited from chaos theory is that prediction, and its ever-present partner prescription is only possible if there is full knowledge of the interrelationships between all of the variables in dynamic systems (Thiétart and Forgues 1995). In practice the reality may be quite different. In a world where the ability of the human mind to compare all the requisite information needed to make sense of a complex and uncertain world is limited (Simon 1997), management tools and techniques may well be only as effective at generating strategic foresight with deep understanding as the quality of the practices, processes and strategists within organizations permit. Turner suggests that strategic foresight is when the precautions that managers, organizations, industries or societies develop are culturally adequate (Turner 1976, p. 380). We suggest that in today's world for strategic foresight to be culturally adequate, it must combine the strongest elements of both prediction and preparation, infused with deep understanding.

In many industries the rules of the game are reconfiguring at ever-increasing rates (Ilinitch et al. 1996). Cultivating deep understanding of the complexity (for example, Brown and Eisenhardt 1997; Boisot and Child 1999; McKelvey 1999), uncertainty (for example, Courtney et al. 1997) and hypercompetive (D'Aveni 1994) conditions that many organizations and industries face, presents enormous challenges for strategic managers and scholars.

Some commentators suggest that the best way of dealing with an uncertain future is to ignore it (for example Hamel 2000, p. 118). Strategic agility, flexibility and resilience, the argument follows, are the best way to cope with uncertain times (Prahalad et al. 1998; Hamel and Valikangas 2003; Skordoulis 2004). A sole reliance on agility, flexibility and resilience for dealing with changing market demand, competitor behaviour, or product innovations, however, has a significant shortcoming; it assumes that strategic adjustment is economical and quick. Large, complex organizations, unlike small, nimble organizations unencumbered by significant capital endowments (financial capital excepted) frequently have millions if not billions of dollars invested in assets including research and development facilities, supply networks, production plants and distribution channels, not to mention the contractual and social obligations to their stakeholders. Changing direction can be a costly and time-consuming affair for many organizations. Organizational resilience is undoubtedly an ingredient in the overall strategic foresight recipe. But, for every turn of the corporate rudder there must first be months and even years of preparation. To paraphrase Einstein, flexibility without foresight is thus blind, while foresight without flexibility is impotent.

Other commentators emphasize a more rigorous approach to analysing uncertainty. McKinsey consultants Courtney, Kirkland and Viguerie, for instance, suggest that there are four levels of uncertainty. They include level one uncertainty where the future is clear enough and strategy can be formulated using tradition strategy tools and single point forecasts. Level two uncertainty is where there is a finite range of alternative futures that can be analysed using a limited number of discreet scenarios and contingency plans. Level three is where a range of different futures are possible. In level three a number of probable scenarios can be developed. Level four uncertainty is true ambiguity. In level four uncertainty it is difficult to identify the variables that will shape the future. To develop strategy, organizations can develop a number of carefully crafted scenarios that give managers a wider perspective on the range of possibilities and that allow them to test the robustness of their organization's strategies (Courtney et al. 1997).

Incorporating a more rigorous analysis of uncertainty into the strategic planning process and paying closer attention to this context when formulating and implementing strategy is a step towards developing strategic foresight. However, analysis of intelligence failures in government and industry (Wilensky 1967), as well as predictable surprises that broadside companies, continue to be responsible for the demise of some of our most reputable corporations and celebrated business leaders (Watkins and Bazerman 2003; Bazerman and Watkins 2004).

In sum, strategic foresight clearly matters. A corporation cannot survive indefinitely without some contemplation of its long-term future any more than a glass canoe can expect to navigate rapids without first scouting them out. What is needed is not less thinking about the future in a turbulent, uncertain and complex world, but more. This necessitates a research agenda that both conserves received wisdom from the past that has relevance for understanding the future today and also challenges traditional dogmas and paradigms constraining the cultivation of strategic foresight for tomorrow.

The objective of this Handbook is to catalyse new thinking and to suggest new directions for cultivating and researching strategic foresight. The idea for the Handbook finds its origins in the British Academy of Management (BAM) Special Interest Group (SIG) on Strategic Foresight, and the Strategic Foresight Caucus at the Academy of Management (AOM) Conference in the United States. Many of the contributions in this book began their intellectual journey at either the BAM or AOM conferences. To meet its objective, the Handbook draws together a collection of research papers contributed by both established and emerging scholars in the field of strategy and foresight. In so doing, it seeks to highlight the latest developments in the field. This Handbook hopes to make its contribution to theory and practice by stimulating disciplined, rigorous and imaginative inquiry into the relationship between strategy and foresight.

Overview
The Handbook is organized into four parts: Probing the Future: Cultivating Strategic Foresight (Part I), Foresight and Organizational Becoming: Strategy Process, Practice and Change (Part II), Shaping the Future: Strategizing and Innovation (Part III), and Responding to the Future: Intuition, Inertia and Strategic Flexibility (Part IV).

In Part I, Bill McKelvey and Max Boisot (Redefining strategic foresight: 'fast' and 'far' sight via complexity science) present a theory of strategy-finding processes against a contextual backdrop of scientific realism's transcendental causality. Using complexity science as an analytical vehicle, they argue that the process of finding strategy stresses 'fastsight', or the speed at which emergent complexity can mobilize social networks that can improve external seeing, and 'farsight', or the processing of focused information from the firm's environmental context. The authors suggest that who looks, how quickly they look and where they look for information is paramount in the strategy-finding processes of firms.

David Seidl and Dominik van Aaken (Anticipating critique and occasional reason: modes of reasoning in the face of a radically open future) present different notions of the future. The authors problematize approaches to strategic foresight by arguing that they are frequently based on a simplistic concept of the future, which limits their usefulness. The authors articulate helpfully the concept of a 'radically open future'. In their conceptualization, they propose a future that might develop in ways that transcend current concepts of the future. This raises questions, they postulate, about reasoning and communicating emerging developments. They therefore advance notions of 'anticipating critique' and 'occasional reasoning' introduced by philosophers Paul Feyerabend and Helmut Spinner as commensurate modes of thinking about a radically open future.

Ajit Nayak (Strategic foresight) argues that to cultivate strategic foresight, analysis needs to be combined with imagination and practical wisdom. To understand foresight, he suggests, traditional assumptions underpinning forecasting approaches to understanding the future, such as intentional action, control and individual autonomy, must be eschewed by both managers and educators in favour of attention to existential experience and philosophical capabilities that incite wonder and coalesce in deep understanding. The author suggests that this forms the basis for understanding notions of precognition and peripheral vision, which are concepts closely associated with strategic foresight and which also links in closely with Part IV.

Jan Oliver Schwarz (The symbolism of foresight processes in organizations) portrays foresight activities as processes of structural learning and communication. The author argues that rather than valuing foresight activities for their prognostic accuracy, they should be valued for their symbolic contribution to generating 'memories of the future'. It is these memories, generated through communication and learning processes, that allow an organization to prepare itself for an unpredictable future. Understanding foresight in this way also provides a criterion for evaluating the mental dexterity of the corporation and its ability to cope cognitively with exogenous surprises.

Coping with exogenous surprises implies a sensemaking component to strategic foresight. Robert Bradley MacKay (Strategic foresight: counterfactual and prospective sensemaking in enacted environments) argues that there is an over-reliance on retrospection and the future perfect in sensemaking frameworks. To refine the sensemaking concept, the chapter draws on research into subjunctive reasoning processes such as counterfactual and prefactual thinking, as cognitive mechanisms that people use to facilitate sensemaking processes. These involve asking 'what ifs', 'if thens', and 'if onlys', particularly after a surprising event. Subjunctive reasoning involves both *retrospective* sensemaking into the past and *prospective* sensemaking into the future. The chapter concludes by suggesting that prospective sensemaking helps to extend sensemaking frameworks and contributes to our understanding of how strategic foresight is cultivated.

Subjunctive reasoning has strong resonance with concepts of modal narratives in disciplines such as history and philosophy. Charles Booth, Peter Clark, Agnés Delahaye-

Dado, Stephen Procter and Michael Rowlinson (Modal narratives, possible worlds and strategic foresight) advance suggestions for a philosophical system that underpins notions of strategic foresight. To do this, the authors discuss concepts of modal narratives including their philosophical and methodological underpinnings. Further, they explore their schemata and advance ways in which they are organized, such as temporal branching and possible worlds. Strategic foresight, they suggest, involves asking questions about strategic options open to managers. These questions require consideration of possibility, impossibility, contingency and necessity. They go on to discuss the implications of these concepts for scenario and strategy development.

Thomas Durand (Scenarios as knowledge transformed into strategic 're-presentations': the use of foresight studies to help shape and implement strategy), argues that at the heart of strategic management is strategic foresight. Foresight, the author suggests, helps to integrate blocs of knowledge that are the product of organizational activities into representations of potential futures. This 'digestive' process contributes to both strategy formulation and implementation by mediating the complexity of the knowledge base and uncertainty of the future that strategists must deal with.

In the final chapter of Part I, George Burt (Researching the organization–environment relationship) probes the epistemological and philosophical debates surrounding the relationship between the organization and its environment. Identifying four distinct perspectives on the 'environment', the author connects them with patterns of organization and management behaviour. He then goes on to discuss the consequential implications for the design and methodological approaches adopted by researchers. Specific insights are elicited from the literature for those that assume a social constructionist epistemological and methodological disposition when researching how managers make sense of and interpret their experiences and enact their environment.

Part II leads with Elena P. Antonacopoulou (Strategizing as practising: strategic learning as a source of connection). Antonacopoulou draws attention to the dynamics of strategizing practice by highlighting the role of learning in the integration of the multiple endogenous and exogenous forces affecting the practice of strategy. For Antonacopoulou, learning can be conceptualized as the cause, context and consequence of strategizing practice.

Miguel Pina e Cunha, João Vieira Da Cunha and Stewart R. Clegg (Improvisational bricolage: a practice-based approach to strategy and foresight) develop the emerging practice-based approach to researching strategy by infusing it with concepts of foresight. Specifically, the authors illustrate how strategic exploration can be integrated with strategic exploitation in the everyday work of the strategist. From the perspective of strategy praxis, foresight becomes an exploratory practice that prepares the organization strategically for shifting market dynamics.

The implications of political practices in organizations for strategic foresight are a neglected area of inquiry. Christoph Dörrenbächer and Mike Geppert (Micro-political strategies and strategizing in multinational corporations: the case of subsidiary mandate change) turn to micro-political strategizing and strategies in MNCs. The authors argue that the quantitative research bias in the study of MNCs has resulted in the neglect of micro political issues. To begin filling this gap, they investigate mandate changes in subsidiary management, which, they argue, helps us to understand the micro processes underpinning organizational change and the development of strategic foresight.

David Weir, Craig Marsh and Wilf Greenwood (How organizational DNA works) study the operational supervisory management processes and mechanisms in a uniformed public-order organization to develop the organizational DNA analogy for organizational change and stability. The authors demonstrate that focusing on the decision-making processes of first-line operational managers can be a fertile research area for understanding how inherently conservative, traditional and bureaucratic organizations resolve the paradox between maintaining their essential *raison d'être* in their core activities while simultaneously *becoming* and evolving into the future.

Ian Colville (Making sense of organizational becoming: the need for essential stabilities in organizational change) amends notions of organizational change that view it as a constant process of becoming. While sympathetic to recent suggestions that organizational change is an ongoing process, the author argues that essential stabilities are also fundamental in our understanding of organizing. Applying a sensemaking perspective, the author proposes that process perspectives must also address the interaction of stabilities and change when (fore)seeing organizing and organization.

Ahu Tatli and Mustafa F. Özbilgin (Agency in management of change: bringing in relationality, situatedness and foresight), in an attempt to both clarify the notion of agency in the change management literature, and to consider it in all of its complexity, reframe the concept using relational, situated and foresight dimensions. The authors argue that agency, as portrayed in the literature, underplays the role of foresight, which, they suggest, is an essential attribute.

Julie Battilana and Bernard Leca (The role of resources in institutional entrepreneurship: insights for an approach to strategic management that combines agency and institution) investigate the process by which institutional entrepreneurs eschew institutional pressures while mobilizing firm resources for organizational change projects. While the discursive practices and the enabling conditions that facilitate the diffusion of institutional entrepreneurial projects have been studied, the authors advance this perspective by injecting the role of agency and resources in the emergence of institutional entrepreneurship.

Part III commences with Laura A. Costanzo and Vicky Tzoumpa (The role of middle managers in enabling foresight). The chapter argues that there are relevant actors, such as middle managers, who, in the wake of organizational downsizing, rather than being claimed to be an expensive organizational burden are increasingly deemed to play a significant role with regard to the processes of facilitating learning both within and outside of their team. Knowledge is generated from a constant learning and unlearning process. It is argued that this process is powerful, as it equips the firm's management with the capability to generate new insights into the future and sense arising market opportunities. In doing so, the firm is better prepared both to take advantage of the new market possibilities and to face the emerging challenges and threats emerging from the external environment.

C. Marlene Fiol and Edward J. O'Connor (Hollow at the top: (re)claiming the responsibilities of leadership in strategizing) begin with an exploration of the dynamics of strategizing in turbulent environments. They argue that for organizations to survive in competitive environments, innovation must be at the core of strategizing activities. Sporadic innovation, however, will result in bursts of activity, but may not lead to organization-wide innovation unless it changes the organization's competencies and cognitive paradigms. While innovation is fundamental to an organization's future, the authors maintain, a balance must be struck between innovation and focus so as not to create either strategic drift or self-destructive rigidities.

Jonathan Sapsed (Visions and innovation strategy) clarifies concepts of vision by differentiating it from other established terms such as strategy, forecasting and planning. To demonstrate what visions are, what they are not, and their tactical and strategic uses, he presents a number of case studies of firms entering the digital media industry in the 1990s. In instances where vision was absent in the digital media innovation strategies of some firms observed, the author brings empirical evidence to bear on explanations for why this occurred.

Constantinos Markides and Wenyi Chu (Innovation through ambidexterity: how to achieve the ambidextrous organization) contribute to innovation theory by debating issues pertaining to ambidexterity in diversified companies operating in organizational environments characterized by high uncertainty. By integrating non-structural elements, such as culture, values, incentives, mindsets and strategic foresight with more traditional notions of resource allocations between divisions in diversified firms, as well as the structural design of organizations, the authors adopt a multi-perspective approach to studying ambidexterity and innovation theory.

V.K. Narayanan (Fast cycle capability: a conceptual integration) extends Bower and Hout's (1988) conceptualization of fast cycle capability by integrating a fragmented literature related to organizational speed by identifying strategic decision making, new product development and primary value chain activities as the key elements determining the permeation of fast cycle capability throughout the organization. The authors point out that while managers have little control over the characteristics of the external environment, they can influence organizational and technologically related factors that can enable fast cycle capability. On this premise, they develop a model of fast cycle capability and relate it to environmental, organizational and technological factors.

C. Annique Un and Alvaro Cuervo-Cazurra (Interactions with customers for innovation) emphasize a customer focus for generating innovations and superior foresight into emerging marketplace trends. The authors differentiate between the types of innovation the firms aim to achieve, such as new product discovery, new product development, product improvement, and product versioning, arguing that each type of innovation has distinct challenges in creating knowledge for the generation of product innovations and fulfilling customer needs and preferences.

In the final chapter in Part III, Faith Hatani (Organizational innovation of the Toyota Group) studies organizational innovation at the interfirm-network level. Drawing on research into the reorganization of the Toyota Group between 1994 and 2004, the author argues that designing interfirm organizations, such as the Toyota supply network, can be accomplished through orchestrating knowledge-sharing processes and structural changes through the creation of an innovative formation that recombines existing resources. The case study suggests that the dominant adaptively rational model of coherent, flexible and progressive coordination through a core firm's strong leadership, acquisitions and mergers is not the only way of re-engineering a firm for the future.

In Part IV, Marta Sinclair, Eugene Sadler-Smith and Gerard P. Hodgkinson (The role of intuition in strategic decision making) analyse intuition from an information processing perspective. Drawing on dual-process theory in social cognition and cognitive psychology, the authors suggest that a critical competence for effective strategizing and decision making is the ability to switch between analytic and intuitive modes of cognition.

Continuing with a cognitive perspective, Rodolphe Durand ((Un) great expectations: effects of underestimations and self-perception on performance), echoes the call by Starbuck and Mezias (1996) for research into the accuracy of perceptions, The author suggests that while foresight permeates everyday strategic activity, and foresight is closely linked with individual and organizational perception, pessimistic estimation is understudied in the management literature. To advance research in this neglected area, the author endeavours to refine our understanding of how underestimations of events, forecasts or environmental trends can manifest as a lack of organizational foresight.

Moving from the cognition of the strategic manager to the cognition of the organization, Stelios C. Zyglidopoulos and Stephanie W.J.C. Schreven (Strategic foresight and the role of organizational memory within a punctuated equilibrium framework) address the relationship between foresight and organizational memory through their presentation of a punctuated equilibrium conceptual model. They identify four factors linking strategic foresight to organizational memory. The first two factors are cognitive. They include speculative imagination and structural understanding. The second two factors are structural. The authors suggest that depending on whether an organization is experiencing a period of punctuation or convergence, the development of strategic foresight can be augmented or constrained by organizational memory.

In some quickly changing environments, prediction becomes very difficult. It is in this turbulence that foresight is exercised through preparation and strategic flexibility. Andrés Hatum and Andrew M. Pettigrew (Adaptation, inertia and the flexible organization: a study of the determinants of organizational flexibility in an emerging economy), focus on issues of adaptation, organizational flexibility and inertia in an Argentinian context. In the chapter, the authors highlight the importance of such attributes as the centralization and formalization of decision-making processes, the level of macrocultural embeddedness within the organization, environmental scanning and the strength of an organization's identity as determinants of a firm's flexibility when responding to a changing environment. In highly volatile environments, the authors suggest, predicting future changes in the external environment can become impossible. Sensemaking and enactment processes thus become paramount, but these can be modified by the heterogeneity of the dominant coalition.

For organizations to be flexible strategically, they must have the option of developing different capabilities. Swapnesh K. Masrani and Peter McKiernan (Addressing path dependency in the capabilities approach: historicism and foresight meet on the 'road less travelled'), challenge the commonly held notion in the capabilities approach, that the development of new capabilities are path dependent on existing capabilities. The chapter suggests that the emphasis in the empirical literature, particularly in resource-based perspectives on strategy, on the development of capabilities being driven entirely by existing technologies is erroneous. The chapter takes the position that organizations must consider several strategic capability development routes including the default 'do nothing'. The authors support their claims with empirical case evidence, which also suggests that, in some instances, technological resources are not a major determinant in the choice of development routes from an option set.

Extending this capability theme, Taman H. Powell and Howard Thomas (Dynamic knowledge creation) argue that hypercompetition, process improvements and innovation speed quickly erodes competitive advantage generated through market positioning and resource-based approaches to strategy. Drawing on examples from consulting, the authors extend these views by linking them with knowledge creation processes in organizations. They suggest that competitive advantage in contemporary organizational environments need to be continually created by focusing on these knowledge creation processes rather than trying to predict future market positions or fortify existing resources.

In the final chapter, Gregory Vit (Foreseeing the problem of conformity in strategy teaching, research and practice) investigates the paradox in the teaching and researching of strategy and foresight. He argues that while many academics and practitioners are engaged in cutting-edge approaches to strategy and foresight, much time continues to be allocated by academics and consultants to building legitimacy for dominant strategic management models which are frequently flawed and inaccurate. Implicit in his argument is a timely call for novel approaches and processes to the teaching and researching of strategy and foresight that reflect the current reality of business and management.

References

Ahuja, G., R. Coff and P. Lee (2005), 'Managerial foresight and attempted rent appropriation: insider trading on knowledge of imminent breakthroughs', *Strategic Management Journal*, **26** (9), 791–808.

Andrews, K. (1971), *The Concept of Corporate Strategy*, New York: Dow Jones–Irwin.

Ansoff, I. (1975), 'Managing strategic surprise by response to weak signals', *California Management Review*, **18** (2), 21–33.

Barnard, C. (1938/1979), *The Functions of the Executive*, Cambridge, MA: Harvard University Press.

Barney, J. (1986), 'Strategic factor markets: expectations, luck, and business strategy', *Management Science*, **32** (10), 1231–41.

Bazerman, M. and M. Watkins (2004), *Predictable Surprises: The Disasters You Should Have Seen Coming and How to Prevent Them*, Boston, MA: Harvard Business School Press.

Boisot, M. and J. Child (1999), 'Organizations as adaptive systems in complex environments: the case of China', *Organization Science*, **10** (3), 237–52.

Bower, J.L. and T.M. Hout (1988), 'Fast-cycle capability for competitive power', *Harvard Business Review*, November–December, 110–18.

Brown, S. and K. Eisenhardt (1997), 'The art of continuous change: linking complexity theory and time-paced evolution in relentlessly shifting organizations', *Administrative Science Quarterly*, **42** (1), 1–34.

Chandler, A. (1962), *Strategy and Structure: Chapters in the History of the American Industrial Enterprise*, Cambridge, MA: MIT Press.

Chia, R. (2004), 'Re-educating attention: what is foresight and how is it cultivated?', in Tsoukas and Shepherd (eds), pp. 21–37.

Courtney, H., J. Kirkland and P. Viguerie (1997), 'Strategy under uncertainty', *Harvard Business Review*, November–December, 67–79.

Cunha, M., S. Clegg and K. Kamoche (2006), 'Surprises in management and organization: concept, sources and a typology', *British Journal of Management*, **17**, 317–29.

D'Aveni, R. (1994), *Hypercompetition: Managing the Dynamics of Strategic Maneuvering*, New York: Free Press.

Drucker, P. (1992), 'The new society of organizations', *Harvard Business Review*, September/October, 95–104.

Durand, R. (2003), 'Predicting a firm's forecasting ability: the roles of organizational illusion of control and organizational attention', *Strategic Management Journal*, **24**, 821–38.

Fayol, H. (1916/1949), *General and Industrial Management*, London: Pitman.

Hamel, G. (2000), *Leading the Revolution*, Boston: Harvard Business School Press.

Hamel, G. and C. Prahalad (1994a), 'Competing for the future', *Harvard Business Review*, **72** (4), 122–8.

Hamel, G. and C. Prahalad (1994b), *Competing for the Future*, Boston, MA: Harvard University Press.

Hamel, G. and L. Valikangas (2003), 'The quest for resilience', *Harvard Business Review*, September, 52–63.

Hart, G. and W. Rudman (Chairs) (1999), *Study Addendum*, Washington, DC: The United States Commission on National Security/21st Century.

Ilinitch, A., R. D'Aveni and A. Lewin (1996), 'New organizational forms and strategies for managing in hyper-competitive environments', *Organization Science*, **7** (3), 211–20.

Loasby, B. (1967), 'Long range formal planning in perspective', *Journal of Management Studies*, October, 300–308.

MacKay, B. and P. McKiernan (2004a), 'Exploring strategy context with foresight', *European Management Review*, **1** (1), 69–77.

MacKay, B. and P. McKiernan (2004b), 'The role of hindsight in foresight: refining strategic reasoning', *Futures*, **36**, 161–79.

Makadok, R. and G. Walker (2000), 'Identifying a distinctive competence: forecasting ability in the fund industry', *Strategic Management Journal*, **21**, 853–64.

Makridakis, S. (1990), *Forecasting, Planning and Strategy for the 21st Century*, New York: Free Press.

Makridakis, S. and S. Wheelwright (1989), *Forecasting Methods for Management*, Chichester: Wiley.

McKelvey, B. (1999), 'Avoiding complexity catastrophe in coevolutionary pockets: strategies for rugged landscapes', *Organization Science*, **10** (3), 294–321.

Mintzberg, H. (1994), *The Rise and Fall of Strategic Planning*, Toronto: Prentice-Hall.

Porter, M. (1980), *Competitive Strategy*, New York: Free Press.

Prahalad, C.K., D. O'Neal, G. Hamel and H. Thomas (1998), *Strategic Flexibility: Managing in Turbulent Environments*, Chichester: Wiley.

Rigby, D. and B. Bilodeau (2007), 'Bain's global 2007 management tools and trends survey', *Strategy and Leadership*, **35** (5), 9–16.

Simon, H. (1997), *Administrative Behavior: A Study of Decision-Making Process in Administrative Organizations*, 4th edn, New York: Free Press.

Skordoulis, R. (2004), 'Strategic flexibility and change: an aid to strategic thinking or managerial distraction', *Strategic Change*, **13** (5), 253–8.

Soanes, C. and S. Hawker (2005), *Compact Oxford English Dictionary*, Oxford: Oxford University Press.

Starbuck, W.H. and J. Mezias (1996), 'Opening Pandora's box: studying the accuracy of managers' perceptions', *Journal of Organizational Behavior*, **17**, 99–117.

Thiétart, R. and B. Forgues (1995), 'Action, structure, and chaos', *Organization Studies*, **18** (1), 119–43.

Toulmin, S. (1961), *Foresight and Understanding: An Enquiry into the Aims of Science*, London: Hutchinson.

Tsoukas, H. and J. Shepherd (eds) (2004), *Managing the Future: Foresight in the Knowledge Economy*, London: Blackwell.

Turner, B. (1976), 'The organizational and interorganizational development of disasters', *Administrative Science Quarterly*, **21** (3), 378–97.

Wack, P. (1985a), 'Scenarios: uncharted waters ahead', *Harvard Business Review*, September–October, 73–89.

Wack, P. (1985b), 'Scenarios: shooting the rapids', *Harvard Business Review*, November–December, 139–50.

Watkins, M. and M. Bazerman (2003), 'Predictable surprises: the disasters you should have seen coming', *Harvard Business Review*, **81** (3), 72–80.

Whitehead, A. (1933), *Adventures of Ideas*, Cambridge: Cambridge University Press.

Wiltbank, R., N. Dew, S. Read and S. Sarasvathy (2006), 'What to do next? The case for non-predictive strategy', *Strategic Management Journal*, **27**, 981–98.

Wilensky, H. (1967), *Organizational Intelligence*, New York: Basic Books.

PART I

PROBING THE FUTURE: CULTIVATING STRATEGIC FORESIGHT

1 Redefining strategic foresight: 'fast' and 'far' sight via complexity science
Bill McKelvey and Max Boisot

Introduction

> The only thing that gives an organization a competitive edge – the only thing that is sustainable – is what it knows, how it uses what it knows, and how fast it can know something new! (Prusak, 1996, p. 6)

It is important to set the competitive circumstances within which we study processes leading to strategic foresight. Good strategy is no longer just picking the right industry; it is being at the right place in the industry – at the cutting edge of industry evolution – new technology, new markets, new moves by competitors. For firms in high-velocity environments (Eisenhardt, 1989), emphasis needs to shift from the competitive dynamics of industry selection and interfirm competition to intrafirm rates of change (McKelvey, 1997). As high-velocity product life cycles and hypercompetition have increased (D'Aveni, 1994), speed of knowledge appreciation has become a central attribute of competitive advantage (Leonard-Barton, 1995), as has organizational learning (Barney, 1991; Argote, 1999). Seeing industry trends (Hamel and Prahalad, 1994) and staying ahead of value migration (Slywotsky, 1996) are also valued. Porter (1996) emphasizes staying ahead of the efficiency curve. Dynamic ill-structured environments and learning opportunities become the basis of competitive advantage if firms can be *early* in their industry to unravel the evolving conditions (Stacey, 1995).

Much of the concern about human capital appreciation bears on high-technology-based industries (Leonard-Barton, 1995). Eisenhardt and colleagues have focused on 'high-velocity' high-tech firms for some time (Eisenhardt, 1989; Eisenhardt and Tabrizi, 1995). In these firms the classic 'organic' organizing style is just too slow to keep pace with changes in high-velocity firms (Brown and Eisenhardt, 1997). In the 21st-century knowledge economy the main danger comes from viscous information flow. Firms need to learn how to speed up knowledge flow (Boisot, 1998). Given high-velocity environments, Hamel and Prahalad (1994) view foresight as seeing economic rents stemming from learning about industry trends before competitors, and imposing 'stretch'. Later we shall equate stretch with the energy differentials of the Bénard (1901) process, and generalize it into 'adaptive tensions' (McKelvey, 2001, 2008). These are defined as imposing contextual tensions strong enough to stimulate discontinuous or 'punctuated' adaptive change within a firm (Tushman and Romanelli, 1985; McKelvey, 1994).

Slywotsky (1996), studying value migration, ostensibly focuses on strategy as a chess game, complete with chess-like patterns managers need to know about. Underlying this, however, he actually tells foresight managers to do the kinds of analysis that uncover *how* customers go about discovering what their needs and priorities are – if you know their prioritizing process, you can uncover their priorities as soon or sooner than they do. Collins and Porras (1994) and O'Reilly and Pfeffer (2000) focus on the core ideologies underlying the foresight management processes that allow some firms to constantly get to new ideas and products before their competitors.

Starting from scientific realism's transcendental causality, our theory about the strategy-finding process stresses the use of (i) *far*sight – pattern processing to simplify and focus information about a firm's environmental context so as to get a grip on where to look, and (ii) *fast*sight – emergent complexity to create and energize the kinds of social networks within a target firm so as to improve its external seeing ability and get a grip on who looks and how quickly. We use complexity science as the analytical engine to unravel both far- and fastsight dynamics. For reasons of exposition, we discuss the farsight process first and then fastsight.

For the 'where to look' question, we turn to the study of longer-run, extant trends at the level above a firm-in-an-industry plane of observation to unravel the firm's environmental context and its potentially dominating adaptive tensions – the supra-forces. We use complexity science to develop a search procedure whereby a firm can process the myriad patterns to simplify down to the more accurate and significant patterns. We do so by focusing on pattern formation and simplification, order parameters, and order creation theory, bringing adaptive tension into greater detail in the process. Here, complexity science is the engine for improving *far*sight.

For the 'who looks' part, we focus on the social network processes comprising distributed intelligence. Especially, we study how to speed up the functioning of the corporate brain and how to sharpen its 'seeing' ability. We use complexity science as it bears on critical values and phase transition effects caused by adaptive tensions (energy differentials) to initiate self-organizing activity aimed at speeding up collective search behaviors. These sub-force dynamics lead to fastsight. Here, complexity science is the engine for improving *fast*sight ability.

This pattern-search, *far*sight procedure, however, requires a well-functioning social network 'seeing' device to deal with the 'who looks' and 'how fast' questions. In a recursive fashion, analyses of where a firm stands with respect to the broader adaptive tensions provides information that can be used to both motivate and steer phase transitions, coevolutionary events, and social networks' self-organizing behaviors. In short, farsight delineation of adaptive tensions motivates self-organization by social networks – improving their fastsight capability. Fastsight development by social networks, in turn, leads to better farsight seeing ability. Why? Broad trends decompose into higher frequency event horizons as one drops down levels of analysis (Simon, 1999) and the events come closer to having impact on a firm. Fastsight becomes a crucial element of farsight as broad, seemingly slow-moving patterns resolve into higher-speed dynamics. Bottom line? Supra-forces and sub-forces coevolve to improve strategic far- and fastsight. Needless to say, reliance on a single visionary CEO is totally inadequate (Marion and Uhl-Bien, 2001; Uhl-Bien et al., 2007).

Defining transcendental foresight
Alfred North Whitehead gives us a fairly elaborate definition of foresight: 'the ability to see through the apparent confusion, to spot developments before they become trends, to see patterns before they fully emerge, and to grasp the relevant features of social

currents that are likely to shape the direction of future events' and being able to 'look for generality where there is variety', and to 'look for idiosyncrasy where there is generality (1967, p. 89). However, the word is a tricky one coming with some hidden baggage. Webster's Dictionary gives the preferred meaning of foresight as 'prescience', defined as: 'foreknowledge of events; a: divine omniscience; b: human anticipation of the course of events'. This view of foresight presages the currently popular concept of the charismatic *visionary* leader (Bennis, 1996; Bryman, 1996) who leads by having a good vision of the future. This orientation toward 'foresight' seems to date back to the days of witch doctoring, and the Oracle at Delphi – some people apparently can see into the future. Strategic thinking is better served by taking a lesson from drunk drivers – the more they drink the slower their brain responds to 'seeing' an approaching curve and, worse, they do not see the curve until they are closer to it than when they are sober. We shall argue that advantageous strategic foresight is better defined as comprising both fast- and farsight.

This chapter is also about 'transcendental foresight'. It builds on the 'transcendental realism' of Roy Bhaskar (1975), one of the founders of modern scientific realist philosophy of science. Foresight is about peering into the future to discern which events are likely to cause other events. By using the term 'transcendental', Bhaskar simply reminds us that causality stems from forces operating at levels different from the plane of our directly observable experience. Given Porter's (1980) characterization of the observable plane of industry competition as consisting of the 'five forces', transcendental foresight calls for focusing on 'sub-forces' and 'supra-forces'.

There are three paths to the future – ordered by foresight feasibility:

1. *Path 1*: Yes, the future – that hasn't happened yet – is uncertain and unknowable, but from the perspective of any given observer, much of what appears to be 'an uncertain future' has already happened and is 'uncertain' only because the observer is lacking information. In this view, foresight is simply learning about the knowable part of what, to the less perspicacious, appears uncertain. No smoke and mirrors here; it is simply a matter of getting out there and studying what has happened before competitors do so. Porter's 'competitive intelligence' fits here – learning about industry-driver effects (already in place) before one's competition.

2. *Path 2*: To the perspicacious, future events are dimly indicated by developments that will become trends and by dots that once filled in will become patterns already in place. This is a sort of pre-trend and pre-pattern view. This presumes a linear, unbroken predictability – the faint glimmerings that we discern now will eventually unfold, as buds slowly turn into flowers. This view assumes that the more perspicacious see the unfolding future sooner than their competitors. This view is closer to the 'let history predict the future' view than one might like to think. Except that instead of from past-to-present it is present-into-the-future. The presumption of the underlying dynamic is the same – linear predictability. This is what econometricians do – make inferences about the future from analyses of the past.

3. *Path 3*: The future is fraught with discontinuities, suggesting that what lies before a discontinuity offers little insight as to what lies beyond. This is the view of chaos and complexity theorists. They see a world of aperiodic, nonlinear, coevolutionary,

discontinuous events. Patterns here do not appear to emerge from historical trends; these cannot be inferentially derived or extended into the future.

We elaborate on fastsight to speed up progress along the second path. We elaborate on farsight to see emerging patterns lying behind the emerging discontinuities of the third path. Complexity science informs both elaborations.

Bhaskar, explanation, and the plane of observation
Bhaskar's transcendental realism is the understructure supporting our notion of transcendental foresight. Bhaskar makes a clear distinction between developing theory based on identified *regularities* – which could be accidental – and experimentally contrived *invariances* in which repeated experiments produce an outcome regularity by manipulating what is hypothesized to be an underlying force, process, mechanism, or structure. Contrived invariances better fit the counterfactual conditional basis of lawlike statements about generative forces that might seldom if ever be naturally discernible in complex open systems (such as organizations) because of the many countervailing influences. Initially, the mental models of idealists and realists both contain 'imagined' (Bhaskar's term, p. 145) conceptual, intangible, unmeasurable theory terms. The difference is that for idealists they remain forever intangible, interpreted, socially constructed, metaphysical, and *unreal*, whereas for realists the better detection of theoretical terms, repeated experiments, and other kinds of empirical research eventually give reason to believe that what were initially imagined metaphysical terms and entities become *real*. Bhaskar notes, however, that the world becomes a construction of the human mind and of a scientific community (pp. 22–7, 148–67). He says:

> [Transcendental realists regard] objects of knowledge [in the models] as the structures and mechanisms that generate phenomena; and the knowledge as produced in the social activity of science. These objects are neither phenomena (empiricism) nor human constructs imposed upon the phenomena (idealism), but real structures which endure and operate independently of our knowledge, our experience and the conditions which allow us access to them. Against empiricism the objects of knowledge are structures, not events; against idealism, they are intransitive . . . (p. 25)

Bhaskar (p. 25) takes an 'updated dynamized' version of Kant's famous transcendental argument that reason and experience presume a priori objectively valid phenomena (Audi, 1995, p. 808). '[I]ntransitive objects of knowledge are in general invariant to our knowledge of them: they are the real things and structures, mechanisms and processes, events and possibilities of the world' (Bhaskar, p. 22). 'Intransitive' means that objects of scientific discovery exist independently of human perceptions, interpretations, and social constructions, and by 'structured', Bhaskar means they are 'distinct from the patterns of events that occur' (p. 35). 'Generating structures' are underlying forces that may occur independent of observed regularities and may not be observable or measurable except via contrived experiments and the creation of invariances.

In this 'transcendental' view, true explanation comes from above or below the plane of direct human observation. To pick a simple example, consider a pot of water coming to the boil on a stove. What we see at the plane of observation is the fire, the pot of water, and the beginning of emergent steam from its spout. What we do not see are the causes (outside the pot) of why the fire occurred and is hot and (inside the pot) why the molecules, as agents,[1] change their governing rules as they go, from (i) mild heat and increased vibration while maintaining position; to (ii) the rolling boil in which they move around in the pot; and finally to (iii) emerging from the pot as steam. It seems logical to us that attempts at gaining foresight should be rooted in philosophical views as to how changing phenomena are best explained – presumably by truthful theories.

Echoing Bhaskar, Salthe (1985) devotes an entire book to his argument that all of science focuses explanation around a 'triadic' structure. A firm ('system') exists in a hierarchy in which there are both upper- and lower-level constraints – environmental 'context' and intrafirm 'agents', as we use these terms in this chapter. Salthe might well have drawn on Bhaskar's (1975) classic discussion of transcendental realism.

Focus on transcendental forces
The term, foresight, obviously, has two parts, 'fore' and 'sight'. We detailed three variants of the 'fore' part above, saying we were going to focus on the second and third variants. We reject the idea of divine omniscience or humans being able to see the future. But strategists can try to look farther down the road faster than competitors and we academics need to offer new ideas that help strategists see beyond the next discontinuity in their competitive landscape.

Besides the feasibility triad, the 'fore' part also subdivides into three levels of 'seeing'. For purposes of exposition, we shall take the 'firm-in-its-industry' level as the plane of observation. Porter's (1980) competitive strategy and its emphasis on the five forces of industry competition is our exemplar. For many people, foresight is nothing other than trying to figure out what the future effects of the five forces are likely to be. The population ecology movement in the study of organizations (Hannan and Freeman, 1989) is another example of attention to the industry (population) plane of observation. Following Salthe and Bhaskar, however, the industry-level plane of observation is the set of top-management agents operating *between* forces above and below their plane of observation – the environmental context *above* the industry plane and coevolving lower-level agents *below*. Building on Porter's language, elements in the environmental context become the *supra-forces* and coevolving agents within a firm become the *sub-forces*. One of the reasons why Hamel and Prahalad's book, *Competing for the Future* (1994), has had such an impact is that it bases its notions of foresight on *both* the supra- and sub-forces. Thus, on the one hand they say, 'Industry foresight must be informed by deep insight into trends in lifestyles, technology, demographics, and geopolitics' (p. 89) – a supra-force orientation. But on the other, they focus on core competencies of the agents within firms (Ch. 10) – a sub-force orientation. We use elements of complexity science to expand on Hamel and Prahalad's 'transcendental' insights.

Farsight   Neoclassical economists view the world as composed of long periods of equilibrium separated by momentary (inconvenient) periods of discontinuous new order creation (Hinterberger, 1994; Rosenberg, 1994), and have patterned their view of good science after that of classical physics (Mirowski, 1989). Their use of linear differential mathematical models has seeped into other social sciences (Henrickson and McKelvey, 2002). The equilibrium assumption allows them to focus on instrumentally predictive variables (Friedman, 1953).

Physics-oriented complexity scientists, in contrast, see order creation in the world as mostly the result of nonlinearities separated by occasional periods of equilibrium. Some complexity scientists focus on nonlinearities resulting from energy differentials (Prigogine, 1955, 1997; Cramer, 1993) and phase transitions (Lorenz, 1963; Haken, 1983). Others, starting from quantum theory, focus on how order emerges from randomness (Gell-Mann, 1988, 2002; Mainzer, 1994/2007). Haken (1983) begins a theory about how order parameters emerge. We elaborate on this stream of complexity theory to develop a theory of pattern formation and then we use the same theory to develop a farsight search process.

Fastsight   The 'sight' part raises the question: 'sight' by whom? Henry Ford[2] is notorious for asking, 'Why is it that whenever I ask for a pair of hands, a brain comes attached?'. In this view, foresight is only possible by the person, or perhaps a few people, at the very top of firms. Leadership gurus such as Bennis (1996), focusing on charismatic visionary leaders, make the same mistake (Uhl-Bien et al., 2007). Since Ford's time, economics has been broadened to include human capital throughout a firm (Becker, 1975) and the social capital that interconnects human capital (Burt, 1992). Even more recently attention has focused on distributed knowledge management (Davenport, 1997), distributed organizational learning (Argote, 1999), and distributed intelligence (McKelvey, 2001, 2008; Stacey, 2001). Distributed intelligence rests on distributed information input, that is, 'distributed seeing'. We use the latter as the technology for speeding up foresight so as to get *fast*sight.

Astronomers use the 'VLA' (Very Large Array) observation system in New Mexico where, instead of one single localized lens (the visionary CEO version), 27 radio telescopes, each movable over a wide geographical area, are distributed so as to maximally 'see' and collect a radio signal coming from some distant quasar – equivalent to a single lens 22 miles across! They get a tremendous advantage from 'distributed seeing'. How to make distributed seeing work better in organizations? Can a CEO produce strategically useful, distributed seeing in a world of nonlinear discontinuities?

Key questions are: Who is looking? How many are looking? How hard are they looking? What are they looking at? Therefore, a study of the strategic foresight process needs to pay as much attention to who is doing the looking and how to manage it, as it does to what they are looking at or looking for. The idea that fastsight comes only from the few people at the top is surely archaic. Given the importance of gaining more fastsight than one's competitors (Hamel and Prahalad, 1994), we begin by outlining some ideas about how to better develop and manage 'distributed seeing' – the 'who is looking' and 'how do they do it collectively' part. For this, we draw on mostly biological and social scientists connected with the Santa Fe Institute – Arthur (1988, 1990), Holland (1988), Kauffman (1988, 1993, 2000) among many others – who see agent coevolution as the primary source of nonlinearities. Unlike classical physicists and neoclassical economists, who assume that agents are homogenous because the math works better, the Santa Fe scholars assume that agents are heterogeneous (Kauffman, 1993; Holland, 1995; Epstein and Axtell, 1996), and use agent-based computational models rather than math models (Casti, 1997; Henrickson and McKelvey, 2002).

Integrating fast- *and* far*sight*   What is most interesting about lessons we draw from complexity theory is that fast- and farsight go hand in hand. Farsight calls for better understanding of the broadest tensions – the supra-forces – imposing on a firm's competitive landscape. Farsight tensions also serve as the adaptive tensions that energize coevolving agents in connectionist networks. This leads the network to function better, leads to distributed intelligence, and sharpens the network's ability to improve its pattern processing capability and, consequently, find patterns faster. This leads to fastsight. But, broad tensions decompose into higher-frequency (faster-moving), more specific tensions as levels of analyses drop (Simon, 1999), and their effects come to have more obvious near-term likelihood of creating discontinuities. When this happens, firms that are prepared with fastsight capability win. Better network functioning – the sub-forces – therefore, improves farsight responsiveness. Farsight and fastsight, therefore, are recursive dynamics. This will become clear as we proceed. Farsight is about finding the right pattern. Fastsight is about finding it in timely fashion. Both are preconditions of effective adaptation.

Translating to transcendental complexity: Ashby's law
In his classic work, *An Introduction to Cybernetics*, Ashby (1956) says:

> When a constraint exists advantage can usually be taken of it . . . Every law of nature is a constraint . . . Science looks for laws . . . Constraints are exceedingly common in the world around us . . . A world without constraints would be totally chaotic . . . That something is predictable implies that there exists a constraint . . . Learning is worth while only when the environment shows constraint. (pp. 130–34)

He also notes that order (organization) exists between two entities, *A* and *B*, only if the link is 'conditioned' by a third entity, *C* (1962, p. 255). If *C* symbolizes the 'environment', which is external to the relation between *A* and *B*, environmental constraints are what cause order (Ashby, 1956). This, then, gives rise to his famous Law of Requisite Variety: 'ONLY VARIETY CAN DESTROY VARIETY' (p. 207; his capitals). It holds that for a biological or social entity to be efficaciously adaptive, the variety of its internal order must match the variety of the environmental constraints.

If Ashby were writing now he would surely update his Law, as follows:

Only variety can destroy variety.
Only degrees of freedom can destroy degrees of freedom.
Only internal complexity can destroy external complexity.

This rephrasing rests on the widely held view that complexity is a function of degrees of freedom.

The first lesson from Ashby is that for strategists to find emerging patterns in what appear to be chaotic environments, they need to uncover the contextual constraints and resources. The second lesson is that internal complexity needs to match the complexity of the environmental context. A third, related lesson comes from Allen (2001). Since it is impossible to know in advance which of a firm's degrees of freedom will actually be relevant to a particular environment, Allen proposes his Law of Excess Variety. A firm cannot simply create internal variety to *match* the environment. It has to create *excess* variety. It follows that a pattern-finding social network within a firm has to be more complex than the complexity of its competitive environment!

Summary
In this section, we drew on Bhaskar's (1975) transcendental realism to define 'transcendental foresight'. Taking a 'firm-in-an-industry' as the plane of observation, we then defined *far*sight as calling for an appreciation of the complexity dynamics in the firm's environment and *fast*sight as calling for distributed seeing within the firm. We then drew on, and updated, Ashby's (1956) Law of Requisite Variety to argue that the complexity of distributed seeing capabilities within the firm have to match the requisite complexity of the firms external competitive environment.

Managing *far*sight dynamics via the supra-forces
We begin by defining forces above the plane of observation and then turn our discussion to how to simplify the quadrillions of impinging patterns.

Supra-forces
To get an idea of what we mean by a firm's supra-forces, about what kind of farsight is desired, we begin with a biological analogy. Consider a species (population) coevolving in some niche along with other competing populations. This is the plane of observation – the level equivalent to Porter's five industry-level forces. What are the forces most crucial to the survival of a niche or most likely to change it? To see these we need to look beyond Darwinian selection processes (Box 1.1).

BOX 1.1   FORCES UNDERLYING BIOLOGICAL DIVERSITY

Lava plumes, plate tectonics, plate subduction
Rising and falling continents
Volcanoes, smoke and ash, and mountains

Emergent rivers, lakes, ponds, and oceans
Climate zones
Emergent forests, plains, deserts, climate zones

These are the supra-forces of biological diversity and speciation that give rise to the 'punctuated equilibrium' of Eldredge and Gould (1972). They argue that these are the forces serving to explain the gaps in the fossil record. If one speeds up a 'movie' of the past 3.8 billion years of life on earth (McKelvey, 2004b), one sees that it is the self-organization of biological agents in the face of the forces mentioned in the box. The plane of analysis has been shifted from local coevolutionary niche dynamics to geological forces.

With this lesson in mind, consider some of the analogous supra-forces for firms (Box 1.2).

Of course, many of these are very broad trends, primarily in the future, and quite unresolved as to their near-term business implications. On the other hand, the 'terrorism trend' has resolved very quickly after the 9/11 World Trade Center attack (Suder, 2006). Many businesses have figured out that there are many fall-outs from this, security, encryption, and protection against weapons of mass destruction being the most obvious. Presumably, each one of the foregoing broad trends will, at some point, resolve just as the terrorist trend recently has. More generally, to the discerning eye, each trend may

BOX 1.2   ANALOGOUS SUPRA-FORCES FOR FIRMS

Basic research and new knowledge
Basic science activities and findings
Cues about trends and implications
  of basic science developments
Technology and knowledge
  applications
Petroleum depletion
Global resource depletion
Global warming
Demography
Globalization
Multicultural
Japan/Europe economic time-bomb –
  low birthrate and low immigration;
  which leads to lower tax base;
  compounded by increasing pension
  costs

Poverty: G7 and vs. Third-World
hunger
Third-World education
Effects of Third-World economic
  development
Global and local politics
Small wars here and there
China, India, Russia, Iraq, Iran, North
  Korea
Changes in economic regimes
Islam and/or terrorism
Third-World nuclear threats
Wall Street's liquidity crisis of 2007

be understood as containing a cascade of more specific, narrow foresight possibilities. Simon (1999) points out that in both natural and social science, as the broad is decomposed into the specific, and the high level decomposed to the low level, the frequency rate increases. Going down almost any hierarchy, what starts as *far*sight eventually calls for *fast*sight! All of these tensions currently impose on some sectors of the world's economies. Entrepreneurship and order creation are nothing more than decomposing these broad tensions down to specific, near-term business opportunities. Each of the broad trends, as they resolve, also can be further subdivided into fast- and farsight-based implications for marketing, production, research and development (R&D), and finance. Boisot and McKelvey (2006a,b) focus on the problem of speeding up fastsight to the point where strategists can see patterns forming – tracks in the sand – that give early clues about forthcoming extreme events like the 9/11 disaster or the London and Madrid bombings before they happen.

There are other hierarchical implications. One can also refine the broad trends into implications for firms at various levels of the SIC code. Thus, perhaps only the largest (2-digit) 'food-production' firms can at this time finance the technological R&D implications and subsequent organizational implications of, say, demographic and world-hunger-related trends. But, as Slywotsky (1996) observes, firms can gain much insight into the future by trying to anticipate how their customer firms are, in turn, going to respond to their customers' needs. Thus, near-term business opportunities for 'supplier' firms resolve from an understanding of how larger firms are trying to anticipate solutions to the broader, long-term trends. It follows that the resolution of one broad trend, say terrorism or hunger, growth in China's economy, Islam's various effects, and so on, resolves into implications for other broad trends such as R&D and technology development, and from there into decomposed, narrower, near-term business opportunities. What should worry any CEO is the prospect that new order-creation discontinuities are in the making at all times – as opportunities for competitors, or problems and opportunities for one's own firm.

Surely useful foresight starts with understanding the long-term effects of these forces on one's firm. Who best to imagine possible outcomes of these forces? This is where the power of distributed seeing comes to play. Presumably, the many lower-level (sub-force) agents have a higher collective probability of seeing these forces and having the intelligence (ideas) to create ideas about how to respond. But, if they look in too many places all at the same time, their seeing ability is out of focus and apt to yield poor results. This is why Hamel and Prahalad (1989) suggest 'refining strategic intent'.

But, what does 'refining strategic intent' mean? By our analysis, long-term trends set in motion broad kinds of pattern formation. These decompose into near-term patterns that become near-term business opportunities. Which competitors see the latter first? Complexity scientists argue that complexity dynamics drive long-term pattern formation and the discontinuities involved. We theorize below that it takes complexity dynamics to unravel patterns set in motion by complexity dynamics. In order for internal connectionist networks to be effective at unravelling external complexity dynamics, they need a search procedure that is, itself, informed by complexity dynamics. We discuss this next.

Pattern-creation theory from complexity science
In defining variety, Ashby (1956, pp. 124–5) pointed to the following series: '*c, b, c, a, c, c, a, b, c, b, b, a*'. He observed that *a*, *b*, and *c* repeat, meaning that there are only three '*distinct* elements' (original italics) – three kinds of variety or three degrees of freedom. In the language of patterns, however, this is variety at the level of 'dots'. Suppose, instead, we define variety in terms of the number of patterns instead of the number of dots. Then, using the formulae from Table 1.1, we see that four dots lead to six possible links; they also generate 64 possible patterns. With 10 dots one gets 45 possible links and approximately 35 trillion possible patterns. Ashby's 12 'variety' dots produce 66 possible links and approximately 4,700 quadrillion possible patterns! Even supposing that 99 percent of these are not worth paying attention to, trillions are left, and one still does not know, up front, which ones are trivial and which are not.

Despite this computational reality, six of America's most experienced intelligence practitioners, writing in *The Economist* (2003, p. 30), about the FBI's failure to 'see' the terrorists' networks (patterns) before the 9/11 event, argue that although there had been 'an inability to connect the dots', what is really needed are more useful dots to connect,

Table 1.1   Relation of dots to patterns

Number of dots: N	Number of possible links: $L = N(N-1)/2$	Number of possible patterns: $P = 2^L$
$N = 4$	$L = 6$	$P = 64$
$N = 10$	$L = 45$	$P = 35$ trillion
$N = 12$	$L = 66$	$P = 4,700$ quadrillion

more fine-grained and better-quality data, and more monitoring based on the data. We believe, however, that foresight does not come from simply pleading for more and better dots. This is to greatly mistake the nature of the problem. An arithmetic increase in the number of 'dots' – high quality or otherwise – leads to a geometric increase in the possible connections that one can establish between them. It also leads to an exponential increase in the number of patterns to decipher.

In quantum-theory language, Gell-Mann (1994, Ch. 11) refers to the trillions of possible patterns among the 12 dots as the 'fine-scale structure'. There are so many interacting correlations among the dots that discernible effects are 'washed out'. His quantum theory focuses on what he calls the 'coarse-graining' process whereby the few dominant patterns that one needs to know about emerge out of the fine-scale structure. He points to the effects of 'context' as causes of coarse-graining.

Haken (1983) takes a closer look at the process by which contextual tensions produce coarse-graining of one kind as opposed to all sorts of other kinds, given the trillions of possible patterns 'out there'. He shows how some contextual elements become the 'order parameters' that drive the formation of new pattern formation – that is, new order. Mainzer ([1994] 2007), then, details how the many possible adaptive tensions, such as all those we listed earlier and many more, are reduced to the very few order parameters that actually drive new pattern formation at some given point in time.

Haken begins by describing a number of physical systems in which a critical temperature, T_c, causes a phase transition: magnetization, Bénard cells, lasers, cell formation in slime molds, chemical reactions such as Belousov–Zhabotinsky, predator/prey growth and decline rates, and so on. The most obvious one for most of us – especially cooks – is the temperature at which a rolling boil begins in a pot of water, that is, when water molecules change their 'rules' so as to transmit heat by moving around the pot rather than increased vibration in a stationary position. Haken is interested in trying to predict how agents – whether atoms, organisms, or social actors – self-organize into some specific pattern when the imposed external energy source exceeds R_{c1} – the 'first critical value' (which we discuss further in more detail in the fastsight section). R_{c1} triggers a phase transition at which point new structure and processes occur in physical systems such as those Haken points to. In Haken's view (1983, pp. 14, 195–9, 249–50), as the environmental energy gradient or adaptive tension approaches R_{c1}, changing external degrees of freedom *enslave* internal degrees of freedom that below R_{c1} were previously independent. As the phase transition completes, the dominant degrees of freedom – what he terms 'order parameters' – essentially negate all of the other degrees of freedom by reducing their relative importance, leaving only one (or a few) remaining as order parameters to define new pattern formation.

Mainzer (1994, pp. 66–8) – reinterpreting Haken considerably – sets the stage for a theory of order creation that builds from Ashby, Gell-Mann, and Haken. We elaborate on Mainzer's basic ideas in the following points to begin an integrative theory of how the more crucial coarse-grained patterns emerge from the fine-scale structure in the domains of physics and biology (we translate into the world of firms later):

1. Start with an existing coarse-grained system. Presumably its internal variety matches external environmental variety, such that each internal degree of freedom corresponds to an external one – otherwise it would not exist (not necessarily true of firms).

External degrees of freedom are uncorrelated, even chaotic, otherwise they would not exist as independent degrees of freedom.

2.   As the one external energy gradient or adaptive tension (degree of freedom; Haken's 'mode') increases toward R_{c1}, adjacent external degrees of freedom recede in *relative* strength, that is, recede back into the fine-grained structure – which is to say their effect becomes randomized or washed out relative to the more dominant mode, and results in environmental effects that are increasingly chaotic – except for the one increasingly dominant mode (force or constraint). Thus, just before a tension parameter increases to the level of R_{c1}, chaotic environmental forces increasingly appear along with the dominant, stable mode.

3.   As the *unstable* external forces multiply, they begin to enslave many of the stable internal degrees of freedom which they influence, thus eliminating the latter as meaningful forces. Consequently, the basis of coarse-graining is increasingly narrowed down to the dominant stable mode. Environmental chaotic-variety produces internal chaotic-variety – that is, fine-grained structure.

4.   At the same time, the more dominant degrees of freedom associated with the imposed adaptive tension are also enslaving some internal degrees of freedom.

5.   The unstable internal degrees of freedom disappear into a stochastic pool of Brownian motion. This leads to a vast reduction in degrees of freedom. Mostly, fine-grained structure dominates.

6.   The last few stable vectors remaining, however, become Haken's 'order parameters', acting to create the emergent patterns of new order as the system tips over R_{c1} into the region of emergent complexity – meaning that the order parameters surviving across the phase transition are totally the result of the dominant mode(s) in combination with the surrounding fine-grained structure. These order parameters become Gell-Mann's contextual effects.

7.   At this juncture, order, complexity, and increased degrees of freedom emerge. The result is emergent coarse-graining.

8.   The region of emergent complexity persists until the energy differential is reduced by virtue of the continuing emergence of new structures – Prigogine (1955) calls them energy 'dissipative structures'. That is, coarse-graining continues until the energy differential is reduced. Of course, if the energy differential is continuously renewed equal to, or even faster than the existing new structures can reduce it, more dissipative structures will continue to emerge.

Needless to say, the foregoing is a very basic pattern formation theory from physics. Still, there are applicable organizational lessons for us:

1.   We need to watch for tension parameters approaching R_{c1}. Even though the broad parameters we listed earlier may not appear to be approaching R_{c1}, quite possibly decomposed elements may be.

2.   For any firm, at any given time, a very few, if not just one, tension parameter(s) will become the order parameter(s) – the basis of an emerging strategic intent.

3.   To find the relevant emerging patterns, a firm has to zero in on the order parameters and decompose broadly defined ones into sub-parameters that have more near-term relevance.

4.   The complexity elements we just used to theorize about new order creation are also the basis for suggesting a search procedure for how intrafirm social networks may go about uncovering the more worrisome or entrepreneurially relevant (sub-)order parameters (more on this in the fastsight section).
5.   Our theory of how order parameters appear and how they cause pattern formation becomes our theory about pattern-search processes.

Academics can try this out at their next faculty meeting. Suppose each person is richly described by 100 variables and has correlated histories with 50 faculty members attending. Given all these variables and all-possible correlated histories, without any task, any probability of predicting a person's behavior would be nil – this is the fine-grained structure. But, add a context – such as 'we are going to vote on hiring person X as a faculty member' – and you can probably predict what most of their colleagues will say! Contextually driven tasks cause coarse-graining to take place.

In the next subsection we detail how our pattern-formation theory translates into a pattern-search theory.

Pattern finding via simplification
As an example to work with, suppose we start with the recent trend of increased consolidation in the telecom and entertainment industries (TE). Chandler's (1962) research on industry formation, combined with Williamson's (1975) transaction cost theory, leads us to expect vertical integration at the beginning of a new industrial era – in this case, one based on emergent fiber optic technology. But as an industry matures and fair markets begin to prevail, Williamson predicts that firms will divest subunits acquired early on so that they can 'buy at the market' rather than administer internal pricing. Here is a broad trend that has not even begun yet. Still, we can imagine the set of agents connected with competitors, technologies, markets, and other institutions as nodes on a search grid, interconnected by links. We know that even for just 10 such agents there are more than 35 trillion possible human capital interaction patterns that could materialize into specific business opportunities or threats. The problem is one of sifting through an overwhelming number of interactions and consequent pattern possibilities. Over time they produce countless correlated histories. In Gell-Mann's terms, this is the fine-grained structure. Is there a way to get some clues about how, where, and when coarse-graining will occur?

Now we take up the problem of how to conduct a search process that works toward uncovering potential order parameters? This calls for thinking of a pattern emerging in a five-dimensional array instead of in a set of lines on paper or in a photo. Our array is i^2 TE agents by k tensions, v vantage points, and t time periods. We begin with the i^2 component.

Defining the i^2 agent set   Since our pattern is not known, we started by asking where does a pattern come from – in the previous subsection – as a way of developing a search procedure that might help our connectionist social network find it sooner rather than later. Let us suppose that our TE agents are scattered over a search space we define as an i^2 array – each of the i agents can communicate with each of the $i-1$ other agents (they may or not all be in one firm). At a bare minimum, distributed seeing is a function of some number of connections among some set of the agents in the i^2 array. Each agent represents some player in the TE arena who could link with some number of other TE players. This linking activity is what could turn into a pattern of emergent social ordering, for example, a new combination of agents working toward a new technology or market approach. In a sea of agents, as the connections increase, a pattern may emerge and become discernible. But, as we saw earlier, there could be many agents and hundreds of connections among them. In this case, there could be quadrillions of patterns to sift through. How to simplify and speed up the search activity?

To begin, part of what the human cellular network inside a firm has to do is define the i^2 array of TE players. Defining an optimal array may be difficult. Presumably, one can begin with a broadly agreed-upon core set of agents and then elaborate as seems appropriate. We could begin by selecting the most innovative agents from the most innovative firms along with possible university-based TE technology and market researchers. A key limitation in a situation of emergent-pattern finding is that parts of, or the entire pattern, may be 'outside the box' of the easily recognized players. Much of this has to do with defining the adaptive tensions that may become the order parameters. The well-known scenario planning process could be one way to do this – it could shift links and nodes from the 'plausible' to the 'possible'. Fortunately, there are ways to expedite this, which we discuss next. We do not mean to discount the difficulty of defining the i^2 array, but we do believe that a well-working cellular network can do this; we pursue this latter point in the fastsight section.

Defining the **k** *adaptive tensions (potential order parameters)*   In the framework of Darwinian selectionist evolutionary theory, the relevant interaction patterns of organisms cannot be defined without understanding the variables defining a system's environmental context – that is, the resources that a better-adapted system could gain access to and the various constraints that might inhibit successful adaptation. One way to narrow the elements of environmental context that are most apt to define the order parameters is to focus on those resources and constraints creating the most adaptive tension. To get a long lead in biology, we would study the geological trends mentioned earlier.

We take a cue from what McKelvey (2004b) calls the '0th law of thermodynamics'. This is a law about where order comes from, that is, what causes new order to appear. We have outlined some of the most basic elements of this law via the previous eight points defining the process by which the many contextual tensions reduce down to one or a few of Haken's order parameters. In the natural world, new order begins with energy differentials of sufficient strength to cause phase transitions. McKelvey (2001, 2008) translates energy differentials as 'adaptive tension' when applied to social systems. Adaptive tension results when a system is at some state, x, and to be fully adapted to one or more environmental states, it needs to be in state y. When the tension defined as $y - x$ exceeds some *critical value*, R_{c1}, a process of new order creation begins and the beginnings of the newly emerging pattern start to appear. Building on the 0th law, we anticipate that searching only where adaptive tensions above their critical values[3] impose upon the target system offers an effective method for reducing many, if not most, agent interactions to fine-grained structure – which can be ignored.

Adaptive tensions inducing learning, improved fitness or performance, innovation, and so on, activate agents to start the coevolution process leading to new order. In the TE system there could be any number of adaptive tensions stemming from its particular context. The tensions have to be high enough that they exceed the threshold gates of each of the many agents. If no agent is activated there cannot be an emergent social-structural pattern. Presumably, in a setting consisting of a list of known resources and constraints, those having the most existing or potential adaptive tension have the highest probability of becoming order parameters. This is to say, of the tensions that are rising toward R_{c1} the fastest are most likely to become order parameters. Tensions that (i) have the most impact on the TE sector; (ii) are least understood by TE agents; or (iii) simply negate the relevance of other tensions for TE, also have high probability of becoming order parameters. The third kind have the effect of lowering the value of R_{c1} – they will activate agents at lower levels of tension. Each one could create tension high enough – that is, above R_{c1} – to activate some number of agents to begin the coevolutionary order-creation process. This results in k adaptive tensions.

The several contextual tensions parallel the roles of different kinds of telescopes or different colored lenses. Each tension could highlight some agent interactions, leaving most unrecognized. Each different kind of telescope highlights different parts of the spectrum. More specifically, for example, a red lens highlights red agents; a yellow lens highlights yellow agents; and so on. If five 'colors' of agents are imagined to be most important in defining the state space of an emergent phenomenon, the five relevant colored lenses could be used to highlight patterns among the relevant agents, leaving all other agents and patterns to be ignored. Pattern finding is only as good as 'seeing'. The different tensions, like different telescopes or different colored lenses, improve seeing ability. This particular seeing ability, then, begins to identify the order parameters, which, in turn, drive the coarse-graining process.

Defining the k tensions depends on the ability of the cellular network to 'see' relevant contexts and their embedded tensions. How to improve 'seeing?'. Members good at defining the agents most relevant to the i^2 array may not be as competent as others in defining the contextual tensions. Presumably some members of the network would specialize on 'seeing' relevant contextual variables. Good seeing is also a function of vantage points.

Defining the v *vantage points*   Part of the problem in seeing is that perception is often biased by the viewer's local situation, existing biases, and learned perspectives. Musicians see different things from physicists; Arabs see different things from Europeans and Americans; poor people see different things from rich ones; travelers see different things from those who do not travel; and so on. People caught up in existing patterns may not see new ones. The continuing availability of heterogeneous agents cannot be taken for granted. There are many forces in organizations that lead to 'groupthink' (Janis, 1972). The control systems that are so prevalent in organizations (Morgan, 1997; Jones, 2000) invariably damp out heterogeneity (March, 1991) and lower-level innovation, and self-organizing capability, as shown in Thomas et al. (2005).

If all the agents are the same, there is no advantage to networking (Holland, 1995). End of story! We cannot overstate the fact that the more that agents in the cellular network view the $i^2 \times k$ part of the array from different vantage points, the more likely they will see emerging patterns. Further, perspectives from different vantage points may lead to more realistic definitions of i and k. This process is essentially a function of how heterogeneous the agents are. We know from biology that when there is very low diversity in a gene pool, the less adaptive a species is[4] – this shows up from inbred members of European monarchies to species such as the California condor or cheetah – all of which are on the edge of extinction. Recall that agent heterogeneity is a founding principle of agent-based computational models. Models by Johnson (2000), Allen (2001), and LeBaron (2002), for example, demonstrate that when agents become less heterogeneous, the systems in which they function lose adaptive capability. Recent research on the importance of biodiversity reported in *The Economist* (2006) supports this point as do two recent books: *The Wisdom of Crowds* (Surowiecki, 2004) and *The Difference: How the Power of Diversity Creates Better Groups, Firms, Schools, and Societies* (Page, 2007). Whereas agent-based model builders can assume agent heterogeneity simply from the process of randomly assigning fitness levels and capabilities, this is not so with human connectionist networks.

How many vantage points are necessary? If the nth vantage point to be added offers no new patterns, then no more are needed.

Defining the **t** *time periods*   Given i^2 dots, k contexts and v vantage points, there could still be a large number of emergent-appearing patterns. An additional way of thinning the field is to look at patterns surviving across some number of time periods. Time periods also act like different colored lenses or different kinds of telescopes in offering different views of patterns. Patterns that appear robust in an early time period may disappear in later ones. Usually, patterns that persist across some number of time periods are the ones to pay attention to. Presumably a connectionist network would start with patterns remaining after the k and v processes have winnowed out many, if not most patterns. These patterns would be tested in as few subsequent periods as necessary to, well, see that the pattern holds up over time.

Summary

In this section we have explicitly used 'complexity to destroy complexity', taking a cue from Ashby's famous phrase, 'It takes variety to destroy variety'. We used complexity theory to outline how patterns form in a complex world. We then used the same theory to develop a farsight search process centered on the i^2, by k, v, t array. In the next section we shall use the same complexity theory to show how contextual tensions motivate and steer the formation of a firm's distributed seeing via connectionist social networks, assuming that they are free enough from top-management control effects to actually form and become robust enough to take on the pattern-search process.

Managing *fast*sight dynamics via the sub-forces

> My work is in a building that houses three thousand people who are essentially the individual 'particles' of the 'brain' of an organization that consists of sixty thousand people worldwide. (Zohar, 1997, p. xv)

Zohar starts her book by quoting Andrew Stone, Director of the retailing giant, Marks and Spencer: each particle has some intellectual capability – Becker's 'human capital'. And some of them talk to each other – Burt's 'social capital'. But, together they comprise 'distributed intelligence'. Human capital is a property of individual employees. Taken to the extreme, even geniuses offer a firm only minimal adaptive capability if they are isolated from everyone else. A firm's core competencies, dynamic capabilities, and knowledge requisite for competitive advantage increasingly appear as *networks* of human capital holders. These knowledge networks also increasingly appear throughout firms rather than being narrowly confined to upper management (Norling, 1996). Employees are now responsible for adaptive capability rather than just being bodies to carry out orders. Here is where networks become critical. Much of the effectiveness and economic value of human capital held by individuals has been shown to be subject to the nature of the social networks in which the human agents are embedded (Granovetter, 1985; Nohria and Eccles, 1992; Burt, 1997).

Intelligence in brains rests entirely on the production of emergent networks among neurons – intelligence *is* the network (Fuster, 1995, p. 11). Neurons behave as simple 'threshold gates' that have one behavioral option – fire or not fire (p. 29). As intelligence increases, it is represented in the brain as *emergent* connections (synaptic links) among neurons. Human intelligence is 'distributed' across really dumb agents! In computer parallel-processing systems, computers play the role of neurons. They are more 'node based' than 'network based'. Artificial intelligence (AI) resides in the *intelligence capability* of the computers as agents, with emergent network-based intelligence rather primitive (Garzon, 1995). AI models increasingly are used to simulate learning processes in firms, though their intelligence capability is not fully connectionist and the intelligence of their agents is minimal – far below that, even, of PCs (Prietula et al., 1998). Our focus on distributed intelligence/seeing places most of the emphasis on the emergence of constructive connectionist networks. Of course, firms that have constructive networks among geniuses usually will fare better than those having great networks among idiots. The lesson from brains and computers is that organizational intelligence is best seen as 'distributed' and that increasing it depends on fostering network development along with increasing agents' human capital. Thus, 'Who is doing the looking?' is a function of the distributed intelligence and seeing capability of an organization. Distributed-seeing ability depends on how well the connectionist networks work. The better they work, the faster the seeing.

We cannot overemphasize our combining of human and social capital. Economists, stressing human capital, and focusing on neoclassical market concepts, assume that intelligence is only in the nodes and not in the emergent system. Sociologists, stressing social networks, assume that intelligence is in the network, and, further, that whatever capabilities nodes have result from their embeddedness in the network. We, along with complexity scientists, assume both: intelligence resides in the connectionist network *and* in its nodes as well.

Fastsight lessons from complexity science dynamics
How to speed up fastsight capability in a firm? How to get insights about a changing environment faster than the competition? How to improve the operating speed of emergent connectionist networks in firms that are playing the role of the astronomers' distributed seeing 'arrays' we mentioned earlier? How can complexity science help?

Complexity science defines the basic process by which connectionist networks form. Connectionist networks are the 'seeing' devices for complexity scientists. They appear most obviously as 'genetic algorithm' (Holland, 1975, 1995; Mitchell, 1996; Pal and Wang, 1996) and 'neural network' pattern recognition devices (Bishop, 1995; Bartlett and Anthony, 1999). Boisot and McKelvey (2006a,b) develop this technology into a basic approach for improving organizational pattern-recognition ability. They also focus on how to improve the speed at which pattern recognition can be accomplished.

Defining agent interaction and emergence dynamics   For complexity theorists, connectionist networks act as the basic pattern-recognition devices in firms. The more complex the external environment, therefore, the more complex the internal network must be – the more complex pattern creation is on the outside, the more sophisticated pattern recognition must be on the inside. Thompson (1967) and charismatic vision leadership theorists (Bennis, 1996) put all the emphasis on top management as the preferred pattern-recognition device. Thompson's argument was that top management absorbed the uncertainty thereby creating predictable, machine-like conditions for lower-level employees to work in. Mélèse (1991) takes the opposite view, as we do here, which is that only a social network matching complexity with that of the environment can reasonably cope with incoming uncertainty. This follows from Ashby's law, which we mentioned earlier.

Holland (1988, p. 117–18) summarizes key elements of complex adaptive systems:

1. 'Dispersed Interaction' – dispersed, possibly heterogeneous, agents active in parallel;
2. 'No Global Controller or Cause' – *coevolution* of agent interactions;
3. 'Many Levels of Organization' – agents at lower levels create contexts at higher levels;
4. 'Continual Adaptation' – agents revise their adaptive behavior continually;
5. 'Perpetual Novelty' – by changing in ways that allow them to depend on new resources, agents coevolve with resource changes to occupy new habitats; and
6. 'Out-of-Equilibrium Dynamics' – economies operate *far from equilibrium*, meaning that economies are induced by the pressure of trade imbalances – individual-to-individual, firm-to-firm, country-to-country, and so on (headings in quotes are from Arthur, Durlauf and Lane, 1997, pp. 3–4).

'Emergent self-organization' begins when three elements are present: (i) heterogeneous agents; (ii) connections among the agents; and (iii) motive to connect – such as mating instincts, improved fitness, performance, and learning. Take any one away and nothing happens. Self-organization results in emergence, that is, new order of some kind. According to Holland (2002) we recognize emergent dynamics when we see multiple levels (hierarchy), intra- and inter-level causal dynamics, and nonlinearity.

We highlight two elements from the foregoing list in italics: 'coevolution' and 'far from equilibrium'. The coevolution term signifies a key nonlinear outcome for biologists and social scientists at the Santa Fe Institute. The 'far from equilibrium' phrase hooks these elements into physical scientists' interest in the triggering of phase transitions and consequent new structure and processes (Prigogine and Stengers, 1984). If the connectionist networks in firms do not have these characteristics, they are not going to serve as effective and timely pattern recognition devices. In short, fastsight depends on a firm having the foregoing network attributes. As you can see, the first critical value, R_{c1}, shows up in internal complexity dynamics as well.

Coevolution dynamics   To understand how connectionist social networks self-organize to create (new pattern recognition) structures, Santa Fe complexity scientists focus on coevolution, nonlinearity, and small instigating events – Holland's (2002) 'levers'. Coevolution of heterogeneous, adaptive learning, agents is the 'engine' of order creation. What instigates bursts of nonlinear order creation via coevolution? Gleick (1987) details chaos theory, its focus on the so-called butterfly effect – a 'butterfly-lever', if you will – (the fabled story of a butterfly flapping its wings in Brazil causing a storm in Texas

(Lorenz, 1972)), and aperiodic behavior ever since the founding paper by Lorenz (1963). Arthur (1990, 2000) focuses on positive feedbacks stemming from levers. In the Santa Fe view, butterfly-levers initiate agent coevolution which results in social networks able to self-organize into kinds of connectionist networks capable of distributed seeing and pattern recognition (Boisot and McKelvey, 2006a,b).

In his classic paper, Maruyama (1963) discusses 'mutual causal' processes mostly with respect to biological coevolution. He also distinguishes between the 'deviation-counter-acting' *negative* feedback most familiar to general systems theorists (Buckley, 1968) and 'deviation-amplifying' *positive* feedback processes (Milsum, 1968). Negative feedback control systems such as thermostats are most familiar to us. Boulding (1968) and Arthur (1990, 2000) focus on 'positive feedbacks' in economies. Positive feedback effects emerge when a microphone is placed near a speaker, resulting in a high-pitched squeal. Mutual causal or coevolutionary processes are inherently nonlinear – large-scale effects may be instigated by very small initiating events, as noted by Gleick (1987), Ormerod (1998) and Holland (2002). McKelvey (2002) discusses the role of damping processes pertaining to coevolutionary behavior – coevolution dynamics can go fast or slow, and in good or bad directions.

The Santa Fe researchers explain how agent interactions can produce nonlinearities of avalanche proportions every now and then. But they do not often explain what activates the agents in ways that are useful for those of us studying firms. In Bak's (1996) sandpiles, for example, a falling grain of sand can be the 'lever' that sets off the movement of a few grains of sand or a large avalanche, but taken for granted in his analysis is gravity – the energy gradient that causes the sand to fall in the first place. We now turn to the physicists' exogenous (adaptive) tension theories to explain how agents become activated. If the levers that instigate coevolution are seen as sparks, adaptive tension can be seen as the cloud of gas waiting to explode into a nonlinearity event. Both are required!

Adaptive tension dynamics   How can CEOs improve distributed seeing connectionist networks in their firms? How can they steer them toward more fruitful directions? Complexity theory points the way. It emphasizes critical values in adaptive tension and consequent phase transitions. By emphasizing one adaptive tension over others, CEOs can steer distributed seeing in one direction or another. Cramer (1993) identifies three levels of complexity – defined in Box 1.3 – depending on how much information is necessary to explain the complexity: Newtonian complexity, emergent complexity, and stochastic complexity. Complexity science (Nicolis and Prigogine, 1989) shows that the separation of the region of emergent complexity from the other kinds is a function of the ambient energy impinging on a system of agents. The region of emergent complexity is the 'melting zone' (Kauffman, 1993) between the first critical value, R_{c1} (the 'edge of order'), and the second critical value, R_{c2} (the so-called 'edge of chaos').

The boundaries of emergent complexity are defined by 'critical values', R_c (Cramer, 1993). Nicolis and Prigogine (1989) describe the function of R_c in natural science. Nothing is so basic to their definition of complexity science as the Bénard cell – two plates with fluid in between (Bénard, 1901) – equivalent to high heat at the bottom of a teapot and less heat at the top. An energy (heat) differential between the plates – defined here as 'adaptive tension', T (Temperature or Tension) – creates a molecular motion of some velocity, R, as hotter molecules move toward the colder plate. The energy differential in the Bénard cell

---

BOX 1.3   DEFINITIONS OF KINDS OF COMPLEXITY BY CRAMER (1993)*

Below the first critical value 'Newtonian complexity' exists where the amount of information necessary to describe the system is less complex than the system itself. Thus a rule, such as $F = ma = md^2s/dt^2$ is much simpler in information terms than trying to describe the myriad states, velocities, and acceleration rates pursuant to understanding the force of a falling object. 'Systems exhibiting subcritical [Newtonian] complexity are strictly deterministic and allow for exact prediction' (1993, p. 213). They are also 'reversible' (allowing retrodiction as well as prediction thus making the 'arrow of time' irrelevant (Eddington, 1930; Prigogine, 1997).

Above the second critical value is 'chaotic complexity'. Cramer lumps both chaotic and stochastic systems into this category, although deterministic chaos is recognized as fundamentally different from stochastic complexity (Morrison, 1991; Gell-Mann, 1994) since the former is 'simple rule' driven, and stochastic systems are random, though varying in their stochasticity. For random complexity, description of a system is as complex as the system itself – the minimum number of information bits necessary to describe the states is equal to the complexity of the system. Probabilistic distributions in stochastically complex systems allow some algorithmic compressibility. Thus, three kinds of stochastic complexity are recognized: *purely random*, *probabilistic*, and *deterministic chaos*. For this chapter we narrow the label to deterministic chaos, at the risk of oversimplification.

In between Cramer puts 'emergent complexity'. The defining aspect of this category is the possibility of emergent simple deterministic structures fitting Newtonian complexity criteria, even though the underlying phenomena remain in the stochastically complex category. It is here that natural forces ease the investigator's problem by offering intervening objects as 'simplicity targets' the behavior of which lends itself to simple-rule explanation. Cramer (1993, pp. 215–17) has a long table categorizing all kinds of phenomena according to his scheme.

Note: * For mnemonic purposes we use 'Newtonian' instead of Cramer's 'subcritical', 'stochastic' instead of 'fundamental', and 'emergent' instead of 'critical' complexity.

---

parallels that between the hot surface of the earth and the cold upper atmosphere – hotter air molecules move upward and if they move fast enough, create storm cells. Complexity science cannot be understood without appreciating the role that T plays in defining the region of complexity between the 'edge of order' and the 'edge of chaos'. If T increases beyond R_{c2}, the agent-system jumps into the region of chaotic complexity. The system may even oscillate between the order and chaos basins of attraction – a chaotic state indeed! Definitions of attractors are given in Box 1.4. Thus, for molecular agents:

BOX 1.4   DEFINITIONS OF ATTRACTORS BY GLEICK (1987)

'Point attractors' act as equilibrium points. A system, even though oscillating or perturbed, eventually returns to repetitious behavior centered around the point attractor – traditional control style management decision structures may act in this manner (appearing as Newtonian complexity).

'Periodic attractors' or 'limit cycles' (pendulum behavior) foster oscillation predictably from one extreme to another – recurrent shifts in the centralization and decentralization of decision making, or functional specialization versus cross-functional integration fit here (also appearing as Newtonian complexity).

If adaptive tension is raised beyond some critical value, systems may be subject to 'strange attractors' in that, if plotted, they show never intersecting, stable, low-dimensional, nonperiodic spirals and loops, that are not attracted by some central equilibrium point, but nevertheless appear constrained not to breach the confines of what might appear as an imaginary bottle. If they intersected, the system would be in equilibrium (Gleick, 1987, p. 140) following a point attractor. The attractor is 'strange' because it 'looks' as though the system is oscillating around a central equilibrium point, but it isn't. Instead, as an energy importing and dissipating structure, it is responding with unpredictable self-organized structure to tensions created by imposed external conditions, such as tension between different heat gradients in the atmosphere caught between a hot surface of the earth and a cold upper atmosphere, or constraints in a fluid flow at the junction of two pipes, or tension created by newly created dissipative structures, such as eddies in a turbulent fluid flow in a canyon below a waterfall, or 'MBA terrorist' structural changes imposed in an attempt to turn around an acquired firm.

As a metaphor, think of a point attractor as a rabbit on an elastic tether – the rabbit moves in all directions but as it tires it is pulled toward the middle by the elastic tether where it lies down to rest. Think of a strange attractor as a rabbit in a pen with a fox on the outside – the rabbit keeps running to the side of the pen opposite from the moving fox but as it tires it comes to rest in the middle of the pen. The rabbit ends up in the 'middle' in either case. With the tether the cause is the *pull* of the elastic. In the pen the cause is *repulsion* from the fox unsystematically attacking from all sides.

- Below R_{c1} – the *edge of order* – agents show minimal response in reducing T – molecules vibrate in place but 'conduct' energy by colliding with each other.
- Above R_{c1} – the *edge of order* – agents show collective action toward reducing T. Gas molecules start bulk currents of 'convection' movement, as the molecules actually circle around from hot to cold and back to hotter plate, or generate strong bulk currents of air flowing up and down from earth's surface to upper atmosphere – the air turbulence and storm cells that create rough airplane rides.

- Above R_{c2} – the *edge of chaos* – the molecular movements become chaotic. For example, if T between hot lower air and cold upper air increases further, perhaps by the conflation of warm moist air from the south and cold air from the north, say over Kansas, R_{c2}, may be exceeded. At this point the storm cell may oscillate between two basins of attraction, order and chaos, that is, tornadic and non-tornadic behavior.

Translating to firms, suppose a large firm acquires another firm needing a turnaround. Suppose T stays below R_{c1}; existing management stays in place and little change is imposed by the acquiring firm. There is little reason for people in the acquired firm to create new structures. Instead, there might be only 'conduction' type changes in the sense that new turnaround ideas percolate slowly from one person to another person adjacent in a network. If T goes above R_{c2}, complexity theory predicts chaos. Suppose that the acquiring firm changes several of the acquired firm's top managers and sends in 'MBA terrorists' to change the management systems 'overnight' – new budgeting and information systems; new personnel procedures, promotion approaches, and benefits packages; new production and marketing systems. And suppose that the acquired firm's culture and day-to-day interaction patterns are changed as well. In this circumstance, two basins of attraction could coincide: one centered around the comfortable pre-acquisition ways of doing business and resistance to change, and the other defined around demands of the MBA terrorists. The activities of the system could oscillate chaotically between these two basins.

Between R_{c1} and R_{c2} lies the organizational equivalent of Cramer's emergent complexity or Kauffman's melting zone. Here, network structures emerge to solve T problems. Using the storm cell metaphor, in this region the 'heat conduction' of interpersonal dynamics between sporadically communicating individuals is insufficient to reduce the observed T. To pick up the adaptive pace, the equivalent of organizational storm cells consisting of 'bulk' adaptive work-flows starts. Formal or informal structures emerge, such as new network formations, informal or formal group activities, departments, entrepreneurial ventures, and so on. Although the Ts in organization science are unlikely to have the precise values they appear to have in some natural sciences (Johnson and Burton, 1994), a probability distribution of such values will exist for individual firms and each of their subunits. Although precise values of T for firms do not exist, we do know about symptoms indicating whether a firm is below R_{c1}, in between, or above R_{c2} (Brown and Eisenhardt, 1998; McKelvey, 2008).

Steps toward better-distributed seeing via emergent complexity[5]

Adaptive tension   For distributed intelligence and seeing to be improved, CEOs need to ensure that the corporate brain is exposed to the full range of 'Ts' 'out there' – that surround the agents – that might energize emergent order. At GE, Jack Welch used 'Be #1 or 2 in your industry' – a very clear motivational valance. Respond to the T or your division 'will be fixed, sold, or closed' (Tichy and Sherman, 1994, p. 108; paraphrased). Thus, Ts are the root motivation causing agents to self-organize.

While agents in a teapot face just one T (heat), the adaptive tension confronting the many agents within a firm – as receivers – could appear as countless Ts. In addition, there are many Ts reflecting forces and constraints in the environment, not to mention

*T*s created by numerous agents within competing firms – from the CEO down to the people in engineering, production, marketing, sales, and so on. An agent network could emerge virtually anywhere in a firm around an initiative to produce a better part, product, marketing approach, new strategy, a cost reduction, and so forth. Consequently, there is danger in a priori trying to focus certain kinds of *T*s toward specific kinds of agents. This might preclude the emergence of the most effective new networks. But there is an equal danger in trying to flood every agent with every kind of *T*. It is also clear that 'selecting' the nature of the incoming *T*s based on preconceived CEO-level notions, as Roger Smith did at GM for a decade (Hunt and Ropo, 1998), puts blinders on the corporate brain. Toyota is well known for its system of increasing the awareness of workers about how well their designs and products compete against the competition – a small set of narrowly defined *T*s. Welch accomplished the same objective by defining *T*s very broadly as, 'Be #1 or 2 in your industry!'. This is a perfect example of using a simple piece of information to focus attention on a particular aspect of the competitive environment – everything is boiled down to one *T* that *drives* the lower-level systems without the command-and-control structure *defining* them. Strong corporate leadership is shown without setting up a suppressive command-and-control structure or otherwise inhibiting emergent distributed intelligence. Hamel and Prahalad's 'strategic intent' (1989) fits this perspective as well and their concept of 'stretch' equates to Welch's 'Be # 1 . . . '.

Critical values   Assuming that agents are confronted by the appropriate *T*s, managing the critical values aspect of adaptive tension requires three basic activities: (i) checking whether behavioral symptoms of *T*s impinging on one or more agents are below, between, or above R_c; (ii) altering motivational valances to move the *T* levels into the region between R_{c1} and R_{c2}; and (iii) widening the distance between R_{c1} and R_{c2}.

As noted above, critical values are not precisely determined in firms – as they are in natural science. Nor does current research indicate what levels of *T*s are below, between, or above the critical values. For now we have to rely on behavioral symptoms for evidence about *T* effects. Brown and Eisenhardt (B/E) (1998) identify some symptoms. For example, as indications that *T* is *below* R_{c1}, B/E point to overbearing structure, fiefdoms, little novelty, and reactive strategizing. For evidence that *T* is *above* R_{c2}, B/E point to random communication, overcoordination, politics, modular structures disconnected, and sporadic intense experimentation too narrowly focused.

There are also direct symptoms of emergence. In general, *T* between R_{c1} and R_{c2} produces emergent dissipative structures, which then start reducing *T*, at which point they dissipate. For example:

1. Emergent social networks such as dyadic or triadic communication channels, informal or formal teams, groups, or other network configurations.
2. More effective networks within or across groups, more structural equivalence, better proportions of strong and weak ties, increased numbers of structural holes (Burt, 1992), more networks emerging between hostile groups – marketing with engineering, or with production, with suppliers, with customers, and so forth.
3. Emergent networks of any kind, networks that produce novel outcomes, new strategies, new product ideas, new directions of knowledge accumulation.
4. Networks that speed up rates of adaptive-event occurrence.

Widening the region of emergence requires operating on the definition of the critical values themselves – lowering R_{c1}, raising R_{c2} – rather than only trying to adjust the Ts to fall in between. Anything that gets networks to form more easily, or sooner, is essentially lowering R_{c1}. Raising R_{c2} requires training agents to develop (i) more effective emergent structures – so tension stops rising and starts dissipating; and (ii) higher 'tension tolerance' to handle higher tension levels before 'going chaotic'. For example, employees in high-velocity firms in Silicon Valley work routinely in an atmosphere of adaptive tension far higher than might ever appear in large dinosauric utility firms or government agencies.

Attractors   The previous two subsections work on the 'fostering-and-speeding-up-emergence' part. Now we turn to the problem of 'steering' without inadvertently fostering the emergence of a suppressive command-and-control bureaucracy. Recall the definitions of 'point' and 'strange attractors' in Box 1.4.

Bureaucratic negative feedback systems center around point attractors. A visionary CEO operates as one – his/her vision is the goal, which becomes the equilibrium point toward which negative feedback-driven managerial control processes define the system. Since firms do need strong leaders, and since some people like being strong leaders and behave like strong leaders, it is pointless to think of avoiding point attractors. The trick is to aim these 'strong leader types' toward using point attractors that 'drive' the system toward reducing the Ts but do not 'define' them in the command-and-control ways that inhibit emergence. Ts *are* point attractors. Activities that serve to reduce Ts, thus, are point attractors. Hamel and Prahalad's 'strategic intent' could inadvertently become a point attractor rather than acting more like Welch's content-*less* tension directive – 'Be #1 or 2 or else . . . '. Mackey et al. (2006) detail how Welch did this, using quotes from Slater (2001) as evidence.

Remaining strong leader activities are best redefined to be strange attractors. This is probably the best way in which to view Bennis's (1996) 'herding cats' metaphor – the 'cage' effect of the rabbit and fox metaphor in Box 1.4. We may use what Morgan (1997, p. 98) refers to as 'cybernetic reference points' and 'avoidance of noxiants' to define the reflective cage of a strange attractor without defining goals that act as point attractors. Strange attractor 'definitions of the cage' must be created without determining specific or repeating paths – characteristics of point attractors and opposite the definition of novelty. Welch did this quite well (Mackey et al., 2006).

Incentives should encourage the proper delineation, separation, and development of point and strange attractors. It is easy to define point attractor incentives – 'Here is the goal and we will pay more if you achieve it'. Saying 'No' is all too easy in firms and seldom needs to be encouraged. Setting up 'inexpensive experiment' strange attractor systems seems more risky. Learning when to discontinue an experimental product development activity is problematic (Royer, 2003). Strange attractors also need to be made attractive for agents 'inside the cage'.

To accomplish this, good strategy depends on having effective strategy production processes inside organizations. We have defined a social information processing model that is a bottom-up and social network-oriented *community* process emphasizing distributed intelligence and social capital. This is very different from the purely *hierarchical organizational* one presented by Galbraith (1973) and Galbraith et al. (1993), which, though decentralized, is still very much a top-down creation.

A good strategy-finding process, then, depends on a CEO's ability to unleash the kinds of forces that produce the right kind of organizational climate – one that allows connectionist social networks to form. Needless to say, the fast- and farsight processes we discuss do not happen in just any old firm. *The Economist* (2001) gives an analysis showing that the CEO firing rate has dramatically increased in recent years – even before the dotcom bust. Bennis and O'Toole (2000) say it is due to the fact that boards cannot find CEOs with the right vision. We think leadership theory is at fault (Marion and Uhl-Bien, 2001; Mackey et al., 2006; Uhl-Bien et al., 2007). If CEOs are listening to leadership theorists such as Bennis (1996), they are applying archaic thinking to 21st-century knowledge economy problems.

Summary
In this subsection we drew from Prigogine, Haken, and Mainzer to explain how energy and/or tension levels exceeding the first critical value, R_{c1}, create dramatic instigations toward change in physical, biological, and organizational situations. We also drew on Holland, Kauffman, and others connected with the Santa Fe Institute to explain how new order emerges in complex adaptive systems composed of heterogeneous agents. We then showed how managers can use adaptive tension to activate the agents so as to create more active or vibrant complex adaptive systems, thereby increasing the possibility that coevolutionary dynamics toward new structure and processes are set in motion. The critical idea is for managers to create melting zones in their firms, that are in between the *edge of order*, R_{c1}, and the *edge of chaos*, R_{c2}. These adaptive systems, then, are more capable of the *fast*sight dynamics needed for a firm to meet the requisite complexity standards we set forth in the *far*sight section. We see Jack Welch as having done this better than most other CEOs.

Charismatic vision versus distributed seeing

Charisma is narcissism looking for an echo. (Max Boisot, Sitges, Spain, 2003)

Could it be that leadership theory is antithetical to CEOs trying to create distributed seeing? Dansereau and Yammarino's (DY) (1998a,b) summary table (1998b, p. xxxix) shows leadership theory to be focused on attributes of leaders and their effects on groups of followers and on individual followers in dyads – corroborated by Klein and House (1998, p. 9). To use Dubin's (1979) phrases, this is mostly 'leadership in organizations' rather than 'leadership of organizations'. In the DY books, only Hunt and Ropo (1998) concentrate on leadership *of* organizations via their case analysis of Roger Smith's years as CEO of General Motors. The Klein and House (1998) chapter on charismatic leadership focuses on leadership of subordinates at different levels *in* firms – leader–subordinate dyads at different levels – rather than leadership *down through* a firm's several levels.

Leadership in the DY books is multilevel. Visionary leadership cascades down one level at a time. Bennis and his colleagues (Bennis and Nanus, 1985; Bennis and Biederman, 1996) zero in on leaders who successfully reorient multilevel sets of followers in organizations. They abandon trait and situational theories for a skill-based theory built around leaders able to get subordinates to follow their vision. Bennis (1996, p. 156) says:

> Leading means doing the right things . . . creating a compelling, overarching vision. . . . It's about *living* [original italics] the vision, day in day out – embodying it – and empowering every other person . . . to implement and execute that vision. . . . The vision has to be shared. And the only way that it can be shared is for it to have meaning for the people who are involved in it. *Leaders have to specify the steps that behaviorally fit into that vision, and then reward people for following those steps* [added italics].

But he also says the opposite: 'The problem facing almost all leaders in the future will be how to develop their organization's social architecture so that it actually generates intellectual capital' (p. 149).

Bennis follows the charismatic leadership theory of House (1977) and Nanus (1992). Klein and House (1998, p. 3) say 'charisma is a fire that ignites followers' energy, commitment, and performance'. In dwelling primarily on the 'mythic', 'heroic', 'visionary', upper echelon leaders, Bennis works at cross-purposes with distributed sensemaking and speeding up the rate of distributed seeing.[6] In the last quote above it is the brain of the leader that creates the vision and followers are rewarded (in the context of command-and-control structure) for carrying it out. And yet, as Bennis himself says, 'people at the periphery of organizations are usually the most creative and often the least consulted' (1996, p. 152). Bennis does not answer the question: 'How to lead the corporate brain without damaging its distributed intelligence or seeing ability?'.

How does the visionary CEO suppress emergent distributed intelligence? First, heroic visionary leaders tend to create 'strong cultures' (Peters and Waterman, 1982; Schein, 1990). The role of entrepreneurs as visionary creators of organizational culture has been noted (Siehl, 1985). Kotter and Heskett (1992) observe that organizational performance is connected to adaptive cultures and that leaders play a key role in culture change. Sorensen (2002) shows that strong cultures are assets in stable environments but liabilities in changing times. Leaders are seen as molding employees' views about a firm and defining their roles within it (Bryman, 1996). Willmott (1993) claims that culture management is simply a new form of managerial control. Bryman (1996, p. 285) notes that Martin's (1992) 'integration perspective' points to leaders who go about 'creating, maintaining or changing cultures' in the normative manner outlined by the foregoing authors.

Second, consider a recent discussion of CEO-level charismatic leadership by Waldman and Yammarino (1999). They focus on strategy formulation by upper echelon managers, that is, leadership *across several levels*. Three propositions are:

- 'Charismatic attributions toward the CEO at lower echelons will result in heightened organizational member effort and intergroup cohesion, especially under conditions of perceived environmental volatility' (p. 276).
- 'Intergroup cohesion will result in linkages regarding the performance objectives of units within an organization so that the subsequent performance of units will be co-coordinated toward higher-level organizational performance' (p. 277).
- 'Coordinated operational performance of subunits will lead to higher organizational performance, especially when units are interdependent' (p. 278).

These propositions are telling because they: (i) focus on leadership across several intervening levels of organization, thus fitting our focus on CEOs leading the entire firm; and

(ii) relate charismatic leadership to group cohesion and coordination which, then, leads to better achievement of 'objectives' – that is, point attractors.

Some leaders may have visions that are correct, innovative, and up to date in high-velocity environments. But what if the heroic leader's one brain is not up to the job? How to get the corporate brain to come to the rescue? Left unsaid, but nevertheless supported by the Waldman/Yammarino propositions, is the idea we wish to stress: upper echelon charismatic leadership produces cohesion and leader-defined 'groupthink' (Janis, 1972) across intervening levels where one would instead want to see emergent distributed seeing ability. Charismatic leadership, thus, produces a corporate brain mirroring the CEO's, and once it is made pervasive via incentive systems, it emerges as a pervasive, rigidifying corporate culture preserving the status quo groupthink.

We note parenthetically that CEOs, in effect, can shape their firm's internal selection environment. A good leader establishes mechanisms for generating variety and mechanisms for selecting from such variety once generated. Given Salthe's (1985) triadic structure, for example, the production of blind variations and selection (Campbell, 1965) occurs at all three levels. The promulgation of a severe selection environment, however, takes on the characteristics of a strong point attractor. If selection is too strong, diversity is driven out at lower levels. Thus, in organisms, a mutation rate remains, which keeps diversity going. If too strong a selection process were to reduce the error rate, species could lose adaptive capability. Argyris (1957) referred to this as 'passive dependence' among lower-level organizational employees (agents). Given Bhaskar's three planes of transcendental realism, too severe a CEO selection process drives causality on the lower planes underground, as it were, bringing to life rebellious informal organizations or, given our perspective, denies the firm the advantages of distributed seeing and intelligence.

Summary
In this section we reviewed basic arguments why current leadership theory works to shut down rather than enable distributed intelligence and fastsight. While it can produce strong followership, control-oriented visionary charismatic leadership can easily produce groupthink. The only way around this is for leaders to enable distributed intelligence by setting the fastsight dynamics in motion, as we discuss in the fastsight section.

Conclusion
We translate strategic foresight into *far*sight and *fast*sight. The former focuses on *supra-forces* operating above the plane of industry competition, which is the plane of Porter's (1980) five forces. The latter focuses on the *sub-forces* operating below the plane, that is, within a firm. Drawing on complexity science, we then pursue a CEO-oriented discussion about how to foster both far- and fastseeing. We first concentrate on farsight, which is a means of helping firms look past emergent discontinuities, see them further down the road, or catch them in the emergent stage. After developing a theory of pattern formation rooted in complexity science, we use the same principle to outline a pattern-search process based on understanding when adaptive tensions become order parameters. This becomes the pattern-finding task facing the emergent connectionist networks. This consists of an i^2 by k, v, t search space. The complexity dynamics leading to efficacious fast- and farsight are recursive. Then we use complexity theory to discuss how energy differentials or adaptive tensions rising above the first critical value, R_{c1}, set off phase transitions that initiate

self-organization among agents comprising social networks in firms. This 'technology' develops connectionist, cellular networks (Miles et al., 1999) of human agents with distributed seeing capabilities. This leads to a firm's fastsight capability. We conclude by briefly mentioning ways in which control-oriented visionary CEOs can inadvertently shut down rather than enable efficacious, emergent, connectionist networks in their firms.

Bennis and O'Toole (2000) argue that lack of vision is what has led to the increased CEO firing rate that they observe. *The Economist* (2001) corroborates that the CEO firing rate has, indeed, gone up – they show that almost 1,600 CEOs had been fired in the 19 months before they published their story. It is obviously tempting for Boards to try to hire CEOs who 'appear' to be visionary leaders, and who 'apparently' can see into the future. But, the idea that Boards can actually tell who has vision and who has not seems ludicrous. The idea that leadership theorists think that Boards can do this seems equally ludicrous.

We take a more scientific approach, arguing that 'foresight' is better translated into fastsight and farsight. This idea builds on Bhaskar's (1975) 'transcendental realism'. It also builds on Salthe's notion of 'triadic structure' as the basic analytical 'unit' in all of science – to wit, that all analysis of any *system* must take into account actions of its *components* (agents) and its *environment*. For us, fastsight is a function of a firm's distributed intelligence from networked employees holding heterogeneous human capital and farsight is a function of using fastsight and adaptive tension to accomplish expedited pattern processing of its exogenous environmental complexity. In this way we use elements of basic philosophy and basic science to decompose the wizard-like concept, foresight, into two component elements, fast- and farsight. Our analysis shows that there is nothing divinely omniscient about either fast- or farsight.

Creating the needed cellular networks (Miles et al., 1999) in firms to pursue the fastsight path is not easy. McKelvey (2004a) and Mackey et al. (2006) present complexity-based 'simple rules' essential to enabling emergent social networks. Boisot (1998) discusses essential organizational conditions for knowledge development. We also present the so-called 'i^2 by k, v, t array' here, which offers a plan for pattern processing under conditions where one can expect vast numbers of possible patterns. We also develop our pattern-processing approach in more depth elsewhere (Boisot and McKelvey, 2006a,b), focusing more on the speed problem.

We conclude by stressing the recursive nature of developing far- and fastsight. Improving the one improves the other. Our use of complexity science shows that CEOs need to focus on environmentally imposed adaptive tensions that, then, may be used to initiate, motivate, and maintain their cellular networks in the fastsight mode. The presence of well-working cellular networks leads to faster pattern processing, which leads to efficacious farsight. Neither can work without the other. The bottom line is that complexity science offers a strategy-finding process *away* from foresight, vision, and witch doctoring or, put more bluntly, the hope of finding modern versions of the Oracle at Delphi. It takes internal complexity to develop strategies suitable for strategic success in a complex external environment.

Notes

1. 'Agent' is a generalized term used in agent-based computational modeling that can refer to atoms, molecules, biomolecules, cells, organisms, species, people, cognitive elements, groups, organizations, societies, and so on.

2. Quoted in Hamel (2000, p. 102).
3. As we detail early in the fastsight section, the region of emergent order (emergent complexity) exists between R_{c1} and R_{c2} (Cramer, 1993; McKelvey, 2004b), but for our purposes here only R_{c1} is important. Tension above this critical value is what activates agents – that is, the tension rate is above the threshold gate value for a sufficient number of agents that the coevolution process begins.
4. Note, however, that adaptability is most likely to occur with 'moderate' diversity (Kauffman, 1993), such as is found on a Galapagos island. Adaptation speeds up if the population's gene pool is attenuated as occurs on each of the Galapagos islands, but virtually stops if the gene pool is grossly attenuated.
5. A more detailed outline – in the form of 'simple rules' – of what CEOs can do to enable emergent, efficacious, connectionist networks in their firms appears in McKelvey (2004a) and Mackey et al. (2006).
6. As noted earlier, Jack Welch got around this problem by promulgating a 'process' vision that was actually based on the 'adaptive tension' we discussed earlier. The trouble emerges when the top-level visionary insists upon specific 'content agendas' that subordinates are incentivized to carry out.

References

Allen, P.M. (2001), 'A complex systems approach to learning, adaptive networks', *International Journal of Innovation Management*, **5**, 149–80.
Argote, L. (1999), *Organizational Learning: Creating, Retaining and Transferring Knowledge*, Norwell, MA: Kluwer.
Argyris, C. (1957), *The Individual and Organization: Some Problems of Mutual Adjustment*, Indianapolis, IN: Bobbs-Merrill.
Arthur, W.B. (1988), 'Self-reinforcing mechanisms in economics', in P. Anderson, K.J. Arrow and D. Pines (eds), *The Economy as an Evolving Complex System*, Reading, MA: Addison-Wesley, pp. 9–31.
Arthur, W.B. (1990), 'Positive feedback in the economy', *Scientific American*, **262**(2), 92–9.
Arthur, W.B. (2000), 'Complexity and the economy', in D. Colander (ed.), *The Complexity Vision and the Teaching of Economics*, Cheltenham, UK and Northampton, MA, USA: Edward Elgar, pp. 19–28.
Arthur, W.B., S.N. Durlauf and D.A. Lane (eds) (1997), *The Economy as an Evolving Complex System*, Proceedings of the Santa Fe Institute, Vol. XXVII, Reading, MA: Addison-Wesley.
Ashby, W.R. (1956), *An Introduction to Cybernetics*, London: Chapman & Hall.
Ashby, W.R. (1962), 'Principles of the self-organizing system', in H. von Foerster and G.W. Zopf (eds), *Principles of Self-Organization*, New York: Pergamon, pp. 255–78.
Audi, R. (ed.) (1995), *The Cambridge Dictionary of Philosophy*, Cambridge, UK: Cambridge University Press.
Bak, P. (1996), *How Nature Works: The Science of Self-organized Criticality*, New York: Copernicus.
Barney, J.B. (1991), 'Firm resources and sustained competitive advantage', *Journal of Management*, **17**, 99–120.
Bartlett, P.L. and M.M. Anthony (1999), *Neural Network Learning: Theoretical Foundations*, Cambridge, UK: Cambridge University Press.
Becker, G.S. (1975), *Human Capital*, 2nd edn, Chicago, IL: University of Chicago Press.
Bénard, H. (1901), 'Les Tourbillons Cellulaires dans une Nappe Liquide Transportant de la Chaleur par Convection en Régime Permanent' (The cellular whirlpools in a liquid sheet transporting heat by convection in a permanent regime), *Annales de Chimie et de Physique*, **23**, 62−144.
Bennis, W.G. (1996), 'Becoming a leader of leaders', in R. Gibson (ed.), *Rethinking the Future*, London: Brealey, pp. 148–62.
Bennis, W.G. and P.W. Biederman (1996), *Organizing Genius: The Secrets of Creative Collaboration*, Reading, MA: Addison-Wesley.
Bennis, W.G. and B. Nanus (1985), *Leaders: Strategies for Taking Charge*, New York: Harper & Row.
Bennis, W. and J. O'Toole (2000), 'Don't hire the wrong CEO', *Harvard Business Review*, **78**(May–June), 170–76.
Bhaskar, R. (1975), *A Realist Theory of Science*, London: Leeds Books, 2nd edn published by Verso (London) 1997.
Bishop, C.M. (1995), *Neural Networks for Pattern Recognition*, New York: Oxford University Press.
Boisot, M. (1998), *Knowledge Assets*, New York: Oxford University Press.
Boisot, M. and B. McKelvey (2006a), 'Speeding up strategic foresight in a dangerous, complex world: a complexity approach', in Suder (ed.) (2006), pp. 20–37.
Boisot, M. and B. McKelvey (2006b), 'A socio/computational method for staying ahead of terrorist and other adversities', in Suder (ed.) (2006), pp. 38–55.
Boulding, K.E. (1968), 'Business and economic systems', in Milsum (ed.), pp, 101–17.
Brown, S.L. and K.M. Eisenhardt (1997), 'The art of continuous change: linking complexity theory and time-paced evolution in relentlessly shifting organizations', *Administrative Science Quarterly*, **42**, 1–34.

Brown, S.L. and K.M. Eisenhardt (1998), *Competing on the Edge: Strategy as Structured Chaos*, Boston, MA: Harvard Business School Press.

Bryman, A. (1996), 'Leadership in organizations', in S.R. Clegg, C. Hardy and W.R. Nord (eds), *Handbook of Organization Studies*, Thousand Oaks, CA: Sage, pp. 276–92.

Buckley, W. (ed.) (1968), *Modern Systems Research for the Behavioral Scientist*, Chicago, IL: Aldine.

Burt, R.S. (1992), *Structural Holes: The Social Structure of Competition*, Cambridge, MA: Harvard University Press.

Burt, R.S. (1997), 'The contingent value of social capital', *Administrative Science Quarterly*, **42**, 339–65.

Campbell, D.T. (1965), 'Variation and selective retention in sociocultural evolution', in H.R. Barringer, G.B. Blanksten and R.W. Mack (eds), *Social Change in Developing Areas: A Reinterpretation of Evolutionary Theory*, Cambridge, MA: Schenkman, pp. 19–49.

Casti, J.L. (1997), *Would-Be Worlds: How Simulation is Changing the Frontiers of Science*, New York: Wiley.

Chandler, A.D., Jr (1962), *Strategy and Structure: Chapters in the History of American Industrial Enterprise*, Cambridge, MA: MIT Press.

Collins, J.G. and J.I. Porras (1994), *Built to Last*, New York: HarperCollins.

Cramer, F. (1993), *Chaos and Order: The Complex Structure of Living Things* (trans. D.L. Loewus), New York: VCH.

D'Aveni, R.A. (1994), *Hypercompetition: Managing the Dynamics of Strategic Maneuvering*, New York: Free Press.

Dansereau, F. and F.J. Yammarino (eds) (1998a), *Leadership: Multiple-Level Approaches: Classical and New Wave*, Stamford, CT: JAI Press.

Dansereau, F. and F.J. Yammarino (eds) (1998b), *Leadership: Multiple-Level Approaches: Contemporary and Alternative*, Stamford, CT: JAI Press.

Davenport, T.H. (1997), *Information Ecology: Mastering the Information and Knowledge Environment*, New York: Oxford University Press.

Dubin, R. (1979), 'Metaphors of leadership: an overview', in J.G. Hunt and L.L. Larson (eds), *Cross-Currents in Leadership*, Carbondale, IL: Southern Illinois University Press, pp. 225–38.

Economist, The (2001), 'Churning at the top', **358**(March 17), 91–101.

Economist, The (2003), 'America needs more spies', **368**(July 12), 30–31.

Economist, The (2006), 'Marine biodiversity: every little fish', **381**(November 4), 89–90.

Eddington, A. (1930), *The Nature of the Physical World*, London: Macmillan.

Eisenhardt, K.M. (1989), 'Making fast strategic decisions in high-velocity environments', *Academy of Management Journal*, **32**, 543–76.

Eisenhardt, K.M. and B.N. Tabrizi (1995), 'Accelerating adaptive processes: product innovation in the global computer industry', *Administrative Science Quarterly*, **40**, 84–110.

Eldredge, N. and J.S. Gould (1972), 'Punctuated equilibrium: an alternative to phyletic gradualism', in T.J.M. Schopf (ed.), *Models in Paleobiology*, San Francisco, CA: Freeman, Cooper, pp. 82–115.

Epstein, J.M. and R. Axtell (1996), *Growing Artificial Societies: Social Science from the Bottom Up*, Cambridge, MA: MIT Press.

Friedman, M. (1953), 'Methodology of positive economics', in *Essays in Positive Economics*, Chicago, IL: University of Chicago Press, pp. 3–43.

Fuster, J. M. (1995), *Memory in the Cerebral Cortex: An Empirical Approach to Neural Networks in the Human and Nonhuman Primate*, Boston, MA: MIT Press.

Galbraith, J.R. (1973), *Designing Complex Organizations*, Reading, MA: Addison-Wesley.

Galbraith, J.R., E.E. Lawler III and Associates (1993), *Organizing for the Future: The New Logic for Managing Complex Organizations*, San Francisco, CA: Jossey-Bass.

Garzon, M. (1995), *Models of Massive Parallelism*, Berlin: Springer-Verlag.

Gell-Mann, M. (1988), 'The concept of the institute', in D. Pines (ed.), *Emerging Synthesis in Science*, Boston, MA: Addison-Wesley, pp. 1–15.

Gell-Mann, M. (1994), *The Quark and the Jaguar*, New York: Freeman.

Gell-Mann, M. (2002), 'What is complexity?', in A.Q. Curzio and M. Fortis (eds), *Complexity and Industrial Clusters: Dynamics and Models in Theory and Practice*, Heidelberg, Germany: Physica-Verlag, pp. 13–24.

Gleick, J. (1987), *Chaos: Making a New Science*, New York: Penguin.

Granovetter, M. (1985), 'Economic action and social structure: a theory of embeddedness', *American Journal of Sociology*, **82**, 929–64.

Haken, H. (1983), *Synergetics, An Introduction: Non-Equilibrium Phase Transitions and Self-Organization in Physics, Chemistry, and Biology*, 3rd edn, Berlin: Springer-Verlag.

Hamel, G. (2000), 'Reinvent your company', *Fortune*, June, 99–118.

Hamel, G. and C.K. Prahalad (1989), 'Strategic intent', *Harvard Business Review*, **67**(May–June), 63–76.

Hamel, G. and C.K. Prahalad (1994), *Competing for the Future*, Boston, MA: Harvard Business School Press.

Hannan, M.T. and J. Freeman (1989), *Organizational Ecology*, Cambridge, MA: Harvard University Press.

Henrickson, L. and B. McKelvey (2002), 'Foundations of new social science', *Proceedings of the National Academy of Sciences*, **99**, 7288–97.

Hinterberger, F. (1994), 'On the evolution of open socio-economic systems', in R.K. Mishra, D. Maaß and E. Zwierlein (eds), *On Self-Organization: An Interdisciplinary Search for a Unifying Principle*, Berlin: Springer-Verlag, pp. 35–50.

Holland, J.H. (1975), *Adaptation in Natural and Artificial Systems*, Ann Arbor, MI: University of Michigan Press.

Holland, J.H. (1988), 'The gobal economy as an adaptive process', in P. Anderson, K.J. Arrow and D. Pines (eds), *The Economy as an Evolving Complex System*, Reading, MA: Addison-Wesley, pp. 117–24.

Holland, J.H. (1995), *Hidden Order*, Cambridge, MA: Perseus Books.

Holland, J.H. (2002), 'Complex adaptive systems and spontaneous emergence', in A.Q. Curzio and M. Fortis (eds), *Complexity and Industrial Clusters: Dynamics and Models in Theory and Practice*, Heidelberg, Germany: Physica-Verlag, pp. 24–34.

House, R.J. (1977), 'A 1976 theory of charismatic leadership', in J.G. Hunt and L.L. Larson (eds), *Leadership: The Cutting Edge*, Carbondale, IL: Southern Illinois University Press, pp. 189–207.

Hunt, J.G. and A. Ropo (1998), 'Multi-level leadership: grounded theory and mainstream theory applied to the case of General Motors', in Dansereau and Yammarino (eds) (1998a), pp. 289–327.

Janis, I.L. (1972), *Victims of Groupthink*, Boston, MA: Houghton Mifflin.

Johnson, J.L. and B.K. Burton (1994), 'Chaos and complexity theory for management', *Journal of Management Inquiry*, **3**, 320–28.

Johnson, N.L. (2000), 'A developmental view of evolving systems: illustrated by a model problem', Working paper, Los Alamos Laboratory, Los Alamos, NM.

Jones, G.R. (2000), *Organizational Theory*, 3rd edn, Reading, MA: Addison-Wesley.

Kauffman, S.A. (1988), 'The evolution of economic webs', in P. Anderson, K.J. Arrow and D. Pines (eds), *The Economy as an Evolving Complex System*, Reading, MA: Addison-Wesley, pp. 125–46.

Kauffman, S.A. (1993), *The Origins of Order: Self-Organization and Selection in Evolution*, New York: Oxford University Press.

Kauffman, S. (2000), *Investigations*, New York: Oxford University Press.

Klein, K.J. and R.J. House (1998), 'On fire: charismatic leadership and levels of analysis', in Dansereau and Yammarino (eds.) (1998b), pp. 3–21.

Kotter, J.P. and J.L. Heskett (1992), *Corporate Culture and Performance*, New York: Free Press.

LeBaron, B. (2002), 'Stochastic volatility as a simple generator of apparent financial power laws and long memory', *Quantitative Finance*, **1**, 621–31.

Leonard-Barton, D. (1995), *Wellsprings of Knowledge*, Boston, MA: Harvard Business School Press.

Lorenz, E.N. (1963), 'Deterministic nonperiodic flow', *Journal of the Atmospheric Sciences*, **20**, 130–41.

Lorenz, E.N. (1972), 'Predictability: does the flap of a butterfly's wings in Brazil set off a tornado in Texas?', Paper presented at the American Association for the Advancement of Science Meeting, Washington, DC.

Mackey, A., B. McKelvey and P.K. Kiousis (2006), 'Can the CEO churning problem be fixed? Lessons from complexity science, Jack Welch and AIDS', Presented at the Academy of Management Meeting, Atlanta, GA, August 14–16.

Mainzer, K. (1994), *Thinking in Complexity: The Complex Dynamics of Matter, Mind, and Mankind*, New York: Springer-Verlag. (Much enlarged 5th edn published in 2007.)

March, J.G. (1991), 'Exploration and exploitation in organization learning', *Organization Science*, **2**, 71–87.

Martin, J. (1992), *Cultures in Organizations: Three Perspectives*, New York: Oxford University Press.

Marion, R. and M. Uhl-Bien (2001), 'Leadership in complex organizations', *Leadership Quarterly*, **12**, 389–418.

Maruyama, M. (1963), 'The second cybernetics: deviation-amplifying mutual causal processes', *American Scientist*, **51**, 164–79. (Reprinted in Buckley (ed.), pp. 304–13.)

McKelvey, B. (1994), 'Evolution and organization science', in J.A.C. Baum and J.V. Singh (eds), *Evolutionary Dynamics of Organizations*, New York: Oxford University Press, pp. 314–26.

McKelvey, B. (1997), 'Quasi-natural organization science', *Organization Science*, **8**, 351–80.

McKelvey, B. (2001), 'Energizing order-creating networks of distributed intelligence', *International Journal of Innovation Management*, **5**, 181–212.

McKelvey, B. (2002), 'Managing coevolutionary dynamics: some leverage points' Presented at the 18th EGOS Conference, Barcelona, Spain, July.

McKelvey, B. (2004a), '"Simple rules" for improving corporate IQ: basic lessons from complexity science', in P. Andriani and G. Passiante (eds), *Complexity Theory and the Management of Networks*, London: Imperial College Press, pp. 39–52.

McKelvey, B. (2004b), 'Toward a 0th law of thermodynamics: order-creation complexity dynamics from physics and biology to bioeconomics', *Journal of Bioeconomics*, **6**, 1–31.

McKelvey, B. (2008), 'Emergent strategy via complexity leadership: using complexity science and adaptive tension to build distributed intelligence', in M. Uhl-Bien and R. Marion (eds), *Complexity and Leadership Volume I: Conceptual Foundations*, Charlotte, NC: Information Age Publishing, pp. 225–68.

Mélèse, J. (1991), *L'Analyse Modulaire des Systèmes* (The modular analysis of systems), Paris: Les Éditions d'Organisation.

Miles, R., C. Snow, J.A. Matthews and G. Miles (1999), 'Cellular-network organizations', in W.E. Halal and K.B. Taylor (eds), *Twenty-First Century Economics: Perspectives of Socioeconomics for a Changing World*, New York: Macmillan, pp. 155–73.

Milsum, J.H. (ed.) (1968), *Positive Feedback: A General Systems Approach to Positive/Negative Feedback and Mutual Causality*, Oxford, UK: Pergamon Press.

Mirowski, P. (1989), *More Heat than Light*, Cambridge, UK: Cambridge University Press.

Mitchell, M. (1996), *An Introduction to Genetic Algorithms*, Cambridge, MA: MIT Press.

Morgan, G. (1997), *Images of Organization*, 2nd edn, Thousand Oaks, CA: Sage.

Morrison, F. (1991), *The Art of Modeling Dynamic Systems*, New York: Wiley Interscience.

Nanus, B. (1992), *Visionary Leadership*, San Francisco, CA: Jossey-Bass.

Nicolis, G. and I. Prigogine (1989), *Exploring Complexity: An Introduction*, New York: Freeman.

Nohria, N. and R.G. Eccles (eds) (1992), *Networks and Organizations: Structure, Form, and Action*, Boston, MA: Harvard Business School Press.

Norling, P.M. (1996), 'Network or not work: harnessing technology networks in DuPont', *Research Technology Management*, **39**(1), 42–8.

O'Reilly, C.A. III and J. Pfeffer (2000), *Hidden Value*, Cambridge, MA: Harvard Business School Press.

Ormerod, P. (1998), *Butterfly Economics: A New General Theory of Social and Economic Behavior*, New York: Pantheon.

Page, S.E. (2007), *The Difference: How the Power of Diversity Creates Better Groups, Firms, Schools, and Societies*, Princeton, NJ: Princeton University Press.

Pal, S.K. and P.P. Wang (1996), *Genetic Algorithms for Pattern Recognition*, Boca Raton, FL: CRC Press.

Peters, T.J. and R.H. Waterman (1982), *In Search of Excellence: Lessons from America's Best-Run Companies*, New York: Harper & Row.

Porter, M.E. (1980), *Competitive Strategy: Techniques for Analyzing Industries and Competitors*, New York: Free Press.

Porter, M.E. (1996), 'What is strategy?', *Harvard Business Review*, **74**(6), 61–78.

Prietula, M.J., K.M. Carley and L. Gasser (eds) (1998), *Simulating Organizations: Computational Models of Institutions and Groups*, Cambridge, MA: MIT Press.

Prigogine, I. (1955), *An Introduction to Thermodynamics of Irreversible Processes*, Springfield, IL: Thomas.

Prigogine, I. and I. Stengers (1984), *Order Out of Chaos: Man's New Dialogue with Nature*, New York: Bantam.

Prigogine, I. (with I. Stengers) (1997), *The End of Certainty: Time, Chaos, and the New Laws of Nature*, New York: Free Press.

Prusak, L. (1996), 'The knowledge advantage', *Strategy and Leadership*, **24**, 6–8.

Rosenberg, A. (1994), 'Does evolutionary theory give comfort or inspiration to economics?', in P. Mirowski (ed.), *Natural Images in Economic Thought*, Cambridge, UK: Cambridge University Press, pp. 384–407.

Royer, I. (2003), 'Why bad projects are so hard to kill', *Harvard Business Review*, **81**(2), 48–56.

Salthe, S.N. (1985), *Evolving Hierarchical Systems*, New York: Columbia University Press.

Schein, E.H. (1990), 'Organizational culture', *American Psychologist*, **45**, 109–19.

Siehl, C. (1985), 'After the founder: an opportunity to manage culture', in P.F. Frost, L.F. Moore, M.R. Louis, C.C. Lundberg and J. Martin (eds), *Organizational Culture*, Newbury Park, CA: Sage, pp. 125–40.

Simon, H.A. (1999), 'Coping with complexity', in Groupe de Recherche sur l'Adaptation la Systémique et la Complexité Economique (GRASCE) (eds), *Entre systémique et complexité chemin faisant . . . Mélange en hommage à Jean-Louis Le Moigne*, Paris: Presses Universitaires de France, pp. 233–40.

Slater, R. (2001), *Get Better or Get Beaten: 29 Leadership Secrets from GE's Jack Welch*, New York: McGraw-Hill.

Slywotsky, A. (1996), *Value Migration*, Boston, MA: Harvard Business School Press.

Sorensen, J.B. (2002), 'The strength of corporate culture and the reliability of firm performance', *Administrative Science Quarterly*, **47**, 70–91.

Stacey, R.D. (1995), 'The science of complexity: an alternative perspective for strategic change processes', *Strategic Management Journal*, **16**, 477–95.

Stacey, R.D. (2001), *Complex Responsive Processes in Organizations: Learning and Knowledge Creation*, London: Routledge.

Suder, G. (ed.) (2006), *Corporate Strategies Under International Terrorism and Adversity*, Cheltenham, UK and Northampton, MA, USA: Edward Elgar.

Surowiecki, J. (2004), *The Wisdom of Crowds: Why the Many Are Smarter than the Few and How Collective Wisdom Shapes Business, Economies, Societies and Nations*, New York: Doubleday.

Thomas, C., R. Kaminska-Labbé and B. McKelvey (2005), 'Managing the MNC and exploitation/exploration dilemma: from static balance to irregular oscillation', in G. Szulanski, Y. Doz and J. Porac (eds), *Advances in Strategic Management*, Vol. 22, Oxford, UK: Elsevier, pp. 213–47.

Thompson, J.D. (1967), *Organizations in Action*, New York: McGraw-Hill.

Tichy, N.M. and S. Sherman (1994), *Control Your Destiny or Someone Else Will*, New York: HarperCollins.

Tushman, M.L. and E. Romanelli (1985), 'Organizational evolution: a metamorphosis model of convergence and reorientation', in L.L. Cummings and B.M. Staw (eds), *Research in Organizational Behavior*, Vol. 7, Greenwich, CT: JAI Press, pp. 171–222.

Uhl-Bien, M., R. Marion and B. McKelvey (2007), 'Complex leadership: shifting leadership from the industrial age to the knowledge era', *Leadership Quarterly*, **18**(4), 298–318.

Waldman D.A. and F.J. Yammarino (1999), 'CEO charismatic leadership: levels-of-management and levels-of-analysis effects', *Academy of Management Review*, **24**, 266–85.

Whitehead, A.N. (1967), *Adventures of Ideas*, New York: Free Press.

Williamson, O.E. (1975), *Markets and Hierarchies*, New York: Free Press.

Willmott, H. (1993), 'Strength is ignorance: slavery is freedom: managing culture in modern organizations', *Journal of Management Studies*, **30**, 515–52.

Zohar, D. (1997), *Rewiring the Corporate Brain*, San Francisco, CA: Berrett-Koehler.

2 Anticipating critique and occasional reason: modes of reasoning in the face of a radically open future
David Seidl and Dominik van Aaken

Introduction

Despite the importance that is generally placed on the investigation of the future, our understanding of the phenomenon of strategic foresight is still rather limited. Traditionally foresight has been framed in terms of extrapolating from past experiences. Such an approach, however, as Ansoff (1975, 1980) and many others have argued, is completely inadequate in the field of strategy, where the focus is less on continuity than on discontinuity. If people base their view of the future exclusively on past experiences, they will not be prepared for new strategic threats or opportunities, which by definition mark a break from the past. Strategic discontinuities are thus systematically out of sight. Particularly in our times of increasingly turbulent environments with accelerated and fundamental changes such approaches are proving more and more inadequate (see Waterhouse 1992; Ansoff and Sullivan 1993; D'Aveni 1994; Kirkbride et al. 1994; Bettis and Hitt 1995; Lombriser and Ansoff 1995).

The faster and the more radically the world changes, the more important does it become for organizations to sense discontinuities as early as possible in order to leave enough time for appropriate reactions. As such, strategic foresight is mostly conceptualized as the ability to pre-sense discontinuities; in particular by being open to so-called 'weak signals' (Ansoff 1975, 1980; Seidl 2004), which point to impending discontinuities. The classical example here is that of the petroleum crises in the 1970s, which could have been foreseen if the organizations had been more responsive to the various reports containing forecasts on possible Arab action. A more recent example is the terrorist attack on the Twin Towers, which took all Western organizations by complete surprise although, as we now hear, there had been signs, albeit weak, pointing to it, which just seem not to have been taken seriously enough at the time. Regarding these and similar approaches, strategic foresight has to do with the attentiveness towards signals indicating future discontinuities. This can be achieved through systematic scanning (and monitoring) of the relevant environments and a meticulous analysis of the data gathered.

The shift of focus from continuity to discontinuity, as exemplified by Ansoff's concept of 'weak signals', has certainly been an important step in the conceptualization of strategic foresight. However, newer approaches have emphasized important issues that had not been appropriately addressed in the past (Chia 2004; Narayanan and Fahey 2004): our cultural–cognitive limitations of perception. The older approaches to strategic foresight implicitly assumed that future developments remained within the present bounds of our imagination. But, as our experience has shown, the world evolves in ways that often transcend what we can imagine with our given cognitive categories at present. For example, two hundred years ago the concept of electricity was hardly imaginable; or, at the beginning of the twentieth century nobody would have been able to conceive a world with computers. In the cases cited, even if there had been some weak signals heralding those developments, we would not have been able to interpret them. Thus, the problem here is rather one of cognitive limitations. While these examples are certainly quite extreme, we should not dismiss the argument as irrelevant. Even if the changes are not that radical they might nevertheless go beyond what we can 'adequately' grasp within our given cognitive categories. Especially within the field of strategy, radical developments are not to be thought of as exceptions; on the contrary, they are surely at its heart. As such, the cognitive limitation can be seen as a central issue of *strategic* foresight.

This chapter is structured as follows. First, we shall present different notions of the 'future'. We argue that many approaches to strategic foresight are based on too simple a concept of the future and thus are only of limited use. Instead we propose the concept of the 'radically open future', where the future might develop in ways that transcend our present cognitive categories. This raises important questions about the ability to think and communicate about such developments at all. Second, we shall introduce the concepts of anticipating critique and of occasional reason, developed by the two philosophers Paul Feyerabend and Helmut Spinner, respectively, which might offer suitable modes of reasoning in the face of a radically open future. Third, we shall show how these two concepts can be applied to the issue of strategic foresight in organizations.

The concept of the future
In almost all areas of business and management studies, the 'future' plays an important role. The way the future is conceptualized, however, varies somewhat. This can best be seen in decision theory, which is underlying much of contemporary business and management thinking. Decision theory usually distinguishes three types of future with regard to the information that the decision maker possesses about it (originally, Knight 1921): (i) decision under certainty, (ii) decision under risk and (iii) decision under uncertainty. The first case describes a situation in which the actor knows exactly what will happen in the future. The future as such is predetermined – even from the perspective of the decision maker. In the second case the decision maker does not know which developments he or she will see in the future but is aware of all possible developments and knows with what probability which development will take place. The future in this case is conceptualized as open, but only within certain limits. In the third case the decision maker merely knows all possible future developments but does not know the likelihood of any of those taking place. The future, here, is more open than in the second case, but the openness of the future remains within the limits of our imaginable world.

Many approaches in business and management studies still assume one of those three types of future. Also Ansoff's concept of 'weak signals' is ultimately based on the notion of a future that is close to the third one described above. He implicitly assumes that if one had the right cues for possible future developments (and if one took them seriously) the conceptualization of these developments would not be a problem. In other words, such approaches presuppose that all possible future developments can be conceptualized already in the present – at least in principle.

The future described in these cases is an *open* future, but it is open only to a certain degree: it excludes any developments that would go beyond what we can presently imagine. We might call this notion the concept of 'a partly open future'. We can contrast this with the notion of a 'radically open future', which is characterized by the fact that the world can evolve in ways that we are not able to conceptualize at present; ways that go beyond our given cognitive categories (see Kirsch 1997a). This concept of future is very much based on the so-called 'linguistic turn' (Rorty 1967) in the social sciences. Briefly summed up, the most important characteristic of the linguistic turn in the social sciences is the notion that focusing on language acts as a way of structuring or conditioning our 'access to reality'. Language determines what we perceive as existing (see Winch 1958; Gergen 1982, p. 101; Rorty 1989). Since the given linguistic categories do not correspond directly to 'the world out there', nor do our perceptions of the world correspond to it. In this sense one can say that language to some extent *produces* a specific reality for us. Whorf explains:

> We dissect nature along the lines laid down by our native languages. The categories and types that we isolate from the world of phenomena we do not find there because they stare every observer in the face; on the contrary, the world is presented in a kaleidoscopic flux of impressions which has to be organized by our minds – and this means largely by the linguistic system in our minds. We cut nature up, organize it into concepts, and ascribe significances as we do, largely because we are parties to an agreement that holds throughout our speech community and is codified in the patterns of our language. (1956, p. 213)

The particular linguistic system – or 'language game' (Wittgenstein 1953; Mauws and Phillips 1995) – that is relevant at a particular time and place, determines the ways in which the world is conceptualized and experienced; different linguistic systems lead to different conceptualizations and experiences. A classic example here is the huge number of different categories of snow that the language of the Eskimos contains. As a result, Eskimos have a different (in particular, a much more differentiated) experience of snow than an average non-Eskimo. On the basis of these particular linguistic categories, the Eskimo sees differences in the world where the average non-Eskimo does not (see Weick and Westley 1996, p. 446).

Linguistic systems, however, are not static but change in the course of time: new linguistic categories are added from time to time while others might disappear. In this sense, our ancestors would have experienced their world – on the basis of the linguistic system of the time – very differently from the way we experience it today with our present linguistic system. But even we might come to see our world differently in the course of our lives as our linguistic system changes.

If we assume that the way we experience the world varies with the development of our linguistic system, we have to acknowledge that our future experiences might not be describable within our present linguistic system, in the same way that we would not be able to conceptualize the many different categories of snow that an Eskimo naturally distinguishes. With regard to strategic foresight this is a much more fundamental problem than the ones described in the older approaches. The problem is not so much one of picking up the right cues for future developments but of limitations in conceptualizing future developments. The linguistic categories available to us at present might not allow us to describe future experiences, for which we shall need to have recourse to as yet undeveloped categories. In other words, the appropriate language for thinking and communicating about the future world might not have been developed yet. A very recent example is the rise of the World Wide Web. For many corporations this development has revolutionized the way they do business. Its introduction in the early 1990s can be described as a classic strategic discontinuity confronting many corporations with substantial strategic opportunities and threats. However, only a couple of years earlier, the World Wide Web had been unimaginable for the average individual, who lacked the linguistic categories for appropriately describing its function and strategic implications.

The philosopher Friedrich Kambartel (1989) describes this phenomenon as a 'transcendence of grammatical borders'. He argues that the world often evolves in such a way as to transcend what our given 'grammar' of language allows us to conceptualize. With the idea of 'grammatical boundaries', Kambartel alludes to Wittgenstein's famous thesis: 'the limits of my language mean the limits of my world' (Wittgenstein 1961, 5.6). As Whorf has already pointed out, a specific linguistic system allows for infinite ways of conceptualizing the world, but it also excludes infinite other possibilities (Whorf 1956, pp. 121–2). A particular language sets the boundaries of what can and what cannot be conceptualized on the basis it provides. In this sense the development of the world might lead to new situations that lie outside our present grammatical boundaries; our existing linguistic categories do not 'fit' the new situation. In order to conceptualize the new situation, a new linguistic system – or as Kambartel says: a new 'grammar' – is needed. In other words, for an 'adequate' grasp of the world the development of the language needs to follow the development of the world. Thus, evolution continuously makes the existing language systems obsolete and demands the proliferation of other and new constructions on the basis of which new developments can be grasped.

If we accept the linguistic turn in the social sciences and the remarks based on Kambartel's ideas, the possibilities of foreseeing radical changes are rather limited. In order to foresee developments that transcend the present grammatical boundaries it would be necessary to 'stretch' the given linguistic possibilities at a particular time. We would have to be able to think and communicate beyond what the linguistic system allowed us to think and communicate. In the following we shall explore possibilities for doing so.

For this we also need to differentiate between thinking and communicating. Until now we have treated the two as one and the same. We assumed that the given linguistic system conditions our thinking and communicating in the same way. Whorf (1956), quoted above, speaks of the linguistic system in our mind much in this vein, while Kambartel conceptualizes our thinking as being bounded by the existing grammar. While our thinking and communicating are certainly very similarly conditioned by the linguistic system, there are some differences that we need to focus on in order to explore possibilities of stretching our grasp of the world.

As Kambartel and others have pointed out, our linguistic system changes over time: some linguistic categories disappear while new ones become integrated into the system; established relationships between categories are broken up and replaced by new ones. In this way the linguistic system allows for certain new conceptualizations while others might become excluded. On that basis, we may hypothesize that the linguistic system guiding our thinking and communicating might be developed at different speeds in each of these two spheres. For individuals it is much easier to 'experiment' in their *thinking* with new categories than to use new categories in their *communication* with others, since 'successful' communication presupposes that the participants are prepared to take on the new categories used (see Bateson 1972, pp. 406–7). In other words, while changes in the 'grammar' used in our individual thinking are merely restricted by our individual minds, changes in the 'grammar' used in our communication are restricted by multiple minds, that is, by the minds of all participants in a particular communication.

In addition to the individual inclinations to accept or reject certain categories, the specific social setting often puts further restrictions on communication. In this respect, formal organizations are particularly restrictive. As many organization theorists have pointed out, the very essence of organizing is the 'reduction of variety' (Weick and Westley 1996). Organizing means the reduction of equivocality (Weick 1979); the organizational context determines acceptable ways in which to conceptualize the different aspects of the world, while excluding alternative possibilities. This phenomenon has also been described as 'uncertainty absorption': organizing means absorbing the uncertainty concerning the ways of interpreting (aspects of) the world (Luhmann 2003; see also March and Simon 1958, p. 165). As such, the organizational context is likely to restrict the speed at which changes in the linguistic system are applied to organizational communication. For members of an organization it is particularly difficult to transfer changes in their 'grammar' of thinking to the level of communication – more difficult than, for example, in an artistic discourse. Undoubtedly, the organizational context affects not only communication but also thinking; nevertheless it can never determine thinking entirely. For that reason, the members of an organization will always experience more flexibility in their thinking than in their communication.

Pulling these arguments together we can say that the individual minds of all members of an organization taken together possess a much greater potential for conceptualizing (aspects of) the world in new ways; this is particularly so considering that different members might develop the 'grammar' of their thinking in different ways, that is, the minds of the different members taken together constitute a 'pool' of different ways of developing the linguistic system. Due to the restrictiveness of communication only a small part of these ways can be realized in the organizational communication: the members' minds encompass a much greater pool of novel categories than the organizational communication does. In other words, the *communicative* categories are only a subset of the *cognitive* categories.

However, the pool of cognitive categories available to the members of an organization is itself only a subset of all the categories that exist within and outside the organization. In other words, outside the organizational context there are other individuals, that is, non-members, with slightly different linguistic systems. There are also other social contexts in which other communicative categories are available, for example, the categories available in the context of artistic discourses are different from those available in an organization. In Figure 2.1 the relation between the three sets of linguistic categories has been represented graphically.

We summarize our argument so far: strategic foresight is possible only to the extent that future developments can be captured at present within the given linguistic categories. Thus, in order for us to be able to grasp new situations, 'grammatically' the present grammar would need to be 'stretched'. In the context of organizations, we argued that while individual members might 'experiment' in their thinking with new linguistic categories, the organizational setting, because of its particular nature, is likely to prevent most of these new categories from being used in communication. As a result of this, organizations slow down the development of their linguistic systems. In order to increase the ability of strategic foresight it would thus be necessary to counteract this tendency: organizations would need to encourage the transfer of new cognitive categories to the communicative domain. This can be done, as we shall argue in the following, by encouraging new modes of reasoning: *anticipating criticism* and *occasional reason*.

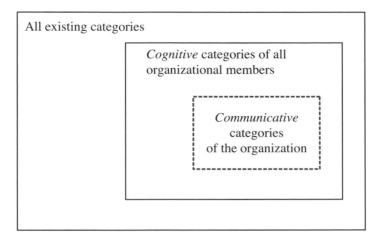

Figure 2.1   Sets of linguistic categories

The concepts of anticipating critique and occasional reason
In this section we shall introduce and explain the philosophical concepts of anticipating critique (Paul Feyerabend) and occasional reason (Helmut Spinner) in their original context (see also Kirsch 1997b) before transferring them to the question of organizational foresight in the ensuing section.

Feyerabend's concept of anticipating critique
Feyerabend developed his concept of anticipating critique in the context of the philosophy of science. He argued that scientific reasoning traditionally has been based on the idea of given, independent criteria such as consistency or the methodology of deduction. Accordingly, scientific statements are expected to be substantiated and evaluated on the basis of such criteria. These independent criteria determine the extent to which statements are seen as 'rational' since 'rationality means: agreement with particular general rules and standards' (Feyerabend 1980, p. 27; our translation).

However, as Feyerabend demonstrated, such independent criteria do not and cannot exist. He thus criticized particularly the rationalists in the tradition of Karl Popper, who placed such independent criteria at the heart of science (see, for example, Feyerabend 1980, 1982). Through his historical reconstructions of the sciences, Feyerabend showed that if scientists had followed such general rules as the rationalists assumed, progress in the sciences would never have taken place. He thus pointed out that all rules and all methodologies 'have their limits' (Feyerabend 1975, p. 32). This does not mean that we should do away with all rules and advocate complete anarchy in the sciences. It rather means that we need a realistic and thus *relativistic* way of handling such rules. In line with this observation, Feyerabend concludes that it is often the refraction of rules, rather than following rules, that leads to progress in the sciences (ibid., p. 23).

This is the particular context in which Feyerabend developed his concept of anticipating critique. On the basis of this concept he argued for a new mode of reasoning, according to which the criteria of criticism (of an argument) need not be given but could be developed in the process of criticism itself. Feyerabend explains:

In the following I will call *anticipating critique* (description, suggestion, etc.) the critique (description, suggestion, etc.) that is based on criteria not yet existing; and I will call *conservative critique* (description, suggestion, etc.) the critique (description, suggestion, etc.) that accords with existing criteria. Anticipating critique always appears somewhat awkward and it is easy for conservatives to prove its absurdity. (Feyerabend 1980, p. 47; our translation; original emphasis)

Thus, rather than basing our arguments on existing criteria, we base them on criteria that are yet to be developed. It is more of an intuitive mode of reasoning, in which the categories for substantiating the argument can be merely vaguely 'sketched' but not clearly explained; we can only hint at the kind of categories that we would need to develop in order to properly clarify an argument. Feyerabend explains this new mode of reasoning by contrasting it with the conventional one:

Arguments, theories, terms, points of view and debates can . . . be clarified in . . . two different ways: (a) in [a] manner . . . which leads back to the familiar ideas and treats the new as a special case of things already understood, and (b) by incorporation into a language of the future, which means *that one must learn to argue with unexplained terms and to use sentences for which no clear rules of usage are as yet available*. (Feyerabend 1975, p. 256; original emphasis)

To make this contrast more explicit: the conventional mode of reason remains within the context of the established categories and thus treats everything as merely a variation of the known; it excludes any type of argument that cannot be captured within this established context and thus inevitably excludes radical novelty. The mode of anticipating critique, in contrast, allows for radically new arguments, as the 'appropriate' context for an argument is developed in the course, and as part, of the argument. Thus, rather than discussing novel ideas within a known context as (a variation of) something already known, they can be treated as something as yet unknown within an as yet unknown context. Anticipating critique, therefore, does not mean doing away with the necessity of substantiating arguments and of placing them in a context on the basis of which they may be evaluated. It only encourages a different kind of substantiation and a different kind of context.

The difference between conservative and anticipating critique can also be seen by looking at the *temporal* relation between an argument and its substantiation or context (see Figure 2.2). In the case of conservative critique, the categories for substantiating an argument precede the argument. In Figure 2.2, we have symbolized the argument itself with a circle and the categories that are drawn upon for its substantiation with squares. If the argument takes place in t_0 the categories for substantiating the argument must have been developed in t_{-1}, t_{-2} and so on. In the case of anticipating critique the temporal relation is reversed: the argument precedes the categories for its substantiation. Thus, if the argument is made in t_0, the categories for substantiating it are developed in t_1, t_2 and so on. This, however, also means that the argument cannot be properly evaluated while being developed, as the substantiation of the argument has not been realized as yet. One could say that the argument is held in suspense.

The type of reasoning implied by anticipating critique puts the participants of the discourse under particular strain. They are expected to (provisionally) accept an argument whose substantiation and integration into an appropriate context are pending. In other words, the participants are expected to (provisionally) accept the argument without even adequately understanding it. Feyerabend acknowledges the difficulties associated with

a) Conservative critique

b) Anticipating critique

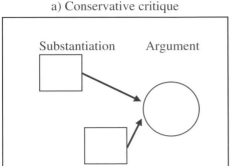
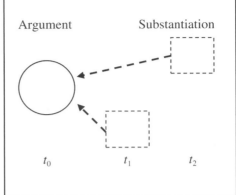

Figure 2.2 Conservative versus anticipating critique

this. He illustrates the situation of the participants in such a discourse with an example from John Stuart Mill (1859), in which a father has a discussion with his young son on logic. The son accepts the arguments of the father although he does not really understand them at the time; only retrospectively is he able to properly appreciate what his father has said. Feyerabend quotes the son's later reflections on the discussion:

> The explanations did not make the matter at all clear to me at the time; but they were not therefore useless; they remained as a nucleus for my observations and reflections to crystallise upon; the import of his general remarks being interpreted to me, by the particular instances which came under my notice *afterwards*. (Feyerabend 1975, p. 257, original italics)

This example is not, of course, about anticipating critique in the proper sense since the father's arguments were based on pre-existing categories (context). However, from the perspective of the son the case is very similar to one where anticipating critique applies, since *for him* the context was developed only afterwards; he did not share it with his father from the beginning.

Feyerabend argues that the sciences could benefit immensely if such new modes of reasoning were more accepted. The traditional mode of reasoning in the sciences adheres blindly to intersubjectively shared criteria, which stifle its development. In view of this, he sees his concept of anticipating critique as merely one new form of reasoning in a more general move towards liberation from the strict rules of the traditional scientific discourse. In this respect he writes:

> Intelligent humans do not adhere to criteria, rules or methods, not even to 'rational' methods; they are opportunists, i.e., they use those mental and material tools, which in a given situation seem most likely to serve their aims. (Feyerabend 1980, p. 9; our translation)

This quote from Feyerabend leads us directly to Spinner's concept of occasional reason, in which the concrete situation – rather than general rules or categories – is taken as the ultimate point of reference for an argument or action.

Spinner's concept of occasional reason

Helmut Spinner developed his concept of 'occasional reason' mainly as a reply to the ideas of Karl Popper and Max Weber (Spinner 1977, 1982, 1994). He criticized the one-sided view of rationality of the Western world, which treats only a specific mode of action as rational, branding all else as 'irrational' (Spinner 1994, pp. 24–5). According to this concept, arguments or actions are only rational to the extent that they can be subsumed under some general principles, for example, the economic principle or Kant's categorical imperative. For Spinner, however, this is not the only form of rationality. He contrasts this traditional 'principle-based' rationality with another form of rationality, which he terms 'occasional rationality' or 'occasional reason'. Every human being usually possesses both of these forms of reason; and everyday action always represents a combination of both in different proportions. In this context, Spinner also speaks of 'double reason' (Spinner 1994), characterizing principle-based rationality as follows:

> [F]ollowing the Weberian model of occidental rationalism, there is the standard concept of the norm-bound, rule-led 'principle-based reason', which manifests itself in general, abstract, anticipating . . . person-independent and situation-independent criteria for *principle-based rational* thinking and acting, seeing and feeling, wishing and deciding – according to principles and rules: in principles (hence its name), norms, rules, maxims, methods, doctrines and other *idées générales*, which apply to all cases of the same kind and which should lead to general solutions to problems. (p. 29; our translation, original italics)

Principle-based reason is subject-independent and its nature is dogmatic. It consists of trans-individual and trans-situational principles, which everybody is supposed to follow. The principles on which a particular action is to be based precede the concrete situation in which the action takes place; the principles 'anticipate' – or better: 'predetermine' – all possible rational actions. According to Spinner, principle-based rationality became the standard mode of reasoning in the Western world, particularly in the scientific, ethical and legal discourses (Kirsch 1985, p. 19; Spinner 1994, p. 47).

In contrast to principle-based reason, in Spinner's theory, occasional reason is conceptualized as a mode of reasoning that pays particular attention to the concrete occasion. As such, it focuses on the surprising and the irregular. Therefore arguments or actions cannot be subsumed under general rules, traditions and so on and are thus in the traditional sense 'irrational'. Spinner himself speaks of

> . . . the *alternative conceptualization* [to principle-based reason] of 'occasional reason', which is uncontrolled, not pre-conceived in [terms of] principles and not bound to general rules. Its *occasional rationality* changes according to the situation from case to case: as specific means . . . without general criteria; for the *occasional rational* solution for the particular individual case – without generalizing and transferring the solution to all comparable cases or similar problems. (1994, p. 29; our translation, original italics)

In contrast to principle-based reason, occasional reason does not presuppose trans-situational principles, according to which individuals may orient themselves in concrete situations. According to occasional reason, every situation is taken to be *unique* and not directly comparable to any other situation. It follows that any trans-situational principle or rule would not take into account the idiosyncrasies of the situation and would thus be seen as inadequate. This suggests that any arguments or actions are determined by the *temporary logic of the concrete situation*. This puts particular emphasis on the way in which the individual *experiences* the concrete situation he or she is in. Due to their different personalities and backgrounds, different individuals might experience the same situation differently. In that sense, different individuals can be expected to display different orientations in the same situation. Thus, while principle-based reason assumes a trans-situational and trans-individual logic, occasional reason is based on a situational and individualistic logic. These two forms of orientation are very different and have very different implications for the way problems in a particular situation are conceived and solved (Spinner 1987, p. 37).

Hypotactic and paratactic styles
Feyerabend's and Spinner's modes of reasoning are closely associated with the way cognitive categories are organized and presented; that is, with the way that these categories are 'held in store' and presented in the concrete communications. Both speak of different (cognitive and presentational) 'styles'. These styles have a significant influence on our thinking and communicating. For example, if two categories are treated as closely connected rather than independent, we tend to use them in combination; that is to say, if we use either category, we are also very likely to use the other. The cognitive style creates dispositions for particular ways of thinking and communicating. In this context, Spinner writes:

> [C]ognitive styles are not a question of truth and method, in the sense of whether specific conclusions or procedures are valid. It rather concerns *cognitive dispositions and tendencies* for distinctive, particular forms of thinking and representing . . . (1994, p. 87, our translation, original italics)

Feyerabend and Spinner ultimately distinguish two types of cognitive styles: the hypotactic and the paratactic style (Feyerabend 1975, p. 223; Spinner 1987, pp. 40–44). The hypotactic style refers to a way of organizing cognitive categories in some sort of hierarchical way. Here categories are systematically integrated with regard to each other, forming a kind of theory. In this sense Spinner also speaks of a 'theoretical' style.[1] There are clear-cut relations between the different categories. If a new category is added to the stock of existing ones it needs to be fitted into the system; its relation to the other categories needs to be clearly defined. Thus, the relations between the existing categories put restrictions on how new categories can be added. Every category is defined in a clear-cut context of other categories. Thus, if we draw on a particular category in our thinking or communicating, we automatically draw on the other categories to which that category is linked.

In contrast to the hypotactic style, in the case of the paratactic style the different categories are not strictly related to any other categories. They are treated as independent, which leaves open the possibility of connecting them to other categories. Thus, contrary to the hypotactic style, where the meaning of a category is defined to a large extent through its relation to other categories, in this case categories are treated as autonomous and 'self-defined'. As such, the different categories are placed next to each other without becoming integrated in any manner. The categories held in store, so to speak, do not form a consistent whole but merely an aggregate of autonomous categories, which are organized sequentially. This also means that new categories can simply be 'added' to the stock of categories without having to be integrated and related to each other – in this sense, Spinner also speaks of an 'additive' style (1994, p. 89). Because of that, this style is also much more open to the incorporation of new categories. Thus, when drawing from a stock of paratactically organized categories in our thinking and communicating, we can pick out individual categories without having to draw on a host of other, interconnected categories.

Closely connected to the hypotactic and paratactic styles of 'holding categories in store' are the presentational styles; that is to say, the styles of presenting or using categories in thinking and communicating in either a hypotactic or a paratactic manner. In the case of the hypotactic style of presentation, the different categories drawn upon are used in a highly integrated way; every category reflects the way it relates to other categories. In contrast, in the paratactic style the various categories are presented as autonomous and sequentially structured. Accordingly, everything is expressed as a sum of 'details', which are shown in their own right without any connection apart from their simultaneousness and their location, which is the same for all (Feyerabend 1975, pp. 235–6; Spinner 1994, pp. 89–92). According to both Feyerabend and Spinner, these two styles are characteristic of different cultural epochs. The paratactic style, for example, can be found in Archaic Greek culture, while our modern Western culture is dominated by hypotactic styles. Feyerabend illustrates these two styles by comparing pictorial representations in different epochs. He gives the example of a scene in which a lion attacks a little kid goat. Hypotactically presented, the picture would present the lion and the kid with regard to each other: the kid would look terrified in expectation of the lion's attack and the lion would be shown in its superiority over the kid. In the paratactic style the scene would be presented very differently as Feyerabend describes:

> The lion looks ferocious, the kid looks peaceful, and the act of swallowing is simply *tacked on* to the presentation of what a lion *is* and of what a kid *is*. (We have what is called a *paratactic aggregate*: the elements of such an aggregate are all given equal importance, the only relation between them is sequential, there is no hierarchy, no part is presented as being subordinate to and determined by others.) The picture reads: ferocious lion, peaceful kid, swallowing of kid by lion. (Feyerabend 1975, pp. 233–4, original italics)

Thus, in contrast to the hypotactic style, in the paratactic style the different elements of the picture do not refer to each other. The relation between the elements is itself an element which is added to the rest. In fact, each element could be taken out and replaced by something else without affecting the presentation of the other elements. Even the relation between the lion and the kid goat could be reversed without it being necessary to change anything in the presentation of the lion and the kid as such. In other words, the element 'swallowing of kid by lion' could be replaced by 'kid biting lion' without anything about the presentation of the lion or the kid having to change. In a hypotactic style, however, such a change would require modifications to *all* elements of the picture.

According to Feyerabend and Spinner these two (cognitive and representational) styles are more or less directly associated with their different modes of reasoning: the hypotactic style is connected with the 'conventional' modes of reasoning (that is, conservative critique and principle-based reason) and the paratactic style with the 'unconventional' modes (anticipating critique and occasional reason). Although not completely impossible, the reverse combinations are rather unlikely (Spinner 1987, p. 37). Anticipating critique and occasional reason are the easier to accomplish, the greater the degrees of freedom in combining categories and the easier the integration of new categories or their addition to the already existing ones.

Modes of reasoning and strategic foresight

In the following we shall discuss the implications of Feyerabend's and Spinner's ideas with regard to the limitations of strategic foresight identified above. Although neither author wrote in the context of organization studies, we would nevertheless argue that their original context is closely related to it. Spinner, on the one hand, was concerned with a philosophical theory of rationality. Because of the important role that rationality plays in organizations, the relevance of his concepts should be obvious. Feyerabend, on the other hand, was mainly concerned with the philosophy of science and the way in which scientific 'truths' are generated. Scientific and organizational discourses, however, share a strong emphasis on the substantiation of any action or argument. In the same way that scientific statements need to be supplemented with evidence for their validity in order to be accepted as 'scientific', organizational communications (usually) need to be justified in order to be accepted as decisions. In both cases the discourses usually refer back to earlier scientific statements or earlier decisions in order to substantiate the current argument – in line with what Feyerabend described as 'conservative critique'.

Going back to our previous analysis, there are two points that are of particular relevance to an organization's ability to employ strategic foresight: (i) the members' propensity for developing new cognitive categories or for accepting new categories from outside and (ii) the probability of the members' cognitive categories becoming available as *communicative* categories in the organization. Feyerabend's and Spinner's modes of reasoning are of direct relevance to both these points.

As Feyerabend and Spinner pointed out, in our Western culture our thinking is dominated by the hypotactic organization of cognitive categories. Our cognitive categories are usually quite tightly integrated in a system of other categories. This, as we argued above, restricts the system's absorptive capacity with regard to new categories. As a result, we might expect that the more open individuals are towards experimenting with new categories, the less hypotactically and, thus, the more paratactically do they organize their cognitive categories. People who 'store' their ideas sequentially are more likely to accept new categories even if the relation to other categories is not defined or even if the various categories seem incompatible. The propensity to organize categories more hypotactically or paratactically probably depends partly on individual psychic dispositions – for more on the topic, see particularly the theory of cognitive types (Maruyama 2003). At the same time it is probably determined to a large extent by the social context in which the individual is integrated (see Berger and Luckmann 1967). Thus, the more paratactically ordered the organizational communications (see below) or the member's other extra-organizational communications are, the more likely is the member also to arrange his or her mind in such a way. In this sense, organizations might increase the likelihood of members' developing new cognitive categories by 'encouraging' a more paratactic ordering of their minds or by selecting members with accordant dispositions. However, to what extent organizations are really able to (indirectly) influence their members' style of thinking has to be left open here. In the following we shall concentrate more on the second point, that is, the extent to which new cognitive categories become available as communicative categories.

We argued above that the members of an organization tend to develop their cognitive grammar faster than the communicative grammar changes; consequently, they might be able to think about certain radical changes in the environment long before they can communicate about them (see Tsoukas and Chia 2002, p. 580). In view of this, the more organizations allow for such cognitive categories to be used in communication, the greater their foresight. A significant obstacle to the use of new categories in communication is the prevailing hypotactic style of organization and presentation: new categories need to be fitted into the system of already accepted categories before they can be legitimately used. Because of that, radically new ideas, which are the most interesting ones in our context, tend to be rejected in the course of communication. Organizations tend to accept only those categories that fit the existing categories and therefore tend to perpetuate the established grasp of the world – a phenomenon comparable to what has been described as 'cognitive dissonance' (Festinger 1957). Different organizations, however, differ in their communicative styles. While a 'pure' paratactic style is certainly very unlikely, one can nevertheless find different combinations of paratactic and hypotactic styles. In fact, one might find that within the same organization certain parts of the various communicative categories are hypotactically arranged, while others are paratactically arranged. It could also be that the hypotactic ordering of categories is not very strict, allowing for variations in relations. An organization might also actively encourage more paratactic styles of communication – for example, through the design of its structures. For example, heterarchical structures (McCulloch 1965) or loose coupling between different parts of the organization (Weick 1976) might contribute to a style of communication that tolerates the coexistence of 'incompatible' ideas. Ultimately, however, the extent to which the communicative categories, concepts, ideas and so on are organized as a consistent whole and whether inhomogeneity and inconsistencies are tolerated is probably a question of organizational culture.

We may now argue that the more paratactically the communicative categories are organized (that is, the less the categories are integrated into a consistent system of categories) the easier it is for members to draw on new cognitive categories in the context of communication. In other words, the more paratactic the communicative style, the more cognitive categories become *potential* communicative categories.

In Figure 2.3 we have tried to represent this idea graphically: we distinguish between the sets of cognitive categories available in the course of communication in the cases of a more hypotactic and a more paratactic style. With the two arrows we have indicated that a highly paratactic style of communication translates into a correspondingly greater number of cognitive categories. Thus, if individual members develop new cognitive categories – which might capture more effectively new developments in the world – they are more likely to be able to use these new categories in the context of communication with other members, even if the relation of the new categories to other, commonly *shared* categories is not clearly defined or if the new categories are inconsistent with those other categories.

The paratactic communicational style, however, does not suffice when an organization attempts to access its members' new cognitive categories in order to significantly 'stretch' its grammatical boundaries. For this purpose, the paratactic style needs to be paired with particular modes of argumentation. New cognitive categories cannot be 'adequately' communicated in the conventional mode of reasoning, where arguments need to be based

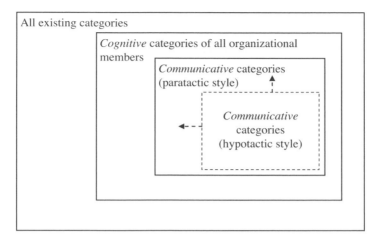

Figure 2.3   The set of communicative categories in hypotactic and paratactic styles

on the established categories. They require alternative modes of reasoning, which do not squeeze them into established contexts but allow them to 'unfold' properly. Anticipating critique and occasional reason, as explained above, are two modes of reasoning that allow breaking with the established 'grammatical rules' and presenting, instead, novel ideas in novel contexts. The important point is that these two modes of reasoning do not do away with the need to justify an argument and as such are compatible with the requirement in organizations that an argument be substantiated.

Feyerabend's anticipating critique more or less explicitly deals with ways of stretching the established communicational grammar. New ideas (categories) are to be allowed into communication even if the appropriate context for them is not developed yet. In this mode of reasoning, the substantiation of an argument is vaguely sketched; it is understood that it will be concretized at some point in the future. To the extent that organizations cultivate such a mode of reasoning – in addition to a conventional mode – the organizational members are in a position to communicate about their individual grasp of new developments in the world even if this is incompatible with the shared worldview. In that respect, new categories can gain access to organizational communications even though their substantiation in yet-to-be-developed contexts is still pending. In this way an organization might go beyond the boundaries of what the established, that is, intersubjectively shared, linguistic system allows it to conceptualize. What is more, the fact that the substantiation of certain arguments is pending might introduce an additional dynamic, encouraging the organization's members to develop (first cognitively and then communicatively) new categories to make up an appropriate context.

Similarly to anticipating critique, occasional reason is a mode of reasoning in which arguments need not be based on the established communicative context. In contrast to the former, however, occasional reason is not explicitly focused on the future but on the present. The particular context for substantiating our arguments or actions is the specific situation in which the argument or action takes place. This focus on the present, however, is ultimately not very different from a focus on the future. As several authors have pointed out (for example, Chia 2004; Tsoukas and Shepherd 2004) foresight, at its very heart, has to do with paying attention to the very concrete present situation. In the mode of occasional reason, then, the attention that a particular, concrete situation receives in its own right (and not merely as a variation of earlier situations) can also be understood as attention to new developments. Where principle-based reason tends to downplay differences between situations, occasional reason tends to highlight them.

As described above, occasional reason puts particular emphasis on the *personal experience* of the concrete situation. In contrast to principle-based rationality, occasional reason acknowledges that different individuals might experience the same situation in different ways. Thus, to the extent that this mode of reasoning prevails in communications, the members of an organization are encouraged to present accounts of their idiosyncratic experiences. They can expect the other participants to display a certain openness to these idiosyncratic accounts, even if others might not be able to comprehend those accounts immediately on the basis of their own experiences. In view of this, the members of an organization might also talk about novel perceptions of the world, introducing their novel cognitive categories into communications. In this way the individual (cognitive) developments of the linguistic system gain access to the communicative realm.

Analogously to the mode of anticipating critique, occasional reason assumes that the context for such arguments is developed in the course of an argument; in this way, we are able to free ourselves from the established categories without having to do away with the substantiation of the argument entirely. In contrast to anticipating critique, here the substantiation of an argument is not deferred to the future but developed within the concrete situation. This requires assembling the linguistic categories in a way that suits the idiosyncrasies of the situation. This might even call forth the development, or integration into the communication, of further novel categories. In other words arguments are substantiated on the basis of a situation-specific logic.

Arguments made in the mode of anticipating critique or occasional reason require a particular style of presentation – above we referred to this as the paratactic style of presentation. In the case of communications these arguments take the form of narratives; we are expected not to present a 'theoretical' argument with clear-cut relations between its elements but rather to tell a 'good story'. It follows that the central criterion for presenting an argument is not its inter-subjective verifiability – which would not be possible in the type of communications described above – but rather its particular kind of believability (see Gioia and Manz 1995). Bruner writes about believability:

> [The] believability of a story is of a different order than the believability of even the speculative parts of physical theory. If we apply Popper's criterion of falsifiability to a story as a test of its goodness, we are guilty of misplaced verification. (1986, p. 14)

The believability of such a story, and thus the likelihood of its being accepted by other members, depends on the internal coherence of its different elements. This, however, is not enough. In addition to internal coherence the narrative has to come across as the *authentic* expression of the speaker's experiences. According to Habermas (1984), the central validity claim connected with the story is not a kind of verifiable truth but its authenticity. In this mode of communication, narratives are accepted by other participants to the extent that the narrator is felt to express his or her real intentions and beliefs.

The narrative mode of communication that focuses on authenticity as the relevant validity claim allows anticipating critique and occasional reason to operate in the context of communication, and as such removes some of the barriers to the transfer of new cognitive categories into the communicative domain. In this way the organization's linguistic system might adjust sooner to changes in the world, increasing the organization's ability of developing strategic foresight. Nevertheless, there can be no doubt that this openness towards new ideas implied by such modes of communication also makes an organization vulnerable to irrational and 'thoughtless' behaviour. As Feyerabend (1980, p. 47, footnote 15) pointed out, in these modes of communication it is hardly possible to distinguish between 'ingenious insights' and incompetence.

Conclusion

In this chapter we drew on the recent developments in the field of strategic foresight, which emphasize the limitations imposed by our socio-cultural context (Chia 2004). We presented the concept of a 'radically open future', which stresses that the world might change beyond what our cognitive categories allow us to conceptualize. As an example of such a change we referred to the development of the World Wide Web at the beginning of the 1990s.

Drawing on linguistic philosophy, we explained how our thinking and communicating are restricted by our linguistic system. To describe this we drew on Kambartel's concept of 'grammatical boundaries'. Because of those boundaries, the current linguistic system allows us to conceptualize a wide array of different things but it excludes the conceptualization of other things, which lie outside its grammatical boundaries. On the basis of this concept we argued that in order to be able to grasp radically new developments in the world, an organization has to await the 'adjustment' of its linguistic system. Thus, the more responsive an organization's linguistic system is and the faster it develops, the more foresightful will that organization be.

We went on to argue that individuals usually develop new linguistic categories in their thinking fairly early on, but are not able to use them in their communications. This means that they are often able to grasp fundamental changes before they can communicate about such changes. From this we inferred that organizations can increase their ability to develop strategic foresight, to the extent that they are able to allow into the organizational communication new cognitive categories used by their members. This, however, requires a different mode of reasoning.

Drawing on Feyerabend and Spinner, we introduced anticipating critique and occasional reason as two modes of reasoning that allow the use of novel cognitive categories in communication. In other words, they make possible the introduction of linguistic developments that have taken place in the members' minds into the realm of communication. The important point about these modes of reasoning is that they allow for different forms of substantiating our arguments. While in the traditional mode of reasoning it would be very difficult to integrate radically new conceptualizations into organizational communication, as the existing categories would be inadequate for substantiating them, anticipating critique and occasional reason assume that the context of substantiation is itself developed as part of the argument.

We explained that these two modes of reasoning are usually associated with a particular way of organizing the linguistic system. In this sense we distinguished between a hypotactic and a paratactic style. According to the latter, cognitive categories are not integrated into a hierarchical order and interrelated in a clear-cut manner. Instead, they are sequentially arranged, which allows for multiple combinations. This provides the linguistic system with the necessary flexibility and openness for accommodating novel cognitive categories.

On the whole we have argued that it is essential to consider separately and carefully different modes of reasoning in the context of strategic foresight. We have shown that Feyerabend and Spinner can offer valuable insights in this respect. Against the background of the argument put forward here, several research questions open up: first, what do these modes of reasoning look like in practice? Although anticipating critique and occasional reasoning might not be very common in organizations today, we should nevertheless be able to find some empirical examples of both. In particular, we need to analyse under what circumstances such modes of reasoning arise and to what extent they can be actively encouraged or even 'managed'. Second, we could ask, to what extent can the different modes of reasoning coexist? Do organizations switch between them? Can these different modes be used in different parts of the organization simultaneously or does one mode prevail across the entire organization? Third, is there empirical evidence that anticipating critique and occasional reasoning result in 'better' (whatever this might mean) foresight? Fourth, what other (positive or negative) effects do these modes of reasoning have on the organization, for example, how do they affect decision making or the enforcement of decisions? All these questions call particularly for more *empirical* studies.

Note

1. To be precise, Spinner uses different terminology for the cognitive style and the presentational style: he refers only to the presentational styles as 'hypotactic' and 'paratactic' and to the cognitive styles as 'theoretical' and 'additive'. In order not to make the text too complex we shall follow Feyerabend, who uses the same terminology for both.

References

Ansoff, H.I. (1975), 'Managing strategic surprise by response to weak signals', *California Management Review*, **18** (2), 21–33.
Ansoff, H.I. (1980), 'Strategic issue management', *Strategic Management Journal*, **1**, 131–48.
Ansoff, H.I. and P.A. Sullivan (1993), 'Optimizing profitability in turbulent environments: a formula for strategic success', *Long Range Planning*, **5**, 11–23.
Bateson, G. (1972), *Steps to an Ecology of Mind: Collected Essays in Anthropology, Psychiatry, Evolution and Epistemology*, New York: Ballantine.
Berger, P. and T. Luckmann (1967), *The Social Construction of Reality*, Harmondsworth: Penguin.
Bettis, R.A. and M.A. Hitt (1995), 'The new competitive landscape', *Strategic Management Journal*, **16**, 7–19.
Bruner, J. (1986), *Actual Minds, Possible Worlds*, Cambridge, MA: Harvard University Press.
Chia, R. (2004), 'Re-educating attention: what is foresight and how is it cultivated?', in H. Tsoukas and J. Shepherd (eds), *Managing the Future: Developing Strategic Foresight in the Knowledge Economy*, Oxford: Blackwell, pp. 21–37.
D'Aveni, R.A. (1994), *Hypercompetition. Managing the Dynamics of Strategic Manoeuvring*, New York: Free Press.
Festinger, L. (1957), *A Theory of Cognitive Dissonance*, Stanford, CA: Stanford University Press.
Feyerabend, P. (1975), *Against Method*, London: New Left Books.
Feyerabend, P. (1980), *Erkenntnis für freie Menschen* (Science in a free society), Frankfurt a. M: Suhrkamp.
Feyerabend, P. (1982), *Science in a Free Society*, London: New Left Books.
Gergen, K. (1982), *Toward Transformation in Social Knowledge*, New York: Springer.
Gioia, D.A. and C.C. Manz (1995), 'Linking cognition and behavior: a script processing of vicarious learning', *Academy of Management Review*, **10** (3), 527–39.
Habermas, J. (1984), *The Theory of Communicative Action*, London: Heinemann.
Kambartel, F. (1989), *Philosophie der humanen Welt. Abhandlungen* (Philosophy of the human world. Treatise), Frankfurt a. M.: Suhrkamp.
Kirkbride, P.S., J. Durcan and E.D.A. Obeng (1994), 'Change in a chaotic post-modern world', *Journal of Strategic Change*, **3**, 151–63.

Kirsch, W. (1985), 'Okkasionelle Rationalität – neu betrachtet' (Occasional reason – reconsidered), working paper, University of Munich.

Kirsch, W. (1997a), *Strategisches Management: Die geplante Evolution von Unternehmen* (Strategic management: the planned evolution of firms), Munich: Kirsch.

Kirsch, W. (1997b), *Kommunikatives Handeln, Autopoiese, Rationalität* (Communicative action, autopoiesis, rationality), Munich: Kirsch.

Knight, F.H. (1921), *Risk, Uncertainty and Profit*, New York: Houghton Mifflin.

Lombriser, R. and H.I. Ansoff (1995), 'How successful top intrapreneurs pilot firms through the turbulent 1990s', *Journal of Strategic Change*, **2**, 95–108.

Luhmann, N. (2003), 'Organization', in T. Bakken and T. Hernes (eds), *Autopoietic Organization Theory. Drawing on Niklas Luhmann's Social Systems Perspective*, Copenhagen: Copenhagen Business School Press, pp. 31–52.

March, J.G. and H.A. Simon (1958), *Organizations*, New York: Wiley.

Maruyama, M. (2003), 'Individual cognitive/cogitative types', *Revue Internationale de Sociologie*, **13**, 546–65.

Mauws, N.K. and N. Phillips (1995), 'Understanding language games', *Organization Science*, **6**, 322–34.

McCulloch, W.S. (1965), *The Embodiments of Mind*, Cambridge, MA: MIT Press.

Mill, J.S. (1859), *On Liberty*, London: Parker.

Narayanan, V.K. and L. Fahey (2004), 'Invention and navigation as contrasting metaphors of the pathways to the future', in H. Tsoukas and J. Shepherd (eds), *Managing the Future: Developing Strategic Foresight in the Knowledge Economy*, Oxford: Blackwell, pp. 38–57.

Rorty, R. (ed.) (1967), *The Linguistic Turn: Essays in Philosophical Method*, Chicago, IL: University of Chicago Press.

Rorty, R. (1989), *Contingency, Irony, and Solidarity*, Cambridge: Cambridge University Press.

Seidl, D. (2004), 'The concept of "weak signals" revisited. A re-description from a constructivist perspective', in H. Tsoukas and J. Shepherd (eds), *Managing the Future: Developing Strategic Foresight in the Knowledge Economy*, Oxford: Blackwell, pp. 151–68.

Spinner, H.F. (1977), *Die Entstehung des Erkenntnisproblems im griechischem Denken und seine klassische Rechtfertigungslösung aus dem Geiste des Rechts* (The emergence of epistemological qusestions in Greek thought and its classical treatment in the spirit of the law), vol. I of *Begründung, Kritik und Rationalität* (Justification, critique and rationality), Braunschweig: Vieweg.

Spinner, H.F. (1982), *Ist der Kritische Rationalismus am Ende? Auf der Suche nach den verlorenen Maßstäben des Kritischen Rationalismus für eine offene Sozialphilosophie und kritische Sozialwissenschaft* (Is critical rationalism dead? – Searching for the lost criteria of critical rationalism for an open social philosophy and critical social science), Weinheim: Beltz.

Spinner, H.F. (1987), 'Vereinzeln, verbinden, begründen, widerlegen. Zur philosophischen Stellung von Begründungs- und Kritikoptionen im Rahmen einer Systematik der Erkenntnisstile und Typologie der Rationalitätsformen' (Separation, connection, justification, refutation. On the philosophical role of alternative options of justification and critique against the background of a systemization of cognitive styles and a typology of forms of rationality), in W.R. Köhler, W. Kuhlmann and P. Rohs (eds), *Philosophie und Begründung* (Philosophy and justification), Frankfurt a. M.: Suhrkamp, pp. 13–66.

Spinner, H.F. (1994), *Der ganze Rationalismus einer Welt von Gegensätzen Fallstudien zur Doppelvernunft* (The entire rationalism of a world of oppositions – case studies on double reason), Frankfurt a. M.: Suhrkamp.

Tsoukas, H. and R. Chia (2002), 'On organizational becoming', *Organization Science*, **13** (5), 567–82.

Tsoukas, H. and J. Shepherd (2004) 'Introduction. Organization and the future: from forecasting to foresight', in H. Tsoukas and J. Shepherd (eds), *Managing the Future: Developing Strategic Foresight in the Knowledge Economy*, Oxford: Blackwell.

Waterhouse, M.F. (1992), 'Managing effectively in turbulent environments', *Journal of Strategic Change*, **3**, 135–46.

Weick, K.E. (1976), 'Educational organizations as loosely coupled systems', *Administrative Science Quarterly*, **21**, 1–19.

Weick, K.E. (1979), *The Social Psychology of Organizing*, Reading, MA: Addison-Wesley.

Weick, K.E. and F. Westley (1996), 'Organizational learning: affirming an oxymoron', in S.R. Clegg, C. Hardy and W.R. Nord (eds), *Handbook of Organization Studies*, London: Sage, pp. 440–58.

Whorf, B.L. (1956), *Language, Thought and Reality*, New York: John Wiley & Sons.

Winch, P. (1958), *The Idea of a Social Science and its Relation to Philosophy*, London: Routledge.

Wittgenstein, L. (1953), *Philosophical Investigations*, Oxford: Blackwell.

Wittgenstein, L. (1961), *Tractatus Logico-Philosophicus*, London: Routledge.

3 Strategic foresight
Ajit Nayak

Introduction

In a remarkably frank admission, Andy Grove the Intel chairman articulates the strategic challenges facing business leaders:

> None of us have a real understanding of where we are heading. I don't. I have senses about it. But decisions don't wait; investment decisions or personal decisions don't wait for that picture to be clarified. You have to make them when you have to make them . . . This is an intuitive process, because the numbers aren't in and the evidence isn't in . . . [One has to] grasp what cannot be spelled out and cannot be shown by data, to be in tune with . . . vague attributes . . . (Grove 2003, pp. 3–4)

There is no doubt that very few in the computing industry are as well placed as Andy Grove to know what the future holds for the industry. Despite this we see that he is unable to forecast or predict how the industry will evolve. What Grove articulates is the increasing importance of strategic foresight in a world where forecasting the future is increasingly problematic. As Wack (1985) states:

> Forecasts are not always wrong; more often than not, they can be reasonably accurate. And that is what makes them so dangerous. They are usually constructed on the assumption that tomorrow's world will be much like today's. They often work because the world does not always change. But sooner or later forecasts will fail when they are most needed. (p. 73)

Wack echoes Andy Grove's predicament. Organizations have developed sophisticated routines and capabilities that are very good at addressing incremental changes but major changes create significant problems. This has been highlighted by various popular management ideas such as hypercompetition (D'Aveni and Gunter 1994) and disruptive innovation (Christensen 1997; Christensen and Raynor 2003) over the last three decades. D'Aveni and Gunter argued that industries are facing an era of hypercompetition that requires them to develop market disruption capabilities. Sony, for example, explicitly state that they aim to disrupt their markets and work on making all their existing products obsolete in the future. Ironically, according to Christensen who popularized disruptive innovation, Sony was a serial disrupter of markets until it started employing MBAs. Christensen implies that the overemphasis on analysis, division of management into various specialisms and the reliance on case studies to provide pseudo-experience on MBA programmes does not prepare managers for the challenges in the real world.

In order to address the challenges of hypercompetition and disruptive innovation, companies need to move away from intense cost-quality competition to creating uncontested market spaces. This is illustrated by popular management ideas such as creating 'blue ocean' strategies (Kim and Mauborgne 2005) and 'breakout' strategies (Finkelstein et al. 2006). Blue ocean strategies highlight the need for companies to innovate in order to create uncontested market spaces that make existing competition irrelevant and create and capture demand from new and non-consumers. Similarly, breakout strategies show how new companies can take an industry by storm and outperform incumbents, how incumbents can go from being laggards to leaders, and how dominant firms can expand the horizons of their industry and shift the shape of existing and emerging markets. What blue ocean and breakout strategies point to is the need to balance our tools and techniques for forecasting with foresight. They demonstrate that the key challenge for managers in an uncertain, ambiguous and hypercompetitive world is to develop a deep engagement with the practices that make up the real world. Being a manager requires an engaging style, one that is experience based, 'quiet and connected, involving and inspiring. . . . Effective managing therefore happens where art, craft, and science meet' (Mintzberg 2004, p. 10).

So what is foresight? Drawing on the philosopher Alfred North Whitehead, Tsoukas and Sheppard (2004) provide a useful definition:

> Foresight is rooted in deep understanding . . . It marks the ability to see through the apparent confusion, to spot developments before they become trends, to see patterns before they fully emerge, and to grasp the relevant features of social currents that are likely to shape the direction of future events. (p. 2)

If we want to take the future seriously we must acknowledge that the future is inherently unknowable, open-ended and genuinely surprising, and that there are cognitive limits to our ability to predict the future. Terms such as 'precognition' (Arthur 1996) and 'peripheral vision' (Chia 2004) aim to articulate the ability to make sense of apparent confusion. For Arthur, what makes someone like Bill Gates such a visionary is that he 'is not so much a wizard of technology as a wizard of *precognition*, of discerning the shape of the next game' (Arthur 1996, p. 104, original italics). Similarly for Chia, what makes someone like Matsushita a visionary is his ability 'to detect those inarticulate forms that conscious attention overlooks' (Chia 2004, p. 31). Chia highlights that strategic foresight is about re-educating attention: 'We learn more fundamentally from *glancing* rather than from *gazing*, from *scanning* and *browsing* than from *looking*; from immersion in *vagueness* than from attending to already-formed *gestalt* figures' (ibid., p. 22, original italics).

What Arthur and Chia point to are the limits of cognitive and activist understanding of human action. Following Arthur and Chia, in this chapter I argue that what is less understood is the role of broader unconscious forces that work through human action and guide strategic foresight and form the basis of understanding terms such as precognition and peripheral vision. It is far too easy to misunderstand peripheral vision and precognition as implying one type or one part of action among others. For example, all the contributors in the special issue on peripheral vision in *Long Range Planning* (2004) take an activist view of human action and agency. The problem with this literature is precisely its source of inspiration – sight. The overemphasis on sight means that they understand the periphery spatially rather than existentially. To truly understand periphery we need to recognize that it is not just the spatial limits of our ability to see, but more fundamentally it lies outside our conditions of intelligibility. Peripheral in the existential sense lies beyond our worldview. The source of the misunderstanding is that management ideas are deeply rooted in the illusion of the rational autonomous actor who is at the centre of the action. In contrast, I articulate a notion of action that emphasizes the broader structuring structures that 'unobtrusively govern' (Heidegger 1978, p. 212) action and work through individual actors.

In this chapter I argue that the coming together of analytical techniques with imagination and practical wisdom prepares the ground for understanding and cultivating strategic foresight. The structure of the chapter is as follows. First, in order to understand foresight, I argue that we need to move away from the underlying assumptions that inform our ideas of forecasting. I identify three main assumptions that are privileged and underpin our theories and models of forecasting – intentional action, bodily control and individual autonomy. Second, I argue that in order to cultivate foresight, managers need to attend to their existential experience of managing and management educators need to complement analytical techniques with a philosophical capability which is paradoxical and incites wonder.

Tacit assumptions of rational action

> The Western conception of the person as a bounded, unique, more or less integrated motivational and cognitive universe, a dynamic centre of awareness, emotion, judgement and action, organized into a distinctive whole and set contrastively against other such wholes and against a social and natural background is, however incorrigible it may seem to us, a rather peculiar idea . . . (Geertz 1979, p. 229)

One consequence of our success in mastering our environment is the privileging of the autonomous self and rational action. Despite numerous reminders in every social science discipline, the rational autonomous person remains 'incorrigible'. Even within topics such as creativity, where one would expect to find ideas that do not privilege rational man, there exists an underlying theme of defining creativity in opposition to non-creative and routine action, and hence re-enforcing rational action (Joas 1996). In opposition to this view, following Joas, I argue that creativity is central to all action by examining three tacit assumptions that underpin rational action. First, rational action presupposes that the actor is, and should be, defined as someone capable of purposive action. If there is a loss or lack of purposiveness, then the actor is not responsible for or assigned the role of the actor. Thus, the notion of action starts with assigning *intentionality*. Second, the actor is assumed to have control over his/her *body*. Along with intentionality, bodily control is seen as a prerequisite of action. If an action occurs without bodily control on the part of the actor, the actor is again seen as not responsible for the action. Third, the actor is seen as being autonomous and separate from other human beings and the situation. The *relationality* among actor–action–situation is seen as secondary to the actor, action and situation.

Critique of intentional action

There has always been a recognition in management theory that rational action is not the only form of action. For example, in *The Functions of the Executive*, Chester Barnard (1938) states that organizational life incorporates logical and nonlogical processes, where the nonlogical processes incorporates intuition, inspiration and enthusiasm. Similarly, March and Simon (1958) view organizational actors as acting according to organizational roles and personal emotions. However, rational action is seen as the better form of action. As a mainstream strategy textbook illustrates,

> Strategy is about winning . . . it is a unifying theme that gives coherence and direction to the actions and decisions of an individual or an organization . . . The key premise that underlies

this book is that there are concepts, frameworks, and techniques that are immensely useful in formulating and implementing effective strategies. (Grant 2005, p. 4)

Strategy establishes the purpose, goals and ends which then enables an individual or an organization to find appropriate means of achieving them. The emphasis establishing the purpose and goals of an organization and on the tools and techniques to achieve those goals takes a means–end view of action as its point of departure. There have been several notable attempts to overcome a means–end approach to action and strategy (March 1988; Wiltbank et al. 2006). In this section I draw on the philosophy of John Dewey to critique a means–end approach. For Dewey, action as it is experienced, is not structured in terms of means and ends, or in terms of chains of means and ends.

However, we can separate out the 'I' of the actor as the source and cause of the action. By doing this we succeed in systematizing the experiential and behavioural potentialities that manifest themselves in natural experience, and interpreting them in such a way that they become available for the purpose of comparison and thus accessible to rationalization. It allows actors to perceive and evaluate the consequences of their action rationally through the means–end schema. In order to avoid an interpretation of action that relies on cause–effect through the division of 'I' from the action, Dewey examines the role of ends in action (Dewey 1939; Visalberghi 1953). Dewey argues that action is infused with meaning. The purpose of action is not to be determined through its effects or causes, but through the moment of maturation and completion that is intrinsic to action. In order to understand action infused with meaning, Dewey distinguishes between goals and results of action. Goals as anticipated results of action do not explain their role in present action. As anticipation, goals are just dreams and do not lead to action. Dewey introduces the concept of 'end-in-view' to define the role of goals in present action. Goals are not given externally to an action but co-determined with the means of action. Goals are usually relatively undefined and only become specific as a consequence of the decision to use particular means. Through the reciprocal relationship between means and goals, we can see the possible goals that are available to us. The means available not only specify the goals, but also expand the scope of possible goals. Ends-in-view are concrete plans of action that guide the choice of possibilities of action as well as being determined by the possibilities. For Dewey, externally determined goals, which are necessary for a means–end schema, are not part of action.

Departing from a means–end approach that privileges intentionality and pre-existent goals has a significant impact on the way we conceptualize action. Action becomes the core of our world. Rather than the world being something external to the self it takes the form of possibilities. As May (1959) explains:

> I do not mean the usual connotation of 'world;' certainly not environment, not the 'sum total' of things around, nor do I refer at all to objects about a subject. All of our English connotations of 'world' are emaciated from the cancer of Western thought, the subject–object split. I use world in the German sense of *Welt*. World is the pattern of meaningful relations in which the person exists and in the design of which he participates. It has objective reality, to be sure, but it is not simply that; world is interrelated to the existing person at every moment. A continual dialectical process goes on between world and self, and self and world; one implies the other, and neither can be defined if we omit the other. (p. 65)

What is generally understood as situationally contingent human action is reformulated as the situation constitutive of action. Thus, situations are not a neutral field of activity for intentions that are conceived outside of the situation, but call forth, to provoke certain actions:

> By 'situation' we – that is, 'we' as human beings who act and who know about action – understand a relationship between human beings and objects, or between a human being and objects, which already precedes the particular action under consideration and which is therefore in each case already understood by the person or people concerned as a challenge either to do or alternatively not to do something. In colloquial speech we talk about 'getting into' situations: they 'befall' us, 'happen to' us and we find ourselves 'confronted' by them. These are ways of expressing that a situation is something which precedes our action (or inaction) but which also provokes action because it 'affects' us, 'interests' us, or 'concerns' us. (Bohler 1985, p. 252, quoted in Joas 1996, p. 160)

The reciprocal relationship between action and situation emphasizes that the situation has to communicate to us, just as we have to communicate to the world:

> Situation orientation and goal-orientation are interlinked with one another from the outset. For if we did not have certain *dispositions towards goals*, no matter how vague, which are given *ante actu* in the form of needs, interests and norms, an event would not occur for us as a situation we are in, but would remain devoid of meaning and mute. (Bohler 1985, pp. 272–3, quoted in Joas 1996, p. 161, original italics)

It is not that the situation was given to us prior to action, but that we can see the givenness of the situation in retrospect. Thus, intentions in action are reflexively present in action. This presence, in Bohler's terms, as vague dispositions, points to the corporeality of action. Although we categorize our world in terms of familiar/unfamiliar, controllable/uncontrollable, self/other, we are still connected to this external world through our capacity to act.

To summarize, in order to overcome the means–end schema, we need to recognize that our practical mediacy of acting in the world and the situation precede all conscious goal setting. Intentions do not precede action but are a phase of action by which action is directed and redirected in its situational contexts. Goals are not determined prior to action, but are a result of a reflection on aspirations, desires and tendencies that are pre-reflective and have already been operative. In order to move beyond the means–end schema, which conceptualizes goals as external to action, we need to recognize that goal setting is not purely a mental activity. This raises the question of how such pre-reflective desires and aspirations of goal setting work. As the next subsection demonstrates, they are at work through the body which encounters the world around us.

The role of the body in action
There is an implicit assumption in action theories that the body is under the control of the actor. Although there is a general recognition that the body plays a major role in action, its use in action is assumed unproblematically. The unquestioningly accepted status of the role of the body has been that 'the growth of civilization requires simultaneously the restraint of the body and the cultivation of character in the interests of social stability' (Turner 1991, pp. 14–15). In this subsection, I examine two critiques of the role of the body in action. First, action theories favour an activist relationship to the world. They emphasize the constant generation of acts, which are culture, if not gender, specific. An activist portrayal of action cannot account for the passivity, sensitivity and receptivity

of action. For example, Indian cultures that accept the notion of destiny and fate or Chinese cultures that '[teach] one to learn how to allow an effect to come about: not to aim for it (directly) but to implicate it (as a consequence)' (Jullien 2004, p. vii) and cultivate aesthetic sensibilities that are not linked to action, cannot be explained by an activist portrayal of action. Second, by considering the body as an instrumental medium that is permanently available for expressing intentions, rationalistic theories confine the role of the body. The body does not have any significance in itself, but is used as a controllable body in communication. In contrast, I draw on 'meaningful loss of intentionality' and 'passive intentionality' to critique the rational approach to the body in action.

Plessner (1970) develops the idea of 'meaningful loss on intentionality' in order to show how laughter and crying cannot be explained within rationalistic theories. He differentiates laughter and crying from intentional control of our bodies in gestures and unintentional bodily action in blushing. For him, during intentional control we have dominance over our bodies, while our limits to the dominance over our bodies is apparent in blushing. However, in laughter and crying, we experience a sudden loss of control, where we lose our relation to our physical existence: 'Bodily processes emancipate themselves; man is shaken by them, buffeted, made breathless. He has lost his relation to his physical existence; it withdraws from him and does with him more or less what it will' (p. 66). Plessner argues that the distance between the 'self' and 'body' is suspended in such action. We revert to our pre-reflective connection with the situation and action. Plessner claims that laughter and crying are not cases where we are overwhelmed by superior forces, but is the result of the loss of that distance which is a precondition of intentional action: 'an absence of distance – not from the actual feeling but from the content which engrosses me in the feeling, which rouses and shakes me' (ibid., p. 143).

Merleau-Ponty (1982) develops the idea of 'passive intentionality' to address the loosening of bodily control and explains this with the example of falling asleep:

> I lie down in bed, on my left side, with my knees drawn up; I close my eyes and breathe slowly, putting my plans out of my mind. But the power of my will or consciousness stops there . . . I call up the visitation of sleep by imitating the breathing and posture of the sleeper . . . There is a moment when sleep 'comes,' settling on this imitation of itself which I have been offering to it, and I succeed in becoming what I was trying to be: an unseeing and almost unthinking mass, riveted to a point in space and in the world henceforth only through the anonymous alertness of the senses. (pp. 163–4)

Merleau-Ponty demonstrates how intentional action needs to be abandoned in order for the pre-reflective intentions of the body to emerge. He develops a concept of intentionality that emphasizes its bodily, 'incarnate' character. He argues that in order to resolve the problem of mind and body or intentions and corporeality we should not presuppose a duality. Using the terms 'pre-reflexive' or 'pre-predicative', he refers to the givenness of the world prior to all acts of reflection or prediction. In order to demonstrate his concept, he addresses the issues of 'phantom organs'. Phantom organs are observed in cases of pathological malfunctioning, where a person feels that an amputated arm or leg is still present, although they 'objectively' do not exist. For Merleau-Ponty:

> The phantom arm is not a representation of the arm, but the ambivalent presence of an arm . . . To have a phantom arm is to remain open to all the actions of which the arm alone is capable; it is to retain the practical field which one enjoyed before mutilation . . . The patient therefore

realises his disability precisely in so far as he is ignorant of it, and is ignorant of it precisely to the extent that he knows of it. (pp. 81–2)

In other words, Merleau-Ponty suggests that there is no a priori distinction between the mind and the body. Thus, 'man taken as a concrete being is not a psyche joined to an organism, but the movement to and fro of existence which at one time allows itself to take corporeal form and at others moves towards personal acts' (p. 88). He distinguishes between 'habitual' and 'actual' body in order to signify the to and fro movement.

Merleau-Ponty develops a philosophical basis for the body in action related to specific situations. Our bodies are not a culmination of sensation that is available to us in action. Reworking the notion of body through the concept of action leads him to how we acquire a sense of body by considering the 'intercorporeite' bodies. By 'intercorporeite' he considers the interrelatedness of our experiences of our bodies to our experiences of others' bodies. By looking at the relations between the subject and others in a pre-linguistic sense, Merleau-Ponty highlights how we move from a stage of 'undifferentiation' to cognising the world as separate. For example, how the mother's care of her infant by means of stance, gesture and voice enables the infant to differentiate between itself and the other.

In order to understand the interrelatedness of the development of the body, we need to look at the role of pre-linguistic communication. In other words, we need to explain how the notion of body is constituted with respect to other bodies before we cognise the difference. George Herbert Mead provides us with insights into such an explanation. Starting with how an infant is able to trace a source to perception, Mead (1934) explains how the infant cannot identify inner experiences as ones from their own body:

> Our bodies are parts of the environment; and it is possible for the individual to experience and be conscious of his body, and of bodily sensations, without being conscious or aware of himself . . . Until the rise of his self-consciousness in the process of social experience, the individual experiences his body – its feelings and sensations – merely as an immediate part of his environment, not as his own, not in terms of self-consciousness. (pp. 171–2)

In order to differentiate between experiences emanating from his/her own body and those from outside, Mead argues, one needs to adopt a stance towards oneself that is conveyed by signifying gestures. This implies that it has, at least in an elementary manner, become possible to experience the unity of the body. Yet, how can the body ever be experienced as unity if each perception only presents one part of it? Mead (1938) points out:

> The body of the percipient individual is not an object as a whole. Different parts of the individual are seen and felt, or are both seen and felt, but there is no experience in which the entire individual appears as an object. That there are peculiar characters that are common to these parts of the body of the individual does not constitute them as a single object, for that arises only in so far as the individual acts with reference to it as a whole. It is only as the objects are fixed in a field of contemporaneity that the individual can be fixed as a persistent whole within such a field, and only as the hypothetical content of the physical object is so identified with the attitudes of the individual that the individual presses against the body's resistance to the object, and the percipient individual becomes an object in the field of physical objects. (p. 226)

For Mead, the formation of the body depends on the constitution of a physical or permanent object. The object and the unity of one's own body is co-determined. Such a co-determination, in Mead's theory, presupposes the existence of elementary structures of role taking.

What Mead emphasizes is that the instrumental nature of our bodies is the result of a primary socialization process. Only through the 'symbolic interaction' can we understand the unity of the body and cognise it as an object. What follows is a process of 'desocialization', through which we recognize inanimate objects as such. Even before we are aware of the boundary between the self and others we are able to react to gestural languages in interaction. In recognizing objects as permanent objects, through the process of desocialization, we are able to co-determine the unity of the body as separate from the social world. In other words, our conception of the body relies on a tacit assumption of how we achieve the unity of the body via socialization. Our ability to act, according to Merleau-Ponty and Mead, rests on relationality, which has not been generated by conscious intentionality but has preceded it.

Relationality

Although the distinction between rational choice structure and individual–social has a long social science tradition, a relational approach draws on a rich philosophical tradition; one that has gained prominence in strategy and organization studies research (Cooper 2005; Chia and Holt 2006). A relational view seeks to explain human actions in terms of broad unconscious forces that form the background of practical coping. These practical engagements precede mental content, reflection or any form of symbolic representation. Heidegger (1962) introduces a new vocabulary to understand our world in terms of relationality. Unusual terms such as 'worldliness', 'readiness-to-hand' and 'for-the-sake-of-which' are Heidegger's way of introducing creative action in place of rational action. In this subsection, continuing the discussion of the body, I examine the work of George Herbert Mead and David McNeill. They offer an excellent refutation of the individualistic and activist notions of human agency and structure.

Mead introduces the autonomous individual in action theory through evolutionary and developmental perspectives on the emergence of the self. Starting with the biological base of the individual, and the stimulus–response theory of action, Mead states that the self is more than its biology because of the human ability to respond to the anticipated behaviour of others. Although the 'biological individual' plays an important part, the self is also a 'socially self-conscious individual'. The distinction between the biological and social can be made, but 'they are not on separate planes, but play back and forth into each other, and constitute, under most conditions, an experience which appears to be cut by no lines of cleavage' (Mead 1934, p. 347). The difference between the purely biological, as in animals, and the biological and social, is the human use of 'symbols' that are interpreted as an intention of action. In humans there is a coordination by means of a shared orientation towards patterns of mutual behavioural expectations. Mead develops the concept of 'role taking', which refers to the anticipation of situation-specific behaviour of others in action. The imaginative completion of an action, which Mead calls 'meaning' and which represents mental activity, necessarily takes place through 'role taking'.

Mead introduces the relationality of the self by starting with the 'social act' in order to explain the individual. Instead of conceptualizing social action as an aggregation of individual action or some holistic notion of action, Mead argues for the irreducible relationality behind all individual acts by examining the importance of language in defining the self.

Language mediates all human action and thought. Language, in the broadest sense, is a communicative act or a 'gesture', which is present in the instinctual form in animals. As Mead states, '[t]he term "gesture" may be identified with these beginnings of social acts which are stimuli for the response of other forms' (ibid., p. 43). Gestures contain information about the future of the whole act, which is communicated. A gesture is meaningful because it carries information that enables others to predict behaviour. The meaning is not dependent on the consciousness of the meaning. Mead reverses the conventional relationship between meaning and consciousness. '[C]onsciousness is an emergent from such behavior; that so far from being a precondition of the social act, the social act is the precondition of it' (ibid., p. 18). Hence, for Mead, meaning is independent of the consciousness of it and exists objectively in the act: '"Meaning" is thus a development of something objectively there as a relation between certain phases of the social act; it is not a psychical addition to that act and it is not an "idea" as traditionally conceived' (p. 76). The objective meaning of a gesture is a triadic relationship between gesture, response and completion.

The objective existence of meaning of the gestures in the act does not imply that the generator is aware of the meaning. For example, when we see an animal that is about to attack, 'we cannot say the animal means it in the sense that he has a reflective determination to attack' (ibid., p. 45). When the generator of the gesture is aware of the meaning, the gesture becomes a 'significant symbol'. For example:

> A man may strike another before he means it; a man may jump and run away from a loud sound behind his back before he knows what he is doing. If he has the idea in his mind, then the gesture not only means this to the observer but *it also means the idea which the individual has.* (p. 45; emphasis added)

When the generator and the receiver of the gesture understand the idea behind the gesture, we reach the stage of 'language':

> [T]hat gesture means this idea behind it and it arouses that idea in the other individual, then we have a significant symbol. . . . [I]n the present case, we have a symbol which answers to a meaning in the experience of the first individual and which also calls out that meaning in the second individual. *Where the gesture reaches that situation it has become what we call 'language.'* (p. 45; emphasis added)

The consciousness of the significant symbol arouses the same meaning and response in the generator and the receiver, and differentiates the animal from the human. It is the shared meaning behind the (vocal or non-vocal) gestures that differentiates the social act as a significant symbol. McNeill (2005), building on Mead's work, demonstrates how gestures are dynamically linked to thought and action. He demonstrates that vocal and non-vocal gestures are inextricably connected in an imagery–language dialectic. This dialectic 'is the key to the evocation, organization, and ultimate execution of meaningful actions shaped to take form in discourse' (ibid., p. 87). McNeill argues that Mead's description of the acquisition of the significant symbol and language in humans is a result of human life being relational, and traces this back to the emergence of family life in human evolution. As McNeill states:

> I suggest that . . . family life, specifically, mother–child interactions, was the setting par excellence. The scenario would had to have been a rich social context in order for Mead's loop

[gesture–response–completion] to be of adaptive value. Human-style scaffolding, in which adults deliberately and closely monitor a child's activity to help him/her acquire and develop activities in an efficient and adaptive way, is a kind of context, and phylogenetically unique and present in all human societies . . . (p. 252)

The relational being-in-the-world of participating in family life is the source of internal mental life. Hence gestures and language are primarily the 'pre-objective space' that connect and relate meaning through agency (Cooper 2005).

To summarize, the self is something that is not present at birth but develops from birth in the process of social experience and activity. The self develops in the given individual as a result of his/her relation to that process as a whole and to other individuals within the process. Starting in childhood the development of the self, as a whole self, continues as s/he internalizes more complex forms of social organization. These complex forms become more generalized and abstract social relations, and the self develops a perspective of him/herself through this generalized other. As Mead states, '[a] person is a personality because he belongs to a community, because he takes over the institutions of that community into his own conduct' (Mead 1934, p. 162). The self starts with the social act of relating, and the person with a personality emerges through this process. Relationality, together with the non-instrumental role of the body and intentions-in-action, shed light on the implicit assumptions that underpin rational action theories. Introducing these implicit assumptions into action theory enables a conceptualization of action that forms the basis for cultivating strategic foresight.

Implications for strategic foresight

In this section I explore two main implications of intentions-in-action, non-instrumental corporeality and relationality of action for cultivating strategic foresight. First, creative action gives primacy to existential experience rather than a tool-based, analytical, simulated, classroom teaching that is commonplace on most MBA programmes. Hence cultivating strategic foresight implies that we need to pay closer attention to lived experience. Second, creative action calls for developing philosophical capability underpinned by a paradoxical way which cultivates a mood of wonder and awe.

Existential experience

In a provocative book, Mintzberg (2004) makes a useful distinction between two mindsets: MBAs and managers. An MBA mindset divides management into a variety of subdisciplines and emphasizes the importance of analytical tools and techniques that a manager can use. In contrast, a manager mindset addresses individuals who accumulate life experiences and develop their capacity to deeply reflect upon the world they dwell in. As Mintzberg observes:

[C]onventional MBA students graduate with the impression that management is analysis, specifically the making of systematic decisions and the formulation of deliberate strategies. This, I argue . . . is a narrow and ultimately distorted view of management that has encouraged two dysfunctional styles in practice: *calculating* (overly analytical) and *heroic* (pretend art). [In contrast management is] a more experienced-based style labelled *engaging* – quiet and connected, involving and inspiring. Put together a good deal of craft with a certain amount of art and some science, and you end up with a job that is above all a *practice* . . . Effective managing therefore happens where art, craft, and science meet. (pp. 10–11, original italics)

Explicit to the manager mindset is the attempt to provide a rich phenomenological account of the events, actions and contexts of managerial life (Watson, 1994; Weick, 1995; Watson and Harris, 1999). While the MBA mindset remains the dominant one, the emphasis within the manager mindset is on the subjective experiences of managers that give rise to actions rather than on the impersonal tools and techniques that are causally linked to organizational success. As such, broader social science approaches that regard being a manager as a practice rather than a science provide the appropriate frame of reference.

The importance of an engaged style of management is illustrated by practices at Toyota. Toyota's ability to consistently set new standards in the auto manufacturing industry has been well documented (Spear and Bowden 1999; Spear 2004). Toyota has demonstrated that there is a causally ambiguous relationship between their success and their resources, capabilities and strategies. Hence, decoding Toyota's DNA does not mean that it is possible for other companies to imitate and replicate it. In order to understand how Toyota themselves replicate their success, Spear (2004) recounts the experience of one American manager, Bob Dallis, hired for their US plant, as he went about learning Toyota's production system (TPS). TPS 'is a system of nested experiments through which operations are constantly improved' (ibid., p. 80). Dallis's training programme involved him understanding not just how to conduct nested experiments but also to learn how to replicate the process by engendering the right mindset in his colleagues. Spear explains how Dallis's training involved deep engagement with practices and the relentless focus on detail and continuous improvements. Dallis is trained to directly observe how things are done and experiment to improve them. Although Spear illustrates the importance of on-the-job experience and deep understanding of practices, for our purposes here, one practice stands out. As part of his training, Dallis was taken to Toyota's famous Kamgo engine plant in Japan. There, Dallis was asked to work with one of the employees to make improvements. Whereas Spear emphasizes the pace and scale of improvements demanded of Dallis, what is instructive to note is that Dallis, who did not speak Japanese, is made to work with the Japanese employee, who did not speak English, without a translator. This reverses the conventional priority given to the spoken part of language as opposed to the gestures and non-vocal articulations that are inherent in how meaning and significance is communicated. Toyota's practices implicitly recognize that meaning, perception and understanding are derived from these non-verbal forms of communication and that at times the verbal can impede a deeper understanding.

Understanding managing as a practice and recognizing the significance of deep engagement with experience is only one side of the coin. Inextricably entwined with a practice-based approach to managing is the need to cultivate a philosophical capability (Chia 1996). As I argue in the next subsection, cultivating such a capability requires us to pay close attention to the vague and the imprecise and to develop a paradoxical way of thinking.

Philosophical capability
In the introduction to Heidegger's (1966) *Discourse on Thinking*, Anderson compares early Hindu thought with the more popular fables of Panchatantra:

> The beast fables of the Panchatantra describe and point up a science of survival, a hard calculative view of life and its possibilities, and an unsentimental evaluation of its content:

Make friends, make friends, however strong
  Or weak they be:
Recall the captive elephants
  That mice set free

How sharply such admonitions contrast with the mystical messages of the Upanishads! How clear they are in formulating the problems and methods of human survival, by casting them in terms of animals and their ways – and how opaque and obscure are the Upanishads in their unremitting efforts to reveal the ultimate nature of things:

The knowing Self is not born, it dies not; it sprang
from nothing, nothing sprang from it.

(Heidegger 1966, pp. 11–12)

This is another way of distinguishing between forecasting and foresight. Whereas forecasts rely on clarity that is akin to the Panchatantra stories, foresight involves engaging with the vague, imprecise and latent (Cooper 2005). The vague, imprecise and latent inherently resists conceptual and practical appropriation, hence the need to understand it as a philosophical capability. In order to do this we need to move away from rational action and calculative thinking.

Paradoxical way   Our fixation with rational action and calculative thinking is accompanied by our emphasis on method. More specifically, it is the scientific method that underpins our attempts to forecast the future. In our conventional understanding, the method provides us with the right direction and a systematic approach. In contrast, a paradoxical way inverts our conventional understanding and emphasizes a more subtle way of thinking rather than a precise method. In order to appreciate a paradoxical way, it is instructive to note that the Greek word 'hodos' gives us our modern-day word 'method'. Hodos means 'way' or 'path' or 'journey'. It can also mean 'a manner'; 'a course of action' or 'speech'. Combined with the prefix meta-, we get methodos, a 'following after, pursuit, esp. pursuit of knowledge, a method of inquiry' (Liddell et al. 1940, quoted in Schur 1998, pp. 16–17). Hence, our modern-day understanding of method, especially the scientific method, hides a more subtle and paradoxical understanding of hodos. This is illustrated by Heraclitus who states, 'The path [hodos] . . . is straight and crooked . . . The way up and the way down are one and the same' (Kahn 1979, pp. 63, 75). For Heraclitus, hodos is a way that is both straight and crooked at the same time. Schur (1998) argues that Heraclitus combines contradictory terms to demonstrate a paradoxical method by inverting our understanding of 'way' or 'path': 'We commonly view [the usage of way or path] as metaphorical rather than literal; in rhetorical terms, the path is a picturesque topos (commonplace) and a vivid trope (figure), turning our attention toward something other than a real road' (p. 17). By inverting this commonsense understanding of 'way' and 'path', Heraclitus exposes us to his paradoxical method in three different ways. First, he inverts the 'way' of verbal expression, which is a topos, an expression of conventionality, something that is customary, captured by our everyday phrases 'of course' or 'that's the way of the world'. Hence, the way describes something that is familiar and methodical. By referring to the way as both straight and crooked, Heraclitus juxtaposes topos with a-topos, which means out of place or strange or paradoxical. Second, he inverts the 'way' as a trope. Tropos means 'turn' and is related to the verbal 'way'. Tropos can mean 'turn' as in 'direction' or 'manner'. By juxtaposing straight and crooked, up and down, Heraclitus raises questions about the status of tropes. The Greek word 'poros' (way) suggests the third paradoxical movement. The topos of the poros becomes an atopos (paradoxical) declaration of the aporia (waylessness). Although the three inversions of 'way' by Heraclitus may seem like a superficial manipulation of ancient words, it serves as an intimation to question our taken-for-granted 'way'. As Schur remarks, Heraclitus' 'descriptions are provocative, challenging our reliance on the metaphor of the way by disturbing the commonplace notions of direction and correctness that it entails' (p. 20).

A paradoxical way with its complexity and 'straight and crooked' approach can appear to be confusing, impractical and far removed from the world of business. However, as I argue in the next subsection, when the paradoxical way inspires awe and wonder it leads to strategic foresight.

Awe and wonder   In his discussions on wonder (*Er-staunen*, *Thaumazein*) Heidegger (1994) distinguishes between the pre-Socratic and our current understanding of the term. Our age confuses wonder with curiosity, hence we are unable to engage in what Heidegger calls 'genuine thinking'. There are three synonyms for wonder that need to be differentiated in order to understand wonder (Stone 2006). First, wonder is confused with amazement (*Sichwundern*). Amazement is 'a certain inability to explain and ignorance from reason' (Heidegger 1994, p. 137). For example, magic tricks are 'wondrous' or amazing when we do not know how they are performed. They are no longer amazing when we learn how the trick is performed. The amazement also reduces the more times we see the trick. Hence what is amazing the first time because it is rare and uncommon becomes habitual, ordinary and boring after repetition. Second, wonder is confused with admiration (*Bewundern*). Popular management literature is full of heroic stories of successful leaders like Jack Welch and Bill Gates whose performance may greatly impress us. We may 'wonder' how they were able to achieve as much as they have. However, such admiration is not wonder because it relies upon the admirers to affirm the admired. Once we stop admiring the successful leaders, they are no longer seen as wonderful. Like amazing magic tricks, in order to continue being admired, we have to chase more and more new things to do that others will admire and not consider boring and ordinary. Third, Heidegger distinguishes between wonder and astonishment. Astonishment leaves the admirer awestruck and dumbfounded. One can be dumbfounded by great acts of nature such as volcanoes or tsunamis or even a great sunset. Unlike admiration and amazement, 'astonishment includes a decisive suspension of position-taking . . . Astonishment allows the unusual to grow, precisely as what is extraordinary, into what overgrows all usual powers and bears in itself a claim to a rank all its own. Astonishment is imbued with the awareness of being excluded from what exists in the awesome' (ibid., p. 143). Great events or acts that leave us dumbfounded exclude us and make us aware of how insignificant we are in comparison to the awesome. However, like amazement and admiration, we are less and less dumbfounded the more we are exposed to the awesome.

For Heidegger, amazement, admiration and astonishment are all variations on curiosity (*Neugier*). They are not wonder because they rely upon the logic of the more and the less. We need to continuously search for 'new' things that can lead to more amazement, more admiration and be more astonishing. Failure to find 'new' things leads to less amazement, admiration and astonishment being experienced. Curiosity (*Neugier*) literally means 'avidity for the new'. In contrast, wonder does not rely on the more and the less. Wonder is not only things that are extraordinary. Nor is it only things that are ordinary. Instead, it lies between and prior to the distinction between ordinary and extraordinary: 'In wonder . . . everything becomes the most unusual . . . Everything in what is most usual (beings) becomes in wonder the most unusual in this one respect: that it is what it is' (ibid., p. 144). Wonder is a broad unconscious disposition that works through individuals and situations and reveals the whole as wondrous. Rather than falling prey (*verfallen*) to the distraction of searching for newer and newer things, wonder implies an attunement to feeling deep awe (*Scheu*): 'Now awe is an ambivalent emotion, compounded of wonder and humility; the wonder keeps the emotion alive and the mind open, while the humility restrains the wonder from slipping into idle curiosity' (Wheelwright 1971, p. 47). Wonder and awe, in this sense, imply that we continually remain on the way rather than moving from one new thing to another. It is a kind of mental questing that moves beyond given categories, contexts and styles (Cooper 2001).

To summarize, a philosophical capability implies engaging with the vague, latent and ambiguous. It implies that managers cannot rely upon a method or rules of analysis to determine direction and plan the future. Instead they need to engage with a paradoxical way that leads to wonder and awe. Philosophical capability deals with one resource that managers often complain about lacking – time. Managers are seen to make bounded-rational decisions because they do not have the time to collect all the information. The incessant search for newness leads to further time pressures. A philosophical capability points to a deeper understanding of time, one that does not fly past and is not susceptible to the highs and lows of newness. To cultivate foresight, managers need to develop the ability to feel wonder and awe that stems from being present in the broader unconscious forces that work through individuals.

Conclusion

Unlike forecasting, foresight is not a concept, framework or toolkit to be used for analysing a situation and predicting the future. Although both aim to address the uncertainties of an unpredictable world, unlike forecasting which privileges scenario planning, mapping possibilities and deliberate action, foresight privileges the existential experience of being and acting in the world by engaging quietly and connectedly with the potentiality and propensity of things and situations (Jullien 1995, 2004). Foresight is not a matter of unifying the myriad of weak signals from the periphery, nor is it a matter of making appearance familiar under the guise of a great principle. Foresight is learning all over again how to see, directing one's consciousness, making of every image a privileged place. Like with terms such as strategy, goals, context and foresight, our Western understanding has a very definite activist and intentional connotation. In comparison, what this chapter has been alluding to is a more subtle, non-activist and non-intentional, yet purposive action. 'There is a very good phrase in Japanese, *kosoryoku* . . . *Kosoryoku* is something like "vision," but it also has the notion of "concept" and "imagination." . . . *kosoryoku* is an ability to see what is invisible and to shape the amorphous' (Ohmae 2005, p. 271). *Kosoryoku* encapsulates this more philosophical and paradoxical way of thinking. The word brings together the latent and vague with the definite and manifest aspects of what it means to act in the world. Strategic foresight is the ability to cultivate this sense of *kosoryoku* that springs from a non-intentional, bodily and relational view of action.

References

Arthur, W.B. (1996), 'Increasing returns and the new world of business', *Harvard Business Review*, **74** (4), 100–109.
Barnard, C.I. (1938), *The Functions of the Executive*, Cambridge, MA: Harvard University Press.
Bohler, D. (1985), *Rekonstruktive pragmatik*, Frankfurt: Suhrkamp.
Chia, R. (1996), 'Teaching paradigm shifting in management education: university business schools and the entrepreneurial imagination', *Journal of Management Studies*, **33** (4), 409–28.
Chia, R. (2004), 'Re-educating attention: what is foresight and how is it cultivated?', in Tsoukas and Sheppard (eds), pp. 21–37.
Chia, R. and R. Holt (2006), 'Strategy as practical coping: a Heideggerian perspective', *Organization Studies*, **27** (5), 635–55.
Christensen, C. (1997), *The Innovator's Dilemma*, Cambridge, MA: Harvard University Press.
Christensen, C. and M.E. Raynor (2003), *The Innovator's Solution*, Cambridge, MA: Harvard University Press.
Cooper, R. (2001), 'Un-timely mediations: questing thought', *Ephemera*, **1** (4), 321–47.
Cooper, R. (2005), 'Relationality', *Organization Studies*, **26** (11), 1689–710.
D'Aveni, R. and R. Gunter (1994), *Hypercompetition: Managing the Dynamics of Strategic Maneuvering*, New York: Free Press.
Dewey, J. (1939), *Theory of Valuation*, Chicago, IL: University of Chicago Press.
Finkelstein, S., C.E. Harvey and T. Lawton (2006), *Breakout Strategy*, London: McGraw-Hill.
Geertz, C. (1979), 'From the native's point of view: on the nature of anthropological understanding', in P. Rabinow and W.M. Sullivan (eds), *Interpretive Social Science*, Berkeley, CA: University of California Press, pp. 225–42.
Grant, R.M. (2005), *Contemporary Strategic Analysis*, 6th edition, Oxford: Blackwell Publishing.
Grove, A. (2003), 'Decisions don't wait', *Harvard Management Update*, **8** (1), 3–4.
Heidegger, M. (1962), *Being and Time*, New York: Harper Row.
Heidegger, M. (1966), *Discourse on Thinking*, New York: Harper Row.
Heidegger, M. (1978), *Basic Writings*, London: Routledge.
Heidegger, M. (1994), *Basic Questions in Philosophy: Selected 'Problems' of 'Logic'*, Bloomington, IN: Indiana University Press.
Joas, H. (1996), *The Creativity of Action*, Cambridge: Polity Press.
Jullien, F. (1995), *The Propensity of Things: Towards a History of Efficacy in China*, London: Zone Books.
Jullien, F. (2004), *A Treatise on Efficacy: Between Western and Chinese Thinking*, Honolulu, HI: University of Hawaii Press.
Kahn, C.H. (1979), *The Art and Thought of Heraclitus*, Cambridge: Cambridge University Press.
Kim, W.C. and R. Mauborgne (2005), *Blue Ocean Strategy*, Cambridge, MA: Harvard University Press.
Liddell, H.G., R. Scott and H. Stuart Jones (1940), *The Greek–English Lexicon*, Oxford: Oxford University Press.
March, J.G. (1988), 'The technology of foolishness', in J.G. March (ed.), *Decisions and Organizations*, Oxford: Blackwell, pp. 253–65.
March, J.G. and H.A. Simon (1958), *Organizations*, New York: John Wiley.
May, R. (1959), 'The nature of creativity', in H.H. Anderson (ed.), *Creativity and Its Cultivation*, New York: Harper Row, pp. 58–65.
McNeill, D. (2005), *Gesture and Thought*, Chicago, IL: University of Chicago Press.
Mead, G.H. (1934), *Mind, Self and Society*, Chicago, IL: University of Chicago Press.
Mead, G.H. (1938), *Philosophy of the Act*, Chicago, IL: University of Chicago Press.
Merleau-Ponty, M. (1982), *Phenomenology of Perception*, London: Routledge.
Mintzberg, H. (2004), *Managers Not MBAs*, London: Pearson.
Ohmae, K. (2005), *The Next Global Stage: Challenges and Opportunities in Our Borderless World*, London: Pearson.
Plessner, H. (1970), *Laughing and Crying: A Study of the Limits of Human Behavior*, Evanston, IL: Northwestern University Press.
Schur, D. (1998), *The Way of Oblivion*, Cambridge, MA and London: Harvard University Press.
Spear, S.J. (2004), 'Learning to lead at Toyota', *Harvard Business Review*, **82** (5), 78–86.
Spear, S.J. and H.K. Bowden (1999), 'Decoding the DNA of Toyota production system', *Harvard Business Review*, **77** (5), 97–106.
Stone, B.E. (2006), 'Curiosity as the thief of wonder: an essay on Heidegger's critique of the ordinary conception of time', *Kronoscope*, **6** (2), 205–29.
Tsoukas, H. and J. Sheppard (eds) (2004), *Managing the Future: Foresight in the Knowledge Economy*, London: Blackwell.

Turner, B.S. (1991), 'Recent developments in the theory of the body', in M. Featherstone, M. Hepworth and B.S. Turner (eds), *The Body: Social Processes and Cultural Theory*, London: Sage, pp. 1–35.

Visalberghi, A. (1953), 'Remarks on Dewey's conception of ends and means', *Journal of Philosophy*, **50** (25), 737–53.

Wack, P. (1985), 'Scenarios: uncharted waters ahead', *Harvard Business Review*, **85** (5), 72–89.

Watson, T.J. (1994), *In Search of Management*, London: Routledge.

Watson, T.J. and P. Harris (1999), *The Emergent Manager*, London: Sage.

Weick, K.E. (1995), *Sensemaking in Organizations*, London: Sage.

Wheelwright, P. (1971), *Metaphor and Reality*, Bloomington, IN: Indiana University Press.

Wiltbank, R., N. Dew, S. Read and S.D. Sarasvathy (2006), 'What to do next? The case of non-predictive strategy', *Strategic Management Journal*, **27** (10), 981–98.

4   The symbolism of foresight processes in organizations*
Jan Oliver Schwarz

Introduction

Organizations face a more complex and dynamic environment than ever, one that is characterized by discontinuities and an uncertain future – a state that is most likely to continue. The major task for managers today is to make decisions, formulate strategies and execute strategic management systems in such an environment. It is obvious that the imperative of 'predict and prepare', as the foundation of the neoclassical school of management (Gharajedaghi 1999), is no longer appropriate for organizations in such an environment.

In the past, many concepts were used to detect 'weak signals' of change, or trends, in the organizational environment. The goal of these concepts was to give organizations the chance to react to or act on these developments in advance. Other concepts have been developed to think about the future of an organization and incorporate that vision of the future into planning processes. These concepts include futures studies (Masini 1993; Cornish 2004), particularly the scenario technique (Fahey and Randall 1998), strategic issue management (Ansoff 1980) or strategic early warning systems (Schwarz 2005), strategic foresight (Tsoukas and Shepherd 2004a), and, in a broader sense, competitive intelligence (Gilad 2004). Overall, these concepts are enjoying greater attention than ever from the corporate world (van der Heijden 2004; Schwarz 2006).

However, referring to the field of organizational symbolism, understanding that symbolism is the production of meaning through the use of symbols (Jones 1996) and that a symbol is a sign which denotes something much greater than itself (Morgan et al. 1983), the question arises, what does a foresight activity symbolize in an organization?

In an attempt to answer this question, this chapter will start by discussing the concept of foresight and then pointing out its limits. Then the role of foresight in organizations will be discussed, followed by an assessment of the symbolism of foresight in an organization.

The limits of foresight

Before discussing what a foresight process can symbolize in an organization, the aim of this section is to elaborate on the limits of foresight, or rather what an organization's foresight process can realistically achieve. This section will begin by defining the concept of foresight.

Defining foresight

Since the late 1980s, the term 'foresight' has been used to describe activities which inform decision makers by improving inputs about an organization's long-term future (Miles et al. 2003). However, the term 'foresight' is often used interchangeably with terms such as 'futurology', 'futures studies', and 'prospective analysis' and there seems to be no

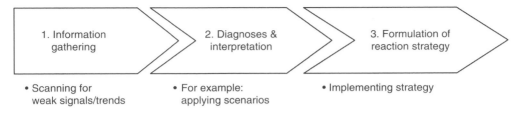

Figure 4.1   Foresight process

consensus on where these terms overlap. It is reported that in a celebrated lecture at the Harvard Business School in 1931, Alfred North Whitehead first used the term 'foresight' to describe the crucial feature of the competent business mind (Tsoukas 2004).

Corporations are now being urged to develop foresight (for example, Hamel and Prahalad 1994; Courtney 2001). Makridakis (2004, p. xiii) states: 'The role of foresight is to provide business executives and government policy makers with ways of seeing the future with different eyes and fully understanding the possible implications of alternative technological/ societal paths'. Foresight is the ability to see developments before they become trends, to recognize patterns before they emerge, and to grasp the features of social currents that are likely to have an impact (Tsoukas 2004); it is not the ability to make predictions.

In the organizational context, foresight is based on the principle that discontinuities do not emerge without warning signs, also known as 'weak signals' (Ansoff 1975), which can also be perceived as trends. When these signals go undetected, they could lead to strategic surprises or an event, which could jeopardize the organizational strategy. Day and Schoemaker (2006, pp. 1–2) describe the value of spotting weak signals as follows: 'The key is to quickly spot those signals that are relevant and explore them further, filter out the noise, and pursue opportunities ahead of the competition or recognize the early signs of trouble before they escalate into major problems'.

There are several ways for an organization to develop foresight, such as the scenario technique (Fahey and Randall 1998), Delphi iterations (Helmer 1983) or business war-gaming (Schwarz 2007b). It appears, however, that a foresight process, incorporating some of these techniques, is most promising for developing foresight. A foresight process (for example, Horton 1999; Liebl 2000), as displayed in Figure 4.1, should consist of three phases: (i) information gathering, achieved by scanning the organizational environment (Aguilar 1967) for weak signals; (ii) diagnosing and interpreting the detected trends; and (iii) formulating responses to these detected and diagnosed trends.

Limits – evidence from the future
The term 'foresight' is interchangeable with terms such as 'futures studies'. While 'foresight' seems to be replacing 'futures studies' in organizational parlance, foresight is still associated with predicting the future. By considering ways of thinking about the future, evidence is collected to determine what a foresight process can realistically achieve.

Handy (1994, p. 18) describes the paradox of dealing with the future: 'Life will never be easy, nor predictable, nor completely predictable. It will be best understood backwards, but we have to live it forwards'. One can understand the future better only when it has become the present. But unfortunately, present decisions, which involve the future, have to be taken and these necessarily require some knowledge about the future (Hansson 1976). Spies (1982, p. 2) is helpful on this point: 'Firstly, the future is not predictable. Secondly, the future is not predetermined. Thirdly, future outcomes can be influenced by individual choices'. Things become even more complicated when a trend has been detected in a foresight process, because such a trend probably has at least one counter-trend (Waters 2006). This leads to the conclusion that it might be more promising not to predict the future course or development of a trend than to try to understand a trend in its context and where or why it has evolved as it has.

The role of foresight in organizations
After pointing out the limits of a foresight process and in particular making the argument that the goal of a foresight process is not to merely predict the future, the following question will now be of interest: what is the goal of a foresight process in an organization?

In general, it can be argued that the role of a foresight process in an organization is not so much to predict the future as to prepare for it (Tsoukas and Shepherd 2004b). Further, Chia (2004) argues that foresight is achieved in an organization through re-educating the attention of management. Foresight activities should be a structured communication processes focusing on mental models, blind spots, and knowledge gaps. These processes should trigger discussions about the future and about current events that might have an impact on the future. This process enables an organization to make sense of its environment and look for weak signals of change, or rather trends. In cognitive terms, a foresight process should enhance an organization's 'memory of the future'.

Communication – fostering strategic conversations
Van der Heijden (1997, p. ix) has put an emphasis on understanding scenarios; this notion is also relevant for foresight processes, as a tool for fostering and initiating strategic conversations in organizations: 'It is my experience that scenarios are the best available language for the strategic conversation, as it allows both differentiation in views, but also brings people together towards a shared understanding of the situation, making decision making possible when the time has arrived to take action'. Following van der Heijden, strategic conversation can be defined as a dialectical process of a scenario planning exercise that aims at forming a shared mental model of the organization, its goals, and the way in which it attempts to achieve them (Ratcliffe 2002). This thought implies that at the heart of foresight lies conjecture, and that at the heart of conjecture is conversation (ibid.).

Grant (2003, p. 511) states that Royal Dutch/Shell's scenario planning process was a vehicle for fostering organizational learning by sharing and integrating multiple knowledge bases from both within and outside the Shell group, with emphasis on communication and knowledge sharing: 'Shell's "scenario-to-strategy" framework involved discussion workshops in which scenarios would provide the foundation for an interactive strategy formulation'. Understanding a foresight process as a vehicle for strategic conversation in an organization helps to define the purpose of such a process in an organization. The value of such a strategic conversation is that mental models in an organization are not only shared but also most likely to be challenged and that an organization is likely to eliminate blind spots from its sensemaking of the environment and of the future.

Learning – enhancing the 'memory of the future'
Understanding a foresight process as a vehicle for strategic conversation is one possible role. The other role is that of learning. Perceiving a foresight as a learning process (Costanzo 2004), allows us to argue that a foresight process can contribute to the 'learning organisation' (Senge 1990). This notion will be underlined with reference to the concept of the 'memory of the future'.

When the future cannot be predicted and trends derived from a foresight process are likely to have at least one countertrend, why even bother with such an activity? The concept of the 'memory of the future' (Ingvar 1985; de Geus 1997; van der Heijden et al. 2002) answers this question. Ingvar (1985) concludes that the human brain is able to store various pictures of the future. The more memories of the future that are stored, the more receptive an individual can be to signals from the outside world.

Reading (2004) remarks that humans can only imagine the future in ways that relate to their own experience and understanding of the past. This thought implies that humans are unable to conceive ideas that do not fit their preconceived models of the world. Van der Heijden et al. (2002, p. 177) emphasize the importance of this concept in reference to the scenario process, which is also applicable to a foresight process:

> In essence, the scenario process enables managers to visit and experience the future ahead of time, thereby creating what is called 'memories' of the future. These visits to anticipated futures are then remembered, creating a matrix in the mind of managers and serving as subconscious guides to make sense of incoming environmental signals and to act on them.

A foresight process fosters learning in an organization. By adding to the memory of the future by considering trends, countertrends and alternative pictures of the future, this process adds greatly to an organization's memory of the future, eventually helping an organization to be better prepared for surprises, new and emerging weak signals, or trends.

The symbolism of foresight
To further assess the symbolism of foresight processes in an organization, we shall consider how organizations deal with the future as such. This task will be achieved by first considering how humans deal with the future and then, second, turning again to the organization. Although the future is not predictable, we cannot ignore the fact that we constantly think about the future, that the future, our inner future, is a natural part of our daily lives, and therefore the future is a natural part of any organization. The concept of future-oriented psychotherapy takes this idea into account. However, the concept of future-oriented psychotherapy will also help to develop a framework to understand the symbolism of foresight processes in an organization.

Evidence from future-oriented psychotherapy
The concept of future-oriented psychotherapy (Melges 1982) relates to the inner future of an individual in psychiatric disorders. Schwarz (2007a) has examined the link between this concept and organizational disorders. Psychiatric illness can cloud a person's future and distort his or her view of that future. Rappaport (1991) states that a person's attitude towards the future determines his or her definitions of the present and the past. This becomes even more evident in the light of the role of foresight or thinking about the future

in cognition. Foresight is an ongoing activity of the human brain (de Jouvenel 1967). Humans have the capacity to imagine future outcomes and to devise the means to handle them (Reading 2004). Cognitive activities are based to a great extent upon concepts of the future (Ingvar 1985).

When the inner future of an organization is distorted, psychiatric disorders in that organization are likely to occur. The future has several implications for an organization:

1. By determining how an organization deals with the future, one can assess the mental state of that organization and diagnose the organization by using psychiatry.
2. The future is not only a central element of diagnosis; it is also central to treating an organizational patient.

However, since thinking about the future is an ongoing activity in a healthy organization, it should not be assumed that organizations that are struggling to bring their future under their control are unhealthy. What still needs to be determined is the reason why an organization is attempting to deal with the future. If the organization deals with the future as an integrated process in an organizational culture that is accustomed to thinking about the future, especially by thinking about alternative futures or challenging mental models, then that organization could appear to be healthy.

In contrast, if the organization implements a foresight activity, but rejects, for instance, that information which is contra-indicative to its strategy (Schwarz 2005), then it is important to know why such a system has been implemented. The obvious reasons would be for the organization to detect weak signals of change in the environment or to deal with the future. Yet, the rejection of information indicates that the organization is struggling with the future or adjusting its goals to accommodate the changes that are occurring. Therefore, the implementation of foresight processes can be a hint that the organization is suffering from a disorder. This line of thought implies that the implementation of such an activity can reveal the mental status of an organization.

Understanding the foresight process
So, what does a foresight process symbolize? The answer to this question is that it depends on the organization and the manner in which the organization implements and eventually runs a foresight process. As we have discussed above and displayed in Table 4.1, the implementation of a foresight process can imply that the organization is suffering from a disorder, which interfered with its future-goal-directed behaviour. If the goal of the process is to derive clear predictions of the future, its implementation can imply that the organization is in danger of acquiring more blind spots and losing its sensemaking capabilities. This is especially true when a strategic conversation is not taking place, or fails to involve enough participants, and if the memory of the future is not leveraged. However, the organization is at even greater danger when it assumes that by implementing a foresight process, foresight is developed and the future is covered by Department or Manager X. This, again, can create blind spots.

Considering the arguments that foresight and thinking about the future are ongoing processes in a healthy organization, one could be tempted to conclude that an organization which is not establishing any kind of foresight activity might be a healthy one and properly prepared for the future. However, this is not the conclusion of this discussion.

Table 4.1   The symbolism of foresight processes in organizations

Foresight process	Possible interpretations	Status
The goal: *clear predictions* It appears that *everything is taken care of*	The organization is in danger, e.g., increasing blind spots, strategic conversations are not taking place	!
No foresight activity	The organization has a healthy inner future and is prepared for the future	?
The process is designed to foster *communication* and *learning* about the future	The organization is developing foresight and preparing for the future	✔

Foresight is perceived as an ongoing process of communication and learning whose goal is not to give easy answers, but to raise questions and awareness concerning an organization's future and especially its environment. Following Daft and Weick (1984), a foresight process could also be a way by which an organization makes sense of its environment, thus making the foresight process one of interpretation.

Conclusion

If dealing with the future and foresight in an organization is more a structured learning and communication process than a prognostic activity, then the organization is able to prepare itself for the unknown, even the unthinkable, for instance, by enhancing its 'memory of the future'. Since the future is unknown and unpredictable, particularly in times of rapid change, the purpose of a foresight activity thus cannot be to predict the future. If it were, a foresight activity would be more likely to increase blind spots and therefore increase the likelihood that the organization will eventually be caught unprepared by the future.

The following notion of business professionals is not unusual: 'We don't work with scenarios or trends because they are never right'. This line of thought completely misses the point of engaging in a foresight activity. And while it is obvious that a prediction or a forecast of the future can never be 100 per cent accurate, it has been emphasized several times how wrong forecasts have been in the past. In this chapter, it has been pointed out that foresight demands communication and learning. Understanding foresight in this way also hints at an answer to the question of how foresight activities can be evaluated, a question that seems particularly significant in corporations (Schwarz 2006). The success of a foresight activity could perhaps then be evaluated in terms of its contribution to communication and learning in an organization, as opposed to the *ex post* analyses of the accuracy of forecasts, trends or scenarios.

Implementing a foresight activity is not simple; it entails increasing the complexity of the organization so that it can deal with its increasingly complex environment. However, it appears that the application and implementation of a foresight process in an organization provides a means of diagnosing its 'mental health'. In other words, it can assess how the organization is adapting and reacting to its environment. Is it increasing its blind spots and putting itself in danger, or is it attempting to mobilize the internal forces in the organization to make sense of what is happening in the environment, and eventually developing foresight and preparing for the future?

It has been emphasized that cognitive barriers (Bazerman and Watkins 2004) hinder foresight. One central goal of a foresight process therefore must be to overcome these barriers, which is most likely achieved by perceiving a foresight activity as a form of strategic conversation and as a vehicle for fostering learning in an organization, adding to the 'memory of the future'. What a foresight process symbolizes in an organization cannot be understood easily. This chapter argues that the value of a foresight process in an organization depends on how foresight is understood, implemented and applied.

Note
*   An earlier version of this chapter was presented at the 25th Standing Conference on Organizational Symbolism, Ljubljana, Slovenia, 1–4 July 2007.

References

Aguilar, F.J. (1967), *Scanning the Business Environment*, New York: Macmillan.
Ansoff, H.I. (1975), 'Managing strategic surprise by response to weak signals', *California Management Review*, **18** (2), 21–33.
Ansoff, H.I. (1980), 'Strategic issue management', *Strategic Management Journal*, **1** (2), 131–48.
Bazerman, M.H. and Watkins, M.D. (2004), *Predictable Surprises*, Boston, MA: Harvard Business School Press.
Chia, R. (2004), 'Re-educating attention: what is foresight and how is it cultivated?', in Tsoukas and Shepherd (eds) (2004a), pp. 21–37.
Cornish, E. (2004), *Futuring: The Exploration of the Future*, Bethesda, MD: World Future Society.
Costanzo, L.A. (2004), 'Strategic foresight in a high-speed environment', *Futures*, **36** (2), 219–35.
Courtney, H. (2001), *20/20 Foresight: Crafting Strategy in an Uncertain World*, Boston, MA: Harvard Business School Press.
Daft, R.L. and Weick, K.E. (1984), 'Toward a model of organizations as interpretation systems', *Academy of Management Review*, **9** (2), 284–96.
Day, G.S. and Schoemaker, P.J.H. (2006), *Peripheral Vision: Detecting the Weak Signals That Will Make or Break Your Company*, Boston, MA: Harvard Business School Press.
de Geus, A. (1997), *The Living Company*, Boston, MA: Harvard Business School Press.
de Jouvenel, B. (1967), *Die Kunst der Vorausschau* (The art of conjecture), Neuwied: Luchterhand.
Fahey, L. and Randall, R.M. (eds) (1998), *Learning from the Future: Competitive Foresight Scenarios*, San Francisco, CA: John Wiley & Sons.
Gharajedaghi, J. (1999), *Systems Thinking*, Boston, MA: Butterworth Heinemann.
Gilad, B. (2004), *Early Warning: Using Competitive Intelligence to Anticipate Market Shifts, Control Risk, and Create Powerful Strategies*, New York: AMACOM.
Grant, R.M. (2003), 'Strategic planning in a turbulent environment: evidence from the oil majors', *Strategic Management Journal*, **24** (2), 491–517.
Hamel, G. and Prahalad, C.K. (1994), *Competing for the Future*, Boston, MA: Harvard Business School Press.
Handy, C. (1994), *The Empty Raincoat: Making Sense of the Future*, London: Hutchinson.
Hansson, B. (1976), 'Some methodological problems in future studies', in Schwarz, S. (ed.), *Knowledge and Concepts in Futures Studies*, Boulder, CO: Westview Press, pp. 65–77.
Helmer, O. (1983), *Looking Forward: A Guide to Futures Research*, London: Sage.
Horton, A. (1999), 'A simple guide to successful foresight', *Foresight*, **1** (1), 5–9.
Ingvar, D.H. (1985), 'Memory of the future: an essay on the temporal organization of conscious awareness', *Human Neurobiology*, **4** (3), 127–36.
Jones, M.O. (1996), *Studying Organizational Symbolism: What, How, Why?*, Thousand Oaks, CA: Sage.
Liebl, F. (2000), *Der Schock des Neuen: Entstehung und Management von Issues und Trends* (Shock of the new: emergence and management of issues and trends), Munich: Gerling Akademie Verlag.
Makridakis, S. (2004), 'Foreword: Foresight matters', in Tsoukas and Shepherd (eds) (2004a), pp. xiii–xiv.
Masini, E.B. (1993), *Why Futures Studies?*, London: Grey Seal Books.
Melges, F.T. (1982), *Time and the Inner Future*, New York: John Wiley & Sons.
Miles, I., Keenan, M. and Kaivo-Oja, J. (2003), *Handbook of Knowledge Society Foresight*, Dublin: European Foundation for the Improvement of Living and Working Conditions.
Morgan, G., Frost, P.J. and Pondy, L.R. (1983), 'Organizational symbolism', in Pondy, L.R., Frost, P.J., Morgan, G. and Dandridge, T.C. (eds), *Organizational Symbolism*, Greenwich, CT: JAI Press, pp. 3–35.

Rappaport, H. (1991), 'Measuring defensiveness against future anxiety: telepression', *Current Psychology: Research and Reviews*, **10** (1&2), 65–77.

Ratcliffe, J. (2002), 'Scenario planning: strategic interviews and conversations', *Foresight*, **4** (1), 19–30.

Reading, A. (2004), *Hope and Despair*, Baltimore, MD: Johns Hopkins University Press.

Schwarz, J.O. (2005), 'Pitfalls in implementing a strategic early warning system', *Foresight*, **7** (4), 22–30.

Schwarz, J.O. (2006), *The Future of Futures Studies: A Delphi Study with a German Perspective*, Aachen: Shaker.

Schwarz, J.O. (2007a), 'Assessing future disorders in organizations: implications for diagnosing and treating schizophrenic, depressed or paranoid organizations', *Foresight*, **9** (2), 15–26.

Schwarz, J.O. (2007b), 'Business wargaming: developing foresight within a strategic simulation', paper presented to the COSTA22 Foresight Conference 'From Oracles to Dialogue: Exploring New Ways to Explore the Future', National Technical University, Athens, Greece, 9–11 July.

Senge, P.M. (1990), *The Fifth Discipline*, London: Century Business.

Spies, P.H. (1982), 'Scenario development: its role and importance in future research', in Spies (ed.), *Scenario Development for Strategic Management*, Stellenbosch: UFR Occasional Paper 82/1, Unit for Futures Research, University of Stellenbosch, pp. 2–9.

Tsoukas, H. (2004), 'Coping with the future: developing organizational foresightfulness', *Futures*, **36** (2), 137–44.

Tsoukas, H. and Shepherd, J. (eds) (2004a), *Managing the Future*, Oxford: Blackwell.

Tsoukas, H. and Shepherd, J. (2004b), 'Introduction: organization and the future, from forecasting to foresight', in Tsoukas and Shepherd (eds) (2004a), pp. 1–19.

van der Heijden, K. (1997), *Scenarios: The Art of Strategic Conversation*, Chichester: John Wiley & Sons.

van der Heijden, K. (2004), 'Afterwords: insights from foresight', in Tsoukas and Shepherd (eds) (2004a), pp. 204–11.

van der Heijden, K., Bradfield, R., Burt, G., Crains, G. and Wright, G. (2002), *The Sixth Sense*, Chichester: John Wiley & Sons.

Waters, R. (2006), *The Hummer and the Mini*, New York: Portfolio.

5 Strategic foresight: counterfactual and prospective sensemaking in enacted environments
Robert Bradley MacKay

Introduction

In a 1989 testimony to the United States' Senate Committee on Commerce, Science and Technology, the 1978 Nobel Laureate in economics, Herbert Simon, argued that the distinction between 'hard' and 'soft' sciences can be misleading. Inquiry into the functioning of competitive markets or into the capacity of human short-term memory is hard because these processes are well researched and understood. They have come to form part of the corpus of knowledge considered to be common sense. Inquiry into how business people and consumers formulate expectations about the future is soft because it is an under-researched phenomenon. A science that is hard all the way through becomes an arid place for furthering knowledge. For science to progress, he postulated, it must push its frontiers into soft areas (Simon 1990, p. 33).

Sensemaking has become one of the signature domains of research in the study of strategic management. While having its roots in the cognitive sciences, in strategic management it refers to the social processes that people use to make their environment sensible (Weick 1995, p. 16). It is portrayed as a retrospective, multifaceted phenomenon whereby managers focus on certain cues in their environment and place them in schematic frameworks (Weick 1995; Brown 2003; Maitlis 2005). It differs markedly from other information processing models advanced by social and cognitive psychologists working from a positivist tradition. Where Simon (1957), for instance, advances a notion of information processing as a rational and sequential affair constrained only by one's limited capacity to compute information elicited from an objective environment in its entirety (that is, bounded rationality), sensemaking perspectives suggest that the perceptions of the manager are socially constructed (for example, Berger and Luckmann, 1966). It thus eschews notions of an objective environment in favor of notions of a perceived environment (Weick 1969 [1979]; Hodgkinson and Sparrow 2002).

While numerous scholars draw on sensemaking perspectives (Anderson 2006), Karl Weick is widely accredited with consolidating the concept (Craig-Lees 2001, p. 513). For Weick (1995, p. 2), sensemaking begins by noticing something unusual in the ongoing flow of events. It could be a discrepant set of cues or a surprise. Whatever form this discrepancy takes, it results in dissonance, or a feeling of equivocality. A successful sensemaking process is where the sensemaker manages to reduce equivocality in these confusing circumstances. They do this by retrospectively constructing a sensible version of what created the dissonance in the first place. Enactment is the action component of the sensemaking concept. People reflexively produce part of the environments that they contend with (ibid.). These enactments, in turn, shape future enactments (Smircich and Stubbart 1985).

Returning to Simon's distinction between hard and soft sciences, an emphasis on the sensemaking process as a fundamentally retrospective one is hardening into an accepted area of Kuhnian 'normal science' (Kuhn 1967, pp. 5–6). Sociologists such as Beck (1999) and Giddens (1990), however, argue that a feature of late modernity is that it is counterfactual and future oriented. Giddens argues, for instance: 'In conditions of modernity, the future is always open, not just in terms of the ordinary contingency of things, but in terms of the reflexivity of knowledge in relation to which social practices are organised' (1990, pp. 83–4). The emphasis on sensemaking as a predominantly retrospective process, as it is currently construed in the literature, does not accommodate contemporary notions of an uncertain future. In sensemaking perspectives, when we do look at the future, we do so in the future perfect tense. In future perfect processes, agents will project their actions into the future as if they have already happened. The future is treated as predetermined. This enables them to make retrospective sense out of anticipated future events (Schütz 1967; Weick 1979, 1995; Gioia and Thomas 1996). Notions of foresight, arguably, approach the future as contingent. This raises a question of whether sensemaking perspectives have anything to add to concepts of strategic foresight.

To advance the sensemaking perspective from a predominantly retrospective process accepted as 'common sense' in strategic management studies into the soft, somewhat ambiguous and certainly uncertain realm of the future, this chapter argues that research needs to be directed at the role that counterfactual and prospective processes play in sensemaking. Sensemaking, the chapter proposes, can be conceptualized as a form of prospecting. Prospecting has traditionally been associated with the search for minerals, oil and precious metals. It depends on a retrospective knowledge of geography, geology, and terrain. However, it is also a highly uncertain process that requires a certain 'negative capability'. The term 'negative capability' was first used by the poet John Keats to express his belief that many people are capable of existing in 'uncertainties, mysteries, doubts without any irritable reaching after fact and reason' (Keats 1817). In circumstances where complexity and uncertainty are predominant, a certain amount of speculating about the past and the future is a common, if under-researched sensemaking phenomenon. It is an important area of inquiry because it can have either deleterious or propitious effects on strategic foresight.

The purpose of this chapter then, is to investigate the role that retrospective and particularly prospective sensemaking processes play in strategic foresight. To do this the chapter begins by elaborating on what is meant by strategic foresight. It goes on to survey selected studies on sensemaking and the future perfect. The future perfect, the chapter contends, is inadequate for understanding prospective sensemaking processes, particularly when faced with a complex future replete with uncertainty and surprising occurrences. Research into counterfactual and prefactual thinking in the cognitive sciences suggests that humans also make sense of the future through mental simulations that are a form of scenario thinking that can either encourage better performance in the future or act as a coping mechanism when surprising events catch strategic managers unaware. The chapter concludes by considering the implications of this research for understanding the role that sensemaking plays in strategic foresight processes in an enacted world.

Strategic foresight and its failures

What is strategic foresight? In a lecture given by Alfred North Whitehead in 1931 at the Harvard Business School, he argued that a feature of the business mind of the future would be foresight involving insight and understanding (Whitehead 1933 [1967], pp. 110–11; Tsoukas and Sheppard 2004, p. 137). He also proposed that foresight is linked with the past, suggesting that a major defect of foresight is incomplete knowledge of facts in the past and present that influence the accuracy of our forecasts of the future. He thus referred to it as 'historical-foresight' (Whitehead 1933 [1967], p. 110–11).

Strategic foresight remains an elusive concept in both theory and practice. In the following paragraphs, the concept of strategic foresight is discussed, its connection with uncertainty and surprising events is investigated and a number of significant failures are identified.

Strategic planning and foresight

Strategic planning is done to varying degrees by most large organizations (Higgins 1981). It normally concerns the long term development of the organization (Chandler 1962; Andrews 1971). While generally assumed to be an important organizational process (for example, Porter 1980, 1985), its pitfalls have been well documented by strategic management scholars (for example, Loasby 1967; Mintzberg 1994a, b). For instance, a distinct cost and numbers orientation and a reliance on static analytical frameworks by many strategic planning processes often has difficulty in accommodating environmental uncertainty (Chae and Hill 1996).

Nevertheless, strategic planning continues to be adopted by firms, particularly (and ironically) as uncertainty increases. Some empirical studies suggest that the greater the environmental complexity and uncertainty organizations face, the more likely they are to adopt comprehensive planning processes (Lindsay and Rue 1980). These findings may help to explain the increase in the corporate usage of strategic planning from 83 per cent in 1993 to 88 per cent in 2006 and scenario and contingency planning from 38 per cent in 1993 to 69 per cent in 2006 according to the annual Bain survey of strategy tools being used by organizations (Rigby and Bilodeau 2007). Strategic planning, however, does not necessarily denote foresight.

Foresight, as an important function of the executive (Barnard 1938 [1979], pp. 201, 282), can be traced back to the writings of early management scholars such as the French management theorist Henri Fayol (1916/1949). Its importance to strategic management rests on the preposition that strategy is concerned with the long-term goals and objectives of the enterprise (Chandler 1962, p. 13), and the long-term development of the firm (Andrews 1987, pp. 13–17). Loasby suggests that there are three reasons for looking at the future in strategic planning processes. He suggests that it is important for firms to look at the future to understand the future implications of present decisions, the present implications of future events, and the final reason is to motivate and facilitate systematically looking at the future, which includes reviewing present assumptions (1967, pp. 301–2).

Foresight, Hamel and Prahalad suggest, is 'based on deep insights into trends in technology, demographics, regulations, and lifestyles, which can be harnessed to rewrite industry rules and create new competitive space' (Hamel and Prahalad 1994a, p. 128; 1994b). It is not something that managers are necessarily naturally endowed with. According to Chia (2004), it is something that must be cultivated. Drawing on a metaphor of vision, he suggests that it consists of a process of re-educating attention towards the nuances of a complex world through strategies of glancing, scanning and browsing, often in our peripheral vision, rather than gazing and looking through our frontal vision. It is the deep insight that is found in vagueness rather than the fully articulated gestalt figures (ibid., pp. 21–2). It is in this 'Platonic fold' (Taleb 2007) that foresight resides, in between what we know and what we think we know. It is also from these places that surprising asymmetries, what Taleb refers to as 'Black Swans', are produced that can be most disruptive to strategic planning efforts.

Despite rigorous strategic planning efforts by many organizations in industry and government, they continue to be disrupted by surprising events. Surprises, Cunha et al. (2006) suggest, can come from a range of endogenous and exogenous sources. Organizational routines, creeping developments and sudden events such as the terrorist attacks on 11 September, 2001, or the sub-prime mortgage crisis of 2007–08 in the United States that engulfed the global financial industry, can seem incomprehensible. Some scholars, however, argue that information normally exists prescient of surprising discontinuities to come (Bazerman and Watkins 2004). Why then do failures in strategic foresight occur?

Failures of strategic foresight
In his study of the use of technological and ideological 'intelligence' in industry and government, Wilensky comments that 'it is remarkable the sociology of complex organizations has so little to say about the conditions that foster the failure of foresight' (1967, p. 121). Taking up this mantle, in his study into the organizational and interorganzational development of disasters, Turner (1976) concludes that there are a number of factors that contribute to failures in foresight including distracting decoy phenomena, multiple information handling difficulties, the exaggeration of hazards by outsiders and the minimizing of dangers inside the organization, institutional rigidities and failures to comply with regulations. Failures in strategic foresight have a propensity of being costly to firms, industries and societies. Indeed, the failure of financial risk models to anticipate the recent sub-prime mortgage crisis is estimated by the Group of Seven to eventually cost about US$400 billion. Even this pales in comparison to the Iraq War, originally forecasted to be a quick and cheap allied victory at a cost of US$200 billion, and which has since been revised by Nobel prize winning economist Joseph Stiglitz and Harvard University budget expert Linda Bilmes to be close to US$3 trillion for the United States alone (Stiglitz and Bilmes 2008). And, as Nicholas Stern (2007) has outlined in the Stern Review, the potential long-term costs of not taking immediate action on climate change – to business, industry and society – could be unfathomable.

Organizations, some scholars suggest (Crozier 1964; Lawrence and Lorsch 1967; Thompson 1975; Turner 1976), are future oriented and designed to cope with uncertainty and unknown events. To address this uncertainty, Turner (1976) argues many organizations develop islands of certainty through habitualized practices, rituals and rules of thumb. In addition, they set goals and objectives for the future and formulate plans to reach them. Other organizations reformulate the problem, ignoring the difficult-to-specify, non-quantifiable features. Disasters can thus go through an incubation stage as factors contributing to them accumulate. Once noticed, they can overwhelm sensemaking processes and result in a cultural collapse within the organization, or indeed, society. Turner thus defines failures in foresight as: 'The collapse of precautions that had hitherto been regarded as culturally adequate' (1976, p. 379).

There may, however, be other reasons that help to explain the manifestation of conditions that foster failures in foresight. The strategies and actions of organizations are predicated, at least in part, on managerial perceptions of their environment (Sutcliffe and

Huber 1998) and the processes used to make sense of them (Weick 1995). In most organizational environments change is relentless (Andrews 1987; Tsoukas and Chia 2002). The ability of organizations to perceive, make sense of and adapt to their changing circumstances has therefore been identified as a significant determinant of corporate longevity (for example, Cyert and March 1963; Duncan and Weiss 1979; Peters and Waterman 1982; Fiol and Lyles 1985; Hodgkinson and Sparrow 2002). Yet clearly, not all organizations manage to adapt to their quickly changing environments. While there are a range of reasons accounting for organizational mortality rates, dysfunctional sensemaking processes and resultant failures of strategic foresight are a significant factor. A study of two railroad firms in the United States, C&NW and Rock Island is illustrative.

In a study of the Top Management Team's (TMT) perceptions and interpretations of change in the railroad industry, Barr et al. drew on archival data to investigate how their interpretations changed over time and their impact on their organization's responses. They found that the perceptions of the TMTs in both railroad companies in 1951 attributes declining performance to exogenous variables in the external environment such as government programs, regulation and the weather. By 1956, however, understanding the need to adapt their strategy to a changing environment, the TMT of C&NW began focusing on issues such as firm-level costs, management issues and productivity. The TMT of Rock Island, by contrast, externalized problems in performance, blaming it on uncontrollable industry-level factors, such as an inflationary economy being responsible for increasing costs throughout the late 1950s and into the early 1960s. The assumption was that their environment would improve. Evidence suggests that the cognitive map of the TMT of Rock Island did not begin to accommodate other factors, such as certain actions taken by the firm resulting in higher costs, until much later in 1964. While the perceptions and mental model of the TMT of Rock Island eventually shifts, it does so a full 8 years after that of C&NW and fails to prevent its ultimate demise (Barr et al. 1992).

As Starbuck and Milliken (1988) have suggested, the perceptual filters of executives consist of what they notice and, equally importantly, how they make sense of it. The C&NW and Rock Island railway companies both noticed changes in their industries, but they made sense of them in different ways. An interpretation of the studies' findings is that the sensemaking processes of C&NW resulted in their management team having the foresight to know that their environment was changing irreversibly and to adapt their corporate strategy to their changing circumstances. The sensemaking processes of the management team of Rock Island, by contrast, short-circuited strategic foresight until it was too late.

The studies' findings are not unusual in the annals of corporate history. In a study of over 50 corporate failures in companies as diverse as Barings Bank, the Boston Red Sox, DaimlerChrysler, Encyclopedia Britannica, Firestone, Fruit of the Loom, Levi Strauss, Motorola, Marks and Spencer, Saatchi & Saatchi, Sony (Columbia Pictures), Tyco and Wang Labs, Finkelstein concludes that there are a range of contributing factors, most centered around the people that lead and manage companies. Some of these factors include fulfilling the wrong vision and executive mindset failures, avoiding reality and having delusions of a dream company, failing to act on signals from the organization's environment as well as vital information available in the organization. From the in-depth interview research into these corporate failures, the studies' principal researcher,

Finkelstein, also elicits seven habits of spectacularly unsuccessful people including: perceiving their companies to be dominating their environments, blurring of the boundary between personal interests and corporate interests, a belief that they have all the answers, elimination of dissent, corporate image obsession, underestimation of major obstacles, and a reliance on past recipes of success (Finkelstein 2003). The major cause of corporate failure that one can infer from this research is what Pierre Wack, a former strategic planner for Royal Dutch/Shell calls the 'microcosm of the manager' – their view of the world (Wack 1985a). Distortions and biases rooted in hindsight (for example, see MacKay and McKiernan 2004a, b; MacKay et al. 2006), can result in sensemaking processes that short-circuit the reception of what Ansoff (1975) terms 'weak signals' in an organization's environment. The result can be failures in strategic foresight and concomitant organizational decline.

Summary
Strategic analysis, Mintzberg (1994a, b) has laboured to convince us, does not necessarily connote synthesis. What differentiates strategic foresight from strategic planning is the ability to go beyond analysis, cultivating experience, intuition, minority views and contrary thinking into the process. Opportunities, risks and new developments are often found on the margins of mainstream thinking. But reception of weak signals that can be prescient of discontinuities to come are prone to being lost in the static of dominant logics and managerial recipes made sense of retrospectively (see also Grinyer and Spender 1979; Hamel and Prahalad 1994a, b; MacKay and McKiernan 2004a, b). Organizations develop strategic planning processes and risk models that they deem to be culturally adequate for making sense of the future. Those same processes can lull the most gifted managers into a false sense of security. When they are caught by surprise, the results can be traumatic, causing a cultural collapse in the organization and instigating sensemaking processes. Sensemaking processes, then, are fundamental for understanding the process of cultivating strategic foresight.

Sensemaking in time
Sensemaking finds its origins in the cognitive sciences. It is a process that involves making sense of confusing, highly uncertain and complex situations that we find ourselves in to facilitate decision making. As a cognitive process, it involves structuring the unknown (Waterman 1990) by generating explanations for confusing circumstances that act as templates for understanding stimuli so that they can 'comprehend, understand, explain, attribute, extrapolate, and predict' (Starbuck and Milliken 1988, p. 51). In this section, selected studies into sensemaking processes that reflect the development of the sensemaking perspective in the study of organizations are surveyed and the relationship between sensemaking and the future is investigated.

Sensemaking in organizations
Sensemaking is a process by which individuals or groups reduce equivocality (Weick 1969 [1979]) (see Box 5.1). Where it diverges from a cognitive perspective is that at the collective level, organizational sensemaking is viewed as fundamentally a social (Maitlis 2005) conversational and narrative (Gephart 1993, 1997; Brown 2003) process involving the interpretation of stimuli, socially constructing (for example, Berger and Luckmann 1966)

BOX 5.1   FEATURES OF SENSEMAKING PROCESSES

Making something sensible:

1.   Identity construction (who the sensemaker is and is becoming).
2.   Retrospective (examination of history – historicizing).
3.   Enactive (we create our own environments for future action).
4.   Social (through conversation, idea exchange, reading communications).
5.   Ongoing (we codify and reflect on specific episodes).
6.   Focuses on extracted cues (we extract elements of our experience).
7.   Driven by plausibility rather than accuracy.

Source: Adapted from Weick (1995, pp. 17–61).

---

identity and producing intersubjective shared meanings explaining situations that deviate from expectations (Leiter 1980; Weick 1995; Brown 2000). In Weick's words:

> To talk about sense making is to talk about reality as an ongoing accomplishment that takes form when people make retrospective sense of the situations in which they find themselves. There is a strong reflexive quality to the process. People make sense of things by seeing a world on which they have already imposed what they believe. (Weick 1995, p. 15)

Sensemaking, particularly in organizations, is normally not portrayed as a solitary process, but one that relies on others. Organizations, which facilitate coordinated action, 'imposes an "invisible hand" on sensemaking' (ibid., p. 3). This is because the socially constructed habituated action patterns and interlocking routines that make up organizations are frequently reconstructed and reaffirmed intersubjectivity (Weick 1995). To understand this, it is helpful to view organizations as open social systems that process information from the environment, and through interpretation, give it meaning from which actions can be chosen (Daft and Weick 1984). Organizations can thus be viewed as distributed information processing systems (Weick and Roberts 1993), or similarly, as distributed knowledge systems (Tsoukas 1996). Both the individual and the collective must therefore be focused on because: 'Only individuals can contribute to a collective mind, but a collective mind is distinct from an individual mind because it inheres in the pattern of interrelated activities among many people' (Weick and Roberts 1993, p. 360). Higher-order patterns emerge from individual actions and the collective mind is actualized in those patterns of behavior, which is 'located' in the process of interrelating (Weick and Roberts 1993).

Sensemaking and surprise

Sensemaking processes are often triggered by a surprise or discrepant set of cues in an ongoing flow of events. Discrepancy is reflected on retrospectively and plausible speculations are offered to explain their occurrence (Weick 1995, p. 2). Surprise, as already discussed, can come in many forms: a bolt from the blue, an issue progressing in an unexpected direction, an event happening at the wrong time, an inaccurate estimation of the duration of an event, or unexpected amplitude of a problem (Kylen 1985 quoted in Weick and Sutcliffe 2001, pp. 36–8).

In a study into the experiences of new employees entering unfamiliar organizations, for instance, Louis (1980) argues that when experiences do not meet the expectations and assumptions of outsiders, surprise will trigger a need to explain the discrepancy. Insiders, on the other hand, will have more accurate expectations about the organization or situation. As a result, they will have less need to sense-make. The sensemaking mechanisms that people will use to deal with new or surprising situations, as opposed to everyday situations, consequently, differ.

Surprising or implausible events will thus require a shifting of analytic focus from probabilities to social construction (Weick 1993). Weick calls this a 'cosmology episode' (Weick 1985, pp. 51–2; Weick 1993, p. 633). He describes such an episode as a feeling of '*vu jàdé*' as opposed to '*déjà vu*'. Rather than a situation feeling as if it is familiar, everything feels confusing (Weick 1993, pp. 633–4). When low probability situations with significant consequences defy interpretations and expectancies, crisis, particularly within organizations, occurs. This leads to severe demands being placed on sensemaking (Weick 1988, p. 305). In some circumstances, the severe demands placed on sensemaking can result in their collapse. In his analysis of the 1949 Mann Gulch fire disaster, Weick (1993) deconstructs one such example of organization unraveling due to a collapse of sensemaking.

Weick's portrayal of the Mann Gulch disaster, where 13 smokejumpers died on August 4, 1949 after being caught by an exploding fire (Weick 1993, 1996), is an example of where the disintegration of organization can lead to disaster. In the incident, as relayed by Weick (1993), the crew leader Dodge saw that the forest fire was bearing down on them in the Mann Gulch at speed and recognized that his crew was in trouble. He ordered the retreating smokejumpers to throw away their tools. None heeded the counterintuitive command. Furthermore, to their astonishment, he then burned a small area of grass, and told his crew to lie in it. None took his advice, and while two men managed to escape through a rock crevice, the rest perished in the exploding fire while trying to outrun it. Some were later found with their heavy packs still on their backs and chain saws in their hands.[1] The story demonstrates that sensemaking is about contextual rationality (ibid.), whereas the world of decision making is about linear strategic rationality.

Senior executive and middle manager sensemaking
Sensemaking processes are particularly important for senior executives as they can provide a minimal structure for making information sensible (Weick 1995, p. 4). Indeed, some researchers have argued that 'shaping interpretive outlooks' may have a greater impact on the positive performance of companies than accurate information does (Sutcliffe and Weber 2003, p. 82). As Gioia and Chittipeddi have demonstrated in the beginning stages of a strategic change program in a large, public university, change processes begin with the CEO making sense of an altered vision of the organization. As this abstract vision of the organization emerges, it must then be communicated to the organization's stakeholders through a process of 'sensegiving' (Gioia and Chittipeddi 1991). Sensegiving is a process where by organizational agents attempt to influence the perceptions of others in the organization (Maitlis and Lawrence 2007).

Sensemaking is not just restricted to senior executives. In a study of middle managers experiencing a change program, Balogun and Johnson (2005) find that both intended and unintended consequences arise from the sensemaking processes of the strategic change interventions. The implementation process was found to be mediated between the evolving interpretations of the middle managers and the planned change interventions. Social interactions between middle managers and senior managers and interactions between the recipients themselves all contributed to the emergence and unpredictability of the change program.

Sensemaking has also been found to influence organizational performance. In a study of 156 hospitals, Thomas et al. (1993) looked at the cognitive tasks of scanning, interpretation and action as reciprocal sensemaking processes. They established a correlation between these processes and the wider performance of organizations.

Enacted sensemaking
Retrospective sensemaking is also linked with an enactment perspective. The concept of enactment directs attention to the reflexive relationship between people's actions and their environments. When people act, their actions result in producing events and structures, constraints and opportunities in their environment (Weick, 1988, p. 305). Key organizational participants enact both the environment and the organization together through social interaction processes (Smircich and Stubbart 1985, p. 726). In other words, the environment that people face is not an objective environment bounded by limited computational ability (for example, Simon 1957) as the behavioral decision theorists portray it (for example, Tversky and Kahneman 1974; Fischhoff 1975; Fischhoff et al. 1977; Kahneman and Tversky 1982), but an environment that is produced by the people who inhabit it (Pondy and Mitroff 1979; Weick 1995).

In their study of the Scottish knitwear industry at Hawick, for example, Porac et al. (1989, 1995) found that the strategic activities of the Scottish manufacturers making up this industry are, as Weick (1969 [1979]) suggests, 'linked together in a loosely coupled "enactment" process in which each is determined partly, but not solely, by the other' (Porac et al. 1989, p. 400). For Porac et al. (1989), the Scottish knitwear producers that they studied came to share a common conception of competition through a process of 'competitive enactment' (Hodgkinson and Sparrow 2002, p. 133). Enacted sensemaking, consequently, is portrayed in the literature as intimately interwoven with action.

While sensemaking is portrayed as being commonly retrospective, and enactment 'is action that produces the raw materials which can then be made sensible' (Weick 1969 [1979], p. 133), there is evidence to suggest that sensemaking is not purely an act of retrospection. In other words, it may also occur with 'an eye to the future' (Gleicher et al. 1995, p. 302).

The future perfect
In the sensemaking literature, people make sense of the future in the future perfect (Weick 1969 [1979], pp. 197–200; Weick 1995, p. 29). The future perfect is a cognitive process where: '[an] actor projects his actions as if it were already over and done with and lying in the past' (Schütz 1967, p. 61; also quoted in Pitsis et al. 2003, p. 574 and Weick 1969 [1979], p. 198). If a future event is treated as over and done with, Weick argues, then it is 'presumably easier to write a specific history based on past experience that could generate that specific outcome' (Weick 1969 [1979], p. 198). After all, Weick points out quoting the

writer E.M. Forster, 'how can I know what I think until I see what I say?' (ibid., p. 207). The future simple, the argument follows, is difficult to work with because any possible outcome might occur. This point is particularly salient for executives who are rewarded for their ability to forecast the future (ibid., p. 199; Ascher 1978).

There has been limited research into the future perfect. In an unpublished study by Webb and Watzke (quoted in Weick 1969 [1979]), the two researchers asked 108 male students at Stanford two questions about the Super Bowl game between Kansas City and Minnesota to be played on January 11, 1970, two days hence. The first group of students was asked the following questions: 'Imagine that it is Saturday, January 10. Kansas City and Minnesota will play tomorrow in the Super Bowl. Please write down the score of tomorrow's game. What will happen during the game?'. The second group of students was asked the following questions: 'Imagine that it is Monday, January 12. Kansas City and Minnesota played yesterday in the Super Bowl. Please write down the score of yesterday's game. What happened during the game to account for the outcome?'. The researchers found that while the accuracy of the predictions did not differ, the students asked to describe the game retrospectively were more detailed and less fanciful than the students asked to describe it prospectively.

In their study of the sensemaking processes in a major change program at a public university, Gioia et al. found that there was an anticipatory character to the phenomena under investigation. The managers that they were studying consciously considered the future consequences of actions and non-actions. The researchers labeled this process as 'prospective sensemaking'. They found that consideration of the future consequences of their actions helped to influence consensual understanding, facilitate decisions and illuminate their present circumstances (1994, p. 378). In a later study of management teams' perceptions of identity and image with 611 executives in 373 colleges and universities, Gioia and Thomas (1996) found that a desired future image is fundamental to sensemaking processes and constitutes an important link between the interpretation of issues and the internal context of the organization. They found that when strategic change is articulated through desired states, or visions, they find people talking in the future tense. A desirable future image, they conclude, helps to prepare employees for a dynamic environment brought about by a change process and can thus ease the launching of a change program (1996, p. 398). In a later paper, Gioia, Corley and Fabbri (2002) argue that history is treated by managers as malleable being constantly revised. The future, drawing on Schütz (1967) and Weick (1969 [1979]), is thought about in the future perfect tense. They suggest that there is interplay between the two. The past is revised to reflect how we see ourselves in the present (our identity) and by invoking the needs of the future (an image of how we want to see ourselves in the future).

Laboratory work conducted by Newby-Clark and Ross (2003, pp. 807, 815) gives some support for thinking in the future perfect. In their study, the researchers found that when asked to consider negative and positive episodes from the past and the future, participants tended to anticipate 'homogeneously ideal futures', even directly after considering mixed episodes in their past history.

In another study into the fast-tracking of a major infrastructural project for the Sydney 2000 Olympics, however, results differed. The researchers analyzed managing through the future perfect with different findings (Pitsis et al. 2003). The researchers adopted Weick's definition that in the future perfect: 'the forward-looking projection of ends is combined with a visualization of the means by which that projected future may be accomplished' (Weick 1969 [1979], p. 198, quoted in Pitsis et al. 2003, p. 574). They reported that when future perfect thinking worked best was when planners had the most control over their material and social contexts. When there was less control, such as when local communities were empowered to question the project's construction, it became more difficult to achieve the future perfect (Pitsis et al. 2003, p. 587).

Evidence for thinking in the future perfect thus comes from the relatively controlled environment of the laboratory. The implications of the Pitsis et al. study are that thinking in the future perfect may be contingent on environments that are relatively stable. Gioia and Thomas (1996), for instance, acknowledge in their study that while the educational industry has become much more competitive, there may still be mimicry (for example, Scott 1987) of emulating a desired future image based on leading organizations in the sector. In this sense, prospective sensemaking is conflated with visioning.

Boje's (2001, p. 3) 'antenarrative' concept, which asserts that storytelling can also involve prospective sensemaking, resonates closely with what is being argued here. Antenarrative re-orientates attention towards the speculative and ambiguity of sensemaking in the flow of experience. Indeed, Boje's (2007) most recent work on narrative and storytelling argues that a complexity perspective allows for retrospective–prospective sensemaking as well as reflexivity and transcendence. In accord with this perspective, there is also evidence that suggests that there may be further cognitive (and social) processes that facilitate retrospective–prospective sensemaking when faced with highly uncertain, surprising or complex circumstances.

Summary
To conclude this section, notions of sensemaking have become pervasive in the literature. They are viewed as: 'an ongoing retrospective development of plausible images that rationalize what people are doing' (Weick and Sutcliffe 2005, p. 409) so that their environment can be comprehended in order to facilitate collective action (Maitlis 2005, p. 21). Research has found that organizational sensemaking and sensegiving are both cognitive (for example, Thomas et al. 1993, p. 262) and social processes that facilitate individuals in their interpretation and enactment of their environments (Weick and Roberts 1993; Maitlis 2005; Maitlis and Lawrence 2007). These processes play primary roles in strategic change initiations (Gioia and Chittipeddi 1991) and the construction of group narratives, such as the legitimating and hegemonic practices embedded in public enquiry reporting (Brown 2000; Brown and Jones, 2000; Brown 2003; Brown and Humphreys 2003). They are also particularly prevalent in crisis situations (Gephart 1993; Weick 1993; Weick and Roberts 1993).

Despite the success of sensemaking theories in the strategic management and organization literature (see Anderson 2006), there have been several criticisms. First, there is little research into the operations underpinning the 'process' of sensemaking (Craig-Lees 2001). Second, the vast literature and developments in cognitive psychology has been left untapped and unintegrated (O'Connell 1998). Finally, there is generally a dismissal of forward-looking 'prospective' sensemaking processes (Gioia and Mehra 1996). In the following section, received research into counterfactual and prefactual mental simulations in psychology is presented. This literature, it is argued, has the capacity to address each of the three criticisms above and to advance notions of prospective sensemaking as a dynamic and temporal process that contributes to the cultivation of strategic foresight.

Received research into counterfactual and prefactual mental simulations

There are two cognitive processes that are particularly relevant for understanding sensemaking processes and their role in the cultivation of strategic foresight. The first is counterfactual reasoning. Counterfactual reasoning is a form of mental simulation that involves asking 'what ifs' about the past that runs counter to the known facts. The second is prefactual reasoning. Prefactual reasoning is a form of cognitive mental simulation that involves asking 'what ifs' about the future. This section examines research into these two processes in psychology for the purpose of developing and extending sensemaking perspectives to include notions of open futures. A prospective dimension to sensemaking that emphasizes its contingent and temporal dimensions will problematize notions of sensemaking as a predominantly retrospective process.

Counterfactual mental simulations

Counterfactual reasoning is a cognitive process where individuals simulate mentally how the past could have evolved differently from how it did. They are a spontaneous mental response for when present realities deviate from expectations of normality. They are used for two primary purposes. Some counterfactual reasoning processes are used as a coping mechanism. For instance, a strategic manager, after a sudden loss of market share, might simulate a world where lost revenues were even worse than in reality. Other counterfactual reasoning processes are used for improving performance in the future. A strategic manager might, for instance, simulate mentally alternative worlds that were much better than in reality so that they can learn from perceived mistakes and develop strategies for improving performance in the future. Researchers have found that counterfactuals influence adaptive learning (Folger 1984; Johnson and Sherman 1990; Roese and Olson 1995b) and, this chapter contends, they can act as both a heuristic and a bias in sensemaking processes and strategic foresight.

Counterfactual reasoning is an integral, if not pervasive cognitive function (Roese and Olson 1995b; Sanna and Turley 1996) and consists of both *prospective* sensemaking processes of speculating, acting and revising, and *retrospective* sensemaking processes that consist of asking what might have been (Sanna and Turley 1996, p. 906), particularly after experiencing a surprising, or episodic event. This functional approach to understanding the reasons people behave as they do (Katz 1960) has considerable potential for understanding sensemaking and how actors' reweave their schematic frameworks and strategic practices when accommodating new experiences, and how they make sense of both the past and the future.

Research demonstrates that counterfactual reasoning affects a wide range of judgments including causal ascriptions (Wells et al. 1987; Gavanski and Wells 1989), assignments of blame (Miller and McFarland 1986; Miller and Gunasegaram 1990) such as when allocating compensation for victims of accidents (Miller and McFarland 1986; Macrae 1992; Turley et al. 1995), how we respond emotionally to unexpected outcomes in our lives (Kahneman and Tversky 1982b; Johnson 1986; Landman 1987; Gleicher et al. 1990), our perceptions of certain types of behavior (Macrae et al. 1993) and our social perceptions (Miller and Gunasegaram 1990). Two studies in particular were important for catalyzing this stream of research.

In the first study, 'The simulation heuristic' (Kahneman and Tversky 1982a), the researchers set out to test a theory of norms and normality. They did this by developing two versions of a story whose chief protagonist is Mr Jones. In one version of the story, Mr Jones leaves work and drives home on his usual route, but he leaves his work at an earlier time. At a traffic light, Mr Jones is struck by another car and killed. In a second version of the story, Mr Jones leaves work at his regular time but takes a more scenic route home. The two narratives were then presented to two groups of participants, who were requested to finish sentences beginning with 'If only . . .'. The researchers discovered that people have a propensity to manipulate variables towards normality. For instance, they might remove a variable that does not conform to their expectations about what is normal, such as 'If only he had left at the normal time or taken his normal route home'.

In a later study entitled 'Norm theory: comparing reality to its alternatives', Kahneman and Miller (1986) develop a theory of normality by establishing that people will construct their own norms by comparing their circumstances with *ad hoc* counterfactual alternatives or similar experiences stored in memory. When events confirm people's anticipations, expectations and predictions, they are deemed to be normal. But when events, particularly abnormal or surprising events, deviate from anticipations, expectations or predictions, violating people's perception of normality, counterfactual alternatives of how the situation could have had a different outcome will be elicited. Events that violate expectations and elicit strong counterfactual alternatives are perceived to be abnormal. If events confirm expectations (which include anticipations and probabilities) then it is perceived as normal. These counterfactuals can affect the choice of strategy for dealing with future events, especially when a subsequent event triggers a trace of a previous event (Schank 1982; Kahneman and Miller 1986). Simulation heuristics such as counterfactual reasoning thus has theoretical import for explaining the cognitive processes that are used to make sense of episodic or surprising events.

Further research into counterfactual mental simulations has also observed that there is a correlation between people's perceptions of prior sets of conditions contextualizing an event and the number of alternative counterfactuals that people imagine (Wells et al. 1987). If there are no prior conditions or inhibiting causes perceived by people, such as legal or resource constraints, social conventions or institutional rules to the game (for example, Meyer and Rowan 1977; DiMaggio and Powell 1983; Mizruchi and Fein 1999), they will imagine a wider range of possibilities. As Wells et al. contend: 'exceptions to the norm epitomize the essence of events that occur in spite of rather than because of these constraints' (1987, p. 429). Consequently, and most importantly for the purposes of this chapter, Wells et al. suggest that the explanations that people generate and the role that imagination plays in the simulation of hypothetical outcomes and the undoing of an event can influence predictions of future outcomes. People have a tendency to undo, or manipulate causes that make the outcome of events easy to explain. Moreover, people may predict a future as most likely to occur if an outcome seems immutable (ibid., p. 429). As Gavanski and Wells state:

> To act purposefully on our physical and social environment, we must not only evaluate reality, but also imagine alternatives to reality. Our thoughts, emotions, and actions are guided not only by what is, but by what might be and what could have been. (1989, p. 315)

While abnormal or surprising events have been shown to elicit counterfactual reasoning as a way of making sense of them, Gavanski and Wells (p. 324) also demonstrate that normal-outcome scenarios can also trigger counterfactual alternatives, often after experiencing a negative outcome. People, they suggest, can be motivated to learn from underperformance and past experiences. They can also have a desire to replicate positive performances in the future. Mental simulations of counterfactual alternatives are one of the heuristics for achieving these ends. Again, quoting Gavanski and Wells: 'The alternative, unrealized outcomes for contrast and comparison hinge on strategies of mutation' (p. 324). Consequently, one can infer that the 'prospective' development of micro strategies for future behavior is tightly coupled with 'retrospective' counterfactual reasoning processes of making sense.

The counterfactuals that individuals generate are a key determinant in emotional and behavioral responses to actual outcomes (Gleicher et al. 1990). Similar to retrospective perspectives on sensemaking, Kahneman and Miller (1986) illustrate that reality is frequently compared to post-computed representations developed *post hoc*, after an event has occurred. Schemas stored in memory as action plans for the future find their basis in these post-computed alternatives to reality. However, retrospective, post-computed mental representations then become the pre-computed schematic templates used for filtering information from the environment and comparing future events with. It is the interplay between the pre- and post-computed schematic representations that determines anticipations, expectations and predictions of normality and, when the future deviates from them, they also determine what is perceived to be abnormal, thus triggering the sensemaking process. Consequently, counterfactual evaluation of experiences is an interpretative, relative and subjective process that depends as much on what did not happen as what did (Miller and Gunasegaram 1990).

Counterfactuals and future performance
The spontaneous generation of counterfactuals can involve mental simulations as better-than-experienced worlds or worse-than-experienced worlds (Markman et al. 1993, pp. 103–7). The generation of 'better-than-experienced' worlds normally take the form of 'if only' statements. Better-than-experienced worlds, which effectively worsen reality, are used as a learning heuristic for the future and 'worse-than-experienced' worlds that worsen reality enhance satisfaction with the events or circumstances experienced, but often at the expense of learning for improved performance in the future (Wells et al. 1987; Taylor and Schneider 1989; Markman et al. 1993, p. 88; Roese 1994, p. 805). As Roese (1994) suggests, 'better-than-experienced' worlds: 'may be taken as schemata for future action, making salient those scripts that are necessary to facilitate success' (p. 806; Johnson and Sherman 1990, p. 512). People imagine alternatives and compare their outcomes to them because there are rarely objective standards for comparison (Boninger et al. 1994, p. 297). As Roese and Olson (1995b) state: 'By manipulating alternatives to past actions, individuals can scrutinize them into prescriptions that may facilitate success in the future' (p. 170).

While the effects of counterfactual mental simulations have been shown to be a cognitive strategy for coping at the expense of preparation for enhancing future performance (for example, Markman et al. 1993), some researchers have found that preparation for the future can also have a positive influence on our emotional reactions to circumstances (Boninger et al. 1994).

In essence, counterfactual mental simulations identify and isolate what we perceive to be 'causally potent antecedent action'. This drives a preparative function (Roese and

Olson 1995b). Identifying and isolating a causally potent antecedent action acts as an expectancy trigger (Sherman et al. 1981; Anderson and Godfrey 1987; Roese and Olson 1995b) for the future consequences of a similar action. Furthermore, intentions of performing the action in the future are heightened, influencing the behavioral intention of that action.

Prefactual mental simulations
Another category of mental simulation that has been identified by psychologists is that of 'prefactuals'. Prefactuals are, in essence, the cerebral component to scenario thinking. They prospectively simulate alternative futures.

   In three studies, one testing counterfactuals and behavioral intentions, the second on prefactuals and condom use, and the third looking at prefactuals and insurance, evidence has been found indicating that there are two positive functions that are served by subjunctive reasoning 'with an eye to the future' (Gleicher et al. 1995). First, prefactuals can ameliorate counterfactually induced negative emotions: 'Thus, the "stink of the past" may well become the sweet smell of the future' (ibid., p. 302). Second, they facilitate adaptive behavioral choices in the future. As Miller and Taylor (1995) state, decision strategies might be affected, 'not [by] people's recollection of the past, but [by] their contemplation of the future' (p. 306). Other researchers, such as Sanna and Turley (1996) agree, arguing that counterfactual thinking involves both a backwards processing from an outcome, and a forward processing from a hypothesis or expectancies to revision or confirmation.

   Returning to our previous discussion of surprises and failures in strategic foresight: 'In the social domain, a long history of disasters of planning and design demonstrates that the impossible sometimes happens and that the inevitable sometimes does not' (Kahneman 1995, p. 380). The 'surprise' element in counterfactuals represents the 'causal texture of an environment' (ibid., p. 376).

Summary
Simulating events prefactually before they occur effectively draws on the same process as simulating counterfactuals. If counterfactuals contribute to the underlying processes of sensemaking, particularly to the sensemaking processes of revising history to conform with perceptions of identity and so on, it stands to reason that prefactuals contribute to the underlying processes behind prospective sensemaking. They may also rely upon the perceptual filters of executives, influencing what is noticed. Far from thinking in the future perfect, depending on the natural disposition of the strategic manager and numerous 'inhibiting' and 'moderating' variables, such as accountability to organizational superiors (Morris and Moore 2000), it seems that prospective sensemaking is a complex and contingent process of 'cultivating' (Chia 2004) strategic foresight through a form of scenario thinking.

Conclusions, implications and further research
Prospecting is normally associated with the search for resource wealth. It consists of exploring new and uncertain terrain and sifting through large amounts of raw material – at one time with pick-axes, shovels and pans – for a trace of mineralization. It provides a useful metaphor for exploring and making sense of equivocality. There may well be something innate in human nature that desires unequivocality, but there is also a side to

humans that understands that the future world is becoming increasingly counterfactual and future oriented.

As sensemaking processes are currently construed in the business and management literature, they remain ontologically bound to a retrospective frame, which is constituted by a relatively 'unreflective' social constructionist idiom (for example, Lash and Wynne 1986, p. 4). Early notions of sensemaking practices (for example, Weick 1969 [1979]) stemmed from an interest in linking human cognition and sensemaking with the social construction (for example, Berger and Luckmann 1966) of organizational realities (Gephart 1978). As sensemaking has become a signature domain of inquiry in strategic management and organization studies, a concept that mainstream psychology has used for decades (Craig-Lees 2001), human cognition has evaporated from the sensemaking equation and, consequently, sensemaking has come to be viewed as synonymous with social constructionism. This has led critics to argue that the vast literature in cognitive psychology that has emerged since its original introduction into organizational studies has remained untapped and unintegrated (O'Connell 1998, p. 207). This may be due, in part, to a perceived incommensurability between the positivist mindset that dominates the cognitive sciences and the social-constructionist mindset that is prevalent in sensemaking perspectives. However, social-constructionists also accept that social realities can be analyzed, reified, compared and ultimately validated by measuring, for instance, communication, narrative and discourse. Social-constructionist approaches to sensemaking have thus been accepted within the positivist paradigm (Craig-Lees 2001, pp. 519–21), but rather than risking becoming ontologically bound to the 'hard' areas of retrospection, new insights from the 'soft' areas of counterfactual and prospective sensemaking may yet yield rich deposits of new wealth.

The argument presented in this chapter is that sensemaking processes are not just retrospective processes 'of reducing equivocality' (Weick 1995, p. 27; 1969 [1979], p. 6). They can also be counterfactual and prospective processes that generate a number of competing interpretations of the past and the future – the raw material – for prospecting. Counterfactual and prospective sensemaking processes are germane to understanding a range of past and future uncertainties that facilitate understanding and strategic foresight. Retrospective sensemaking may indeed reduce equivocality, but it can also erase other causal sequences 'that complicate and obscure the present and future' (Starbuck and Milliken 1988, p. 37; Fischhoff 1975, pp. 298–9). Sensemaking processes that attempt to reduce hegemonic accounts of phenomena through multiple interpretations, both counterfactually into the past or prospectively into the future, heighten understanding of the reflexive consequences of managing strategically in an enacted world. This remains underinvestigated in the study of strategy and organization, and constitutes an important area of future research.

Implications for theory
Research into counterfactuals and prefactuals has found that they are a pervasive cognitive function. If they can also be shown to be evident in intersubjective narrative and conversational processes in strategic management, notions of sensemaking as a predominantly retrospective process become problematized (for example, see Boje 2007). There is some evidence that the 'strategic conversation' (van der Heijden 1996) and 'strategizing as lived experience' (Samra-Frederichs 2003) in organizations include both retrospective

and prospective processes when trying to shape strategic direction. Moreover, prospective prefactual simulations in the subjunctive mood have been shown to be a function used to make sense of an uncertain future (Gleicher et al. 1995, p. 294; Byrne and Egan 2004, p. 113). Strategies and decisions are affected by more than mere recollection of the past, but also by contemplation of the future (Miller and Taylor 1995, p. 306). Prospective sensemaking thus involves making sense for, and structuring the future in order to identify opportunities for action and to propel ourselves forward (Gioia and Mehra 1996, p. 1229). Concepts of prospective counterfactual and prefactual reasoning help to refine and extend notions of sensemaking into the vast and daunting realm of the counterfactual past and prospective future.

Sensemaking then, as both a cognitive and social process, is arguably important for the cultivation, and perhaps at times the short-circuiting, of strategic foresight. Foresight is not simply a process of understanding the future. Whitehead's (1933 [1967]) suggestion that an attribute of the business mind of the future would be a philosophical disposition towards understanding the nuances of a complex world through 'historical-foresight' is no less salient, if perhaps unrealized, today. These insights also have implications for arguments in the strategic management literature that suggest that identifying strategies is primarily a retrospective process. Andrews, for instance, proposes that corporate strategy is: 'the pattern of decisions in a company' (1987, p. 13). Similarly, Mintzberg and Waters describe strategy as: 'a pattern in a stream of decisions' (1985, p. 257). In both cases strategy must be recognized restrospectively. Again, the evidence presented here suggests that it is much more likely that strategy formulation is a process of prospecting for patterns both retrospectively and prospectively through historical foresight.

Weick (2002) argues that while we understand the reflexive liabilities that seem to threaten the validity of understanding the world retrospectively, in hindsight, we do not know how these 'threats' influence our prospective disposition, or strategic foresight. He uses Heidegger's language (Dreyfus 1995) to deconstruct the observation that life is understood backwards but lived forwards. It has been argued that when people attempt to 'vision' the future, they do so in the future perfect (Schütz 1967; Weick 1969 [1979], 1995). However, future perfect thinking works best – one might even argue only works – when there is a high degree of control over changing social, technological and material contexts for future action (Pitsis et al. 2003, p. 587). More research into the correlation between sensemaking processes and environmental complexity and uncertainty needs to be done.

Clearly there is interplay between retrospective and prospective sensemaking. Sensemaking may be both a trip-wire and a trigger for strategic foresight. At times, particularly in times of severe crises, when 'low probability/high consequence events . . . threaten the most fundamental goals of an organization' (Weick 1988, p. 305), or when cognitive dissonance is at its highest, prospective sensemaking may well decline, and depending on the severe demands placed on retrospective sensemaking, a combination of improvisation and enactment sensemaking may take over. It may also be that the requisite variety that Weick (1995) talks about being necessary for sensemaking out of complex situations will partly come from *ex ante* mental simulations of past and future. As Smircich and Stubbart (1985, pp. 731–2) suggest, managing in an enacted world encourages the generation of multiple realities and testing and experimenting, which, it is argued here, is often done virtually through a combination of counterfactual and prefactual prospecting.

Implications for practice

Many sensemaking processes manifest themselves as spontaneous mental simulations, or in social contexts, conversations and interactions among managers. This leads to the question of whether insights from this chapter can have any normative possibilities for improving sensemaking in organizations? The answer is yes. Strategic planning techniques such as scenario planning can help reduce surprises that lead to confusion by understanding the range of complexities and uncertainties in an organization's external environment.

But scenarios are not a panacea for failures in strategic foresight and can themselves be vulnerable to a range of biases, some embedded in hindsight and others driven by sensemaking processes discussed in this chapter. The results can be missing weak signals of emerging patterns and asymmetries that can be disastrous for strategic planning efforts and lead to failures of strategic foresight (see MacKay and McKiernan 2004a, b for a wider discussion).

A second implication for managers, then, is that sensemaking processes often involve revision of the past (Gioia et al. 2002). Research in psychology suggests that incorrect causal analysis can diminish accurate understanding of a situation and perpetuate poor judgment, decision making and performance in the future (Sherman and McConnell 1995). The implications for strategic foresight as a temporal process are that spontaneous revisions of the past can lead to strategic foresight failures. As Nystrom and Starbuck suggest, 'Organizations can succumb to crisis largely because their top managers, bolstered by recollections of past successes, live in worlds circumscribed by their cognitive structures. Top managers misperceive events and rationalize their organization's failures' (1984, p. 59). Historians Neustadt and May, in their study of the uses of history by decision makers, have found that decision makers not only use history in their decision making processes, but also that incorrect application of history, through analogies, rhetoric and reliance on past recipes of success, can lead to poor decisions. They suggest testing the sense that we have made from the past through the asking of journalistic questions such as who, what, why, where and when something happened to ensure contextual commensurability with current circumstances (Neustadt and May 1986). Explicit counterfactual analysis can also help to expose assumptions and investigate causality in our strategic foresight processes (see MacKay 2008 for a wider discussion of the use of counterfactual history in organizations), thereby giving structure and rigor to sensemaking processes.

Modernity has been accompanied by considerable progress in science. It also brings with it unintended consequences, future risks and uncertainties that we have yet to contemplate fully. The future is no longer a benign and distant place that can be understood retrospectively by making sense of our experiences of the past *ex post*. The challenges and potential consequences for the firm, industry and nation of modern technology and the productive (and destructive) forces that it has unleashed make the study and application of strategic foresight practices and processes an imperative.

Note

1. See Weick (1993, 1996) for a full discussion of the disaster and its implications for management theory and practice. For the full story, see Norman Maclean, *Young Men and Fire*, Chicago: University of Chicago Press, 1992.

References

Anderson, C. and S. Godfrey (1987), 'Thoughts about actions: the effect of specificity and availability of imagined behavioural scripts on expectations about oneself and others', *Social Cognition*, **5**, 238–58.

Anderson, M. (2006), 'How can we know what we think until we see what we said? A citation and citation context analysis of Karl Weick's *The Social Psychology of Organizing*', *Organization Studies*, **27** (11), 1675–92.

Andrews, K. (1971), *The Concept of Corporate Strategy*, Homewood: Irwin.

Andrews, K. (1987), *The Concept of Corporate Strategy*, New York: Dow Jones–Irwin.

Ansoff, I. (1975), 'Managing strategic surprise by response to weak signals', *California Management Review*, **18** (2), 25–33.

Ascher, W. (1978), *Forecasting*, Baltimore, MD: Johns Hopkins University Press.

Ayres, R. (2000), 'On forecasting discontinuities', *Technological Forecasting and Social Change*, **65**, 81–97.

Balogun, J. and J. Johnson (2005), 'From intended strategies to unintended outcomes: the impact of change recipient sensemaking', *Organization Studies*, **26** (11), 1573–601.

Barnard, C. (1938 [1979]), *The Functions of the Executive*, Cambridge, MA: Harvard University Press.

Barr, P., J. Stimpert and A. Huff (1992), 'Cognitive change, strategic action, organizational renewal', *Strategic Management Journal*, **13**, 15–36.

Bazerman, M. and M. Watkins (2004), *Predictable Surprises: The Disasters You Should Have Seen Coming and How to Prevent Them*, Boston, MA: Harvard Business School Press.

Beck, U. (1986) (ed.), *Risk Society: Towards a New Modernity*, London: Sage.

Beck, U. (1999), *World Risk Society*, Cambridge: Polity.

Berger, P. and T. Luckmann (1966), *The Social Construction of Reality*, London: Penguin.

Boje, D. (2001), *Narrative Methods for Organizational and Communication Research*, London: Sage.

Boje, D. (2007), *Storytelling Organization*, London: Sage.

Boland, R. (1984), 'Sense-making of accounting data as a technique of organizational diagnosis', *Management Science*, **30**, 868–82.

Boninger, D., F. Gleicher and A. Strathman (1994), 'Counterfactual thinking: from what might have been to what may be', *Journal of Personality and Social Psychology*, **67** (2), 297–307.

Brown, A. (2000), 'Making sense of inquiry sensemaking', *Journal of Management Studies*, **37** (1), 45–75.

Brown, A. (2003), 'Authoritative sensemaking in a public inquiry report', *Organization Studies*, **25** (1), 95–112.

Brown, A. and M. Humphreys (2003), 'Epic and tragic tales: making sense of change', *Journal of Applied Behavioral Science*, **39** (2), 121–44.

Brown, A. and M. Jones (2000), 'Honourable members and dishonourable deeds: sensemaking, impression management and legitimation in the "Arms to Iraq" affair', *Human Relations*, **53** (5), 655–89.

Byrne, R. and S. Egan (2004), 'Counterfactual and prefactual conditionals', *Canadian Journal of Experimental Psychology*, **58** (2), 113–20.

Chae, M. and J. Hill (1996), 'The hazards of strategic planning for global markets', *Long Range Planning*, **29** (6), 880–91.

Chandler, A.D., Jr. (1962), *Strategy and Structure: Chapters in the History of the American Industrial Enterprise*, Cambridge, MA: MIT Press.

Chia, R. (2004), 'Re-educating attention: what is foresight and how is it cultivated?', in H. Tsoukas and J. Shepherd (eds), *Managing the Future: Foresight in the Knowledge Economy*, London: Blackwell, pp. 21–37.

Craig-Lees, M. (2001), 'Sense making: Trojan horse? Pandora's box?', *Psychology and Marketing*, **18** (5), 513–26.

Crozier, M. (1964), *The Bureaucratic Phenomenon*, London: Tavistock.

Cunha, M., S. Clegg and K. Kamoche (2006), 'Surprises in management and organization: concept, sources and a typology', *British Journal of Management*, **17**, 317–29.

Cyert, R. and J. March (1963), *A Behavioral Theory of the Firm*, Englewood Cliffs, NJ: Prentice-Hall.

Daft, R. and K. Weick (1984), 'Toward a model of organizations as interpretation systems', *Academy of Management Review*, **9** (2), 284–95.

DiMaggio, P. and W. Powell (1983), 'The iron cage revisited: institutional isomorphism and collective rationality in organizational fields', *American Sociological Review*, **48**, 147–60.

Dreyfus, H. (1995), *Being-in-the-world*, Cambridge, MA: MIT Press.

Duncan, R. and A. Weiss (1979), 'Organizational learning: implications for organizational design', in B. Staw (ed.), *Research in Organizational Behavior*, Greenwich, CT: JAI Press, pp. 283–304.

Erman, B. and D. Decloet (2008), 'Miscalculating the risks', *Globe and Mail*, February 22.

Fayol, H. (1916/1949), *General and Industrial Management*, London: Pitman Publishing Company.

Finkelstein, S. (2003), *Why Smart Executives Fail: And What You Can Learn from Their Mistakes*, New York: Portfolio.

Fiol, C. and M. Lyles (1985), 'Organizational learning', *Academy of Management Review*, **10**, 803–13.

Fischhoff, B. (1975), 'Hindsight and foresight: the effect of outcome knowledge on judgment under uncertainty', *Journal of Experimental Psychology: Human Perception and Performance*, **1**, 288–99.

Fischhoff, B., P. Slovic and S. Liechtenstein (1977), 'Knowing with certainty: the appropriateness of extreme confidence', *Journal of Experimental Psychology: Human Perception and Performance*, **3**, 552–64.

Folger, R. (1984), 'Perceived injustice, referent cognitions, and the concept of comparison level', *Representative Research in Social Psychology*, **14**, 88–108.

Gavanski, I. and G. Wells (1989), 'Counterfactual processing of normal and exceptional events', *Journal of Experimental Social Psychology*, **25**, 314–25.

Gephart, R. (1978), 'Status degradation and organizational succession: an ethnomethodological approach', *Administrative Science Quarterly*, **23** (4), 553–81.

Gephart, R. (1993), 'The textual approach: risk and blame in disaster sensemaking', *Academy of Management Journal*, **36**, 1465–514.

Gephart, R. (1997), 'Hazardous measures: an interpretive textual analysis of quantitative sensemaking during crisis', *Journal of Organizational Behavior*, **18**, 583–622.

Giddens, A. (1990), *The Consequences of Modernity*, Cambridge: Polity.

Gioia, D. and K. Chittipeddi (1991), 'Sensemaking and sensegiving in strategic change initiation', *Strategic Management Journal*, **12**, 433–48.

Gioia, D. and A. Mehra (1996), 'Book Review: *Sensemaking in Organizations*', *Academy of Management Journal*, **21** (4), 1226–40.

Gioia, D. and J. Thomas (1996), 'Identity, image, and issue interpretation: sensemaking during strategic change in academia', *Administrative Science Quarterly*, **41**, 370–403.

Gioia, D., K. Corley and T. Fabbri (2002), 'Revising the past (while thinking in the future perfect tense)', *Journal of Organizational Change Management*, **15** (6), 622–34.

Gioia, D., J. Thomas, S. Clark and K. Chittipeddi (1994), 'Symbolism and strategic change in academia: the dynamics of sensemaking and influence', *Organization Science*, **5** (3), 363–83.

Gleicher, F., D. Boninger, A. Strathman, D. Armor and M. Ahn (1995), 'With an eye toward the future: the impact of counterfactual thinking on affect, attitudes, and behaviour', in N. Roese and J. Olson (eds) (1995a), pp. 283–304.

Gleicher, F., K. Kost, S. Baker, A. Strathman, S. Richman and S. Sherman (1990), 'The role of counterfactual thinking in judgments of affect', *Personality and Social Psychology Bulletin*, **16** (2), 284–95.

Grinyer, P. and J.-C. Spender (1979), *Turnaround: Managerial Recipes for Strategic Success: The Fall and Rise of the Newton Chambers Group*, London: Associated Business Press.

Hamel, G. and C. Prahalad (1994a), 'Competing for the future', *Harvard Business Review*, **72** (4), 122–8.

Hamel, G. and C. Prahalad (1994b), *Competing for the Future*, Boston, MA: Harvard University Press.

Higgins, R. (1981), 'Long range planning in the mature corporation', *Strategic Management Journal*, **2**, 235–50.

Hodgkinson, G. and P. Sparrow (2002), *The Competent Organization*, Buckingham: Open University Press.

Johnson, J. (1986), 'The knowledge of what might have been: affective and attributional consequences of near outcomes', *Personality and Social Psychology Bulletin*, **12**, 51–62.

Johnson, M. and S. Sherman (1990), 'Constructing and reconstructing the past and the future in the present', in E. Higgins and R. Sorrentino (eds), *Handbook of Motivation and Cognition: Foundations of Social Behaviour*, New York: Guilford Press, pp. 482–526.

Kahneman, D. (1995), 'Varieties of counterfactual thinking', in Roese and Olson (eds) (1995a), pp. 375–96.

Kahneman, D. and T. Miller (1986), 'Norm theory: comparing reality to its alternatives', *Psychological Review*, **93** (2), 136–53.

Kahneman, D. and A. Tversky (1982a), 'The psychology of preferences', *Scientific American*, **246**, 160–73.

Kahneman, D. and A. Tversky (1982b), 'The simulation heuristic', in D. Kahneman, P. Slovic and A. Tversky (eds), *Judgment Under Uncertainty: Heuristics and Biases*, Cambridge: Cambridge University Press, pp. 201–10.

Katz, D. (1960), 'The functional approach to the study of attitudes', *Public Opinion Quarterly*, **24**, 163–204.

Keats, J. (1817), 'Negative capability', Letter to George and Thomas Keats, dated December 21.

Kuhn, T. (1967), *The Structure of Scientific Revolutions*, Chicago, IL: University of Chicago Press.

Landman, J. (1987), 'Regret and elation following action and inaction: affective responses to positive versus negative outcomes', *Personality and Social Psychology Bulletin*, **13** (4), 524–36.

Lash, S. and B. Wynne (1986), 'Introduction', in Beck, pp. 1–8.

Lawrence, P. and J. Lorsch (1967), *Organizations and Environment: Managing Differentiation and Integration*, Boston, MA: Harvard University Press.

Leiter, K. (1980), *A Primer on Ethnomethodology*, New York: Oxford University Press.

Lindsay, W. and L. Rue (1980), 'Impact of the organization environment on the long-range planning process: a contingency view', *Academy of Management Journal*, **23** (3), 385–404.

Loasby, B. (1967), 'Long-range formal planning in perspective', *Journal of Management Studies*, October, 300–308.

Louis, M. (1980), 'Surprise and sensemaking: what newcomers experience in entering unfamiliar organizational settings', *Administrative Science Quarterly*, **25** (2), 226–51.

Macrae, C. (1992), 'A tale of two curries: counterfactual thinking and accident related judgments', *Personality and Social Psychology Bulletin*, **18**, 84–7.

Macrae, C., A. Milne and R. Griffiths (1993), 'Counterfactual thinking and the perception of criminal behaviour', *British Journal of Psychology*, **84**, 221–6.

MacKay, B. (2008), 'What if? Synthesizing debates and advancing the prospects of using virtual history in management and organizational theory', *Management and Organization History*, **2** (4), 295–314.

MacKay, B., S. Masrani and P. McKiernan (2006), 'Strategy options and cognitive freezing: the case of the Dundee jute industry in Scotland', *Futures*, **38**, 925–41.

MacKay, B. and P. McKiernan (2004a), 'Exploring strategy context with foresight', *European Management Review*, **1** (1), 69–77.

MacKay, B. and P. McKiernan (2004b), 'The role of hindsight in foresight: refining strategic reasoning', *Futures*, **36**, 161–79.

Maitlis, S. (2005), 'The social processes of organizational sensemaking', *Academy of Management Journal*, **48**, 21–49.

Maitlis, S. and T. Lawrence (2007), 'Triggers and enablers of sensegiving in organizations', *Academy of Management Journal*, **50** (1), 57–84.

Markman, K., I. Gavanski, S. Sherman and M. McMullen (1993), 'The mental simulation of better and worse possible worlds', *Journal of Experimental Social Psychology*, **29**, 87–109.

Meyer, J. and B. Rowan (1977), 'Institutionalized organizations: formal structure as myth and ceremony', *American Journal of Sociology*, **83**, 340–63.

Miller, D. and S. Gunasegaram (1990), 'Temporal order and the perceived mutability of events: implications for blame assignment', *Journal of Personality and Social Psychology*, **59** (6), 1111–18.

Miller, D. and C. McFarland (1986), 'Counterfactual thinking and victim compensation: a test of norm theory', *Personality and Social Psychology Bulletin*, **12** (4), 513–19.

Miller, D. and B. Taylor (1995), 'Counterfactual thought, regret, and superstition: how to avoid kicking yourself', in Roese and Olson (eds) (1995a), pp. 305–32.

Mintzberg, H. (1994a), 'The fall and rise of strategic planning', *Harvard Business Review*, **72** (1), 107–14.

Mintzberg, H. (1994b), *The Rise and Fall of Strategic Planning*, Toronto: Free Press.

Mintzberg, H. and J. Waters (1985), 'Of strategies, deliberate and emergent', *Strategic Management Journal*, July–September, 257–72.

Mizruchi, S. and C. Fein (1999), 'The social construction of organizational knowledge: a study of the uses of coercive, mimetic, and normative isomorphism', *Administrative Science Quarterly*, **44**, 653–83.

Morris, M. and P. Moore (2000), 'The lessons we (don't) learn: counterfactual thinking and organizational accountability after a close call', *Administrative Science Quarterly*, **45**, 737–65.

Neustadt, R. and E. May (1986), *Thinking In Time: The Uses of History for Decision Makers*, New York: Free Press.

Newby-Clark, I. and M. Ross (2003), 'Conceiving the past and future', *Personality and Social Psychology Bulletin*, **29** (7), 807–18.

Nystrom, P. and W. Starbuck (1984), 'To avoid organizational crises, unlearn', *Organizational Dynamics*, **12**, 53–65.

O'Connell, D. (1998), 'Book review: *Sensemaking in Organizations*', *Administrative Science Quarterly*, March, 205–8.

Peters, T. and R. Waterman (1982), *In Search of Excellence*, New York: Harper & Row.

Pitsis, T., S. Clegg, M. Marosszeky and T. Rura-Polley (2003), 'Constructing the Olympic dream: a future perfect strategy of project management', *Organization Science*, **14** (5), 574–90.

Pondy, L. and I. Mitroff (1979), 'Beyond open systems models of organization', in B. Staw (ed.), *Research in Organizational Behavior*, Greenwich, CT: JAI, pp. 3–39.

Porac, J., H. Thomas and C. Baden-Fuller (1989), 'Competitive groups as cognitive communities: the case of Scottish knitwear manufacturers', *Journal of Management Studies*, **26** (4), 397–416.

Porac, J., H. Thomas, F. Wilson, D. Paton and A. Kanfer (1995), 'Rivalry and the industry model of Scottish knitwear producers', *Administrative Science Quarterly*, **40**, 203–27.

Porter, M. (1980), *Competitive Strategy*, New York: Free Press.

Porter, M. (1985), *Competitive Advantage: Creating and Sustaining Superior Performance*, New York: Free Press.

Rigby, D. and B. Bilodeau (2007), 'Bain's global 2007 management tools and trends survey', *Strategy and Leadership*, **35** (5), 9–16.

Roese, N. (1994), 'The functional basis of counterfactual thinking', *Journal of Personality and Social Psychology*, **66** (5), 805–18.

Roese, N. and J. Olson (eds) (1995a), *What Might Have Been: The Social Psychology of Counterfactual Thinking*, Hillsdale, NJ: Lawrence Erlbaum.

Roese, N. and J. Olson (1995b), 'Counterfactual thinking: A critical overview', in Roese and Olson (eds) (1995a), pp. 1–56.

Samra-Fredericks, D. (2003), 'Strategizing as lived experience and strategists' everyday efforts to shape strategic direction', *Journal of Management Studies*, **40** (1), 141–74.

Sanna, L. and K. Turley (1996), 'Antecedents to spontaneous counterfactual thinking: effects of expectancy violation and outcome valence', *Personality and Social Psychology Bulletin*, **22** (9), 906–20.

Schank, R. (1982), *Dynamic Memory: Learning in Computers and People*, New York: Cambridge University Press.

Schütz, A. (1967), *The Phenomenology of the Social World*, Evanston, IL: Southwestern Press.

Scott, R. (1987), 'The adolescence of institutional theory', *Administrative Science Quarterly*, **32**, 493–511.

Sherman, S. and A. McConnell (1995), 'Dysfunctional implications of counterfactual thinking: when alternatives to reality fail us', in N. Roese and J. Olson (eds), *What Might Have Been: The Social Psychology of Counterfactual Thinking*, New Jersey: Lawrence Erlbaum, pp. 199–232.

Sherman, S., R. Skov, E. Hervitz and C. Stock (1981), 'The effects of explaining hypothetical future events: from possibility to probability to actuality and beyond', *Journal of Experimental Social Psychology*, **17**, 142–58.

Simon, H. (1957), *Administrative Behavior*, New York: Macmillan.

Simon, H. (1990), 'Herbert A. Simon testimony on the social sciences: Senate Committee on Commerce, Science, and Technology, September 29, 1989', *Political Science and Politics*, **23** (1), 33–4.

Smircich, L. and C. Stubbart (1985), 'Strategic management in an enacted world', *Academy of Management Review*, **10** (4), 724–36.

Stacey, R. (1995), 'The science of complexity: an alternative perspective for strategic change processes', *Strategic Management Journal*, **16** (6), 477–95.

Starbuck, W. and F. Milliken (1988), 'Executives' perceptual filters: what they notice and how they make sense', in D. Hambrick (ed.), *The Executive Effect: Concepts and Methods for Studying Top Managers*, Greenwich, CT: JAI, pp. 35–56.

Stern, N. (2007), *The Economics of Climate Change: The Stern Review*, Cambridge: Cambridge University Press.

Stiglitz, J. and L. Blimes (2008), *The Three Trillion Dollar War*, New York: Allen Lane.

Sutcliffe, K. and G. Huber (1998), 'Firm and industry as determinants of executive perceptions of the environment', *Strategic Management Journal*, **19**, 793–807.

Sutcliffe, K. and K. Weber (2003), 'The high cost of accurate knowledge', *Harvard Business Review*, May, 74–82.

Taleb, N. (2007), *The Black Swan: The Impact of the Highly Improbable,* London: Penguin.

Taylor, S. and S. Schneider (1989), 'Coping and the simulation of events', *Social Cognition*, **7**, 174–94.

Thomas, J., S. Clark and D. Gioia (1993), 'Strategic sensemaking and organizational performance: linkages among scanning, interpretation, action, and outcomes', *Academy of Management Journal*, **36** (2), 239–70.

Thompson, J. (1967), *Organizations in Action*, New York: McGraw-Hill.

Tsoukas, H. (1996), 'The firm as a distributed knowledge system: a constructionist approach', *Strategic Management Journal*, **17** (Winter), 11–25.

Tsoukas, H. and R. Chia (2002), 'On organizational becoming: rethinking organizational change', *Organizational Science*, **13** (5), 567–82.

Tsoukas, H. and J. Shepherd (2004), *Managing the Future: Foresight in the Knowledge Economy*, London: Blackwell.

Turley, K., L. Sanna and R. Reiter (1995) 'Counterfactual thinking and perceptions of rape', *Basic and Applied Social Psychology*, **17**, 285–303.

Turner, B. (1976), 'The organizational and interorganizational development of disasters', *Administrative Science Quarterly*, **21** (3), 378–97.

Tversky, A. and D. Kahneman (1974) 'Judgment under uncertainty: heuristics and biases', *Science*, **198**, 1124–31.

van der Heijden, K. (1996), *Scenarios: The Art of Strategic Conversation*, Chichester: John Wiley & Sons.

Wack, P. (1985a), 'Scenarios: uncharted waters ahead', *Harvard Business Review*, September–October, 73–89.

Wack, P. (1985b), 'Scenarios: shooting the rapids', *Harvard Business Review*, November–December, 139–50.

Waterman, R. (1990), *Adhocracy: The Power to Change*, Memphis, TN: Whittle Direct Books.

Weick, K. (1969 [1979]), *The Social Psychology of Organizing*, New York: Random House.

Weick, K. (1985), 'Cosmos vs. chaos: sense and nonsense in electronic contexts', *Organizational Dynamics*, **14** (Autumn), 50–64.

Weick, K. (1988), 'Enacted sensemaking in crisis situations', *Journal of Management Studies*, **25** (4), 305–17.

Weick, K. (1993), 'The collapse of sensemaking in organizations: the Mann Gulch disaster', *Administrative Science Quarterly*, **38** (4), 628–52.

Weick, K. (1995), *Sensemaking in Organizations*, Thousand Oaks, CA: Sage.

Weick, K. (1996), 'Drop your tools: an allegory for organizational studies', *Administrative Science Quarterly*, **41** (2), 301–13.

Weick, K. (2002), 'Essai: Real-time reflexivity: prods to reflection, *Organization Studies*, **26** (6), 893–8.

Weick, K. and K. Roberts (1993), 'Collective mind in organizations: heedful interrelating on flight decks', *Administrative Science Quarterly*, **38** (3), 357–81.

Weick, K. and L. Sutcliffe (2001), *Managing the Unexpected*, San Francisco, CA: Jossey-Bass.

Weick, K. and K. Sutcliffe (2005), 'Organizing and the process of sensemaking', *Organization Science*, **16** (4), 409–21.

Wells, G., B. Taylor and J. Turtle (1987), 'The undoing of scenarios', *Journal of Personality and Social Psychology*, **53** (3), 421–30.

Whitehead, A. (1933 [1967]), *Adventures of Ideas*, London: Cambridge University Press.

Wilensky, H. (1967), *Organizational Intelligence*, New York: Basic Books.

6 Modal narratives, possible worlds and strategic foresight*

Charles Booth, Peter Clark, Agnès Delahaye-Dado, Stephen Procter and Michael Rowlinson

There is at all times enough past for all the different futures in sight, and more besides, to find their reasons in it, and whichever future comes will slide out of that past as easily as the train slides by the switch.

(William James, *The Meaning of Truth*, 1909)

Introduction

In this chapter we advance suggestions for a philosophical system to underpin strategic foresight. In an editorial for a forthcoming special issue of the journal *Futures*, Mermet et al. (2009) argue that, because of the indeterminate and uncertain nature of the object and subject of the futures studies field, futurists have consistently demonstrated a concern for methodology, in part to defend the field against external criticism of its legitimacy and of its practices. The existence of the field as one concerned with practical application (and with the conjoining of efforts of academics and practitioners) has also arguably tended to result in an overemphasis on methodological codification and with it a proliferation of approaches (Bradfield et al., 2005), at a cost of sacrificing theoretical and philosophical underpinnings of sufficient depth. This chapter therefore seeks to address Mermet's and his colleagues' call for such underpinnings. The chapter is thus not concerned primarily with the practices and methods of strategic foresight, but with the delineation of a potentially useful, supportive and transformational conceptual approach, drawn from outside the futures studies domain.

Most strategy textbooks (for example, Johnson et al., 2005) place strategic choice at the centre of the strategy process. This canonical account of strategizing divides the strategy process into three linearly organized sets of activities: strategic analysis (of resources and the external environment), strategic choice and strategy implementation. Strategic choice involves generating a number of alternatives for the organization, and then selecting the strategic option that best fits the objectives, resources and environmental position determined as an outcome of the prior analysis. Such choices may be driven by decisions concerning the basis for competitive advantage and the competitive scope of the organization (as in Porter's (1985) generic strategies framework, for example); or concerning the optimum product-market configuration (see Ansoff's (1965) product-market matrix). Whatever the genealogy of the decision space concerned, however, what is involved is the generation, specification and selection of future strategic actions within a fairly limited range of realizable possibilities.[1]

Organizational foresight exercises, such as scenario planning, focus more tightly on the generation of possible futures for the organization. Although used in a wide variety of contexts and using a considerable range of methodologies (van Notten et al., 2003), such exercises would normally concern themselves with plausible future states of affairs.

Although the precise nature and meaning of plausibility in this context may be contestable, it is likely that scenario planners will not invest time and effort in generating futures which, for example, involve the contravention of physical laws. Thinking about the future in strategy and organizational foresight, then, involves at least the implicit and perhaps the explicit consideration of such questions as: 'What options are open to us?', 'Which options cannot be realized under any circumstances?', 'What would it take to make this option possible?', and 'Do we have any choice but to do this?'.

These questions concern, respectively, possibility, impossibility, contingency and necessity. In philosophy (Divers, 2002), these are the four cases of modality. We have elsewhere (Clark et al., 2007) coined the term 'modal narratives' to describe analytically structured narratives which are driven by modal questions and issues. Such 'what if' accounts include scenario and other foresight narratives; other cases are counterfactuals or alternate histories (if past rather than future oriented). In this chapter we explore the philosophical and methodological underpinnings of modal narratives, with special reference to strategy and foresight.

The chapter is organized as follows. Following this introduction, we discuss the concept of modality in more detail, before explicating our conception of modal narratives. We then explore two fundamental schemata for organizing modal narratives, those of temporal branching and possible worlds, with different ontological, epistemological and methodological implications. Finally, we discuss the ramifications of these concepts for scenario and strategy development.

Modality and modal narratives

In philosophy (Beall and van Fraassen, 2003), modality concerns issues such as necessity, possibility, impossibility and contingency: in other words, 'what the world obliges, forbids or merely permits' (Fuller, 1995, p. 121). *Possibility* implies linguistic constructions like 'can', 'may', 'could', 'might'; *impossibility*, 'cannot', 'must not', 'could not'; *necessity*, 'must be', 'has to have been', 'could not be otherwise'; and *contingency*, 'maybe if', 'might have been if', 'could have been otherwise if' (Divers, 2002, p. 3; Booth et al., 2009). These four *cases* of modality are thus interrelated: possibility implies necessity or contingency, but negates impossibility; impossibility negates possibility, contingency or necessity; necessity requires possibility but negates impossibility or contingency; and contingency requires possibility and rules out necessity and impossibility (Divers, 2002, pp. 3–4)

As well as these cases, philosophers recognize different *kinds* of, or reasons for modality. A very wide range of kinds has been variously proposed. In terms of strategy, for example, a choice might be impossible for a firm to adopt because it contravenes deeply held cultural values of senior managers, because it is illegal, because of technological lock-in, because the organization lacks the necessary resources and the means to acquire them, because it does not even appear as an option because of organizational myopia or rapid environmental change, or for many other reasons. A system of modalities has been developed by Doležel (1976; Ryan, 1991a) which we reproduce here as Table 6.1. It should be noted that this system omits some other modal relations, such as the metaphysical, nomological and apodeictic (Divers, 2002; Beall and van Fraassen, 2003), but its characterization is robust, informative and persuasive.

Within this framework of modal systems *alethic* modality refers to the truth value of statements about the world, and in this sense to the world itself, ontologically speaking:

Table 6.1 Doležel's systems of modalities

System	Operators		
Alethic system	Possible	Impossible	Necessary
Deontic system	Permitted	Prohibited	Obliged
Axiological system	Indifference	Wrong	Right
Epistemic system	Uncertainty	Ignorance	Knowledge

Source: Adapted from Ryan (1991a, p. 111).

issues of 'causation, time–space parameters, and the action capacities of persons' (Doležel, 1998a, p. 115); *deontic* modality concerns proscriptive or prescriptive rules and norms about the world; *axiological* modality involves agents' values and ethics and the possible (and so on) actions and states of affairs arising as a result; and *epistemic* modality relates to degree of the knowledge of the world possessed by agents, and the consequent actions and states of affairs possible or otherwise. Although in principle these systems and their operators are separable, in practice, as Doležel (ibid., p. 114) points out: 'agents of the actual world have to deal with a tangled bundle of modal restrictions' – that is, the world is modally heterogeneous. The implications of this complexity and heterogeneity for the production of actionable knowledge in strategic foresight are discussed in later sections and in the conclusion to the chapter.

As Ronen (1994) points out, philosophy is the reference discipline for discussions of modality, yet modality, in its broadest sense, is a pluralistic and interdisciplinary topic of scholarly enquiry, as well as one enjoying a prominent place in popular culture. The subject is explored (implicitly or explicitly) in disciplines as diverse as quantum mechanics, artificial intelligence, philosophy and semantics, as well as psychology, political science, organization studies, futurology, history and literary studies (Clark et al., 2007); and in genres as diverse as popular science texts, popular history, journalism, and alternate history and science fiction novels, television programmes and films; as well as in academic knowledge artefacts such as books, refereed journals, conference proceedings, and the like. As Booth et al. (2009) point out, any literary, historical and scientific narratives that engage with causation, in particular, are saturated with modality. In addition, as Roese and Olson (1995b, p. 1) argue: '[t]he ability to imagine alternative . . . versions of actual occurrences appears to be a pervasive, perhaps even essential, feature of our mental lives'. Modality is thus a rich and nuanced aspect of human discourse and existence.

However, we restrict our definition and present discussion of what we have called 'modal narratives' to two particular instantiations: counterfactuals – and, in passing, the associated concept of the superfactual, and the counterfactual's popular culture counterpart, the alternate history – and scenarios. However, before we do so, we need to distinguish modal narratives from other kinds of modal discourse. The social psychologist's (for example, Roese and Olsen, 1995a) concern with individuals' counterfactual thinking downplays narratives, instead focusing on the use and effect of statements such as: 'If I had exercised more frequently during graduate school, I would not have gained weight as I approached the age of 30' (Roese, 1997, p. 143). In philosophy, for example, modality is also often voiced through propositions, such as: 'If kangaroos had no tails, they would topple over' (Lewis, 1973, p. 1). These examples are not modal narratives in the sense we have developed. Clark (2000, p. 113) argues that in organization studies and strategy, approaches to temporality and history often invoke the genre label of 'narrative', implying 'that the readers can relax their critical, sceptical facilities'. In this sense, by insisting on counterfactuals and scenarios as analytically structured narratives, we are not only making a claim as to their mode(s) of analysis and narration (see Booth et al., 2009, on how 'modal narratives work') but retrieving narrative from the mainstream's attempt to marginalize it as 'mere' genre. In emphasizing the narrative element of counterfactuals and scenarios, we stress, among other things, the descriptive, evocative and expressive roles of narrative (Bermejo Barrera, 2005).

Turning to our two types of modal narrative, we first examine counterfactuals and the related concepts of superfactuals and alternate histories, before briefly discussing scenarios as modal narratives. In logic, a counterfactual conditional is an 'if *p*, then *q*' sentence where the antecedent clause (*p*) is a statement describing an event which did not in fact occur (Booth, 2003). The use of counterfactual explanation therefore requires the analyst to consider the questions: 'What if . . . ?' or 'What might have happened if . . . ?'. Counterfactual narratives (extended narrative examples of counterfactual inquiry and explanation) have recently received increasing attention in a wide variety of literatures (for examples in different fields, see Bulhof, 1999; Hassig, 2001; Tetlock and Lebow, 2001; Cowan and Foray, 2002; and Winthrop-Young, 2006). The disciplines in which this attention has been longest lasting are historiography and political science. Until relatively recently, however, counterfactual thinking has aroused considerable controversy in both disciplines (Ferguson, 1997; Tetlock et al., 2006).

The disciplinary area where the most detailed theoretical and methodological discussion of counterfactual narratives[2] has taken place is the history of politics and international relations (for example, Tetlock and Belkin, 1996a; Tetlock et al., 2006). Tetlock and Belkin (1996b) argue that counterfactuals may be used in a number of different modes, the three most important of which we sketch out here.[3] *Idiographic counterfactuals* are explorations of a particular historical case to explore modal themes within a specific context: 'in each case, the investigators want to know what was historically possible or impossible within a circumscribed period of time and set of relationships' (Tetlock and Belkin, 1996b, p. 7). As Booth et al. (2009) point out, such counterfactuals are held valuable in challenging linear, teleogical and deterministic assumptions about temporality and history, in evaluating the significance of particular historical actions and choices, and in assessing the roles and reputations of individual historical actors. *Nomothetic counterfactuals*, on the other hand, are counterfactuals that seek to test theoretical or empirical generalizations by applying them to specific historical situations, typically by combining well-defined antecedent conditions with a covering-law model – 'the goal is not historical understanding: rather, it is to pursue the logical implications of a theoretical framework' (Tetlock and Belkin, 1996b, p. 9). The final counterfactual mode is that which Booth et al. (2009) label *doxastic-axiological counterfactuals*. The aim of this approach – the most important of the three for Booth et al. – is to highlight gaps or contradictions in belief (doxastic) or value (axiological) systems by creating thought experiments which challenge the 'certainties' generated by those systems. In this mode the counterfactual operates as a 'surprise machine' (DiMaggio, 1995). In particular, such approaches work by: 'revealing double standards in moral judgement, contradictory causal beliefs, and the influence of unwanted biases such as certainty of hindsight' (Tetlock and Belkin 1996b, p. 13).

There is one other form of modal narrative which is closely related to counterfactuals; the semifactual, or as Clark et al. (2007) prefer, the superfactual (see also Clark, 2006; Clark and Blundel, 2007). If counterfactuals are 'What ifs?', semifactuals are 'Even ifs': such as 'Even if Henry Ford had started from Birmingham, the British motor industry would still have suffered eventual decline' (Clark et al., 2007). Clark et al. characterize narratives employing semifactual logic as superfactual narratives, whereby structural and contextual factors tend to prevail over or limit the actions and choices of agents. For them, the key question is: what role does pre-existing stratified reality and social structure play in constraining, or enabling, organizational dynamics and zones of manoeuvre? The superfactual is thus a form of modal narrative which is related but opposed to counterfactuals. While the latter arguably tend to emphasize contingency and possibility in presupposing human agency as relatively less bounded by context, superfactuals might be said to emphasize the limitations – necessity, impossibility – placed on agency by pre-existing structures; and thus, have direct potential connection with those foresight exercises which adopt similar emphases. Nevertheless, superfactuals share with other modal narratives a concern to explore the zones of manoeuvre that are potentially open to agents-in-the-world.

Finally, before considering scenarios, we should briefly mention alternative histories as modal narratives. Such fictionalized counterfactuals are set in worlds in which Germany won the Second World War, in which the Confederacy triumphed in the American Civil War, in which the Spanish Armada was successful, and so on. In other words, like counterfactuals, 'alternative histories revolve around the basic premise that some event in the past did not occur as we know it did, and thus the present has been changed' (Hellekson, 2000, p. 248). Alternate histories are thus firstly concerned by the mechanisms by which the textual world is tipped away from the actual world, and secondarily with the unfolding of the textual world's path following the point of departure. Rosenfeld (2002) deems alternate histories to be a sub-genre of the broader category of counterfactual narratives, although he does make limited reference to their status as fiction, by distinguishing between 'academic' and 'dramatic' alternate histories. Like other forms of modal narratives, alternate histories are fundamentally concerned with temporality, historicity, linearity, contingency and determinism. They have received rather fitful attention from historical and literary theorists (see Booth et al. (2009) for a more extended discussion of this literature). In this context (both thematically and theoretically), despite their negligible status as scholarly artefacts, as an important sub-genre of modal narratives they may potentially contribute to developing a theoretical underpinning of other forms of modal narrative.

The second major form of modal narrative, and the more important for this chapter, is scenario analysis. In this discussion we shall confine our attention in this section to outlining some aspects of scenario thinking as they relate to modality, and so demonstrating that these issues indicate that scenarios are inherently modal in nature. This is inevitably, therefore, a very selective review of a large and diverse (van Notten et al., 2003; Bradfield et al., 2005) literature. Scenario analysis and other organizational foresight exercises have become increasingly influential in organizational practice since their introduction by Shell and other firms in the mid-to-late 1970s, although in broader policy terms scenario planning can be traced back to RAND and other policy institutes in the USA in the early Cold War period, and to groups of futurists working in firms, government and institutes in France during the late 1950s and early 1960s (Bradfield et al., 2005).

A number of studies have explored the connections between history and foresight, both from a historical perspective (for example, Staley, 2002) and many others (for example, Kaivo-oja et al., 2004) from varying perspectives within the futures studies field. Indeed, some futures research (for example, Krishna, 1992; Atherton, 2003) has implicitly or explicitly used counterfactual analysis as a methodological tool. MacKay and McKiernan (2004a, 2004b) link counterfactual and scenario thinking in connecting organizational hindsight and foresight: counterfactual analysis, they argue, stands in relation to hindsight as does scenario analysis to foresight. Both the past and the future are indeterminate and modal. In particular, complex scenario building (characterized by 'wicked problems', multidimensional concerns, and multilevel processes – van Notten et al., 2003) raises questions of complex chains of causality and of potentially intractable combinations of deterministic and contingent elements within the actor-network. No one would claim that scenarios *predict* the future, or tell the unvarnished truth about what is to come. Rather, they sensitize agents to possible contingencies or possible outcomes, in what Borges (quoted by Ferguson, 1997, p. 70) calls 'a garden of forking paths'. In some real and important sense they are a history of the future (Staley, 2002).

In their typology of scenarios, van Notten et al. (2003) raise a number of questions central to modality, of case and kind. In distinguishing between exploratory and decision-support project goals, between intuitive and formalized process designs, and between complex and simple scenario content, they describe a field with significantly diverse methodological predilections, and with potentially serious tensions between nomothetic and ideographical methodologies. Distinctions between contrast/peripheral scenarios on the one hand, and surprise-free/trend scenarios on the other, reveal the analytical choices to be faced in predicting the modal behaviour of complex, nonlinear systems operating under conditions of discontinuity and in punctuated, multiple equilibria. Moreover, the relationship between peripheral and trend, alternative and conventional scenarios clearly mirrors debates among counterfactualists about plausible-worlds and miracle-worlds, and likely reflects deeply conflicting beliefs concerning appropriate outcomes and processes of foresight methodologies. Similarly, differences between what Van Der Heijden (2000) characterizes as critical realist and social interactionist perspectives on scenarios and forecasting reflect possibly incommensurable judgements about methodology, epistemology and ontology that are reflected, for example, in differences between nomothetic and idiographic styles of counterfactual thinking. Finally, a common emphasis on the transformative effects of scenario thinking, and on scenarios as provoking deep learning (see Chermack and van der Merwe, 2003, for example) reflects strong connections to the doxastic–axiological approach to counterfactuals.

Modal narratives are thus about what might have been, or what might yet be. They are not assessed as true or false, but rather as sensitizing agents to the multiple possible worlds that might have been and that could still emerge. Counterfactuals, for example, can thus be a heuristic device to understand the circumstances, events and actions of organizational history: scenarios, devices for sensitizing managers and analysts to possible future paths and trajectories of organizational or policy development. Modal narratives' governing trope is the suggestion that the indeterminacy of the past and future provides opportunities (or barriers) for alternative trajectories. Modal narratives are thus, we argue, a form of conditional account based on the logic of possible worlds. Their role is to keep explanations open by introducing multiple possibilities; while at the same time – particularly in the case of superfactuals – emphasizing that many of these possibilities are or were likely to prove unrealizable (Clark et al., 2007).

Finally, we see modal narratives as occupying a space framed by the interaction of social science and imagination, between cognition and estrangement. As discussed in the next section, some philosophers adopt a position of strong (or 'genuine') modal realism – possible worlds do really exist beside our actual one. We have no access to these worlds, yet assuming their existence allows us to work fruitfully with a number of problems in our actual world. Similarly, we have no access to the reality that was the past: yet as Dening (1996, p. xvi) argues, history should restore to the past those qualities of the present which it once possessed: 'giv[ing] back to the past its present'. We have no access to the future; yet organizational foresight demands we attach a modal genealogy to possible future outcomes, trends and developments.

Temporal branching and possible worlds
Booth et al. (2008) argue that there are two fundamental schemata for organizing modal narratives, with different ontological and epistemological implications (see also Elster, 1978; Cowan and Foray, 2002). In this section of the chapter we discuss and distinguish these schemes. The first position – which Booth et al. (2009) label the 'temporal branching' paradigm – focuses on temporal sequentiality, in that time (past, present and future) is envisaged as a tree with many branches (see Figure 6.1), the bifurcation of which represent points where different events present agents with choices: 'we proceed up the tree, moving higher and higher, never descending, as decisions are made and history unfolds' (Cowan and Foray, 2002, p. 548). Past-oriented modal narratives, such as counterfactuals and alternate history, look back down the tree, identifying branching points (points of divergence or nexuses) where, if different choices had been made or different events occurred, history would have been different. Alternate history, in particular, then focuses on the development of the 'new' history in a speculative fashion: to 'bring this alternative history up to date and ask how the alternative present differs from our own' (ibid., p. 548). Despite the apparent low status of counterfactuals and alternative histories in mainstream academic terms, such narrative thought experiments can be claimed to perform important functions:

> The alternate history as a genre speculates about such topics as the nature of time and linearity, the past's link to the present, the present's link to the future, and the role of individuals in the history making process. Alternate histories question the nature of history and causality; they question accepted notions of time and space; they rupture linear movement . . . and they foreground the 'constructedness' of history and the role narrative plays in this construction. (Hellekson, 2000, pp. 254–5)

Future-oriented modal narratives, such as scenarios and other foresight exercises, instead look up the tree to consider possible future nexus points and their likely outcomes. In this sense, the temporal branching paradigm allows analysts to trace and delineate the genealogies which make a future 'futurible' (de Jouvenel, 1967, p. 18). A very simplified schematic of temporal branching is depicted in Figure 6.1. Here, a number of branches

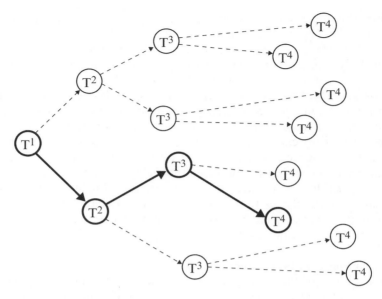

Figure 6.1   Temporal branching

and nexus points link the present (T^1) to multiple futurible futures (T^4). In this diagram, the bold line indicates that the temporal branching perspective assumes that only one future will eventually transpire, with other possibilities remaining unactualized. In so far as explicit questions of (alethic) modality are concerned, Ryan (1991a, p. 273) points out:

> Given a tree of the future developments allowed by the physical laws of the world, a state or event is temporally necessary if it occurs on all the branches, possible [or contingent] if it occurs on some of them, and impossible if it is excluded from all branches.

In addition, and in a more general sense, the foresight analyst's judgement of the degree of plausibility to be accorded to each of the possible states of T^4 will depend on his/her judgement as to modalities operating on the various potential choices available (or perceived to be available) at each nexus point.

The second perspective identified by Booth et al. (2009) and others, is that of possible worlds (see Figure 6.2). As indicated in the previous section, much of the present discussion of modal issues in philosophy and literary theory has concentrated on realist and actualist approaches to possible worlds. Talk of possible worlds in philosophy was originated by Gottfried Wilhelm Leibniz in the late seventeenth and early eighteenth centuries, but it is only since the early 1960s that it has become prominent. Kripke's (1963, 1980) treatment of possible worlds as a tool in semantic logic and Lewis's (1973, 1986) use of possible worlds in modal realism have shaped debates which have spread far outside their original disciplinary base (see, for example, Climo and Howells, 1976; Allén, 1989; Ryan, 1991a, b; Ronen, 1994; Doležel, 1998a, 1998b; Ginsberg and Smith, 1998).

The possible-worlds paradigm explores the possibilities afforded by modal thinking if it is assumed that (in some views, an almost infinite) number of worlds exist, each

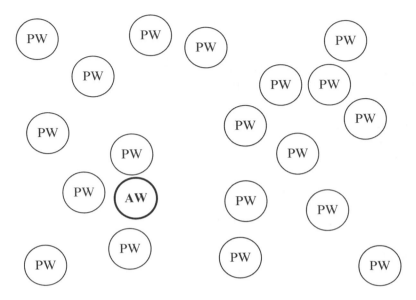

Figure 6.2   Possible worlds

different from our own – inasmuch as in these different worlds, different states of affairs have obtained. What is possible is the case in some worlds, what is contingent may be the case in some worlds, what is necessary is the case in all worlds, what is impossible is the case in no world. At the risk of oversimplifying the debate, it can be said that opinion is divided between modal realists (like Lewis, 1973 and 1986, for example) for whom possible worlds are real, though relativized to our own actual world, and modal actualists (such as Stalnaker, 2003, for example) who argue that the actual world is the only real world, although possible worlds exist as unactualized states of affairs – possibilities, stipulations, sets of propositions, abstract theoretical entities – in the actual world. In this respect, actualism towards possible worlds is perfectly compatible with the temporal branching perspective, with the broken lines in Figure 6.1 representing unactualized possible worlds:

> [H]ad things been different, an alternative state of affairs would not only have been possible but there would have been such a state of affairs . . . The actual world has the distinction of actually obtaining while all other possible worlds exist in the actual world, yet they do not actually obtain. (Ronen, 1994, p. 23)

From this perspective, possible worlds exist within the actual world, but they do not obtain: there is only one actual world, but possible worlds are all the ways it might have been or might yet be.

In order to clearly differentiate the possible-worlds perspective from temporal branching, therefore, it is necessary to explore the ontological extravagance (Booth et al., 2009) of Lewisian modal realism. Here, as simplified in Figure 6.2, 'all modal possibilities we might stipulate, as well as the actual world, are equally realised in some logical space where they possess a physical existence' (Ronen, 1994, pp. 21–2). Possible worlds are relativized to our own actual world, just as our actual world is a possible world relativized to our counterparts in another world to whom their world is actual. A major difference between modal realism and temporal branching is that there is no spatio-temporal relationship between actual and possible worlds, or between possible worlds themselves; and no trans-world identity between agents in different worlds. The Bill Gates who founded Microsoft in our actual world shares no trans-world connection with the Bill Gates who completed his studies at Harvard, and went on to develop an undistinguished career in computer sales management in a possible world.

This conceptual complexity and the lack of a spatio-temporal connection between worlds creates certain methodological issues for the use of this perspective in foresight studies and in strategizing. If the number of possible worlds is in principle almost infinite, foresight analysts require conceptual and methodological tools to manage this infinitude. As Doležel (1998b, p. 786) suggests:

> The infinite size, number, and variety of possible worlds can be handled by logical formalisms, but they are beyond the reach of empirical theories and research methods. Two heuristic moves have been suggested to overcome this problem: (a) choose as your universe of discourse a manageable subset of possible worlds, which is pertinent to your problem; (b) design small worlds ('miniworlds') comprising a finite number of elements and characterized by a limited number of parameters.

We suggest that the first of these heuristic tools is connected with the idea of accessibility or proximity relations between worlds. It seems clear that some possible worlds are 'closer' to the actual world than are others. The world in which Gates dropped out of Harvard a day later than he did in the actual world is likely to be far more proximate to the actual world, than the possible world in which he completed his studies. Given the uncountable proliferation of worlds, the analyst is, we suggest, required to stipulate the relative proximity of the selected worlds under consideration. Indeed, for purposes of comparison between different possible worlds, the specification of a proximal set of worlds might be necessary, from very close (minimal deviation) to more distant. We propose that such a specification involves considering a range of accessibility relations. While it may be, in principle, possible to specify a generic range of accessibility relations (for example, Ryan, 1991a, 1991b)[4] governing possible worlds, it is more appropriate in the foresight context to recognize that analysts will specify the parameters of accessibility according to the analytical object of interest. For example, to take a very simple case, PEST (political, economic, socio-cultural and technological) analysis and its variants (PESTEL, STEEP, and so on) are commonly used in the strategic analysis of a firm's external environment. In a possible-worlds context using this kind of approach, analysts might specify a range of scenarios based on variations in PEST accessibility relations; that is, a set of worlds is stipulated in which possible worlds are P-relative to the actual world, E-relative, S-relative, and so on. As we argue that the actual world is modally heterogeneous, however, this first deconstructive stage would then be followed by a reconstructive second step that bundled or combined selected accessibility relations to generate a limited number of plausible worlds.

In considering plausibility and access, it should also be apparent that foresight exercises concern themselves in the main with 'small worlds'; that is, that they also utilize the second of Doležel's heuristic tools. Rather than imagining and narrating the entirety of their limited range of possible worlds, including their pasts, presents and futures, analysts

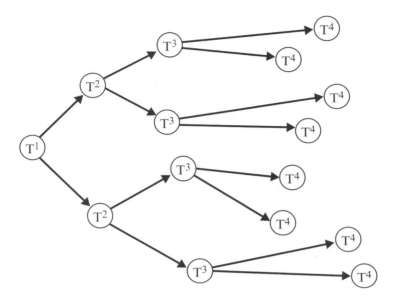

Figure 6.3 Many worlds

present worlds which have been lightly sketched in, as it were, with only salient aspects germane to the object of analysis (firm, market, industry, technology, and so on) dealt with in any detail. In this sense, we are suggesting that use of possible-world thinking in foresight exercises is simultaneously both broad and narrow. The breadth of imaginative thinking involved in embracing and assimilating the possible-worlds idea is potentially emancipatory and transformative, while on the other hand focus, parsimony and discipline is required to render the exercise manageable. These aspects very strongly relate to the interrelated elements of estrangement and cognition in Suvin's (1979) conception of *cognitive estrangement*, elaborated upon in a futures context by Booth et al. (2009).

Finally in this section of the chapter, we discuss very briefly the many-worlds or Everett interpretation (Everett, 1957; DeWitt and Graham, 1973) of quantum mechanics (see Figure 6.3). The many-worlds thesis holds:

> [W]henever there is doubt about what can happen, because of quantum uncertainty, the world multiplies so that all possibilities are actually realised. Persons of course multiply with the world, and those in any particular branch world experience only what happens in that branch. (Bell, 1989, p. 366)

Such worlds, unlike Lewis's possible worlds, are connected, at least prior to the point of multiplication (or 'decoherence'): 'David Lewis requires that possible worlds have no causal or spatiotemporal relationship at all. They are utterly distinct. So, the possible worlds of David Lewis are not the many worlds of quantum theory' (Girle, 2003, p. 153). Notwithstanding this important distinction, however, adopting a many-worlds perspective on foresight analysis carries with it many of the same benefits as utilizing a modal realist possible-worlds approach, and may be developed through the same methodology that we sketch out in this chapter. Although the many-worlds thesis remains a 'bizarre proposal' for futurists (for example, Peat, 2007, p. 922) its very bizarreness opens up possibilities for dialogue, reflexivity and learning that enable us to question and reflect upon the foundations of our values and assumptions. This point is elaborated upon in the conclusion to the chapter.

Conclusion

In this chapter we have argued that scenarios and related strategic planning exercises are fundamentally concerned with issues of modality – that is, questions of possibility, impossibility, necessity and contingency. We elucidated these cases of modality and argued that understanding of these issues could be refined by an appreciation of different kinds of modality, namely alethic, deontic, axiological and epistemic; proposing, however, that as the world is modally heterogeneous, analysts and other actors are required to deal with complex modal bundles of systems and operators. That is, that the 'possibility' (for example) of a particular scenario arises from a complex blend of structural, systemic and agentic factors.

In so far as these foresight exercises are expressed in a narrative form, we therefore characterize them as modal narratives and argue that they share common underpinnings with other forms of modal narrative, such as counterfactual narratives and alternate histories. We have argued that counterfactuals and some other forms of modal narrative possess three fundamental methodological and theoretical purposes and have argued, here and elsewhere, that potentially the most fruitful of these is the doxastic–axiological. That is, modal narratives are most valuable, in our view, when employed as 'surprise machines', highlighting gaps or contradictions in belief (doxastic) or value (axiological) systems by creating thought experiments which challenge the 'certainties' otherwise generated by those systems, rather than striving towards inaccessible mimetic goals such as prediction. In this respect, the aims of our approach has much in common with endeavours in the futures studies field which share such objectives, such as those, for example, of Chermack and van der Merwe (2003), Peat (2007) and others.

We have argued that these aims may be facilitated by adopting a philosophical system for strategic foresight which is based on possible-worlds thinking. We outlined a number of related approaches, or underpinning paradigms, for understanding modality in the past, present and future. In particular, we contrasted a temporal branching paradigm and a strong possible-worlds paradigm, which, in philosophical terms, equate to actualist and realist approaches to modality. We are, in a sense, agnostic about which approach might better serve the interests of foresight practice. However, the ontological extravagance of modal realism leads us to suggest that this system might be helpful in accomplishing the estrangement required to challenge mental and cultural presuppositions and assumptions. However, estrangement must be balanced by an ability to make sense of the alternative reality under consideration. We therefore proposed, loosely following Doležel (1998a) and Ryan (1991a, 1991b), a heuristic process for managing the bewildering possibilities engendered by possible-worlds thought experiments: first involving the specification of accessibility to possible worlds, and second by the stipulation that the worlds of the foresight analyst are necessarily small worlds; that is, the situations depicted in scenario narratives, for example, focus only on the characteristics of the imagined world central to the desired unit(s) and level(s) of analysis.

The chapter represents only the outline of a possible-worlds approach to scenario analysis. In particular, more work is required on the relationship between cases and kinds of modality in foresight narratives, and on providing more finely developed tools to assist analysts in unpacking the complex bundles of modality that is implied by the approach we have outlined. A more nuanced and deeper understanding of the processes involved in stipulating accessibility relations and thus of the meaning and implications of plausibility in scenario analysis is required, and will be of central importance in the development of a possible-worlds approach to foresight. Finally, the approach outlined in the chapter, although philosophically compelling, awaits empirical and practical validation. Nevertheless, despite these necessities for further development, we consider that we have successfully outlined a novel and compelling philosophical system to underpin strategic foresight, which emphasizes the commonality of foresight with other related endeavours in modal narrative.

Notes

*   This chapter is part of the research project on 'Corporate History, Narrative, and Business Knowledge' (RES-334-25-0013), funded by the Economic and Social Research Council under the Evolution of Business Knowledge programme (http://www.ebkresearch.org/). We are also very grateful to the editors for their support. The chapter reprises and extends material contained in earlier papers (specifically, Clark et al., 2007, and Booth et al., 2009) and we are very grateful for the help and encouragement of a number of colleagues for the project as a whole, especially Ted Fuller, Laurent Mermet, Ruud van der Helm, Riel Miller, Judith Jordan, Kyle Bruce, Geoffrey Winthrop-Young, Tom Shippey and Marie-Laure Ryan.
1.   Alternative strategy paradigms, such as those informed by evolutionary (Aldrich, 1999) or institutional theories (Powell and DiMaggio, 1991) will differ sharply from this canonical account in downplaying the importance of objective or intended rationality in the strategic choice process. Nevertheless, whether the focus is on rational option selection criteria, on variation, selection and retention mechanisms, or on pressures for isomorphism within institutional fields, choices emerge through the mediation of the strategizing process which reflect potentially realizable outcomes for the organization.
2.   The disciplines in which counterfactuals *generally* have received most attention are social psychology (for example, Roese and Olsen, 1995a) and philosophy (for example, Divers, 2002). However, see our discussion of the importance of narrative, above.
3.   We focus on these three modes of counterfactual analysis because they are the most often encountered and because they relate relatively closely to different approaches to foresight.
4.   Ryan (1991a, 1991b) proposes a far more wide-ranging taxonomy of relations between worlds than we indicate here. We have deliberately chosen to be parsimonious in this respect to illustrate the utility of this methodology for foresight analysts and strategists, not because these are the only possible relations between worlds. For example, Ryan proposes a relation of physical compatibility (worlds share the same physical laws) and a relation of logical compatibility (worlds share the same logical principles, such as of non-contradiction and of excluded middle). As we say in our introduction, we consider it unlikely that worlds that do not share these relations will be of interest to scenario analysts; but readers who are interested in these broader potentialities of possible-world modal thinking are directed to Ryan's work.

References

Aldrich, Howard (1999), *Organizations Evolving*, London: Sage.
Allén, Sture (ed.) (1989), *Possible Worlds in Humanities, Arts and Sciences*, Berlin: Walter de Gruyter.
Ansoff, H. Igor (1965), *Corporate Strategy: An Analytic Approach to Business Policy for Growth and Expansion*, New York: McGraw-Hill.
Atherton, Andrew (2003), 'A future for small business? Prospective scenarios for the development of the economy based on current policy thinking and counterfactual reasoning', *Futures*, **37**, 777–94.
Beall, J.C. and Bas C. van Fraassen (2003), *Possibilities and Paradox: An Introduction to Modal and Many-Valued Logic*, Oxford: Oxford University Press.
Bell, John S. (1989), 'Six possible worlds of quantum mechanics', in Allén (ed.), pp. 359–73.
Bermejo Barrera, José C. (2005), 'On history considered as epic poetry', *History and Theory*, **44** (2), 182–94.
Booth, Charles (2003), 'Does history matter in strategy? The possibilities and problems of counterfactual analysis', *Management Decision*, **41**, 96–104.
Booth, Charles, Michael Rowlinson, Peter Clark, Agnès Delahaye and Stephen Procter (2009), 'Scenarios and counterfactuals as modal narratives', *Futures*, **41**, forthcoming.

Bradfield, Ron, George Wright, George Burt, George Cairns and Kees Van Der Heijden (2005), 'The origins and evolution of scenario planning techniques in long range business planning', *Futures*, **37**, 795–812.

Bulhof, Johannes (1999), 'What if? Modality and history', *History and Theory*, **38**, 145–68.

Chermack, Thomas J. and Louis van der Merwe (2003), 'The role of constructivist learning in scenario planning', *Futures*, **35**, 445–60.

Clark, Peter (2000), *Organisations in Action: Competition between Contexts*, London: Routledge.

Clark, Peter (2006), 'Superfactuals, structural repertoires and productive units: explaining the evolution of the British auto industry', *Competition and Change*, **10** (4), 393–410.

Clark, Peter and Richard Blundel (2007), 'Penrose, critical realism and the evolution of business knowledge: a methodological reappraisal', *Management & Organizational History*, **2** (1), 45–62.

Clark, Peter, Charles Booth, Michael Rowlinson, Stephen Procter and Agnès Delahaye (2007), 'Project hindsight: exploring necessity and possibility in cycles of structuration and co-evolution', *Technology Analysis & Strategic Management*, **19** (1), 83–97.

Climo, T.A. and P.G.A. Howells (1976), 'Possible worlds in historical explanation', *History and Theory*, **15**, 1–20.

Cowan, Robin and Dominique Foray (2002), 'Evolutionary economics and the counterfactual threat: on the nature and role of counterfactual history as an empirical tool in economics', *Journal of Evolutionary Economics*, **12** (5), 539–62.

de Jouvenel, Bertrand (1967), *The Art of Conjecture*, New York: Basic Books.

Dening, Greg (1996), *Performances*, Chicago, IL: University of Chicago Press.

DeWitt, Bryce S. and Neill Graham (eds) (1973), *The Many-Worlds Interpretation of Quantum Mechanics*, Princeton, NJ: Princeton University Press.

DiMaggio, Paul J. (1995), 'Comments on "What theory is not"', *Administrative Science Quarterly*, **40** (3), 391–7.

Divers, John (2002), *Possible Worlds*, London: Routledge.

Doležel, Lubomír (1976), 'Narrative modalities', *Journal of Literary Semantics*, **5**, 5–14.

Doležel, Lubomír (1998a), *Heterocosmica: Fiction and Possible Worlds*, Baltimore, MD: Johns Hopkins University Press.

Doležel, Lubomír (1998b), 'Possible worlds of fiction and history', *New Literary History*, **29**, 785–809.

Elster, Jon (1978), *Logic and Society: Contradictions and Possible Worlds*, London: Wiley.

Everett, Hugh (1957), '"Relative state" formulation of quantum mechanics', *Review of Modern Physics*, **29** (3), 454–62.

Ferguson, Niall (1997), 'Virtual history: towards a "chaotic" theory of the past', in Ferguson (ed.), *Virtual History: Alternatives and Counterfactuals*, London: Macmillan, pp. 1–90.

Fuller, Steve (1995), 'A tale of two cultures and other higher superstitions', *History of the Human Sciences*, **8** (1), 115–25.

Ginsberg, Matthew L. and David E. Smith (1988) 'Reasoning about action I: A possible worlds approach', *Artificial Intelligence*, **35** (2), 165–95.

Girle, Rod (2003), *Possible Worlds*, Montreal: McGill/Queen's University Press.

Hassig, Ross (2001), 'Counterfactuals and revisionism in historical explanation', *Anthropological Theory*, **1**, 57–72.

Hellekson, Karen (2000), 'Towards a taxonomy of the alternate history genre', *Extrapolation*, **41** (Fall), 248–56.

Johnson, Gerry, Kevan Scholes and Richard Whittington (2005), *Exploring Corporate Strategy*, 7th edn, London: Prentice-Hall.

Kaivo-oja, Jari Y., Tapio S. Katko and Osmo T. Seppälä (2004), 'Seeking convergence between history and futures research', *Futures*, **36**, 527–47.

Kripke, Saul A. (1963), 'Semantical considerations on modal logic', *Acta Philosophica Fennica*, **16**, 83–94.

Kripke, Saul A. (1980), *Naming and Necessity*, Cambridge, MA: Harvard University Press.

Krishna, Sakaran (1992), 'Oppressive pasts and desired futures: re-imagining India', *Futures*, **24**, 858–66.

Lewis, David K. (1973), *Counterfactuals*, Oxford: Blackwell.

Lewis, David K. (1986), *On the Plurality of Worlds*, Oxford: Blackwell.

MacKay, R. Bradley and Peter McKiernan (2004a), 'The role of hindsight in foresight: refining strategic reasoning', *Futures*, **36**, 161–79.

MacKay, R. Bradley and Peter McKiernan (2004b), 'Exploring strategy context with foresight', *European Management Review*, **1**, 69–77.

Mermet, Laurent, Ted Fuller and Ruud van der Helm (2009), 'Re-examining and renewing theoretical underpinnings of the futures field: a pressing and long-term challenge', *Futures*, **41**, forthcoming.

Peat, F. David (2007), 'From certainty to uncertainty: thought, theory and action in a postmodern world', *Futures*, **39**, 920–29.

Porter, Michael E. (1985), *Competitive Advantage: Creating and Sustaining Superior Performance*, New York: Free Press.

Powell, Walter W. and Paul J. DiMaggio (1991), *The New Institutionalism in Organizational Analysis*, Chicago, IL: University of Chicago Press.

Roese, Neal J. (1997), 'Counterfactual thinking', *Psychological Bulletin*, **121**, 133–48.

Roese, Neal J. and James M. Olson (eds) (1995a), *What Might Have Been? The Social Psychology of Counterfactual Thinking*, Mahwah, NJ: Lawrence Erlbaum.

Roese, Neal J. and James M. Olson (1995b), 'Counterfactual thinking: a critical overview', in Roese and Olson (eds), pp. 1–55.

Ronen, Ruth (1994), *Possible Worlds in Literary Theory*, Cambridge: Cambridge University Press.

Rosenfeld, Gavriel (2002), 'Why do we ask "what if?": reflections on the function of alternate history', *History and Theory*, **41** (4), 90–103.

Ryan, Marie-Laure (1991a), *Possible Worlds, Artificial Intelligence, and Narrative Theory*, Bloomington, IN: Indiana University Press.

Ryan, Marie-Laure (1991b), 'Possible worlds and accessibility relations: a semantic typology of fiction', *Poetics Today*, **12**, 553–76.

Staley, David J. (2002), 'A history of the future', *History and Theory*, **41** (4), 72–89.

Stalnaker, Robert C. (2003), *Ways a World Might Be: Metaphysical and Anti-metaphysical Essays*, Oxford: Clarendon Press.

Suvin, Darko (1979), *Metamorphoses of Science Fiction: On the Poetics and History of a Literary Genre*, New Haven, CT and London: Yale University Press.

Tetlock, Philip E. and Aaron Belkin (1996a), 'Counterfactual thought experiments in world politics: logical, methodological, and psychological perspectives', in Tetlock and Belkin (eds), pp. 3–38.

Tetlock, Philip E. and Aaron Belkin (eds) (1996b), *Counterfactual Thought Experiments in World Politics: Logical, Methodological and Psychological Perspectives*, Princeton: Princeton University Press.

Tetlock, Philip E. and Richard Ned Lebow (2001), 'Poking counterfactual holes in covering laws: cognitive styles and historical reasoning', *American Political Science Review*, **95**, 829–43.

Tetlock, Philip E., Richard Ned Lebow and Geoffrey Parker (eds) (2006), *Unmaking the West: 'What-if'? Scenarios that Rewrite World History*, Ann Arbor: University of Michigan Press.

Van Der Heijden, Kees (2000), 'Scenarios and forecasting: two perspectives', *Technological Forecasting and Social Change*, **65**, 31–6.

van Notten, Paul W.F., Jan Rotmans, Marjolein B.A. van Asselt and Dale S. Rothman (2003), 'An updated scenario typology', *Futures*, **35** (5), 423–43.

Winthrop-Young, Geoffrey (2006), 'The Third Reich in alternate history: aspects of a genre-specific depiction of Nazism', *Journal of Popular Culture*, **39** (5), 878–96.

7 Scenarios as knowledge transformed into strategic 're-presentations': the use of foresight studies to help shape and implement strategy
Thomas Durand

Introduction

Future studies contribute to gaining insight into the context in which organizations maneuver. In this sense, future studies are essential inputs to the strategy process, when an organization envisages its future activities and its competitive positioning. It may be argued that 'future studies' are as important ingredients of the making of strategy as competitive intelligence, market surveys, technology assessment or identification of core competence.

Future studies and foresight will be used as equivalent terms here. However, the French tradition of future studies is known as '*La Prospective*', and it derives from Gaston Berger's work in the 1950s (Berger, 1957, 1958, 1964). Berger wrote about '*l'attitude prospective*' (the foresight stance) which soon became as substantive as *La Prospective*:

> Observing an atom modifies the atom; watching a person affects the person; looking at the future transforms the future.

> Tomorrow will not be like yesterday. It will be new and shaped by us. The future is less to be discovered than invented.

> The past, the present and the future are intricately interwoven as they impact each other. (1964)

Subsequent contributions came from Jacques Lesourne (1981) and Michel Godet (1977, 1985, 1991, 2001) from their years at Sema, or André Gros and Armand Braun (2001) known as '*conseillers de synthèse*' at Sics. Gros founded the journal *Prospective* with Gaston Berger in 1957. In turn Bertrand de Jouvenel (1967) founded the review *Futuribles* in 1975. Over the years, this became one of the vehicles of publications on future studies in the French-speaking arena. The public sector, for example, education, regional governments, public utilities (energy such as EdF, or the railway, SNCF) have been significant users (and thus indirect contributors) of the methodologies developed over the years. A specific subset of future studies also developed on the theme of technology foresight (Durand 1992, 2003; Durand and Dubreuil, 2001). 'Key technologies', or similar exercises in various countries (see Salo and Cuhls, 2003) led the EU Commission to launch a series of initiatives such as the Institute for Prospective Technological Studies (IPTS) or Foren.

Yet, future studies are less common in industry practice as these have often been perceived as laborious and time-consuming exercises, with sometimes vague results that are not easy to implement. More precisely, the typical cognitive stance of *La Prospective*, and future studies in general, is to think of a plurality of futures (the 'futuribles'). The intent is to grasp the variety of potential outcomes, not just the most probable or the most desirable future. This clearly departs from the forecasting perspective which aims at evaluating what the most probable outcome is likely to be. This cognitive shift from forecast to foresight is not easy for decision makers and managers who tend to ask for less uncertainty, not more complexity. Many managers feel that they are better off with a carefully computed forecast. They tend to dislike a variety of scenarios crafted to describe – not reduce – uncertainty. This is an important issue as the strategic process needs more, not less, insight into the future. This is the heart of the matter which this chapter addresses.

The chapter aims at a better understanding of how strategy builds upon knowledge, and more specifically knowledge about potential futures, existing within and around organizations. The chapter argues that some form of meta-knowledge, or 'representations', stems from the knowledge base of the organization through a complex transformation process. The making of these representations both informs and partakes in the strategy process.

In turn, this leads to the question of what exactly is meant by representations, how they emerge from bits and pieces of knowledge and how they help the strategist to think about a 'desired' future of the organization. The chapter attempts to address these questions through concrete examples and thus throws some light on the difficult task of constructing strategies out of knowledge through foresight exercises. (In other words, this chapter aims at contributing to the legitimization of the themes of knowledge and foresight in strategic management, if need be.)

As a result, the core argument of the chapter is as follows: one important task of the strategists is to collect/scan/assemble/recombine/digest the many pieces of knowledge which resulted from various kinds of learning taking place in and around the organization through action and interaction. This re-processing of internally available (or externally reachable) knowledge results in meta-knowledge, recombining intermediate 'blocks of knowledge' into representations. The chapter argues that foresight studies are a good way to build such representations of existing and future challenges, strategic issues and dilemmas for an organization facing contradicting pressures within its system. Foresight scenarios are typical representations useful to the strategists. From a documented understanding of the current state of the system, its inherent internal dynamics, the influence of exogenous forces, these representations capture some form of description of potential future states of the system. The chapter further argues that representations are better fit to the construction, formulation and implementation of strategies than the elementary pieces of knowledge from which the representations emerged.

The chapter first defines the various concepts used: strategy, foresight, knowledge, representations and scenarios. It then presents a theoretical framework based on the concept of 'social interaction', 'interpretative frames' and the 'duality of structuring'. The chapter suggests that foresight scenarios should be viewed as cognitive representations (which are seen as an extension of the concept of interpretative frames). The scenarios are designed to capture and integrate elements of knowledge which may be available about potential futures of the environment, the competitive arena and the focal organization. Three typical cases of foresight studies are then briefly presented to illustrate 'the making of scenarios'. The cases deal with public utilities in electricity, the future of business schools, and road and air transportation. Through the case studies, the chapter discusses the process of dealing with elementary pieces of knowledge gathered from different sources, partly contradictory, highly uncertain and extremely diverse. It shows how the emergence of scenarios can occur, including through ad hoc techniques, and how this may subsequently help the strategic thinking process of the participants. Concrete implications emerge: in most instances, the process of building the representation ('representing') turns out to be more important than the representations themselves. In addition, the involvement of participants in the foresight exercise is an important element which facilitates subsequent implementation of the strategy. The final section concludes.

Theoretical concepts
Strategy is about how to reach a desirable future. This means first, thinking about the potential futures (in a foresight sense, as discussed below), second, assessing which of these potential outcomes may be more desirable than others, and third, identifying ways and making decisions to influence the outcome in the desired direction.

In contrast, foresight is about attempting to grasp the diversity of potential futures. Foresight corresponds to the field of future studies, that is, studies about the future. It should be stressed that foresight is not equivalent to forecasting (Wack, 1985a, 1985b; Martin and Irvine, 1989; Godet, 2001; Salo, 2001). Unlike forecasting, foresight is not about predicting the most probable future. Foresight is not prediction. Rather, foresight is about describing the variety of potential futures, in order to allow stakeholders to prepare for this variety and to contribute to shaping the outcomes in the direction they wish. In this sense, foresight is an input for strategy. Foresight thus lies at the heart of strategic management. This point is rarely recognized as such but this Handbook clearly conveys the message.

The French school of thought known as *La Prospective* is typically a branch of foresight thinking, with tools and methods designed to grasp the potential futures, namely the 'futuribles' (possible futures), for example, through the construction of scenarios.

Two main types of foresight exercises can be distinguished. Foresight may be intended to raise awareness and generate debates among experts or even beyond, possibly reaching a large audience including the general public. In such circumstances, the process followed during the foresight work is crucial. The exercise, however, may be used primarily as a tool to define priorities for the future. In this case, it is the content of the foresight results that becomes crucial. This distinction among objectives is critical as it radically shapes the work to be conducted.

In this context, a scenario is a coherent, self-sustained and meaningful description of a potential state of the future of a given system, its environment, the industry, the competitive landscape, and/or of a combination of part or all of the above.

At this stage, it is important to relate this idea of scenarios to the concepts of knowledge and representations. Organizational competence results from the various learning processes taking place within and around organizations. These processes include learning through (i) the generation of or access to information, and its assimilation, (ii) action and (iii) interaction. These three complementary processes interact and contribute to building (a) cognitive knowledge, (b) know how and (c) attitudes in the organization, thus building, reinforcing or transforming the competence base, Durand (1998).

In other words, knowledge in organizations may be viewed as the cognitive part of

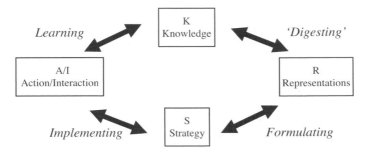

Figure 7.1   Representation as part of the strategy loop

organizational competence. This does not mean that all organizational knowledge is fully explicit and articulated. Part of it may in fact be tacit. However, organizational knowledge covers the cognitive aspects of competence, corresponding to both articulated and 'articulatable' parts of competence, while the other parts, for example, the management routines and the culture, are more embedded in the depth of the organization.

It is now possible to connect knowledge, foresight scenarios as representations, and strategy. This is illustrated in Figure 7.1. Strategy stems from representations resulting from 'digested knowledge'. Focusing on the knowledge dimension within organizational competence, it may be further suggested that strategies are built through some 'use' of the knowledge available in the organization. This is done via representations, in the sense of social representations which emerge in organizations through the process of interaction: in this sense, representations are the result of some form of digestion of various pieces of knowledge, yielding a vision or a story of a 'higher explanatory level'. Building representations requires an ability to shape meaningful stories about the future. This is, as is argued here, where foresight comes into the knowledge–strategy interaction.

In other words, the loop of organizational learning operates as follows: new knowledge is created via learning occurring through action and interaction. The processing or digestion of these elements of knowledge lead to some representations which help elaborate and formulate strategies. In turn, strategy feeds into action which stands as the concrete form of strategy. And action (with its associated interactions) inherently leads to new learning. This is summarized in the loop shown in Figure 7.1.

The focus of the chapter is to better understand how strategic representations – in this context, representations about potential (and desirable) futures – emerge from elementary pieces of knowledge. The chapter thus deals with one specific part of the loop of Figure 7.1, namely the 'digesting' process by which knowledge feeds into representations. (Conversely, one should also recognize that representations tend to operate as a bias, filtering subsequent learning and thus new knowledge. This relates to Giddens's (1987) duality of structuring.)

Also note that formulating and implementing are key elements of the strategy process. Strategy is not just about building representations. However, the chapter focuses on the foresight dimension of strategy. The attention here is on the building of intermediate strategic productions, that is, representations about the variety of potential futures, in the form of scenarios which are seen as instrumental to the strategic process.

Theoretical framework
The overall theoretical background model stems from Drisse (2001) and more specifically de la Ville's work (1996) and operates in three layers. The first layer calls upon social interactions as the founding mechanism of knowledge and thus representations (Moscovici, 1988). This suggests that individual learning takes place as actors interact in their social context (Gibbert and Durand, 2006). The second layer borrows from Goffman's (1991) interpretative frames which both support and channel subsequent learning taking place among actors throughout their joint activities. Learning is in turn increasingly constrained and structured, thus becoming shared, at least to a certain extent. Obviously, along the way, interpretative frames evolve as they are adapted and reshaped. The third layer deals with the process of 'memorizing'. Indeed interpretative frames cannot constitute the basis of knowledge if they are volatile. Some form of permanence is needed. This is what the concept of routinization (Nelson and Winter, 1982) had to offer for management processes, together with Giddens's (1987) idea of the duality of structuring which suggests that interpretative frames tend to reinforce themselves in time as they channel, structure and thus constrain subsequent learning. In other words, interpretative frames emerge and shape up over time through learning while at the same time they structure and condition the learning taking place, thus building some form of permanence.

All in all, social interaction among actors, interpretative frames and institutionalization through routines, reinforcement and dual structuring constitute the architecture of the theoretical framework (Figure 7.2). Thus, one may attempt to grasp how Goffman's idea of interpretative frames may be adapted and extended to help better understand the concept of strategic representations. This requires a better understanding of knowledge transformation in organizations, which in turn requires a better understanding of the nature of organizational knowledge. The granularity and nature of the knowledge fabric – that is, the size and form of the knowledge grains – is a difficult issue. Bits and pieces of

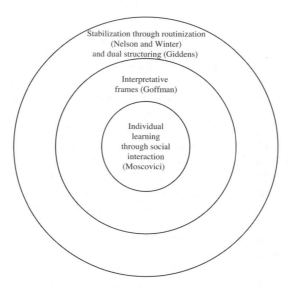

Figure 7.2   Theoretical framework

knowledge are heterogeneous in many ways. The old entrenched piece of knowledge may differ from recent disturbing learning, the uncertain rumor blurs the established beliefs, the narrow precise bit of information may contradict one of the well-documented basic 'visions' prevailing in the organization, and so on.

How can the strategist sort out this complex, heterogeneous and contradictory set of elements in the knowledge base? The chapter hypothesizes that compatible bits and pieces of knowledge naturally come together to consolidate into some 'aggregates' or blocks of knowledge which, grouped, tend to make sense, at least to a certain extent. (Durand, 2006, called these 'leaves', using the metaphor of the foliage of a tree to describe organizational knowledge and competence.) This grouping mechanism takes place naturally within the organization and leads to the interpretative frames: these 'blocks of knowledge' filter new learning, thus reinforcing existing beliefs and rejecting incompatible new information. (Yet, incompatible blocks of knowledge may also coexist in the same organization – as leaves overlap in a fuzzy way in the foliage of a tree.) This view suggests that elements of knowledge tend to assemble naturally into compatible sub-blocks, generating elements of interpretative frames which are then self-reinforcing as they filter new learning.

However, one can go one step further and follow Pierre Wack (1985a, b) (former head of strategic planning at Shell) who argued that 'when carefully looking at the data, for periods of time long enough, new visions may emerge'. These 'new visions' are no longer naturally formed sub-blocks of knowledge. Instead, they are intentionally integrated, articulated stories which recombine previously available sub-blocks and pieces of knowledge in a way that gives more meaning. These new visions, these stories add value for the strategist. This is why scenarios may be viewed as strategic representations, 're-presenting' the knowledge, that is, presenting it differently, thus helping the strategist at work.

Keeping in mind that foresight scenarios are viewed here as strategic representations (Durand et al., 1996), the core argument of the chapter is now explicit. Strategy is about how to reach a desirable future. Foresight is the way to integrate pieces and sub-blocks of knowledge stemming from the organization activities (action and interaction) into useful representations about potential futures. Scenarios are coherent, self-sustained and meaningful stories describing the potential future states of a given system. In this sense, scenarios are the strategic representations built through a foresight exercise from the accessible knowledge of an organization. As strategic representations, the scenarios mediate the complexity of the knowledge base, the uncertainty of future outcomes and the work of the strategist.

In addition, as the foresight exercise may call upon a number of stakeholders from the organization, these will most probably learn from the foresight work that there is not a single straightforward strategy that can be utilized to face the many issues at hand. As a result, it is very likely that the participants to the foresight exercise will show more understanding for the strategy subsequently adopted, whatever it may be, as well as for its implementation in the form of a series of concrete decisions. These players may thus become advocates of strategies which they might not have otherwise supported, thus giving momentum to the implementation of strategy. In this sense, beyond improved strategy formulation, foresight can directly contribute to the implementation of strategy.

At this point, one may object that emergent strategies, *à la* Mintzberg (Mintzberg and Waters, 1985), are not properly dealt with through the linear chain below:

'knowledge; digesting via foresight; representations as scenarios; strategy; implementation'. Recognizing the importance of emergent strategies, it may in fact be argued that scenario building is an excellent way to prepare the strategist to be quick to recognize new opportunities and new strategic ways that were not identified earlier. In other words, foresight is a state of mind, not a source of rigidity, nor a planning process. An understanding of the wide variety of potential states of the future of the system may be one of the best ways to prepare for unexpected outcomes and thus emergent strategies. In this sense, scenario building helps strategic reactivity and flexibility. Scenario building helps the strategist to recognize emergent strategic options.

Case studies
This section presents three typical examples of foresight studies which served as a basis for strategic thinking in their own context.

Public utility in electricity: demand-side management
This is a case where two very large companies, Electricité de France (EdF) and HydroQuébec (HQ), decide to share their experience about demand-side management (DSM). HQ had invested heavily in DSM, while EdF was used to conducting foresight exercises. The two public utilities decided to launch a joint foresight exercise on the future of DSM.

DSM is a strange concept. In a way, through DSM, companies try to limit the use of their offerings and thus their sales. The rationale is as follows: producing electricity requires investing in new power plants (dams, nuclear plants, and so on). This may damage the environment and thus usually faces opposition from surrounding populations. As a result, some large public utilities develop paradoxical strategies: they do their best to reduce the use of electricity. Then, when faced with capacity shortages despite the consumption reduction programs, they open public debates to justify their investments in new plants, showing how much effort they have made to avoid or postpone these investments by 'managing the demand side'. At that point, they usually succeed in circumnavigating public opposition to the investment. All in all, it may seem rather strange to see a company try to reduce or at least limit its own sales. This difficult and complex matter was typically selected as the topic for the joint foresight exercise.

The foresight exercise took the form of a joint working group. The group was composed of 12 participants. These were high-level managers combining mostly seasoned profiles with a few younger colleagues. They came from a variety of departments: strategic planning, marketing, regulation, and operations (distribution); six were from EdF and six from HQ. The expertise of additional managers was called upon when needed. The method used was Godet's 'Mactor' approach (Appendix 7A; Godet 2001).

Five scenarios were built through the foresight work. Each is presented as a column in Table 7.1. The variables used for the first four rows of the matrix progressively emerged from the foresight work as key dimensions of the system (dominant driver, lead player, regulatory conditions and structure of the electricity sector).

An important element of the description of the scenarios is an example that portends what this future could look like, that is, a situation which somehow pre-illustrates what the system could like look, should that scenario prevail in the future. This is shown as the fifth row of Table 7.1. The corresponding market conditions are also described in

Table 7.1   Scenarios for demand side management

	Status quo 'Sell better, to sell more!'	Deregulation 'Sell cheaper and better, to sell more!'	Green world 'Sell better, to sell less!'	Capacity bottlenecks 'Sell better to face demand growth!'	Green deregulation 'Sell better'
Dominant driver	Status quo	Liberalism	Environment preservation	Capacity shortages	Liberalism plus pragmatic green
Lead player	Electric utilities	EU Commission	Green regions and cities	The green	EU, regions and cities
Political and institutional context	Status quo, Nuclear OK	Market logic: environment is secondary	Pragmatic green policies, local authority influence	Local authorities & green against nuclear	Green decentralized production unit
Structure of electricity sector	Independent power production but regulated distribution	Unbundling	Nuclear stopped, smaller units	IPP n ne Nuclear plants	Unbundling, local companies
Portentous situation	France	UK	Denmark	Italy	California, and Netherlands
Market conditions	Limited slack Slow price decrease Slow demand growth	Price war, especially large accounts, overcapacity and market oscillations	Overcapacity Co-generation Lower consumption	Shortages	Overcapacity Price war Quality improvements
DSM	No incentive for more marketing Customer service	No DSM Limited DSM differentiation	Systematic DS Public debates	DSM regulates capacity, new providers	Government drives DSM tax on electricity sales, R&D investment

the sixth row. Finally, the last row of the table shows the likely role of DSM in each of the scenarios. In addition, the mapping shown on Figure 7.3 helped to visualize the five scenarios.

The mapping offers a visual representation of the relative positions of the five scenarios (the columns of Table 7.1). Three of them have been given subtitles as a way to capture the core of the matter: the 'status quo' in both HQ and EdF was a situation with a central monopoly, *à la* Colbert, while the 'green world' was nicknamed 'ecolo-local' as it is the combination of locally embedded environmentally-driven regulation, a situation close to what can be found in part of Scandinavia, especially Denmark and, at least to a certain extent, in the Netherlands. The 'deregulation' scenario was named after Margaret Thatcher who had led the change in the UK. California exemplifies the idea of a 'green deregulation', in between the regulated 'green world' and 'deregulation', thus opposing

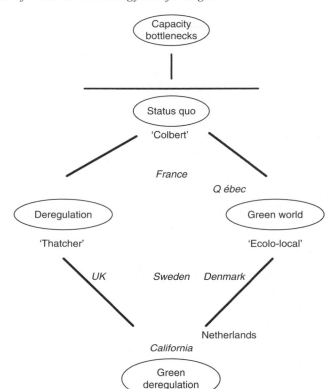

Figure 7.3   Scenarios for demand side management

the Colbert centrally driven model. The shortages of the 'Capacity bottlenecks' scenario were seen as a situation of crisis radically departing from the other four scenarios – thus the line of divide shown graphically as the horizontal bar on the figure. (Although not identified at the time of that study, a typical example of this situation today would be China facing considerable demand growth with a centrally planned model, *à la* Colbert, having difficulty coping with demands.)

On that basis, strategic discussions took place to assess what both EdF (not yet involved in DSM) and HQ (with significant past investments in DSM) could do. This thus illustrates the foresight–strategy connection, via the building of scenarios. The final results of the foresight exercise (scenarios, implications and recommendations for action) were discussed at the executive committee level in both companies.

The case of a foresight study concerning the future of business schools
This study was sponsored by the French Foundation for Management Education and Research (FNEGE), and led to a report published in 2005, and a book (Durand and Dameron, 2008).

The study was conducted through (i) a literature review, (ii) interviews in Europe and North America, together with (iii) the contribution of a working party composed of

12 academics, deans and faculty of several management schools, who met five times for half a day over a 9-month period to build scenarios.

The approach used was again the Mactor method (Appendix 7A). The analysis of the future of business schools in Europe led to the identification of a set of 10 families of actors: private business schools, universities, faculty, students, alumni, business executives, firms, new entrants, state authorities (including the EU Commission) and quality assessment bodies (those providing accreditation and rankings). A set of nine dilemmas was also identified, for which the above players could have converging or diverging views: is management a science? Can business schools educate the managers of tomorrow? Towards more institutional autonomy for universities? Towards more market orientation in academia? Towards internal battles around branding? Towards the emergence of a European specificity in management? A reshuffling of the value chain due to e-learning? Back to teaching? When and how to address managers' learning needs? This made it possible to assess how often families of actors would diverge or converge on dilemmas, thus providing a map of de facto alliances/oppositions. Exogenous forces affecting the system were also identified (the construction of the EU, the development of Asia, aging population in Europe, and so on). On that basis, participants in the working party were invited to formulate scenarios. This generated a set of 17 candidate scenarios from which five were finally recomposed and retained. These five scenarios were described and illustrated in a report in the form of Table 7.2 and Figure 7.4.

Table 7.2   Five scenarios for business schools

	1 Drifting away	2 European management stands up	3 Unbundling business schools as vendors	4 M&As	5 Reactive adaptation
Funding	Mostly public and insufficient	Awareness about the financial issue: EU invest + National public Resources + Foundations + Companies	Diversified sources of funding Payment for services	Combining public and private resources, including from local/regional governments	Public basic funding, some foundations, executive education, local and regional additional fundings
Attractiveness of careers for faculty	Low. 60% only of retiring papy-boomers are replaced. Quality of recruits is mediocre	Significant upgrading of careers Attractiveness Good level of recruits	Clear segmentation of career paths	Segmentation of careers	Faculty produce to generate/reinforce institutional visibility. Importance of Executive education
Alliances and mergers	Limited deals, ad hoc. Essentially in best 'Grandes écoles'	Promoted by EU A European job market emerges for business professors	The value chain breaks Some professors create, exploit and maintain their own brand	Exclusive alliances Search for critical mass, or geographic coverage	Some deals, Some go for volume, some for quality

Table 7.2   (continued)

	1 Drifting away	2 European management stands up	3 Unbundling business schools as vendors	4 M&As	5 Reactive adaptation
Role of market	Increasing for 'Grandes écoles'	Strong but kept under control	Dominant	Complementary to the dominance of institutional logic	Increasing
Role of institutions	Dominates in universities	Positive dynamics of universities with some autonomy	Weakened Universities as distribution channels	Still strong	Status quo with margins of maneuver Local pressures and incentives
New entrants	Corporate universities Consultants	Limited role of new entrants as incumbents are in better shape	Many new entrants in opening spaces of the value chain	Limited Incumbents institutions control the market	Moderate involvement
Management as a science?	A widening gap with practitioners	European Social Sciences are mobilized. More clinical/project research.	Debated Consultants and practitioners sell their best practices as theories	Business seen as a science	Bipolarity: researchers who publish/ teachers who train
E -learning	Limited development, lack of resources to invest	Some initiatives	Makes it possible to distribute same content in many classrooms at once	Institutions remain the dominant design	Some initiatives
Foreboding / signaling examples	Some European universities in bad financial trouble	Germany creating Business Schools CEMS Program	Strategy Academy (Bob de Witt and Ron Meyer), Theseus, Univ. Phoenix	Insead-Wharton, Polytechnicum Normandie. ICN-Mines-Art (Nancy)	Sciences Po Dauphine, Leading 'Grandes écoles'

Source: Durand and Dameron (2005).

Each of the five scenarios (presented as a column of Table 7.2) was named with a catchy title and described by means of key variables which appeared in the course of the foresight work (funding, attractiveness of faculty careers and so on; see Table 7.2). The scenarios were also developed in the form of a one page description. Finally a mapping was constructed as a way of offering a visual representation of the variety of potential futures identified for the system of university education in management at the 2015–20 horizon. This is shown in Figure 7.4.

It was felt that the five scenarios captured most of the knowledge available about the future of business schools and made it simpler for deans to think about their strategies.

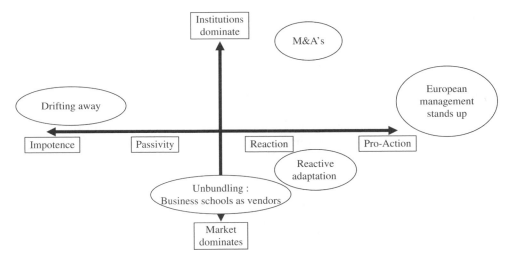

Source: Durand and Dameron (2005).

Figure 7.4   Mapping of five scenarios

It appeared that the process of building the scenario was an essential part of the added value of the representations. In that sense, 'representing' (building the representation) was more important and more useful to think through the strategy than the representation itself.

The case of a foresight study on road and air transport technologies
The French railway company, SNCF, was interested in learning from potential future innovations in competing sectors (road and air transport). Rail transport in Europe is significant both for passengers and for freight. SNCF has been deploying TGV quite successfully since the early 1980s and intended to pursue the search for innovative strategies in railways. This led to the idea of conducting a foresight study about potential new technologies and services in other (competing) transport sectors.

In this instance, the foresight exercise did not mean building systemic, comprehensive scenarios. Instead, it meant looking for external (and sometimes internal) information to construct micro-scenarios about a new feature, a new piece of technology, a new service in road and air transportation. (For example, one option was identified to transport passengers to and from airport terminals by air balloons which would land on the top of tower buildings in the heart of the cities. Another option was the automatic guiding of buses approaching a bus stop so as to minimize the gap between the sidewalk and the bus platform, thus providing easy access to elderly passengers. Another example was the concept of 'truck trains', with trucks electronically connected on a specific highway lane.) The idea was still to improve the description of potential evolutions in the competitive landscape, but in a more focused way than was discussed in the two previous cases. The exercise largely led to collecting external information through various means (literature search, interviews, and so on) plus a systematic Delphi enquiry.

Interestingly, it is the subsequent phase of exploitation of the results of the external investigation that is illuminating. When confronted with structured foresight views of potential innovations in competing companies, even from other industries, internal participants tend to change their own perspective. In a way, the foresight exercise which focused on outside players (from connected, though different, transport sectors) turned out to be a detour to force some form of reflexive thinking about the future of railways.

Rail transportation was facing deregulation and SNCF had to prepare for it. At the same time, SNCF was not just another monopoly quietly sitting behind regulatory barriers. Competition had been a reality for many decades for rail (both road and air transport had been gaining market share heavily against rail for more than 50 years). The development and deployment of the TGV had clearly been a competitive move against this continuous erosion of market share. While a more innovative response from rail was needed to face the competition from air and road, it appeared that a complementary intent behind the foresight study was to help the organization prepare for the direct rail competition which would soon stem from deregulation.

This is a classical trick. Looking at other businesses is a means of better understanding one's own. What has humankind really learned from space exploration so far? It has been argued that what we got back was essentially the image of our blue planet, isolated in the universe. That is, we travelled that far just to look at ourselves. Thus foresight studies are about revisiting 'ourselves', in context, which is what strategy is all about.

Discussion

The brief presentation of case studies aimed at illustrating the practice of constructing foresight scenarios as a way of feeding into strategic thinking. (Thus, foresight is actually part of the strategic process.) Several lessons emerge from experience gained from scenario building.

Foresight exercises tend to be laborious. A typical exercise requires 6–9 months of data collection, group work, maturation of ideas, reformulation of challenges and issues, identification of main drivers, generation of candidate scenarios, choice of final scenarios and formal reformulation, and so on. This requires time. While strategy is known to be a lengthy process too, lead times in business life may not be fully compatible with the typical duration of foresight exercises. Once an issue is identified, managers tend to prefer to tackle the matter quickly. This may be why this type of approach has been mostly implemented in large public or semi-public organizations. The examples of public utilities in electricity or rail as well as the case of management education typically illustrate the point.

Another important contribution of foresight exercises is that they bring stakeholders into a debate. It may be argued that the best foresight works are participative, calling upon a variety of competence and perspectives and putting them in a position to look at issues in their full complexity. A foresight process helps every participant become aware of the truly complex nature of the matter at hand. These will thus subsequently have a much more supportive stance when strategic decisions are made, as they will have learned from the process that there is no clear-cut answer, no one-best-way, no simple response. Thus, foresight contributes not only to the formulation of strategy but also to implementation. In addition, regarding the emergent side of strategy, one could argue that an organization which adopts a foresight culture is more likely to be quick to react when facing unexpected situations, precisely because it made the effort to prepare for a variety of futures. A direct consequence of the above is that it may be relevant to prepare future strategic decisions on difficult matters by launching foresight exercises early on, with a variety of managers and staff from various layers of the organization. This process will help to prepare informed supporters for sensitive future strategic decisions.

Foresight is not decision making. Foresight is not about selecting the 'best' scenario. As the future is uncertain, foresight thinking suggests accepting a variety of potential futures, including those that would not naturally come to mind. Foresight is about contributing to strategic decisions. In this sense, foresight is about bringing insight. Thus the clearer the conflicting visions, the sharper the scenarios, the better. This chapter argues that strategists and decision makers can benefit from a rich variety of perspectives, only as long as the resulting 're-presentations' are documented and organized. This is why the main argument of this chapter is that scenarios may be seen as organized knowledge (re-presentations) of potential futures.

Thus, experience suggests that visual maps help participants in foresight exercises to convey their re-presentations to strategists and top management. Obviously, scenarios need to be delicately crafted and worded. Semantics is a key element, which means that language barriers can be very detrimental to foresight exercises. A full description of the potential futures is important. Yet, experience indicates that many of the participants involved tend to relate more easily to some form of mapping. While some may argue that this is a sign of shallow thinking, it can also be argued that texts and diagrams are complementary. Although this is a complex and much debated topic, in Microsoft language, PowerPoint complements Word, and vice versa. In any case, communicating through the use of maps is as important as naming scenarios with clear and easy-to-memorize titles.

Finally, a foresight exercise needs to be properly guided with adequate tools. It is not just another refreshing, future-oriented, loose creativity game. Building scenarios means in-depth analysis, repeated iterations, active interaction and debate. It is about systematically trying to grasp complexity, by analyzing the drivers and the chains of interactions in the system studied, as well as the exogenous pressures exerted on the system. This requires method and willingness to understand, openness and rigour, continuity and persistence. Half-baked foresights are of little use.

Conclusion

This chapter raised the issue of the process of strategy building based on available or accessible knowledge, and more specifically knowledge about potential futures. It argued that if strategy is about how to reach a desirable future, foresight is the way to integrate pieces and blocks of knowledge stemming from action into useful representations about potential futures. Scenarios are self-sustained and meaningful stories describing the potential future states of a given system. In this sense, scenarios are the strategic representations built through a foresight exercise from the accessible knowledge of an organization. In other words, scenarios are a foresight way of 're-presenting' the knowledge accessible to an organization about its future. As strategic representations, the scenarios mediate the complexity of the knowledge base, the uncertainty of future outcomes and the work of the strategist.

The theoretical framework presented was built on the concepts of social interaction, the duality of structuring, the interpretative frames and the process of routinization. Action and interaction generate knowledge via learning. Knowledge is digested into representations which feed strategy via a formulation process. The strategy implementation in turn generates action and interaction, and thus new knowledge. The chapter focused on the 'digesting' part of the loop.

The main findings of the three case studies discussed have concrete implications for practitioners: the laborious nature of foresight exercises, the relevance of adopting a participative approach, the importance of viewing foresight as a way of recognizing the plural character of futures (strategy is thus required to be capable of facing a variety of potential futures), the importance of both semantics and visual mapping, and the need to rely on foresight methods and tools. More importantly, the discussion suggested that re-presenting is in many instances more important to the strategic process than the resulting re-presentations. In addition, the case studies showed how foresight contributes not only to strategy formulation but also to strategy implementation.

More work on the 'knowledge about the futures' – 'strategy' connection is needed. Typically, we are still lacking empirical studies on larger samples in order to get a broader picture of the processes at hand. At the same time, careful longitudinal studies about the use of foresight studies in strategy formulation and implementation would also contribute to gaining more insight into the strategy–foresight connection, adopting the viewpoint of this chapter, that is, foresight as knowledge transformation processes.

Appendix 7A
The first two case studies used the Mactor method. The third case study used a survey technique derived from the Delphi method.

The Mactor method requires listing the players of a given system and then grouping them in families. The next step is to identify the objectives and strategic levers available to each family of players to influence the others. On that basis (note that there is no logical step here), key issues in the system are listed. For each issue, each category of players is analyzed to assess their preference regarding the issue. This makes it possible to identify how often two different categories of players converge, diverge or are neutral, across all issues. Once this is done (note again that there is no logical step here), participants are invited to build scenarios to describe potential futures. For more on the Mactor method, see Godet (2001).

The survey technique used in the third case is based on an internet questionnaire to about 600 experts, complemented by phone interviews, followed by an internet-iteration to challenge the key suggestions stemming from the first round. All items identified were finally reviewed by a panel of referents via face-to-face interviews. This was not a pure Delphi exercise but the idea of iteration was used to generate some form of cross-checking among the participating experts (second round) before a third and final iteration with a review panel which essentially helped to clarify and document the items resulting from the survey.

References
Berger, G. (1957), 'Sciences humaines et prévision' (Human sciences and forecasting), *La Revue des Deux Mondes*, no. 3, February.
Berger, G. (1958), 'L'attitude prospective' (The foresight stance), *Prospective*, no. 1, May.
Berger, G. (1964), *Phénoménologie du Temps et Prospective* (Phenomenology of Time and Foresight), Paris: PUF.
Braun, Armand (2001), 'Le CRC', Working Paper, Institut de l'Entreprise, Paris.

de Jouvenel, B. (1967), *The Art of Conjecture*, translated from French by Nikita Lary, New York: Basic Books.
de la Ville, Inès (1996), 'Apprentissages collectifs et structuration de la strategie dans la jeune enterprise de haute technologie (Organizational learning and structuring of the strategy in a high-tech start-up), Phd thesis, Lyon III University.
Drisse, L. (2001), *Le Management stratégique en représentations* (Strategic management in representation), Paris: Ellipses.
Durand, Thomas (1992), 'The dynamics of cognitive technological maps', in P. Lorange, J. Roos, B. Chakravarty and A. Van de Ven (eds), *Strategic Processes*, Cambridge, MA: Blackwell Business, pp. 165–89.
Durand, Thomas (1998), 'The alchemy of competence', in G. Hamel, C.K. Prahalad, H. Thomas and D. O'Neal (eds), *Strategic Flexibility: Managing in a Turbulent Environment*, New York: John Wiley, pp. 303–30.
Durand, Thomas (2003), '12 lessons drawn from key technologies 2005, the French Technology Foresight Exercise', *Journal of Forecasting*, **22**, March, 161–77.
Durand, Thomas (2006), 'The making of a metaphor: developing a theoretical framework', in Jan Löwstedt and Torbjörn Sternberg (eds), *Producing Management Knowledge*, London: Routledge, Ch. 11.
Durand, T. and S. Dameron (2005), *Prospective 2015 des établissements de Gestion: cinq scenarios pour agir* (Foresight study of business schools: five scenarios for action for 2015), Paris: FNEGE, www.fnege.org.
Durand, T. and S. Dameron (2008), *The Future of Business Schools: Scenarios and Strategies for 2020*, London: Palgrave Macmillan.
Durand, Thomas and Marie Dubreuil (2001), 'Humanizing the future: science and soft technologies', *Journal of Future Studies, Strategic Thinking and Policies*, **3** (4), August, 285–95.
Durand, Thomas, Eléonore Mounoud and Bernard Ramanantsoa (1996), 'Uncovering strategic assumptions: understanding managers' ability to build representations', *European Management Journal*, **14** (4), 389–98.
Gibbert, M. and T. Durand (eds) (2006), *Strategic Networks: Learning to Compete*, Oxford: Blackwell.
Giddens, A. (1987), *La Constitution de la société*, Paris: PUF.
Godet, M. (1977), *Crise de la prévision, essor de la prospective* (Crisis of forecasting, rise of prospective), Paris: PUF, translated into English, Oxford: Pergamon, 1979.
Godet, M. (1985), *Prospective et planification stratégique* (Prospective and strategic planning), Paris: CPE Economica.
Godet, M. (1991, 2001), *De l'Anticipation à l'Action: Manuel de Prospective et de Stratégie* (Creating futures: scenario planning as a strategic management tool), Paris: Dunod (two volumes).
Godet, M. (2001), *Creating Futures: Scenario Planning as a Strategic Management Tool*, Paris: Economica-Brookings.
Goffman, E. (1991), *Les cadres de l'expérience*, Paris: Ed de minuit.
Lesourne, J. (1981), *Les mille sentiers de l'avenir* (One thousand paths into the future), Paris: Seghers.
Martin, B.R. and J. Irvine (1989), *Research Foresight: Priority Setting in Science*, London: Pinter.
Mintzberg, H. and J.A. Waters (1985), 'Of strategies, deliberate and emergent', *Strategic Management Journal*, **6**, 257–72.
Moscovici, S. (1988), 'Notes towards a description of social representations', *European Journal of Social Psychology*, **18**, 211–50.
Nelson, R. and S. Winter (1982), *An Evolutionary Perspective of Economic Change*, Cambridge, MA: Harvard University Press.
Salo, A. (2001), 'Incentives in technology foresight', *International Journal of Technology Management*, **21** (7–8), 711–25.
Salo, A. and K. Cuhls (2003), Special Issue on Technology Foresight, *Journal of Forecasting*, **21** (7/8).
Wack, P. (1985a), 'Scenarios: uncharted waters ahead', *Harvard Business Review*, September–October.
Wack, P. (1985b), 'Scenarios: shooting the rapids', *Harvard Business Review*, November–December.

8 Researching the organization–environment relationship
George Burt

Introduction

What is the environment, and would we recognize it if we saw it? Simple questions, yet they have profound implications for those interested in researching the organization–environment (and environment–organization) relationship. These questions have been and are increasingly being posed by researchers as they continue to develop contemporary theoretical explanations of the organization and environment relationship (and the environment and organization relationship) (Emery and Trist, 1965; Child, 1972; Boyd et al., 1993; Weick, 1995; Scott, 2003; Burt et al., 2006). However, there are two differing (and dichotomous) perspectives about how to understand the organization–environment relationship, which have important implications for any research in this domain.

In the first perspective, the environment is traditionally understood as exogenous, that is, external to and detached from managers and organizations (Hatch, 1997), and it is continually imposing opportunities and constraints upon an organization. Under these circumstances, managers are challenged to respond quickly to such opportunities and constraints in an attempt to ensure survival and adaptation in the first instance (Boisot and Child, 1999) and competitive advantage in the second instance (Lawrence and Lorsch, 1967; Porter, 1985; March, 1991). The ability of management to adapt their organization to the drivers of change in the environment has been the focal concern for researchers (Burt et al., 2006).

In the second perspective, the environment is understood as being endogenous (Dill, 1958; Duncan, 1972), that is, subjective and internal in the mind of the managers and socially constructed (Berger and Luckmann, 1966; Weick, 1979, 1995; Dilley, 1999) through conversation (van der Heijden, 1996). Environment is therefore the socially negotiated outcome of the experiences of managers (Eden, 1992), implying that environment can only be interpreted and understood from their perspective (Guba and Lincoln, 1985) as they make sense of such experiences (Weick, 1979, 1995). Managerial processes and activities for ongoing perceiving, interpreting and understanding of the organization–environment (and environment–organization) relationship in and through their conversation becomes the focal concern for researchers (Ford, 1999; Mir and Watson, 2000; Brown and Duguid, 2001; McKiernan, 2006).

These two dichotomous approaches bring the organization–environment debate to the fore: which, if either, has the primary influence over the other? It is not the intention in this chapter to resolve such a dichotomy, it is the intention to keep these debates, tensions and arguments open to help researchers consider these perspectives and their impact on their own research.

The purpose of this chapter is to explore the philosophical and epistemological arguments surrounding the organization–environment relationship, identifying four perspectives on 'environment', the nature of organizational and managerial behaviour in each of these four perspectives on environment, and the consequential implications for research design and methodology. The discussion will include a review of the seminal papers on environment, developing an understanding of their contribution to date, as well as identifying their limitations from a contemporary perspective of the literature and practice. The discussion will then move to methodological issues for those who argue for a constructionist perspective (Berger and Luckmann, 1966; Eden, 1992; Mir and Watson, 2000) when researching 'our' environment, and are interested in researching the organization–environment relationship as management perceive, interpret and make sense of their experiences and enact their environment (Daft and Weick, 1984; Smircich and Stubbart, 1985; Brown and Duguid, 2001).

The ontological and epistemological nature of the organization–environment relationship

Before reviewing the literature to appreciate the evolution of the organization–environment relationship, it is important to first consider questions about ontology and epistemology generally, then subsequently discuss the implications of ontology and epistemology on the various perspectives presented here on the organization–environment relationship. By doing so it is possible to articulate the fundamental assumptions about the organization–environment relationship as part of the rationale to conduct research.

Burrell and Morgan (1979) proposed and discussed opposing ontological extremes that could be held about the nature of the world and our understanding of it – is reality external from our consciousness or a product of individual consciousness? These extreme positions that Burrell and Morgan proposed are (i) whether a true reality can exist and be found (realism) or (ii) if reality is perceived and created by individuals and communicated socially, therefore truth(s) is (are) unique to each individual based on his or her experience (relativism or subjectivism). Building from the debate about the extreme ontological positions, Burrell and Morgan again pose questions about the epistemology of knowledge, including: how can knowledge be understood, what forms of knowledge can be obtained, and how can truth be determined from falsehood? Can knowledge be acquired, or must it be determined from our experiences? The extreme epistemological positions that Burrell and Morgan propose are based on whether knowledge about the world can be (i) proved or not, resulting in the uncovering of laws about its working: objectivism or positivism at one extreme or, alternatively, (ii) with knowledge held by individuals, the uncovering of the individual's subjective knowledge from his/her experience being the key to understanding: relativism or anti-positivism (see Figure 8.1).

In developing the debate further, we shall consider the realism and relativism perspectives in more detail, and their implications for research into the organization–environment relationship.

The realism and relativism perspectives
The realism perspective is based on the view that phenomena such as universal and moral facts and theoretical scientific entities exist independently of people's thoughts and perceptions (Burrell and Morgan, 1979). The realism perspective holds that although there is an objectively existing world, not dependent on our minds, people are able to understand aspects of that world through their perception and they and their actions can be studied independently (Frishammar, 2006).

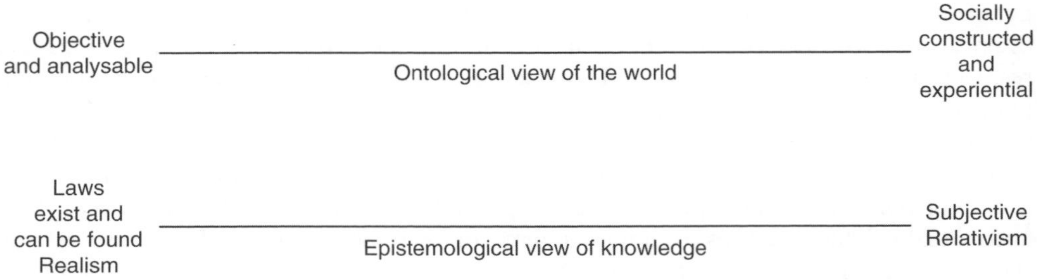

	Socially
Objective	_____	constructed
and analysable	Ontological view of the world	and
	experiential

Laws		
exist and	_____	Subjective
can be found	Epistemological view of knowledge	Relativism
Realism		

Figure 8.1   Ontology and epistemology for organization–environment

Cromby and Nightingale state:

> [R]ealism is the doctrine that an external world exists independently of our representations of it. Representations include perceptions, thoughts, language, beliefs and desires, as well as arte- facts such as pictures and maps, and so include all the ways in which we could or do know and experience the world and ourselves. Relativism repudiates this doctrine, arguing that since any such external world is inaccessible to us in both principle and practice, it need not be postulated or considered. (1999, p. 6)

The realism perspective is based on the belief that the world has structures and objects that have a cause and effect relationship with each other, and that these structures and objects are universal in their properties. Bohm (1996) considers such phenomena as 'presented realities' (p. 55), which is defined as the physically demonstrable and publicly discernible characteristics, qualities or attributes of a thing, event or situation. Presented realities 'are composed of uninterpreted facts and data that are accessible (i.e. in the world), measurable and empirically verifiable' (Ford, 1999, p. 481). They require a range of pre-established and agreed constructs to be widely available, known and understood, which are the basis of everyday life.

The realism perspective therefore leads us to conclude that it is possible for the researcher to be independent of the organization in time and place, study it and 'the' envi- ronment in a detached manner, and then draw out conclusions about the organization– environment relationship (Easterby-Smith et al., 1991). The researcher is not required to be in close proximity to the phenomena that are to be studied.

The relativism perspective is based on the belief that concepts such as right and wrong, goodness and badness, or truth and falsehood are not absolute but change from culture to culture and situation to situation. This perspective holds that people can only have knowl- edge of what they experience directly. Each organization's management is unique, each organization operates in a unique context, which can only be understood from the perspec- tive of the managers, by an understanding of their individual and shared experiences of 'our' environment. Bohm (1996) described such a situation as 'represented realities' that are not 'in' the facts or data of the situation itself, but are interpretations put there by observers including their opinions, judgements, assessments, evaluations and accounts (Watzlawick, 1976; Harre, 1980; Ford, 1999, p. 481). There are no universal properties (Burrell and Morgan, 1979) and that order emerges out of sensemaking activities (Weick, 1995).

Represented reality emerges from the individual and group interpretations, conceptualization and agreement through dialogue; thus, studying sensemaking activities becomes the focus for the researcher. Therefore to undertake research here it is argued that the researcher needs to develop an understanding of the processes by which managerial understanding of context emerges by 'occupying the frame of reference of the participant in action' (Burrell and Morgan, 1979, p. 5).

Understanding the differences between one manager's worldview and that of another is just as important as understanding the areas of agreement in their worldviews. The notion of consistency in worldviews is a contrary point for researchers (Huff et al., 1992), as many managers believe that there is commonality between them, when there is in fact fragmentation and equivocality (Harvey, 1974).

Weick (1979, 1995) has argued that there are three interrelated elements to moving towards a situation of unequivocality. First, enactment, which involves a stream of experiences and reflects the creative nature of 'the' environment where there is ongoing dynamic interaction between the organization and 'its' environment. Management impose their will onto the environment and the environment imposes its will onto the organization. Second, selection, which is the development of shared meanings about their joint experiences. Such a process involves 'sensemaking', where managers together impose their cognitive frameworks upon (enacted) events to understand such events as they attempt to reduce equivocality about those events. Third, retention, where managers extract and retain key insights generated from the process of consensus and agreement.

Micro research is required to probe and understand such experiences. Undertaking such micro research is complex and involves developing a rich understanding of the intricacies of the process of shared understanding, as it reveals itself in 'both a temporal and contextual manner' (Pettigrew, 1990, p. 268).

The challenge for the researcher here is the issue of intersubjectivity in the micro worlds of managers. Intersubjectivity is the resolution of understanding between two or more people, who have their personal subjective views based on their experiences, to the point where they have shared meaning and understanding (Eden et al., 1981). Intersubjectivity can arise at three levels (ibid.):

1. between people if they agree on a given set of meanings or definition of a situation;
2. between people where the shared meanings constructed by people in their inter-actions with each other are used as an everyday resource to interpret the meaning of elements of social and cultural life; and
3. between people where they have a shared, or partially shared, understanding of the divergences of meaning about seemingly familiar issues.

Researching the organization–environment relationship can therefore only be achieved from the manager's perspective, with the researcher following a hermeneutic methodology (Guba and Lincoln, 1985) inside the organization (Denzin, 1997). A hermeneutic methodology involves following the trends or processes of understanding that emerges between people as they come to a shared understanding of their context. The process is likely to include the surfacing and resolution of dilemmas, tensions and also the potential for reframing individual and collective worldviews.

The Burrell and Morgan framework (1979), while producing different ontological and epistemological positions, is not intended to be a prescriptive framework, but one that challenges the researcher to consider and question his/her view of the world and the impact it has on framing their research design and methodology. The ontological and epistemological assumptions that we make have a major impact on the nature of the organization–environment relationship research – is the environment 'known to' or 'known by' managers? 'Known to' implies that context is external to the manager and it can be determined through a process of analysis and investigation. 'Known by' implies that context is subjective and emerges from sharing and making sense of experiences that constitute our *unique* context. Making sense of our experiences implies that an understanding of the past emerges and that that understanding is linked to the present. From such an understanding, insights and conclusions can be derived about context that influence future actions as managers enact their environment.

This leads to another aspect of this debate, that is, whether managers have the ability to make choices that affect their future (Child, 1972) or whether their future is determined by externalities (Pfeffer and Salancik, 1978). Cyert and March argue 'that the posture towards the environment which those in control of organisations attempt to adopt will reflect their perception of environmental conditions in relation to their desire to attain with some certainty the goals they have set for the organisation' (1963, pp. 118–20). This section will now explore the issues surrounding the choice–determinism debate, and we shall return to the ontological and epistemological debate later in the chapter. The following section will discuss the evolution of the literature on 'environment' and how it is determined in the world of management, identifying gaps in current knowledge.

The managerial choice–environmental determinism debate

Having explored issues surrounding ontology and epistemology generally, it is possible now to pose questions about the ability management has to exert strategic choice (Child, 1972) in terms of whether that can or cannot be done to shape their future destiny. 'Strategic choice' extends to cover the relationship between context, organization structure, organizational performance and decision making (ibid., p. 2). Do managers have a 'free will' (Burrell and Morgan, 1979) to make choices and take decisions or are they constrained by their context?

Emery (1977, p. 67) states: 'men are not limited simply to adapting to the environment as given. Insofar as they understand the laws governing their environment they can modify the conditions producing their subsequent environments and hence radically change the definition of "an adaptive response"'. 'Free will' manifests itself in other forms, such as technological innovation where new products create markets that did not exist previously. How else can we explain phenomena such as SatNav or home bread makers or iPod?

The organizational learning literature would support such a position, arguing that learning is based on a trial-and-error approach allowing the organization to evolve through the discovery of what works (Galer and van der Heijden, 1992; Wall and Wall, 1995). Galer and van der Heijden argue that learning in groups is based on three interrelated activities. First, 'joint review of their experience of what has been going on in the world in which their business operates; second, internalize this experience against the background of new information (e.g. new scenarios) and also to internalize the scenarios themselves; and third, infer conclusions, at least of a preliminary nature' (p. 9). The key element to such learning is 'the art of organizational conversation' (p. 10) or dialogue. Dialogue is a form of consciously constructed conversation in which participants engage in a sustained and collaborative investigation into the underlying assumptions and certainties that underlie their everyday experiences and relationships with the intent of creating more effective interactions. Dialogue provides an opportunity for people to examine and authentically deal with their conversations as the fundamental presumptions, presuppositions, assumptions and backgrounds in which they dwell and to reflect on the implication of those conversations (Bohm, 1996).

In contrast, Child (1972) states: 'the environment has normally been regarded as the primary source of constraint upon organisational design' (p. 8). If the environment is seen as a primary constraint on the organization, as the variables that constitute the environment are outside the influence of management, then the environment will determine which organizations are successful and which organizations fail. There is little that management can do to determine their future. Resource dependency theory also suggests that organizations are constrained by the network of relationships and contracts that lock in organizations to other organizations and major stakeholders limiting their choice (Pfeffer and Salancik, 1978; Christensen, 1997), thus reducing the ability of managers to decide and act. In addition, a systems perspective on environment would also argue for environmental constraint due to feedback loops, both positive and negative, interacting to create another, although different situation from the previous paragraph, of lock-in. A manager who was unaware of these positive and negative feedback loops would find the organization facing the same challenges time after time (Senge, 1990).

So tensions are again evident in the literature around the management choice and environmental determinism debate, adding to the challenge for researchers interested in researching the organization–environment relationship. What becomes evident from this debate is on the one hand the perceptual ability of management to understand the context within which they are operating. Do managers perceive, interpret, construct and enact their environment? Do managers work collectively to reach agreement on their perceptions? The outcome of such processes is likely to be a greater development of common language and concepts in the dialogue that has emerged from their conversations. The manifestation is the negotiated agreement of future direction of the organization, with attendant agreement on subsequent supporting individual and organizational actions. On the other hand, do managers wait for events to occur, hoping that they have the ability to respond over time? Are managers limited by what they can perceive and take action on? As managers are unable to have omniscient knowledge about their context, then it is inevitable that they will regularly be taken by surprise. Do they understand why were taken by surprise and did they have time to react? The manifestation is likely to be changes to systems and structures to cope with their new circumstances.

Again, acknowledging these tensions and their impact will impact on any research design for those studying the organization–environment relationship. The researcher has a choice of either studying the unfolding development of manager's conversations, in formal and informal settings as they occur, or alternatively, studying the external events that managers recognize retrospectively, which will reveal different understandings of the organization–environment relationship.

Summarizing the organization–environment relationship debate
Two different perspectives on environment begin to emerge from this debate. In the first perspective, the environment is socially constructed and emerges through the ongoing

Table 8.1   Summarizing the organization–environment relationship

	Realism	Relativism
Environment	Exists separately from the organization	Exists in the minds of managers
Mode of understanding environment	Discovery from existing laws	Constructed from experiences
Adaptation	See change and adapt	Enact environment from actions
Strategic choice	Free will	Move from equivocality to unequivocality through conversation

managerial dialogue, conversation and sensemaking processes. The environment is ebbing and flowing with the passage of time, changing continually due to the organization's actions, the actions of other independent third party actors, as well as the impact of these actions impacting back on themselves. The key for managers (and researchers) is not the alignment of the organization with the environment; it is shaping and changing the conversation that is the key. As Ford (1999, p. 484) argues:

> [C]onversations bring history and future into the present utterance by responding to, reaccentuating, and reworking past conversations while anticipating and shaping subsequent conversations. When we are asked to justify or explain our linguistic characterisations, we respond with other linguistic characterisations which are themselves based on still other linguistic characterisations, etc.

In the second perspective, the environment can only be known retrospectively, as events manifest and impose themselves onto the organization and are recognized by management from the well-established laws and rules that exist to explain such phenomena. Such a situation is described by Bohm (1996) in his 'presented realities'. Management's ability to quickly recognize such events will determine the organization–environment relationship.

The organization–environment debate is summarized in Table 8.1.

Four perspectives on the organization–environment relationship
To consider these two perspectives on the organization–environment relationship further, a framework is developed that synthesizes the issues discussed so far in this chapter. To help conceptualize the organization–environment relationship it is proposed to juxtapose the ontological and epistemological assumptions about environment – objective or subjective – with the differing views about managerial choice – proactive and perspective or reactive and retrospective (see Figure 8.2).

Exploring the four organization–environment perspectives
The above conceptualization of the organization–environment relationship presents four different perspectives, with differing implications for the research and research design: (i) the imposed environment (known retrospectively), (ii) the analysable environment (known retrospectively), (iii) the enacted environment, which is created from our actions

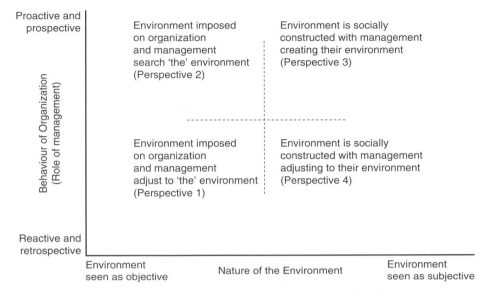

Figure 8.2   Conceptualizing the organization–environment relationship

and reflections on those experiences and (iv) the performance-divergent environment, which is constructed retrospectively, usually when the organization is not performing as intended.

The discussion that follows explains each perspective in turn, starting with perspective 1 and working through to perspective 4, as well as developing the implications of each perspective for those interested in researching the organization–environment relationship. For each perspective there is a note of some of the key research that has been published to date about that perspective.

Perspective 1   The first perspective, 'environment imposed onto an organization and management adjust to the environment', suggests that the environment is knowable and the challenge for management is to spend time working out the laws of the environment, when there are environmental pressures imposing themselves on the organization. However, management do not recognize that they can search for and identify the environment; they wait for it to emerge. Such a situation would imply that researchers would study the impact on management of environmental-led change. Understanding the retrospective cues and their link to the actions that created organizational adjustment processes to outside-in imposed change would be the key to research design. Examples of some of the research on perspective 1 are as follows:

- Miller and Friesen (1980) studied a wide range of organizations and key events that indicated that a process of change (rather than resistance) had occurred, and identified the relationship between the variables that were key to the change in direction.
- Pettigrew (1985) studied ICI to identify the changes that brought about a turnaround in its fortunes.

- Johnson (1987) investigated a situation where management were locked into a particular recipe that they followed against the signs for change in their context that ultimately brought about their demise.
- Grinyer et al. (1988) considered a number of exemplar companies that, at the time, demonstrated a turnaround of their financial performance, from decline to growth.
- Miller (1990) analysed a wide range of successful American companies to reveal the decisions and actions that management took that brought about the downfall.
- MacKay et al. (2006) highlighted the impact of soft systems, such as procedures, structures and processes, that underpin managerial thinking; and the inability of the industry to perceive itself in the wider, global textile industry resulting in its consequent decline.

Perspective 2   The second perspective, 'environment imposed onto an organization and management search for the environment', again suggests that the environment is analysable and knowable, and the challenge for management is to spend time working out the laws of the environment; however, in this perspective management are able to engage in law-establishing activities to identify the environment. Such a situation would imply that researchers should study the efficiency of management in determining the environment and the consequent impact of the laws that govern their organization. Understanding the reactive organizational adjustment processes to outside-in imposed change would be the key to research design. Examples of research on perspective 2 are:

- Quinn (1978) studied management in order to understand the (retrospective) understanding of recent change that their companies had experienced in an attempt to better understand the role of planning in organizations.
- Mintzberg and Waters (1985) presented in-depth case studies across 11 settings of how strategies formed in organizations, identifying the patterns of decisions that gave rise to different types of strategy – intended and realized/unrealized and unintended and emergent in nature.

Perspective 3   The third perspective, 'environment is socially constructed with management creating their environment', suggests that the environment is determined from an inside-out perspective. Managerial sensemaking and meaning-giving of their subjective experiences would be the focus for the researcher. Management would be continually enacting their environment and the researcher would be studying the interpretative and negotiation activities of management as they agree upon and enact their environment. Understanding the ongoing process of managerial perception, thinking and consensus-building (Weick, 1979, 1995) that determines an ongoing inside-in approach would be the key to research design. Examples of research on perspective 3 are:

- Meyer (1982) combined ethnographic research with survey-based research to study the impact of a hospital strike on decision makers to identify the propitious opportunities that occurred from an unexpected exogenous event.
- Brown and Eisenhardt (1998) put forward the argument that the environment is unpredictable and uncontrollable and that successful organizations use these conditions to their advantage to take action to lead rather than follow change.

- Burt (2003) studied (elements of the) formal and informal strategic conversation in three organizations to reveal how they coped with the identification of external change during their sensemaking activities.
- Cairns et al. (2004) presented two case studies with similar contexts, where the strategic conversation enabled one organization to overcome fragmentation between members and stakeholders, and the other where key actors were unable to craft the strategic conversation, resulting in a continuation of fragmentation.

Perspective 4   The fourth perspective, 'environment is socially constructed with management adjusting to their environment', again suggests that the environment is determined from an inside-out perspective; however, the difference between this perspective and the previous one is that management are likely to engage in a process of consensus-building only when they perceive a mismatch between expected and actual performance of the organization. There are experiences that management have still to make sense of and these experiences are impacting on the organization. Understanding the retrospective process of managerial sensemaking and consensus-building that determines a punctuated inside-in approach would be the key to research design. Examples of research on perspective 4 are:

- Gioia and Chittipeddi (1991) tracked change processes in a university, revealing four interrelated phases of envisaging, signalling, re-visioning and energizing that show the interplay between inside-out and outside-in forces.
- Burt et al. (2006) reveal the outcome of a dialectic process between managers where they identified a dramatic position on impending change, if no new future action were taken to prevent the inevitable happening.

The conceptualization of the ontological and epistemological assumptions about environment with the differing views about managerial choice has resulted in the development of four perspectives on environment, each with differing implications for those interested in researching the organization–environment relationship. It would now make sense to review briefly the literature to understand the extent of knowledge in each of the four perspectives.

Evolution of the literature on the organization–environment relationship

Categories of environment literature
So what does the literature tell us about the organization–environment relationship? Over the last 50 years many researchers have been interested in the environment–organization relationship, discussing the impact of the environment on structure, performance and managerial choice (Dill, 1958; Lawrence and Lorsch, 1967; Child, 1972; Miles and Snow, 1978; Grinyer et al., 1988). The essence of the debate surrounds management's ability to have the ability to make choices about their organization's destiny, or whether the structures that make up the environment constrain management's ability to make decisions that affect the future (Pfeffer and Salanick, 1978; Romanelli and Tushman, 1994). The early literature on environment can be classified into two categories: the first is concerned with providing descriptions of the different types of environment that an organization

may experience; the second with an organization's behaviour in the environment it experiences. Both of these categories will be discussed.

Descriptions or types of environment   The nature of the environment has been studied over the past 40 years in an attempt to understand different contexts, their impact on organizations, and the behaviour of the organization in response to their changing context. The question raised earlier, 'In the organization–environment debate, which is the primary influence over the other?', is central to considering the evolution of our understanding of environment.

A starting-point in the literature for the evolution of the environment is the work of Emery and Trist (1965), who identified four types of environment or 'causal textures'. These are approximations of the environment that may be thought of as existing in the real world of organizations (Fahey and Narayanan, 1986):

1. 'placid and randomised' in which the environment is stable and unchanging;
2. 'placid and clustered' in which the environment is stable but with greater connectedness between organizations and environmental variables;
3. 'disturbed and reactive' in which the environment is changing and organizations engage in an ongoing process of competition; and
4. 'turbulent' where the environment is constantly changing and redefining the basis of organizational success.

In the 1960s when Emery and Trist were writing such descriptions, organizations were experiencing less stable conditions in their environment. Technological-driven change was emerging as a key factor. In addition, the environment was more volatile with the emergence of the Arab–Israeli seven day war; the fluctuation in world oil prices being examples of the surprises that were experienced at that time. The essence of these descriptions was to provide managers with a theoretical explanation of the environment they were experiencing, which at that time was moving from the first causal texture to the fourth causal texture over time.

Ansoff (1965), meanwhile, identified that turbulence is a major feature of the environment, and further provided five distinct categories describing environmental conditions faced by an organization:

1. 'stable' in which the environment is placid and non-turbulent;
2. 'reactive', in which the environment is slow changing and repetitive;
3. 'anticipatory', in which the environment is changing incrementally;
4. 'exploratory', in which the environment is changing infrequently but unexpectedly; and
5. 'creative', in which the environment is highly turbulent.

Ansoff's categories are a subsequent development of Emery and Trist's 'causal textures', where the nature of change in the environment is refined. Turbulence was entering the language of strategic management due to the recognition of ambiguity, complexity and uncertainty in the contextual environment.

Further descriptions of the environment were provided by Duncan (1972), who essentially re-cast Emery and Trist's four causal textures and Ansoff's five environment types into categorizations based on the polar extremes of two dimensions:

1. simple/static, in which the environment undergoes little change; and
2. complex/dynamic, in which the environment is characterized by uncertainty.

All of these descriptions are helpful; however, they could only be known retrospectively, which is likely to be too late for the organization!

Ansoff (1965), in defining the characteristics of turbulence, stated that it was 'determined by a combination of numerous factors including changeability of market environment, speed of change, intensity of competition, fertility of technology, discrimination by customers and pressures from governments and influence groups' (p. 203). The increased recognition of turbulence as a key factor in 'context' is recognized by the impact of technological, market, economic, regulatory and trade changes that have occurred across the world.

Instead of the previous stable environments in which organizations operated, they now find that they are facing hypercompetitive contexts (D'Aveni, 1994), where time and rate of change are major influences on context. Hypercompetition is 'characterized by intense and rapid competitive moves, in which competitors move quickly to build new advantages and erode the advantages of rivals' (ibid., pp. 217–18). Bourgeois and Eisenhardt (1988) developed a similar idea with the idea of high-velocity environments, which are characterized by 'changes in demand, competition, and technology are so rapid and discontinuous that information is often inaccurate, unavailable or obsolete' (Eisenhardt, 1989b, p. 544).

In these circumstances the nature of context is always changing, stable context is illusory, turbulent context is becoming the norm for many organizations and strategizing and reframing the environment are becoming an ongoing challenge for management (Fenton and Pettigrew, 2000).

Organizational behaviour in the environment   After the mid-1970s, the emphasis in the literature moved to understanding the relationship between the organization and the environment (Bourgeois, 1980; Miles and Snow, 1978). The outcome of this examination was the development of definitions of the environment and of the behaviour of firms in their environment(s), which were subdivided at two levels:

1. *the contextual (or general) environment* which is understood in terms of macro factors such as political, economic, societal and technological ones, giving birth to the PEST taxonomy; and
2. *the task (or transactional) environment* which is understood in terms of the actors, such as trade unions, bankers, suppliers and so on who have an interest and power over the organization's choice of strategy.

The contextual environment that organizations operate in is usually understood as the variables arising from *p*olitical, *e*conomic, *s*ocietal, *t*echnological, *l*egal, *e*cological and *d*emographical factors. These factors are universally understood as PEST or PESTLED, and have been critiqued for their generality and lack of clarity about their cross-disciplinary interaction (Burt et al., 2006).

The task environment gave rise to the classification of 'domain definition' (of the contextual environment) and 'domain navigation' (within the task environment) (Bourgeois, 1980) and they focus the debate on the organization's ability to shape the environment through its decisions. Within the task environment there is a well-established theory about the various forces that impact on management's ability to make any such decisions (Porter, 1980).

Miles and Snow (1978) provide a taxonomy that summarizes organizational behaviour that helps provide a set of explanations for behaviour in different contexts. The types of behaviour are prospector, analyser, defender and reactor, with each one fitting the four perspectives on the organization–environment relationship set out earlier: prospector situated in perspective 3; analyser situated in perspective 4; defender situated in perspective 2; and reactor situated in perspective 1.

From these descriptions the environment could be considered as either proactive (opportunistic and uncertain) or as determined (Child, 1972). If proactive or opportunistic, the environment could be seen as a source of information for members of an organization, so that the fast-moving members of the organization could arguably create its environment. However, if the environment were conceived as deterministic, then the environment would be seen as a stock of (scarce) resources, which would lead to organizational dependence (Aldrich and Pfeffer, 1976; Aldrich and Mindlin, 1978; Pfeffer and Salancik, 1978). So what does this imply for our understanding of environment (adaptation and organizational change)?

Implications of evolution of the literature
A number of researchers have questioned what we understand as 'the' environment (Smircich and Stubbart, 1985; Weick, 1995; Mintzberg and Waters, 1985; Scott, 2003; Burt et al., 2006). If we consider environment as 'the' environment, there is recognition that it exists independently of people and that it can be discovered through analysis. Yet, organizations have suffered from 'strategic drift' (Johnson, 1987) where they imperceptibly lose their relevance to the market, as well experience exogenous 'jolts' (Meyer, 1982) where the environment brings about unexpected surprises which reduce management's ability to manage and therefore change the destiny of the organization.

It is posited here that there are two reasons for the continued dichotomy between these perspectives on environment and the organization–environment relationship. The first reason concerns the few opportunities for researchers to gain access to organizations in times of the social interaction that facilitates managerial sensemaking (Gioia and Chittipeddi, 1991). Second, the misalignment between published research and strategy textbooks, with the misalignment between the published research that is moving towards organization-specific understanding of the environment and contemporary strategy textbooks that continue to reflect the classic, general taxonomies discussed above (Burt et al., 2006). Smircich and Stubbart (1985, p. 724) stated: 'environments . . . are enacted through the social construction and interaction processes of organized actors' are, in the main, ignored in the textbooks, thus reinforcing the notion of the environment objective and 'out there'.

As Weick argued:

> [T]here is not some kind of monolithic, singular, fixed environment that exists detached from and external to people. Instead, people are very much a part of their own environments because they act and, in doing so, create the materials that become the constraints and opportunities

they face. There is not some impersonal 'they' who puts these environments in front of passive people. Instead, the 'they' is the people who think and act, creating their own environment. (1995, p. 32)

These debates about our understanding the environment have grown recently from a combination of the dissatisfaction with the universal taxonomies to categorize elements of the environment (Burt et al., 2006); as well as the impact that environment was having on organizations (Mir and Watson, 2000; McKiernan, 2006) resulting in a renaissance of research on context and the organization–environment relationship.

In considering the evolution of the debates about the organization–environment relationship, recognition is given in this chapter to the need to undertake research with organizations that are making sense of their experiences and enacting their environment. The focus of research has moved from understanding the causal textures of environment (Emery and Trist, 1965) to one where researchers are studying processes and activities surrounding sensemaking as managers as they socially construct and negotiate their environment (Berger and Luckmann, 1966; Eden, 1992; McKiernan, 2006).

Impact of ontological and epistemological debates on research design and methodology
It is argued in this chapter that one of the initial considerations facing researchers as they think about researching context is the relationship between the organization and the environment. Researchers need to address both the ontological and epistemological debates that were discussed above, as they consider appropriate research design and interaction with an organization and how it interacts with context and enacts its environment.

In this section, the discussion moves towards research design and research methodology. Given the lack of research on management as they create and enact their environment, the focus here will be on perspective 3. This perspective is identified as it is most closely linked to the current status on the evolution of the organization–environment literature, and there are many opportunities for researchers to develop, and contemporary contributions to, the organization–environment relationship. We shall discuss the stages that researchers are likely to address in helping them design and undertake research that develops a contemporary, constructionist understanding of the organization–environment relationship.

With regard to researching perspective 3, the challenge in the research design will be to ensure that the research process and findings 'can stand up to outside scrutiny and be believed' (Easterby-Smith et al., 1991, p. 40), which raises questions of reliability, validity and generalizability of the findings. Easterby-Smith et al. (p. 41) set out three tests for those interested in researching perspective 3:

1. *Validity* – has the researcher gained full access to the knowledge and meanings of the informants?
2. *Reliability* – will similar observations be made by different researchers on different occasions?
3. *Generalizability* – how likely is it that the ideas and theories that are generated in one setting will also apply in other settings?

For validity, the researcher can gain confidence through field data gathered using multi-method approaches (Miles and Huberman, 1984). A multimethod approach can include pre- and post-sensemaking interviews, observations, critical incidents (Flanaghan, 1954), field notes and memos (Burgess, 1984), and member checks (Stake, 1995) with regular discussions with participants to explore the impact of sensemaking from their perspective. By not imposing a rigid a priori theory on the empirical data, it is possible for the researcher to stay open to emergent ideas that will be captured in the complex set of data gathered during the fieldwork (Glaser and Strauss, 1967; Strauss and Corbin, 1990).

For reliability, the researcher needs to be concerned about triangulation across methods and cases (Miles and Huberman, 1984; Yin, 1994). Triangulation of methods can be based on within-case structuring of empirical evidence, looking for consistencies and contradictions in the empirical evidence. Such triangulation is achieved by researchers searching for patterns that occur in interviews, and that similarly occur in data captured by other methods, for example, observations, and critical incidents, which can be further understood from member checks. Triangulation of cases is intended to help comparison of findings from one case study to another. Are the emergent findings consistent or divergent? Consistent empirical findings suggest that there is growing confidence in the reliability of such findings.

For generalizability, the findings that emerge from the data analysis phase can be developed and strengthened by comparison with the literature. The literature can be either similar or contradictory (Eisenhardt, 1989a). Literature that is similar helps the researcher to tie together emergent findings with a body of established concepts and ideas, thus providing greater internal validity of the concepts and theories. Contradictory literature is important as it helps the researcher to further analyse the findings to develop plausible explanations of such differences.

Researching 'our' environment
This subsection sets out an approach that will address the validity, reliability and generalizability questions more fully as part of an integrated research design. The overall approach to guiding the research design is Eisenhardt's (1986b) eight-step framework for building theory from case study research. Eisenhardt's framework is chosen as it provides a broad range of concerns that need to be considered by a researcher no matter what perspective they may be working with. The eight steps are as follows: (i) getting started; (ii) selecting cases; (iii) crafting instruments; (iv) entering the field; (v) analysing data; (vi) shaping hypotheses; (vii) enfolding literature; and (viii) reaching closure (p. 553).

Each of these steps is now discussed, bringing out issues that researchers need to consider and resolve for their own research design with regard to validity, reliability and generalizability.

Step 1: getting started   On designing the research the first issue to consider is the extent of knowledge in the literature about the focal area to be researched. Is there extensive or little empirical evidence on the focal area? If there is little empirical evidence on the focal area, such as researching sensemaking as it happens, then the researcher is likely to be faced with a number of dilemmas at the outset of the research design.

Dilemma number one – focus on one case study site or multiple case study sites? Dilemma number two – start in-depth case analysis at the conclusion of data gathering in one case study and influence the outcome of the data collection in the other case study sites or analyse cases when the research is concluded? The resolution of these dilemmas will inform the overall research design, with the researcher considering research trade-offs to overcome these dilemmas. Single-site research cases have the advantage of being studied incrementally in-depth as the researcher builds up his/her relationship with the participants over time. However, single-site research cases are potentially more limited in their generalizability. Multiple-site cases have the advantage of cross-case comparison of findings, however, they will require more time in the field, gathering data.

Step 2: selecting cases   The second step in the process concerns the theoretical basis of 'selecting cases' (Eisenhardt, 1989a, p. 536):

> The first decision to be made concerns the population from which the cases will be selected. The concept of population is crucial, as the population defines the set of entities from which the research sample will be drawn. Selection of an appropriate population helps in controlling extraneous variation, as well as helping to define the limits for generalization of the findings. (ibid., p. 537)

Eisenhardt argues:

> [S]tatistical sampling of cases from the chosen population is unusual when theory building from case studies. Such research relies on theoretical sampling, i.e. cases chosen for theoretical, not statistical, reasons (Glaser and Strauss, 1967). The cases may be chosen to replicate previous cases or extend emergent theory, or they may be chosen to fill theoretical categories and provide examples of polar types. (Ibid., p. 537)

As 'n' is likely to be small, it is important to identify cases that are theoretically different from each other, but encompass a broad territory of organizational characteristics to aid the generalization process. This in an attempt first to overcome bias in selection of participating organizations, and second, to support generalization of findings to a wider population. Repertory grid is a method that can be adopted to identify organizational characteristics.

Repertory grid is devised to help elicit the system of *constructs* that a person uses to make sense of a repertoire of *elements* in a situation (Stewart and Stewart, 1982). In this context, repertory grid is used to understand individuals' perceptions in making sense of their organization (Easterby-Smith et al., 1991). A wide range of characteristics should be identified to help the researcher understand the nature and characteristics of the organization. For example: global versus local operations; autocratic leadership versus democratic leadership; people as assets versus people as resources. If multiple cases are being researched it is possible to rank each case against these characteristics.

Step 3: crafting instruments   The third step is concerned with data collection methods and the need for multiple data collection opportunities. Eisenhardt (1989a) argues that 'triangulation is made possible by multiple data collection methods [which] provide stronger substantiation of constructs and hypotheses' (p. 538). So which combination of methods should the researcher consider adopting?

Most likely the researcher will consider observations, interviews, critical incidents and historical documents as some of the data collection methods to be included in the research design. Each of these data methods has its own strengths and limitations, which the researcher should acknowledge and accommodate in the research design. The data collected can be captured as field notes in a research field book (Burgess, 1982). These field notes will be kept in chronological order, with reflective notes being captured about the issues and tensions that are emerging. These emergent issues and tensions can be discussed with the actors to seek out their interpretations and understanding of such phenomena.

Step 4: entering the field   On entering the field the researcher needs to be able to gather data from the research site(s) as well as being able to analyse the data gathered. The detailed field note write-up can be summarized in the form of key concepts. This helps in developing an understanding of the emergent findings. Such an understanding is likely to be achieved as the researcher engages with the structuring of the data.

In addition, none of the field data has been deleted or thrown out as it is unlikely that there will be complete clarity of findings at such an early stage in the fieldwork.

Step 5: analysing data   Eisenhardt (1989a) states: 'analysing data is at the heart of theory building from case studies, but it is the most difficult and least codified part of the process' (p. 539). As Miles and Huberman (1984, p. 16) highlight: 'one cannot ordinarily follow how a researcher got from 3600 pages of field notes to the final conclusions, sprinkled with vivid notes and commentary'. The researcher must ensure that there is a clear and documented audit trail to show the incremental progression of analysis, findings and conclusions.

To undertake the initial analysis and coding of the field data, the researcher is likely to use the themes identified from the literature review, or possibly a research agenda already established by another researcher, which has not been applied in the focal area of the research. Using such identified concepts, the researcher can then re-visit the field data annotating the relevant notes in the field book about the categories identified from the literature. These can then be captured in a database with the relevant explanatory information, and cross-referencing back to the original source.

By undertaking such a process, it is possible to develop a systemic understanding of the impact of the sensemaking from the perspective of the participants. Such an approach will enable the researcher to develop 'thick descriptions' (Geertz, 1973; Denzin, 1978) of the participants' (actors') interpretative procedures. Such empirical data is concerned with the 'intentions, motives, meanings, contexts, situations, and circumstances of action' (Denzin, 1978, p. 39) rather than a purely descriptive set of research notes.

There is one further issue to address in the data analysis stage, which is discussed in the next step.

Step 6: shaping a hypothesis   On completion of the data analysis and coding phase, the next step is a systematic and detailed search for patterns in the structured data. This phase involves conceptualizing and categorizing concepts in the data and their emergent (causal) relationship. Such an approach is likely to initially be on a trial and error basis, with multiple iterations of conceptualizations out of which patterns emerge from the data. The researcher will develop further databases about the key findings, recording the nature of the iterative understanding that is emerging from the process.

From these patterns the researcher is able to develop and shape a hypothesis about the patterns. The hypothesis would then be the basis of further analysis of the data, searching for issues relevant to the hypothesis, to refine existing or develop further hypotheses, as well as prove or disprove any hypothesis. Such a process is an important phase of the research in developing a holistic understanding of the emergent theorizing that is occurring.

Step 7: enfolding literature   Once a clear pattern of concepts emerges from the data analysis, together with an understanding of the causal relationships linking the concepts, the researcher is able to focus on the significance of the findings. At this stage it is likely that there will be more questions and answers in the theorizing process.

The researcher will undertake a review of the literature about the concepts emerging from the data analysis. The researcher will be exploring both literature adjacent to the original focus of the research as well literature in a domain that is unlikely to be related to the original focus of the research in an attempt to develop a broader understanding of the emergent findings.

By reading widely about the emergent findings, the researcher is able to anchor the emergent theorizing in established theory, even if that established theory is in a domain outside of the focal area of the research. Such an outcome helps the researcher with the generalizability of the findings.

Step 8: reaching closure   As the researcher continues to interact with the structured data, reading of the literature and building up of theoretical explanations of the findings, there comes a point when there is no further incremental advantage to be gained from further iterations of analysis–literature–theorizing. Once the theoretical concepts are stabilized in the literature, with the findings supported by the literature, and the causal linkages and explanations have been completed, the researcher is able to finalize the contribution to knowledge.

Finalization of the contribution to knowledge can take a number of forms. First, the emergent theory could set out a model with an explanation of the causal relationships and interaction between the theoretical constructs that have emerged from the research. Second, the emergent theory could be a new explanation of an existing theory interpreted in a different context. Third, the emergent theory could be a new theoretical explanation about a phenomenon that is not well understood or explained.

Discussion and conclusion

The purpose of this chapter was to explore the philosophical and epistemological arguments surrounding the organization–environment relationship. The initial question posed was: what is the environment, and would we recognize it if we saw it? Is 'the' environment objective or subjective? What alternative ways are possible to conceptualize and understand 'environment', and what are the implications of the alternative conceptualization of 'the' environment for researchers and research design?

The discussion that has evolved in this chapter is based on the conceptualization of four perspectives of environment, which were developed from the epistemological and ontological discussion on the nature of reality and management's ability to have (strategic) choice on their decisions. The conceptualization of the four perspectives is intended to help researchers as they strive to understand the circumstances of their research.

Within the wider strategic management literature there is a linked debate about the nature of strategy and strategy development, with tensions between the planning and emergent schools (Mintzberg, 1990; Ansoff, 1991). The debate is summarized by Weick (1979) when he stated:

[O]rganisations persistently spend time formulating strategy, an activity that literally makes little sense given the debates about selection, retention and enactment. Organisations formulate strategy after they implement it, not before. Having implemented something – anything – people can then look back over it and conclude that what they implemented is strategy. (p 188)

Although Weick's comments were made some time ago, they provide a summary of the challenges and opportunities open to researchers interested in studying the organization–environment relationship.

The four perspectives provide a framework to help researchers consider critically the nature of the environment and then to position and design their research based on the nature of the environment. Each perspective has a different set of assumptions about environment, which in turn have different implications for research design. Some of the perspectives have a well-founded research tradition, yet there is limited understanding on others, especially perspective 3. Perspective 3 offers opportunities to engage and study proactive, rather than retrospective, managerial sensemaking and consensus building with a management team as they move from equivocality to unequivocality among themselves.

A clear agenda begins to emerge for researchers interested in studying 'context' from perspective 3. First, if environment is increasingly recognized as an outcome of managerial thinking rather than an input to managerial thinking, then how do managers recognize the past? How do managers reconcile their understanding of the past to the present? What set of linked actions do managers take to enact their future? Second, what do we mean by 'stable environment' and 'turbulence' in the environment? Are these terms redundant? Processes of organization–environment change have been conceptualized as 'punctuated equilibrium' (Romanelli and Tushman, 1994); is such a description still relevant if context is socially constructed, with the organization–environment relationship changing continuously? How do managers learn to change their organization continuously? Third, research on the organization–environment relationship requires the researcher to undertake micro-activity research, focusing on dialogue and significant events. How do managers frame and reframe their organization, which links constancy with change? This chapter sets out methods to engage with such managerial micro activity.

While there are many well-established characterizations and definitions about 'the' environment in the literature, these classifications and definitions are retrospective and therefore are too late to be of benefit to managerial practice. Greater theoretical explanation, as well as codified guidance, is required to develop the contemporary organization–environment relationship.

The chapter has set an agenda for research on context and its impact on organizations. While the wider strategic management literature recognizes the role of context on organizations, context research has lost ground to other areas of interest. The arguments put forward here are designed to encourage researchers interested in the organization–environment relationship to regain momentum.

References

Aldrich, H.E. and Mindlin, S. (1978), 'Uncertainty and dependence: two perspectives on environment', in L. Kerpit (ed.), *Organisation and Environment*, Beverly Hills, CA: Sage, pp. 149–70.

Aldrich, H.E. and Pfeffer, J. (1976), 'Environments of organisations', in A. Inkeles, J. Coleman and N. Smelser (eds), *Annual Review of Sociology*, Vol. 2, Palo Alto, CA: Annual Reviews, pp. 79–105.

Ansoff, I. (1965), *Corporate Strategy*, London: Penguin Books (revised edn 1987).

Ansoff, I. (1991), 'Critique of Henry Mintzberg's "The design school: reconsidering the basic premises of strategic management"', *Strategic Management Journal*, **12** (6), 449–61.

Berger, P.L. and Luckmann, T. (1966), *The Social Construction of Reality: A Treatise in the Sociology of Knowledge*, New York: Anchor Books–Doubleday.

Bohm, D. (1996), *On Dialogue*, London: Routledge.

Boisot, M. and Child, J. (1999), 'Organisations as adaptive systems in complex environments: the case of China', *Organization Science*, **10** (3), 237–52.

Bourgeois, L.J. (1980), 'Strategy and environment: a conceptual integration', *Academy of Management Review*, **5** (1), 25–39.

Bourgeois, L.J. and Eisenhardt, K.M. (1988), 'Strategic decision processes in high velocity environments: four cases in the microcomputer industry', *Management Science*, **34**, 816–35.

Boyd, B.K., Dess, G.G. and Rasheed, A.M.A. (1993), 'Divergence between archival and perceptual measures of the environment: causes and consequences', *Academy of Management Review*, **18** (2), 204–28.

Brown, J.S. and Duguid, P. (2001), 'Knowledge and organization: a social practice perspective', *Organization Science*, **12** (2), 198–213.

Brown, S.L. and Eisenhardt, K.M. (1998), *Competing on the Edge, Strategy as Structured Chaos*, New York: Free Press.

Burgess, R.G. (1982), *Field Research: A Sourcebook and a Field Manual*, London: Routledge.

Burgess, R.G. (1984), *In the Field: An Introduction to field Research*, London: Routledge.

Burrell, G. and Morgan, G. (1979), *Sociological Paradigms and Organizational Analysis*, London: Heinemann.

Burt, G. (2003), 'Epigenetic change: new from the seeds of the old', *Journal of Strategic Change*, **12**, 381–93.

Burt, G., Wright, G., Bradfield, R., Cairns, G. and van der Heijden, K. (2006), 'The role of scenario planning in exploring the environment in view of the limitations of PEST and its derivatives', *International Studies of Management and Organisations*, **36** (3), Fall, 50–76.

Cairns, G., Wright, G., Bradfield, R., van der Heijden, K. and Burt, G. (2004), 'Exploring e-government futures through the application of scenario planning', *Technological Forecasting and Social Change*, **71** (3), 217–38.

Child, J. (1972), 'Organisation, structure, environment and performance: the role of strategic choice', *Sociology*, **6**, 1–22.

Christensen, C.M. (1997), *The Innovator's Dilemma*, Cambridge, MA: Harvard Business School Press.

Cromby, J. and Nightingale, D.J. (1999), 'What's wrong with social constructionism?', in Nightingale and Cromby (eds), *Social Constructionist Psychology: A Critical Analysis of Theory and Practice*, Buckingham: Open University Press, pp. 1–19.

Cyert, R.M. and March, J.G. (1963), *A Behavioral Theory of the Firm*, Englewood Cliffs, NJ: Prentice-Hall.

D'Aveni, R.A. (1994), *Hypercompetition: Managing the Dynamics of Strategic Manoeuvring*, New York: Free Press.

Daft, R.L. and Weick, K. (1984), 'Toward a model of organisations as interpretation systems', *Academy of Management Review*, **9** (2), 284–95.

Denzin, N.K. (1978), *The Research Act*, 2nd edn, New York: McGraw-Hill.

Denzin, N.K. (1997), *Interpretive Ethnography: Ethnographic Practices for the 21st Century*, Thousand Oaks, CA: Sage.

Dill, W. (1958), 'Environment as an influence on managerial autonomy', *Administrative. Science Quarterly*, **2** (4), 409–43.

Dilley, K.M. (1999), *The Problem of Context: Perspectives from Social Anthropology and Elsewhere*, Oxford: Berghahn Books.

Duncan, R.B. (1972), 'Characteristics of organisational environments and perceived environmental uncertainty', *Administrative Science Quarterly*, **17**, 313–27.

Easterby-Smith, M., Thorpe, R. and Lowe, A. (1991), *Management Research: An Introduction*, London, Sage.

Eden, C. (1992), 'Strategic management as a social process', *Journal of Management Studies*, **29**, 799–811.

Eden, C., Jones, S., Sims, D. and Smithin, T. (1981), 'The intersubjectivity of issues and issues of intersubjectivity', *Journal of Management Studies*, **18**, 37–47.

Eisenhardt, K.M. (1989a), 'Building theories from case study research', *Academy of Management Review*, **14** (4), 532–50.

Eisenhardt, K.M. (1989b), 'Making fast strategic decisions in high velocity environments', *Academy of Management Journal*, **32** (3), 543–76.

Emery, F.E. (1977), *Futures We Are In*, Leiden: Martinus Nijhoff.

Emery, F.E. and Trist, E.L. (1965), 'The causal texture of organisational environments', *Human Relations*, **18**, 21–32.

Fahey, L. and Narayanan, V.K. (1986), *Macroenvironmental Analysis for Strategic Management*, St Paul, MN: West Publishing.

Fenton, E.M. and Pettigrew, A.M. (2000), 'Theoretical perspectives on new forms of organizing', in Pettigrew and Fenton (eds), *The Innovating Organization*, London: Sage, pp. 1–46.

Flanaghan, J.C. (1954), 'The critical incident technique', *Psychological Bulletin*, **51**, 327–58.

Ford, J.D. (1999), 'Organizational change as shifting conversations', *Journal of Organizational Change Management*, **12** (6), 480–95.

Frishammar, J. (2006), 'Organizational environment revisited: a conceptual review and integration', *International Studies of Management and Organisations*, **36** (3), Fall, 22–49.

Galer, G. and van der Heijden, K. (1992), 'The learning organisation: how planners create organizational learning', *Marketing Intelligence and Planning*, **10** (6), 5–12.

Geertz, C. (1973), *The Interpretation of Cultures: Selected Essays*, New York: Basic Books.

Gioia, D.A. and Chittipeddi, K. (1991), 'Sensemaking and sensegiving in stratgeic change initiation', *Strategic Management Journal*, **12** (6), 443–8.

Glaser, B.G. and Strauss, A. (1967), *Discovery of Grounded Theory: Strategies for Qualitative Research*, Chicago, IL: Aldine.

Grinyer, P.H., Mayes, D. and McKiernan, P. (1988), *Sharpbenders: The Secrets of Unleashing Corporate Potential*, Oxford: Basil Blackwell.

Guba, E. and Lincoln, Y. (1985), *Naturalist Inquiry*, London: Sage.

Harre, R. (1980), *Social Being: A Theory for Social Psychology*, Totowa, NJ: Littlefield Adams & Co.

Harvey, J.B. (1974), 'The Abilene paradox and other meditations on management', *Organizational Dynamics*, **3** (1), 17–34.

Hatch, M.J. (1997), *Organization Theory*, New York: Oxford University Press.

Huff, J.O., Huff, A.S. and Thomas, H. (1992), 'Strategic renewal and the interaction of cumulative stress and inertia', *Strategic Management Journal*, **13**, 55–75.

Johnson, G. (1987), *Strategic Change and the Management Process*, New York: Basil Blackwell.

Lawrence, P.R. and Lorsch, J.W. (1967), *Organisation and Environment*, Homewood, IL: Irwin.

MacKay, R., Masrani, S. and McKiernan, P. (2006), 'Strategy options and cognitive freezing: the case of the Dundee jute industry in Scotland', *Futures*, **38** (8), 925–41.

March, J.G. (1991), 'Exploration and exploitation in organizational learning', *Organization Science*, **2** (1), 71–87.

McKiernan, P. (2006), 'Understanding environmental context in strategic management', *International Studies of Management and Organisations*, **36** (2), Fall, 7–21.

Meyer, A.D. (1982), 'Adapting to environmental jolts', *Administrative Science Quarterly*, **27**, 515–37.

Miles, M.B. and Huberman, A.M. (1984), *Qualitative Data Analysis*, Thousand Oaks, CA: Sage.

Miles, R.E. and Snow, C.C. (1978), *Organizational Strategy: Structure and Processes*, New York: McGraw Hill.

Miller, D. (1990), *The Icarus Paradox*, New York: Harper Business.

Miller, D. and Friesen, P.H. (1980), 'Momentum and revolution in organizational adaptation', *Academy of Management Journal*, **23**, 561–614.

Mintzberg, H. (1990), 'The design school: reconsidering the basic premises of strategic management', *Strategic Management Journal*, **11** (3), 171–95.

Mintzberg, H. and Waters, J.A. (1995), 'Of strategies, deliberate and emergent', *Strategic Management Journal*, **6** (3), 257–72.

Mir, R. and Watson, A. (2000), 'Strategic management and the philosophy of science: the case for a constructionist methodology', *Strategic Management Journal*, **21** (9), 941–53.

Pettigrew, A.M. (1985), *The Awakening Giant*, Oxford: Blackwell.

Pettigrew, A.M. (1990), 'Longitudinal field research on change, theory and practice', *Organization Science*, **1** (3), 267–92.

Pfeffer, J. and Salancik, G.R. (1978), *The External Control of Organisation: A Resource Dependency Perspective*, New York: Harper & Row.

Porter, M.E. (1980), *Competitive Strategy: Techniques for Analyzing Industries and Competitors*, New York: Free Press.

Porter, M.E. (1985), *Competitive Advantage: Creating and Sustaining Superior Performance*, New York: Free Press.

Quinn, J.B. (1978), 'Strategic change: logical incrementalism', *Sloan Management Review*, **20** (Fall), 7–21.

Romanelli, E. and Tushman, M.L. (1994), 'Organisational transformation as punctuated equilibrium: an empirical test', *Academy of Management Journal*, **37** (5), 1141–66.

Scott, W.R. (2003), *Organisations, Rational, Natural, and Open Systems*, 5th edn. Englewood Cliffs, NJ: Prentice-Hall.

Senge, P. (1990), *The Fifth Discipline*, London: Century Business.

Smircich, L. and Stubbart C. (1985), 'Strategic management in an enacted world', *Academy of Management Review*, **10** (4), 724–36.

Stake, R.E. (1995), *The Art of Case Study Research*, London: Sage.
Stewart, V. and Stewart, A. (1982), *Business Applications of Repertory Grid*, London: McGraw-Hill.
Strauss, A. and Corbin, J. (1990), *Basics of Qualitative Research: Grounded Theory Procedures and Techniques*, Newbury Park, CA: Sage.
van der Heijden, K. (1996), *Scenarios, The Art of Strategic Conversation*, Chichester: John Wiley & Sons.
Wall, S.J. and Wall, S.R. (1995), 'The evolution (not the death) of strategy', *Organization Dynamics*, Autumn, 7–19.
Watzlawick, P. (1976), *How Real is Real?*, New York: Random House.
Weick, K.E. (1979), *The Social Psychology of Organising*, Reading, MA: Addison-Wesley.
Weick, K.E. (1995), *Sensemaking in Organizations*, London: Sage.
Yin, R.K. (1994), *Case Study Research: Design and Methods*, Beverly Hills, CA: Sage.

PART II

FORESIGHT AND ORGANIZATIONAL BECOMING: STRATEGY PROCESS, PRACTICE AND CHANGE

9 Strategizing as practising: strategic learning as a source of connection

*Elena P. Antonacopoulou**

Introduction

In recent years, we have witnessed a turn in strategy research towards a greater emphasis on the processual nature of the phenomenon (Pettigrew, 1992; Langley, 1999; Khanna et al. 2000). The concern with capturing the dynamic nature of strategy formulation and implementation has prompted a greater attention towards the micro foundations of strategizing with a particular focus on the social and situated nature of the phenomenon (Chakravarthy and Doz, 1992; Hendry, 2000; Levy and Alvesson, 2003). This is best reflected in the upsurge of 'strategy-as-practice' as a new perspective for thinking about and researching strategic issues. This new perspective focuses on micro processes such as strategic activities, episodes and other forms of strategic routines (Johnson et al., 2003; Jarzabkowski, 2005). A practice focus is also consistent with (and extends) recent contributions which have stressed that routines (intended as repeated application of a specific practice) can be a source of change and adaptation (Feldman, 2000; Feldman and Pentland, 2003). All these developments have also significantly affected the language we use to describe the strategy process and it is now more common to refer to 'strategizing' (Whittington, 2003) as a way of illustrating the dynamic nature of the process and practice of performing strategy.

These trends can also be seen in the context of a wider effort in strategy research to pay more attention to the subtle and often invisible resources that can account for the competitive advantage of organizations (Barney, 1991). Among such resources, knowledge and learning are emerging as key contributors to competitive advantage and those promoting a 'knowledge-based view' of the firm (Kogut and Zander, 1992; Grant, 1996) have drawn attention to the role of learning and knowledge in capability development and absorptive capacity (Zahra and George, 2002; Zollo and Winter, 2002). Several contributions (Burgelman, 1988; Szulanksi and Amin, 2001) have already recognized the role of learning as a central feature of the strategy process and have posed critical questions about the ways in which managers become strategists and learn to strategize (Liedtke, 1998; Whittington, 2001).

It is in the context of these debates in strategy research that the idea of strategic learning (Sanchez and Heene, 1997; Kuwada, 1998; Pietersen, 2003) is also beginning to receive attention. Current perspectives on strategic learning focus mainly on the process of strategic capability acquisition and modification as a means of designing effective organizational strategic behaviours. Moreover, definitions of strategic learning tend to adopt a limited view of learning, embracing predominantly a cognitivistic perspective, thus neglecting recent developments in organizational learning research which seek to more fully engage with the social complexity of learning (see Antonacopoulou, 2006a).

There is therefore, a need to enhance our understanding of the nature of strategic learning both in the context of its strategic role in supporting organizational renewal and competitiveness, as well as in relation to other micro processes which define learning as a practice within organizations. This chapter responds directly to this need and examines the relationship between learning and strategizing practice.

The analysis in this chapter will argue that strategic learning can be conceptualized as a 'strategizing practice' where tensions between strategic and operational issues across different levels and perspectives in the organization are exposed such that they can be reconnected in ways that their interdependencies can be strengthened. For the purposes of this analysis strategic learning is defined as a cause, consequence and context of strategizing practice because *practising* is one of the central elements. By focusing on practising we extend our understanding of practice as a mode of institutionalization of activities and routines. Instead, when reference is made to 'practice' and 'practising' the focus is on the holistic and emergent nature of the social interactions, actions and activities and the social context in which these are performed (ibid.).

This new conceptualization of strategic learning highlights that the focus of attention is neither only the practice (as a set of action rules) nor only the routine of learning as a deliberate, conscious and systematic process. Learning is also a dynamic flow as part of the ongoing socio-political connections embedded in practising attempts as part of the various processes, practices and routines that constitute strategizing (Antonacopoulou and Chiva, 2007). This perspective provides better scope for more fully capturing the strategic role of learning in strategizing practice.

The chapter organizes the ideas on these issues in three main sections. First, we begin with an overview of the relationship between learning and strategizing from a practice perspective. Second, we elaborate on the idea of strategizing as practising and explore in particular the generative dance between strategic intentions and operational realities. This perspective provides better scope for combining multiple units and levels of analysis (from macro to micro) in exploring the interconnectivity of endogenous and exogenous forces affecting strategizing practice. Third, we examine strategic learning as a source of connection between the micro and macro aspects of strategizing practice. The analysis builds on the conceptualization of strategic learning as a context of strategizing practice and also positions strategic learning as a strategizing practice itself. The chapter concludes with some suggestions for future research in strategic learning and research concerned with the micro foundations of organizing more generally.

The relationship between strategizing and learning: a practice perspective
The strategic management and organizational learning literatures seem to be developing in parallel a practice-based view of strategizing and learning, yet the two communities do not seem to interact sufficiently so that they can inform each other's research. This focus on practice parallels what Schatzki et al. (2001) discuss as the practice turn in contemporary theory, a point which has been supported much earlier by De Certeau (1984), Bourdieu (1990) and Turner (1994).

In the strategy literature, the resulting vibrant practice-based thinking (Hendry, 2000; Johnson et al., 2003; Whittington, 2006) places the emphasis on the micro dynamics embedded in human action and interaction. Therefore, attention is given to activities of all kinds in the pursuit of what strategists actually do.

An equally vibrant debate is taking place in the organizational learning field (Wenger,

1998; Brown and Duguid, 2000; Gherardi, 2000, 2006; Nicolini et al., 2003) where learning as practice embraces not only actions and activities in relation to learning, but also the role of language and other cultural and material artefacts, the nature of social interactions and not least the tacit, situated and almost instinctive responses of actors in the socially networked worlds in which they live. This perspective also emphasizes the importance of communities of practitioners as the space where the social dynamics of learning are negotiated, thus reinforcing principles of interconnectedness and interdependence between agency and structure. This is a point which is central both in structuration theory (Giddens, 1984) and in actor network theory (Law, 1999).

Efforts to integrate these streams of research and to provide a more holistic understanding of the nature of practice have resulted in new conceptualizations of practice, which emphasize the fractal and holistic nature of the phenomenon as a continuous flow of multiple adjoining and interlocking practices that form the heart of their evolution (Antonacopoulou, 2007, 2008a). This view of practice focuses on the ongoing emergence and co-evolution of practice as different aspects of practice interact. The existing literature provides a number of different aspects of practice by virtue of how practice is defined. Some of the most common interpretations are: practice as *action* (Bourdieu, 1990); practice as *structure* – language, symbols, tools (Turner, 1994); practice as *activity system* (Engeström et al., 1999); practice as *social context* (Lave and Wenger, 1991); practice as *knowing* (Nicolini et al., 2003).

These multiple interpretations of practice reveal the coexistence of a plurality of interlocking practices which co-evolve in dynamic interaction with one another. Therefore, the everyday execution of practice becomes the context of tensions among different practices and the groups that embody them. This tension is no better evident than in the dualisms that we often create to distinguish strategic intent from operational reality when in essence both coexist as part of a continuum of ongoing strategizing attempts. However, tensions capture both the socio-political forces as well as the 'elasticity' and fluidity of organizing, as different processes and practices connect to provide new possibilities (Antonacopoulou, 2008b). This view opens the possibility that practices behave fractally and the tensions between them provide the basis of 'ex-tension' of a practice.

Therefore, if we understand practice as a self-organizing process connecting multiple routines and actions, then the definitions of practice need to become more elastic as well. This also suggests that our focus needs to shift from institutional representations of practices as the end result of a practice, to the flow that underpins the way practices unfold and are constantly reconfigured. By focusing on the emergence of *the practise of practice* it is possible to map the social network of connections in the way practices are orchestrated, through practising attempts (Antonacopoulou, 2008a).

Therefore, practice conceptualized as a dynamic social process that emerges over time and across space entails at its core practising attempts, which seek to accommodate endogenous and exogenous forces, brought about by ecological, economic, social and political dynamics. This dynamic view of practice is useful in reconceptualizing 'strategy-as-practice' (Jarzabkowski, 2005) and 'learning-as-practice' (Nicolini et al., 2003) and exploring the relationship between learning and strategizing as a continuous flow of *practising*. Placed in the context of the current view of strategizing, greater attention to the practising attempts of strategic intention in relation to operational reality provides scope for understanding the role of learning, given the upsurge of dynamic capability development which assumes that learning can be deliberate. This is discussed further in the next section.

Strategizing as practising
A hot topic in current strategic management debates is the issue of capability development. The emphasis on capability results from recent developments in theorizing how organizations achieve sustainable competitive advantage over the medium to long term. In particular, the dynamic capability (Teece et al., 1997) and strategic learning (Kuwada, 1998) approaches, both drawing sustenance from the resource-based view of the firm, present the impression that organizational success is intimately linked to the capabilities developed and deployed.

The dynamic capabilities concept is developed on the assumption that 'competences can provide competitive advantage and generate rents only if they are based on a collection of routines, skills, and complementary assets that are difficult to imitate' (Teece et al., 1997: 524), and are hence, distinctive. Recent developments (Eisenhardt and Martin, 2000; Zollo and Winter, 2002) suggest that although idiosyncratic to a firm, dynamic capabilities may exhibit commonalities across firms, allowing 'best-practice' recommendations to be developed and dynamic capability to be learned. This argument has subsequently been developed by Zollo and Winter (2002) through the notion of deliberate learning where organizations strategically decide to intervene in operational routines and associated capability development. To demonstrate their argument, Zollo and Winter present experience accumulation, knowledge articulation and knowledge codification as key learning mechanisms. These three mechanisms are described as having direct effects on the evolution of operating routines and an indirect effect via the creation of dynamic capabilities. How these mechanisms are operationalized is not discussed by Zollo and Winter.

Reflecting on the current attempts to capture learning processes that can support strategic action, both dynamic capabilities and strategic learning view capability development through a functionalist lens where both capability and competence are assumed to be easily achieved (Alvesson, 2004). Through such functionalist positioning, it could be argued that organizations are presented as attempting to secure/impose a hegemonic bloc, a historically specific alignment of economic, political and ideological forces that coordinates major social groups into a dominant alliance (Levy and Alvesson, 2003: 101). Following Levy and Alvesson it could be argued that attempts to secure a relatively stable hegemonic bloc may require material payoffs, political compromises, and the projection of moral and intellectual leadership. However, this line of inquiry is conspicuous by its absence.

This analysis highlights one of the most important limitations of our conceptualization of macro-level perspectives. We tend to refer to macro-level perspectives predominantly with a focus on path dependency and rent appropriation (Blyler and Coff, 2003). In doing so, we limit the possibilities for enhancing absorptive capacity through learning from both exogenous and endogenous sources through existing internal processes of sharing information as well as the existing capability and experience (Van den Bosch et al., 2003). Zahra and George (2002) recognize exogenous and endogenous learning as antecedents to absorptive capacity. While they do recognize the temporal aspects of capability development and point to the need for research which examines the role of managers in the development of absorptive capacity and the potential of the organization to absorb learning from internal and external sources, they do not fully account for the socio-political dynamics of knowledge. Based on recent empirical evidence in three organizations, Easterby-Smith et al. (2008) show that politics influence the ability of a firm to learn from external sources, which also depends on the extent to which the new knowledge is seen as complementary to the existing knowledge of the firm. Similarly, internal learning takes place through experience over time where the ability to absorb new ideas depends on the memory of the successes and failures of past experiments and innovations.

Consequently this chapter argues that our current conceptualizations of both dynamic capability and strategic learning pay scant regard to the situatedness of learning to develop capability. Situatedness not only sensitizes us to the particularities of context that shape praxis, practitioners and their practices (Wenger, 1998; Brown and Duguid, 2000), but it also highlights that socio-political forces are central to participative learning (Coopey, 1995; Antonacopoulou, 2001). Equally situated is the practice of strategizing. The interaction between strategic intent and the actual operationalization of strategy is a key feature of the *dynamic* underpinning capability development. In performing a practice or in developing capability we cannot casually assume that all participants in a practice will share the same objectives, nor can we assume that they have the same level of knowledge and expertise. Equally we cannot assume that they will have the same level of position or by implication power to own the practice and its transformation. This, however, does not mean that they will also lack the power to learn.

As Antonacopoulou (1998, 2000, 2006b) showed through longitudinal studies of managerial learning practices in the banking sector in the UK, managers performing their learning practices frequently adopt an institutional identity in learning, presenting themselves as powerless (helpless) when their very attitudes to learning determine what they learn and whether they learn what they say they learned. The political nature of learning, therefore, lies in the power of learning to commit one to responsible action by working towards overcoming defensive routines rather than treating them as undiscussable (Argyris, 2004). This point also reflects the power of learning to steer a whole host of emotions and to participate in practices through different degrees of engagement.

Practices therefore, manifest as much actions and activities as they also illustrate behaviours, states of emotion and desire to act based on one's knowing. All these issues form part of the experience and know-how one brings as resources in the process of performing one's practice on an ongoing basis. Thus, knowledge and learning are critical to practice as they create the capacity to connect previous and current experiences in perfecting one's practice. By tapping into both micro activities and the wider context on a macro level in which such activities are performed, we can better appreciate the flow that is so central to organizing attempts, such as strategizing practice.

This brings us to the long-debated relationship between 'practice' and 'field' that has been at the core of Bourdieu's work on practice. In a recent review, Warde (2004: 13) provides an interesting account of the orientation and distinction between 'practice' and 'field'. He points out specifically that fields by their nature are competitive, strategic and oriented towards external goods. The characteristics of practices, on the other hand, are their pluralism, cooperative nature and orientation towards internal goods. In a similar tone, Reckwitz (2002: 249) distinguishes practice from practices ('*praktik*') where practice refers to praxis – the whole of human action – while practices are routine behaviours which consist of several interconnected elements including bodily and mental activities, artefacts, background knowledge, states of emotion and know-how. Schatski (1996: 89–98) offers yet another distinction between 'dispersed practices' and 'integrative practices'. The former focus on general aspects of social life that require understanding, while the latter focus on more complex practices constitutive of particular domains of social life. More recently, Whittington (2001, 2003) drawing on Turner (1994: 8) provides further distinctions between praxis, practice, practices and practitioners. Practice refers to activities in relation to the goal-seeking drives of the actors who engage in such activities, whereas practices are the norms governing behaviour and social conduct. Finally, praxis refers to actual events while a practitioner is the performer of a practice.

All these distinctions seek to position practice both on a micro and a macro level. In other words, practice operates both in relation to endogenous (what McIntyre 1985: 195 calls 'internal goods') and exogenous forces (what he refers to as 'external goods'). These forces are in positive tension, because they provide different dimensions that feed a practice in the way it is represented when performed. This would suggest that the same practice has always the potential to be both performed and represented in diverse ways depending on the way different internal and external goods of a practice are connected. Extending the fractal view of practice discussed earlier, different internal and external goods of a practice operate as actants which may be attracted to different actants, thus creating multiple possibilities in the way a practice emerges. These ideas draw from a complexity science perspective which has hitherto proven useful in engaging with the coexistence of seemingly oppositional forces such as order and chaos (see Stacey, 1995; Antonacopoulou and Chiva, 2007).

In the context of our analysis, such a perspective provides us with an avenue for exploring the diversity of practice in relation to the multiple and competing forces that it entails. At the same time, this perspective could help us to explore the interconnectivity of practices by focusing on the elasticity they create when they interlock thus, stretching a practice to different dimensions through the possibilities such interlockings create. Therefore, when we seek to understand the micro and macro aspects of a practice we need to be mindful of the dynamics that the connections between them create that both define the practice and the way it is engaged with in action and interaction with others.

An example illustrating these ideas would be the experience of an opera singer performing an aria. What one finds is that the same aria is performed differently, by the same opera singer at different times, subject to the way the very practice of singing is refined. Performing a practice, however, is not only a matter of competence and the practising entailed in perfecting one's art. It is also a matter of the moment in which the practice is represented. Practising one's practice, as already pointed out in the earlier section, is central to refining the intricate qualities of a practice. However, despite the dictum 'practice makes perfect', it is also important to acknowledge that practice is always subject to imperfections at the critical moment of its representation in action. This alerts us to the fact that no performance of a practice is ever guaranteed to lead to the desired outcome. There are always a whole host of forces that have a bearing on the way a practice is embodied and enacted.

For example, an opera singer may be practising her vocal techniques and may be in full command of the intricacies of the specific piece of music she will be delivering during her performance. In delivering an aria she would be both using her knowledge and skills as much as she would be relying on her internal goods – mentally, emotionally, physically – in giving this particular aria her own special touch. She may have other things on her mind, she may have a bad throat, she may be tired or be in a bad mood. All these factors could influence the outcome of her delivery. The success of the performance would also be largely affected by her interaction with the audience. As is commonly known, the success of a performance is in the applause! The external goods of her practice are not only the audience but also the conductor and the orchestra who are in constant coordination with her, her colleagues on or off stage, the journalists and music critics that will be assessing and reporting on her performance drawing on their own experience and views of the performance and the established standards and rules that would distinguish a good from a bad performance.

This example seeks to demonstrate that the internal goods of a practice such as emotions would be in constant interaction with external goods such as the mood of the audience in defining how a practice is delivered and received. This places the performer and the audience in a mutual context of co-creation.

Therefore, the tensions between micro and macro forces in practices are critical in the way a practice is formed and the way it unfolds over time and across multiple contexts. These tensions, therefore, can extend the elasticity of a practice to bend, adapt and at the same time be transformed in the way endogenous and exogenous dynamics interact to define and redefine the practice. In other words, tensions become the basis for *ex-tensions* of current reality. These ongoing permutations of practice remind us that no practice is ever the same. The same performer can perform the same practice very differently at different times and across space. Moreover, different performers in the same context can perform the same practice very differently. These variations in practice and its delivery may be explained by the *learning dynamics* embedded in practice. Learning is not only an activity; it is also a flow, a flexible, ever-changing process that connects actors, systems and artefacts. This view of learning in relation to practising could prove useful in helping us appreciate further the heterogeneity of practice when enacted. Practising attempts are not only reflective of the fluidity of a practice as we discussed in the previous section. They may also account for the flow of learning that underpins practising attempts. Therefore, if we are to fully tap into the emerging, fluid nature of practices we need to focus on the way practices are practised.

Placed in the context of strategizing practice we need to find ways of examining the interactions between strategic intent and operational realities to identify the process of strategy re-formulation in the process of strategy implementation. As Whittington (2001) points out with reference to his notion of 'learning to strategize', from a practice perspective, it provides greater scope for asserting the interdependence of the micro- and macro-level strategizing. While micro strategizing on the one hand, points to activities of actions within organizations, macro strategizing on the other, points to wider practices and strategies. Connecting micro and micro levels would aim to embrace social space and its transformations in its full complexity. This point suggests that instead of punctuating strategy into phases to more fully engage with the complexity of strategizing, we need to be mindful of not only strategizing practice but also the practising of strategizing.

This very process of trying things out could help us encounter more closely the social and political tensions when competing forces may stand in the way of translating intent into reality. At the same time, such an analysis would also help us come closer to the multiplicity of alternatives that form part of strategizing as it is enacted. Alternative courses of action are explored in community and the practising attempts by actors performing such a practice derive meaning in the course of action and interaction. This point also has the potential to better place strategy as an integral part of working life, therefore, strategizing can be afforded as a practice that is performed in multiple contexts and by multiple players, not only top managers.

With that view in mind, we can focus more on the practising of strategizing which would enable us to tap into the ways in which actors learn to perform strategizing as a process and a practice. By focusing on the learning practices of strategic actors, we can also come closer to the way connections are made between micro and macro aspects of strategizing practice. This too would be a critical foundation for better capturing the nature of strategic learning and the strategic role that learning can play in organizations. This point is discussed in the next section of the chapter.

Strategic learning as connecting
In the previous section we focused on the strategic role of learning in its capacity to support capability development not as a deliberate process but as an integral aspect of the way a practice is performed. By facilitating the learning across levels and perspectives, through practising attempts, the strategic role of learning becomes critical in providing the seamless flow of action that practices tend to reflect. By revealing the underlying tensions within and across practices, in its strategic role, learning explores the interdependencies of interlocking practices and can create new possibilities by motivating new connections. In the context of strategizing practice, the strategic role of learning is reflective in its ability to connect resources such that multiple alternatives can be explored in the course of strategizing attempts.

Acknowledging the strategic role of learning, we also appreciate the fluid nature of learning, which is central to the social complexity that it reflects and in which it is embedded. Dominant views in learning theory, however, tend to neglect this important aspect and instead present learning as an acquisitional process based on the accumulation of experience, knowledge and skills over time. A large body of the current literature both in organizational learning and in workplace learning discuss learning with reference to the *experiential* issues (Kolb, 1984; Argote, 1999), the *behavioural* aspects (Cyert and March, 1963), the *cognitive* issues (Duncan and Weiss, 1979), the *socio-cultural* dimensions (Cook and Yanow, 1993), the *reflective and emotional* dimensions (Schön, 1983; Antonacopoulou and Gabriel, 2001) and more recently the *practice-based* view (Nicolini et al., 2003).

However, even studies which claim to take a processual approach to the study of learning within organizations have not examined the nature of learning as a flow. We are only now beginning to engage with the social complexity of learning, and some of the early insights that are emerging from such analyses (see Fenwick, 2003; Antonacopoulou, 2004, 2006a; Antonacopoulou and Chiva, 2007) are starting to highlight some of the neglected dimensions of learning in the context of work organizations.

Among the neglected aspects, Antonacopoulou (2006a: 239–44) identifies four dimensions that to date have not been fully discussed: 'Inter-connectivity, diversity, self-organisation/emergence and politics'. While inter-connectivity highlights the relational nature of learning, diversity embraces heterogeneity and possibility, and self-organization highlights the inherent nature of social systems to renew themselves. Finally, the political dynamics of learning highlight the inequalities of power and control and the power of learning to make a difference through responsible action. A common theme that runs through these additional dimensions of learning is *surprise*. In other words, contrary to the view of learning as intentional and deliberate, these dimensions of learning leave room for the unexpected. This lies at the core of appreciating that learning is not only a practice but it is also a transactional space where practising takes place. This means that learning is always emergent and negotiated. By virtue of this it also means that learning is also by definition incomplete.

Therefore, the strategic role of learning creates connections and possibilities through practising. Connections between practices form the core of 'learning-in-practise' (Antonacopoulou, 2006a: 244–7), the co-evolution of practice and the unfolding learning through the repeated enactments which configure multiple arenas for negotiation of order. The ongoing experimentation and exploitation of multiple possibilities as part of the strategic role of learning, also positions learning as a strategizing practice.

From this perspective, strategic learning can be conceptualized as a strategizing practice where local learning practices are reflexively engaged with, maximizing their capacity to provide internal goods in the form of new capabilities. At the same time, in these strategizing attempts the approach of strategic learning practice is exposed to a wider set of principles more globally as part of the field of action and variety of interactions across communities of practitioners.

Strategic learning can therefore, be seen as a *cause for strategizing practice*, as a *consequence of practising strategizing* and itself a *strategizing practice*. Over and above the strategic role of learning in the context of strategizing practice, strategic learning as a strategizing practice provides scope for self-organization in ways that can renew practice through the connections of internal and external goods. Consequently, strategic learning highlights that the focus of attention is neither only the practice (as a set of action rules) nor only the routine of learning in a deliberate, conscious and systematic process. It is also a dynamic outcome of the ongoing socio-political connections embedded in practising attempts as part of the various macro and micro processes that constitute strategizing.

Therefore, a greater understanding of this interaction between strategic intent (geared towards a macro perspective in response to external pressures) and operational reality (geared towards a micro perspective in response to internal integration) of strategizing may be afforded by concentrating on the actual strategic learning practices of organizational and extra-organizational groups and individuals.

This approach could provide a more informed understanding of strategic learning practice by focusing on the learning aspects, as well as the socio-political dynamics that underpin capability development, itself a strategizing practice. Consequently, it is suggested that the implicit and explicit negotiations among the differing perspectives serve to create an array of balancing acts between strategic intent and operational realities. Fundamentally, balancing acts are reflective of learning practice where the strategizing process of human agents takes shape in the context of social structures which frequently define the boundaries of learning (that is, knowing – tacitly and explicitly – how to respond to competing priorities; see Antonacopoulou, 2001). Strategic learning practices, provide an important lens for understanding the dynamics of the interaction between human intend and social structures as the two reinforce and recreate each other (Latour, 1987).

This analysis is intended to help us to rethink the strategic nature of learning as a process of connecting and the centrality of learning in strategizing practices. Moreover, the dynamics underpinning the way learning is practised in the context of socio-political relations broaden the scope of understanding strategizing not only as the institutionalization of strategic practices but also as a reflection of their self-organizing nature. This is best captured by the inherent quality of learning to forge new connections through unlearning (Antonacopoulou, 2009).

Conclusions and implications for future research
In this chapter a new conceptualization of strategic learning is presented as a source of connecting the micro and macro forces of strategizing practice. Strategic learning as an emerging theme in the strategic management debates according to this analysis holds a vital role in helping us understand and engage with the intricacies of fluid organizational practices such as strategizing practice. Strategic learning not only reveals more powerfully the strategic role of learning as a key organizational resource for competitiveness. It also reveals the relational nature of learning in the way it exposes socio-political tensions and employs these tensions as a foundation for extending the scope of core business practices such as strategizing. The strategic role of learning to connect the strategic intentions and the operational realities not only provides new avenues for rethinking strategic reformulation as part of strategy implementation in an ongoing continuum of strategizing. It also broadens strategizing practice beyond the realm of path dependency and a prerogative of top managers into a practice performed in diverse ways by heterogeneous actors across multiple context as an integral part of working life.

The strategic role of learning expands strategizing practice by focusing on the relationships binding multiple actors, multiple practices and multiple performances together in a complex set of social dynamics that unfold in time and across space. Strategizing practice unfolds in a self-organizing process by virtue of practising attempts which are the balancing acts providing continuity in the ongoing stream of discontinuity. Therefore, strategizing as an unfolding practice is in flow when in *practise*. Therefore, central to the flow of strategizing beyond an appreciation of the processual nature of strategy and the need to focus on the micro practice of strategy in the activities and actions of strategic actors, this analysis highlights also the importance of *practising* attempts.

The introduction of practising as distinct from practice is important not only because it clarifies language, but also because it encourages strategy researchers to both talk about the enactment of strategy and also engage with its embodiment in the way strategy is performed. This perspective can also support our efforts to engage foresight as a fundamental aspect of strategic activity. Foresight embraces the complexity of the unknown and does not rely on past knowledge as a foundation for future learning. Foresight in this regard is an illustration of strategic learning in action. This is so because foresight employs actionable knowledge to construct viable possibilities for strategic action. In short, foresight is commitment to strategic learning.

The focus on the relationship between strategizing and learning in this chapter marks a step forward in process research in organization studies. It reveals the need to challenge our basic epistemological and ontological assumptions in relation to the flow of organizing practices that form organization. It invites us to look beyond agents and their structures and the way these interact in a working net of activities and actions. It fundamentally invites us to explore the flow of organizing-in-flow. In other words, it introduces us to an epistemology of connectivity and an ontology of embeddedness. This relational orientation is a powerful means of capturing the dynamics of the social complexity that constitutes processes such as learning and strategizing.

This suggests that in studying organizational processes such as strategizing practice, it is not enough that we only focus on micro processes such as actions. It is equally critical that we also focus on the micro foundations of practice in the way internal and external goods of practice co-evolve through practising.

The ongoing permutations of practice in relation to other practices and in relation to the array of internal forces such as emotions, behaviours and knowledge, reveal chance and ambiguity as an integral aspect of flow. Flow cannot be controlled by taking intentional measures (such as learning) to define the outcome. For when we seek to control the way practice unfolds, we limit the possibilities for unexpected connections to be made which could reconfigure strategic practice. Instead, engaging with practice could provide scope for practising where the strategic role of learning (to connect) is itself acknowledged as a strategizing practice.

These ideas call for greater attention to the way learning as a micro process is understood in relation to strategizing and in the context of work organizations more generally. Instead of treating learning as a commodity to be manipulated at will, it can be a powerful means of tapping into the social complexity of practices by revealing the intricate connections that form conditions affecting the systemic/fractal nature of practices.

In relation to future strategy research, these ideas call for greater attention to avoid dualities between macro and micro perspectives in studying strategizing practices intended to support competitiveness. Competitiveness as we have already acknowledged is not only a matter of identifying a firm's unique resources at a certain point in time and developing capabilities that enhance distinctiveness. Competitiveness is also about the ongoing reconfiguration of these resources in the way routines and core practices are constantly interconnected, placing the firm in competition with itself!

Note

* The author would like to acknowledge the support of the ESRC/EPSRC Advanced Institute of Management Research under grant number RES-331-25-0024 for this research. I also thank Paula Jarzabkowski and Richard Whittington for feedback to an earlier version.

References

Alvesson, M. (2004), *Knowledge Work and Knowledge-Intensive Firms*, Oxford: Oxford University Press.
Antonacopoulou, E.P. (1998), 'Developing learning managers within learning organisations', in M. Easterby-Smith, L. Araujo and J. Burgoyne (eds), *Organisational Learning and the Learning Organisation: Developments in Theory and Practice*, London: Sage, pp. 214–42.
Antonacopoulou, E.P. (2000), 'Employee development through self-development in three retail banks', *Personnel Review*, Special Issue on 'New Employee Development: Successful Innovations or Token Gestures?', **29**(4), 491–508.
Antonacopoulou, E.P. (2001), 'The paradoxical nature of the relationship between training and learning', *Journal of Management Studies*, **38**(3), 327–50.
Antonacopoulou, E.P. (2004), 'On the virtues of practising scholarship: a tribute to Chris Argyris a timeless learner', *Management Learning*, **35**(4), 381–95.
Antonacopoulou, E.P. (2006a), 'Working life learning: learning-in-practise', in Elena Antonacopoulou, Peter Jarvis, Vibeke Andersen, Bente Elkjaer and Steen Hoeyrup (eds), *Learning, Working and Living: Mapping the Terrain of Working Life Learning*, London: Palgrave, pp. 234–54.

Antonacopoulou, E.P. (2006b), 'The relationship between individual and organisational learning: new evidence from managerial learning practices', *Management Learning*, **37**(4), 455–73.

Antonacopoulou, E.P. (2007), 'Practice', in Stewart Clegg and James Bailey (eds), *International Encyclopaedia of Organization Studies*, London: Sage, pp. 1291–8.

Antonacopoulou, E.P. (2008a), 'On the practise of practice: in-tensions and ex-tensions in the ongoing reconfiguration of practice', in David Barry and Hans Hansen (eds), *Handbook of New Approaches to Organization Studies*, London: Sage, pp. 112–31.

Antonacopoulou, E.P. (2008b), 'Practise-centred research: the study of interconnectivity and fluidity', in Richard Thorpe and Robin Holt (eds), *Dictionary of Qualitative Management Research*, London: Sage, pp. 165–9.

Antonacopoulou, E.P. (2009 forthcoming), 'Impact and scholarship: unlearning and practising to co-create actionable knowledge', *Management Learning*, **40**.

Antonacopoulou, E.P. and Chiva, R. (2007), 'The social complexity of organizational learning: dynamics of learning and organising, Special Issue, *Management Learning*, **38**(3), 277–96.

Antonacopoulou, E.P. and Gabriel, Y. (2001), 'Emotion, learning and organisational change: towards an integration of psychoanalytic and other perspectives', *Journal of Organisational Change Management*, Special Issue on 'Organisational Change and Psychodynamics', **14**(5), 435–51.

Argote, L. (1999), *Organizational Learning: Creating, Retaining and Transferring Knowledge*, Boston, MA: Kluwer Academic.

Argyris, C. (2004), *Reasons and Rationalizations: The Limits to Organizational Knowledge*, Oxford: Oxford University Press.

Barney, J.B. (1991), 'Firm resources and sustained competitive advantage', *Journal of Management*, **17**(1), 99–120.

Blyler, M. and Coff, R.W. (2003), 'Dynamic capabilities, social capital, and rent appropriation: ties that split pies', *Strategic Management Journal*, **24**, 677–86.

Bourdieu, P. (1990), *The Logic of Practice*, Stanford, CA: Stanford University Press.

Brown, J.S. and Duguid P. (2000), *The Social Life of Information*, Boston, MA: Harvard Business School Press.

Burgelman, R. (1988), 'Strategy making as a social learning process: the case of internal corporate venturing', *Interfaces*, **18**(3), 74–85.

Chakravarthy, B.S. and Doz, Y. (1992), 'Strategy process research: focusing on corporate self-renewal', *Strategic Management Journal*, Special Issue, **13**, 5–16.

Cook, S.D.N. and Yanow, D. (1993), 'Culture and organisational learning', *Journal of Management Inquiry*, **2**(4), December, 373–90.

Coopey, J. (1995), 'The learning organisation: power, politics and ideology', *Management Learning*, **26**(2), 193–213.

Cyert, R.M. and March, J.G. (1963), *A Behavioral Theory of the Firm*, Malden, MA: Blackwell.

De Certeau, M. (1984), *The Practice of Everyday Life*, Berkeley, CA: University of California Press.

Duncan, R. and Weiss, A. (1979), 'Organizational learning: implications for organizational design', *Research in Organizational Behavior*, **1**, 75–123.

Easterby-Smith, M., Graça, M., Antonacopoulou, E.P. and Ferdinand, J. (2008 forthcoming), 'Absorptive capacity: a process perspective', *Management Learning*, **39**(5), 483–501.

Eisenhardt, K.M. and Martin, J.A. (2000), 'Dynamic capabilities: what are they?', *Strategic Management Journal*, **21**, 1105–21.

Engeström, Y., Miettinen, R. and Punamäki, R.L. (1999), *Perspectives on Activity Theory*, Cambridge: Cambridge University Press.

Feldman, M.S. (2000), 'Organizational routines as a source of continuous change', *Organization Science*, **11**(6), 611–29.

Feldman, M.S. and Pentland, B.T. (2003), 'Reconceptualizing organizational routines as a source of flexibility and change', *Administrative Science Quarterly*, **48**, March, 94–118.

Fenwick, T. (2003), 'Reclaiming and re-embodying experiential learning through complexity science'. *Studies in the Education of Adults*, **35** (2), 123–41.

Gherardi, S. (2000), 'Practice-based theorizing on learning and knowing in organizations', *Organization*, **7** (2), 211–23.

Gherardi, S. (2006), *Organizational Knowledge: The Texture of Organizing*, London: Blackwell.

Giddens, A. (1984), *The Constitution of Society*, Cambridge: Cambridge University Press.

Grant, R.M. (1996), 'Towards a knowledge-based theory of the firm', *Strategic Management Journal*, Special Issue, **17**, Winter, 109–22.

Hendry, J. (2000), 'Strategic decision-making, discourse and strategy as social practice', *Journal of Management Studies*, **37**(7), 955–77.

Jarzabkowski, P. (2005), *Strategy as Practice: An Activity Perspective*, London: Sage.

Johnson, G., Melin, L. and Whittington, R. (2003), 'Micro-strategy and strategising', *Journal of Management Studies*, Special Issue, **40**(1), 3–20.

Khanna, T., Gulati, R. and Nohria, N. (2000), 'The economic modelling of strategy process: clean models and dirty hands', *Strategic Management Journal*, **21**(7), 781–90.

Kogut, B. and Zander, U. (1992), 'Knowledge of the firm, combinative capabilities and the replication of technology', *Organization Science*, **3**(3), 383–97.

Kolb, D.A. (1984), *Experimental Learning: Experience as the Source of Learning*, Englewood Cliffs, NJ: Prentice-Hall.

Kuwada, K. (1998), 'Strategic learning: the continuous side of discontinuous strategic change', *Organization Science*, **9**(6), 719–36.

Langley, A. (1999), 'Strategies for theorizing from process data', *Academy of Management Review*, **24**(4), 691–710.

Latour, B. (1987), *Science in Action: How to Follow Scientists and Engineers through Society*, Milton Keynes: Open University Press.

Lave, J. and Wenger, E. (1991), *Situated Learning: Legitimate Peripheral Participation*, New York: Cambridge University Press.

Law, J. (1999), 'After ANT: complexity, naming and topology', in John Law and John Hassard (eds), *Actor Network Theory and After*, Oxford: Blackwell, pp. 1–14.

Levy, D.L. and Alvesson, M. (2003), 'Critical approaches to strategic management', in Mats Alvesson and Hugh Willmott (eds), *Studying Management Critically*, London: Sage, pp. 92–110.

Liedtke, J.M. (1998), 'Strategic thinking: can it be taught?', *Long Range Planning*, **31**(1), 120–29.

McIntyre, A. (1985), *After Virtue: A Study in Moral Theory*, London: Duckworth.

Nicolini, D., Gherardi, S. and Yanow, D. (2003), 'Introduction: towards a practice-based view of knowing and learning in organizations', in Davide Nicolini, Silvia Gherardi and Dvora Yanow (eds), *Knowing in Organizations: A Practice-Based Approach*, London: M.E.Sharpe, pp. 3–31.

Pettigrew, A.M. (1992), 'The character and significance of strategy process research', *Strategic Management Journal*, **13**, 5–16.

Pietersen, W.G. (2003), *Reinventing Strategy: Using Strategic Learning to Create and Sustain Breakthrough Performance*, New York: John Wiley.

Reckwitz, A. (2002), 'Towards a theory of social practices: a development in culturalist theorizing', *European Journal of Social Theory*, **5**(2), 243–63.

Sanchez, R. and Heene, A. (1997), *Strategic Learning and Knowledge Management*, Chichester: John Wiley.

Schatzki, T.R. (1996), *Social Practices: A Wittgensteinian Approach to Human Activity and the Social*, Cambridge: Cambridge University Press.

Schatzki, T.R., Knorr Cetina, K. and Von Savigny, E. (2001), *The Practice Turn in Contemporary Theory*, London: Routledge.

Schön, D.A. (1983), *The Reflective Practitioner*, New York: Arena.

Stacey, R.D. (1995), 'The science of complexity: an alternative perspective for strategic change processes', *Strategic Management Journal*, **16**, 477–95.

Szulanksi, G. and Amin, K. (2001), 'Learning to make strategy: balancing discipline and imagination', *Long Range Planning*, **34** (5), 537–56.

Teece, D.J., Pisano, G.P. and Shuen, A. (1997), 'Dynamic capabilities and strategic management', *Strategic Management Journal*, **18**(7), 509–33.

Turner, S. (1994), *The Social Theory of Practices: Tradition, Tacit Knowledge and Presuppositions*, Cambridge: Polity.

Van den Bosch, F.A.J., Van Wijk, R. and Volberda, H.W. (2003), 'Absorptive capacity: antecedents, models and outcomes', in Mark Easterby-Smith and Marjorie A. Lyles (eds), *The Blackwell Handbook of Organizational Learning and Knowledge Management*, Oxford: Blackwell, pp. 278–301.

Warde, A. (2004), 'Practice and field: revising Bourdieusian concepts', CRIC Discussion Paper, 65, University of Manchester.

Wenger, E. (1998), *Communities of Practice: Learning, Meaning and Identity*, Cambridge: Cambridge University Press.

Whittington, R. (2001), 'Learning to strategize: problems of practice', SKOPE Research Chapters Series, 20.

Whittington, R.E. (2003), 'The work of strategizing and organizing: for a practice perspective', *Strategic Organization*, **1** (1), 117–25.

Whittington, R. (2006), 'Completing the practice turn in strategy research', *Organization Studies*, **27**(5), 613–34.

Zahra, S.A. and George, G. (2002), 'Absorptive capacity: a review, reconceptualisation, and extension', *Academy of Management Review*, **27**(2), 185–203.

Zollo, M. and Winter, S.G. (2002), 'Deliberate learning and the evolution of dynamic capabilities', *Organization Science*, **13**(3), 339–51.

10 Improvisational bricolage: a practice-based approach to strategy and foresight

Miguel Pina e Cunha, João Vieira Da Cunha and Stewart R. Clegg

Introduction

The tension between exploration and exploitation of knowledge is one of the most discussed topics in the strategic and change management literatures (Gersick 1991; Romanelli and Tushman 1994; Eisenhardt and Tabrizi 1995; Tushman and O'Reilly 1996). Too much of either is regarded as a bad thing: too much exploration and the risk is that there is too little that can be exploited routinely, as routines are projected into an uncertain and indeterminate future; too much exploitation and the risk is that as the knowledge assets wear out they will not be replenished in a present that is rapidly fading into a nonrenewable past. In this chapter we contribute to this discussion by explaining how improvisational bricolage allows organizations to integrate these two processes and by discussing an approach to foresight that supports the capability to engage in exploitative exploration.

The dilemma inherent to the relation between exploration and exploitation can be succinctly stated as follows. Exploitation is necessary because it allows organizations to reap benefits from present knowledge and past strategy. Exploration is necessary because it allows organizations to construct new knowledge, create new markets, and build new sources of competitiveness. Some strategy literature views these two approaches as opposites, stating that one can only be pursued at the cost of the other (see Sastry 1997), while some argues that both exploration and exploitation are necessary conditions for strategic viability in fast-changing markets (Levinthal 1997). The paradoxical relation between these two approaches to organization materializes in a number of central concepts in strategy research, such as the winner's curse (Miller 1993), the need for ambidextrous organizations (Duncan 1976) and the risks of an opportunity trap (see Paich and Sterman 1993). In this chapter we draw on the concept of improvisational bricolage to address how the paradoxical tension might be used productively. Improvisational bricolage can be defined as the practice of drawing on available resources to address challenges as they unfold (Weick 1993; Cunha et al. 1999). When engaging in this practice, organizations are able to integrate exploration and exploitation into a mutually constituted duality, instead of keeping them as two poles of a dualism. We explore the consequences of this role of improvisational bricolage in both strategy making and foresight.

We start by summarizing the tension between exploration and exploitation before discussing how improvisation can turn this tension into a mutually reinforcing dynamic. We end by looking at how improvisation allows for real-time foresight, the process through which organizations make sense of their future as they deal with present competitive challenges.

Exploration versus exploitation

The difference between exploration and exploitation is deceptively simple to explain. Exploration is about seeking new sources of revenue. Organizations explore in the future perfect tense, when they strengthen their competitive position by entering new markets or creating new opportunities, which they imagine in terms of positive outcomes; thus, exploration concerns developing current strategies designed to optimize revenue and organizational activity in the future. Organizations exploit here and now; in classical theories of surplus value it is present-day exploitation of labor and its knowledge which enables profit to be realized. In contemporary theories, organizations exploit not just by securing additional value from existing resources, such as labor, usually through improving the capital to labor ratio in the form of technological inputs, but by other means of increasing revenue or reducing costs in current markets.

Theoretically, both exploration and exploitation are time dependent: the former on an as yet unrealized future perfect, the latter on a present which, the longer it remains as it is, will be imperceptibly ebbing with increasing velocity into a past which will threaten the organization's survival. The subtlety is that the past is continuously being prepared in the present. Insufficient exploration renders the present into a future past full of missed opportunities; insufficient exploitation in the present renders the future imperfect as a past that scuttled the best-laid plans. An excess of exploration leads organizations to spread themselves too thinly across a number of opportunities, succumbing to an opportunity trap (Miner et al. 2001). These organizations have the right product ideas for the right markets but lack the commitment and often the resources to produce and market their ideas efficiently enough to make them competitive. To caricature, exploring organizations may be designing an increasingly better product that no one can afford. For exploitation, the passage of time means obsolescence. Organizations excessively specialized in exploiting are highly efficient at making and marketing their products, but they lack the commitment and resources to innovate and follow shifts in market needs and wants, succumbing to a simplicity trap (Kelly and Ambrugey 1991). At the extreme, organizations focused on exploitation can be increasingly efficient at making a product or delivering a service that is rapidly diminishing in use value. And, just as Marx ([1844] 1975) argued for production so it is for consumption: when the use value of knowledge and features embodied and embedded in either products or services diminishes, the surpluses that it can yield decline precipitously.

Ideally, organizations should be able to combine exploration and exploration in their strategy. However, this integration is difficult to achieve. The best-known attempt to do so is the concept of the ambidextrous organization (Duncan 1976; Tushman and O'Reilly 1996). An organization is said to be ambidextrous when it has a portfolio of units where some are focused on exploration, and the others are focused on exploitation as a result of deliberate top management choices. 'Exploitation' units provide resources for 'exploration' units to seek new sources of revenue and competitive advantage. If an 'exploration' unit is able to generate revenue, then it is transformed into an 'exploitation' unit to fund further exploration. Such an approach is problematic both practically and theoretically. In practice, such an arrangement succumbs to the political dynamics of organizations (Jackall 1989). Managers are loath to lead exploring units because, even in cultures that tolerate failure as a source of learning, there is always more political clout to be gained from success. In the future they may control the necessary nodal points through which success passes, but right now they are desperately seeking for those ways to the future that they should stabilize. Those few organizations that have adopted the ambidextrous form (for example, Microsoft and Hewlett Packard), have turned their 'exploring' units into permanent research centers. Although some knowledge spillovers occur between these units and the 'exploitative' units, most mainstream innovations and new markets come from deliberate search efforts conducted by the 'exploiting' side of the organization (von Hippel 1987). Such an approach neither conceptually nor practically integrates exploitative and exploratory learning. Instead, it separates them as two opposites by locating them in different nodes of the organization (see Poole and Van de Ven 1989). As a solution it fails for all but the most resource-rich organizations. First, it is difficult to apply to small organizations because these seldom have the breadth of resources necessary to sustain several units with different stances (see Mintzberg and Waters 1982). Second, as a result of divorcing exploration from exploitation nodes, some organizations may fall into a simplicity trap, where a simple strategy fails to adjust to changing environmental conditions and others an opportunity trap, where potential innovations are spurned because they do not seem to fit with the way that node defines present realities. To avoid these nodal blockages, top management has to foster a level of communication among exploratory and exploitative units that is very difficult to achieve in practice (Morrow 1981).

Improvisational bricolage and strategy

Improvisational bricolage allows organizations to integrate exploration and exploitation at the level of practice, thus ensuring that these processes are continually in a relationship of mutual constitution. Improvisational bricolage is a practice that thrives on novelty and aims to generate innovation. However, it differs from other change-inducing practices in that it draws on available resources and skills. It is thus an exploitative form of exploration (Barrett 1998).

Improvisational bricolage as exploration

Improvisational bricolage came into organization studies via jazz. Modern jazz thrives on creativity, non-repetition, and switching between loosely coupled soloists, who, to challenge each other, extemporize and improvise around any given chord structure with a sometimes ferocious intensity. In doing so, the musicians in an ensemble (such as the Ornette Coleman Trio or one of the many great Miles Davis ensembles) have to understand how to address the unexpected, urgent and important challenges that their collaborators will develop. Adapted from jazz to organizational practice, improvisational bricolage seeks to use even the smallest of challenges to produce innovation and change the organization's strategy, even if only through very small increments (Crossan et al. 2005). Thus, in fast-changing environments in which organizations need to address competitive challenges quickly if they are to remain viable, improvisation is an especially effective approach. Improvisation allows organizations to use challenges to craft a strategic theme that allows them to follow an incremental path to radical change (Eisenhardt and Tabrizi 1995). Thus, the jazz metaphor is apposite: the chord structure of 'How High the Moon' became the basis for an entirely new theme, 'Ornithology', in Charlie Parker's hands, diverting his fellow soloists from any plans they might have had based on the original chord structure. In fast-changing competitive environments, there is simply no time to plan and the equivalent of the chord structure – the underlying themes – change rapidly. Research on crises, new product development and competitive dynamics in such environments has consistently shown that strategic planning – the business equivalent of scoring a chart for all the instrumentalists – is too slow a process to be of any use in such environments (Brews and Hunt 1999; Repenning et al. 2001). Some studies even suggest that the uncertain nature of fast-changing markets forecloses the very possibility of strategic planning because market conditions are very difficult to pin down with the accuracy needed for this process. In such conditions, equivalent to an avant-garde jazz performance, none of the players appears to be following the same, or indeed any, script: there are as many inventors as players who will sometimes hit rich and rewarding themes while others will languish in the margin, missing the opportunities to fly high with their creativity and innovation. Studies such as those of Lane and Maxfield (1996) and Mintzberg and McHugh (1985) have shown the inadequacy of planning to advocate action as the most effective mode with which to deal with competitive challenges in fast-changing competitive markets. There is some empirical evidence (for example, Eisenhardt 1989) and plenty of anecdotal evidence (for example, Peters 1992) for the merit of an action orientation, meaning one that focuses on addressing each threat and opportunity as it comes and forfeiting long-term strategy making as an impossible, if not futile, exercise. Authors arguing for this approach emphasize the role of emergent strategy in deciding the course of an organization (Levinthal and Warglien 1999). They underscore the small impact of deliberate and planned strategies relative to everyday adaptations in defining the actual strategic path of an organization. In jazz terms, the contrast is between the tightly written charts of a Stan Kenton big band and the loose improvisation of the late John Coltrane and Archie Shepp sessions. However, if the planning approach overemphasizes the value of a long-term consistent strategy, or the tightly scored charts, then the action approach underemphasizes the thematic utility of some underlying structure, as many critics would allege of some of Coltrane's late, most avant-garde, works. Any attempts at systematizing an explicit strategy are written off as futile (Anderson 1999). In organizational terms, an avant-garde strategy conceptualizes organizations and their markets as self-organizing systems whose evolution is, at the same time, a product of the player's actions and a dynamic beyond the grasp of any single agent.

Research on improvisational bricolage, in line with the action approach, sees predefined plans as being of little use in guiding organization action in fast-changing competitive environments (Crossan 1998). However, in line with the planning approach, improvisation understands the value of a shared conception of competitive dynamics – a common sense of the chord structure underlying improvisation – and the organizations' path through the challenges presented by fast-changing markets. When they improvise, organizations are not only responding to urgent challenges, they are also making sense of those challenges and their improvisations to craft a dynamic understanding of their competitive environment and their own path in it (Weick 1987). In improvisational bricolage, planning and action are mutually constituted. Action is taken not only to address competitive challenges but also to make sense of the competitive environment. The interpretations built in such a way are, however, not used to constrain action in much the same way as plans are used in the planning approach. Instead these interpretations are used to enable action, keeping the organization flexible enough to take advantage of other players' threats and opportunities to innovate creatively and successfully (Eisenhardt 1997). Sensemaking in improvisation is centripetal, not centrifugal.

Improvisational bricolage is also distinct from the planning and the action approaches in how it approaches threats and strategic mistakes. Both the planning and the action approaches interpret threats as negative (Starbuck and Milliken 1988). Threats are to be eliminated: they distract the organization from its plans, and divert its members from taking advantage of competitive opportunities. Threats are crises that the organization needs to address to return to routine just as many big bands found that the soling proclivities of emergent Bop players threatened the orderly business of producing dance-hall routines; thus, whether that routine is implementing a plan or taking whatever action is needed to change and innovate, deviation from it is perceived as a threat (Ashmos et al. 1997). In improvisation, competitive threats are as valued as opportunities (Kamoche and Cunha 2001). (A band such as the mid-1960s Miles Davis Quintet was metaphorically fired by the prodigious threats to rhythm of the young Tony Williams.)

Improvising organizations do not interpret threats and opportunities as one and the same. Research has shown that improvising organizations see threats with the same sense of alarm as do planning and acting organizations. However, improvising organizations look at threats as opportunities to disturb routine practices that members have slipped into, without much reflexive everyday awareness. Improvising organizations look at threats as opportunities to increase their members' motivation and commitment to innovation and change (Peplowski 1998). Threats are also interpreted as opportunities for a quantum leap in the organization's competitive position. If a threat affecting the players in a competitive context is used as an opportunity to craft a unique competitive position, the other players in the market will suddenly be faced with a loss in their competitive position which outweighs the original threat (Eisenhardt and Bourgeois 1988).

Improvisational bricolage is also different from the action and the planning approaches in how it uses errors. In the planning approach, errors are due to either inaccuracy in plans or failure in implementation. Inaccuracies in plans are deviations to be corrected by redesigning the planning process so that competitive information is more accurate and so that it is used more effectively in mapping the organization's future (Miller and Cardinal 1994). In the action approach, errors represent lost opportunities or breaches in the organization's resilience against competitive threats. They represent either a failure that becomes a threat in itself to be addressed immediately or a loss that needs to be recovered through future action (Sitkin 1992). Mistakes and errors are not rehashed. They are interpreted as an unavoidable cost of approaching competition through action. In improvisational bricolage, errors are seen as an important part of the process of innovation. As Weick put it, improvisation espouses an 'aesthetic of imperfection' (Weick 1999), occasions for improvisation inasmuch as errors can be starting-points for change and on-the-spot strategies. In improvisational bricolage, errors are thus not to be avoided or corrected. Instead they are encouraged and appropriated as a source of pre-emptive transformation.

Improvisational bricolage thus shares with exploratory approaches to strategy a focus on innovation and change as the driving forces in adaptation to fast-changing markets. It differs from both these forms of exploration in the extent to which it embraces change and innovation. Improvising organizations change not only when their competitive environments present them with opportunities to do so but also when they are faced with threats either from competitive dynamics or from their own errors.

Improvisational bricolage as exploitative exploration

The feature of improvisational bricolage that allows it to integrate exploration and exploitation is its use of existing resources for change and innovation. In the planning approach the focus is on acquiring and developing the optimal resources for each strategy (Beer 1996; Beer and Eisenstat 2000). When planning for change and innovation, this approach emphasizes the need to ascertain the resources that fit with the process and goals of change and innovation and put those resources in place before launching this process. The action approach has a similar interpretation of resources (Pascale 1984; Slocum et al. 1994). When responding to competitive challenges through action, organizations need resources fit for the task. However, this approach downplays the need to obtain these resources through formal processes and channels. Instead it emphasizes members' ability to obtain these resources through informal processes and channels. Focusing on the fit between, on the one hand, the goals and the process of innovation and change, and on the other, the resources available to the organization, is a defining difference separating exploration from exploitation. Exploration requires new resources whereas exploitation entails the repeated use of existing resources.

Improvisational bricolage turns this dualism between exploration and exploitation into a relationship of mutual constitution (see Giddens 1986). When improvising, organizations do not seek new resources to change and innovate. Instead, they seek to use available resources in new ways (Berry and Irvine 1986; Cunha and Cunha 2001), such as the chord structure of 'How High the Moon'. The process of change and innovation through improvisational bricolage turns into a process both exploratory and exploitative. As they explore, improvising organizations use the same resources in multiple ways, deploying them to take advantage of multiple competitive challenges. Available resources get used repeatedly but not repetitively, maximizing efficiency while striving for effectiveness.

Improvisational bricolage is an adaptive use of resources in fast-changing competitive environments because it matches the time pressure and the bias for action imposed by such contexts, while matching the complex nature of their market dynamics.

Fast-changing markets seldom allow the time needed to procure new resources by organizations to meet demands raised by competitive challenges (Eisenhardt 1989). Even when these resources can be procured informally, without wasting time by going through formal resource allocation processes, time is still needed to activate informal ties and to learn how to use them (for example, Lanzara 1983). Improvisational bricolage is entrained with the dynamics of fast-changing markets because it draws on resources that are already available and familiar to organizational members. When engaging in improvisational bricolage, members make do with their available resources, that is to say with the tools and materials that they use in their everyday work and with which they are familiar and skilled (Johnson and Rice 1984). Improvisational bricolage allows members to take advantage of resources that are already available locally at their point of contact with competitive dynamics (Machin and Carrithers 1996). By making do with everyday resources, members are able to draw on tacit knowledge to engage in important and unexpected strategic challenges.

Improvisational bricolage is a challenging practice. As Weick (1996) and others (for example, Orlikowski 1993a) have shown, using everyday resources in new ways and to address new challenges is far from being a trivial process. Instead it is a demanding creative process that can only be learned through practice, and that varies among individuals (see chapters in Heath and Luff 2000). Moreover, this challenge is not only cognitive but also emotive inasmuch as it calls upon members to bricolate with artefacts that are attached to their professional identity (Kondo 1990). Indeed, whereas members do not use most of their work tools and materials to make sense of their professional trajectory and identity, some artefacts are used to this end. These artefacts and their use are central to members' professional identity. Therefore using them in ways other than those sanctioned by members' views and enactments is very challenging (Weick 1996), due to the level of creativity that novel uses require. However, much of the difficulty resides in employees experiencing increased uncertainty in their professional identity through novel uses of what have been identity-rich tools and materials (Whyte 1948; Gouldner 1954; Goffman 1967). Improvisational props lose their old meanings and what their new ones are is uncertain. Improvisational bricolage is nonetheless a practice attuned to fast-changing markets because creativity and identity challenges are addressed in action. The creativity and identity work that bricolage demands are socially enacted as members jointly take advantage of opportunities, threats and imperfections to innovate and change (Orr 1990). Identity challenges are situated and thus do not require any enduring changes to the way members make sense of themselves nor do they require any enduring changes to the way members present themselves to others (Thevenot 1999). As far as identity goes, bricolage is more flexible than any other approach to competitive challenges.

There is another important feature of bricolage that makes this especially fit for fast-changing competitive environments – the match between the uncertainty and complexity of such contexts and the indetermination of resources. If there is a feature that distinguishes competitive challenges in fast-paced markets from those in other competitive contexts, it is their level of complexity and uncertainty (Hedberg et al. 1976). Fast-changing markets are complex environments in the sense that they challenge organizations with an erratic flow of incremental opportunities and threats that in time interact to provoke discontinuous peaks of creative destruction (Foster and Kaplan 2001). These moments of creative destruction are seldom independent environmental occurrences. Instead, these discontinuities are the outcome of the interpretation of sets of incremental changes in competitive dynamics (Kiesler and Sproull 1982). These interpretations are enacted in episodes of creative destruction in two ways. In some cases, organizations interpret their environments as undergoing a discontinuity and fall into a self-fulfilling prophecy (Haveman 1992). In such instances, organizations take a discontinuity for granted and act on it as if it were an objective market dynamic. In other cases, an organization, or a small set of organizations, interpret incremental market changes as a consistent business opportunity. In such instances, the process of creative destruction is intentionally triggered by a set of organizations as they attempt to reap the benefits of a creative interpretation of market dynamics (Christensen 1997).

Both processes of creative destruction underscore that competitive dynamics are the outcome of a structuration process (see Giddens 1986). This means that competitive dynamics result from the interplay between discrete market changes and the way organizations interpret those changes and incorporate them into their strategy (Daft and Weick 1984). Market dynamics shape organizations both to the extent that organizations enact and pay attention to those changes, and in the ways in which they transform the conditions within which sense is made, even if the same old sense continues to be made until the changing circumstances sabotage it completely. The specific features of the way market dynamics shape organizations are the outcome of the process through which organizations use those changes to decide their future position in the market and the path they choose to reach it. Structuration of competitive dynamics is carried out as members enact market challenges (Eisenhardt 1997). Organizations interpret challenges as they act on them and thus make sense of competitive dynamics as they make sense of their situated decisions and actions and how these are received by the market (Weick 1987). Organizations cannot necessarily determine competitive opportunities and threats beforehand and if competitive challenges cannot be interpreted before organizations act, knowing in and by their acting, then they cannot decide, a priori, the resources needed (Ansoff et al. 1970). Organizations need to be able to shape their mix of resources as they make sense of market dynamics by enacting and acting on them. Market dynamics become evident in the flows and relations that surround and surge through organization members and stakeholders, which is exactly what the practice of improvisational bricolage allows organizations to achieve (Cunha et al. 2002). Improvisational bricolage allows organizations to change their resources as the competitive situations they face change, not by procuring new resources but by putting available resources to new uses (Weick 1993). Thus, given resources have neither objective features nor canonical purposes. Instead, they are artefacts that agents use with specific properties enacted in their uses (Suchman 1987). Of course, just as the members of any given organization enact some uses other members, perhaps of other, competitive organizations, enact other uses that may, in the future, be more successful. As members of any given organization enact, they do so within a context where other organizations are enacting artefacts, resources and meanings that shape the environments within which the initial enacting is being done; even as members do not enact effects themselves they cannot help but be themselves enacted within the environments of others that may shape them in ways that they have not even dreamed – or had nightmares – about. Bricolage offers a structurational approach to resources that meshes with the dynamics of enacted and enacting environments, thus establishing a mutually constitutive relationship between exploration and exploitation.

Developing improvisational bricolage
Improvisational bricolage depends on practical skills and dispositions. New members of organizations acquire these by engaging in simple tasks and with little if any improvisational content, and progressively take on more demanding tasks in which improvisational bricolage plays a more important role. Newcomers are allowed and encouraged to work together with experienced members who model the skills and dispositions that newcomers are expected to acquire. Lave and Wenger (1991) term this 'legitimate peripheral participation', which they see as differing from other forms of learning because it integrates action learning and social learning in a centering learning process (that is, a learning process which matches increasing task complexity with decreasing task structure). Bricoleurs become improvisational through legitimate peripheral participation, developing their improvisational skills and disposition through embodied, distributed and situated practice (Bastien and Hostager 1991; Lewin 1998).

Improvisational bricolage often begins, experientially, as a material accomplishment that conceives creative solutions to competitive challenges by experimenting and enacting using available resources. Even when challenges and resources are nonmaterial, the central role that artefacts play in memory and cognition means that when carrying out improvisational bricolage, employees use material resources to act on nonmaterial challenges as they unfold (Hutchins 1996). Learning to use resources in such a way sometimes involves more than knowing how to manipulate them, enacting a relationship between material artefacts and the body, pushing the bodily movements below declarative consciousness, into the realm of practical consciousness (Lave 1988). At this level, members can focus on improvising in terms of the challenges at hand without having to think about the specific manipulations they have to carry out with artefacts to perform those improvisations. The relationship between the body and local artefacts cannot be created away from the situated conditions in which newcomers, once they attain full membership, will carry out their everyday work because improvisational bricolage is a situated, 'sticky' skill that cannot be easily transported to different sets of conditions for action (von Hippel 1994). Newcomers thus need to engage in their actual work once they begin learning. The social nature of legitimate peripheral participation together with its commitment to a progressive escalation of the need to improvise allows newcomers to acquire the skill of improvisational bricolage *in vivo* but without jeopardizing the organization's goals. The corollary of these remarks is that organizations should develop 'hands-on' skills even among those who may ultimately be required to use their hands – and bodies – in other, perhaps less material, ways. As newcomers go through the increasing simplification of the structure of the process of legitimate peripheral participation, their disposition to engage in, and their skill at doing improvisational bricolage become increasingly situated (Brown and Duguid 1991).

   The motivation to respond to a challenge through improvisational bricolage increases when employees have a stake in addressing a challenge. When challenges do not carry sizeable stakes for employees, alternatives to improvisational bricolage become more attractive. In such instances, employees 'fake' the resolution of competitive challenges – they improvise to create the representation of addressing those challenges, instead of improvising to address them head on (Cunha and Cunha 2001). As employees develop stakes in competitive challenges that they interpret as important, they often develop a disinterest for those challenges that are interpreted as being marginal to their everyday work (Bourdieu 1990; Ibarra 1999), encouraging a situated disposition for improvisational bricolage as newcomers are encouraged to focus on those challenges relevant for their role, and disregard others as less relevant. As they enact their role on a variety of increasingly demanding conditions for action, newcomers develop socially constructed classifications of situations which they draw on to support their improvisational bricolage (Bowker and Starr 2000). These socially constructed classifications include interpretations of importance, urgency and level of surprise, and views about resource uses, including culturally sanctioned accounts of likely flexibility and spatial deployment. Again, it is difficult to develop this skill outside everyday work and actual competitive challenges. Organizations can develop explicit classifications from members' categorization devices (Sacks 1972). As knowledge of the conditions for action becomes more institutionalized, then organizations can teach them to new employees. Those classifications that work best are appropriated in and from practice to incorporate the complexity that members experience in their everyday work and to match the interests that employees develop as they gain full membership (Orr 1990). When situations for action are classified in the course of everyday work, newcomers are able to appropriate them *in vivo*, as they observe others improvising to deal with competitive challenges. Moreover, the increasing level of complexity enforced by legitimate peripheral participation allows employees to develop increasingly complex interpretations of the different challenges that they face as they enact their role, allowing them to develop the skill to perform improvisational bricolage early on in their affiliation to the organization without rendering them useless while they do so (George et al. 1995).

The routinization of improvisational bricolage
Improvisational bricolage allows not only for integration of exploration and exploitation in action but also their integration in the organization's structure through the routinization of specific improvisations. Routinization of improvisation is, in essence, evolutionary (Aldrich 1999). As employees enact specific improvisational bricolages, some of these improvisations are likely to become a routine as they are enacted in different conditions for actions and adopted by different groups of people. These improvisational bricolages are those that are enacted frequently enough to be able to command the necessary procedural memory to be retained (Moorman and Miner 1998b), and which become a part of the behavioral repertoire of devices with which members classify and confront their organizational worlds. Other instances of improvisational bricolage that are enacted less frequently or with limited visibility to others are more likely to be forgotten due to the limitations of human memory (Anderson 1983). As an evolutionary dynamic, a population of entities (procedures, be they instances of improvisational bricolage or not), compete for limited resources that each entity needs for survival (memory); in the process, there are identifiable mechanisms for variation, selection and retention of entities in the population, whose parameters are set at a macro-population level (Van de Ven and Scott 1995). Entities in this population are procedural routines, improvised or not, that address the variety of tasks the organization has to handle over time. The limited resources for which procedural routines compete are memory and usage. If a given routine is not used for a considerable time it is likely to be gradually dropped from memory because of human and organizational cognitive limitations, bounding rationality, and hence will become redundant (Tversky and Kahneman 1974; Moorman and Miner 1998a). Mechanisms of variation, selection and retention do not only relate to active consciousness and memory but also to those minimal structures supporting them (Brown and Eisenhardt 1997) that serve as centripetal but variety-inducing elements, through which members conceive novelty (Weick, 1998, 1999). By acting within the bounds of the minimal structure, organizational members are able to create the necessary variety for tackling urgent, unexpected and important competitive challenges demanding rapid action which, via sensemaking, allow for new procedural routines to emerge (Orlikowski 1996).

The selection of variations emerging from this process obeys a simple mechanism. If the improvisational bricolage appears to work, it will be selected; if it appears to fail, it will not (Barrett 1998; Crossan 1998). Of course, appearances are heavily socially nuanced and can often be deceptive. Retention comes from the storage of a newly created routine into procedural memory and its use in future problems and opportunities with a similar set of triggers, thus becoming a standard routine/procedure. Such usage may also take the form of bricolage when the routine becomes used as an input for creating new (composite) routines (Scribner 1986).

Those instances of improvisational bricolage that become part of the organization's memory, distributed across practices and artefacts, become standard, albeit unprescribed, procedures for the organization which create new resources for improvisation by expanding the interpretation of current resources and their uses. They allow the organization to obtain what are de facto new resources without having to acquire them.

Foresight as exploitative exploration

The literature on foresight treats it as a specific instance of organizational exploration (Slaughter 1989, 1996; Godet and Roubelat 1996). Foresight is seen as a process through which the organization makes sense of the future and creates the conditions for a long-term, sustainable competitive position. Recently, it has been framed as a problem of managerial cognition in environments that change through punctuated equilibrium dynamics (Greeve 1998; Tripsas and Gavetti 2002). Research has shown that in such contexts, impending radical change sends many 'weak signals' that fail to catch the attention of managers of organizations that hold dominant competitive positions in an industry (Mendonca et al. 2004). Once the competitive actions producing these 'weak signals' accumulate into discontinuities in the bases of industry competition, dominant players are replaced by firms that have generated or quickly adapted to the innovations that define the new market landscape (Romanelli and Tushman 1994; Edelman and Benning 1999). The purpose of foresight is to take advantage of these competitive dynamics by reading 'weak signals' to anticipate discontinuities and either preempt them to defend the firm's current competitive position or put a strategy in place to ensure that the firm can ride the discontinuity to a dominant market position once the basis of competition shifts (Stubbart 1989).

There are three major processes to anticipate competitive dynamics, each matching an approach to competitive discontinuities. The first focuses on detecting and interpreting weak signals (Hodgkinson 1997), framing market discontinuities as changes that incumbents respond to or not. They are the outcome of the actions of new entrants into the industry which can only be preempted, but not generated, by established firms. These firms suffer from what Miller (1993) called the 'curse of success': they are unwilling and unable to imagine different futures for their markets and even to change if a new future presents itself to them. The only possible course of action in this case is to detect changes early so that they can be preempted by strategic action or acquisition. Executives need to detect these market discontinuities when they are only hinted at by 'weak signals' and decide how to act on them so as to avoid the threat that, imaginatively, they can be enacted to represent.

The second major process to anticipate competitive dynamics relies on market experiments to detect emerging changes in market dynamics (Brown and Eisenhardt 1997). This view interprets market discontinuities as opportunities that every firm in the industry can take advantage of, *if* they detect them in time. Discontinuities are the outcome of the interplay between organizations' actions and changing consumption patterns (Tushman and Anderson 1986). If incumbents leave these changes unaddressed, a tipping-point is reached that turns into a market discontinuity. However, incumbents can detect these changes by engaging in low investment experiments (probes) to interpret views of the future that they can seek to validate against their competitive environment. The goal is to help executives decide which experiments to conduct and design these probes to maximize their validity and the knowledge gained from the market (Cohen and Levinthal 1990; Miner et al. 2001).

The third major process for anticipating competitive dynamics sees competitive landscapes as social constructions by industry incumbents, which can be changed through reinterpreting the bases of competition (Henderson and Clark 1990; Berger and Luckmann 1991; Dougherty 1992). Discontinuities are thus the outcome of companies enacting a different social construction of the market than that held by other industry members. If this reinterpretation of the competitive landscape is widely adopted in the market, those companies that fail to follow it will be left, at best, to serve a small niche of customers. Executives need to be able to re-imagine their industry and play not only an active but also a leading role in creating its future.

Overall, each of these three processes seeks to know what the future of organizations' competitive landscape holds for its incumbents. Foresight, in this view, is a window on a possible future which helps the organizations' top management team decide what to do in the present to achieve a sustainable and enduring competitive position – a future perfect. Independently of how the organization sees its future, the ultimate outcome of foresight will be a long-term strategic plan to ensure that the necessary resources are in place to sustain and improve the organization's competitive position in the future, without being distracted by strategic challenges in the present (McGrath and MacMillan 1995; Lane and Maxfield 1996). In this sense, foresight is an exploratory practice which seeks to carve a strategic path for the organization by preparing it for changes in market dynamics. If foresight is oriented towards discovering the future of the organization and away from discovering the future of the market, it can be used to integrate exploitation and exploration.

Independently of whether an organization is flexible and adaptive, flexibility and adaptability are part and parcel of employees' everyday practice (Mirvis 1998; Tyre and von Hippel 1999). As research has consistently shown, employees routinely adapt prescribed rules and procedures to customers' needs and demands (Blau and Scott 1962; Orr 1990). These micro processes of adaptation often include improvisations to match changes in situated interactions. These everyday improvisations are, however, often invisible to managers because the interpersonal and computer-aided information systems that managers use are not designed to capture unprescribed adaptations to prescribed processes and outcomes (for example, Orlikowski 1996). Nonetheless, if managers are able to observe these improvisations systematically, they not only learn about market changes first-hand but also learn about how these changes can be addressed and taken advantage of using the organizations' internal resources (Mintzberg and McHugh 1985). Drawing on existing company resources to make sense of the future and to address the challenges and opportunities that it harbors, enables foresight to integrate exploration and exploitation. To manage the organization's future in such a way is to delegate strategic cognition to employees, focusing on articulating and systematizing the knowledge they acquire in their everyday interactions with customers and competitors, and in sharing the improvisations they enact in these interactions (Brown and Duguid 1991). To look inside the organization to make sense of the future does not so much adopt an autopoietic view of markets as social constructions of specific organizations (see Maturana and Varela 1980) as take employees' ability to learn from everyday experiences seriously. Competitive intelligence is at least as abundant in the lower echelons of the organization as in its top management team (Mintzberg and Waters 1982; Ciborra 1996). Managers need only to create processes that allow them to access this information and make sense of it, developing heterarchical spaces rather than blocking these through hierarchical conduits (Fairtlough 2005), so that employees can craft strategies as the organization's environment changes (Kidder 1981; Dutton et al. 2001). The emergent side of strategy needs to be taken seriously and the situated improvisations of employees need to be acknowledged as constituting a strategy-making process whose collective intelligence is capable of addressing strategic challenges more effectively than a top-down planning process could ever hope to produce (Hedberg et al. 1976; Picken and Dess 1997). The managers' role in the foresight and strategy process is not simply to craft a strategy, relying on simplified inputs. Instead, their role consists in making others' improvisations visible to the organization so that they can be adopted and appropriated by employees addressing similar strategic challenges.

Institutionalizing improvisations
There are two approaches to managing exploitative and exploratory forms of foresight: formalizing improvisations and formalizing diffusion. When formalizing improvisations, the managers' role is to learn about and prescribe improvisations (Orlikowski 1993a, 1993b). Learning about improvisations is difficult. Improvisations are variations on pre-scribed practice and can thus be interpreted as a threat to managers' professional sense of self-worth and their identity. Prescribed procedures are, after all, sanctioned, if not designed, by managers. Deviations from them can be seen as a negative comment on man-agers' ability to make and implement those processes that best serve organizational goals (see Goffman 1969). This means not only that managers may be unwilling to learn about improvisations but also that employees may be reluctant to make these practices visible to avoid challenging the managers directly. Learning about improvisations requires what Weick (1999) called an 'aesthetic of imperfection', a culture that values and celebrates errors and deviations. Such a culture is a necessary condition for managers to see improv-isations, but it is not sufficient. An aesthetic of imperfection makes managers willing to seek and value employees' improvisations, but it fails to address the challenge of actually finding them in the organization. Research suggests that it is hard to find a more effective way of seeing employees' improvisations than being close to their work (Suchman 1995). Even when employees use sophisticated information systems, improvisations are hard to detect (Orr 1990). Some studies suggest that formal knowledge management systems may help, but this information is likely to be more limited than first-hand observation (Lyles and Schwenk 1992). Prescribing improvisations to other organizations is also difficult. Improvisations can hardly be made explicit, especially if its element of bricolage is an embodied practice not easily transmitted outside joint action (Orr 1990). The managers' role in spreading foresight is closer to that of crafts masters who teach and learn from their apprentices as they attempt to continuously enhance the competence, knowledge and skills of their workshop.

When formalizing the diffusion process, managers focus on making sure that empl-oyees have an opportunity to share their improvisations with each other. Their role is to create and maintain the organizational conditions to support improvisation and to ensure that it is shared across the communities of practice in the organization (Hedberg et al. 1976; Kamoche and Cunha 2001). In this approach, the challenge for managers is to relinquish most of their control over the strategic process – a considerable identity challenge, inasmuch as control is at the core of the social construction of the managers' role. Formalizing the diffusion process is not, however, an effort at organizational design. Research has shown that attempting to 'design' emergent groups often backfires with disastrous results. Instead, formalizing the diffusion of improvisations means creating a minimal structure that guides and energizes the emergent process of strategy making through improvisation without constraining it (Weick 1993). Minimal structures are typically constituted by compatible goals, such as deadlines, which do not prescribe outcomes but prescribe when outcomes need to be achieved. They are structures that foster minimal consensus, attempting to maximize variety and diversity by creating the conditions where these can thrive without causing entropy or dissipation, such as an aesthetic of imperfection and a bias for action. Such structures are not easily put in place and maintained but need managers whose leadership enforces these minimal requirements and draws on employees' identity as a motivator for improvisation. These managers push down the content of foresight and focus on managing its process. Their goal is to ensure that their organization is able and willing to find its futures as its present unfolds.

Conclusion

The purpose of this chapter was to contribute to the literature on the tension between strategic exploration and strategic exploitation. Our contribution was to bring the integration between the two poles of this tension to the level of everyday action. In accomplishing this, the goal was to complement other approaches that address the exploration/ exploitation debate, seeking integration through macro-level organizational design and through the process of deliberate strategy making.

Integrating exploration and exploitation at this level raised the issue of the role of foresight in the strategy process. Foresight has been declared obsolete in fast-changing competitive contexts. Indeed, it is challenging to rely on foresight as a practice focused on attempting to assemble the future of the organization from weak signals in the market to change the strategy of organizations. However, managers can strengthen their company's competitive position if they help the organization to look inside and find its future in the weak signals embedded in everyday instances of improvisational bricolage. These micro-level adaptations hold not only hints about the future of competitive dynamics but also situated attempts to deal with the challenges this future will bring. For researchers, the challenge is to understand the practices that managers draw on to learn about these weak signals and make sense of them to enact their organization's futures. For practitioners, the challenge is to lead their organization in a way that enables them to learn from and diffuse successful instances of improvisational bricolage, thereby creating the conditions to follow and even anticipate changes in their market. Fostering improvisational bricolage and engaging in inward-looking foresight is not easily accomplished, but if managers are able to nurture these practices they open the possibility of learning about and creating new futures.

References

Aldrich, H. (1999), *Organizations Evolving*, London: Sage.
Anderson, J.R. (1983), *The Architecture of Cognition*, Cambridge, MA: Harvard University Press.
Anderson, P. (1999), 'Complexity theory and organization science', *Organization Science*, **10**(3), 216–32.
Ansoff, H. Igor, J. Avner, R.G. Brandenburg, F.E. Portner and R. Radosevich (1970), 'Does planning pay off? The effects of planning on success of acquisitions in American firms', *Long Range Planning*, **3**(2), 2–7.
Ashmos, Donde P., Dennis Duchon and Wayne D. Bodensteiner (1997), 'Linking issue labels and managerial

actions: a study of participation in crisis vs. opportunity issues', *Journal of Applied Business Research*, **13**(4), 31–45.

Barrett, Frank J. (1998), 'Coda: Creativity and improvisation in organizations: implications for organizational learning', *Organization Science*, **9**(5), 605–22.

Bastien, David T. and Todd J. Hostager (1991), 'Jazz as social structure, process and outcome', in Reginald T. Buckner and Steven Weiland (eds), *Jazz in Mind: Essays on the History and Meanings of Jazz*, Detroit, MI: Wayne State University Press, pp. 148–65.

Beer, Michael (1996), 'Developing an organization capable of implementing strategy and learning', *Human Relations*, **49**(5), 597–619.

Beer, Michael and Russell Eisenstat (2000), 'The silent killers of strategy implementation and learning', *Sloan Management Review*, **41**(Summer), 29–40.

Berger, Peter and Thomas Luckmann (1991), *The Social Construction of Reality: A Treatise in the Sociology of Knowledge*, London: Penguin Books.

Berry, J.W. and S.H. Irvine (1986), 'Bricolage: savages do it daily', in R.J. Sternberg and R.K. Wagner (eds), *Practical Intelligence: Nature and Origins of Competence in the Everyday World*, Cambridge: Cambridge University Press, pp. 271–306.

Blau, Peter M. and Richard Scott (1962), *Formal Organizations*, San Francisco, CA: Chandler.

Bourdieu, Pierre (1990), *The Logic of Practice*, Stanford, CA: Stanford University Press.

Bowker, Geoffrey C. and Susan Leigh Starr (2000), *Sorting Things Out: Classification and Its Consequences*, Cambridge, MA: MIT Press.

Brews, Peter J. and Michelle R. Hunt (1999), 'Learning to plan and planning to learn: resolving the planning school/learning school debate', *Strategic Management Journal*, **20**, 889–913.

Brown, John Seely and Paul Duguid (1991), 'Organizational learning and communities-of-practice: toward a unified view of working, learning and innovation', *Organization Science*, **2**(1), 40–57.

Brown, Shona L. and Kathleen M. Eisenhardt (1997), 'The art of continuous change: linking complexity theory and time-paced evolution in relentlessly shifting organizations', *Administrative Science Quarterly*, **42**, 1–34.

Christensen, Clayton M. (1997), *The Innovator's Dilemma: When New Technologies Cause Great Firms to Fail*, Boston, MA: Harvard Business School Press.

Ciborra, Claudio U. (1996), 'The platform organization: recombining strategies, structures and surprises', *Organization Science*, **7**(2), 103–18.

Cohen, Michael D. and Daniel A. Levinthal (1990), 'Absorptive capacity: a new perspective on learning and innovation', *Administrative Science Quarterly*, **35**, 128–52.

Crossan, Mary M. (1998), 'Improvisation in action', *Organization Science*, **9**(5), 593–9.

Crossan, Mary M., Miguel P. Cunha, Dusya Vera and João Cunha (2005), 'Time and organizational improvisation', *Academy of Management Review*, **38**(1), 129–45.

Cunha, João Vieira, Ken Kamoche and Miguel P. Cunha (2002), 'Once again: what, when, how, and why?', in Ken Kamoche, Miguel P. Cunha and João Vieira Cunha (eds), *Organizational Improvisation*, London: Routledge, pp. 296–308.

Cunha, Miguel P. and João Vieira Cunha (2001), 'Managing improvisation in cross-cultural virtual teams', *International Journal of Cross Cultural Management*, **1**(2), 187–208.

Cunha, Miguel Pina, João Vieira Cunha and Ken Kamoche (1999), 'Organizational improvisation: what, when, how and why', *International Journal of Management Reviews*, **1**(3), 299–341.

Daft, Richard L. and Karl E. Weick (1984), 'Toward a model of organizations as interpretation systems', *Academy of Management Review*, **9**(2), 284–95.

Dougherty, Deborah (1992), 'Interpretive barriers to successful product innovation in large firms', *Organization Science*, **3**, 179–202.

Duncan, R. (1976), 'The ambidextrous organization: designing dual structures for innovation', in R. Kilman and L. Pondy (eds), *The Management of Organizational Design*, Amsterdam: North-Holland, pp. 167–88.

Dutton, Jane E., Susan J. Ashford, Regina M. O'Neill and Katherine A. Lawrence (2001), 'Moves that matter: issue selling and organizational change', *Academy of Management Journal*, **44**(4), 716–37.

Edelman, Linda F. and Anne Louise Benning (1999), 'Incremental revolution: organizational change in highly turbulent environments', *Organization Development Journal*, **17**(4), 79–93.

Eisenhardt, Kathleen M. (1989), 'Making fast strategic decisions in high-velocity environments', *Academy of Management Journal*, **32**, 543–76.

Eisenhardt, Kathleen M. (1997), 'Strategic decision making as improvisation', in Vassilis Papadakis and Patrick Barwise (eds), *Strategic Decisions*, Norwell, MA: Kluwer Academic, pp. 251–7.

Eisenhardt, Kathleen M. and L.J. Bourgeois III (1988), 'Politics of strategic decision making in high velocity environments: toward a midrange theory', *Academy of Management Journal*, **31**(4), 737–70.

Eisenhardt, Kathleen M. and Behnam N. Tabrizi (1995), 'Accelerating adaptive processes: product innovation in the global computer industry', *Administrative Science Quarterly*, **40**, 84–110.

Fairtlough, G. (2005), *The Three Ways of Getting Things Done: Hierarchy, Heterarchy and Responsible Autonomy in Organizations*, Greenway, UK: Triarchy.

Foster, Richard and Sarah Kaplan (2001), *Creative Destruction: Why Companies that are Built to Last Underperform the Market and How to Successfully Transform Them*, New York: Doubleday.

George, J.F., S. Iacono and R. Kling (1995), 'Learning in context: extensively computerized work groups as communities-of-practice', *Accounting, Management and Information Technologies*, **5**(3), 185–202.

Gersick, Connie J. (1991), 'Revolutionary change theories: a multilevel exploration of the punctuated equilibrium paradigm', *Academy of Management Review*, **32**, 274–309.

Giddens, Anthony (1986), *The Constitution of Society: An Outline of the Theory of Structuration*, Berkeley, CA: University of California Press.

Godet, Michel and Fabrice Roubelat (1996), 'Creating the future: the use and misuse of scenarios', *Long Range Planning*, **29**(2), 164–71.

Goffman, Erving (1967), *Interaction Ritual: Essays on Face-to-Face Behavior*, New York: Pantheon Books.

Goffman, Erving (1969), *Strategic Interaction*, Philadelphia, PA: University of Pennsylvania Press.

Gouldner, Alvin W. (1954), *Patterns of Industrial Bureaucracy*, New York: Free Press.

Greeve, H.R. (1998), 'Managerial cognition and the mimetic adoption of market positions: what you see is what you do', *Strategic Management Journal*, **19**, 967–88.

Haveman, H (1992), 'Between a rock and a hard place: organizational change and performance under conditions of fundamental environmental transformation', *Administrative Science Quarterly*, **37**, 48–75.

Heath, Christian and Paul Luff (2000), *Technology in Action*, Cambridge and New York: Cambridge University Press.

Hedberg, Bo L.T., Paul C. Nystrom and William H. Starbuck (1976), 'Camping on seesaws: prescriptions for self-designing organizations', *Administrative Science Quarterly*, **21**, 41–65.

Henderson, Rebecca M. and Kim B. Clark (1990), 'Architectural innovation: the reconfiguration of existing product technologies and the failures of established firms', *Administrative Science Quarterly*, **35**, 9–30.

Hodgkinson, G.P. (1997), 'The cognitive analysis of competitive structures: a review and critique', *Human Relations*, **50**(6), 625–54.

Hutchins, Edwin (1996), *Cognition in the Wild*, Cambridge, MA: MIT Press.

Ibarra, Herminia (1999), 'Provisional selves: experimenting with image and identity in professional adaptation', *Administrative Science Quarterly*, **44**, 764–91.

Jackall, Robert (1989), *Moral Mazes: The World of Corporate Managers*, Oxford and New York: Oxford University Press.

Johnson, Bonnie McDaniel and Ronald E. Rice (1984), 'Reinvention in the innovation process: the case of word processing', in Ronald E. Rice (ed.), *The New Media*, Beverly Hills, CA: Sage, pp. 157–83.

Kamoche, Ken and Miguel P. Cunha (2001), 'Minimal structures: from jazz improvisation to product innovation', *Organization Studies*, **22**(4), 733–64.

Kelly, D and T.L. Ambrugey (1991), 'Organizational inertia and momentum: a dynamic model of strategic change', *Academy of Management Journal*, **34**(3), 591–612.

Kidder, Tracy (1981), *The Soul of a New Machine*, Boston, MA: Little Brown.

Kiesler, S. and L. Sproull (1982), 'Managerial response to changing environments: perspectives on problem sensing from social cognition', *Administrative Science Quarterly*, **27**, 548–70.

Kondo, Doreen (1990), *Crafting Selves: Power, Discourse and Identity in a Japanese Factory*, Chicago, IL: University of Chicago Press.

Lane, David and Robert Maxfield (1996), 'Strategy under complexity: fostering generative relationships', *Long Range Planning*, **29**(2), 215–31.

Lanzara, Giovan Francesco (1983), 'Ephemeral organizations in extreme environments: emergence, strategy, extinction', *Journal of Management Studies*, **20**(1), 71–95.

Lave, Jean (1988), *Cognition in Practice: Mind, Mathematics, and Culture in Everyday Life*, Cambridge: Cambridge University Press.

Lave, Jean and Etienne Wenger (1991), *Situated Learning: Legitimate Peripheral Participation*, Cambridge: Cambridge University Press.

Levinthal, D.A. (1997), 'Adaptation on rugged landscapes', *Management Science*, **43**(7), 934–50.

Levinthal, D.A. and M. Warglien (1999), 'Landscape design: designing for local action in complex worlds', *Organization Science*, **10**(3), 342–57.

Lewin, Arie Y. (1998), 'Jazz improvisation as a metaphor for organizational theory', *Organization Science*, **9**(5), 539.

Lyles, M.A. and C.R. Schwenk (1992), 'Top management, strategy and organizational knowledge structure', *Journal of Management Studies*, **29**(2), 155–74.

Machin, David and Michael Carrithers (1996), 'From "interpretative communities" to "communities of improvisation"', *Media, Culture and Society*, **18**, 343–52.

Marx, K. ([1844] 1975), *Early Writings*, Ontario: Penguin.

Maturana, Humberto R. and Francisco J. Varela (1980), *Autopoiesis and Cognition: The Realization of the Living*, Dordrecht: D. Reidel.
McGrath, Rita Gunther and Ian C. MacMillan (1995), 'Discovery-driven planning', *Harvard Business Review*, July–August, 44–54.
Mendonca, Sandro, Miguel P. Cunha, Jari Kaivo-oja and Franks Ruff (2004), 'Wild cards, weak signals and organisational improvisation', *Futures*, 36(2), 201–18.
Miller, C.C. and L.B. Cardinal (1994), 'Strategic planning and firm performance: a synthesis of more than two decades of research', *Academy of Management Journal*, 37(6), 1649–65.
Miller, Danny (1993), 'The architecture of simplicity', *Academy of Management Review*, 18(1), 116–38.
Miner, A.S., P. Bassoff and C. Moorman (2001), 'Organizational improvisation and learning: a field study', *Administrative Science Quarterly*, 46(2), 304–37.
Mintzberg, Henry and Alexandra McHugh (1985), 'Strategy formation in an adhocracy', *Administrative Science Quarterly*, 30, 160–97.
Mintzberg, Henry and James A. Waters (1982), 'Tracking strategy in an entrepreneurial firm', *Academy of Management Journal*, 25, 465–99.
Mirvis, Philip H. (1998), 'Practice improvisation', *Organization Science*, 9(5), 586–92.
Moorman, Christine and Anne Miner (1998a), 'The convergence between planning and execution: improvisation in new product development', *Journal of Marketing*, 62, 1–20.
Moorman, Christine and Anne Miner (1998b), 'Organizational improvisation and organizational memory', *Academy of Management Review*, 23(4), 698–723.
Morrow, P.C. (1981), 'Work-related communication, environmental uncertainty, and subunit effectiveness: a second look at the information processing approach', *Academy of Management Journal*, 24, 851–8.
Orlikowski, Wanda J. (1993a), 'CASE tools as organizational change: investigating increment', *MIS Quarterly*, 17(3), 309–39.
Orlikowski, Wanda J. (1993b), 'Learning from notes: organizational issues in groupware implementation', *Information Society*, 9(3), 237–50.
Orlikowski, Wanda J. (1996), 'Improvising organizational transformation over time: a situated change perspective', *Information Systems Research*, 7(1), 63–92.
Orr, J. (1990), 'Sharing knowledge, celebrating identity: war stories and community memory in a service culture', in D.S. Middleton and D. Edwards (eds), *Collective Remembering: Memory in Society*, Beverly Hills, CA: Sage, pp. 35–47.
Paich, M. and J.D. Sterman (1993), 'Boom, bust, and failures to learn in experimental markets', *Management Science*, 39(12), 1439–58.
Pascale, Richard T. (1984), 'Perspectives on strategy: the real story behind Honda's success', *California Management Review*, 26, 47–62.
Peplowski, Ken (1998), 'The process of improvisation', *Organization Science*, 9(5), 560–61.
Peters, Thomas J. (1992), *Liberation Management: The Necessary Disorganization for the Nanosecond Nineties*, New York: Alfred A. Knopf.
Picken, Joseph C. and Gregory G. Dess (1997), 'Out of (strategic) control', *Organizational Dynamics*, 25(1), 35–47.
Poole, Marshall Scott and Andrew H. Van de Ven (1989), 'Using paradox to build management and organization theories', *Academy of Management Review*, 14(4), 562–78.
Repenning, N.P., P. Goncalves and L.J. Black (2001), 'Past the tipping point: the persistence of firefighting in product development', *California Management Review*, 43(4), 44–63.
Romanelli, E. and M.L. Tushman (1994), 'Organizational transformation as punctuated equilibrium: an empirical test', *Academy of Management Journal*, 37(5), 1141–66.
Sacks, H. (1972), 'An initial investigation of the usability of conversational data for doing sociology', in D. Sudnow (ed.), *Studies in Social Interaction*, New York: Free Press, pp. 31–74.
Sastry, M.A (1997), 'Problems and paradoxes in a model of punctuated organizational change', *Administrative Science Quarterly*, 42, 237–75.
Scribner, Sylvia (1986), 'Thinking in action: some characteristics of practical thought', in R.J. Sternberg and R.K. Wagner (eds), *Practical Intelligence: Nature and Origins of Competence in the Everyday World*, Cambridge: Cambridge University Press, pp. 13–30.
Sitkin, Sim B. (1992), 'Learning through failure: the strategy of small losses', in B.M. Staw and L.L. Cummings (eds), *Research in Organizational Behavior*, Greenwich, CT: JAI Press, pp. 231–66.
Slaughter, R.A. (1989), 'Probing beneath the surface: review of a decade's futures work', *Futures*, 21(5), 447–65.
Slaughter, R.A. (1996), 'Mapping the future: creating a structural overview of the next 20 years', *Journal of Futures Studies*, 1(1), 5–25.
Slocum, John W., Jr, Michael McGill and David T. Lei (1994), 'The new learning strategy: anytime, anything, anywhere', *Organization Science*, 22(2), 33–47.

Starbuck, W. and F. Milliken (1988), 'Challenger: fine-tuning the odds until something breaks', *Journal of Management Studies*, **25**, 319–40.

Stubbart, Charles I. (1989), 'Managerial cognition: a missing link in strategic management research', *Journal of Management Studies*, **24**(4), 325–47.

Suchman, Lucille Alice (1987), *Plans and Situated Actions: The Problem of Human–Machine Communication*, Cambridge: Cambridge University Press.

Suchman, Lucille Alice (1995), 'Making work visible', *Communications of the ACM*, **38**(9), 56–61.

Thevenot, Laurent (1999), 'Pragmatic regimes governing the engagement with the world', in K. Knorr-Cetina, T. Schatzki and Eike v. Savigny (eds), *The Practice Turn in Contemporary Theory*, London: Routledge, pp. 56–74.

Tripsas, Mary and G. Gavetti (2002), 'Capabilities, cognition, and inertia: evidence from digital imaging', *Strategic Management Journal*, **21**, 1147–61.

Tushman, M.L. and P. Anderson (1986), 'Technological discontinuities and organizational environments', *Administrative Science Quarterly*, **31**, 439–65.

Tushman, Michael L. and C.A. O'Reilly (1996), 'Ambidextrous organizations: managing evolutionary and revolutionary change', *California Management Review*, **38**(4), 8–30.

Tversky, A. and D. Kahneman (1974), 'Judgement under uncertainty: heuristics and biases', *Science*, **185**, 1124–31.

Tyre, M. and E. von Hippel (1999), 'The situated nature of adaptive learning in organizations', *Organization Science*, **8**, 71–83.

Van de Ven, A.H. and Poole M. Scott (1995), 'Explaining development and change in organizations', *Academy of Management Review*, **20**(3), 510–40.

von Hippel, Eric (1987), *The Sources of Innovation*, Oxford and New York: Oxford University Press.

Von Hippel, Eric (1994), '"Sticky information" and the locus of problem solving: implications for innovation', *Management Science*, **40**(4), 429–39.

Weick, Karl E. (1987), 'Substitutes for strategy', in D.J. Teece (ed.), *Competitive Challenge*, Cambridge, MA: Ballinger, pp. 221–33.

Weick, Karl E. (1993), 'Organizational redesign as improvisation', in George P. Huber and William H. Glick (eds), *Organizational Change and Redesign*, Oxford and New York: Oxford University Press, pp. 346–79.

Weick, Karl E. (1996), 'Drop your tools: an allegory for organizational studies', *Administrative Science Quarterly*, **41**, 301–13.

Weick, Karl E. (1998), 'Introductory essay: improvisations as a mindset for organizational analysis', *Organization Science*, **9**(5), 543–55.

Weick, Karl E. (1999), 'The aesthetic of imperfection in organizations', *Comportamento Organizacional e Gestão*, **5**(1), 5–22.

Whyte, W.F. (1948), *Human Relations in the Restaurant Industry*, New York: McGraw-Hill.

11 Micro-political strategies and strategizing in multinational corporations: the case of subsidiary mandate change

Christoph Dörrenbächer and Mike Geppert

Introduction

Like all other forms of politics, micro politics are a strategic attempt to exert a formative influence on social structures and human relations. The aim of micro-political strategies is to secure options, to realize interests, and to achieve success through efforts that are often but not exclusively motivated by interests or individual career plans of key actors. Micro-political strategizing is thus an everyday occurrence at large multinational corporations (MNCs), and understanding and anticipating actors' strategizing is a key to developing strategic foresight (Tsoukas and Chia, 2002; Costanzo, 2003). However, the question of which actors are involved in micro-political strategizing in MNCs is still largely debated. In the early 1960s, James G. March devised a general list of relevant political actors in firms including investors, investment analysts, suppliers, customers, governmental agents, employees, trade associations, political parties and labor unions (March, 1962, pp. 672f.). Taking the perspective of a large and differentiated MNC this list would seem to be an oversimplification which, in particular, does not do justice to management, with their different hierarchical, functional and organizational backgrounds, not to mention their national and intercultural ties that are especially important here.

The large number of potential micro-political actors in MNCs as well as their heterogeneity indicates first the specific significance of coalition building. According to March (ibid.), negotiations between political coalitions determine the composition and goals of an organization. Second, the heterogeneity of the actors involved in the political processes at a business firm illustrates that micro-political strategies can have very different thematic reference points and ranges. Micro-political strategies can affect an MNC as a whole, for example, when global business strategy is their concern. However, this can also apply to medium-range issues, for example, when key actors disagree on which subsidiaries and/or countries are set to be up- or downgraded. Finally, micro-political strategies can also occur at the department level of any unit of an MNC, for example, on the issue of boundary spanning (the sovereignty to develop exclusive internal and external relations to powerful stakeholders). Following Tom Burns (1961/62), who is credited as being the author who coined the term 'micro politics', micro-political processes create and change organizational structures. In early studies on micro-political processes, the restructuring of private enterprises and public organizations used to be the focus of attention. However, the specific areas of reorganization studied varied significantly. Along with the question of technology diffusion, strategic human resource management as well as issues related to strategic business planning, quality management and ecological management have been investigated. However, micro-political strategies associated with corporate internationalization have been largely neglected so far (Bélanger and Edwards, 2006). Addressing this gap is a main purpose of this chapter.

In this chapter we shall screen the relevant literature and discuss the strengths of micro-political approaches so far. The chapter thereby provides a short discussion of relevant strands of literature, encompassing the behavioral theory of internationalization, and institutionalist and contingency theory approaches discussing strategies of corporate internationalization. In line with scholars recently calling for a 'practice turn' in strategic management studies, we propose a more actor- and activity-centered approach as well as to have a closer and more in-depth look at the political dimension of strategic change and the strategizing process. We shall propose that especially mandate changes in MNCs are a particularly interesting field of empirical research since these micro events have consequences both at the micro (activity) and the macro (structural) levels. Here we also refer to the first findings of a current empirical study. We shall conclude by discussing methodological issues on how the ideas developed here can be related to some more recent institutionalist studies, and raise a few questions and considerations for future research on micro-political strategies and strategizing in MNCs.

Theoretical starting points
The fact that MNCs – like other organizations – are rational actors only to a certain extent was already pointed out by the behavioral internationalization theory in the 1970s. Compared to other internationalization theories that follow the rational choice paradigm (for example, the eclectic theory of foreign direct investment, which is presumably the most widely received theory today), behaviorist studies have searched for explanations to internationalization processes that contradict rationality expectations in the narrow sense. This is exemplified in the fact that strategically many companies do not or only very hesitantly invest abroad, although the expected earnings far outweigh the expected risks (Aharoni, 1966; Johanson and Vahlne, 1977). Another example is the fact that companies in oligopolistic markets do not pursue the most promising investment possibilities abroad, but practice a follow-the-leader strategy that may imitate the suboptimal investment strategies of their competitors (Knickerbocker, 1973; Graham, 1974).

Like the behavioral theory of internationalization, more recently comparative institutionalist research also portrays the actors in multinational organizations as failing to follow consistently rational strategies of economic efficiency (Morgan, 2001). Unlike mainstream strategic management approaches, it places more emphasis on the social and institutional embeddedness of MNCs, but like these it does assume weak actors with little strategic choices. Moreover, in the institutionalist approach (as in the behavioral theory of internationalization), researchers tend to focus on the dimension of cross-border business activities and primarily discuss convergence- and divergence-related developments. The core questions are: what characterizes the internationalization strategies of businesses, and what are the essential national institutional influences? Quite a few authors presume that the country of origin possesses a dominant influence. Hu (1992, p. 107), for example, defines MNCs as 'national firms with international operations'. Similarly, Sally (1995), Ruigrok and van Tulder (1995), and Whitley (2001, 2005) assume that MNCs are forced to make a more or less one-to-one transfer of organizational and production strategies that were effective in their country of origin to the situation abroad because of isomorphic environmental pressures and sunk costs. This view, which is at heart against research predicting the existence of a 'one best way', has meanwhile proved to be too undifferentiated. Depending on which strategic aspects of internationalization are studied,[1] one can identify universal factors, home-country effects, host-country effects, third-country effects as well as intra-organizational and extra-organizational effects.[2] As pointed out by proponents of institutionalist theories, these effects normally are not exerted smoothly, but rather, in processes charged with variable degrees of friction. However, a detailed analysis of this clash of genuinely micro-political strategies underpinning internationalization processes has not fit into their field of knowledge (at least up to now).

Advocates of the organization structure tradition more closely investigate the question of micro-political strategies in MNCs. Here, the relevant literature focuses on headquarters–subsidiary relationships in MNCs. While almost all of the older works on this subject investigate this relationship from the parent company perspective, Hedlund's (1986) concept of MNCs as 'heterarchies' (a company with more than one center of gravity) triggered a veritable flood of publications in which the viewpoints of MNC subsidiaries were examined more intensely. Their basic assumption is that subsidiaries of MNCs are by no means mere executive organs of the headquarters, but strategically important business units that systematically contribute to the competitiveness of the overall corporation.[3] According to Birkinshaw et al. (1998), the level of importance a subsidiary can attain depends on three factors: (i) the subsidiary's socioeconomic environment, (ii) the attitude of the headquarters towards the subsidiary, and (iii) the subsidiary management's ability to make the headquarters aware of its achievements and capabilities. The last two points are particularly important issues where micro-political strategies of headquarters and subsidiaries clash. According to Sölvell and Zander (1998), the headquarters' desire to maintain control is always in latent opposition to the subsidiary's desire to become as autonomous as possible. According to Forsgren and Johanson (1992a), the distribution of profits and decisions regarding the direction of development of the MNC in general or of the subsidiary in particular are further fundamental sources of strategy conflicts between headquarters and subsidiaries. These basic strategic conflicts can take place in different forms that are often related to each other or overlap: for example, they occur as investment conflicts, status or role conflicts of key players in strategic decision making (Johanson and Vahlne, 1977; Hofstede, 1997), or as strategic conflicts about knowledge transfer (see below).

Strategic conflicts about knowledge transfer in MNCs have been a particularly frequent focus of attention in recent years – from an institutional as well as an organizational perspective. This is due to the special importance of cross-border knowledge transfer processes in increasingly integrated MNCs strategically controlled by global product divisions: cross-border transfers make it possible to use more complex firm-specific advantages that are too risky or impossible to transfer to other countries via market control (Hymer, 1960; Dunning, 1979).[4] Furthermore, the strategic impetus from foreign markets and subsidiaries can only be incorporated and evaluated through such transfers (Hedlund, 1986; Sölvell and Zander, 1998).[5] Until now, empirical studies have mainly been concerned with micro-political issues and conflicts emanating from the strategic transfer projects initiated by headquarters. According to Forsgren et al. (1995) and Edwards et al. (1999), the corresponding resistance within the foreign subsidiaries towards certain knowledge transfer strategies is essentially fueled by the so-called 'not-invented-here syndrome', that is, by subsidiaries' seemingly illogical (from the headquarters' perspective) refusal to adopt certain knowledge, technologies or practices that originate from outside their own business unit (Katz and Allen, 1982). Other studies have implicated the nonconformity of the strategic content to be transferred as cause of conflicts (Jankowicz, 2001; Michailova, 2002), whereas others blame the affected subsidiary's lack of critical involvement (Hetrick, 2002) or absorptive capacity (Cohen and Lewinthal, 1990). However, quite a few authors (for example, Sharpe, 2001; Becker-Ritterspach et al., 2002; Fichter 2003) interpret the blockade, modification and avoidance strategies of subsidiaries as a necessary cultural, institutional or organizational politics-related ways to 'fine-tune' overly standardized directives from the headquarters. This exemplifies that the effects of strategy conflicts on organizations can be functional or dysfunctional, and is also an interesting starting-point for research on conflict management in MNCs. According to the characterizations of Morgan (2001), Pries (2001) or Geppert and Clark (2003), MNCs are pluri-local, intrinsically heterogeneous transnational social spaces, the internal dynamics of which calls for differentiated conflict management mechanisms.

Compared to the former approaches theorizing about micro-political strategies, the discussion about the social construction of transnational social spaces requires a different perspective. Former studies had a structuralist bias, focused mainly on how macro structures of the economic or institutional environments influence micro-political strategic decision making or cause certain micro-political conflicts. However, what is missing is to develop a better understanding of what managerial actors do, with whom they interact and why some of these interactions are political or have political implications. Thus, in line with arguments stressing the need of a 'practice turn' in strategy research (Johnson et al., 2003; Whittington, 2006), we believe that in order to understand the 'micro' dimension of strategic processes in MNCs we need to study strategies in the MNC from the bottom up. Thus, we propose the analysis of micro-political strategies of key actors at the subsidiary level. Furthermore, we agree that it is important not only what headquarters and subsidiary managers do, for example, what kind of knowledge they transfer, what kind of strategic resources they acquire to enable subsidiary entrepreneurship (see, for example, Birkinshaw, 2000) whether subsidiaries win or lose certain strategic roles (see, for example, Taggart, 1998), but also 'how' this is done (Johnson et al., 2006; Geppert and Mayer, 2006). Thus, research on micro-political strategies in the MNC sheds some light on the question how certain practices, for example, of key actors, influence the development of subsidiary mandates and how – whatever happened in practice – it is influenced by the actors' skills and political activities (Johnson et al., 2006).

In summary, we propose an activity-based (ibid.) view on micro politics, which means we must address the strategy content (for example, mandate change) in relation to certain organizational structures and institutions (for example, a subsidiary of an MNC and its location), and to the political activities of key actors developing and pursuing certain politically motivated strategies to influence others and gain and/or maintain power resources (in mandate change processes). We call the latter 'strategizing', and will discuss this in more detail after the next section. In the following section, however, we first want to shed some light on the issue of micro-political game playing in general and in the context of the MNC.

Strategies in micro-political games as social spaces of strategizing
Various features distinguish a micro-political approach to study internationalization and strategizing in MNCs from the structuralist approaches described above. One relatively

obvious distinction is that a bottom-up micro-political approach takes not just actors first but is interested in developing an activity-based view of strategy. The focus lies on the processes of strategy building and strategizing. These are conceived as social practices in the context of MNC and subsidiary management (see also Geppert and Mayer, 2006) and not so much as a 'property of organizations' (Whittington, 2006, p. 613). Additionally, a more differentiated view of actor relationships and the consideration of different interaction levels in the context of the MNC are further important advantages of the micro-political approach. This is important because 'life is lively' in organizations (Ortmann, 1988b, p. 7), especially when individuals or groups of actors with different (sub-)organizational, national and cultural backgrounds interact across borders as they typically do in MNCs. These important aspects are neglected in many of the institutionalist studies on MNCs.[6] Together with common international business research, macro structures and institutions are understood as the point of departure, when micro issues of political strategies and strategizing are addressed.

Probably the clearest and therefore potentially most fertile difference between the micro-political approach and the others is that the micro-political approach conveys two major paradigms of social theory, namely, volunteerism and determinism (Neuberger, 1998). The integrated structural and action perspective is realized by the conceptualizing of micro-political strategizing processes as games. These games, which are played both simultaneously and successively, are seen as characterizing an organization. Crozier and Friedberg (1980) define organizations as the sum of interconnected games.

When playing these games, actors are bound by rules, restrictions and resources. However, these structural limitations also provide certain liberties (with actor-specific differences) that can be used to implement one's own tactics and strategies. Hence, there are limitations but also liberties that create 'social spaces'[7] for micro-political game playing. According to Mintzberg (1983), authority games, power-building games, rivalry games and change games are of special significance in organizations. Ortmann et al. (1990) distinguish between routine and innovative games. A rather functional list includes budget games, career games and reorganization games. Further investigation is required to determine more precisely whether there are one or more genuine internationalization games and to identify their characteristic features.

Strategizing in the context of corporate internationalization plays a particularly important part in other types of games too. In career games, for example, this is evident when one considers how important it was and still is to be assigned to and to successfully manage the (strategically) best subsidiaries abroad to make the leap into the top management level of an MNC (Stahl et al., 2002). Budget games are another example. A German headquarters manager responsible for the company's East European subsidiaries summed up its experiences with micro politics in cross-border budget negotiations as follows:

> Now you have to slow down the Hungarians. They create lots of paperwork and know precisely where and what they are hiding. Another thing is also clear: we can't finance all the wishes of Mr. Works Director or make golden doorknobs. What we maintain with them is a sort of open relationship with a culture of friendly conflict. (Author interview with German corporate manager)

However, there are also arguments in support of the assumption of genuine internationalization games. For example, the loyalty of foreign subsidiaries' general managers to the headquarters, on the one hand, and to the foreign subsidiary, on the other, is a situation that requires a great power of integration and a high tolerance of ambiguity (Black et al., 1992). This is also a situation that presents tactical and strategic options that would otherwise be unavailable within the national framework. In certain situations, subsidiary managers can weaken, modify or ward off disagreeable and unreasonable requests from the headquarters by citing the institutional structures in their country or the political power of local actors as the reason (for examples, see Tempel, 2001 and Becker-Ritterspach et al., 2002). They can either exploit existing differences, for example, in national labor law, or they can capitalize certain 'insecurity zones', related to the need to locally adapt certain practices and relationships with key local practitioners. For example, for several months a French subsidiary of a German beverage manufacturer managed to pursue the foundation of a subsidiary in North America without the head-quarters' knowledge. Only the need to register the new subsidiary in the commercial register ultimately made it unavoidable to inform the headquarters (author interview with German expatriate in France). Although this sort of 'hidden' power-building strategy of subsidiaries rarely gets so far, it is still undisputed that such activities that functionalize the peculiarities of the 'insecurity zone' in an MNC take place at almost all foreign (and domestic) subsidiaries.

According to Crozier and Friedberg (1980), the extent to which such projects can proceed in secret, that is, the extent of the assertive power of micro-political actors, depends on the degree of their control over the 'insecurity zone' in question. Activities related to and around 'insecurity zones' within an organization usually emerge due to the fact that key actors, or groups of powerful actors, are in charge of setting rules and often also control resources that other actors require to develop projects and strategies successfully, for example, from the bottom up. According to this hypothesis, the manner in which the key actors are able to exert their influence across the geographical, political, socioeconomic, cultural and religious boundaries associated with internationalization is generally difficult to assess and even more difficult to control. However, one can expect to find different communication and influence strategies from those seen in co-located nationally and culturally and institutionally homogeneous settings.

In summary, micro-political strategizing takes places in a contested social space in which actors compete over resources or negotiate about setting rules and agendas through multi-layered games, be it specific internationalization games or games that take place within national borders. In the next section we explore more deeply the specific game emerging in and around the change of subsidiary mandates. The change of a subsidiary mandate is an organizational micro event that often triggers micro-political strategizing, because critical resources might be at stake and/or the established division of labor and power might be questioned.

Mandate changes as organizational micro events that trigger micro-political strategies and strategizing

Since MNCs operate across national, cultural, institutional and religious borders, they are organizations which contain different rationalities that underpin strategizing processes. We can, therefore, assume that there is a high potential for micro-political conflicts. Thus, for example, competitive pressure to achieve strategic and functional integration generates interest-driven conflicts not only between the company's individual units, but usually also between key individual and/or collective actors with dissimilar interests, norms and value systems (Kostova, 1999). In this respect, mandate changes in MNCs can be understood as critical 'micro events'[8] triggering micro-political strategizing. This has received surprisingly little attention in the international business literature so far. Mandates are time- and content-limited tasks assigned to a subsidiary by the headquarters, or acquired independently by the subsidiary, that define the internal division of labor within an MNC (Birkinshaw, 1996, 2001). Since mandates are usually associated with the control of resources or potential courses of action, mandates also define a business unit's level of 'clout' (Cyert and March, 1963; Pfeffer and Salancik, 1974; Birkinshaw and Ridderstråle, 1999). Changes (gains or losses) in mandates therefore have a distinct, intrinsic conflict potential in MNCs, especially when they lead to (or could lead to) long-term up- or downgrading of a subsidiary.[9] Upgrading occurs when a subsidiary of an MNC is assigned more demanding tasks, or gains increasing economic significance within the company over the course of time while maintaining the same tasks. Inversely, downgrading is said to occur when a subsidiary is allocated to less demanding tasks or loses its economic significance within the company over the course of time while maintaining the same tasks (Dörrenbächer and Gammelgaard, 2006).

Naturally, mandate changes are also of great strategic importance to the various key actors in MNCs. Careers, clout and jobs (at the headquarters as well as at subsidiaries at home and abroad) are influenced by the distribution of mandates among the different corporate units. Therefore, mandate assignments or changes are also subject to the orientation-related motives of the key actors involved. These motives which drive strategizing processes remain more or less latent since mandates are normally limited with respect to time and content. Furthermore, because of the internal and external dynamics of corporate changes, mandate assignments can be challenged once they are implemented. It is therefore in the interest of the headquarters at least occasionally to have a more or less open competition (bids from inside and outside the company) for the assignment of existing or new mandates (Birkenshaw and Lingblatt, 2005). The rationale for this might be adaptation to changes on the market or standardization of products, efforts to increase corporate or shareholder value and/or the desire to obtain greater control of a specific subsidiary. Simultaneously, the individual domestic and foreign subsidiaries strive to acquire new or expand existing mandates, either in response to changes on the market or customer relations, or to secure and improve their position and influence within the corporation.

According to strategic organizational analysis theories (Crozier and Friedberg, 1980; Ortmann, 1988a), headquarters and subsidiary managers of MNCs are primarily involved in conflicts related to mandate change. Depending on the importance and content of the desired mandate change as well as on the size of the corporation, actors involved at the headquarters may include the board of directors, members of the strategic planning staff, and managers with regional or divisional (product-specific) responsibilities; below this level, managers with functional responsibilities (for example, for personnel, production, marketing or research and development: R&D) are also involved. At the subsidiary level, the corresponding actors are normally the general managers (that is, managing directors) and/or managers in functional but strategically important areas (for example, personnel, production, marketing or R&D). Various other actors may also play an important part in the process of mandate change. Some of them may be directly affiliated with the company, for example, employee representatives who accept concessions to avoid the relocation of production and other activities. Some may be stockholders pushing to exploit international cost, service and regulatory advantages by changing the corporation's internal division of labor. Others, however, may be relatively company-independent stakeholders, such as investment-promoting government organizations exerting their influence to push the transfer of mandates to their region as well as non-governmental organizations attempting to block certain mandates that they feel are associated with undesirable production or R&D activities. A common trait of these unaffiliated stakeholders is that they normally do not intervene directly in processes of mandate change. However, their interests and positions target the strategies of the managerial actors and have permissive or restrictive effects on their strategizing processes.

Thus, in summary, to understand the micro-political underpinnings of actors' strategies and strategizing in the multinational firm we propose to focus on critical micro events in the organizational development of subsidiaries, such as mandate change. We argue that these events, no matter whether they are initiated by the headquarters or by an individual subsidiary, cause critical situations in which key actors feel strongly inclined to micro-political strategizing due to potentially strong and strategic gains or losses in influence and resources. At the same time, newly introduced mandate changes always require local acceptance and need to be legitimized in both directions internally in the subsidiary itself and externally in relation towards the headquarters, other subsidiaries of the MNC as well as important stakeholders such as customers, suppliers and shareholders. Thus, in contrast to institutionalist studies which see the importance of legitimacy for organizational development and predict isomorphic convergence of organizational structures and institutions, we stress that gaining legitimacy for, for example, mandate changes in an MNC is a micro-political process. As we shall see in the mini case studies we shall describe in the next section, the implementation of financial performance measures is isomorphic and can be found in MNCs even when they are operating in different host countries and industrial sectors. However, how these measures translate into mandate change processes and how they are strategically interpreted and enacted by key subsidiary managers differs considerably.

Micro-political strategies and strategizing in the processes of mandate change

Given the scope of this chapter, the activities of the actors involved in mandate assignment-related conflicts, the significance of various institutional circumstances, corporation-wide practices and routines, as well as organizational (or sub-organizational) and individual interests will be described only cursorily, based on the example of one key actor's perspective and interpretations, namely, foreign subsidiary managers. Nevertheless, the ensuing accounts will go beyond the so far dominant structuralist approaches that attribute mandate change processes in MNCs solely either to structural or to institutional influences. In this context, it must first be noted that turning to an action theory perspective by no means negates the fact that strategizing patterns of certain actors within the corporation can only be understood with reference to the conditions of their structural constitution and the strategic position of the subsidiary in the MNC. However, on the other hand this does not mean that actors in organizations are entirely compliant executive instruments of structural and institutional constraints. The concept 'that every action in, for and in regard to organizations is always an action in consideration and in pursuit of the actor's own interests' appears to be more realistic (Küpper and Felsch, 2000, p. 149; own translation). The questions of how structural and institutional circumstances and/or constraints and an actor's individual room to operate correlate with and influence each other are interesting but still largely empirically underexplored issues.

The basic structural and institutional forces that influence the potential and actual strategic interactions of subsidiary managers in the case of mandate change events can be defined as host-country-, subsidiary-, and headquarters-context factors:

- *Host-country-context factors* are essentially determined by the national institutions, economic structures, resources and foreign investment policies of the host nation. Host-country factors have been the key focus of analysis in the standard literature on the strategic management of MNCs (for example, Ietto-Gillies, 2005) as well as in the rapidly growing institutionalist literature on the internationalization of business (see above).
- *Subsidiary-context factors* that influence the potential course of strategic action or interactions of subsidiary managers are mainly based on the resources and capabilities at a subsidiary's disposal (Mariotti and Piscitello, 1999). These are primarily determined by the functional role of the respective subsidiary, in other words, by the strategic and functional tasks assigned to the subsidiary. According to the resource-dependence concept, these potential courses of action depend mainly on 'discrete resources', that is, resources that bring added value and that are hard to imitate or replace (Barney, 1991).
- *Headquarters-context factors* are the third and last group of relevant structural factors. The potential course of strategic action that subsidiary managers can take within the process of mandate change also depends on MNC structure and headquarters policy regarding the assignment of mandates. The question of whether there are other competing subsidiaries within the MNC is particularly relevant. Additionally, the outsourcing of work to extra-organizational contractors has an important influence on the actions of subsidiary managers. In conflicts surrounding mandate changes in MNCs, one can generally assume the presence of structural asymmetry between the headquarters and the subsidiaries involved in and/or affected by the change.[10] In spite of decentralization tendencies, decisions regarding mandate changes are some of the most strategically significant prerogatives of the headquarters that lay the foundations for unified corporate management. Comparative institutionalists have also stressed that the country of origin of the MNC significantly affects strategy building (Whitley, 2001).

The specific features and impact of host-country-, subsidiary- and headquarters-context factors vary from one case to another; these factors lay the basic structural and institutional foundations for subsidiary managers' potential actions in mandate conflicts, but directly shape the strategies and strategizing of subsidiary managers only in part. Following the micro-political premise, their personal interests also have a relevant impact on their strategizing and which strategic approach they develop. This is especially obvious in cases where the key subsidiary player's strategic orientations contradict with those of the subsidiary as a whole.[11] For example, it is problematic to assume that the subsidiary management as a whole is always interested in playing in line with the rules set in certain mandates and maintaining the status quo, as especially assumed by scholars promoting the development of the 'transnational solution' (for example, Bartlett and Ghoshal, 1989). It is not unusual for a career-oriented subsidiary manager – especially for expatriates – to develop her/his own political agenda and decline mandate requests of the headquarters as smoothly as possible or even decide to shut down a site if that helps to improve the current power position and develop career prospects (see also Flecker, 2000). National loyalties and career interests are thus relevant *actor-specific factors* that may also influence micro-political strategic approaches of subsidiary managers in disputes over mandate changes and will therefore be examined more closely next.

According to a widely accepted framework, foreign subsidiary managers are citizens of the host country, the home country or a third country. The actions of home-country nationals (expatriates), host-country nationals (inpatriates) and third-country nationals are thereby alleged to be guided by different loyalties (Harzing, 1999). Home-country nationals (*expatriates*) are assumed to be loyal to the headquarters. Expatriates presumably work to ensure sufficient control of the subsidiary and implement the central policies of the headquarters in a generally consistent fashion – that is, as long as they do not assimilate in the host country through marriage, change of religion, extended stays abroad, and so on. Home-country nationals (*inpatriates*) are presumably more concerned with local interests, that is, the continued development of the subsidiary. Following Petersen et al. (1996, 2000), this assumption holds only as long as the inpatriate does not have international career plans (which depends on the MNC's career development policies and the abilities and qualification of the individual manager). Last but not least, *third-country nationals* are presumed to have a more balanced outlook on headquarters and subsidiary interests. However, research (for example, Black et al. 1992) indicates that compared to the number of expatriates and inpatriates, the total number of foreign subsidiary managers who are citizens of neither the home country nor the host country is extremely small. Likewise, only a few subsidiary managers have binational, bilingual or bicultural biographies.

As indicated above, the national loyalty-based actions of subsidiary managers are not unchanging, but appear to be significantly influenced by the subsidiary managers' career ambitions and orientations. While classical career models have long presumed that career ambitions were relatively strongly age dependent (Hall and Nougain, 1968), the increasing de-standardization of professional biographies has now led to the opinion that career ambitions are determined by the level of professional success one has achieved (Hall, 2002). To what extent a subsidiary manager will think s/he has arrived at his/her end career goal or will have further career ambitions depends on a number of personal factors, such as age, marital status, health, self-assessment, and assessment of one's current professional status. The organizational context of the MNC, for example, its career, incentive, pay and professional support systems, and so on (Peltonen, 1992; Stahl et al., 2002), together with situational conditions, for example, geographic mobility and possible changes in work conditions and responsibilities (Moss Kanter, 1989; Schein, 1990), and last but not least national institution-related differences, for example, differences in the educational backgrounds of key managers between headquarters and subsidiary managers, might also play an important role in understanding the strategizing processes of subsidiary managers.

The weight and influence of these factors on their strategic choices, however, is closely related to the question of whether managers' career ambitions are directed towards their climbing the hierarchical ladder within the MNC or towards further developing the economic and political standing of the local subsidiary, as we shall discuss next. We shall introduce three mini cases from a current research project in order to illustrate and discuss the subsidiary managers' strategizing and strategic choices during the process of mandate change. Thus, we are especially interested in shedding some light on the question of how the strategists' career interests shape their mandate change strategies and how these strategizing processes are intertwined with the specific organizational structural and institutional context factors of the multinational firm and subsidiary. First, we provide a brief storyline of the mandate change game, including the managers' personal backgrounds as well as their interpretations of their own role in the mandate change process. We especially focus on the question of whether they present their strategic approach as a rather successful or positive scenario, as in cases 1 and 2, or whether, as in case 3, a more negative or prone to conflict scenario has been drawn. Second, we interpret and discuss the efforts of the actors to micro-politically influence mandate changes at the subsidiary level. Here, we especially focus on the question of how these strategic approaches of particular key actors are both shaping and being shaped by specific organizational and institutional features of the MNC and the subsidiary itself.

- *Case 1* With his career at the headquarters in mind, a young manager of a German service company's French subsidiary exploited his subsidiary's mandate to operate on the French market to develop a detailed restructuring proposal with huge rationalization potential for the overall corporation. The recent restructuring of an important French competitor gave the subsidiary manager the idea for this proposal. The manager carefully observed and analyzed this restructuring process with his career at headquarters in mind. Assisted by a broad coalition of internal and external stakeholders, he finally succeeded in convincing the headquarters to adopt 'his' idea.
- *Case 2* This manager, whose career plans were strongly oriented towards entrepreneurial initiative (entrepreneurship), pursued the continuous expansion and upgrading of the activities of a Hungarian subsidiary of a German software company. The manager, a Hungarian software engineer, about 35 years old, first put forward the idea of transferring Hungarian market sales assignments originally assigned to Austrian companies to Budapest. In addition to taking over and continuously expanding these sales activities, the manager prevailed over major competitors from the MNC's home country and was authorized to establish a Hungarian call center for the software company's German-speaking clients, and he subsequently succeeded in expanding the activities of the call center. The manager also tried to get more and more of his Hungarian subsidiary's managers to work in international teams in order to improve the subsidiary's performance potentials. His long-term goal was to have a greater share in central product development in Germany.
- *Case 3* Profession-oriented career ambitions were the basic motivation for a soon-to-retire manager of a German automotive supplier's French subsidiary to greatly expand the technical expertise of the subsidiary under his management. Without support from the headquarters, the manager, who had several years of

experience as an engineer, and his staff succeeded in implementing significant process modifications. However, company headquarters blocked a proposed expansion of the subsidiary's mandate that would afford a better utilization of this knowledge base but would require additional financial investment. In this case, the decisive factor was that the gains to be expected were medium to long range and thus incompatible with the headquarters' growing goal of producing short-term increases in shareholder value.

These three empirical spotlights illustrate how strongly personal career interests and orientations affect the way in which subsidiary managers try to carry out or develop their subsidiaries' mandates. They also point out the importance of specific organizational and institutional factors. In cases 1 and 2 we see two relatively young and ambitious subsidiary managers playing the game of mandate change. Both are interested in improving their own overall standing and reputation. In case 1 the manager benefited from the shift of the overall strategies of the German telecommunication MNC from an engineering and technological leadership focus towards a finance and shareholder value-driven organization. It can be assumed that the former state-owned and now stock market listed company supported a new generation of managers who understand the new rules of the game. In other words, changes in the traditionally bank-based German financial system (for example, Lane, 2000) towards shareholder capitalism initiated micro-political game playing in the French subsidiary which obviously favors managers with professional backgrounds in accounting to secure a powerful position and get involved in rewriting the rules of the game. As we have seen, this 'rewriting' process was partly based on copying the best practices of the French competitor. However, contrary to institutionalist scholars, for example, DiMaggio and Powell (1983), who fall short by mainly focusing on mimetic isomorphic structural changes, our case shows that structural changes are actively shaped by key actors also pursuing their own micro-political strategies when playing these games. Strategizing was either actively supporting the implementation of new rules of the game, or resisting these rules, as, for example, in case 3. Thus, stressing that the overall strategic approach of all three German MNCs is in line with the institutionalist argument of isomorphic pressures (global industrial and home-country effects) is only one part of the story. The other part is how actors interpret these events, what personal interests and esteem come into play and what kind of micro-political strategies they develop. Thus, to argue that changes in the financial system will influence the management, especially of stock market listed firms, is right, but it does not mean, for example, that it has the same effect in all firms. Actors react differently to the same isomorphic pressures. Thus, case 2 shows similarities to cases 1 and 3 in terms of the increasing importance of financial performance measures. This was obviously one reason why the German MNC invested in Hungary in case 2. However, while strategizing in case 1 was concentrated mainly on coalition building within the MNC mainly involving key actors within the headquarters, strategizing in case 2 was more embedded in the organizational and institutional context of the subsidiary. Thus, the availability of German language skills and lower labor costs in Hungary provided sufficient resources which enabled the subsidiary manager in case 2 to negotiate mandate upgrading and to enhance the strategic position and future prospects of the Hungarian site. However, both performance management and upgrading of the strategic position of the company went hand in hand with the career interests of the strategist.

The focus of playing the game was different for each player. The French subsidiary manager in case 1, bilingual and a native German, was pushing towards a position in the headquarters. The Hungarian subsidiary manager's strategizing, on the other hand, was more entrepreneurially oriented and looking more towards improving his local career prospects, which indirectly of course also support his and the subsidiary's position in future mandate change games. The third case is more complex and the storyline of the key player has a more negative tone. Similarly to the other two cases, the strategic move of the German headquarters towards shareholder value and tighter financial control mechanisms is an important part of the micro-political game. However, the role of the actors, their personal as well professional backgrounds and thus the institutional embeddedness, do influence how subsidiary managers' approach and play the mandate change game. Compared to the first two cases, the subsidiary manager in case 3 acted less as an accountant who gets involved in rewriting the new rules of the game (as in case 1) and also less as an entrepreneur interested in upgrading certain strategic functions of the mandate (as in case 2). Instead, he acted as a typical German engineer who is used to balancing social, technological, and economic requirements of a flexible specialized production system. In short, the headquarters approach of one-dimensionally focusing on financial performance measures was just not acceptable for him, because it undermined the core elements of the established high-quality and R&D-led production system of the subsidiary. Compared to the two key players in cases 1 and 2, he did not accept the new rules of the game and was not interested in playing the game to improve his career prospects and reputation with regard to the headquarters. Thus, personal interests together with his strong orientation towards a traditional engineering culture led to severe conflicts with the headquarters, which was interpreted as an escalating no-win situation by the strategist. However, based on his long-established embeddedness in Franco-German professional social networks, he was to a certain extent able to maintain the flexible production system. This approach has been called 'subversive' by Morgan and Kristensen (2006). Comparing different micro-political games of subsidiary managers with the headquarters, they show that local embeddedness of the subsidiary is important to resist financial performance-related mandate changes, providing social spaces for more autonomous and often subversive strategizing.

Concluding discussion and outlook

In this chapter we have shed some light on micro-political strategies and strategizing in MNCs, a topic which is often neglected, but which has a key relevance to developing strategic foresight (Costanzo, 2003) and understanding organizational change (Tsoukas and Chia, 2002). We have especially concentrated on mandate changes, because they are critical events in the organizational development of the MNC, in general, and, in particular, for the subsidiary management. One reason for the wide neglect of micro-political issues in the study of the MNC, is without doubt a quantitative bias of many international business scholars and core publication outlets (for example, Welch and Welch, 2004). Taking the call for a 'practice turn' in strategic management seriously, however, requires alternative methodological approaches that place greater focus on case studies and comparative research of national, industrial sector and company-specific differences. In short, in order to fully understand micro-political activities intertwined with organizational and institutional change processes a more qualitative research, based on in-depth and longitudinal case studies, is needed.

There are various reasons why research on micro politics tends to be rare and projects are difficult to conduct. Micro-political activities are sensitive issues in every organization and proper company access and the willingness of the key players is crucial, but not always possible to achieve. To understand the micro-political underpinnings of, for example, mandate change processes, researchers need to enter the 'community of practice' for a certain period of time and ideally to be present as, for example, participant observers when micro-political conflicts occur. However, such research strategies are not just time-consuming but also require solid funding, which is often difficult to get given the bias of various funding bodies towards larger surveys and statistical methods of analysis.

Nevertheless, despite these limitations there are a few examples of recently published research which show that the study of micro-political issues in MNCs is possible and useful. For instance, there is a very interesting paper by Sharpe (2006) comparing green- and brownfield subsidiaries of Japanese firms in the UK, which demonstrates that industrial relations traditions are important to understand the micro-political implications of knowledge transfer. There is also an equally interesting paper by Moore (2006), who carried out an in-depth case study of cultural change processes and emerging micro-political problems in a British subsidiary of a German bank. Furthermore, Kristensen and Zeitlin (2005) focus on micro-political issues emerging between the British headquarters and some foreign subsidiaries of an engineering firm. Just like the first two studies cited, the work by Kristensen and Zeitlin stresses that the course of organizational and institutional change in internationally operating firms is importantly shaped by micro-political activities.

Having emphasized that the study of strategizing requires qualitative methods, we also believe that quantitative research methods can be useful, if they are solidly based on qualitative groundwork and fine-grained enough to cope with the facets of micro-political strategizing. A combination of quantitative and qualitative methods would be useful to show larger international and/or industry-wide trends. Thus, for example, with regard to our discussion in the previous section, a larger survey of the relationship between financially driven mandate changes and its underlying micro-political consequences would provide very interesting insights.

Future research in micro-political strategies and strategizing can contribute to current debates on internationalization and the MNC. In particular, links to institutionalist approaches should be developed. We have stressed that using a bottom-up approach and starting at the subsidiary level is useful, because subsidiaries are arenas for various micro-political games which are of course influenced by changes at the macro (transnational) and meso (national) levels, but which have their own dynamics and players with their own personal interests. The latter can be related, as we have demonstrated in our mini cases, to career interests, on the one hand, and the social embeddedness in close-knit local networks, on the other, which provide resources for resistance and for the development of subversive strategies to maintain and widen the decision-making autonomy of local managers. Thus, we need more in-depth studies about who are the key players in mandate change processes, and how and why they initiate, support and resist certain mandate changes, such as the introduction of benchmarking or financial performance measures.

In our mini cases we found evidence that changes in the financial institutions, especially in large German firms (see, for example, Lane, 2000), led to modifications of the overall strategic approach, which result in internal strategizing processes to 'rewrite' the rules of the game. We examined the power resources of traditional powerful players such as engineers (as in case 3), which leads to micro-political games around 'insecurity zones' and provides 'social space', for example, for younger entrepreneurially minded managers (as in case 2) or for managers with an accounting and controlling background (as in case 1). However, the discussion on home-country impacts on host-country subsidiaries needs to be more open for dynamic change processes than assumed, for example, in comparative studies of national business systems (Whitley, 2001). Both actor groups and institutions are more loosely coupled to home-country institutions than is usually assumed by institutionalist research. In other words, home-country effects are coming into play only through certain more or less powerful actors. Thus, changes in financial performance measures might be more easily resisted when the company is strongly locally embedded. This is shown by Morgan and Kristensen (2006) in the case of a British MNC where the managers of the Danish subsidiary were able to benefit from strong national institutional support and to negotiate more local autonomy. However, the example given by Morgan and Kristensen also shows that resistance to coercive financial performance measures led to increasingly 'unorganized' strategic processes at the subsidiary level, because global standardization of subsidiary mandates and/or the introduction of corporate-wide benchmarking systems tend to increase competition between subsidiaries and lead to non-reversible downgrading spirals for some of them. This interesting single case study evidence needs corroboration by more comparative research on how changes in the home- and host-country settings influence the strategizing of local subsidiary managers regarding mandate changes and how (vice versa) they promote or resist changes at the macro-institutional level, such as transnational capital market pressures.

Notes

1. Until now, empirical research has mainly concentrated on the internationalization of human resource management strategies (for example UNCTAD, 1994; Edwards et al., 1999; Almond et al., 2005) and the cross-border transfer of production and organization models (for example, Abo, 1994; Clark and Soulsby, 1999; Freyssenet et al., 2003).
2. See Westney (1993) on the coexistence of home- and host-country effects, Mueller (1994), Dörrenbächer (2000) and Harzing and Sorge (2003) on the coexistence of universal, societal and organizational effects, and Dörrenbächer (2004) on the existence of third-country and extra-organizational effects.
3. Management theory perspective: see Ghoshal and Nohria (1989), Gupta and Govindarajan (1994), Taggart (1998), Birkinshaw (2000); organization sociology perspective: see Kristensen and Zeitlin (2001, 2005), Becker-Ritterspach et al. (2002), Geppert et al. (2003); macroeconomic perspective: see Birkinshaw and Hood (1997), Pearce (1999) and contributions in Jungnickel (2002).
4. This permits better use of the available knowledge base. Benchmarking studies within individual businesses demonstrated that the efficiency potentials here are considerable (Szulanski, 1997).
5. According to Birkinshaw and Hood (2001), the many geographically scattered business units of large MNCs generally have a much greater innovation potential than their headquarters.
6. This contributes to the often seemingly anemic and construed argumentation in institutionalist contributions on the internationalization of businesses.
7. In the context of the MNC these can be, of course, more or less transnationally spread (Morgan, 2001).
8. In line with Weick (1993) we understand micro events such as mandate change as closely interrelated with macro events, for example, capital market pressures which, as we shall discuss later, trigger micro-political strategizing. However, the dialectics between interactive strategizing processes legitimizing or de-legitimizing certain structures and institutions is often ignored by structuralist studies, which mainly discuss the influence of macro structures on strategic behavior. However, narrowly focused micro-level studies (for example, ethnographic studies) addressing strategic interactions often suffer from neglecting larger societal consequences.
9. This includes different mandate-awarding situations (awarding of supplementary mandates, redistribution of existing mandates) and different mandate types (product, regional and functional mandates).

10. There are, of course, exceptions to the rule.
11. However, the literature on mandate change in MNCs consistently assumes that such a concurrence exists.

References

Abo, Tetsuo (ed.) (1994), *The Hybrid Factory: The Japanese Production System in the United States*, Oxford and New York: Oxford University Press.
Aharoni, Yair (1966), *The Foreign Investment Decision Process*, Boston, MA: Harvard University Press.
Almond, Phil, Tony Edwards, Trevor Colling, Antony Ferner, Paddy Gunnigle, Michael Müller-Camen, Javier Quintanilla and Hartmut Wächter (2005), 'Unraveling home and host country effects: an investigation of the HR policies of an American multinational in four European countries', *Industrial Relations*, **44** (2), 276–305.
Barney, Jay B. (1991), 'Firm resources and sustained competitive advantage', *Journal of Management*, **17** (1), 99–120.
Bartlett, Christopher A. and Sumantra Ghoshal (1989), *Managing Across Borders: The Transnational Solution*, Boston, MA: Harvard Business School Press.
Becker-Ritterspach, Florian, Knut Lange and Karin Lohr (2002), 'Control mechanisms and patterns of reorganization in MNCs', in Mike Geppert, Dirk Matten and Karen Williams (eds), *Challenges for European Management in a Global Context: Experiences from Britain and Germany*, Basingstoke: Palgrave, pp. 68–95.
Bélanger, Jaques and Paul Edwards (2006), 'Towards a political economy framework: TNCs as national and global players', in Anthony Ferner, Javier Qunitanilla and Carlos-Sánchez-Runde (eds), *Multinationals, Institutions and the Construction of Transnational Practices*, Basingstoke: Palgrave, pp. 24–51.
Birkinshaw, Julian (1996), 'How multinational subsidiary mandates are gained and lost', *Journal of International Business Studies*, **27**, 467–95.
Birkinshaw, Julian (2000), *Entrepreneurship in the Global Firm*, London: Sage.
Birkinshaw, Julian (2001), 'Strategies for managing internal competition', *California Management Review*, **44** (1), 21–38.
Birkinshaw, Julian and Neil Hood (1997), 'An empirical study of development processes in foreign-owned subsidiaries in Canada and Scotland', *Management International Review*, **4**, 339–64.
Birkinshaw, Julian and Neil Hood (2001), 'Unleash innovation in foreign subsidiaries', *Harvard Business Review*, March, 131–7.
Birkinshaw, Julian, Neil Hood and Stefan Jonsson (1998), 'Building firm-specific advantages in multinational corporations: the role of subsidiary initiative', *Strategic Management Journal*, **19**, 221–41.
Birkinshaw, Julian and Jonas Ridderstråle (1999), 'Fighting the corporate immune system: a process study of subsidiary initiatives in multinational corporations', *International Business Review*, **8**, 149–80.
Birkinshaw, Julian and Mats Lingblatt (2005), 'Intrafirm competition and charter evolution in the multibusiness firm', *Organization Science*, **16** (6), 674–86.
Black, Steward J., Hal B. Gregersen and Mark E. Mendenhall (1992), *Global Assignments: Successfully Expatriating and Repatriating International Managers*, San Francisco, CA: Jossey-Bass.
Burns, Tom (1961/62), 'Micropolitics: mechanisms of institutional change', *Administrative Science Quarterly*, **6**, 257–81.
Clark, Ed and Anna Soulsby (1999), *Organizational Change in Post-communist Europe: Management and Transformation in the Czech Republic*, London: Routledge.
Cohen, Wesley M. and Daniel A. Lewinthal (1990), 'Absorptive capacity: a new perspective on learning and innovation, *Administrative Science Quarterly*, **35**, 128–52.
Costanzo, Laura A. (2003), 'Strategic foresight in a high-speed environment', *Futures*, **36**, 219–35.
Crozier, Michel and Erhard Friedberg (eds) (1980), *Actors and Systems: The Politics of Collective Action*, Chicago, IL: University of Chicago Press.
Cyert, Richard Michael and James G. March (1963), *A Behavioral Theory of the Firm*, Englewood Cliffs, NJ: Prentice-Hall.
DiMaggio, Paul J. and Walter W. Powell (1983), 'The iron cage revisited: institutional isomorphism and collective rationality in organizational fields', *American Sociological Review*, **48**, 147–60.
Dörrenbächer, Christoph (2000), 'Between global market constraints and national dependencies: the internationalisation of the world leading telecommunication equipment manufacturers 1980–1995', *Transnational Corporations*, **9** (3), 1–35.
Dörrenbächer, Christoph (2004), 'Fleeing or exporting the German model? The internationalisation of German multinationals in the 1990s', *Competition and Change*, **8** (4), 443–56.
Dörrenbächer, Christoph and Jens Gammelgaard (2006), 'Subsidiary role development: the effect of micro-political headquarters – subsidiary negotiations on the product, market and value-added scope of foreign-owned subsidiaries', *Journal of International Management*, **12** (3), 266–83.

Dunning, John H. (1979), 'Explaining changing patterns of international production: in defense of the eclectic theory', *Oxford Bulletin of Economics and Statistics*, **41**, 269–95.

Edwards, Tony, Chris Rees and Xavier Coller (1999), 'Structure, politics and the diffusion of employment practices in multinationals', *European Journal of Industrial Relations*, **5** (3), 286–306.

Fichter, Michael (2003), 'Internationalization of production: options and responses. Evidence from German enterprises in Hungary', AICGS/DaimlerChrysler Working Paper Series, Washington, DC: American Institute of Contemporary German Studies, Johns Hopkins University.

Flecker, Jörg (2000), 'Transnationale Unternehmen und die Macht des Ortes', in Christoph Dörrenbächer and Dieter Plehwe (eds), *Grenzenlose Kontrolle. Organisatorischer Wandel und politische Macht multinationaler Unternehmen*, Berlin: Edition Sigma, pp. 45–70.

Forsgren, Mats, Ulf Holm and Jan Johanson (1995), 'Division headquarters go abroad: a step in the internationalization of the multinational corporation', *Journal of Management Studies*, **32** (4), 475–91.

Forsgren, Mats and Jan Johanson (eds) (1992a), *Managing Networks in International Business*, Philadelphia, PA: Gordon & Breach.

Forsgren, Mats and Jan Johanson (1992b), 'Managing in international multi-centre firms', in Forsgren and Johanson (eds), pp. 19–31.

Freyssenet, Michel, Koichi Shimizu and Guiseppe Volpato (eds) (2003), *Globalization or Regionalization of the European Car Industry?*, London: Palgrave Macmillan.

Geppert, Mike and Ed Clark (2003), 'Knowledge and learning in transnational ventures: an actor-centred approach', *Management Decision*, **41** (5), 433–42.

Geppert, Mike, Dirk Matten and Karen Williams (2003), 'Change management in MNCs: how global convergence intertwines with national diversities', *Human Relations*, **56** (7), 807–38.

Geppert, Mike and Michael Mayer (2006), 'Introduction', in Geppert and Mayer (eds), *Global, National and Local Practices in Multinational Companies*, Basingstoke: Palgrave, pp. 1–14.

Ghoshal, Sumantra and Nitin Nohria (1989), 'Internal differentiation within multinational corporations', *Strategic Management Journal*, **10**, 323–37.

Graham, Edward M. (1974), *Oligopolistic Imitation and European Investment in the United States*, Boston, MA: Harvard Business School Press.

Gupta, Anil K. and Vijay Govindarajan (1994), 'Organizing for knowledge within MNCs', *International Business Review*, **3** (4), 443–57.

Hall, Douglas T. (2002), *Careers in and out of Organizations*, Thousand Oaks, CA: Sage.

Hall, Douglas T. and K. Nougain (1968), 'An examination of Maslow's need hierarchy in an organizational setting', *Organizational Behavior and Human Performance*, **3**, 12–35.

Harzing, Ann-Wil (1999), *Managing the Multinationals: An International Study of Control Mechanisms*, Cheltenham, UK and Northampton, MA, USA: Edward Elgar.

Harzing, Ann-Wil and Arndt Sorge (2003), 'The relative impact of country of origin and universal contingencies on internationalization strategies and corporate control in multinational enterprises: worldwide and European perspectives', *Organizational Studies*, **24** (2), 187–214.

Hedlund, Gunnar (1986), 'The hypermodern MNC: a heterarchy?', *Human Resource Management*, **25**, 9–25.

Hetrick, Susan (2002), 'Transferring HR ideas and practices: globalization and convergence in Poland', *Human Resource Development International*, **5** (3), 333–51.

Hofstede, Geert (1997), *Lokales Denken, Globales Handeln. Kulturen, Zusammenarbeit und Management*, Munich: Deutscher Taschenbuch Verlag.

Hu, Yao-Su (1992), 'Global or stateless corporations are national firms with international operations', *California Management Review*, Winter, 107–26.

Hymer, Stephen H. (1960), *The International Operations of National Firms*, Boston, MA: Harvard Business School Press.

Ietto-Gillies, G. (2005), *Transnational Corporations and International Production, Concepts, Theories and Effects*, Cheltenham, UK and Northampton, MA, USA: Edward Elgar.

Jankowicz, Devi A. (2001), 'Limits to knowledge transfer: what they already know in the post-command economies', *Journal of East–West Business*, **7** (2), 37–59.

Johanson, Jan and Jan-Erik Vahlne (1977), 'The internationalization process of the firm: a model of knowledge development and increasing foreign market commitments', *Journal of International Business Studies*, **8** (1), 23–32.

Johnson, Gerry, Leif Melin and Richard Whittington (2003), 'Introduction: micro-strategy and strategizing: towards an activity-based view', *Journal of Management Studies*, **40** (1), 3–22.

Jungnickel, Rolf (ed.) (2002), *Foreign-owned Firms. Are They Different?*, Basingstoke and New York: Palgrave.

Katz, Richard S. and Thomas Allen (1982), 'Investigating the not invented here (NIH) syndrome: a look at the performance, tenure, and communication patterns of 50 R&D project groups', *R&D Management*, **12** (1), 7–19.

Knickerbocker, Frederick T. (1973), *Oligopolistic Reaction and the Multinational Enterprise*, Boston, MA: Harvard University Press.

Kostova, Tatiana (1999), 'Transnational transfer of strategic organisational practices: a contextual perspective', *Academy of Management Review*, **24** (2), 308–24.

Kristensen, Peer Hull and Jonathan Zeitlin (2001), 'The making of a global firm: local pathways to multinational enterprise', in Glenn Morgan, Peer Hull Kristensen and Richard Whitley (eds), *The Multinational Firm: Organizing across Institutional and National Divides*, Oxford: Oxford University Press, pp. 172–95.

Kristensen, Peer Hull and Jonathan Zeitlin (2005), *Local Players in Global Games: The Strategic Constitution of a Multinational Corporation*, Oxford: Oxford Univeristy Press.

Küpper, Willi and Anke Felsch (2000), *Organisation, Macht und Ökonomie: Mikropolitik und die Konstitution organisationaler Handlungssysteme*, Wiesbaden: Westdeutscher Verlag.

Lane, C. (2000), 'Globalization and the German model of capitalism: erosion or survival?', *British Journal of Sociology*, **25** (2), 207–34.

March, James G. (1962), 'The business firm as a political coalition', *Journal of Politics*, **24**, 662–78.

Mariotti, Sergio and Lucia Piscitello (1999), 'Is divestment a failure or part of a restructuring strategy: the case of Italian transnational corporations', *Transnational Corporations*, **8** (3), 25–53.

Michailova, Snejina (2002), 'When common sense becomes uncommon: participation and empowerment in Russian companies with Western participation', *Journal of World Business*, **37**, 80–187.

Mintzberg, Henry (1983), *Power in and around Organizations*, Englewood Cliffs, NJ: Prentice-Hall.

Moore, F. (2006), 'Governing the outposts? Exploring the role of expatriate managers in a multinational corporation', in Mike Geppert and Michael Mayer (eds), *Global, National and Local Practices in Multinational Companies*, Basingstoke: Palgrave, pp. 167–88.

Morgan, Glenn (2001), 'The multinational firm. Organizing across institutional and national divides', in Glenn Morgan, Peer Hull Kristensen and Richard Whitley (eds), *The Multinational Firm: Organizing across Institutional and National Divides*, Oxford: Oxford University Press, pp. 1–24.

Morgan, Glenn and Peer Hull Kristensen (2006), 'The contested space of multinationals: varieties of institutionalism, varieties of capitalism', *Human Relations*, **59** (11), 1467–90.

Moss Kanter, Rosabeth (1989), 'Careers and wealth of nations: a macro-perspective on the structure and implications of career forms', in Michael B. Arthur, Douglas T. Hall and Barbara Lawrence (eds), *Handbook of Career Theory*, Cambridge: Cambridge University Press, pp. 506–21.

Mueller, Frank (1994), 'Societal effect, organizational effect and globalization, *Organization Studies*, **15** (3), 407–28.

Neuberger, Oswald (1998), 'Spiele in Organisationen, Organisationen als Spiele', in Willi Küpper and Günter Ortmann (eds), *Mikropolitik: Rationalität, Macht und Spiele in Organisationen*, Opladen: Westdeutscher Verlag, pp. 53–86.

Ortmann, Günther (1988a), 'Macht, Spiel, Konsens', in Willi Küpper and Günter Ortmann (eds), *Mikropolitik: Rationalität, Macht und Spiele in Organisationen*, Opladen: Westdeutscher Verlag, pp. 13–26.

Ortmann, Günther (1988b), 'Vorwort: mikropolitik – das handeln der aktevre und die zwänge der systeme', in Willi Küpper and Günter Ortmann (eds), *Mikropolitik: Rationalität, Macht und Spiele in Organisationen*, Opladen: Westdeutscher Verlag, pp. 7–9.

Ortmann, Günther, Arnold Windeler, Albrecht Becker and Hans-Joachim Schulz (1990), *Computer und Macht in Organisationen. Mikropolitische Analysen*, Opladen: Westdeutscher Verlag.

Pearce, Robert (1999), 'The evolution of technology in multinational enterprises: the role of creative subsidiaries', *International Business Review*, **8**, 125–48.

Peltonen, Tuomo (1992), 'Managerial careers in multinational organisations: towards a typology', CIBR Working Paper Series, 2/1992, Helsinki: HSE Press.

Peterson, Richard B., Nancy Napier and Won Shul Shim (1996), 'Expatriate management: the differential role of national multinational corporation ownership', *International Executive*, **38**, 543–62.

Peterson, Richard B., Nancy Napier and Won Shul Shim (2000), 'Expatriate management: a comparison of MNCs across four parent countries', *Thunderbird International Business Review*, **42**, 145–66.

Pfeffer, Jeffrey and Gerald R. Salancik (1974), 'Organizational decision making as a political process: the case of a university budget', *Administrative Science Quarterly*, **19**, 135–51.

Pries, Ludger (2001), 'The approach of transnational social spaces. Responding to new configurations of the social and the spatial', in Pries (ed.), *New Transnational Social Spaces: International Migration and Transnational Companies in the Early Twenty-first Century*, London: Routledge, pp. 3–33.

Ruigrok, Winfried and Rob van Tulder (1995), *The Logic of International Restructuring*, London: Routledge.

Sally, Razeen (1995), *States and Firms: Multinational Enterprises in Institutional Competition*, London: Routledge.

Schein, Edgar H. (1990), *Career Anchors* (Revised), San Diego, CA: University Associates.

Sharpe, Diane R. (2001), 'Globalization and change: organizational continuity and change within a Japanese multinational in the UK', in Glenn Morgan, Peer Hull Kristensen and Richard Whitley (eds), *The*

Multinational Firm: Organizing across Institutional and National Divides, Oxford: Oxford University Press, pp. 196–222.

Sharpe, D. (2006), 'Shop-floor practices under changing forms of managerial control: a comparative ethnographic study of micro-politics, control and resistance in a Japanese multinational', *Journal of International Management*, **12** (3), 318–39.

Sölvell, Örjan and Ivo Zander (1998), 'International diffusion of knowledge: isolating mechanisms and the role of the MNE', in Alfred Chandler, Peter Hagström and Örjan Sölvell (eds), *The Dynamic Firm: The Role of Technology, Strategy, Organization, and Regions*, Oxford: Oxford University Press, pp. 402–17.

Stahl, Günter K., Edwin Miller and Rosalie L. Tung (2002), 'Toward the boundaryless career: a closer look at the expatriate career concept and the perceived implications of an international assignment', *Journal of World Business*, 37, 216–27.

Szulanski, Gabriel (1997), 'Intra-firm transfer of best practices', in Andrew Campbell and Kathleen Sommer-Luchs (eds), *Core Competency-based Strategy*, London: International Thomson Business Press, pp. 208–35.

Taggart, James H. (1998), 'Strategy shifts in MNC subsidiaries', *Strategic Management Journal*, **19**, 663–81.

Tempel, Anne (2001), *The Cross-national Transfer of Human Resource Management Practices in German and British Multinational Companies*, Munich-Mering: Rainer Hampp Verlag.

Tsoukas, Haridimos and Robert Chia (2002), 'On organizational becoming: rethinking organizational change', *Organization Science*, **13** (5), 567–82.

UNCTAD (1994), 'World Investment Report 1994, Transnational Corporations, Employment and the Workplace', United Nations, Geneva.

Weick, K.E. (1993), 'Sensemaking in organizations: small structures with large consequences', in J. Keith Murnighan (ed.), *Social Psychology in Organizations: Advances in Theory and Research*, Englewood Cliffs, NJ: Prentice-Hall, pp. 10–37.

Welch, Denise E. and Lawrence S. Welch (2004), 'Getting published: the last hurdle?', in Rebecca Marschan-Piekkari and Catherine Welch (eds), *Handbook of Qualitative Research Methods for International Business*, Cheltenham, UK and Northampton, MA, USA: Edward Elgar, pp. 551–69.

Westney, Eleanor D. (1993), 'Institutionalization theory and the multinational corporation', in Sumantra Ghoshal and Eleanor Westney (eds), *Organization Theory and the Multinational Corporation*, New York: St Martin's Press, pp. 1–23.

Whitley, Richard (2001), 'How and why are international firms different? The consequences of cross-border managerial coordination for firm characteristics and behaviour', in Glenn Morgan, Peer Hull Kristensen and Richard Whitley (eds) (2001), *The Multinational Firm: Organizing across Institutional and National Divides*, Oxford: Oxford University Press, pp. 27–68.

Whitley, Richard (2005), 'Developing transnational organizational capabilities in multinational companies: institutional constraints on authority sharing and careers in six types of MNC', in Glenn Morgan, Richard Whitley and Eli Moen (eds), *Changing Capitalisms: Internationalization, Institutional Change, and Systems of Economic Organization*, Oxford: Oxford University Press, pp. 235–76.

Whittington, Richard (2006), 'Completing the practice turn in strategy research', *Organization Studies*, **27**(5), 613–34.

12 How organizational DNA works
David Weir, Craig Marsh and Wilf Greenwood*

Beyond structure and agency

The debate about the relative significance of structure and agency continues to be at the heart of much organizational analysis, and has largely been polarized around two antonymic positions – the so-called 'macro' and 'micro' theories, 'structure' versus 'agency'.

The theoretical framework for this chapter attempts to move beyond these antonymic positions by building on theories which are inclusive rather than exclusive of both the 'micro' and 'macro' positions – the critical realism of Bhaskar (1975), the sociology of Bourdieu (1977, [1982] 1990) and the autopoietic organization theory of Luhmann (Luhmann 2003; Hernes and Bakken 2003; Mingers 1995).

Our framework, assumes, first of all, social structures which precede individual interpretation and action and that therefore exist independently of that action. We are persuaded by the critical realist position which argues that there are aspects of social reality which are unknown and unknowable by actors, and which have material influence on their interpretations and their practices. What exists is therefore conceptually, at least, distinct from what can be known.

For a description of the relationship between practice and structure, we find Bourdieu's concept of the 'intermediary' of 'habitus' persuasive. Pre-existing social conditions act as conditioner of a series of 'predispositions' in the agent that orient, subconsciously, practice without the practice being the unreflective following of predetermined norms. These predispositions also serve to reconstruct an infinite (but nevertheless determined) number of possibilities for future social structures, in the way that the grammar and syntax of a language both limits, and creates unlimited options for, individual speech practice.

There are, however, two areas in which Bourdieu's sociology appears unable to explain adequately empirical phenomena emerging from the data. The first is in the precise nature of the causal effect of pre-existing structure on human action; the second area is the relative stability of the social structures he describes.

A key question would seem to be: which part of practice is causally influenced by structure through predisposition, and which parts are the results of autonomous action? On Bourdieu's interpretation, it would not be clear how much the accounts of the first-line managers are to do with their circumstances (through predisposition), and how much of what they say is about themselves. There appears to be a mediating influence missing, allowing a more precise understanding of the effects of the enabling and constraining mechanisms of structure; and for this Archer's (2003) account of the 'inner conversation' is persuasive.

She argues for the importance of the ability of actors to reflect upon themselves in relation to their circumstances, and for the centrality of this reflexivity to the process of mediation between structure and agent. This position entails that there is a pre-existing social world different from that of the actor, and that equally the actor has subjectivity that is 'causally efficacious in relation to himself and his society' (ibid., p. 14). This allows the actor to adopt a particular position in relation to his or her social circumstances, and make choices of courses of action accordingly (without assuming that these choices, or the position adopted, is correct or even optimal to the circumstances or 'interest' of the actor (in Bourdieu's terms)).

How does this mediation occur? Archer differs from Bourdieu in that she does not attach any predictive power to the dispositions (or, as she refers to them – 'distributional positions' (ibid., p. 138)), at least without knowing more about the human projects upon which the constraints and enablements of these dispositions 'act'. It is through reflexive deliberation, or 'internal conversation' that the agent subjectively determines courses of action in relation to their objective circumstances.

Three types of 'reflexive' practice are defined by Archer according to the precise mediating function of the internal conversation between structure and practice. It is not directly our concern to describe in detail each of these 'types', but what is of interest is how in one of them, referred to by Archer as the 'autonomous' reflexive, the individual is able, through their reflexivity, to 'articulate projects that would carry them away from their original social backgrounds' rather than replicate them (ibid., p. 228).

It seems to us that herein lies one of the most persuasive elements of Archer's sociology. Whereas Bourdieu seemed concerned with explaining how the habitus enables the reproduction of existing or historical social structures, and thus perpetuates existing power relations, Archer delineates the circumstances in which the actor is able to develop strategies, through reflexivity, for overriding the enablements and circumventing the constraints imposed by historical social structures.

Archer's argument also entails that we consider the social world to be an open system which 'consistently enables us to conceive of alternative futures for ourselves' (ibid., p. 73). The reproducing nature of this system (which Archer refers to as 'morphogenetic') would seem to answer the second limitation of Bourdieu's sociology, namely to explain how the social structure itself evolves in its interaction with agency. Here, we turn to the autopoietic theory of Maturana and Varela (1980) as interpreted by Niklas Luhmann.

Bourdieu's sociology was constructed in a particular social and political context which orients it toward explaining and describing relatively stable structures which preserve power relations through the mechanisms of habitus. It seems less useful for describing a rapidly evolving social context, as is the case with both sets of empirical data in my thesis. The autopoietic organization theory of Luhmann appears to fill this gap.

In this chapter we attempt a description of some classes of managerial action that can be perceived in some 'real situations' in which the managers find themselves. In so doing we hope to illuminate the ways in which action as expressed in critical incidents creates the conditions for organizational change.

Complex adaptive systems

In a recent paper, Hernes and Bakken (2003) make a case for the utility of certain ideas of Luhmann in organization theory. They draw out similarities in Luhmann's conceptual framework with the approach of Maturana and Varela in recommending biological rather than mechanical models for organizational systems. We accede in their conceptualization of autopoeisis (Maturana and Varela, 1980).

Stafford Beer (1980) also saw the potential of autopoetic models of organization. Giddens is referenced as a further warrant for these ideas in his claim that 'the most relevant sources of connection between biological and social theory . . . concern recursive or self-producing systems' (Giddens, 1973, p. 75).

Giddens goes on to argue: 'Society only has form, and that form only has effects on people, in so far as structure is produced and reproduced in what people do' (Giddens and Pierson, 1998, p. 77). We take the point and accept that the mechanism of organizational structural reproduction is located and may therefore be discovered in what people *do*.

Hernes and Bakken review Luhmann's work in relation to three epistemological foundations of organizational theory, which they identify as equilibrium-based, process-based and recursivity-based theory and conclude that its complementarity with Giddens's structuration theory provides a 'promising basis' for recursivity-based organization theory.

The generic and systematic nature of Luhmann's work is acknowledged, but likewise Maturana and Varela's and Giddens's work stands somewhat aloof from such questions as '*how* does this happen?' and '*what* changes in the process of autopoiesis allow us to understand "before" from "after"?', or *a fortiori* '*why* do only some changes become incorporated into the fabric of organizational systems in such a way as to change their very nature?'. So we are left to consider whether it is possible to frame an account of autopoiesis that permits us to focus on the context, texture and content of organizational decision making.

Hennes and Bakken discuss the conventional distinction between open and closed systems, noting that systems may be characterized as more or less permeable. This distinction is also relevant to our research. According to van Krogh and Roos (1995, p. 181): 'the complex adaptive organization is simultaneously open and closed. It must have a natural order and structure to embody high scale processes that are defined and understood, while at the same time being open to signals (or data) from the environment'.

But these openings and closures to environmental signals and data do not occur at random or in predictable response patterns to environmental stimuli. They are the product of managed processes that nonetheless do not produce predictable responses because the social actors in these positions have the experience, responsiveness and authority to adapt to the specific situation. Certain roles have the responsibility for maintaining both the structural aspects that guarantee survival in the short term, and to enable what van Krogh and Roos call 'advancement activities'.

These advancement activities fall into the categories of organizational process identified by Maturana and Varela as autopoietic. Access to the choices which constitute these autopoietic elements is central to the ways in which organizations recreate themselves to face new and to some extent unknown challenges. So we require a more precise and situated account of the circumstances under which autopoiesis is likely to occur.

But we would wish to take this line of argument further and note that systems may be open at some points and times and closed at others, and that systems move through a characteristic cycle of open-ness depending on their interaction with the external environment. Educational systems, for example, schools and universities, regulate their open-ness through quite rigorous protocols for identifying when (for example) parents, governors and other stakeholders may access organizational processes and personnel. Parents can visit for degree ceremonies but not enter classrooms, and governors have to learn to access staff through the head teacher or vice-chancellor.

Hennes and Bakken state that Luhmann goes further than Weick when discussing these boundary-maintaining enactments, 'although the boundary cannot be observed from the outside, the outside might be "co-interpreted" as an actuality' (p. 1516). In many organizations, responsibility for these 'co-enactments' is vested in certain quite specific roles. So closure and open-ness are not logically distinguishable but coexist with and presuppose the other. This creates a situation of 'double contingency' and one of considerable interest for organization theorists operating in the practical realms of operational management, for it is the existence of this double contingency that permits the autopoietic process to operate.

The most important knowledge for managing advancement activities is not necessarily located at the top of organizations. As Luhmann puts it: 'the increasing need for specialist knowledge results in subordinates often being more knowledgeable than their superiors' (2003, p. 31). In practice there typically exist lacunae in higher management's knowledge map of the enterprise which create pools of 'subterranean knowledge', accessible to those who share the inner secrets of the enterprise but are unwilling to share it on a free access basis to the higher echelons (Weir, 2004). Experienced middle managers may not necessarily know precisely 'what is going on'. But they normally develop a good nose for suspecting that 'something is going on'. Management is about knowing something; not about knowing everything.

Luhmann points out: 'in addition to their specialised knowledge, subordinates may be independent in other ways, for example their personal dealings with the outside world, which cannot be completely supervised . . . the exploitation of this knowledge and of these relations cannot simply be commanded' (Luhmann, 2003, p. 31). Luhmann concedes (almost with a sigh): 'the issuance of commands may have little causal influence on decision-making' (p. 34).

But if the causal chain is not clear it must be broken or at least interfered with by what lies in between. That in an organizational context is middle management. This is the level that interferes to get things right or to stop the organization getting things wrong. In the case of new projects or changing plans, this is a most significant level. The everyday experience of most consultants and managers tends to support these conclusions. Certainly from the perspective of those responsible for the implementation of organizational change it is the willing support or at least the supportive acquiescence of the middle management cadres that is the *sine qua non* of successfully managed organizational change rather than the ponderous repetition of vision statements, however inspirational. It is the middle management roles that embody and have especial responsibilities for the organizational DNA that helps to guarantee the survival of the enterprise.

The organizational DNA can exist because of the existence of parallel systems of decision and the recording of decision and the existence of processes of transformation. This is equally the case for systems of human and non-human actors as it is for mixed systems in which typically humans take responsibility for the outcomes of decisions even if they did not have physical responsibility for them at the time. In imperatively coordinated associations in Dahrendorf's ([1959] 1976) sense, middle managers are responsible for what happens on their shift even if they did not do anything or were not aware that anything was being done.

This is equally true in respect of the virtual domain and of the mixed virtual and real domains that are increasingly the central stuff of contemporary operational middle management. Thus Sowunmi et al. (1996, p. 168) write:

Decision support systems with a knowledge base containing specific past decision situations regarding an organization may be referred to as organizational memory systems. A record of these past decisions is assumed to be beneficial to decision-makers and their organization. Building such systems involves collecting past decision situations from a decision-maker. This is analogous to knowledge acquisition where an expert's knowledge is elicited and modelled.

They go on to offer a description of a methodology for 'eliciting past decision situations (cases) and their characteristics from an expert decision-maker (to provide) case-based organizational memory to support decision-making' (p. 168)

In practical terms this is what middle managers do all the time. It is the substance of their job. But as well as embedding historical sequences of decision making in their own patterns, they have to be aware of current contexts as well. Thus Grimshaw et al. (1997, p. 170) point out: 'Where decision making is carried out by several people, perhaps in several different locations for different purposes the same data is used in multiple decision contexts. . . . the role of context is vital'.

We seek to modify the general direction of this thinking in order to approach some possibilities for creating an operationalizable basis for empirical work along these lines. While significant reference (indeed in some ways we could almost say 'reverence') has been made (paid) to this general approach, it is evident that much less empirical work has been undertaken using these frameworks. This interest derives from our general research concerns in operational management and our sense that in much of the contemporary literature the level of operational leadership and the practices of supervision of people and processes are somewhat neglected. The discourse of 'leadership' tends to stress great men. The discourses of strategy, system and evolution seem to favour the organizational bravehearts rather than the procedural plodders of the middle range.

Yet it is at the level of operational leadership that confrontations between different versions of organizational and social reality may most decisively occur and where the conditions for autopoetic transformation may be most clearly met and closely studied. We have previously pointed to the relative neglect of research on this organizational level and argued for more empirical work to focus on the nature of 'street-level' decision making (Weir, 1976; Marsh, 2003).

Operational middle management
It would appear to be consistent with the logic of formal organizations as applied, for example, to bureaucracies in the civil service or local government that there would in practice be very tight constraints on action, and very strict delimitations of appropriate decision, effectively limiting originality, responsiveness and flexibility and thus inhibiting the conditions in which autopoietic response could emerge. Indeed, some characterizations of classical Weberian bureaucracy have noted this criterion of the defensibility of decision as being associated with a generally conservative and inhibited style of decision making.

But this does not inevitably seem to be the case, for one of the common findings of research into first-line supervision in this type of organization is that there exist considerable opportunities for the operation of discretion, in both a positive and a negative sense. Moreover, in these roles proactivity is positively defined as a desideratum of the role, but is cited regularly by role occupants as one of its attractive and desirable features.

What are the special qualities of this level of management that renders it especially important? It is precisely because they operate at the *interface* between a number of organizational subsystems each with specialist concern for a range of definable activities that these operational middle managers have a special role as decision-making generalists. To be a generalist implies a number of responsibilities and these can in principle be arrayed and documented and even in our present times are capable of being subject to audit. But the principal unifying characteristic is that they are open-ended with respect to both clients and actions. That is what it means to be a 'manager'.

Thus a middle manager interfaces between higher and lower levels. Passing on messages is not prima facie a 'management' task. Interpreting what senior managers expect to happen and reframing these expectations in terms of a range of deliverables within the actual or potential competences of junior levels, undoubtedly is.

A middle manager interfaces conversely between lower and higher levels. Upward transmission of every worker plaint and motivational withdrawal is not a management task. Using trained experience to interpret the subtle creaks and groans of the delivery systems as they strain to perform, and knowing which signs of organizational stress predict impending rupture of vital system members, undoubtedly is.

A middle manager interfaces between product and customer. Knowing the fine detail of the product characteristics in a scientifically accurate sense is a task for a specialist; being able to interpret those attributes in terms of experienced performance in order to plausibly satisfy a customer complaint, undoubtedly is.

A middle manager interfaces between the generalities of a legal framework and their organizational application. Being able to pass legislation or to frame a critique of social policy in respect of health and safety issues is not a management task; chairing a Health and Safety Committee in the knowledge that only one person may be liable to go to prison in respect of an infringement of the relevant law and that this person is you, undoubtedly is.

Because organizational life is full of surprises, the role of management may be defined in short as the 'management of surprises'. From the perspective of senior levels it may equally as plausibly be represented as the 'management of non-surprises'. Senior ranks tend to prefer dogs that do not bark in the night. Inevitably, therefore, there are considerable opportunities for the operation of discretion in middle management, in both a positive and a negative sense. First-line managers operate with their relevant publics at the interface between a number of distinct structures creating a multiple contingency that frames their actions. Proactivity is cited regularly by these role occupants as an attractive and desirable feature of their job. But this proactivity can of its nature adversely or positively affect the life chances and success opportunities of others, whether above or below, inside or outside the organization.

We claim therefore that we must see middle management as intrinsically rooted in its essential tasks, which are typically not the big decisions and heroic stances beloved of leadership case writers but a stream of actions which tend to be discontinuous, detailed, specific and subject to interruption from pressing claims from above and below. But even the most pressing claims have to be interrogated by the middle manager as he/she strains to distil the important from the merely urgent.

The study: data collection
All of these considerations affect our choice of methodology in this study. The initial phase of the research was to examine in depth, and in their own words, what police sergeants

do and how they go about doing it. The in-depth study was conducted in April 2004. The data were collected through open-ended interviews with a sample of 72 respondents and supplemented with data from focus groups, in which a further 25 respondents participated. The topics used for discussion in the focus groups came from an analysis of the themes raised in the in-depth interviews. There was reasonable representation by gender, ethnicity and other aspects of diversity.

Each evening, as a team, we reviewed the interviews completed, noting key points and writing research notes for future reference. We focused from the outset on the 'critical incidents' in which the decisions made by our respondents had 'made a difference'.

In the 72 direct interviews we used a guide to key areas of interest as an *aide-mémoire* rather than a formal questionnaire. The interviews usually started with a descriptive account of the respondent's job and moved into career issues, so that descriptive material was gathered early on in the process, thus relaxing the interviewee before topics involving analysis and judgement themes were developed. Mostly, the interviews developed at a natural and unforced pace with the respondents in command of their subjects and at ease with the situation. The 'critical incidents' were usually volunteered quite naturally in the course of the interview. The atmosphere in the interviews was invariably positive and serious with a strong sense from the respondents that the research was worthwhile and focused on important issues for their job, rank and career.

Our intention was to learn how to see through the eyes of our respondents, capture their verbalizations, and glimpse their logics of explanation and ways of making sense of the situations they were describing.

Our approach in framing the questions was therefore to introduce headings, areas, issues and frameworks in an open-ended manner to permit the respondents to follow their own path through the meaning. Thus the accounts should make psychological sense. This technique is quite common in other fields of work and relies heavily on open-ended questions, a non-judgemental stance by the interviewer, and regular summary questions of a non-directive nature.

In essence we were trying to establish – in the respondents' own words – the answers to 'What is going on here? How do you see it? How would you explain that?'. In principle, 'How', 'What', 'Where' and 'When' questions were used as well as 'Tell me about' and similar probes to elicit shades of meaning.

All interviews were taped, culminating in over 100 hours of recordings, and complete transcripts and the initial analysis was conducted through the NVivo qualitative data analysis software. This enables researchers to code words, phrases or complete sections of text. The programme works by storing and organizing files, searching for themes and relating these themes to others in the text. It permits the identification and recording of units of meaning, called 'nodes'.

This theoretical approach can broadly be subsumed under the rubric of 'critical realism'. In essence we accept the ontological objectivity of our object of study and yet remain sensitive to the interpretative nature of much of what passes for relevant knowledge about it. While being aware of the probability that our roles as observers/researchers were an element in the discovery of this knowledge, we attempt to 'bracket' our role sufficiently to create the opportunities for a plausible interpretation. But essentially these analyses remain our interpretations of the accounts given by our respondents.

Thus, our approach to the interview situation was to continually probe until we considered that we had understood what it was the respondent was trying to convey, rather than to terminate the questioning when a prestructured information box could be coded and completed. Thus the interviews varied in length, but some strong themes emerged consistently.

The 'critical incidents' emerged from and in the context of a focused discussion around the decision-making experiences of the respondents in their natural attitude in the domain of discourse in which they were expert. In the next section we give two examples of the types of critical incident with which we are concerned.

Case 1: the boy with the knife

In this first case, the sergeant is aware of the need to attempt to accommodate the potentially conflicting demands of bureaucracy, and what he sees as 'the bigger picture'. This sergeant we shall quote at some length, to maintain the complexity of the position he adopts, and the actions he takes. First, the basic facts of the case and what should have happened according to strict procedure:

> This job we went to last night. It was a report of a child threatening some other children with a knife. As it turns out, yes, an 11 year old child threatened an 11 year old and a 12 year old child with a leather working tool cum knife. Now, if I'd dealt with that absolutely by the book, I should have arrested that 11 year old then, I should have arranged video interviews with the other 2 kids, because I couldn't interview them, and bailed the lad, who's got no previous convictions whatever, pending the outcome of the interviews, brought him back in, and all this needed to be done. Put a crime . . . recorded it as a crime.

Next, what the sergeant actually did:

> But I didn't. What I did was speak to the lad who was crying his eyeballs out, in front of his parents, then I went to speak to the two complainants' parents who were perfectly satisfied with the course of action I'd taken, to speak to the lad, warn him of any repercussions etc. etc. Made a note of everything, seized the knife, got a disclaimer for it. Booked into property. But what you have to do then is go to the incident log and write it up . . . can't tell why, write it up in such a way that it's not going to be questioned as to why you didn't arrest that juvenile. Because if I say that that juvenile threatened somebody with a knife, the DI or DCI will be on my back saying 'you should've arrested him'. And they'd be quite right, right in the sense that if I was following the National Crime Reporting System, then that was a crime. It was at least a Public Order, if not, an Offensive Weapon, because it was the way he was actually using it. So there is . . . in the strictest sense of the word, there's a criminal offence, and therefore a crime, and therefore a suspect for a crime. And that lad would now have a record.

Then, the internal dialogue of the sergeant, highlighting the conflict between 'right decision' and 'expedient decision-following procedure':

> Perhaps he deserved it? But he's an 11 year old for God's sake. I think that it was the most appropriate way to deal with the situation. From what the parents wanted, what the complainants wanted, it's an altercation between 11 year olds. I mean OK it's a bit more than that, because there's this knife, it wasn't a stabbing, there wasn't even a likelihood of a stabbing, it was just a bit of bravado, to my mind, I'm satisfied that that lad has learnt his lesson.

And finally, negotiating the post-action report:

The art of doing something like that now is writing it properly on the incident log. Because if you don't . . . the trouble is, many officers don't have the knack or the art of writing properly. What you can do is you don't tell lies, but you can write it in such a way, it's the 'glass half empty or half full' syndrome. It depends on how you describe the incident as to the way the questions are going to be asked. You could say it's part of policing, but it's . . . it is a back covering exercise. I don't know how you feel about that, I mean I'm only giving you my version of events. (Price)

There are several interesting aspects to this narrative, enhanced perhaps by its currency (it had happened 24 hours before the date of the interview), and therefore the lack of time available to 'refine' it in any substantial way. We can see again the sergeant dealing with the conflict between what he perceives to be the demand for the right course of action in the particular circumstance, and the demand by the 'system' for standardized responses which should theoretically eliminate any need for discretion on his part.

What is particularly noticeable with this sergeant is his acceptance that the 'bureaucratic' response (arrest the child) would have been technically 'right'; had he done so, there would have been no criticism of his action; but because he understands this, he also perceives the need to reflect the record of the incident in a way that minimizes the chances of senior officers 'finding out' what 'really happened' and asking him some awkward questions; a 'back covering exercise', as he says. He doesn't 'lie', but manages to describe what happened in a way that does not attract unnecessary attention. He later says that part of his role as a supervisor is to help his officers learn how to write reports in this fashion.

Asked what he would expect of his officers in the same circumstances, he said they would call him to ask his advice. These may be circumstances which are faced by all operational personnel, but it is the sergeant who has to make the choice, to 'negotiate the terrain'. There is an element of resistance – resistance to the temptation to follow blindly any particular course of action – but that resistance is not associated simply with an automatic rejection of the performance management 'regime'.

Case 2: the gold chain
This is a verbatim extract from an interview with a sergeant in an urban area:

Our divisional priority is robbery. Any robbery that occurs, we must deal with it positively. A robbery came in which was a nasty one. Two juveniles had been subjected to robbery at knife point. A gold chain and mobile phone was stolen. The two juveniles came home and told their father, and he turned up at one of the offenders' addresses and he recovered the chain, but not the phone. We know everything and we should respond to it.

   Just before this, there had been an incident where an old lady had been subjected to an aggravated burglary. And one of the offenders had been chased and we had secured him in an area, and two of my operators were in control in that area. I was the only operational manager on duty; all other operators were busy on other essential tasks.

   Then this 'robbery' comes in. As my procedures tell me I have to 'look around your division' so I asked – is there any other operator who is available?' and the answer is that there was not. So I waited until the night shift came on. I then directed an operator to go to the house, locate the offender if he was still there, secure the missing property and lock up the offender.

   When I come back on the day after, I'm told by one of my operators that the boss is furious and that I'm 'for the ******* high jump' for not responding to the robbery when it came in. So I go up there [to the Inspector's office]. I'm not too impressed when I go in there and its no 'Hello, how are you'. It's just a piece of paper pushed across the desk and 'What do you know about that?'.

So I don't say anything and then he says 'Are you aware of the Divisional Priorities about Robbery? and how you should respond to it?' and he went on about this and that and I said 'Have you finished?' and he said 'Yes', and I told him, 'Can you have a look at the incident? This incident log tells you the actions that I have taken'. As I've said, there were no operators available . . . if you want to carry out a resource check on what these operators were doing, then that's your prerogative but I will tell you what they were doing because I am responsible for these operators. These operators were doing this, this, this and this . . . and there were no others available. That's why we didn't attend this incident, but I did direct the operator coming on shift'.

So he said 'Right, I was going to b*****k you but now I understand why you did what you did'.

This case illustrates the way in which the operational manager has to translate generic policy instructions into practical actions. He has to make sense of the higher-level policies and make sure that his operators understand what is the realistic and appropriate way to deal with complex situations, while remaining in charge of evolving sequences of events. He is thus the linch-pin in this organization of forces.

The decisions of the operational manager may well be challenged by higher authority so he has to be sure of his ground and able to justify his actions. But he is empowered to take decisions in a way that is creative and develops the apparent possibilities available.

He is clearly operating as the operational manager, with the ability to promote the best use of the resources available on the spot at that precise time. Thus he has to be able both to manage inexperienced operators, with a due sense of the health and safety aspects of their supervision, and also to directly control the actions of more experienced operators, who may have a tendency to cut corners if left to their own devices. Almost certainly in this kind of situation, a senior operator could not have handled the situation in the same way. It is the rank of the operational manager that enables him both to handle the complexities of the situation, but also to be able to defend it later as a successful outcome.

Now let us work through the choices that the operational manager has had to make in order to achieve the desirable outcome, sequentially, as these choices have been presented to him.

First, there is the decision about what constitutes a significant event. The apparent organizational priority is that the first event was of more significance than the second. The operational manager has the opportunity to adopt a purely temporal scheme for prioritizing, which could have finessed the decision and have given him another basis for choice: he could adopt a policy of 'first things first' and this might well be defensible in any later questioning. But he drops his interest in the first incident when news comes in of another situation requiring decision.

Second, there is a set of choices relating to the prioritization of resources. The operational manager has finite resources and he has both to solve the problems that occur on his watch and to keep enthusiasm and morale high as potential resources for what tomorrow may bring.

Third, he has a choice about the time and nature of his reporting of the incidents. He chooses not to make the instant report which complies with the hierarchy's perception of priorities but to leave some writing up for more mature reflection on the morrow when he has had the opportunity to see what has actually happened in the case of each incident, given the natural effluxion of time.

Fourth, he is faced on the next morning with a potential threat to his organizational rank and authority, for it is a junior operator, one of his subordinates, who advises (surely with a rebellious smirk) that he, the operational manager is 'for the ******* high jump'.

The sergeant has to make a major choice with potentially negative consequences for the role. Instead of dealing with this situation in due course when it is brought home to his turf, in a face-to-face confrontation that might have the potential for the threat to his position to become crystallized in a damaging interpersonal encounter, the sergeant makes the choice to escalate the threat and raise the stakes by leaving his post to confront the inspector who is apparently the source of the 'high jump' threats. He has to move out of his defensible space and into threatening territory. This is not a necessary move but it is a clear purposive choice. He has to meet his superior on his turf. A victory there will be the more significant. He then has to make the choice as to how to defend the decisions he has taken, all the time on the basis of imperfect knowledge, incomplete factual basis and uncertainty as to the hierarchical support he can expect. He does this in a confident, assured way that compels his superior to acknowledge that he might have handled this complex situation in the same way.

Finally the sergeant positions the choices he had to make in the defensible choice he made that the better use of the resources available was to have an officer attend the incident he had judged to be the more serious, even if it did not evidently conform to the senior management's expressed priorities. What might have started out as a purely tactical choice turns out to have potentially strategic consequences. Although the main parameters of decision making in this organization have not apparently or transparently changed, in practice the outcomes of decisions after these events are likely to be different in character and substance from those that might have been made before these events occurred. These circumstances have altered these cases. What is 'robbery' and what is 'priority' are different in connotation afterwards though not necessarily in denotation. Thus the criteria for mutative autopoiesis are satisfied.

The sergeant's confidence is assured by his figuring after the event as the key player in a relevant story. What he has shown is not just that he knows the rules of engagement but that he can make them and break them. He is becoming the hero of his own lunchtime, and has defended his turf, but he has also moved the confrontation to away turf where a victory may be the more significant. But he is also changing the way the organization does business; he is creating case law for handling these kinds of situation in future. On the basis of these encounters with the changing reality of the street and its challenges, the organization evolves. This has been an autopoietic sequence.

When he tells the story later in an organizational setting and his respondent affirms 'I see what you mean', we are witnessing a rather complex utterance. Both 'I see' and 'what you mean' have been redefined by what this operational manager has *done*. Events have changed options. The past has become the prisoner of an evolving present in which this operational manager is empowered and reinforced in his empowerment. The organization has mutated and added to its repertoire of action possibilities for this operational manager and others.

This outcome had involved the sergeant in taking a dangerous, exposed position that could have wrecked his standing in this community had he not turned out to have been right. So his assumption of personal risk created an opportunity for moral redefinition as well as reinforcing his own hierarchical position.

He became strengthened in his control, even dominance, of his own personal space and his ability to influence the surrounding spatial domains. There is little doubt either that as this story and its outcome becomes part of the totality of community understandings of 'how we do things around here' that this person's penumbra of influence is also strengthened. He may become known as 'X (who did Y)', and the subsequent myth itself becomes incorporated as an element in the socialization of others.

In interpreting the decision sequence, the sergeant has been replaying the 'inner conversation' he has surely already had, at least three times, at the close of the previous shift when he logs the report in such a way as to leave the certain possibility of a hierarchical challenge to his priorities, overnight when he considers what is likely to be required on the morrow by way of explanation, and doubtless in the car as he drives up to his confrontation with his superior. For this is not mere 'rule-following' behaviour, but it has the possibility to be rule improving. He has to think about this and be sure in his own mind that this is how he wishes the sequence to develop.

But most importantly, this situation has created the possibility of a transformation of the organization's own decision-making parameters. The inspector now has to take on board this new knowledge. He has to understand more clearly how generic strategic dictates prioritizing a certain class of offence, in this case robbery, can distort good decision making. The sergeant has shown how the organization can evolve and make better decisions.

The resulting outcomes form part of a stream of decisions that reinforce and transmute the relevant organizational structures, redrawing boundaries as to the appropriateness and morality of procedures, influencing policy and also norms, procedures and also values. This is how the autopoietic process works. This is where the organizational DNA is located, in the middle.

Discussion: criteria for autopoietic transformation
As far as we are aware, there have been rather few attempts to operationalize what could be implied by the discourse of autopoetic processes. Yet if these concepts are to influence future research, this attempt must be made. In Box 12.1 we attempt a rough schematization of the elements that seem to us to relate to situations in which autopoietic transformations can be anticipated.

BOX 12.1   PROPOSED CRITERIA FOR AUTOPOIETIC TRANSFORMATION

- Dynamic motion
- Visibility
- Dangerous exposure
- Probability of minimal support in case of failure
- Impact on life chances of others
- Normative flexibility
- Justifiability
- Location

We deal with these points briefly.

The first point to note is that autopoiesis takes place in a dynamic rather than a static context. DNA is a living thing. It evolves over time and it evolves in ways that are not totally predictable. We use the language of 'mutation' to describe these processes as they lead to changed forms of the organism. It is a changing phenomenon throughout time periods. It has 'befores' and 'afters'. In short, it is involved in dynamic motion.

Second, these processes and these evolutions should nonetheless in principle be visible to some type of observation. However embedded in organizational substance they are, the difference they make should be susceptible to some type of recording and description. They are empirical, not mystical, however small and insignificant they may appear to be to the casual observer.

Third, and this is not a trivial point, they exist in a dangerous environment. If we accept the viability of the mammalian and biological macro metaphor that is autopoiesis, and we wish to use concepts like 'organizational DNA' in a realistic sense, we need to accept that, like the spermatozoa and ova that are the carriers of human DNA, they are prone to environmental pressures and threats, sometimes of a potentially catastrophic nature.

Fourth, these small weak entities that carry organizational DNA are not surrounded by mechanisms and tissues that guarantee their survival. Many a small Adam falls by the wayside. Many a small decision does not get supported by the hierarchy. Much of the decision making that is of interest to the researcher is of this kind. It is tentative and vulnerable at its inception. Its future life chances depend on circumstances outside its own direct control.

Fifth, and despite all of the above considerations, the impact of a successfully achieved autopoietic sequence may potentially be very great. In the case of mammalian DNA this is how the species is carried on. In the case of the organizational DNA with which we are concerned here, there is the possibility of these apparently small events having an influence far beyond their scale.

Sixth, as in the events and sequences that surround the processes of the transmission of mammalian DNA, there are profound ethical penumbrae. Some of the most apparently insignificant events are subject to the most demanding moral inhibitions. Again it is important not to overstate the obvious, but it is in small incidents that the researcher can see how the organization actually works and why what is right is right and why what is wrong is wrong. But these judgements are not static and timeless. They too are continuously evolving. As decisions change actions so their outcomes change norms.

Seventh, it is part of organizational reality that judgements have to be justified after their enactment and the justification will itself evolve as situations vary. 'Circumstances', we say, 'alter cases' and we note a borderline decision that 'that has not come up before' and after a decision that may have been the object of interpersonal confrontation at the time, that 'now I see why you did what you did, I can see that, although I was critical of your decision at the time, I now see that it was, in fact, the right thing to do'.

Finally, as far as this brief review is concerned, the likelihood is that many of the decisions that are of interest to us in this context have a spatial implication. They take place somewhere and they exert influence over some terrain. Elsewhere, dealing with other aspects of these findings we do indeed talk of 'negotiating the terrain' and we give some examples of how that is done in this milieu. Here we only seek to note that these decisions tend indeed to be spatially referenced and that the location of events can be of significance for considering their autopoietic character.

Conclusion

In conclusion we submit that analysis of what we have termed 'critical incidents' is important for understanding the processes through which organizations evolve towards better quality decisions, changing with changing circumstances while still providing a framework of certainty. Structure is transformed by agency but the opposite is also true.

Many of our respondents were very conscious that it was mainly at the level of sergeant that the greatest opportunities for exercising discretion of this kind existed. One sergeant, a graduate with nearly 20 years experience, a specialist in murders, explained that although she was regularly advised to go for promotion and take her inspector exams, she regularly declined because 'this is the last level in the police in which you can do real police work'.

The middle manager does not act in a deterministic way in the sense that choices and actions are entirely driven by the structural characteristics of the organization. In the work of translating structural elements (targets, objectives, tasks, performance measures and so on) into something that works, the manager is presented with a choice – broadly, the choice to act within the constraints and enablements of structure, or not – a choice mediated by the inner conversation of the individual (Archer, 2003).

Having made this choice, there is then an additional potential choice presented to the manager, wherein lies one of the main conditions for autopoiesis, namely to make visible to the wider organization how the results of action may modify future structures. The organization may, or may not, be receptive to the information generated by the manager in this way; the more receptive it is to future modification of structures, the more likely it is that autopoiesis will occur.

We argue therefore that an autopoietic system is not simultaneously open and closed (van Krogh and Roos, 1995), nor is the autopoietic system inevitable. The system seems to work in a way that allows the sequential opening and closing of the system according to the choices made by its agents, the managers. The organization may, or may not, be open to reproduction, depending on the openness of its members to structural modification. Moreover, as in mammalian reproduction, the autopoietic mechanisms operate in relatively specialized organs and are not necessarily obvious in all parts of the system. They operate some, but not all of the time. Thus, they are spatially and temporarily intermittent.

We have therefore tentatively identified the mechanisms and criteria by which structure is translated into agency – and back again. We believe that in many of these interviews the methodology we adopted permitted the respondents to rehearse the 'inner conversations' that they had had at the time of the original experience. The inner conversation both mediates experience and also provides the opportunity to expand the discourse. It is not just a mulling over of a predetermined or predictable outcome.

We remain convinced that the most likely locus of these sequences that we have identified as 'autopoietic' is in the middle of the organization, but we do not wish to privilege this research locus arbitrarily. The most appropriate way to resolve these issues is by extending this methodology to higher and lower ranks in the police service and also to other types of operational middle management in other types of organization.

Finally we argue that the processes we are describing are not accounts of persistent states of organizational functioning that are always as it were open for business. While autopoiesis is a process, it is a sequential rather than a persistent one, intermittent in operation and only surfaced in critical situations. But the individuals who star in these accounts are purposive, they have intentions and they aim to behave in certain ways. But these are not the automata-like responses of pre-programmed role occupants. These players are also agents.

Note

* An earlier version of this chapter was given at the track on foresight and organizational becoming: British Academy of Management Conference: Queens University, Belfast, September 2006. The authors express their appreciation for the feedback from colleagues at the meeting.

Bibliography

Archer, M. (2003), *Structure, Agency and the Internal Conversation*, Cambridge: Cambridge University Press.

Beer, S. (1980), 'Introduction' in Maturana and Varela.

Bhaskar, R.A. (1975), *A Realist Theory of Science*, London: Version.

Bourdieu, P. (1977), *Outline of a Theory of Practice*, Cambridge: Cambridge University Press.

Bourdieu, P. ([1982] 1990), *In Other Words: Essays Towards a Reflexive Sociology*, trans. M. Adamson, Stanford, CA: Stanford University Press.

Dahrendorf, R. ([1959] 1976), *Class and Class Conflict in Industrial Society*, London: Routledge & Kegan Paul.

Dahrendorf, R. (1977), *Class and Class Conflict in Industrial Society*, Stanford, CA: Stanford University Press.

Giddens, A. (1973), *The Class Structure of the Advanced Societies*, London: Hutchinson.

Giddens, A. and Pierson, C. (1998), *Conversations with Anthony Giddens: Making Sense of Modernity*, Cambridge: Polity Press.

Grimshaw, D.J., Mott, P.L. and Roberts, S.A. (1997), 'The role of context in decision making: some implications for database design', *European Journal of Information Systems*, **6**(2), 1 June, 122–8.

Hernes, T. and Bakken, T. (2003), 'Implications of self-reference: Niklas Luhmann's autopoiesis and organization theory', *Organization Studies*, **24**(9), 1511–35.

Luhmann, N. (2003), 'Organization', in T. Bakken and T. Hernes (eds), *Autopoietic Organization Theory: Drawing on Niklas Luhmann's Social Systems Perspective*, Oslo: Copenhagen Business School Press, pp. 31–52.

Marsh, Craig (2003), 'Values-driven performance management systems and the authoritarian leader', paper presented at the Management Theory at Work conference, Lancaster University, 14–16 April.

Maturana, H.R. and Varela, F.J. (1980), *Autopoiesis and Cognition: The Realization of the Living*, Vol. 42 in Boston Studies in the Philosophy of Science, Dordrecht: D. Reidel.

Mingers, J. (1995), *Self-Producing Systems: Implications and Applications of Autopoiesis*, New York: Plenum Press.

Sowunmi, A., Burstein, F.V. and Smith, H.G. (1996), 'Knowledge acquisition for an organisational memory system', 29th Hawaii International Conference on System Sciences (HICSS), Vol. 3, *Collaboration Systems and Technology*, pp. 168–77.

van Krogh, G. and Roos, J. (1995), *Organizational Epistemology*, London: St Martin's Press.

Weir, D.T.H. (1976), 'Radical managerialism', *British Journal of Industrial Relations*, **14**(3), 324–38.

Weir D.T.H. (2004), 'Lice and icebergs: a reminder of subterranean knowledge', paper presented at the Organizational Discourse Conference, Amsterdam Free University.

13 Making sense of organizational becoming: the need for essential stabilities in organizational change
Ian Colville

It is in the realm of the glimpsed potential that the future takes shape.

Seamus Heaney

Sensemaking is in the nature of the reflective glance.

Karl Weick

Introduction

A driving assumption behind process thinking is that social reality is not a steady state but a dynamic process (Pettigrew, 1997) which in turn, leads us to questions of organizational change. These emphases on process and dynamism are most clearly brought together in Tsoukas and Chia's (2002) recent rethinking of organizational change. Traditional approaches to change, they say, have been dominated by assumptions privileging stability, routine and order, giving rise to the view of stability being the norm and change being the exception.

However, if you assume that the essence of life is its continuously changing character, as Tsoukas and Chia argue, then change rather than stability is the norm. This reversal of ontological priorities from stability to change sensitizes us to how pervasive change already is and allows us to see that change is always potentially there, if only we care to look for it (2002: 568). This looking for change involves searching for micro processes that make change constitutive of reality. The ongoing and dynamic aspect of change is conveyed by Tsoukas and Chia through the term 'organizational becoming'. This parallels Pettigrew's observation that human conduct is perpetually in a process of becoming, hence the overriding aim of the process analyst is to 'catch reality in flight' (1997: 338).

This chapter is sympathetic to a view which recognizes the becoming of change because it allows us to (fore)see organizing and organization as an ongoing present shaped through the glimpses of a potential future and the glances of a potential past. Over and above this, however, the chapter argues for two important amendments that suggest all is not process and that there are goings as well as becoming(s), and how they are taken into account is crucial to our understanding as to exactly what is organized in an organization. The first amendment suggests that even a process view of change has to address the issue of stability. To journey hopefully as a process may be better than arriving but without destinations or stability, journeys lose definition (or anything against which to define themselves). This is not to say that stability functions in the same way when it is the ontological priority, just that in reversing priorities so that change is 'seen' does not imply that stability should disappear. The second amendment counsels that Lewin (1951) may have captured some *thing* about change, if not every *process*, and that we should

234

think twice before abandoning the event sequence associated with stability. It suggests that there is theoretical and practical learning to be had in how the ontologies of stability and change interact. These amendments are proposed from within an organizing and sensemaking perspective (Weick, 1979, 1995).

The chapter proceeds by outlining the two ontological positions as reflected in episodic and continuous change, before considering how even a process view of change, consistent with a continuous model of change, requires stability (characteristic of an episodic change ontology) for making sense of change. To see only process is to blind us to the essential stabilities without which we cannot detect flow, change and process (Colville et al., 1999a). This is briefly illustrated by considering the energy company AES and its four core values of integrity, fairness, social responsibility and fun which act as essential stabilities. This is followed by an examination of how and why ongoing processes of change in organizations do not result in organizational change (Tsoukas and Chia, 2002: 580) and is elaborated in more depth, drawing on an ethnographic study of safety culture in a Norwegian aluminium plant.

The conclusions suggest that a fuller understanding of organizational change requires process researchers not only to have a sense of stability within an ontology which prioritizes change, but perhaps more importantly, that they should seek to adopt an ambivalent position with regard to ontologies that prioritize stability or change. An ability to engage in such ontological oscillation provides insights as to how glimpses of the becoming of organization interact with glances of its going, allowing us to make sense of the present.

Conceptual setting

In their review of the organizational change literature, Weick and Quinn (1999) note an important and emerging contrast in change research between change that is episodic, discontinuous and intermittent and change that is continuous, evolving and incremental. This contrast is sufficiently pervasive in research and sufficiently central to the conceptualization of change that it forms the organizing framework for their review. And while it is always dangerous to simplify into two camps, it does seem that each of these affords a different view of change and its relationship to stability which helps us locate and differentiate more traditional approaches from more recent work, exemplified by Tsoukas and Chia (2002). Our purpose here is to use this framework as a means of focusing more clearly on what follows if you see 'process as ultimate' and you adopt a 'strong version of process'.

Van de Ven and Poole (1995) and Poole and Van de Ven (2004) argue that process refers to the progression and unfolding of events in an organizational entity's existence over time. If this is the case, then both episodic and continuous change have process. In episodic change, the flow of events appears to observers to look like repetitive action, routine and intertia dotted with occasional episodes of discontinuous change (Weick and Quinn, 1999: 362). Change is thus intermittent and is captured by the classical Lewinian model of unfreezing, changing and refreezing. This is not so much a model of change as a model of how equilibrium or order can be reattained after inertia has generated disequilibrium when an organization loses fit with its environment. Realignment occurs through deliberate intervention strategies for bringing about change and which tend to be programmatic and top down (Beer and Nohria, 2000).

The fact that Hendry (1996) can argue that the whole theory of change can be reduced to Lewin's idea that change is three stages which begins with unfreezing testifies to the durability and centrality of this view. This is what Tsoukas and Chia (2002) have in mind when they say that traditional approaches to change are dominated by assumptions privileging stability, routine and order in which stability is the norm and change is the exception. Change is thus not considered in its own terms, but is reified: it is treated as the unexpurgated middle of the Lewinian sandwich between unfreezing and refreezing. The question Tsoukas and Chia pose is what does change look like if you reverse the ontological priorities, such that change is the norm and stability is the exception?

If you take Heraclitus seriously that everything changes and nothing abides, if like William James, you see the essence of life as its continuously changing character, as Tsoukas and Chia do, then reversing ontological priorities sensitizes us to how pervasive change already is, if only we care to look for it (p. 568). One has to look closely, though, to see this incessant change because the modifications and adjustments are small. What looked like routine from the macro, episodic perspective reveals itself on closer inspection to comprise ongoing adaptation and adjustment. Some researchers (Colville et al., 1993; Orlikowski, 1996) hold that these ongoing adjustments are the essence of organizational change and that while they are small, ongoing changes are cumulative and can alter strategy and structure, such that incremental processes of first-order change can accumulate and give rise to second-order change outcomes.

When viewed from this perspective, change is not an interruption to anything – it is constitutive of reality. And because change is continuous, it makes little sense to talk of deliberate and dramatic interventions to initiate change, rather it is more a case of building on what is already in the making. For Tsoukas and Chia (2002), the dynamic and ongoing nature of change is conveyed by the phrase, 'organizational becoming'. Meanwhile, change becomes the reweaving of actors' webs of beliefs and habits of action to accommodate new experiences obtained through interactions (2002: 567). Weick and Quinn (1999) conclude their review by saying that change starts with failures to adapt and that change never starts because it never stops. That is, episodic change is characterized by inertia, and the challenge of getting change started and of returning the organization to equilibrium. Continuous change, however, suggests that by definition, getting change going is not an issue as it is always already present and change is an endless modification of work processes and social practice (ibid.).

Each represents different perspectives on change: literally, a different way of seeing change. The episodic framing takes a more macro perspective and fails to see fine-grained change which, in the continuous change, micro perspective, is the essence of change. Note, however, that because change in this perspective is constitutive of organization, then micro processes of change are also the essence of organization. To deal with the theory of process is also, in this view, to deal with the process of theorizing about organizing. This is the 'strong view of process' as articulated by Tsoukas and Chia (2002).

Certainly, as acknowledged by Van de Ven and Poole (1995), the organizing/ sensemaking model was one of the first and most influential models to underscore the importance of a process perspective. And it was a strong process view: 'the point is that the crucial events to be explained are processes; their structuring, modification and dissolving. It is not the tangible fixtures in an organization that are crucial. They merely provide the media through which processes are expressed' (Weick, 1979: 15).

The dynamic quality of process was underscored by developing a vocabulary that stressed verbs and verb forms which would allow people to see movement, change and flow (ibid.: 44). Thus the talk was of organizing rather than the more static organization. Organizing has to do with the process by which people make sense of their worlds by reducing equivocality. This is difficult though because the organizing/sensemaking perspective assumes that people continually live within streams of organizing events and as such, change rather than stability is the rule in any organization (ibid.: 117). This so far is compatible with Tsoukas and Chia. Change or, more appropriately, changing, is the norm and ongoing process is constitutive and organization is the outcome of actors' attempts to make sense of and act coherently in the world.

This is the becoming of change, the directly apprehended perception of change that allows us in Pettigrew's phrase, to 'catch reality in flight'. Of course, you have to get very close to catch something which is constantly on the move and to see change for what it is. But the organizing/sensemaking model, while acknowledging the dynamic nature of change, also suggests that we make sense of perception through concepts gained from prior experiences or previous attempts to reduce equivocality and which are stored in the form of recipes. This is why in the sensemaking perspective, a sensible event is one that has happened before (Weick, 1995: 170). And that history/memory/structure is the natural and first attitude taken in sensemaking and that attention to process is the unnatural and second attitude in sensemaking with the basic question being, 'is it still possible to take things for granted?' (Colville et al., 1999b).

In sum, while process theories allow us to see the dynamics of change in a way that was not possible from a Lewinian-type model based on the ontological assumption of stability, from an organizing/sensemaking perspective process is not enough. Process always has been present and, important in change but so too has order and, more importantly, the process of creating sense from fragments of order. Change may be the rule and people may continually live within streams of ongoing events but their aim (just like process theorists) is to impose some patterning on the stream of events (Langley, 1999).

They do this, not from within the stream, but by stepping out of the flow to freeze, bracket, single out and generally stabilize some portion of the ongoing events. Heraclitus in addition to asserting that all is flux, claimed equally famously that you cannot step into the same river twice. This is correct in terms of the doing of change as pure *durée* or pure process but it is false in terms of sensemaking. You do put your feet in the stream of events twice; prospectively at t_0 and retrospectively at t_1. This brackets the interval between t_0 and t_1 and singles out what has happened for closer inspection. Schütz articulates why this closer inspection and sensemaking are in the reflective glance:

> When, by my act of reflection, I turn my attention to my living experience, I am no longer taking up my position within the stream of pure duration, I am no longer simply living within that flow. The experiences are apprehended, distinguished, brought into relief, marked out from one another; the experiences which were constituted as phases within the flow of duration now become objects of attention as constituted experiences. What had first been constituted as a phase now stands as a full-blown experience, no matter whether the Act of attention is one of reflection or of reproduction. . . . *For the Act of attention* – and this is of major importance for the study of meaning – presupposes an elapsed, passed-away experience – in short, one that is already in the past. (Schütz, 1967: 51, original italics)

What this comes down to saying is that process, if viewed as ultimate, directs attention away from 'stepping aside to retrospect', from 'bracketing', from any notion of stability.

This blinds us to essential stabilities without which we cannot detect flow, change and process itself.

The point is not that change is a discrete event that shifts from one unfreezing state to another, but if change is 'too' continuous, it becomes difficult to make sense of what is happening unless the person is able to freeze, break up or recycle portions of this flow (Weick, 1979: 117). That is, making sense of process requires some notion of stability: Watzlawick et al. (1974) argue that change and stability are opposite sides of the same coin rather than being opposite in nature. They operate by comparison and contrast and this relativity is reflected in the idea that instead of having a theory of change and a theory of stability, what is required are theories of stability and change (ibid.: 1–2). Appropriately enough, Watzlawick et al. argue for the comparative approach by relating how originally philosophers of science saw change as such a pervasive and immediate element of our experience that it could be the subject of thought only after early Greek philosophers had been able to conceptualize the antithetical concept of invariance or persistence. Until then, there was nothing that change could be contrasted with and the situation must have been like one proposed by Whorf: that in a universe in which everything is blue, the concept of blueness cannot be developed for lack of contrasting colours (ibid.: 2).

If process is ultimate and the ontological priorities are reversed to one of change, are there any contrasting colours? Is there any place for a notion of stability in such a world-view? The organizing/sensemaking model argues that the contrasting colours are provided by essential stabilities. To adopt a more familiar metaphor for change, if process is about journeys and journeying, then the essential stabilities define those journeys by providing comparison and contrast. Journeys (processes) require destinations (stabilities) and the view adopted here is that if you lose sight of stabilities, you also lose sight of change.

It is thus possible, and indeed as argued here, essential to interrupt the continuous flow of experience, the doing of changing, in order to make sense of it. This is not to deny that reality is a dynamic process or that the overriding aim of the process analyst therefore is to catch reality in flight. What it does suggest however, is that *you* have to stop the flow/flight in order to achieve this. The 'you' applies to process analysts as much as it does to human actors conducting their affairs. If catching reality in flight is about process, pure *durée* and becoming(s), making sense of reality is about grounding that reality by finding discrete events that terminate, and because sense is made retrospectively, it is about lapsed time and going(s).

It may be objected that in turning flow into phases, process into structures, becomings into goings, we are merely smuggling Lewin back into the equation. But this does not equate with Lewin so much as turn him on his head. The issue here is not one of unfreezing to overcome inertia and stability but of freezing in order to reveal the patterns, schemas, stories (Weick and Quinn, 1999: 379) that provide the essential stabilities that lie at the heart of sensemaking and understandings of ongoing, micro-based continuous change. To this end, the next section provides a selection of empirical examples to illustrate these ideas.

Change in organization and organizational change: empirical insights into change and changing

In developing their argument that change is an ongoing process and the norm in organizations, Tsoukas and Chia make a distinction between change in organization and organizational change. This section seeks to explore that distinction to suggest that just as we sought to develop an imagery that kept change and stability in play at the same time, so it is possible to consider coexisting ontologies that honour change and stability.

According to Tsoukas and Chia, while there are ongoing processes of change *in* organizations, this should not be taken to mean that organizations constantly change (p. 580, emphasis in original). That is, while there is continuous change at the micro level with variations begetting variations, they may not be formally taken up – 'they may not break through existing culture' (p. 580). The source of this confusion is said to be language where organizational change is often used to refer to both phenomena. And while there are issues of developing a vocabulary of process (Pettigrew, 1997), things become less confused if we refer to changes in organization as 'changing'. The issue explored here is not only one of language but one of adopting an ontology that prioritizes either change or stability.

Here we offer two particular and contrasting case examples which give some empirical illustration of these ideas. The first is from AES, the global energy company (co-founded by Robert Waterman) which was, in part, from where these ideas began to gestate; the second, which is a much more substantial and micro-detailed case, is drawn from an ethnographic study of an aluminium plant in Norway.

AES, has, since its inception, been developed around four key values – fairness, integrity, social responsibility and fun – which provide the essential stability. It is these four values which provide continuity, identity and meaning against which change is not only recognized but also framed. The values are so central to understanding not only 'who' AES is but how it will act such that the Securities and Equities Commission made it clear in a note to investors: 'that if the company perceives a conflict between its values and profits, the company will try to adhere to its values, even if it means a diminishment of profits'. Employees who become tightly coupled to these values are given autonomy to act because they will do 'the right thing' (Weick and Sutcliffe, 2001: 144). In a sense, employees at AES have first been centralized around focused rhetoric and values, so that they can then be decentralized to deal with unexpected events in ways framed by this internalized rhetoric and values.

The four values thus provide continuities that anticipate discontinuities and also provide a rough map of how to deal with them. And if the bare bones of sensemaking are that people stay in motion, have a direction, look closely, update often and converse candidly, then these values provide a perfect resource for sensemaking (Colville et al., 1999a; Weick, 2001).

However, Tsoukas and Chia fear that if we see change only as formal organizational change, then it will be as if the micro changes that always go on in the bowels of organizations and do not get translated into structures, never existed. The question then becomes, how do we acknowledge the knowledge of the micro changing, particularly if it does not result in organizational change? This returns us to having to get close up and to visiting the bowels of organizations, away from the formal management areas of the organization, to see what is *really* going on. This is where ethnography reveals itself as a means of getting up close so that you can see the movement:

> If we were to take an ethnographic look at what is really going on *in* organizations . . . we would most likely see some sort of Brownian motion taking place with actors constantly reweaving their webs of belief and actions to accommodate new experiences . . .

... Whether the reweaving of individual webs of belief and habits of action leads to microscopic changes becoming *organizational* is a different issue. It may or may not happen or, to be more precise, the extent to which it happens is an interesting topic for empirical research and further theoretical development. (Tsoukas and Chia, 2002: 580, original italics).

In an ethnographic study of 'safety culture' in a Norwegian aluminium plant (Langåker, 2002; Colville and Langåker, under review), we see aspects which may contribute to this topic. We have already seen how in the organizing/sensemaking perspective, the ongoing process of continuous change or now, more appropriately, changing, was tempered by essential stabilities as exemplified in the case of AES by its four core values.

The aim of the research was to provide a culturally informed view as to how safety was practised and made sense of in a hazardous environment. The core production at the plant studied was one of fashioning extruded aluminium profiles used in shipbuilding and the oil industry. It was a tough, physically demanding environment and heavy machinery and acid baths provided constant reminders that safety was not a peripheral or insignificant issue: that safety was something that went to the heart of everyday life, not to say, survival. This was the bowels of the organization and it felt and smelt like it.

'Excellent safety' was a widely stated core organizational value and one that was repeated and expanded on by management.

As a member of the management put it :

Safety is our first priority. The most important issue for us is that all workers leave the plant every day without injuries, and we never compromise where safety is concerned. (Plant Manager)

The plant workers (that is, non-managerial roles) also echoed and shared this emphasis on safety:

Today, safety considerations are central issues in our daily work. We think safety, we talk safety and our managers constantly remind us about it. (Plant Worker)

It is the way that all of us think about safety, whatever job operations we are involved in. It is in our blood in a way. (Plant Worker)

These quotations and other data collected illustrated how workers and management alike had shared interpretations as to the history and development of safety over the years; shared perceptions as to what causes accidents; shared views as to the importance of the formal safety structure; a shared delegation to comply with safety procedures; and a shared belief in the importance of accident reporting. There was, in short, a consensus and unifying view about safety.

Shared belief is another way of saying it is part of the culture – at least, part of what Martin (1992, 2002) would recognize as an integrationist view of culture which stresses harmony, homogeneity and consensus. Make no mistake, the workers were not cultural dopes or dupes of management (Willmott, 1993). This organization had a positive image and reputation for safety which was uniformly enjoyed and co-presented by workers as much as management. This then is a strong culture, the strength of which derives from the provision of coherence and order. In terms of the present discussion, its ontological assumption is one of stability.

The weakness of the strong culture, however, lies in its simplicity. In order to act individually and/or collectively, people adopt simplifying assumptions (Turner, 1978). Effectively these come culturally inscribed but the problem with these simplifications is that because they ignore aspects of the environment, they can become a *trap* – a possible source of blind spots:[1]

> [T]he central difficulty, therefore, lies in discovering which aspects of the current set of problems facing an organization are prudent to ignore and which should be attested to, and how an acceptable level of safety can be established as a criterion in carrying out this exercise. (Turner, 1978: 379)

The simpler the simplifying assumptions, the greater the likelihood of creating a vision that is capable of being shared or 'united' among organizational members. The potential cost is that in the promotion of order through simplicity, the organization becomes blind to small failures that are incubating and possibly compounding.

In terms of the organizing model, the safety culture lacks the requisite variety to register and/or make further sense of the small changes: a situation that is compounded when change is viewed against a background assumption of stability. In short, the formal safety culture/ organization fails to see what is really going on. Or rather, there were other interpretations as to what was going on in terms of safety in the organization among the plant workers but these were in a different space (or province). This was no 'smash and grab' ethnography, with some 13 months of observation spread out over the course of two years. During the course of the fieldwork, one hundred in-depth interviews were carried out with 92 production workers and eight managers out of a total population of the plant of 115 (Langåker, 2002).

As the research progressed, it became more and more evident that alongside a shared safety culture, there was also evidence of other cultural characteristics that were not so much 'shared', as in 'held in common', but as in 'shared out' and distributed (Weick, 1995). This was more consistent with Martin's differentiation perspective on culture (1992) with its emphasis on differences and ambiguities. For example, while there was a shared commitment to using the safety reporting system, some deliberately failed to report accidents:

> I don't like to see my name in reports, so I guess I don't report as much as is wanted by management. (Plant Worker)

This casts doubt on management claims that the safety culture is reflected in the statistics:

> We all know that the more years a shift has recorded no injuries leading to work absence, the greater the pressure to keep the shift record clean. When the statistics proclaim many injury-free years, I think there is reason to be suspicious about the production of those statistics. (Plant Worker)

Alongside the pressures for underreporting of injuries, more pragmatic workers argued that recording 'trade mark' injuries was simply being too scrupulous:

> It is absurd to argue that all types of injuries ought to be reported. I mean, almost daily, someone gets a cut or a small burn – what we call, 'trade mark' injuries. There is no sense in reporting these because they will always happen and cannot be prevented in a plant like this. (Plant Worker)

Hence, it can be concluded:

> The safety statistics which they constantly brag about don't represent the real safety situation at all. (Plant Worker)

So what is actually going on? What is the 'real' safety situation? And how do people make sense of it?

Pidgeon (1998) sees the dilemma of 'safety culture' as being between the need for a unified version of safety culture and diversity of thought to deal with change. Our case suggests that there are two different yet coexisting safety cultures that each address a different horn of the dilemma. Both cultures can be said to exist and both of them work, it is just that they do different work. And while there are similarities between an integrated and differentiated culture, these tend to be understood as competing perspectives (Martin and Frost, 1996). So instead, we turn to Goffman's idea of frontstage and backstage arenas as a means of understanding how the two safety cultures can coexist.

Goffman (1959: 17) says that when one's activity occurs in the presence of others, some aspects of the activity are expressively accentuated and other aspects which might discredit the fostered impressions are suppressed. Accentuated facts make their appearance in a front region, or frontstage, but there may be another region, a back region or backstage, where the suppressed facts may make an appearance: 'A back region or backstage may be defined as a place relative to a given performance, where the impression fostered by the performance is knowingly contradicted as a matter of course' (Goffman, 1959: 114). What we take from this is that while the frontstage is presented as unified, there is a sheltered area backstage where membership is restricted. It is here backstage that performers can 'let drop' speaking and acting their unitarist lines:

> Since the vital secrets of a show are visible backstage and since performers behave out of character while there, it is natural to expect that the passage from front to back will be kept closed to members of the audience or that the entire back region will be kept hidden from them. (Ibid.: 116)

Translated to the context of the plant, the frontstage comprised a strong safety culture in which management and workers joined to present a coherent and consistent impression of safety culture. Based on strong social order, this satisfies Pidgeon's (1998) requirement for a unified vision of safety. However, it is the strong social order and the assumption of stability that goes with it which means that the formal safety culture may be blind to small changes. Small changes are particularly important in safety because as defined by Reason (1997), safety is a dynamic non-event. That is, when safety works, there is no product or event to examine – the outcome is one of stability or no change. But as Reason points out, what produces the stable outcome (safety) is constant change rather than continuous repetition (p. 37).

This clearly resonates with the assumptions of continuous change and of adopting an ontology that prioritizes change. It also chimed with the culture that was found backstage. When viewed up close, the backstage culture was found to be more variegated, had more requisite variety and complexity and was based more clearly on day-to-day working practice, as regards safety. This is a weak culture (as defined in contrast to a strong one) but its lack of a strong social order and diversity of beliefs creates a likelihood that blind spots will be fewer and more likely to be detected at an earlier stage in the incubating process. There were thus two cultures, or provinces of meaning (Schütz, 1967) in existence which were based on different assumptions about order and change. Taken together they satisfied the needs of a safety culture to be able to provide a unified vision of safety and diversity of thought to deal with change, but if taken together, there were contradictions.

As indicated, the plant prided itself on the quality of its safety culture and the regard with which this was held externally. Yet backstage, there existed more and more varied views, for example, whether the statistics reflected the actual situation. What was interesting was that the very same workers could hold differing and contradicting views on safety at the same time without any signs of dissonance. The answer to this was that they could hold them at the same time but not in the same place. Goffman alerts us to the idea that appropriate behaviour depends on the region, and what is appropriate frontstage make be inappropriate backstage. This regional behaviour was accompanied by provinces of meaning and just as Pascal has said, that what is truth on one side of the Pyrenees can be error on the other. So is it the case here.

This form of cultural relativity is not a problem, so long as you are aware of what the meanings are and you know where you are. In mapping the provinces of meaning, we found that organizational members were well aware of the borderlines between the provinces of meaning and the different types of 'thinking-as-usual' that were contextually appropriate in each. As long as the front and back stages were kept separate, then it was most unlikely that the wrong interpretations would be promoted in the wrong province.

Occasionally, however, issues arose that breached the boundary lines between front and back stages and this caused problems for the heavily espoused frontstage consensus and unity. For example, on one occasion a plant worker who had been off work with a work-related injury, was encouraged to return to work before the injuries had been completely healed, with the promise of lighter job tasks. Management's frontstage sense-making in such instances was that it was important for social reasons for people to return quickly to work after an injury. Most plant workers though had a backstage interpretation that contradicted this:

> This is a good example of how managers try to manipulate key safety figures. Their main goal is to keep the statistics nice-looking, and they don't care a damn if this collides with health concerns. And they talk about safety?! – what kind of safety is it to have a man drive his car to work when his foot is so badly damaged that he becomes a dangerous driver? These incidents have to be stopped. (Plant Worker)

Management's response to such breaching of the lines between frontstage and backstage is to enter into negotiations and this can result in changes to what is deemed an appropriate or inappropriate practice.

Discussion

The point that needs emphasizing is that it requires a major contradiction for the lines between backstage and frontstage to be breached. The formal, managerially endorsed frontstage, as we have seen, is based in more simple and unifying assumptions that reflect an ontological priority of organization and stability. Change does not come easily as this risks undermining the coherent and consistent vision of safety culture. And this is why it requires a major breach to be seen in the first place and for it to overcome the inertia of the frontstage portrayal of safety culture. Change thus tends to follow the unfreezing/changing/refreezing stages of Lewin.

Backstage, the province of meaning does not extend to having to take management's considerations into account and is more firmly focused on developing local everyday knowledge that allows the employees to remain safe. Achieving this dynamic non-event requires continuous change which itself requires a more complex and differentiated culture or province of meaning. The ontological assumption is one of continuous changing, minor modifications and adjustments which lead to a dynamic non-event of safety. Note that the achievement of a non-event can itself be seen from the frontstage as a success for the formal safety culture and for stability in the organization. Backstage, it is the constant, local and particular changing which produces the dynamic non-event. Organization, or rather organizing, is not prior to change, a stable back*ground* against which the *figure* of change takes place, but is itself the *outcome of changing*. The dynamic non-event of stability or safety is an accomplishment. This view of change is consistent with the continuous change model.

The suggestion here is that rather than posit an ontology that prioritizes change over stability or vice versa with episodic change in contrast to continuous change, it is possible to find representations of both in the one organization at the same time. In our case, the frontstage would represent an ontology that favours stability and change requires overcoming inertia and resistance with episodic or radical change. The backstage operates on an ontology that favours change, where change or changing is continuous. Stability is still implicated and important but in the organizing model, it is the result of attempts of sensemaking.

Such changing involves the constant reweaving of actors' webs of beliefs and habits of action to accommodate new experiences obtained through interactions as defined by Tsoukas and Chia (2002). It was such local and particular knowledge that kept the employees safe but because of the separation of the front and back stages, such change did not translate to the frontstage. And in as much as the frontstage represented the formal safety culture, then these ongoing processes of changing did not break through existing culture and do not amount to organizational change: backstage changing (in organization) does not get translated into frontstage organizational change.

Stevenson et al. (2003) also utilize Goffman's distinction between backstage and frontstage to comment on organizational change and conclude:

> Organization change attempts occur within an already established set of rhythms and routines within an organization that typically are backstage, taken for granted, and not even noticed. It is important to pay attention to these routine processes. (2003: 256)

Our position is that because it is backstage, taken for granted and not even noticed, it is unlikely that it will be taken into account. Indeed, if our case is representative, it is unlikely that management would be very concerned because the micro changes never reach the frontstage. And because it is management who have the power to instigate formal change interventions, these will be largely based on frontstage understandings which, while not wrong, simply do not take account of the backstage micro changes: we suggest that this may perhaps explain the high failure rate of around 70 per cent of planned change efforts (Kotter, 1995; Beer and Nohria, 2000).

But if management were reluctant to see or acknowledge the micro-level knowledge, then the employees were also reluctant to share their backstage practice with the management. If the employees work life is balanced and 'orderly' due to a separation of the provinces of meaning which allows them to participate comfortably frontstage as well as backstage, there seems to be no compelling reason as to why people on the shopfloor would try to promote backstage definitions of safety in the wider organization. Rather it seems quite sensible to keep such knowledge to themselves as this gives them powers in and out of their daily work life which are largely beyond managerial sight and influence. So for different reasons, neither management nor employees sought to bring backstage micro changes to the frontstage. This had the effect of affirming the validity of the formal safety culture and keeping the backstage at a very real but an informal level.

The conclusion we draw from this is that in order to make sense of change, it is helpful to work with both the episodic and continuous change models. Rather than see the two as mutually exclusive with one based on the ontological assumption of stability and the other of change, it is possible to see them as coexisting. According to Weick, sensemaking begins with the basic question 'is it still possible to take things for granted?' (1995: 14). Is it still possible to proceed with the thinking-as-usual and the 'of course' assumptions in the cultural recipes, or will they have to be changed to find a line of action that makes better sense? If the ontological priority is one of change or as is argued here, *changing*, then the answer is more likely to be no – you cannot proceed with automatic routines – than it is when the assumption is one of stability. But the necessary action required to move the answer back to yes – if only fleetingly because change is the rule – will involve incremental modification and improvisation of existing work processes.

If the ontological priority is one of stability, that is, order is the rule, then the answer is more likely to be yes – you can continue to take things for granted – because such an assumption fails to see micro changes and as a result, inertia builds. When change is recognized as necessary, it is usually later in the day (or even too late in the day to prevent a crisis from happening) and as a result, requires radical change involving the replacement of work processes and the establishment of a new order.

The frontstage seems more in keeping with the latter while the backstage seems closer to the former. The most interesting facet of this is that the plant employees who participated both front and back stages were capable of behaving in line with both cultures – both models of change – as long as they were kept separate. To make sense of this requires the adoption of not one ontology or the other but of both. There may be objections to this but people who study sensemaking oscillate ontologically because that is what helps them understand the actions of people in everyday life who could not care less about ontology (ibid.: 35).

This does not mean that researchers should not care about ontology, or that they can be careless when talking about it. It merely says that in trying to make sense of how people make sense, you should not draw your theoretical boundaries too narrowly but have a framework that is loose enough to accommodate inductive/data-driven research and tight enough to provide directions and clues for deductive/theory-driven research. This requirement is well served by the sensemaking model, because it is a 'low paradigm', best described as a developing set of ideas with explanatory possibilities, rather than a body of knowledge (ibid.: xi). The organizational (battle) field is littered with the remains from previous wars over paradigms and ontologies. It would be interesting to see what follows, if only for the purpose of discussion, if we can entertain the idea of coexisting ontologies.

Conclusions

Following Tsoukas and Chia's (2002) process-inspired rethinking of organizational change, this chapter has sought to provide a corrective of that position. This critique is from the organizing/sensemaking perspective (Weick, 1979, 1995) and because the perspective is regarded as one of the first process models of change and organization to treat change seriously (Van de Ven and Poole, 1995), it is largely sympathetic. However, if Tsoukas and Chia suggest that sensemaking does not 'go far enough' in developing a processual view of change and that, for example, it is 'ambivalent about the ontological status of continuous change' (p. 569), then the position outlined here suggests that from a sensemaking perspective they are replacing one category mistake for another. You can have process that accommodates stability, and indeed it is essential both conceptually and empirically.

Pettigrew (1997) noted that when participants at a special conference on process analysis were asked to say what were the key phrases/words associated with process, the list, for example, flow, chronology, unfolding, language, change and so on was such that it gave rise to the remark, 'if process is all that, what is NOT process?' (ibid.: 338). The Special Issue was silent on the matter. This chapter has attempted to outline the beginnings of such answer. This is important because as Van Maanen (1995) says, the very process of theorizing helps create the organizational properties we find in an all-too-real world. But he also reminds us that while theory works by making sense of times and situations because it always involves rhetoric, it is a matter of words not worlds; of maps not territories; and of representations, not realities.

The map created by the organizing/sensemaking perspective provided two amendments to the process view of Tsoukas and Chia, as it relates to their rethinking of organizational change. The first amendment argues that process theories of change require some notion of stability. This is not to argue against the idea that social reality is a dynamic process and that human conduct is perpetually in a process of becoming (Pettigrew, 1997). What it does say is that just as T.S. Eliot tells us that mankind cannot bear too much reality, so too much process becomes overwhelming. People make sense of flow by stepping outside to bracket, stabilize and find events that terminate. In other words, just as is the case with chapters in books, people like things brought to a conclusion, however temporary or transient, in the interests of sensemaking. The ontological priority is still one that sees change as the rule in organization but the background to this figure, a background that allows the figure to be seen, is provided by history, memory and structure.

Becomings are shaped and made sense of against historical goings. This was illustrated by the way AES, the power company, used its four core values as essential stabilities which acted as continuities: continuities that anticipated future change with a rough map for dealing with them – thus embedding change with essential stabilities (Colville et al., 1999b). In other words, goings shape becomings. However, if process is about becoming, how do we take into account goings and what does it mean for ideas of process?

The second amendment suggests that a fuller understanding of organizational change could require holding an ontology that privileges order/stability and another that privileges change/changing. This was illustrated with the front and back stages of safety culture in a Norwegian aluminium plant. The backstage seemed to reflect micro processes of changing that were consistent with the continuous change model. A close-up view revealed constant improvisations and modifications to achieve the dynamic non-event of safety. The frontstage reflected a more integrated and uniform safety culture that was the formal representation of the safety culture. Its coherence meant that stability was the guiding ontology.

What this effectively meant in this case was that local knowledge derived from practical continuous learning did not translate because it was not seen or recognized by the frontstage, the province of management. Yannow (2004) has commented on how local experiential knowledge tended to be disparaged by managers more interested in more abstract and strategic knowledge. She makes the point that such knowledge, if it crosses organizational borders, can be disturbing to the natural organizational–structural order of things (p. 18). This was certainly the case here with the frontstage based on the order of things and the backstage reflecting the disorder of constant organizing. And just as the plant employees could oscillate ontologically, so to speak, then it behoves researchers to be able to do likewise. Adopting an ambivalent attitude to change was not a weakness, but a sign of sophisticated and discriminatory views of change. We conclude that the real conceptual and empirical lacuna is how we understand not only the role of essential stabilities in a process theory of changing, but also that of ontological oscillation. Is that how people can simultaneously hold a view of change that is typified by discriminatory detail about changing, while also acting according to a more simplistic and coarse-grained Lewinian view that sees the non-event of safety as a triumph of the status quo? Is that how can theorists and safety workers make sense of mindful changing and mindless routine (Weick and Sutcliffe, 2006) at the same time? How can we hear more often about foresight rather than its lack without resorting to forecasting an unknowable future? How can we see change as the glimpses of becoming(s) and the glances of going(s)? This chapter has suggested a view compatible with a process approach in which we may begin to take such questions seriously – and ultimately make sense of them.

Note

1. Turner (1978) described a number of stages in the development of man-made disasters. The first stage comprised the initial belief and simplifying assumptions of the organization and because the organization cannot attend to everything, this generates blindspots, that is, aspects of the environment that the organization does not attend to and therefore simply does not see. Thus organizations are defined by what they ignore (Weick, 1998). This means that blindspots can potentially incubate and grow undetected until a disaster draws their existence to the attention of members of the organization.

References

Beer, M. and Nohria, N. (2000), *Breaking the Code of Change*, Boston, MA: Harvard Business Press.
Colville, I.D., Bartunek, J., Bate, S.P., Langåker, L., Pye, A.J. and Weick, K.E. (2003), 'Making sense of organizational change', Joint ODC/OMT Symposium to the AoM, Seattle.
Colville, I.D., Dalton, K. and Tomkins, C.R. (1993), 'Developing and understanding cultural change in HM Customs & Excise: there is more to dancing than knowing the next steps', *Public Administration*, **71**: 549–66.
Colville, I.D. and Langåker, L. (under review), 'Safety and sensemaking in a Norwegian aluminium plant: a cultural perspective from the backstage'.
Colville, I.D., Waterman, R.H. and Weick, K.E. (1999a), 'Organizing and the search for excellence: making sense of the times in theory and practice', *Organization*, **6**(1): 129–48.
Colville, I.D., Waterman, R. and Weick, K.E. (1999b), 'Making sense of change: essential stabilities in breathless journeys', Showcase Symposium to the AoM, Chicago, 6–11 August.

Goffman, E. (1959), *The Presentation of Self in Everyday Life*, Garden City, NJ: Doubleday.
Hendry, C. (1996), 'Understanding and creating whole organizational change through learning theory', *Human Relations*, **49**: 621–41.
Kotter, J. (1995), 'Leading change: why transformation efforts fail', *Harvard Business Review*, **73** (2): 59–67.
Langåker, L. (2002), 'Reframing organisational safety: a multi-perspective cultural approach', unpublished PhD dissertation, University of Bath.
Langley, A. (1999), 'Strategies for theorizing from process data', *Academy of Management Review*, **24**(4): 691–710.
Lewin, K. (1951), *Field Theory in Social Science*, New York: Harper & Row.
Martin, J. (1992), *Cultures in Organizations: Three Perspectives*, Oxford: Oxford University Press.
Martin, J. (2002), *Organizational Culture: Mapping the Terrain*, London: Sage.
Martin, J. and Frost, P. (1996), 'The organizational culture war games: a struggle for intellectual dominance', in S. Clegg, C. Hardy and W. Nord (eds), *Handbook of Organizational Studies*, Newbury Park, CA: Sage, pp. 598–621.
Orlikowski, W.J. (1996), 'Improvising organizational transformation over time: a situated change perspective', *Information Systems Research*, **7**(1): 63–92.
Pettigrew, A.M. (1997), 'What is processual analysis?', *Scandinavian Journal of Management*, **13**(4): 337–48.
Pidgeon, N. (1998), 'Safety culture: key theoretical issues', *Work and Stress*, **12**(3): 202–16.
Poole, M.S. and Van de Ven, A. (2004), 'Theories of organizational change and innovation processes', in M. Scott Poole and A.H. Van de Ven (eds), *Handbook of Organizational Change and Innovation*, Oxford: Oxford University Press, pp. 1377–404.
Reason, J.T. (1997), *Managing the Risks of Organisational Accidents*, Aldershot: Ashgate.
Schütz, A. (1967), *The Phenomenology of the Social World*, trans. G. Walsh and F. Lehnert, Evanston, IL: Northwestern University Press.
Stevenson, W.B., Bartunek, J.M. and Borgatti, S.P. (2003), 'Front and backstage processes of an organizational restructuring effort', *Journal of Applied Behavioral Science*, **39**(3): 243–58.
Tsoukas, H. and Chia, R. (2002), 'On organizational becoming: rethinking organizational change', *Organization Science*, **13**(5), September–October: 567–82.
Turner, B.A. (1978), *Man-Made Disasters*, London: Wykeham.
Van de Ven, A. and Poole, M. (1995), 'Explaining development and change in organizations', *Academy of Management Review*, **20**(3): 510–40.
Van Maanen, J. (1995), 'Style as theory', *Organization Science*, **6**: 133–43.
Watzlawick, P., Weakland, J. and Fisch, R. (1974), *Change: Principles of Problem Formation and Problem Resolution*, New York: Norton.
Weick, K.E. (1979), *The Social Psychology of Organizing*, 2nd edn, Reading, MA: Addison-Wesley.
Weick, K.E. (1995), *Sensemaking*, London: Sage.
Weick, K.E. (1998), 'Foresights of failure: an appreciation of Barry Turner', *Journal of Contingencies and Crisis Management*, **6**(2): 72–5.
Weick, K.E. (2001), *Making Sense of Organization*, Oxford: Blackwell.
Weick, K. and Quinn, R. (1999), 'Organizational change and development', *Annual Review of Psychology*, **50**: 361–86.
Weick, K.E. and Sutcliffe, K. (2001), *Managing the Unexpected*, Beverly Hills, CA: Jossey-Bass.
Weick, K.E. and Sutcliffe, K. (2006), 'Mindfulness and the quality of organizational attention', *Organization Science*, **17**: 514–24.
Willmott, H. (1993), '"Strength is ignorance: slavery is freedom": managing culture in modern organizations', *Journal of Management Studies*, **30**(4): 515–52.
Yannow, D. (2004), Translating local knowledge at organizational peripheries', *British Journal of Management*, **15**: S9–S25.

14 Agency in management of change: bringing in relationality, situatedness and foresight
Ahu Tatli and Mustafa F. Özbilgin

Introduction

There is an overwhelming preoccupation in the management literature with predicting the future and capitalizing on the opportunities that such a vision may offer. This is due to a recognition of the primacy of foresight in economic development (Harper and Georghiou, 2005). Decades of unprecedented growth of the literatures on foresight (Costanzo, 2004; Tsoukas and Shepherd, 2004), forecasting (Chuls, 2003) and intuition (Simon, 1987; Agor, 1986) in management is indicative of this preoccupation. However, we contend that this very literature is littered with conceptions of foresight which do not attend to interplay of foresight and change agency. Indeed, foresight is often considered as an organizational and strategic issue, rather than a phenomenon which essentially resides at the level of the individual, as an essential part of individual agency. We focus on foresight as an aspect of change agency in the management of change literature and explore: (i) what deems framing of change agency weak in the management of change literature and (ii) whether it is possible to address inadequacies of the change agency literature through reframing of foresight. Finally, we call for a framework which captures the multidimensional nature of change agency, and which refers to change agency in contextual, relational and temporal terms.

Agency is a central theme in change management scholarship. However, we demonstrate in this chapter that change management literature's portrayal of agency does not do justice to the complexity of the concept. We try to disentangle the concept of agency by exposing the problems with its current treatment in the change management literature and question whether it is possible to reframe agency in a way true to its nature. In order to achieve this, we refashion agency with relational, situated and foresight dimensions and explore foresight as an essential, but yet severely underplayed, component of change agency. Therefore, the chapter makes a theoretical contribution to the field of organizational change, by bringing contextual and relational insights into micro-level strategy making.

The chapter is organized as follows. First, we define agency, drawing on sociological literature. Next, we critique the models of agency in the process of organizational change. Third, we introduce foresight as a central concern of organizational change process. The final section concludes.

Defining agency

'Agency' is an ephemeral concept which often evades definition. Efforts to define and frame agency have engaged scholars from all disciplines of social sciences. However, the disciplinary polarization has meant that agency is often conceptualized either from explicitly individualized or from highly context-dependent perspectives. Nevertheless, increased attention to structure, agency and action debates in the social sciences has recently yielded the emergence of broadly syncretic conceptions of agency. For example, in their authoritative paper titled, 'What is agency?', Emirbayer and Mische (1998: 970) define agency as: 'the temporally constructed engagement by actors of different structural environments – the temporal relational contexts of action – which, through the interplay of habit, imagination, and judgment, both reproduces and transforms those structures in interactive response to the problems posed by changing historical situations'.

Emirbayer and Mische's definition of agency sets it in a social interaction, structural environment, temporal relational context, in which action is both situated and creative. This definition provides an ideal measure against which we assess the treatment of agency in the change management literature. In the next section, we examine the models of change agency and reflect on the problems in their theorization.

What is wrong with the models of agency in the change management literature?
The survey of the change management literature reveals an overfragmented research area crowded with various disconnected works, each piece focusing on a specific aspect of the phenomenon without articulating it in the totality of the subject or situating it in a wider theoretical framework of change agency. In addition to the lack of theoretical rigor, the works in the field also suffer from a lack of empirical grounding. As noted by Huy (2001), most of the works are examples of predominantly prescriptive models of change agents established on scientifically vulnerable theoretical and empirical bases. In addition to this general flaw in the literature, there are four other problematic areas: (i) a rational, autonomous and individualistic conceptualization of change agency, (ii) an a-contextual and disembodied focus on change agents' competencies and traits, (iii) a lack of consideration for power dynamics in the change process and (iv) an inattention to the link between change agency and foresight, the issue which this chapter explores further.

Change agents as rational and autonomous individuals
First, there are several competing models of change agency that treat the concept as an individualized phenomenon. Until the 1980s, the work on change agency was confined to organizational development (OD) research inspired by the works of Lewin (1951). Within the OD tradition, the conception of change was that of a linear and rational process of planned change in relatively stable organizations, and understanding of the role of change agent was that of unbiased external or internal consultant as facilitator armed with counseling, consensus building, listening and coaching skills (Beckhard, 1969; Tichy, 1974). These rationalized and individualized understandings of the change process and change agency were later identified as main weaknesses of the OD perspective (Dawson, 1994, 2003; Caldwell, 2003).

Another strand in the literature that presents such a linear process of change focuses on the tempo of change for understanding change agency. Weick and Quinn (1999: 375) define two types of change corresponding to different tempos of the process: episodic or radical change, which is discontinuous and intermittent; and continuous change, which is incremental and evolving. Drawing on that typology of organizational change, change agents are associated with different types of roles and competencies. In episodic change, change agents assume a proactive role as 'prime movers' in the process which is governed by the 'logic of replacement' (ibid.: 375). On the other hand, the basis of continuous change is described with reference to the 'logic of attraction' and the role of the change agent is that of a facilitator where she or he acts as a 'sense-maker'(ibid.: 380). These two distinct logics, which epitomize change agents' roles and strategies, correspond to two different types of leadership conceptualized by Bass (1995, cited in Munduate and Gravenhorst, 2003: 4); transactional (logic of replacement) and transformational (logic of attraction). The common vulnerability of these contributions is their tendency to analyze the strategies and activities of change agents as linear processes which are coordinated by autonomous individuals, who act on their rational calculations, drawing on 'perfect' information on organizational resources for change. Indeed, this approach is insufficiently detailed to capture the reality of organizational processes of change, which is characterized by layers of negotiated and politicized forms of access to resources.

Change agents as a-contextual and disembodied actors
Our second concern is over decontextualized and disembodied understanding of change agency in the literature. In the 1980s, associated with the rhetoric of the flexible, competitive and innovative organization (Atkinson, 1985; Volberda, 1998), a new stream of literature, which is fed by leadership research and which primarily focuses on the role of senior managers and organizational leaders throughout the change process, has begun to grow outside of the OD tradition (Kanter, 1984, 1999). In this literature, the role and skills of change agents, such as personal drive, energy, courage and vision, the desire to lead, honesty and integrity, cognitive ability, self-confidence and knowledge of business, flexibility and risk taking, have become almost identical with those of effective leaders (Kirkpatrick and Locke, 1991; Dulewicz and Herbert, 2000). Due to its reliance on a single individual as the focus of the change process, that is, the extraordinary qualities of a charismatic leader, this approach was criticized by many change agency scholars (Nadler and Tushman, 1990; Caldwell, 2003).

Posing a challenge to the 'change leader' approach, the 'contingency perspective' claims that there is not a universal, standard formula for change agency; rather it is contingent upon business and organizational environment (Dunphy and Stace, 1993: 905). Nadler and Tushman (1990) argued that there is not a single type of organizational change and an associated style of leadership. They proposed a typology of four different change types based on the pace of and motivation for change, each requiring different types of leadership styles. Ironically, although the contingency perspective is based upon a critique of the 'charismatic leader' approach, it is also centered on the idea of the individual leader as the focal point of the organizational change process (Westley and Mintzberg, 1989).

However, in both 'change leader' and 'contingency' perspectives, change agents are ontologically situated as disembodied and a-contextual individuals. Correspondingly, the level of exploration of change agency is overwhelmingly reduced to that of individual psychology. Caldwell (2003: 132), in his critical review of change agent literature, asserts that the inclination to associate change agents with extraordinary qualities, traits and attributes, endures in different models of change agency. This ontological attribution leads to the omission of contextual analysis of change and excessive focus on change agents' competency and traits, which essentially results in inflation of prescriptions regarding the necessary competencies for change agents and recipes for success. Consequently, the change agency literature is packed with a series of presumably universal lists of competencies and skills required by change agents. Some lists include skills in specific areas such as forecasting, anticipating, counseling, consensus building, listening, coaching and facilitating (for example, Beckhard, 1969; Bass, 1995; Weick and Quinn, 1999) or more professional competencies such as being trained in work process analysis, process consultancy or organizational development training (for example, Tichy, 1974; Huy, 2001). Elsewhere, personal traits such as the desire to lead, honesty and integrity, cognitive ability, problem solving, self-confidence, expertise, information and flexibility and risk taking are also included in these lists (for example, Kanter, 1984, 1999; Kirkpatrick and Locke, 1991; Buchanan and Boddy, 1992; Dulewicz and Herbert, 2000; Munduate and Gravenhorst, 2003). Other lists (for example, Buchanan and Boddy, 1992; Muir, 1996; Huy, 2001) include interpersonal skills such as team building, negotiation, authority, effective communication, building trust, being sympathetic, and competency in interpersonal inquiry. Hence, most of the works attempt to present blueprint models of change agency in the form of advice and guidelines. Although these may be considered useful from the practitioners' point of view as they specify possible individual strategies that may be employed by the change agents, they add up to an unsatisfactory attempt at scientific inquiry due to the lack of a robust multilayered analysis of the conditions in which change agency takes place.

Failure to recognize power dynamics in the change process
Third, although some models of change agency seek to contextualize the role of change agents within the organizational framework, these works overlook the power dynamics involved in the change process. An example of this is the model of change agency which is proposed by Huy (2001). Focusing on the planned change process, he constructs a model exploring two dimensions of organizational change: time and content. Four ideal types of intervention that come out of the time–content matrix of change are commanding, engineering, teaching and socializing, each corresponding to a change in different spheres of organization, that is in formal structures, work processes, beliefs and social relationships, respectively (ibid.: 604). Accordingly, Huy (p. 604) argues that corresponding to these four ideal types, change agents will be different organizational actors in each intervention: namely, the people from the higher echelons of organizations assisted by external consultants will be change agents in the commanding type of interventions. The professional task analysts will be change agents in the engineering type. The process consultants and psychoanalysts will act as change agents in the teaching type. Finally, the organizational members themselves will adopt change agent roles in the socializing type. Huy's model of ideal types furthers the debate on the role of change agents by pointing out the various personal competencies and styles of leadership required for intervening in different aspects of organization. However, the model still shares the mainstream change agency tradition's myopic tendency to limit the study of the subject to the construction of 'ideal types' and assignment of some trait and competency requirements to change agents.

Another work on change agency that deserves to be mentioned in this context is Muir's 'system readiness approach' (1996: 478). Here, the author attempts to situate the change process in the external macro-environmental situation and internal organizational context such as formal and informal networks and procedures, as well as pointing to the importance of assessing the impact of different ranks of organization on the process. Muir's work presents a valuable contribution by including external and internal contextual factors as the factors affecting the success of change process. However, after the discussion of the contextual nature of change, change agents are again depicted as a-political individuals with some skill and ability requirements.

Alternatively, Munduate and Gravenhorst (2003) draw a model for exploring the power bases of change agents within the organizational change process which is based on a dual typology of episodic and continuous change. Focusing on the continuous change process and relying on the social psychology tradition, they note that the individuals who are targeted through change programs display three possible reactions to the change process: public compliance, private acceptance or identification and internalization. Citing French and Raven (1959) and Raven (1965), Munduate and Gravenhorst (2003: 6) state that change agents have six bases of power and that each will elicit different reactions by organizational members: reward, coercion, legitimacy, expertise, reference and information. Use of reward and coercion as the power bases by the change agent leads only to public compliance, leaving the value systems of the targets of change intact. On the other hand, use of legitimacy (belief in the legitimate right of the change agent to exert influence on the target), reference (the situation where targets identify themselves with the change agent) and expertise (targets perceive the change agent as having expertise in the area) as power bases induces private acceptance on behalf of the target. The only base of power which creates a sustained change independent of surveillance by and presence of the change agent is noted by the authors as information that will lead to a cognitive change in the target's beliefs, attitudes, or values (ibid.: 7).

The model of power bases of change agents proposed by Munduate and Gravenhorst offers an original approach for understanding the impact of leadership style on the organizational members during the change process. However, overemphasis of the interpersonal relationship between the change agents and change targets as the basis of the evaluation of the success of the change process renders the model deficient in explaining the change at the organizational level and the associated role of the change agent. Change of interpersonal relations corresponds to the micro level of organizational change, while, for instance, organizational culture establishes the meso level of change process. Neglecting any reference to organizational culture which is more than the sum of the actions, values, attitudes or beliefs that are held by the individual organizational members and of the interpersonal relationships, the model proposes an oversimplified notion of the potential power bases of change agency and impact of their use on the change process. Moreover, the rather implicit assumption of change agent as a rational decision maker in the previous research on change agency, here becomes explicit with the presentation of change agent as the leader who utilizes the power bases he or she has on the basis of rational cost–benefit calculations.

The role of change agents is not limited to the publicly visible activities associated with seemingly rational and linear change processes on which the prescriptive models in the literature are based; but more importantly it involves what Buchanan and Boddy (1992: 27) call 'backstage activities' where the activities of the change agent are focused on bargaining and negotiation with different interest groups in the organization. Unfortunately, this publicly covert and inherently political dimension of change management is often ignored in the change agency research.

Inattention to the link between change agency and foresight
Building on these three problems in the change management literature's framing of agency, the poor treatment of temporal and in particularly foresight dimensions of change agency in this literature is one of our central concerns. Meyerson and Scully point

to the depoliticized nature of foresight in change agency in the organizational studies literature as follows:

> Change agents in organizational literature generally do not have broader visions of change in mind. Although terms like 'revolutionary' and 'deep' are sometimes used to describe change, those terms rarely refer to system change that challenges the embedded assumptions of the status quo. (1995: 594–5)

In the final analysis, owing to all these implicit assumptions on change agents, which reduce them to a-political, disembodied, decontexualized, autonomous and rational actors, foresight of change agents is framed without reference to the political, economic and history context. When context, history and relationships are absent or reduced to a set of moderating influences, foresight becomes an individual property of disembodied creativity. That is, foresight becomes an individual attribute or a skill that is independent of the contextual circumstances and network of relations which also inform an agent's ability to foresee and identify path dependencies, disjunctures and temporal fluctuations, as well as direction of contextual and relational shifts over time.

We argue that foresight has two dimensions: *reflexive* and *futuristic*. The reflexive dimension involves use of retrospection to identify temporal patterns, trends and shifts in contextual and relational phenomena with a view to forecast what may come if the temporal patterns remain the same. Therefore, the reflexive dimension of agentic foresight involves a historical and situated perspective recognizing routines, path dependencies and patterns of change over time. Authors such as Bourdieu (1980), Giddens (1984) and Fairclough (1992) have attempted within the sociological tradition to explain the foresight from this situated perspective, using terms such as habitus, and routinized and normalized behavior to denote the predictable routines of human behavior which delineates foresight in the domain of retrospection. However, it is important to note that their formulations of foresight in this way have not been widely adopted within management literature.

Instead, in the mainstream literature of change management, change agents are envisaged as a-political, disembodied, decontexualized, autonomous and rational actors. Therefore, this *reflexive* dimension of foresight is predictably missing in formulations of change agency. What remains in abundance then is the *futuristic* dimension of foresight. In this dimension, change agency is viewed as an individual trait or skill, either innate or learned, which involves prediction without recourse to history. This kind of foresight is therefore disembodied. It does not refer to present and past but provides a routemap for the future. The next section questions whether the above problems associated with change agency can be addressed.

Is it possible to address the contextual, relational, performative and temporal inadequacies of the change agency literature?

There are notable exceptions to our characterization of change management literature in terms of its treatment of change agency. For example, an exception to the pattern to overlook power relations as well as other embedded processes taking place throughout the change process is offered by Agocs (1997). She maintains that organizational change is political in that the exercise of power and control by different parties involved is central in the process. This, in turn, means that change agents may need to confront institutionalized resistance by the power holders in the organization. However, prescriptive models of change agency or 'guidelines' for success, which dominate the literature, are designated as tools for dealing with the resistance from middle or lower ranks, not from the higher echelons of the organization. The lack of consideration for potential resistance by power holders, it can be argued, is largely due to the blindness towards the organizational power dynamics. Others (Collinson et al., 1990; Acker, 2000; Lawrence, 2000; Dawson, 2003) also point to the contradictory status of change agents in the organization, which stems from the friction between their job responsibilities and organizational position when they, as a part of their job, need to monitor and control those who hold a higher rank than themselves. In stark contrast with other literature on change agency, which focuses on necessary skills and competencies of change agents, Agocs claims:

> It is not the knowledge or expertise in itself that is the source of power and a resource for organizational change: it is the knowledge upon which authorities have conferred legitimacy and assimilated into the organization's ideological framework. Whether a change message will be accorded legitimacy is the choice and decision of authorities. (1997: 925)

Hence Agocs incorporates the micro politics of interpersonal relations into her framework of the potential power sources for the change agents. Accordingly, six potential strategies that change agents may make use of are: (i) to resist; (ii) to create allies; (iii) to make a case for change; (iv) to make effective use of existing resources; (v) to mobilize politically; and (vi) to build new parallel organizations (ibid.: 929). With Agocs's contribution, the field gains a politicized notion of change agency as opposed to the abstract idea of agency dominating the mainstream literature. However, in that article, where she aims to 'assist change advocates' by offering strategies to struggle with institutionalized resistance, Agocs (p. 917) does not offer a comprehensive contextual analysis of change agents. Nevertheless, as Acker (2000) emphasizes in her interpretation of the success and failure of gender equity intervention projects, competencies, capacities and strategies of the change agent are only a few among many factors that affect the outcome of the change process.

In addition to the political nature of organizational relations, change agents themselves are also political beings who strive to act according to their own personal values. For example, Tichy (1974: 164) explained change agency on the basis of the interplay between the role assumed by change agents, their personal values and life projects. Based on the survey of 91 social-change agents, he formulated what he calls 'change agents' general change model' which covers three components: value, cognitive and change technologies, all of which refer to the qualities and traits of change agents. He looks at the congruence of values and actions and of cognition and action. The model that Tichy proposes makes an important contribution to the change agency research since it is not limited to competencies of the change agents, but it also takes into account their values and cognitions. In addition, Tichy's model sheds light on some possible sites of self-contradiction that change agents may experience while they are realizing their role throughout the change process.

One of the most original contributions to change agency literature in recent years has been Meyerson's (2001a) book, *Tempered Radicals: How People Use Difference to Inspire Change at Work*. The basic contribution of the work to the organizational change literature is the introduction of a new type of change agents, 'tempered radicals', who are both the insiders and the outsiders to the organization due to the conflict of their personal values with the dominant organizational culture (ibid.: xi). The term is defined by Meyerson and Scully as follows:

> The individuals who identified with and are committed to their organization, and are also committed to a cause, community or ideology that is fundamentally different from, and possibly at odds with the dominant culture of their organization. (1995: 586)

Being an insider in the organization equips tempered radicals with information regarding the dynamics of the organizational system and the ability to act confidently within that familiar system (ibid.: 596). Moreover, tempered radicals are aware of the importance of gaining allies among those representing the majority perspective which will provide them with 'a sense of legitimacy, access to resources and contacts, technical and task assistance, emotional support, and advice' (Meyerson, 2001b: 99). This new understanding of change agency allows for the investigation of power relations not only to situate the role of change agent, but also to examine the potential strategic power sources, which are shaped by their life projects and which they may exploit in order to mould and promote change. Another work that provides an alternative perspective to organizational change and agency is an edited book by Ledwith and Colgan (1996a), *Women and Organizations: Challenging Gender Politics*, which is a collection of empirical studies from different sectors. Throughout the book, strategies used by women to challenge the status quo and gender order in their organizations are explored. Ledwith and Colgan (1996b: 30–31) argue that women as change agents need to have political skills and to be aware of the organizational power relations. Neither Meyerson's study, nor Ledwith and Colgan's edited work focus on a specific functional category in organizations, but conceptualize change agency as a quality which is rather dispersed through different levels of an organization. However, within the scope of this chapter, we limit our discussion to change agents, although this in no way suggests that we see organizational change as solely the property or responsibility of a small set of individuals.

Discussion: Reclaiming foresight in change agency
Returning to our earlier discussion on reflexive and futuristic archetypes of foresight may be useful in positioning foresight in agency. In recent years, there has been extensive critique of explicitly retrospective and a-historically futuristic conceptions of human agency. In order to understand the complexity of foresight as an aspect of agency, we need to question the issue of both history and future. There is a tradition in social sciences which perceives the history and the future as immutable objective realities (see Giddens, 1974). This approach to the temporal spectrum means that through careful and robust study of our past we can reveal time-bound patterns and changes. However, this understanding of foresight fails to recognize the infinitely subjective configurations of history as recorded by individuals and the immense capacity of agents for transformation, and their strategic deployment of resources and relationships in order to affect changes, which may ultimately disrupt the temporal order that our careful calculations suggest. Berkhout and Hertin (2002: 39) explain: 'humans are uniquely capable of shaping their futures and acting reflexively in response to new knowledge about what the future may hold'.

While there is the problem of treating history and future as immutable objective realities, treating history and the future as domains of infinite possibility is also problematic.

This leads to what Paulo Freire (1968), in his masterpiece, *Pedagogy of the Oppressed*, so aptly calls 'verbalism', as evidenced by absence of action. Considering past and future as a seamless series of possibilities may absolve us from the burden of planning a future that is better than today. What is required then is a conception of foresight in agency that combines a conception of time as possibility and time as certainty.

In order to operationalize this ideal, we can give the example of most card games which embody elements of luck (possibility) and mastery (immutable knowledge). While it is possible for luck or mastery to dictate the final outcome of each game, it is expected that mastery would help an individual to overcome poor luck over a number of rounds. Translating this to agency in the context of management of change would be useful. While some aspects of organizational change yield well to future planning based on reflexivity and retrospection, some aspects of change may not be foreseen. Fischhoff (2003: 311) elaborates that unforeseen occurrences should be considered in assessing work and performance in organizational settings:

> In situations where information is limited and indeterminate, occasional surprises – and resulting failures – are inevitable. It is both unfair and self-defeating to castigate decision makers who have erred in fallible systems, without admitting to that fallibility and doing something to improve the system.

Recognizing that some changes cannot be foreseen allows the change agents to prepare for the unexpected. Although 'preparing for the unexpected' sounds a misnomer or an oxymoron, an expectation of the 'unexpected' allows for individuals to develop a capacity for flexibility, through which they can readjust their strategies and consider redeployment of their resources and amend their future plans. In framing our syncretic model of foresight which draws on immutable and chance aspects of time, we contend that such syncretism also requires a keen awareness of the agent's own capabilities, resources, relationships and context. Indeed, Fischhoff et al. (2005) argue that even emotional capital impacts on an agent's capacity for foresight. Only through such an awareness of their own circumstances and capacities, can agents, prepare for both the path-dependent changes and the unexpected. Although Fink et al. (2005) provide such a syncretic model, their formulation resides at the organizational foresight level, and does not relate to foresight of the agency.

Recent reports suggest that foresight is becoming an integral requirement for professional work. For example, Conde (2004) increased litigations from customers against professional workers based on their failure to act proactively and deliver foresightful action. The implication of this is that foresight is now expected in wider constituent domains of life. The modern-day obsession with long-range planning diffuses the responsibility for foresight in change agency from specialized change agents in organizations to all members of the organization. This is supplemented with mechanisms of individual professional responsibility and systems of accountability which now increasingly demand that individuals develop foresight.

Conclusion

It is important to note that foresight is only one of the elements of agency; the resources, strategies, relationships and contexts of agents also frame the volume and scope of their agentic power. Therefore, shifting of emphasis from specialized foresight, which was expected of change agents, to individual foresight, which is now expected of professional workers, should be considered in the context of the general individualization of working life in industrialized countries. Diffusion of foresight as a required professional competence across the organization means that foresight is likely to become more common a concern for understanding agency that is power, influence, competences and resource deployment strategies of people at work.

In this chapter, we examined foresight in the context of change agency. In order to achieve this, we examined the change agency literature and questioned the possibility of addressing its weaknesses through the lens of foresight. We offered a multidimensional conception of change agency, which refers to it in contextual, relational and temporal terms. Finally, we presented foresight as a central concern of the organizational change process.

References

Acker, J. (2000), 'Gendered contradictions in organizational equity projects', *Organization*, **7**(4): 625–32.
Agocs, C. (1997), 'Institutionalized resistance to organizational change: denial, inaction and repression', *Journal of Business Ethics*, **16**: 917–31.
Agor, W. (1986), *The Logic of Intuitive Decision Making: A Research-based Approach for Top Management*, Westport, CT: Quorum Books.
Atkinson, J. (1985), *Flexibility, Uncertainty and Manpower Management*, Brighton: Institute of Manpower Studies.
Bass, B.M. (1995), 'From transactional to transformational leadership: learning to share vision', *Organizational Dynamics*, **18**(3): 19–31.
Beckhard, R. (1969), *Organizational Development: Strategies and Methods*, Reading, MA: Addison-Wesley.
Berkhout, F. and Hertin, J. (2002), 'Foresight futures scenarios: developing and applying a participative strategic planning tool', *Greener Management International*, **37**: 37–52.
Bourdieu, Pierre (1980 [1990]), *The Logic of Practice*, trans. Richard Nice, Stanford, CA: Stanford University Press.
Buchanan, D. and Boddy, D. (1992), *The Expertise of the Change Agent*, London: Prentice-Hall.
Caldwell, R. (2003), 'Models of change agency: a fourfold classification', *British Journal of Management*, **14**: 131–42.
Chuls, K. (2003), 'From forecasting to foresight processes – new participative foresight activities in Germany', *Journal of Forecasting*, **22**(2–3): 93–111.
Collinson, D.L., Knights, D. and Collinson, M. (1990), *Managing to Discriminate*, London and New York: Routledge.
Conde, C. (2004), 'The foresight saga: risk litigiousness and negligence law reforms', *Policy*, **20**(3): 28–34.
Costanzo, L. (2004), 'Strategic foresight in a high-speed environment', *Futures*, **36**(2): 219–35.
Dawson, P. (1994), *Organizational Change: A Processual Approach*, London: Paul Chapman.
Dawson, P. (2003), *Understanding Organizational Change: The Contemporary Experience of People at Work*, London: Sage.
Dulewicz, V. and Herbert, P. (2000), 'Predicting advancement to senior management from competencies and personality data: a seven-year follow-up study', *British Journal of Management*, **10**(1): 13–23.
Dunphy, D. and Stace, D. (1993), 'The strategic management of corporate change', *Human Relations*, **46**(8): 905–18.
Emirbayer, M. and Mische, A. (1998), 'What is agency', *American Journal of Sociology*, **103**(4): 962–1023.
Fairclough, Norman (1992), *Discourse and Social Change*, Cambridge, MA: Polity.
Fink, A., Marr, B., Siebe, A. and Kuhle, J.-P. (2005), 'The future scorecard: combining external and internal scenarios to create strategic foresight', *Management Decision*, **43**(3): 360–81.
Fischhoff, B. (2003), 'Hindsight ≠ foresight: the effect of outcome knowledge on judgment under uncertainty', *Quality and Safety in Health Care*, **12**: 304–12.
Fischhoff, B., Gonzalez, R.M., Lerner, J.S. and Small, D.A. (2005), 'Evolving judgements of terror risks: foresight, hindsight, and emotion', *Journal of Experimental Psychology*, **11**(2): 124–30.
Freire, Paulo (1968), *Pedagogy of the Oppressed*, New York: Seabury.
Giddens, A. (1974), *Positivism and Sociology*, London: Heinemann.
Giddens, A. (1984), *The Constitution of Society: Outline of the Theory of Structuration*, Berkeley, CA: University of California Press.

Harper, J.C. and Georghiou, L. (2005), 'Foresight in innovation policy: shared visions for a science park and business–university links in a city region', *Technology Analysis and Strategic Management*, **17** (2): 147–60.

Huy, Q.N. (2001), 'Time, temporal capability and planned change', *Academy of Management Review*, **26**(4): 601–23.

Kanter, R.M. (1984), *The Change Masters*, London: Allen & Unwin.

Kanter, R.M. (1999), *Leading Change*, London: Simon & Schuster.

Kirkpatrick, S.A. and Locke, E.A. (1991), 'Leadership: do traits matter?', *Academy of Management Executive*, **5**(2): 48–60.

Lawrence, E. (2000), 'Equal opportunities officers and managing equality changes', *Personnel Review*, **29**(3): 381–401.

Ledwith and F. Colgan (eds) (1996a), *Women and Organizations: Challenging Gender Politics*, London: Macmillan.

Ledwith, S. and Colgan, F. (1996b), 'Women as organizational change agents', in Ledwith and Colgan (eds), pp. 1–43.

Lewin, K. (1951), *Field Theory in Social Science*, New York: Harper & Row.

Meyerson, D.E. (2001a), *Tempered Radicals: How People Use Difference to Inspire Change at Work*, Boston, MA: Harvard Business School Press.

Meyerson, D.E. (2001b), 'Radical change, the quiet way', *Harvard Business Review*, October: 92–100.

Meyerson, D.E. and Scully, M.A. (1995), 'Tempered radicalism and the politics of ambivalence and change', *Organization Science*, **6**(5): 585–600.

Muir, C. (1996), 'Workplace readiness for communicating diversity', *Journal of Business Communication*, **33**(4): 475–86.

Munduate, L. and Gravenhorst, K.M.B. (2003), 'Power dynamics and organizational change: an introduction', *Applied Psychology: An International Review*, **52**(1): 1–13.

Nadler, D.A. and Tushman, M.L. (1990), 'Beyond the charismatic leader: leadership and organizational change', *California Management Review*, Winter: 77–97.

Simon, H. (1987), 'Making management decisions: the role of intuition and emotion', *Academy of Management Executive*, **1**(1): 57–64.

Tichy, N.M. (1974), 'Agents of planned social change: congruence of values, cognitions and actions', *Administrative Science Quarterly*, **19**(2): 164–82.

Tsoukas, H. and Shepherd, J. (2004), 'Coping with the future: developing organizational foresightfulness', *Futures*, **36**(2): 137–44.

Volberda, H.W. (1998), *Building the Flexible Firm: How to Remain Competitive*, Oxford: Oxford University Press.

Weick, K.E. and Quinn, R.E. (1999), 'Organizational change and development', *Annual Review of Psychology*, **50**: 361–86.

Westley, F. and Mintzberg, H. (1989), 'Visionary leadership and strategic management', *Strategic Management Journal*, **10**: 17–32.

15 The role of resources in institutional entrepreneurship: insights for an approach to strategic management that combines agency and institution

Julie Battilana and Bernard Leca

Introduction

The take-off in France of a market for socially responsible investment (SRI) corresponds to the creation, in 1997, of the first social rating agency, ARESE. SRI existed long before ARESE's creation but was not recognized as legitimate by the financial community, which perceived it to be a marginal activity led by idealists who lacked seriousness. ARESE managed to develop a measure of companies' corporate social performance that would resemble well-established ways of evaluating organizational performance and could be integrated within fund managers' traditional decision-making processes. Rather than provide monographs about companies, ARESE formulated quantitative measures with which to generate the 'ARESE notation', which financial executives regarded as more serious and legitimate. Using this new tool, which was more in conformance with the dominant logic of the financial world, fund managers willing to develop SRI funds were able to legitimize themselves in the financial community and set up those funds. The SRI market subsequently developed such that by the end of 2001, SRI assets in France totaled €1000 million. ARESE held that same year 85 percent market share of the market for social rating (Déjean et al., 2004). The first social rating agency in France, ARESE, in developing a measure of companies' corporate social performance, diverged from the existing norms of the financial market sector, yet framed its measure in such a way that it appeared to be congruent with the existing models. In contributing to the development of new practices in the financial market sector in France, ARESE thus acted as an institutional entrepreneur.

Institutional entrepreneurs are actors, whether individuals or organizations that mobilize resources to either create new or transform existing institutions (DiMaggio, 1988). They contribute by breaking with existing institutions to design and diffuse new rules and practices that might subsequently become institutions. Institutional entrepreneurs envisage radically new ways of organizing that might in the future become the dominant norms in a field of activity. Hence, institutional entrepreneurs are characterized by their projective capacity (Emirbayer and Mische, 1998; Seo and Creed, 2002), that is, the capacity to imaginatively generate possible future trajectories of action that diverge from institutionalized structures of thought and action in response to their hopes, fears, and desires for the future. In other words, they are able to foresee radically new ways of doing things and getting organized in a field of activity. For example, ARESE's founders foresaw the emergence of a new maket for SRI in France as well as the need to articulate it using well-established practices of the financial community rather than develop an alternative model that might be perceived to be in opposition to the traditional financial approach.

The strategies that institutional entrepreneurs use to implement their projects not only effect change within a given organization, but also might contribute to changing practice across an entire sector of activity. Such strategies tend to be more complex and demanding than the usual organizational strategies, which require only that their implementers be able to enact already legitimized practices or leverage existing rules. Institutional entrepreneurs, on the other hand, must be able to articulate, sponsor, and defend particular practices and organizational forms as desirable and legitimate (Lawrence, 1999). To better account for the specificity of the strategies implemented by institutional entrepreneurs, Lawrence (1999: 162) developed the concept of 'institutional strategies' that is: 'patterns of action that are concerned with managing the institutional structures within which firms compete for resources'. Actors who would implement institutional strategies must be able to foresee not only radically new ways of doing things and getting organized but also potential obstacles to the implementation of their change project both within their organizations and, more broadly, within their field of activity.

Organization studies have explored the conditions that enable actors to be institutional entrepreneurs (for a review, see Battilana, 2006) and examined the discursive strategies they use to diffuse their new institutional projects (see, for example, Fligstein, 1997; Creed et al., 2002), but little research has been conducted into how institutional entrepreneurs mobilize resources both to emancipate themselves from institutional pressures and to implement an institutional change project. The few studies that have attempted to account for the processes of resource mobilization by institutional entrepreneurs have been conducted at the organizational and field levels of analysis (for example, Rao et al., 2000). In failing to take into account intra-organizational dynamics, they have neglected the role of organizational resources in the process of institutional entrepreneurship. The purpose of this chapter is to fill this gap by exploring the question: how do institutional entrepreneurs leverage their organizational resources?

Institutional entrepreneurs, unlike other actors, do not use all their available resources to comply with institutional pressures, but rather commit some to projects that diverge from existing institutional arrangements. The purpose of this chapter is to analyze the role that organizational resources play in actors' development and the implementation of their institutional strategies. We first examine how institutional pressures might influence the mobilization of organizational resources and, reciprocally, how institutional entrepreneurs might mobilize resources to change their institutional environment. Next, we explore the key role that organizational resources play in the emergence of institutional entrepreneurship. We then examine how institutional entrepreneurs mobilize resources to support the development and diffusion of their institutional change projects. We end the chapter by emphasizing the need for further research that would extend Oliver's (1997) efforts to bridge strategic management theory and institutional theory by investigating how actors mobilize organizational resources to develop, initiate, and diffuse changes that diverge from the existing institutions in a field of activity.

Institutional entrepreneurship and resources

Institutional embeddedness

Institutions are patterns of action or organization that eventually become taken for granted in a given field of activity. Marriage and the corporate form are examples. Institutions are characterized by their self-activating nature (Lawrence et al., 2002: 282; Jepperson, 1991: 145) and enforcement by social mechanisms that prevent deviation (Douglas, 1986). Actors commonly require neither repeated authoritative intervention nor collective mobilization to reproduce institutions in a given field of activity (Berger and Luckmann, 1967; Clemens and Cook, 1999: 445). Institutional theory emphasizes the influence on organizational behavior of institutional pressures that stem from the environment.

The degree to which actors are embedded in their context (that is, 'embeddedness') is a central variable in the explanation of why actors tend to reproduce existing institutions (Dacin et al., 1999). Although some researchers have begun to consider actors' embeddedness as a potential source of opportunity (for example, Baum and Dutton, 1996; Powell, 1996; Dacin et al., 1999), most research thus far has treated embeddedness as a constraining force that explains actors' limited ability to act in ways that diverge from the norms of existing institutions (Reay et al., 2006). Being institutionally embedded, actors' decisions are influenced not only by what is economically optimal, but also by what they see as socially appropriate according to existing social justification and social obligations (Zukin and DiMaggio, 1990).

Institutional entrepreneurship
Institutional embeddedness interpreted as a constraint on actors' courses of action was used by institutional theory to explain organizational isomorphism within organizational fields (for example, DiMaggio and Powell, 1983). Thus, it put an emphasis on convergence and stability within organizational fields. However, institutional change has become a central issue for institutional theorists (*Academy of Management Journal*, 2002), and one way to account for institutional change is to analyze the role that exogenous forces play in the disruption of the institutional order (for example, Krasner, 1984). But this explanation is unsatisfactory because, as Zucker (1988) has emphasized, it leads, to a logical fallacy in that infinite regression results as institutional change always comes from a higher level. This emphasis on exogenous forces has likely contributed to the image of institutional theory as being of little practical use (Miner, 2003).

To become more actionable, institutional theory must develop, as a complement to exogenous explanations, endogenous explanations that account for the possible role of actors in institutional change. The notion of institutional entrepreneurs, organized actors with sufficient resources who see in new institutions an opportunity to realize interest that they value highly (DiMaggio, 1988: 14), is one way to account for institutional change endogenously. Such research as has been conducted on institutional entrepreneurs (for example, DiMaggio, 1988; Holm, 1995; Fligstein, 1997; Rao, 1998; Beckert, 1999; Garud et al., 2002) has aimed at understanding the mechanisms by which they are able to conceive and impose institutional change projects. How do institutional entrepreneurs manage to envisage and diffuse a different approach when so many other actors persist in abiding by rules that are widely perceived to be 'taken for granted?'. In other words, how is it that some actors can foresee radically new ways of doing things and getting organized when others cannot?

Although the literature on institutional entrepreneurship has begun to address these questions, it has tended to neglect the role of organizational resources. This is surprising, resources being central to the definition of institutional entrepreneurship proposed in DiMaggio's seminal study:

Creating new institutions is expensive and requires high levels of both interest and resources. New institutions arise when organized actors with sufficient resources [institutional entrepreneurs] see in them an opportunity to realize interest that they value highly. (1988: 14)

According to this definition, the likelihood that actors will act as institutional entrepreneurs is a function of willingness and ability. Willingness to act is dependent on actors' interest, ability to act determined mostly by the resources they possess or to which they have access (Lawrence, 1999). The potential for institutional entrepreneurship would thus seem to depend in part on the availability of resources. Yet, as Lawrence (p. 162) notes, most of the connections that have been established between strategic management theory and institutional theory have so far focused on organizations' strategic responses to institutional pressures. The focus of research has consequently been on how the institutional environment influences the acquisition and use of resources (for example, Oliver, 1997) rather than on how actors strategically mobilize organizational resources to change the institutional environment. Indeed, most research has examined how actors develop and manage organizational resources in order to comply with institutional pressures.

Institutional compliance and resources
Resources are assets that can be used to ensure the survival and growth of an organization. There are both tangible resources such as employees and financial and material assets, and intangible resources such as knowledge, reputation, and social capital. Organizations' accumulation of resources depends on various stakeholders. Qualified employees must be willing to join, shareholders to invest in, business partners to engage in relations with, and consumers to acquire the products or services of an organization. To attract the respective inputs from these stakeholders an organization must somehow earn their trust.

Building such trust is tricky, particularly for new ventures that lack an established record and must cope with the 'liability of newness' (Stinchcombe, 1965); newcomers can gain legitimacy and reduce the 'liability of newness' by complying with the existing social norms and institutional practices these stakeholders share and value (Aldrich and Fiol, 1994). Evidence that an organization will play 'according to the rules' facilitates interactions with incumbents, enhances its reliability in the eyes of potential partners and employees, and promotes access to the resources needed to survive and develop (ibid., 1994; Zimmerman and Zeitz, 2002; Déjean et al., 2004).

Institutional studies have shown that new entrants are not the only organizations that must comply with institutional pressures; compliance affords all organizations a number of advantages. It increases an organization's legitimacy and thereby its chance of survival (Baum and Oliver, 1991); it enables an organization to maintain elaborate displays of confidence, satisfaction, and good faith, and minimize inspection and evaluation, both internally and externally (Meyer and Rowan, 1977); and it minimizes risk and ensures average performance, thereby concomitantly reducing the risk of underperformance (Kondra and Hinings, 1998).

An organization that deviates from established rules not only forgoes the benefits of compliance, but might also incur penalties. Non-compliance is risky for organizations. It can reduce their legitimacy and damage their relations with key stakeholders (ibid.) as well as generate opposition from actors whose interests and values are supported by the existing intuitional arrangements (DiMaggio, 1988; DeJordy and Jones, 2006). Regulatory bodies, professional associations, and field members whose interests and values are at stake are among those who are likely to act as 'institutional guardians' and oppose the diffusion of institutional change projects (DeJordy and Jones, 2006). Finally, when non-compliance intersects with mandatory rules, be they regulatory or professional, an actor might be prevented from continuing to pursue the deviant activity and even driven out of business.

The institutional approach suggests that the implications of compliance versus non-compliance dictate that managers develop and manage organizational resources in accordance with institutional pressures (Meyer and Rowan, 1977; Oliver, 1997). Rao and Sivakumar (1999), for example, showed how stakeholder pressures on the Fortune 500 industrials led to the widespread diffusion of investor relations departments that diverted resources from other possible uses.

Despite pressure to comply with norms and practices that have been institutionalized, some actors, namely institutional entrepreneurs, use part or all of their resources not to comply, but to break, with existing institutions.

How do institutional entrepreneurs use resources?
Research on institutional entrepreneurship has so far addressed two central questions that mirror two sequences of the institutional entrepreneurship process. The first question has to do with the emergence of institutional entrepreneurs. How can actors whose beliefs and actions are shaped by the institutional environment in which they are embedded, change this environment? This question captures the paradox of embedded human agency (Holm, 1995; Seo and Creed, 2002), or the contradiction between actors' agency and institutional determinism. The second question has to do with how the process of institutional entrepreneurship unfolds over time. What strategies are used by institutional entrepreneurs? In the following sections, we highlight the importance of resources in addressing both questions.

The role of resources in the emergence of institutional entrepreneurship
The paradox of embedded agency inherent in neo-institutional theory becomes particularly salient when dealing with the notion of institutional entrepreneurship. This notion has consequently been a source of controversy among institutional scholars. The controversy revolves around the ability of actors, who are supposed to be institutionally embedded, to distance themselves from institutional pressures, foresee radically new ways of doing things and getting organized, and act strategically to implement change. Overcoming the paradox of embedded agency is crucial because it is prerequisite to laying the foundations for a theory of institutional entrepreneurship (for example, Battilana, 2006; Greenwood and Suddaby, 2006; Leca and Naccache, 2006). To resolve this paradox, it is necessary to identify the conditions that enable actors to act as institutional entrepreneurs.

Researchers have already identified a number of organization (for example, Leblebici et al., 1991; Rao et al., 2000; Greenwood and Suddaby, 2006) and organizational field-level (for example, Oliver, 1991; Holm, 1995; Clemens and Cook, 1999; Greenwood et al., 2002) conditions that enable actors to act as institutional entrepreneurs. Most of the studies (for example, Leblebici et al., 1991; Kraatz and Zajac, 1996; Rao et al., 2000; Garud et al., 2002; Greenwood and Suddaby, 2006) that have examined the role of organization-level enabling conditions for institutional entrepreneurship have focused on the relationship between the position of an organization in the field and the likelihood that it will act as an institutional entrepreneur.

Organizations' incentives and ability to change the institutional status quo have been shown to be dependent on their position in the field. Research has shown that organizations at the periphery of organizational fields, most often lower-status organizations, are more likely to introduce new practices that diverge from those of existing institutions, and more central, often higher-status, organizations are more likely to mobilize resources to maintain the status quo (Leblebici et al., 1991; Haveman and Rao, 1997; Palmer and Barber, 2001; Kraatz and Moore, 2002). Some studies (Sherer and Lee, 2002; Greenwood and Suddaby, 2006) have, however, identified conditions under which higher-status organizations might also act as institutional entrepreneurs.

Resources play a key role in explaining these behavioral differences across organizations. Resources can operate in two ways in the emergence of an institutional change project. The lack of resources needed to succeed according to the field's established 'rules of the game' is likely to increase agents' willingness to change those rules (for example, Leblebici et al., 1991). But even agents who have access to the necessary resources might, if they consider their overall organizational resources to be underexploited in the existing institutional context, conclude that other rules would enable them to make more out of the available resources (Sherer and Lee, 2002; Greenwood and Suddaby, 2006). In both cases, it is the perceived inadequacy of the resources in relation to the institutional environment that leads the agents to initiate changes that diverge from those of existing institutions.

Apart from playing a role in the emergence of institutional entrepreneurship initiatives, organizational resources might also play a key role in the elaboration of the institutional change project. In other words, organizational resources might influence actors' ability to envisage radically new ways of doing things and getting organized.

The use of resources in the elaboration of the institutional change project

The design of an institutional change project partly determines the likelihood of its diffusion. To increase projects' chances of diffusion, institutional entrepreneurs must consider the situations of potential allies and specify both the weaknesses of existing institutions and why the proposed alternatives serve potential allies' interests and values better than the existing arrangements (Tolbert and Zucker, 1996). The institutional project must be 'framed' (McAdam et al., 1996; Rao et al., 2000; Lounsbury et al., 2003) so as to align with the interests and values of the maximum number of potential allies (for example, Déjean et al., 2004).

Frames define the grievances and interests of aggrieved constituencies, diagnose causes, assign blame, provide solutions, and enable collective attribution processes to operate (Snow and Benford, 1992: 150 in Rao et al., 2000). Institutional entrepreneurs use frames to define, justify, and push the theory and values that underpin their institutional change project, and to convince others that what will happen is in their best interests. Fligstein and Mara-Drita (1996), for example, show how Jacques Delors, acting as an institutional entrepreneur, used a broad cultural frame to build support from the different countries of the European Union for the Single Market program. Other studies (for example, Strang and Meyer, 1993; Tolbert and Zucker, 1996; Greenwood et al., 2002) have analyzed the key role played by the theorization phase in institutionalization processes. Theorization is the process by which organizational failings are specified and potential solutions corresponding to new institutional projects are justified. Greenwood et al. (2002) show that institutional entrepreneurs justify their institutional change projects by appealing to the particular values embedded in their fields of activity.

Institutional entrepreneurs need to possess social skills (Fligstein, 1997), that is, the ability to read the current level of organization in the field and to respond to it by taking into account, when framing their institutional change initiative, the positions of other actors. Theorization (or framing) thus plays a key role in the mobilization of resources by increasing the legitimacy of the actors and thereby facilitating their access to other resources (Zimmerman and Zeitz, 2002). But framing also requires resources.

The mobilization of resources is implicit in the elaboration and framing of an institutional change project. Several subunits of an organization are likely to be involved in the definition of a project, and top managers, who are in charge of the organization strategy, are likely to be responsible for developing and implementing the institutional change project. However, these managers are likely to be more focused on what will happen within the boundaries of the organization than on any obstacles they might encounter at the field level during implementation of the change project. They are also likely to consider the interests of their organizations over those of potential allies. The design of change projects that diverge from the practices of existing institutions is thus likely to involve in addition to top managers the public relations and legal, or other, departments. The latter will be responsible for identifying which institutions need to be changed, who must be convinced that such change is desirable and necessary, and what sort of arguments must be developed to do so. Companies might decide to outsource some of the support for the change project by engaging the services of a lobbyist.

ARESE provides an example of the use of resources by an institutional entrepreneur to elaborate and frame the institutional change project. As a start-up, it benefited from the financial backing of the Caisses d'Epargne and Caisse des Dépôts et Consignations, two of France's most prominent financial institutions. Thanks to this financial support, it was able to hire personnel to develop its method and rating one year before introducing it to the market. Specifically, founding CEO Geneviève Férone used the money to hire individuals with both a knowledge of the financial markets or rating processes and a sensitivity to corporate social responsibility who could work on the development of a hybrid model that employed traditional quantitative measures to account for a non-traditional dimension: corporate social performance. In using quantitative measures to generate the 'ARESE notation', ARESE effectively framed its new model of company evaluation so as to appear to be congruent with the existing quantitative models.

Although we have so far highlighted the role of resources in the initial stages of the institutional entrepreneurship process, that is, the emergence of institutional entrepreneurship and elaboration and framing of the institutional change project, organizational resources also play a key role in the unfolding of the institutional entrepreneurship process.

The role of resources in the unfolding of the institutional entrepreneurship process

Institutional entrepreneurship is a complex political and cultural process. The main challenge for institutional entrepreneurs is to mobilize resources to gain legitimacy and support for their institutional change projects (Lawrence, 1999). Legitimacy becomes more difficult to acquire the more a project diverges from the practices of existing institutions (Zimmerman and Zeitz, 2002). Institutional entrepreneurs implementing a change project can use resources in two interrelated ways: to overcome resistance to institutional change, and to help diffuse the institutional project.

Using resources to overcome resistance to institutional change
That they are enforced by social mechanisms that sanction deviation being central to the definition of institutions, institutional entrepreneurs are likely to face opposition. Two kinds of actors are likely to oppose them: those that are statutorily in charge of enforcing the institutional practices (including regulatory and professional bodies), and field members whose values or interests are in opposition to the institutional change project. The latter group includes members whose dominant position is threatened by the institutional entrepreneur, high-status professionals in multi-professionalized fields being an example (Starr, 1982; Abbott, 1988). These organizations are likely to try to impose penalties on the institutional entrepreneur. Other members might not so much oppose the change as be simply risk adverse; fear of uncertainty might put such members into the opposition camp.

Institutional entrepreneurs must thus command sufficient resources to resist their opponents and 'ride out the negative economic costs of the transitional period in which unpopular new ideas are initially promoted' (Greenwood and Suddaby, 2006). Greenwood et al. (2002) suggest that larger players are more likely to act as institutional entrepreneurs because they are more likely to have at their disposal the resources needed to buffer them from the sanctioning organizations. Such organizations are also more likely to have the resources needed to engage in the essentially political process of changing the accepted scripts of legitimacy (for example, by negotiating with professional and state agencies).

This is not to say that players with fewer resources cannot act as institutional entrepreneurs. But the shortage of resources might lead them to develop strategies that involve reliance on others. Organizations with limited financial resources, for example, can seek additional debt or equity capital. A common example of such a strategy is the start-up company that would impose new technical standards likely to disrupt existing rules in technological industries, which seeks from venture capitalists seed money needed to establish itself and resist the pressure exerted by incumbents to prevent the diffusion of its innovation.

The trade-off that organizations must strategically manage involves the level of resources that the organization is ready to commit to ensure the success of the institutional change project, the importance of reactions opposing the change, and the time needed to gain the support of a critical mass of allies willing to provide resources to those committed to advancing the new institution (Dorado, 2005). This critical mass will neutralize the negative costs generated by the opposition, nurture the institutional change project, and provide a basis for its diffusion.

Using resources to diffuse the institutional change project
In the use of resources in the diffusion of a change project, two cases must be distinguished: that of institutional entrepreneurs with sufficient resources to impose the institutional

change without having to seek outside support; and that of institutional entrepreneurs in need of external support that must mobilize resources to secure that support.

There is a relationship between dependence on access to resources and power (Crozier, 1964; Perrow, 1970; Pfeffer and Salancik, 1978; Porter, 1980). The more other agents depend on an institutional entrepreneur for access to resources, the more power the institutional entrepreneur exerts over them. Institutional entrepreneurs that control access to key resources are sufficiently powerful to impose institutional change on other field members. Such cases have not been documented by existing research save that of Dorado (2005), who points to the case of John D. Rockefeller who, having acquired most of the oil refineries in the United States, was enabled by his dominant position and control of resources to change how the oil market operated by controlling prices (as reported in Chernov, 1998). Meyer and Rowan (1977: 348) consider a similar case in a related industry:

> Powerful organizations force their immediate relational networks to adapt to their structures and relations. For instance, automobile producers help create demands for particular kinds of roads, transportation systems, and fuels that make automobiles virtual necessities; competitive forms of transportation have to adapt to the existing relational context.

Often, institutional entrepreneurs cannot impose an institutional change without the support of other agents in the field. Sun Microsystems, for example, relied on a coalition of systems assemblers, software firms, and computer manufacturers to help it disrupt the hegemony of Microsoft's Windows, promote a network-centric view of computing, and impose its Java product in 1995. Sun was able to impose Java by providing free access to both collaborators and potential competitors in order to create a community and initiate a bandwagon effect (Sawhney and Prandelli, 2000; Garud et al., 2002). Microsoft resisted, but Sun, with the support of the coalition it had created, prevailed and Microsoft eventually had to license Java. This is illustrative of the case of institutional entrepreneurs mobilizing resources to secure the support of other agents in the field.

Resources can be used to pressure other agents to comply with an institutional change project in much the same way that institutional entrepreneurs with sufficient resources can impose the institutional change on less powerful agents that depend on them for access to resources. Institutional entrepreneurs can also use resources as incentives to motivate others to support and endorse an institutional change project. Financial resources, for example, can be used both to support and to convince potential allies. Research on corporate political strategies has long documented companies' use of financial resources to influence public authorities and the media in order to shape regulation (Dahan, 2005 provides a synthesis). Central to those strategies is the use of financial resources to fund political campaigns as well as 'study' trips and seminars.

Institutional entrepreneurs can also leverage their formal authority and leadership to mobilize support for their institutional change projects. Fligstein (1997, 2001) and Phillips et al. (2004) documented uses of institutional entrepreneurs' formal authority. Fligstein (2001) showed how it can help in framing stories, Phillips et al. (2004) how it can abet the diffusion of institutional entrepreneurs' discourse so that it is increasingly acknowledged and 'consumed' by other actors. Phillips et al. also suggest that an institutional entrepreneur's leadership position in the field favors institutionalization.

Reputation and expertise can be leveraged as well. Suggestions for change that emanate from an organization with a good reputation are more likely to be followed. DiMaggio and Powell (1983) maintain that organizations are likely to imitate competitors perceived to be the best performers in the organizational field. 'Trickle down' or legitimate innovations diffuse from the actors with better reputations in a field (Abrahamson and Fombrun, 1994). For example, because of its reputation for innovation in a highly uncertain industry, IBM's decisions are often analyzed by other actors as important strategic moves to be considered and potentially imitated (Rindova and Fombrun, 1999), and Sherer and Lee (2002) showed how an incumbent law firm with a good reputation managed to change the way lawyers' careers were organized and convince other firms to adopt this new model.

Social capital, that is, one's position in a web of social relations that provide information and political support, is also quite important, as is the ability to draw on that standing to influence others' actions (Fligstein, 1997). In networks with multiple structural holes, centrality provides exclusive control over information flows (Burt, 1992), which might facilitate the diffusion of an institutional change project. Freeman (1979: 221) observes that actors 'in such a position can influence the group by withholding or distorting information in transmission', and Fligstein suggests that institutional entrepreneurs can use this position to sever links between some groups, which can then be enlisted as allies, and the rest of the field. Phillips et al. (2004) suggest that being central in the field also increases the likelihood that a project will be acknowledged by other agents. Finally, Maguire et al. (2004) insist that institutional entrepreneurs must attain positions that enable them to bring together diverse stakeholders and then champion, and orchestrate collective action around, their change projects. Social capital was crucial in the development of ARESE. Although the framing of the rating largely accounts for the organization's success, to the extent that Geneviève Férone's charisma and ability to network among powerful decision makers also proved instrumental, her social capital can be said to have played a key role in the success of ARESE as well. Invited to international forums such as the World Forum in Davos, she was acknowledged by the French financial community to be a leader in the development of the market for SRI.

Discussion

Although they play a central role in the definition of institutional entrepreneurship (see DiMaggio, 1988), resources have not occupied the center of the stage in most research about institutional entrepreneurship. We believe that examining more carefully how actors mobilize organizational resources throughout the institutional entrepreneurship process can provide a number of benefits and open new avenues for research. We do not mean to understate the importance of other factors such as field- and organization-level conditions in the process of institutional entrepreneurship. Our analysis of the role of organizational resources is intended to be articulated within the existing literature on institutional entrepreneurship.

This chapter makes two contributions. First, we show that organizational resources play a key role in the different stages of the institutional entrepreneurship process. They are key enabling conditions for the emergence of institutional entrepreneurship, and they are central to the strategies institutional entrepreneurs use to develop and diffuse their change projects. Taking into account the role of resources thus contributes to a better understanding of the mechanisms that underlie institutional entrepreneurship. Indeed, it helps us to better understand how some actors can foresee radically new ways of doing things and getting organized, and subsequently impose changes, despite institutional pressures for stasis.

Second, this chapter contributes further to the bridging of strategic management theory and institutional theory. It provides new insights that suggest an approach to strategic management that accounts for both actors' agency and the influence of the institutional environment in which the actors are embedded, thereby pursuing and extending the line of research initiated by Oliver (1997), who first attempted to bridge strategic management theory and institutional theory by highlighting the influence of the institutional environment on the acquisition and use of resources. In the present chapter, we extend this line of research by examining how actors can mobilize organizational resources to change the institutional environment.

Bridging strategic management theory and institutional theory is particularly challenging because they are based on different views of human agency. Strategic management theory assumes a high degree of human agency, institutional theory a limited degree of human agency. To reconcile these views, one must adopt a relational view of human agency (Emirbayer, 1997; Emirbayer and Mische, 1998). Rather than consider that human agents pursue lines of conduct in a solipsistic manner, or that their line of conduct is largely determined by institutional pressures, one must regard them as being embedded in a social context and as responding to the situations they encounter in that context (Emirbayer, 1997). Such a conception of agency accounts for the fact that actors are not only shaped by existing institutions, but might also, under certain conditions, shape those institutions (Berger and Luckmann, 1967; DiMaggio and Powell, 1991). Whereas Oliver (1997) accounted for the influence of the institutional environment on actors' use of organizational resources, this chapter highlights how actors can use resources to change their institutional environment, and thereby more fully accounts for the relation between actors and their environment.

The analysis presented in this chapter also suggests new avenues for research. First, it calls for reflection on the different forms of resources that must be considered. Resources used by institutional entrepreneurs range from tangible to intangible, including financial and human resources as well as social resources such as social capital, legitimacy, and reputation. Although we do not intend in this chapter to develop an exhaustive list of all existing resources, we suggest that future research on institutional entrepreneurship account for the variety of resources that might be mobilized by institutional entrepreneurs, which would effectively constitute the institutional entrepreneur's tool kit. The types of resources institutional entrepreneurs mobilize might be contingent on a number of factors, including the stage of the institutional entrepreneurship process that is considered (emergence of institutional entrepreneurship, development or diffusion of the institutional change project), the type of institutional change project being implemented (Battilana, 2007), and the characteristics of the field in which they are embedded (Fligstein, 1997).

Second, a number of key questions about the role of resources in institutional entrepreneurship remain unanswered. Regarding the role of resources in the emergence of institutional entrepreneurship, we need to know more about the interaction between actors' willingness and ability to act. We noted earlier that the lack of resources needed to succeed according to a field's established 'rules of the game' is likely to increase agents' willingness to change those rules (for example, Leblebici et al., 1991), but those agents are less likely to be able to change the rules because of their lack of resources (Greenwood and Hinings, 1996). Those with access to the resources needed to succeed in a field, on the other hand, although more able to change the rules of the game, are likely to be less willing to do so. We need to know more about the conditions under which these different categories of agents are likely to act as institutional entrepreneurs. When are actors with fewer of the appropriate resources able to change the rules of the game? Reciprocally, when are actors with more of the appropriate resources willing to change the rules of the game? We need more studies about the emergence of institutional entrepreneurs to be able to answer these questions.

We also need to know more about why certain resource mobilization strategies work and others do not. The extant literature has largely examined winning strategies, leaving the reasons for failure understudied. In reporting only successful cases of institutional entrepreneurs, the literature has not heeded DiMaggio's (1988) observation that, logically, institutional entrepreneurs must fail most of the time. This bias in the sampling makes it difficult now to understand how institutional entrepreneurs can misuse resources. More diversified and comparative studies are called for.

Finally, examining the use of organizational resources appears to be an interesting way to open the 'black boxes' to which organizations correspond in institutional theory. There has been little response to Greenwood and Hinings's (1996) call for more studies that would account not only for the organizational and organizational field levels of analysis, but also for the intra-organizational level of analysis (for a few exceptions, see Wicks, 2001; Reay et al., 2006; Battilana, 2007). Because most studies that analyze the processes of resource mobilization employed by institutional entrepreneurs have been conducted at the organizational and field levels of analysis (for example, Rao et al., 2000), there is little understanding of how individual actors might mobilize resources in their organizations to implement changes that diverge from the practices of existing institutions. To improve our understanding of the strategies used by such actors, we need to know which resources they mobilize when they develop and implement their institutional change projects and how they use them. Not taking into account the individual level of analysis risks disembodying action and thereby neglecting the role of individual agency in institutional change.

Conclusion

In this chapter, we highlight the role of organizational resources in the different stages of the institutional entrepreneurship process, specifically, the emergence of institutional entrepreneurship and elaboration and diffusion of the institutional change project. We need to better understand what resources institutional entrepreneurs use in these various stages and how they use them. To do so, we need to open the 'black boxes' to which organizations very often correspond in institutional theory. We also need to conduct more comparative research that examines the resource mobilization strategies of institutional entrepreneurs. Such studies will enable us to answer such key questions as: to what extent are institutional entrepreneurs' resource mobilization strategies contingent on the environment in which they evolve? Is it possible to identify 'best practices' for a type of environment with respect to mobilizing resources to implement an institutional change project? Answers to these questions will have important managerial consequences because they will help us to better understand why, among the actors who foresee radically new ways of doing things and getting organized, some succeed in developing and diffusing new practices while others do not.

References

Abbott, A. (1988), *The System of the Professions: An Essay on the Division of Expert Labor*, Chicago, IL: University of Chicago Press.

Abrahamson, E. and Fombrun, C. (1994), 'Macrocultures: determinants and consequences', *Academy of Management Review*, **19** (4): 728–55.

Academy of Management Journal (2002), 'Institutional Change', special issue.

Aldrich, H. and Fiol, C.M. (1994), 'Fools rush in? The institutional context of industry creation', *Academy of Management Review*, **19** (4): 645–70.

Battilana, J. (2006), 'Agency and institutions: the enabling role of individuals' social position', *Organization*, **13** (5): 653–76.

Battilana, J. (2007), 'Initiating divergent organizational change: the enabling role of actors' social position', Harvard Business School working paper.

Baum, J.A.C. and Dutton, J.E. (1996), 'Introduction: the embeddedness of strategy', in Baum and Dutton (eds), *Advances in Strategic Management: The Embeddedness of Strategy*, vol. 13, Greenwich, MA: JAI Press, pp. 1–15.

Baum, J.A.C. and Oliver, C. (1991), 'Institutional linkages and organizational mortality', *Administrative Science Quarterly*, **36**: 187–218.

Beckert, Jens (1999), 'Agency, entrepreneurs, and institutional change: the role of strategic choice and institutionalized practices in organizations', *Organization Studies*, **20** (5): 777–99.

Berger, P. and Luckmann, T. (1967), *The Social Construction of Reality*, New York: Doubleday.

Burt, Ronald S. (1992), *Structural Holes: The Social Structure of Competition*, Cambridge, MA: Harvard University Press.

Chernov, Ron (1998), *Titan: The Life of John D. Rockefeller, Sr.*, New York: Random House.

Clemens, Elisabeth S. and Cook, James M. (1999), 'Politics and institutionalism: explaining durability and change', *Annual Review of Sociology*, **25** (1): 441–66.

Creed, Douglas, Maureen, W.E., Scully, A. and Austin, John R. (2002), 'Clothes make the person? The tailoring of legitimating accounts and the social construction of identity', *Organization Science*, **13** (5): 475–96.

Crozier, M. (1964), *Le Phénomène Bureaucratique*, Paris: Le Seuil.

Dacin, M.T., Ventresca, M. and Beal, B. (1999), 'The embeddedness of organizations: debates, dialogue and directions', *Journal of Management*, **25** (3): 317–56.

Dahan, N. (2005), 'A contribution to the conceptualization of political resources utilized in corporate political action', *Journal of Public Affairs*, **5** (1): 305–29.

Déjean, Frédérique, Gond, Jean-Pascal and Leca, Bernard (2004), 'Measuring the unmeasured: an institutional entrepreneur's strategy in an emerging industry', *Human Relations*, **57** (6): 741–64.

DeJordy, R. and Jones, C. (2006), 'Institutional guardianship: protecting and preserving existing institutional orders from change', paper presented at the Academy of Management Meetings, Atlanta, GA, 11–16 August.

DiMaggio, Paul J. (1988), 'Interest and agency in institutional theory', in L. Zucker (ed.), *Research on Institutional Patterns and Organizations*, Cambridge, MA: Ballinger, pp. 3–22.

DiMaggio, P.J. and Powell, W.W. (1983), 'The iron cage revisited: institutional isomorphism and collective rationality in organizational fields', *American Sociological Review*, **48**: 1750–62.

DiMaggio, P.J. and Powell, W.W. (1991), 'Introduction', in Powell and DiMaggio (eds), *The New Institutionalism in Organizational Analysis*, Chicago, IL: University of Chicago Press, pp. 1–38.

Dorado, Silvia (2005), 'Institutional entrepreneurship, partaking, and convening', *Organization Studies*, **26** (3): 383–413.

Douglas, M. (1986), *How Do Institutions Think?*, Syracuse, NY: Syracuse University Press.

Emirbayer, M. (1997), 'Manifesto for a relational sociology', *American Journal of Sociology*, **103** (2): 281–317.

Emirbayer, Mustafa and Mische, Ann (1998), 'What is agency?', *American Journal of Sociology*, **103** (4): 962–1023.

Fligstein, Neil (1997), 'Social skill and institutional theory', *American Behavioral Scientist*, **40** (4): 397–405.

Fligstein, Neil (2001), 'Social skills and the theory of fields', *Sociological Theory*, **19** (2): 105–25.

Fligstein, Neil and Mara-Drita, Iona (1996), 'How to make a market: reflections on the attempt to create a single market in the European Union', *American Journal of Sociology*, **102** (1): 1–33.

Freeman, Linton C. (1979), 'Centrality in social networks: conceptual clarification', *Social Networks*, **1**: 215–39.

Garud, R., Jain, S. and Kumaraswamy, A. (2002), 'Institutional entrepreneurship in the sponsorship of common technological standards: the case of Sun Microsystems and Java', *Academy of Management Journal*, **45** (1): 195–214.

Greenwood, Royston and Hinings, Christopher R. (1996), 'Understanding radical organizational change: bringing together the old and new insitutionalism', *Academy of Management Review*, **22**: 1022–54.

Greenwood, Royston and Suddaby, Roy (2006), 'Institutional entrepreneurship in mature fields: the big five accounting firms', *Academy of Management Journal*, **49** (1): 27–48.

Greenwood, Royston, Suddaby, Roy and Hinings, C. Robert (2002), 'Theorizing change: the role of professional associations in the transformation of institutionalized fields', *Academy of Management Journal*, **45** (1): 58–80.

Haveman, Heather A. and Rao, Hayagreeva (1997), 'Structuring a theory of moral sentiments: institutional and organizational coevolution in the early thrift industry', *American Journal of Sociology*, **102** (6): 1606–51.

Holm, Petter (1995), 'The dynamics of institutionalization: transformation processes in Norwegian fisheries', *Administrative Science Quarterly*, **40** (3): 398–422.

Jepperson, R. (1991), 'Institutions, institutional effects and institutionalism', in W.W. Powell and P.J. DiMaggio (eds), *The New Institutionnalism in Organizational Analysis*, Chicago, IL: University of Chicago Press, pp. 143–53.

Kondra, A.Z. and Hinings, C.R. (1998), 'Organizational diversity and change in institutional theory', *Organization Studies*, **19** (5): 743–67.

Kraatz, M. and Moore, D. (2002), 'Executive migration and institutional change', *Academy of Management Journal*, **45**: 120–43.

Kraatz, M.S. and Zajac, E.J. (1996), 'Exploring the limits of the new institutionalism: the causes and consequences of illegitimate organizational change', *American Sociological Review*, **61**: 112–36.

Krasner, S.D. (1984), 'Approaches to the state: alternative conceptions and historical dynamics', *Comparative Politics*, **16** (2): 223–46.

Lawrence, Thomas B. (1999), 'Institutional strategy', *Journal of Management*, **25** (2): 161–88.

Lawrence, Thomas B., Hardy, Cynthia and Phillips, Nelson (2002), 'Institutional effects of interorganizational collaboration: the emergence of proto-institutions', *Academy of Management Journal*, **45** (1): 281–90.

Leblebici, Huseyin, Salancik, Gerald R., Copay, Anne and King, Tom (1991), 'Institutional change and the transformation of interorganizational fields: an organizational history of the U.S. radio broadcasting industry', *Administrative Science Quarterly*, **36** (3): 333–63.

Leca, B. and Naccache, P. (2006), 'A critical realist view of institutional entrepreneurship', *Organization*, **13** (5): 627–51.

Lounsbury, Michael, Ventresca, Marc and Hirsch, Paul M. (2003), 'Social movements, field frames and industry emergence: a cultural–political perspective on US recycling', *Socioeconomic Review*, **1**: 71–104.

Maguire, Steve, Hardy, Cynthia and Lawrence, Thomas B. (2004), 'Institutional entrepreneurship in emerging fields: HIV/AIDS treatment advocacy in Canada', *Academy of Management Journal*, **47** (5): 657–79.

McAdam, Doug, McCarthy, John D. and Zald, Mayer N. (eds) (1996), *Comparative Perspectives on Social Movements*, Cambridge and New York: Cambridge University Press.

Meyer, J.W. and Rowan, B. (1977), 'Institutionalized organizations: formal structure as myth and ceremony', *American Journal of Sociology*, **83** (2): 340–63.

Miner, J.B. (2003), 'The rated importance, scientific validity, and practical usefulness of organizational behavior theories: a quantitative view', *Academy of Management Learning and Education*, **2** (3): 250–68.

Oliver, Christine (1991), 'Strategic responses to institutional processes', *Academy of Management Review*, **16**: 145–79.

Oliver, C. (1997), 'Sustainable competitive advantage: combining institutional and resource-based views', *Strategic Management Journal*, **18** (9): 697–713.

Palmer, D. and Barber, M. (2001), 'Challengers, elites and owning families: a social class theory of corporate acquisitions in the 1960s', *Administrative Science Quarterly*, **46**: 87–120.

Perrow, C. (1970), *Organizational Analysis: A Sociological View*, Belmont, CA: Wadsworth.

Pfeffer, Jeffrey and Salancik, Gerald (1978), *The External Control of Organizations: A Resource Dependence Perspective*, New York: Harper & Row.

Phillips, Nelson, Lawrence, Thomas and Hardy, Cynthia (2000), 'Interorganizational collaboration and the dynamics of institutional fields', *Journal of Management Studies*, **37** (1): 23–45.

Phillips, Nelson, Lawrence, Thomas B. and Hardy, Cynthia (2004), 'Discourse and institutions', *Academy of Management Review*, **29** (4): 635–52.

Porter, M. (1980), *Competitive Strategy*, New York: Free Press.

Powell, W.W. (1996), 'On the nature of institutional embeddedness: labels vs. explanation', in J.A.C. Baum and J.E. Dutton (eds), *Advances in Strategic Management: The Embeddedness of Strategy*, vol. 13, Greenwich, CT: JAI Press, pp. 293–300.

Rao, Hayagreeva (1998), '*Caveat emptor*: the construction of nonprofit consumer watchdog organizations', *American Journal of Sociology*, **103** (4): 912–61.

Rao, Hayagreeva, Morrill, Calvin and Zald, Mayer N. (2000), 'Power plays: how social movements and collective action create new organizational forms', *Research in Organizational Behavior*, **22**: 239–82.

Rao, Hayagreeva and Sivakumar, Kumar (1999), 'Institutional sources of boundary-spanning structures: the establishment of investor relations departments in the Fortune 500 industrials', *Organization Science*, **10** (1): 27–42.

Reay, T., Golden-Biddle, K. and GermAnn, K. (2006), 'Legitimizing a new role: small wins and micro-processes of change', *Academy of Management Journal*, **49** (5): 977–98.

Rindova, V.P. and Fombrun, C.J. (1999), 'Constructing competitive advantage: the role of firm–constituent interactions', *Strategic Management Journal*, **20** (8): 691–710.

Sawhney, M. and Prandelli, E. (2000), 'Communities of creation: managing disruptive innovations in turbulent markets', *California Management Review*, **42** (4): 24–54.

Seo, M.-G. and Creed, W.E.D. (2002), 'Institutional contradictions, praxis and institutional change: a dialectical perspective', *Academy of Management Review*, **27** (2): 222–47.

Sherer, P.D. and Lee, K. (2002), 'Institutional change in large law firms: a resource dependency and institutional perspective', *Academy of Management Journal*, **45** (1): 102–10.

Starr, P. (1982), *The Social Transformation of American Medicine*, New York: Basic Books.

Stinchcombe, A.L. (1965), 'Social structures and organizations', in J.G. March (ed.), *Handbook of Organizations*, Chicago, IL: Rand McNally, pp. 142–93.

Strang, D. and Meyer, J.W. (1993), 'Institutional conditions for diffusion', *Theory and Society*, **22**: 487–511.

Tolbert, P. and Zucker, L. (1996), 'Institutionalization of institutional theory', in S. Clegg, C. Hardy and W. Nord (eds), *Handbook of Organizational Studies*, London: Sage, pp. 175–90.

Wicks, D. (2001), 'Institutionalized mindsets of invulnerability: differentiated institutional fields and the antecedents of organizational crisis', *Organization Studies*, **22** (4): 659–92.

Zimmerman, Monica A. and Zeitz, Gerald J. (2002), 'Beyond survival: achieving new venture growth by building legitimacy', *Academy of Management Review*, **27** (3): 414–31.

Zucker, L. (1988), 'Where do institutional patterns come from?', in L.G. Zucker (ed.), *Research on Institutional Patterns and Organizations: Culture and Environment*, Cambridge, MA: Ballinger, pp. 23–49.

Zukin, S. and DiMaggio, P.J. (1990), 'Introduction', in Zukin and DiMaggio (eds), *Structures of Capital: The Social Organization of the Economy*, Cambridge: Cambridge University Press, pp. 1–36.

PART III

SHAPING THE FUTURE: STRATEGIZING AND INNOVATION

16 The role of middle managers in enabling foresight
Laura A. Costanzo and Vicky Tzoumpa

Introduction

Hamel and Prahalad (1994: 82–3) in their groundbreaking book *Competing for the Future* state that foresight is more than a vision. While a 'vision connotes a dream', industry foresight goes beyond a simple vision, as 'it requires a deep understanding of the current trends' in society. They argue that without a solid factual foundation in the current trends a vision is going to remain fantastical. We agree with Hamel and Prahalad's view of foresight and conceptualize foresight as a learning process, which enacts the future by a mechanism of 'probing and learning', an evolving process as managers' sensemaking of the future evolves over time (Costanzo, 2004).

In start-up companies, managers' attention to the unfolding events occurring across the industries' boundaries is critical as managers are exposed to a wide range of information, through which they can develop sensemaking of arising market opportunities or new market gaps to fill (Hamel and Prahalad, 1994; Kim and Mauborgne, 1999). Moreover, the knowledge of the current trends is useful to build managers' confidence in their sensemaking of the future. In established companies, this outside perspective (market based) is complemented by an inside perspective (resource based) which posits that the existence of limited structures helps people to make sense of a fast-changing environment. Semi-structures can help people to get an understanding of the environment and build the confidence to make quick decisions (Brown and Eisenhardt, 1997). Also, it is argued that a stable top management team may act as a bridge between the actors who learn and the organizational structures and routines in dynamic business environments where attempts of future analysis prove to be inaccurate or inadequate (Rindova and Kotha, 2001).

On the other hand, it is argued that many established organizations find it hard to change and/or anticipate future events regardless of the abundant amount of information to which established organizations are exposed. Bettis and Prahalad (1995) argued that this inability is due to the dominant coalition's inability to unlearn the dominant logic. Levinthal and March (1993) identified three types of major learning myopia that constrain the contribution of learning to organizational intelligence: temporal myopia, spatial myopia and failure myopia. They argue that all three elements of learning myopia compromise the effectiveness of learning and, particularly, the need of a balance between the two fundamental types of learning, exploration and exploitation.

A number of recommendations, mainly based on organizational changes, have been suggested in order to elicit organizational learning and, therefore, make the organization ready for the future challenges. For instance, Prahalad and Bettis (1986) proposed interventions at the top management level, such as including top managers with diverse backgrounds; allowing members of the top management team to take a sabbatical so that they can enrich their experiences; rehearsing as a management team for a broad range of future industry scenarios; rewarding executives for experimenting even when projects fail; and legitimizing dissent. Brown and Eisenhardt (1997) suggested the adoption of semi-structures which balance the need of continuous change with stability. O'Reilly and Tushman (2004) emphasized the role of developing ambidextrous organizations to ensure both continuity with the past (stability based on exploitation learning) and change for the future (innovation based on exploration learning). Given the disruptive nature of exploration learning, it has been suggested that the setting-up of newly independent business units would resolve the tension existing between exploitation learning and exploration learning (Christensen, 1997).

While we do not disagree with this literature, we argue that the organizational measures outlined above are limiting as they are imposed, abstracted organizational changes which neglect the contextual and social nature of learning. We conceptualize learning as a process stemming from the social interactions among people and their dynamic relationships situated in the context where learning take place (that is, work settings, project team and so on). Ultimately, it is people – the repository of both codified and tacit knowledge (Nonaka, 1991) – who must learn. Drawing on the social construction of learning, the chapter argues that there are relevant actors, such as middle managers, who, in the wake of organizational downsizing, rather than being claimed to be an expensive organizational burden are increasingly deemed to play a significant role with regard to the processes of facilitating learning both within and outside of their team. Therefore, in order to facilitate knowledge integration within the team and from the team to the rest of the organization, new managerial roles are claimed for middle managers. By being situated at the intersection of both horizontal and vertical flows of information within the company (Nonaka and Tacheuchi, 1995), middle managers are best positioned to reconcile the tension that exists between the two problematic processes of learning, *interpreting–integrating* versus *institutionalizing–intuiting* (Crossan et al., 1999). Drawing on these conceptualizations, it is argued that foresight is a proactive learning process which filters and evolves across the organizational boundaries through the key roles deployed by relevant actors.

In the next sections, first an overview of the theory of organizational learning is provided with an emphasis on the different types of learning and the stages involved in the learning process and their relevance for foresight; then, the tension that exists between exploitation and exploration learning is discussed with a focus on the key reasons for such tension; subsequently, the focus is on the context where learning take places – the team – and the barriers to knowledge sharing and integration within and outside the team's boundaries. This leads to focus on the evolving nature of the role of the middle manager and his/her influence in overcoming the barriers to knowledge integration across the organizational boundaries. Finally, the chapter will focus on the managerial roles of middle managers in facilitating team and organizational learning and the specific managerial processes involved for facilitating knowledge integration across the organizational boundaries.

Organizational learning

We draw on the theory of organizational learning in order to develop a better understanding of foresight conceptualized as a learning process. Early conceptualizations viewed organizational learning as an adaptive process whereby goals, attention rules and search rules are adapted to the experiences that are made within the organization (Cyert and March, 1963). Further developments made a clear distinction between two types of learning: 'adaptive' and 'proactive'. While the former denotes an automatic organizational response to changes in the external conditions of the environment, the latter is concerned with planned organizational changes that extend far beyond simple reactions to environmental changes. Thus, some scholars (Argyris and Schön, 1978; Fiol and Lyles, 1985; Senge, 1990; Dodgson, 1991) have considered proactive learning to be superior to adaptive learning given the fact that it is more cognitively induced. Drawing on this argument, we conceptualize foresight as a proactive learning process aimed at anticipating changes in the external environments. Within this perspective, foresight goes beyond the technical aspects of the learning process, which consist of effective processing, interpretation of, and response to, the information, mostly available in explicit form, either within or outside the organization. A classical representation of the technical aspects of learning can be found in Argyris and Schön's (1978, 1996) work on single- and double-loop learning. Instead, we mainly draw on the social perspective of learning. Lave and Wenger (1991) and Wenger (1998) provide a fascinating example of the social construction of learning in their studies of apprenticeship and communities of practice. Schön (1983, 1987) also provides some insights into the use of the 'tacit' sources of learning in the exploration of reflective practice. By adopting the social construction of learning, foresight is considered as a proactive learning process enacted by the way people make sense of their experiences at work. It is a process which unfolds within the social interactions taking place among people in the natural work setting and the related dynamics of power and/or as a cultural artefact (Easterby-Smith et al., 1999).

Furthermore, organizational learning theorists distinguish between 'observational' (what is achieved/results-based product knowledge) and 'experimental' learning (how it is achieved/processes/procedural knowledge). The former refers to 'vicarious' learning, that is, the second-hand acquisition of new behaviours or knowledge structures as a consequence of observing others (Weiss, 1990). It is argued that observational learning presents some limitations. For instance, it is inadequate in the presence of dramatic changes in the external environments, where adaptation of new knowledge to new conditions requires complete new understanding (Van de Ven and Polley, 1992). Also, observational learning does not contribute to developing full understanding in circumstances such as strategic partnerships, when one of the knowledge partners is not willing to share its knowledge base with the other partners (Zahra et al., 2000). In contrast, experimental learning can lead to developing new knowledge and behaviours that are in accordance with existing cultural values, resources and routines (Kogut and Zander, 1996). Rather than focusing on 'product knowledge', the focus of experimental learning is on 'procedural knowledge'.

Experimental learning has its roots in experiential learning theory (Kolb, 1984). Kolb (p. 41) defines experiential learning as 'the process whereby knowledge is created through the transformation of experience. Knowledge results from the combination of grasping and transforming experience'. Experiential learning theory portrays two dialectically related modes of grasping experience, concrete experience (CE) and abstract conceptualization (AC), and two dialectically related modes of transforming experience, reflective observation (RO) and active experimentation (AE). Experiential learning is a process of constructing knowledge that involves a creative tension among the four learning modes. This process is described as a spiral learning cycle where the learner 'touches all the bases' – experiencing, reflecting, thinking, and acting – in a recursive process that is responsive to the learning context and what is being learned. Immediate or concrete experiences are the basis for observations and reflections. These reflections are assimilated and distilled into abstract concepts from which new implications for action can be drawn. These implications can be actively tested and serve as guides in creating new experiences. Drawing on experiential learning theory (Kolb, 1984), we argue that foresight is a proactive experimental learning process whereby individuals make sense of their experience and modify their behaviours as a result of their interpretations of the unfolding events derived from those experiences. Clearly, it is an articulated process which consists of the development or creation of skills, insights, relationships (knowledge acquisition), the dissemination to others of what has been acquired by some individuals (knowledge sharing), and integration of the learning so that it is assimilated, is broadly available and can also be generalized to new situations (knowledge utilization) (Dibella et al., 1996). Such a process is iterative and dynamic as it requires a firm's competence in (i) engaging in experiences, (ii) drawing inferences from them and (iii) storing the inferred material for future experience (Hayward, 2002). Therefore, we argue that foresight is an interactive and dynamic social process – a dynamic capability – that requires both organizational and individual skills and joint contributions to the understanding of complex problems (Teece et al., 1997).

Crossan et al.'s (1999) 4I framework of learning provides a useful framework to refer to, for the conceptualization of foresight as the process of change in thought and action, where cognition affects action (and vice versa). Crossan et al.'s 4I framework disentangles the process through which learning occurs within firms by adopting a three-level perspective, which include individual, group and organizational. The three levels of organizational learning are linked by social and psychological processes: intuiting, interpreting, integrating and institutionalizing. To begin with, *intuiting* is the preconscious recognition of a pattern and/or possibilities inherent to a personal stream of experience. This initial phase of learning affects the intuitive individual's behaviour, but it only affects others as they attempt to interact with that individual. Second, *interpreting* is the explanation of an insight, or idea to one's self and to others. This process goes from the preverbal to the verbalization of the idea or insight and requires the development of a language for communication purposes. Third, *integrating* is the process of developing a shared understanding of an insight or idea among a group of individuals and involves a coordinated action through mutual adjustment. Enough consensuses around a set of diverse interpretations by the members of a group are required, so that organized collective action can follow (Fiol, 1994). This collective action can be powerful enough to challenge established cultural values (Contu and Willmott, 2003) and people's cognitive maps or understandings (Nicolini and Meznar, 1995); all leading to a complete new range of organizational behaviours that are potentially available to an organization (Huber, 1991). Last, *institutionalizing* is about the embedding of the learning within the wider organization through the definition of tasks, specification of actions and the setting up of adequate organizational mechanisms, which include systems, structures, procedures and strategy.

Drawing on Crossan et al.'s (1999) framework, we argue that some specific learning processes, such as the preconscious development of an insight or idea, are more likely to occur at the individual level. Furthermore, it is only through social processes and group dynamics that individuals start to share their insights or ideas with the other group members (integrating process). This integrating process via socialization facilitates collective organizational learning (ibid.). Crossan et al. use the example of Apple to illustrate how the three levels and four processes of organizational learning work in practice. Steve Jobs, through an intuitive process, had the insights upon which Apple was founded. As insightful as Jobs was, he could not accomplish his vision alone. He needed to involve others. The conversation and dialogue with the others, which served to develop his understanding, also helped to integrate the cognitive maps of the group – to develop a shared understanding. In the Apple situation, John Sculley was brought in to provide, at least in part, needed systems, structures, and other formal mechanisms. Individual and communal learning became institutionalized in the hope that the learning could be exploited more systematically. Institutionalization of learning contributed to more efficient operations, enabling the organization to better deliver on the founder's original vision. Therefore, we argue that foresight as a proactive learning process is initially enacted by the intuitive mode of the individual and then evolves (i) through common interpretation shared between the individual and the other members of the group and (ii) through integration of the learning within the group and from the group to the wider organization. The dynamics of the group context are relevant as they affect the outcomes of the integration process.

The tension between exploitation and exploration learning
A dynamic view of organizational learning recognizes that there may be bottlenecks in the ability of the organization to absorb the feed forward of learning from the individual to the group and to the organization (Cohen and Levinthal, 1990). For instance, it is argued that there is a continuous tension between exploration learning – assimilating new knowledge – and exploitation learning – using what has already been learned (Crossan et al., 1999). Exploitation and exploration learning are in tension because while the former involves refinement, choice, production, efficiency, selection, implementation and execution, the latter is a risk-taking activity, which involves experimentation, flexibility, discovery and innovation. Exploration and exploitation learning pose a constant trade-off as they both compete for scarce resources, with the consequence that an organization has to make a choice with regard to which activities will have to be supported more and which activities will have to be neglected. Given the high level of uncertainty and risk associated with exploration learning and the fact that its impact on performance is only observable in the long term, there is a natural tendency of the management to focus primarily on the exploitation learning activities, which contribute to superior returns in the short term. Thus, the process of resource allocation is a problematic area in that it tends to inhibit the development of new insights given its great emphasis on track record and proven success. In this way, exploration learning becomes progressively neglected by the firm management. March (1991) argues that this learning approach is unbalanced and potentially self-destructive as an excessive focus on exploitation learning will merely privilege the improvement of the current existing competences to the expenses of developing new skills and competencies for the future.

On a similar line of reasoning, Levinthal and March (1993) identified three types of learning myopia which limit the contribution of learning to organizational learning: temporal myopia, spatial myopia and failure myopia. Temporal myopia consists in the fact that over time the difficulty of sustaining exploration learning is accentuated by learning. As learning develops distinctive competencies it simultaneously compromises capabilities outside those competencies and niches. When the conditions change, the learned skills become an impediment. Spatial myopia consists in the fact that learning tends to favour effects that occur near to the learner and which the latter is familiar with. Failure myopia consists in the fact that learning tends to oversample successes and eliminate failures. This tendency is accentuated by the way learning produces confidence and confidence tends to produce favourable anticipations and interpretations of outcomes. Drawing on Levinthal and March's theory of learning myopia, we argue that all three elements of learning myopia compromise the effectiveness of learning and particularly compromise the balance between exploration and exploitation learning.

On the basis of the above discussion of the social perspective theory of learning, we argue that while exploration learning is enacted by the intuitive mode of the individual and enough consensuses generated among people at the group level, the three modes of learning myopia exacerbate the constraints on exploration learning at the organizational level. This might explain the inability of many organizations to adapt themselves to changes in the external environment or anticipate these changes, despite the presence of very creative and highly intuitive managers situated across different organizational levels. In this regard, Prahalad and Bettis's (1986) theoretical perspective of the dominant logic provides a useful theoretical framework that enables us to further understand the failure of many organizations to learn and anticipate changes or shape changes in the external environment. The dominant logic can be viewed as a fundamental aspect of organizational intelligence, which is about the capability of a firm to learn; what is learned is then transformed into organizational knowledge. Prahalad and Bettis argue that at the organizational level, learning can be thought of as occurring at the level of the strategy, systems, values, expectations and reinforced behaviours, which then shape the dominant logic through a feedback process. In order for learning to take place, the dominant logic will have to be unlearned (ibid.). Yet, organizations seem to lack the intelligence to appropriately interpret and act on the flood of information (ibid.). For Prahalad and Bettis this issue revolves around the inability of the firm's dominant coalition to learn.

Furthermore, drawing on Crossan et al.'s (1999) and Crossan and Berdrow's (2003) research, we argue that the organizational incapability to interpret and act on the unfolding information explains some of the challenges that established organizations face in undertaking strategic renewal. Since established organizations have past learning embedded within them, they have to manage the tension between institutionalized learning and the processes of intuiting, interpreting and integrating. Crossan et al. (1999) refer to these processes as the 'feed-forward' and 'feedback' processes of learning. Learning not only occurs over time and across the three levels, but it also creates a tension between assimilating new learning (feed forward) and exploiting or using what has already been learned (feedback). Through feed-forward processes, new ideas and actions flow from the individual to the group to the organization levels. In addition to the feed-forward learning processes, learning that has been institutionalized feeds back and impacts on individual and group learning. These interactions exhibit two problematic relationships: interpreting–integrating (feed forward) and institutionalizing–intuiting (feedback). The tension between assimilating new learning (feed forward) and using what has already been learned (feedback) arises because the institutionalized learning (what has already been learned) impedes the assimilation of new learning. For example, rules and routines that once captured the logic and learning of how to facilitate learning at the individual level may no longer apply in a changed circumstance; yet the systems still focus an individual's energy and attention in ways that impede the assimilation and feed forward of new learning (Mintzberg, 1994). Also, an organization structure that is vital to establishing the communication channel (who talks to whom) in the organization may impede conversation that could develop valuable new shared understandings. Thus, any dynamic theory of organizational learning needs to recognize the different levels and processes involved in the learning process and the fact that these differences create a tension between the feed-forward and feedback processes of learning. Clearly, this tension also impacts on the evolving nature of foresight.

A number of recommendations have been suggested in order to elicit exploration learning at the organizational level and, therefore, make the organization ready for future challenges. Adequate organizational systems should be in place in order to ensure that institutionalized exploitation learning (feedback) does not drive out exploration learning (feed forward). For instance, some firms, for example, 3M, have recognized this problem and have institutionalized a different resource allocation process that provides funding for new projects and also holds the business accountable for having a significant portion of the revenue derived from new products (Hurst and Zimmerman, 1994). Other mechanisms include interventions that have a direct impact on people. For instance, Prahalad and Bettis (1986) proposed specific interventions at the top management level, such as including top managers with diverse backgrounds, allowing members of the top management team to take a sabbatical so that they can enrich their experiences; rehearsing as a management team for a broad range of future industry scenarios; reward executives for experimenting even when projects fail; and legitimizing dissent. On a similar line of reasoning, Dibella et al. (1996) argue that firms may improve their learning capability by adopting adequate organizational structures and processes. The latter should allow for more efficient information processing and the identification of market opportunities and related resources, which are needed to exploit those opportunities (ibid.). Clearly, all the firms' activities, which include people's creative and technical skills, intuition, group interpretations of an idea, insight, communication of ideas to others, getting support from the top, setting up of adequate organizational processes for information processing and so on, mutually reinforce and complement one another (Miller, 1987). For instance, creative skills available within an organization can be used to interpret future customer needs and respond to emerging market trends and opportunities; technical skills may enable a company to develop understanding of the opportunities and challenges that a new emerging technology poses to the organization; collaborative skills may enable access to unique resources that otherwise would not be available to an organization. We argue that such critical knowledge-based resources are greatly influenced by exploration learning, as they are all developed and nurtured through a process of experimentation, constant refinement and reconfiguration.

Yet, it is the task of managers to invest significant efforts in integrating learning and achieving the internal consistency and strategic flexibility necessary to take advantage of recognized market opportunities (Spicer et al., 2000). Knowledge within firms resides in many forms and places, but it is ultimately people who must learn new ways of doing things while being prepared to unlearn the past. It is a top priority of individuals to undertake this learning as they are the primary repository of both codified and tacit knowledge (Grant, 1996).

Therefore, drawing on the dynamic theory of organizational learning and the above discussion, we are interested in constructing a unified framework that enables us to better define and understand the roles of key organizational actors with regard to facilitating learning from the individual to the rest of the organization. In particular, given the social perspective adopted in this chapter, at the group level we focus on the team, which represents 'a shared context in which individuals can interact with each other, and engage in the constant dialogue on which reflection depends' (Nonaka, 1991: 104). The team is an important context for the creation of tacit knowledge and its externalization via the social and work relationships that exist between the manager and the team members (ibid.: 104). Team working, however, presents a number of inefficiencies which represent barriers to learning and knowledge sharing beyond the team context. This is further discussed in the next section.

Barriers to knowledge sharing across the organizational boundaries
Organizations seem to lack the intelligence to appropriately interpret and act on the flood of information (Prahalad and Bettis, 1986), despite flatter organizational structures, which should bring key organizational actors closer to the sources of information. For Prahalad and Bettis, this issue revolves around the inability of the firm's dominant coalition to learn. While we do not disagree with this view, we argue that the causes of this organizational inability to learn are deeper and are to be found in the organizational inner. For instance, at the group level of learning, it is noticed that although an abundance of free-flowing communication exists within the organization via cross-functional project teams, communication back to the enterprise is limited, with very little collective knowledge captured and retained at an institutional level. This is due to the fact that cross-functional project teams do not last for a long time. As soon as the objectives of the projects are achieved, the cross-functional team is disbanded and both collective intelligence and experience of the team quickly dissipate, with the consequence that some new relevant knowledge that has been learned is lost and no new knowledge is created at the institutional level (Huang and Newell, 2003). We argue that the way that teams operate contributes to this loss of new knowledge. For instance, research suggests that in most project teams, time is spent on capturing learning in terms of 'what' the projects have achieved, which is termed 'product knowledge', while a more useful type of learning would be learning 'how' knowledge has been achieved; in other words, focusing on the 'procedural' content of knowledge (Newell, 2004). Similarly, Neale and Homes (1990) emphasize the importance of capturing procedural knowledge for enhancing learning in cross-project work. Garrick and Clegg (2001) refer to this as the problem of conflating project performance with project learning, simply because too much emphasis is put on project performance rather than on the actual learning that occurred. In a way, the cross-functional teams, which have become a common way of organizing people with the purpose of bridging organizational boundaries, facilitating knowledge transmission and quick response to the market, represent a limitation in themselves. The members of the cross-functional team work with a mindset that it is limited by the project framework. In our own terminology we call this limitation 'project myopia', which clearly restricts learning to the team context.

Furthermore, wide organizational learning is limited by the cross-functional team members' unwillingness to share their power. Also, the diverse nature, the dissimilar languages and backgrounds of the team members may generate a knowledge gap that requires adaptation time before thinking of the issue of sharing learning via team integration (Mirghany et al., 2004). In this respect, Scarbrough et al. (2004) suggest that there are 'learning boundaries' which represent barriers to knowledge sharing, in the sense that the knowledge accumulated in cross-functional projects cannot simply be captured and retained under a different set of new circumstances determined by new projects. Carlile (2002) referred to these boundaries as 'knowledge boundaries', which consist of a syntactic (language) boundary, where the flow of knowledge is inhibited by the lack of a common syntax between the individuals or groups involved, implying the need for creating knowledge redundancy (Nonaka and Takeuchi, 1996) or common understanding to enable knowledge transfer; a semantic (meaning) boundary, where relevant groups are unable to share knowledge because they bring different interpretations to it; and a pragmatic (practice) boundary, where the flow of knowledge is constrained by differences invested in the interests between individuals and groups. Thus, without this common understanding, knowledge is lost because the recipients are not able to understand the new knowledge, particularly when the latter is in conflict with individually held beliefs. Scarbrough et al. (2004) argue that these knowledge boundaries are tied to social practices and the bounded nature of such practices across organizational units. Similarly, Tsai and Ghoshal (1998) emphasize the role of social ties as channels of knowledge sharing which influence positively the creation and diffusion of innovations.

Other barriers to knowledge sharing within the wider organization are to be found in the intrinsic characteristics of knowledge, which is distributed, ambiguous and disruptive (Newell, 2005). Knowledge is 'distributed' in the sense that team members are not aware that there is knowledge available that could possibly be useful to them. Thus, teams are said to wear 'blinkers' and even if useful knowledge is available to them, it remains unused because no one looks for it (ibid.). The second problematic characteristic of knowledge is that it is 'ambiguous', whereby it creates barriers to knowledge sharing and acceptance when it does not fit with one's current view of the world (Tsoukas, 1996). Teams exist in a 'cognitive cage' meaning that they do not trust the transferred knowledge unless it fits with their pre-existing mental view of the world (Polanyi, 1996). Boland and Tenkasi (1995) refer to the need to get into the head or world of the other in order to understand and use knowledge that they can provide, respectively (Nonaka and Takeuchi, 1996). Third, 'disruptive' knowledge (Vaughan, 1997; Christensen et al., 2000) creates problems for getting acceptance, especially if this undermines a recipient's knowledge powerbase. As Carlile (2002) points out, teams wear a 'straight-jacket' that makes them resistant to knowledge that would bring change practice and potentially undermine the knowledge base of the team, so that knowledge is blocked by that team in order to maintain their power/knowledge base. We argue that knowledge is situated, whereby the characteristics of knowledge of being ambiguous and disruptive are determined by the contextual situation of the team. The contextual circumstances of the team, the mindset of people and their power relations affect knowledge sharing.

Under the circumstances outlined above, we argue that the ability of organizations to learn and act on the basis of the flood of information is constrained twice: first, at the top organizational level (dominant coalition) where learning myopia prevents the dominant coalition from recognizing and anticipating changes in the external environment before these changes take place; and second, at the group level (cross-functional teams), where project myopia and knowledge boundaries (Carlile, 2002; Scarbrough et al., 2004; Newell,

2005) prevent the sharing of new knowledge outside the team boundaries, from team to team. These constraints put restrictions on wide organizational proactive learning with the consequence that foresight, although residing in a few organizational pockets, unfolds within a restricted scope, determined by the project objectives, which are very specific and short-term oriented. In this way, foresight neither spans nor evolves across the organizational boundaries. In order to facilitate this process, we argue that key actors – middle managers – who are situated at the intersection of the vertical and horizontal flows of information (Nonaka and Takeuchi, 1995) are deemed to play a relevant role with regard to the transmission of learning from the team to the rest of the organization. In the next sections, we look at how middle managers can contribute to knowledge sharing across organizational boundaries. However, before discussing this, in the next section we look closely at the evolution of the role of middle managers, with a particular emphasis on examining the reasons for which middle managers are deemed to deploy an important role with regard to organizational learning and, therefore, foresight.

The evolution of middle managers' role
The definition of middle managers' roles has traditionally been derived from the position that they physically occupy within the organization. For instance, early studies (Fletcher, 1973; Dickson, 1977) described middle management as one layer of management isolated from the key decision-making processes (Scase and Goffee 1989; Dopson and Stewart, 1990). Dopson et al. (1992) and Livian (1997) identify middle managers as those who occupy all those positions between 'top strategic managers' and 'first-level supervisors'. Similarly, Heckscher (1995: 9) defined middle managers as 'those below the general manager's executive team and above the level of supervisor'. Wai-Kwong et al. (2001) argued that the unique nature of middle managers' role derives from the unique position that they occupy between the strategic apex and the operating core of the organization. This position impacts on the function that middle managers play in the organization. In this regard, Heckscher's (1995: 9–10) research indicated that 'the middle managers of several levels shared a common view of themselves as the operational core, holding the business together at a practical level while the top managers thought long-range thoughts and the supervisors dealt with the workers'. On a similar line of interpretation, Sethi (1999: 10) proposed that middle managers held the organization together by simply acting 'as a bridge between the visionary ideals of the top and the often chaotic reality of those on the front line of business'.

However, in the wake of organizational downsizing due to widespread corporate restructuring, the position of the middle manager has been seen as particularly at risk of becoming redundant, while being increasingly threatened by developments in information and communication technology (ICT) (Burke and Cooper, 2000). The flatter, less hierarchical structures of the 'flexible firm' (Child and McGrath 2001; Kalleberg, 2001) or the 'network corporation' (Castells, 2000) have required increasing cuts of layers of middle management. Therefore, middle managers do not derive their power from the hierarchical position of authority that they occupy within the organization, but rather from having specific knowledge that enables them to influence both strategic and operational organizational priorities (Wai-Kwong et al., 2001: 1325). Critically, middle managers have been increasingly involved in wide organizational activities, which range from the strategic management of the organization as a whole (Floyd and Wooldridge, 1994;

Huy, 2001) to the operational management of a front-line work unit (Hales, 2006). Yet, despite the increasing strategic and change management role, Floyd and Wooldridge, and Huy argued that middle managers should not to be considered as a miniature version of top managers, but they play a crucial role in ensuring that the activities inside an organization are carried out; and by balancing organizational change and stability they ensure that the organization is able to generate creative alternatives to its problems. We argue that by balancing stability with change, middle managers can facilitate relevant learning activities, including both exploration and exploitation learning.

Middle managers are usually found to be leading cross-functional project teams (Claydon and Doyle, 1996). Given the fact that a team represents 'a shared context in which individuals can interact with each other, and engage in the constant dialogue on which reflection depends', it is an important forum for the creation and transfer of tacit knowledge occurring within the social and work relationships between the manager and the team members (Nonaka, 1991: 104). In order to develop high-performing teams and cover the wider spans of control left in the wake of downsizings, middle managers need increased skills (Klagge, 1998). Fewer in number, middle managers have been given wider spans of control, resulting in a dispersion of their focus and a dilution of their ability to respond to the complexities and dynamics of today's organizational environment (Pinsonnealut and Kraemer, 1993). In taking more leadership roles, middle managers have become less personally productive. In order to compensate for this loss of productivity, middle managers have asked for more creativity and innovation from their team members (Skagen, 1992). Hence, the efficient transfer of knowledge between the team manager and the rest of the team is a challenge for the new manager and requires new skills and practices (Floyd and Wooldridge, 1994), such as the ability to lead change through team building, systems thinking and organizational visioning (ibid.).

The role of middle managers in facilitating team and organizational learning

Drawing on the social construction of learning as discussed in the previous sections, we turn now to examine the different roles and practices that middle managers should adopt in order to facilitate the integration of learning within teams and across the organizational boundaries. Particularly, we draw on Nonaka and Takeuchi's (1995) spiral model of organizational learning, which consists of four stages that alternate between tacit knowledge and explicit knowledge. Nonaka and Takeuchi suggest that knowledge is created through the conversion between two forms of knowledge: the transformation from tacit to explicit knowledge, from explicit to tacit, and, within each one, the transfer between individual, group, organizational, and inter-organizational levels. According to this model, organizational learning and knowledge creation take a path of socialization, externalization, combination, internalization, socialization, externalization and so on in an infinite spiral. Tacit knowledge, which tends to be personal subjective and context specific, resides in a few key individuals. Such knowledge is shared through socialization and can be made explicit via codification in manuals so that it is incorporated into new activities, for example, new products and processes. This process is termed 'externalization'. Through combination, codified knowledge is then disseminated to the rest of the organization. The reverse process from explicit to implicit knowledge takes place through key individuals who internalize an organization's formal rules and procedures and other forms of explicit knowledge.

Drawing on Nonaka and Takeuchi's spiral model of organizational learning, Asllani and Luthans (2003) identify two major groups of middle managers as knowledge managers: 'explicit knowledge managers' and 'tacit knowledge managers'. While the former carry over processes such as knowledge generation, knowledge codification, and knowledge transfer, the latter mostly provide the necessary interaction between knowledge experts. Particularly, tacit knowledge managers are those managers who subscribe to Nonaka's thinking of increasing managers' tacit knowledge through internalization and socialization. Drawing on Nonaka and Takeuchi's (1995: 125) proposition that 'knowledge is created by middle managers at the intersection of the vertical and horizontal flows of information within the company', middle managers are best positioned to identify the knowledge gaps and communication problems between groups and bridge them. This bridging activity creates a network organization. The coordination and management of people through networking activities contribute to extracting further tacit knowledge (Schaafsma, 1997; Gold et al., 2001). Furthermore, through the use of personal networks, middle managers are *knowledge seekers*, in that they are able to gather both explicit and tacit knowledge by simply looking for insights, judgement and understanding through the use of their personal networks (Davenport and Prusak, 2000).

On a similar line of reasoning, Leonard-Barton (1995), who focused on the interaction between the activities pursued in the course of developing new products and processes and the organization's core technological capabilities, identified two categories of important key actors, respectively, 'gatekeepers of knowledge' and 'boundary spanners'. These actors contribute to expanding an organization's own absorptive capacity. Existing knowledge is exploited by sharing creative problem-solving skills and new knowledge is explored by importing, experimenting with and integrating such knowledge into organizational capabilities. Furthermore, in extending Zahra and George's (2002) work, Jones (2006) refers to the role deployed by 'change agents' with regard to the impact of managerial agency on absorptive capacity and ultimately, the transfer of knowledge between functions and organizations.

Given their position within the organization, a critical task of middle managers is to facilitate learning and knowledge transfer in cross-functional project teams (CFTs) and from the team to the rest of the organization. Middle managers can facilitate the integration of new knowledge beyond the boundary of the group dynamics, by encouraging project team members to focus on 'procedural knowledge' rather than on 'product knowledge' (Huang and Newell, 2003). For instance, middle managers can motivate CFTs to think about what procedural-type problems they might face and recognize possible ways of overcoming these problems, either by referring to other past projects, or simply by learning from the experience of others. The knowledge gained can then be transferred through social networks, which is actually what community approach to cross-project learning entails. In this way, the middle manager contributes to overcoming the learning project myopia as he/she becomes a key link in the learning process and a channel through which knowledge is transferred; also he/she is an important *gatekeeper* through which ideas and insights are not dispersed, but transmitted within the group and from the group members to the others within the rest of the organization. Thus, although the intuitive skills of individuals are the starting inputs into the process of foresight, middle managers enrich this process through two modes:

1. *Externalization of knowledge* Middle managers facilitate the development of a shared interpretation and integration of new knowledge within the team through their gatekeeping and agency roles; and from the team to the rest of the organization through their boundary spanning role. Through externalization the new knowledge gained within the team is codified and disseminated to the rest of the organization. The new codified knowledge can be re-adapted to other organizational contexts. In this way, middle managers facilitate the institutionalizing of learning within the wider organization.
2. *Internalization of knowledge* Middle managers, through a process of socialization, facilitate the interactions between knowledge experts situated in different organizational contexts. In their role of knowledge seekers, they look for new insights, judgements and understanding, which is primarily subjective and personal until they are not shared with other individuals through a process of socialization. This process leads to the development of further insights, until a common interpretation is shared among the members of a group. Integration of the new knowledge within the team is then externalized via dissemination of the codified knowledge.

Thus, foresight is not confined to the team boundary; it evolves and spans across the three levels – individual, group and organizational – as ideas and new insights unfold into a continuum spiral of knowledge externalization and internalization. Clearly, this is a self-generated process which stems from the psychological and social processes enabled by the middle managers' new roles. It follows that middle managers can contribute to overcoming the knowledge boundaries by taking on new managerial roles (Newell, 2005). For instance, they could contribute to removing the 'knowledge blinkers' by acting as 'knowledge brokers' and as a kind of 'bridge' between the existing and the new knowledge (Pawoloski and Robey, 2004). They can overcome the barrier of 'knowledge ambiguity' by building team relationships through team-building exercises and intense social interactions with the aim of creating trust, mutual respect and understanding. By doing so, they open the cognitive cage of teams (Newell, 2005). Last, the challenge represented by 'disruptive knowledge' will require middle managers to become negotiators, to ensure that change in practice is accepted (Kolb, 1984). In this case, middle managers will need to engage in a political process in which the negotiation will depend primarily on norms of reciprocity rather than one team imposing power on another (Gouldner, 1960). In order for knowledge transfer to occur, middle managers will have to build close social and professional working relationships among the teams, developed through face-to-face interactions.

From the above discussion, it clearly emerges that middle managers' practices are primarily derived from the social construction of learning. Thus, we argue that in order to facilitate knowledge transfer and learning across projects, middle managers should place more emphasis on social capital (Nahapiet and Ghoshal, 1998) and community development (Brown and Duguid, 2001), rather than excessively focusing on investments in ICTs.

Managerial processes facilitating the integration of learning
In addition to the above-identified preferable practices, middle managers can become facilitators of learning integration within projects by adopting one or more of the

following managerial processes or 'knowledge modes': analytic, intuitive and pragmatic (Janczak, 2004). In his study, Janczak identified that managers behaved differently in each of the three identified phases of project development: (i) awareness, (ii) exploring versus exploiting knowledge, and (iii) codifying and assessing results.

Specifically, managers who adopt an analytic mode (the so-called 'analysts') perceive the projects as problems to be solved. As far as the project phases are concerned, in the awareness phase middle managers act as *knowledge seekers* as they engage in search activities, such as 'selecting people', 'clarifying a goal', and 'clarifying a mandate' with the aim of generating efficient solutions for their organizations. In the exploring versus exploiting knowledge phase of the project process, analysts focus their actions on searching and collecting new knowledge from outside their departments through the acquisition of explicit knowledge (contained in reports and other documents) and contracting consultants, and training themselves or their employees. In the assessing and codifying phase (standardizing), analysts focus their attention on describing the efficiency of the product or service delivered rather than the implementation process. In particular, analysts focus on describing product codification, which facilitates internal and external knowledge transfer. Since they are only interested in the diffusion of a solution, they do not describe feedback activities (procedural knowledge), whereby organizational learning is limited to the learning of each member who participated in the project phases.

Intuitive managers perceive the projects as personal challenges and proactively pursue projects from which they can derive pleasure once such projects are successfully completed. Intuitive managers mainly believe in intuition and influence organizational members by using emotional adjectives in their arguments, such as enthusiasm, pleasure and trust. With regard to the project phases, in the awareness phase intuitive managers are mainly preoccupied with discovering and generating new ideas, exploring the environment and trying to discover opportunities for creating new organizational knowledge. In the exploring versus exploiting phase, intuitive managers experiment with new knowledge through trial and error processes. Intuitive managers stress the importance of having trust in other members, and the necessity of having freedom (autonomy) to experiment without top management approval. Thus, only after experimentation are intuitive managers able to influence top managers. In the assessing and codifying phase, intuitive managers celebrate the newly created knowledge from the previous phase, and then start another original process in which new knowledge can be created. Unlike analysts, who focus their attention on codifying knowledge in documents and software, intuitive managers encode knowledge in people, fostering knowledge to be transmitted collectively.

Last, under the pragmatic mode, managers describe each project as a negotiation process intended to settle an organizational issue. Pragmatic managers have neither clear goals nor a range of solutions at the beginning of their negotiations. Unlike analysts, pragmatics negotiate the scope of organizational issues that are part of an organizational and political system. In the awareness phase, pragmatic managers develop activities primarily with top managers and with peers. Then, in building a network of contacts, pragmatic managers interact with different organizational levels and with departments outside the normal chain of command, frequently crossing departmental and organizational boundaries. In the exploring versus exploiting knowledge phase, they develop a network of contacts through which they adapt existing knowledge to new uses, by applying the knowledge that exists inside or outside a department to a specific context.

Pragmatic managers adopt an incremental approach through which they either combine existing knowledge to create new expertise within a department or introduce changes to the existing knowledge to solve problems that are of a similar nature to the ones dealt with in the past. In the assessing and codifying phase, pragmatic managers hold a debriefing so that the activities within this phase can lead to future successful negotiations. Debriefing entails learning from experience by discussing the results afterwards. Although pragmatic managers do not create new knowledge, the continuous adding of incremental pieces of knowledge helps their organization to perform effectively. Pragmatic managers do not focus on the results, instead they focus on a constant evaluation of their activities and performance, even before completing the projects. Thus, pragmatic managers engage in an interactive and iterative approach in which they conciliate multiple interests through-out their projects, implying the constant sharing of knowledge with their peers and top managers

In summary, in each of the three knowledge modes, middle managers perform a set of typical knowledge processes through which external and internal knowledge interact to create completely new knowledge. With regard to knowledge integration, analysts are important because they provide new external solutions for the organization and although no new knowledge is created, the continuous renewal of external input allows for organizational learning. Intuitive middle managers, instead, create new knowledge within organizations, and discover new opportunities and approaches. By empirically testing new ideas, intuitive middle managers create learning processes which focus on using previous solutions and on incrementally extending the knowledge base. Pragmatic managers, rather than collecting external knowledge, adopt existing knowledge and focus on implementing changes to the knowledge learned from previous experiences inside or outside of a department.

Discussion and conclusions

This chapter draws on the dynamic theory of organizational learning and posits foresight as a proactive learning process, which is enacted by the social interactions taking place in the normal work settings. Particularly, drawing on Crossan et al.'s (1999) 4I framework of organizational learning, foresight is conceptualized as a process of change in thought and action where cognition impacts on action (and vice versa). It is a process occurring at the individual, group and organizational levels via psychological and social processes that include intuiting, interpreting, integrating and institutionalizing. The consideration of the 4I framework leads us to propose that foresight is a proactive learning process in-itially enacted by the intuitive mode of the individual; then it evolves (i) through common interpretations shared between the individual and the other members of the group and (ii) through integration of the learning within the group and from the group to the wider organization. The dynamics of the group context are relevant as they affect the outcomes of the integration process.

Furthermore, it is recognized that constant tension exists between the feed-forward (interpreting and integrating) and feedback (institutionalizing and intuiting) processes of learning. The tension between assimilating new learning (feed forward) and using what has already been learned (feedback) arises because the institutionalized learning (what has already been learned) impedes the assimilation of new learning. This tension may explain the inability of many firms to interpret and act on the relevant explicit information and anticipate changes in the external environment. This inability to learn proactively (exploration learning), which is rooted in the organizational inner, contributes to exacerbating the learning myopia induced by the dominant logic of the top management (Prahalad and Bettis, 1986; Levinthal and March, 1993). Although a number of specific interventions at the top management and organizational levels have been suggested, we argue that these might not be effective on their own if they are completely detached from people's actions. It is argued that ultimately it is the individuals – the primary repository of both codified and tacit knowledge (Grant, 1996) – who must embrace exploration learning, undertake new ways of doing things while being prepared to unlearn the past.

In particular, given the social perspective adopted in this chapter, at the group level the team is an ideal context for the social interactions taking place among individuals in the normal work settings. The team represents 'a shared context in which individuals can interact with each other, and engage in the constant dialogue on which reflection depends' (Nonaka, 1991: 104). We argue that the context in which a team operates and the relational dynamics among its members lead to some well-known inefficiencies – project myopia, learning boundaries and knowledge boundaries – which prevent the interpretation and integration of new knowledge within the team and the sharing of new knowledge outside the team boundaries, from team to team and to the wider organization, with the consequence that wider proactive learning at the organizational learning is inhibited. These learning restrictions also limit foresight; although residing in a few organizational pockets (that is, key individuals and special groups), foresight unfolds within a restricted scope, which is mainly determined by the context of the team and the project objectives. The latter tend to be very specific and short-term oriented. In this way, foresight neither filters nor evolves across the organizational boundaries. In order to overcome these barriers, the chapter argues that key actors – middle managers – who are situated at the intersection of the vertical and horizontal flows of information (Nonaka and Takeuchi, 1995) are deemed to play a relevant role with regard to the transmission of learning from team to team and to the organization. Given their position within the organization, middle managers formulate 'process triggers' and create a context for knowledge creation (ibid.). By acting as knowledge seekers, gatekeepers and boundary spanners, middle managers contribute to overcoming the barriers to knowledge sharing both within and outside the group.

Finally, drawing on Janczak's (2004) research findings, it is argued that middle managers contribute to the integration of the knowledge flows and learning by using three different processes – analytical, intuitive and pragmatic – the choice of which depends mostly on how middle managers perceive their activities. For instance, analysts focus on the technical conformity and standardization of the solution (product knowledge); intuitive managers focus on new methods and procedures (procedural knowledge) that would generate satisfaction; and pragmatic managers focus more on the process of change and the utility of their actions to achieve personal recognition instead of the technical quality of their decisions (procedural knowledge). By managing the knowledge flows, middle managers contribute to organizational learning – both exploration and exploitation learning – and the development of new skills and capabilities within their organizations. In doing so, middle managers influence the development of foresight and the way this evolves throughout organizational boundaries. For instance, analysts solve problems by seeking external knowledge and developing their own knowledge and understanding of the problems. Ultimately they contribute to the integration of learning within their own organizations by introducing external knowledge and by standardizing solutions (exploitative learning). Intuitive managers explore their environment for new opportunities and undertake experimental learning, whereby new knowledge for their departments and clients is created through social interactions (explorative learning). Intuitive managers facilitate such interactions during the whole process by promoting collaboration, accepting mistakes and increasing trust among team members. Pragmatic managers adapt existing knowledge to new uses in their departments and clients. Pragmatic managers act as missionaries of knowledge by interacting with a large number of people in order to facilitate the introduction of a new use of the existing knowledge and they achieve learning by debriefing their experiences in order to be prepared for subsequent negotiations (adaptive and experiential learning). We argue that the three process modes are complementary and help the integration of learning both within and outside the team. Thus, middle managers contribute to both the externalization of tacit knowledge and the internalization of explicit knowledge by being analytical, intuitive and pragmatic. The prevalence of one mode over the others will depend on the manager's preferences. Yet, the coexistence of the three mode processes will help to loosen the tension between exploration and exploitation knowledge, thus ensuring that the process of foresight is enriched through the analytical analysis of knowledge and the development.

References

Argyris, C. and D. Schön (1978), *Organizational Learning: A Theory of Action Perspective*, Reading, MA: Addison-Wesley.

Argyris, C. and D.A. Schön (1996), *Organizational Learning*, Reading, MA: Addison-Wesley.

Asllani, A. and F. Luthans (2003), 'What knowledge managers really do: an empirical and comparative analysis', *Journal of Knowledge Management*, **7** (3), 53–66.

Bettis, R.A. and C.K. Prahalad (1995), 'The dominant logic: retrospective and extension', *Strategic Management Journal*, **16**, 5–14.

Boland, R.J. and R.V. Tenkasi (1995), 'Perspective making and perspective taking in communities of knowing', *Organization Science*, **6** (4), 350–72.

Brown, J.S. and P. Duguid (2001), 'Knowledge and organization: a social practice perspective', *Organization Science*, **12**, 198–213.

Brown, S.L. and K.M. Eisenhardt (1997), 'The art of continuous change: linking complexity theory and time-paced evolution in relentlessly shifting organizations', *Administrative Science Quarterly*, **42**, 1–34.

Burke, R.J. and C.L. Cooper (eds) (2000), *The Organization in Crisis: Downsizing, Restructuring, and Privatization*, Oxford: Blackwell.

Carlile, P.R. (2002), 'A pragmatic view of knowledge and boundaries: boundary objects in new product development', *Organization Science*, **13** (4), 442–55.

Castells, M. (2000), *The Rise of the Network Society*, 2nd edn, Oxford: Blackwell.

Child, J. and R.G. McGrath (2001), 'Organizations unfettered: organization form in an information-intensive economy', *Academy of Management Journal*, **44** (6), 1135–48.

Christensen, C.M. (1997), *The Innovator's Dilemma: When New Technologies Cause Great Firms to Fail*, Boston, MA: Harvard Business School Press.

Christensen, C., R. Bohmer and J. Kenagy (2000), 'Will disruptive innovations cure health care?', *Harvard Business Review*, 102–12.

Claydon, T. and M. Doyle (1996), 'Trusting me, trusting you: the ethics of employee empowerment', *Personnel Review*, **25** (6), 13–25.

Cohen, W. and D. Levinthal (1990), 'Absorptive capacity: a new perspective on learning and innovation', *Administration Science Quarterly*, **35** (1), 128–52.

Contu, Alessia and Hugh Willmott (2003), 'Re-embedding situatedness: the importance of power relations in learning theory', *Organization Science*, **14** (3), 283–96.

Costanzo, L.A. (2004), 'Strategic foresight in a high-speed environment', *Futures*, **36**, 219–35.

Crossan, Mary M. and Iris Bedrow (2003), 'Organisational learning and strategic renewal', *Strategic Management Journal*, **24** (11), 1087–105.

Crossan, M.M., H.W. Lane and R.E. White (1999), 'An organizational learning framework: from intuition to institution', *Academy of Management Review*, **24** (3), 522–37.
Cycert, R.M. and J.G. March (1963), *A Behavioral Theory of the Firm*, Englewood Cliffs, NJ: Prentice Hall.
Davenport, T.H. and L. Prusak (2000), *Working Knowledge: How Organizations Manage What They Know*, Boston, MA: Harvard Business School Press.
Dibella, Anthony J., Edwin C. Nevis and Janet M. Gould (1996), 'Understanding organizational learning capability', *Journal of Management Studies*, **33** (3), 361–79.
Dickson, J. (1977), 'Plight of the middle manager', *Management Today*, 66–9.
Dodgson, M. (1991), 'Technology, learning, technology strategy and competitive presssures', *British Journal of Management*, **2/3**, 132–49.
Dopson, S., A. Risk and R. Stewart (1992), 'The changing role of the middle manager in the United Kingdom', *International Studies of Management and Organization*, **22** (1), 42–53.
Dopson, S. and R. Stewart (1990), 'What is happening to middle management?', *British Journal of Management*, **1**, 3–16.
Easterby-Smith, M., J. Burgoyne and L. Araujo (eds) (1999), *Organizational Learning and the Learning Organization*, London: Sage.
Fiol, C.M. (1994), 'Consensus, diversity, and learning in organizations', *Organization Science*, **5** (3), 403–20.
Fiol, C.M. and M. Lyles (1985), 'Organizational learning', *Academy of Management Review*, **10** (4), 803–13.
Fletcher, C. (1973), 'The end of management', in J. Child (ed.), *Man and Organization: The Search for Explanation and Social Relevance*, London: Allen & Unwin, pp. 135–57.
Floyd, S.W. and B. Wooldridge (1994), 'Dinosaurs or dynamos? Recognizing middle management's strategic role', *Academy of Management Executive*, **8** (4), 47–57.
Garrick, J. and S. Clegg (2001), 'Stressed-out knowledge workers in performative times: a postmodern take on project-based learning', *Management Learning*, **21** (1), 119–35.
Gold, A.H., A. Malhorta and A.H. Segars (2001), 'Knowledge management: an organizational capabilities perspective', *Journal of Management Information Systems*, **18** (1), 185–214.
Gouldner, A. (1960), 'The norm of reciprocity: a preliminary statement', *American Sociological Review*, **25**, 161–78.
Grant, R.M. (1996), 'Toward a knowledge-based theory of the firm', *Journal of Strategic Management*, **17**, 109–22.
Hales, C. (2006), 'Moving down the line: the shifting boundary between middle and first-line management', *Journal of General Management*, **32** (2), 31–55.
Hamel, H. and C.K. Prahalad (1994), *Competing for the Future*, Boston, MA: Harvard Business School Press.
Hayward, Mathew L.A. (2002), 'When do firms learn from their acquisition experience? Evidence from 1990–1995', *Strategic Management Journal*, **23** (1), 21–39.
Heckscher, C. (1995), *White Collar Blues Blues: Management Loyalties in an Age of Corporate Restructuring*, New York: Basic Books.
Huang, J.C. and S. Newell (2003), 'Knowledge integration processes and dynamics within the context of cross-functional projects', *International Journal of Project Management*, **21** (3), 167–76.
Huber, G.P. (1991), 'Organizational learning: the contributing processes and the literatures', *Organization Science*, **2** (1), 88–115.
Hurst, D.K. and B.J. Zimmerman (1994), 'From life cycle to eco-cycle: a new perspective on the growth, maturity, destruction, and renewal of complex systems', *Journal of Management Inquiry*, **3** (4), 339.
Huy, Q.N. (2001), 'In praise of middle managers', *Harvard Business Review*, **79** (8), 72–9.
Janczak, S. (2004), 'How middle managers integrate knowledge within projects', *Knowledge and Process Management*, **11** (3), 210–24.
Jones, O. (2006), 'Developing absorptive capacity in mature organizations: the change agent's role', *Management Learning*, **37** (3), 355–76.
Kalleberg, A. (2001), 'Organizing flexibility: the flexible firm in a new century', *British Journal of Industrial Relations*, **39** (4), 479–504.
Kim, W.C. and R. Mauborgne (1999), 'Strategy, value innovation, and the knowledge economy', *Sloan Management Review*, **40**, 41–54.
Klagge, J. (1998), 'Self-perceived development needs of today's middle managers', *Journal of Management Development*, **17** (7), 481–91.
Kogut, Bruce and Udo Zander (1996), 'Knowledge and the speed of the transfer and imitation of organizational capabilities: an empirical test', *Organization Science*, **6** (1), 76–92.
Kolb, D.A. (1984), *Experiential Learning*, Englewood Cliffs, NJ: Prentice-Hall.
Lave, J. and E. Wenger (1991), *Situated Learning: Legitimate Peripheral Participation*, Cambridge: Cambridge University Press.
Leonard-Barton, D. (1995), *Wellsprings of Knowledge: Building and Sustaining the Sources of Innovation*, Boston, MA: Harvard Business School Press.

Levinthal, D.A. and J.G. March (1993), 'The myopia of learning', *Strategic Management Journal*, **14**, 95–112.
Livian, Y.-F. (1997), *Middle Managers in Europe*, London: Routledge.
March, J.G. (1991), 'Exploration and exploitation in organizational learning', *Organization Science*, **2** (1), 71–87.
Miller, D. (1987), 'The genesis of configuration', *Academy of Management Review*, **12** (4), 686–701.
Mintzbert, H. (1994), 'Rounding out the manager's job', *Sloan Management Review*, Fall, 11–26.
Mirghany, M., M. Stankosky and A. Murray (2004), 'Applying knowledge management principles to enhance cross-functional team performance', *Journal of Knowledge Management*, **8** (3), 127–42.
Nahapiet, J. and S. Ghoshal (1998), 'Social capital, intellectual capital, and the organizational advantage', *Academy of Management Review*, **23**, 242–66.
Neale, C. and D. Homes (1990), 'Post-auditing capital projects', *Long Range Planning*, **23** (40), 88–96.
Newell, S. (2004), 'Enhancing cross-project learning', *Engineering Management Journal*, **16** (1), 12–20.
Newell, S. (2005), 'Knowledge transfer and learning: problems of knowledge transfer associated with trying to short-circuit the learning cycle', *Journal of Information Systems and Technology Management*, **2** (3), 275–90.
Nicolini, D. and M. Meznar (1995), 'The social construction of organizational learning: conceptual and practical issues in the field', *Human Relations*, **48**, 727–46.
Nonaka, I. (1991), 'The knowledge-creating company', *Harvard Business Review*, **69**, 96–104.
Nonaka, I. and H. Takeuchi (1995), '*The Knowledge-Creating Company: How Japanese Companies Create the Dynamics of Innovation*, Oxford and New York: Oxford University Press.
Nonaka, I. and H. Takeuchi (1996), *The Knowledge-Creating Company*, 2nd edition, Oxford: Oxford University Press.
O'Reilly III, C.A. and M.L. Tushman (2004), 'The ambidextrous organization', *Harvard Business Review*, **82**, 74–81.
Pawoloski, S. and D. Robey (2004), 'Bridging user organizations: knowledge brokering and the role of IT professionals', *Management Information Systems Quarterly*, **28** (4), 645–73.
Pinsonnealut, A. and K.L. Kraemer (1993), 'The impact of information technology on middle managers', *Management Information Systems Quarterly*, **17**, 271–90.
Polanyi, M. (1996), *The Tacit Dimension of Knowledge*, London: Routledge & Kegan Paul.
Prahalad, C.K. and R.A. Bettis (1986), 'The dominant logic: a new linkage between diversity and performance', *Strategic Management Journal*, **7**, 485–501.
Rindova, V.P. and S. Kotha (2001), 'Continuous morphing: competing through dynamic capabilities, form and function', *Academy of Management Journal*, **44**, 1263–80.
Scarbrough, H., J. Swan, S.P. Laurent, M. Bresnen, L. Edelman and S. Newell (2004), 'Project-based learning and the role of learning boundaries', *Organization Studies*, **25** (9), 1579–600.
Scase, R. and R. Goffee (1989), *Reluctant Managers: Their Work and Lifestyles*, London: Unwin Hyman.
Schaafsma, H. (1997), 'A networking model of change for middle managers', *Leadership and Organization Development Journal*, **18** (1), 41–9.
Schön, D.A. (1983), *How Professionals Think in Action*, New York: Temple Smith.
Schön, D. (1987), *Educating the Reflective Practitioner*, San Francisco, CA: Jossey-Bass.
Senge, P. (1990), 'The fifth discipline: the art and practice of the learning organization', in *The Knowledge-Creating Company*, Oxford: Oxford University Press, p. 413.
Sethi, D. (1999), 'Leading from the middle', *Human Resource Planning*, **22** (3), 9–10.
Skagen, A. (1992), 'The incredible shrinking organization: what does it mean for middle managers?', *Supervisory Management*, **37**, 1–3.
Spicer, A., G. McDermott and B. Kogut (2000), 'Entrepreneurship and privatization in Central Europe: the tenuous balance between destruction and creation', *Academy of Management Review*, **25**, 630–49.
Teece, D.J., G. Pisano and A. Shuen (1997), 'Dynamic capabilities and strategic management', *Strategic Management Journal*, **18**, 509–33.
Tsai, W. and S. Ghoshal (1998), 'Social capital and value creation: the role of intra-firm networks', *Academy of Management Journal*, **41** (4), 464–76.
Tsoukas, H. (1996), 'The firm as a distributed knowledge system: a constructionist approach', *Strategic Management Journal*, **17**, 11–25.
Van de Ven, A.H. and D. Polley (1992), 'Learning while innovating', *Organization Science*, **3** (1), 92–116.
Vaughan, D. (1997), 'The trickle-down effect: policy decisions, risky work, and the *Challenger* tragedy', *California Management Review*, **39** (2), 80–102.
Wai-Kwong, F.Y., R.L. Priem and C.S. Cycyota (2001), 'The performance effects of human resource managers' and other middle managers' involvement in strategy making under different business-level strategies: the case in Hong Kong', *International Journal of Human Resource Management*, **12** (8), 1325–46.
Weiss, H.M. (1990), 'Learning theory and industrial and organizational psychology', in M.D. Dunnette and L.M. Hough (eds), *Handbook of Industrial and Organizational Psychology*, Consulting Psychologists Press.

Wenger, E. (1998), *Communities of Practice*: *Learning, Meaning and Identity*, Cambridge: Cambridge University Press.
Zahra, S.A. and G. George (2002), 'Absorptive capacity: a review, reconceptualization, and extension', *Academy of Management Review*, **27** (2), 185–203.
Zahra, S.A., D.R. Ireland, I. Gutierrez and M.A. Hitt (2000), 'Privatization and entrepreneurial transformation: emerging issues and a future research agenda', *Academy of Management Review*, **25**, 509–24.

17 Hollow at the top: (re)claiming the responsibilities of leadership in strategizing

C. Marlene Fiol and Edward J. O'Connor

Introduction

Leaders in charge of their organization's strategy face turbulent times that seem to demand more than they can deliver. Forecasts seem pretty useless as a basis for strategic decisions. The business landscape is changing too rapidly for leaders to keep their fingers on the pulse of what is happening in their markets. It is hardly surprising that strategizing has shifted in the past several decades from formal top-down strategic planning either to (i) more emergent bottom-up strategy making, which derives from decisions made by line managers (Grant 2003), or even more extreme, to (ii) the pursuit of whatever fleeting opportunities arise, with virtually no centralized oversight (Eisenhardt and Sull 2001).

On the face of it, the shift from centralized strategizing to emergent opportunity seizing makes sense in a volatile world of uncertainty and turbulence.[1] The emergent and less formal processes of largely bottom-up decision making may foster greater adaptability to market forces in ways not possible in more formal top-down processes. And the freedom for line managers to pursue opportunities that lie before them may foster pockets of great innovativeness. But what are organizations sacrificing in order to gain greater adaptability and pockets of innovation?

This chapter presents the argument that in the process of shifting the strategizing functions down to line management or even largely eliminating them, many leaders have abdicated what we shall argue are their most basic responsibilities, to (i) ignite organization-wide passion for innovation, and (ii) provide focus in the form of an overarching definition of 'who we are' and 'who we want to be' as an organization. These two responsibilities fall squarely on the shoulders of a company's leadership. And when they are ignored, no amount of opportunity-seizing is likely to lead to sustainable success.

Organizations are not made up of structures and functions. They are not even made up of their products and services. Organizations are groups of people. And while the business environment seems to be marked by increasing turbulence, the dynamics of human beings in groups are not that different from what they have always been: a *passion* for innovation and winning gets people moving and *focus* gets them moving in a similar direction.

The chapter builds on three basic premises. The first premise is that organizational innovation is a requirement for survival and competitiveness, and thus should be at the core of an organization's strategizing. We agree with Hamel (2000), who noted that innovation is the defining competitive advantage of the twenty-first century. Following prior researchers, we define organizational innovation as a process that involves changes in an organization's competencies (Mezias and Glynn 1993) and cognitive paradigms (Anderson and Tushman 1990). Sporadic pockets of innovation, though they may create short and isolated bursts of new activity, do not lead to organization-wide innovation without the integration of the new insights into the rest of the firm's activities. Huber

(2004) pointed to the challenge of producing such integration, given the rate of increase in knowledge and specialization in organizations, and described the structures and processes needed to support integration efforts. Although structures and processes are critical for new knowledge integration within a firm, our second premise is that structures and processes will have little impact, unless and until the firm's leadership instills a focus around which to integrate the disparate efforts. Collins (2001, p. 95) referred to such a focus as a 'hedgehog' concept, 'a simple crystalline concept that guides all their efforts'. These two premises as they relate to each other, lead to our third premise: innovation without focus is likely to lead to the organization spinning out of control; and focus without innovation is likely to lead to destructive rigidities.

We begin with a brief history of what strategizing has looked like over time, from highly formal strategic planning processes in the 1960s and 1970s, to more emergent bottom-up decision making in the late 1980s and into the 1990s, and finally to the most recent trend of 'managing on the edge', which replaces strategizing as we have known it with unplanned pursuits of fleeting opportunities as they arise. The purpose of reviewing the different phases of strategizing is to examine whether and how each of the phases has managed to drive passion for innovation and focus down throughout the organization.

To foreshadow our arguments, we shall describe the strategizing phases as a progression from centralized top management owning the process to a completely decentralized process today in which leadership in many organizations is only minimally involved. We identify the 'hollowness at the top' that has been created by the shift from formal top-down planning to emerging bottom-up decision making, and ultimately to the encouragement of 'designed chaos'. To inject organization-wide innovation into the planning process, leaders must (re)claim their responsibilities as primary facilitators for determining and communicating the company's passion for innovation and its focus.

Three phases of strategizing

Phase 1: formal top-down strategizing
Early strategic planning efforts grew out of the need to control the increasing number of large and diversified companies in the 1950s and 1960s. As businesses grew too large and too diverse to manage as a whole, strategic planning processes were decomposed into categories of specific steps and formalized procedures. The primary task of early planning departments was to forecast business trends and make predictions about the future, to prepare for the inevitable, to pre-empt the undesirable, and to control the controllable (Starr 1971, p. 315). The role and formality of planning departments grew significantly in the 1970s and early 1980s largely based on the assumption that the planning activities (forecasting trends, establishing goals, generating alternative strategies, and managing the annual strategic planning cycle) would allow these organizations to outperform firms that were not similarly engaged in planning.

Did these strategic planning efforts really pay off? Hofer (1976, p. 262) summarized it well when he stated,

> For a substantial time, those involved in the strategic planning area have had to accept as a tenet of faith the belief that strategic planning was indeed worthwhile. This belief was justified with the theoretical arguments of Ansoff and others, but there was not research evidence to provide support for these beliefs.

In the subsequent decades, numerous studies examined the impact of planning on firm performance. Overall, the findings suggested that the effect of planning on performance was, in fact, very weak (Ramanujam et al. 1986; Boyd 1991). Collins (2001) similarly found no evidence that the 'great' companies in his sample spent any more time on strategic planning than the less successful comparison companies.

Mintzberg (1994) argued that formal strategic planning was in decline and would further decline because of a number of 'fallacies': the fallacy that one can predict, the fallacy of the detachment of planners from real business issues, and the fallacy that formalized systems can detect discontinuities and provide creativity. He suggested, in fact, that the term 'strategic planning' is an oxymoron (p. 321) because 'no amount of elaboration will ever enable formal procedures to forecast discontinuities, to inform managers who are detached from their operations, to create novel strategies'.

Of course, these formal planning systems were not developed primarily for the purpose of stimulating novel strategies. Companies were growing so rapidly and diversifying so widely that focus and stability, not innovation, were the desired outcomes. As the environment became less munificent and the need for change and innovation more apparent during the 1990s, so also did the pitfalls of formal planning become more obvious.

Phase 2: emergent bottom-up strategizing
An interesting pattern emerged around the time of Mintzberg's (1994) prediction of the demise of strategic planning. Formal strategic planning techniques (for example, Porter-type industry analysis, SWOT, PIMS) continued to be some of the most widely used of any management tools throughout the 1990s (Rigby 1999). However, the techniques were being applied differently from the highly formal top-down processes of the 1960s and 1970s. In 1996, *Business Week* ran an article stating that 'strategic planning is back with a vengeance . . . but with a difference' (p. 46). The planning tools were being applied by line management with far less centralized involvement. To cope with the increasing unpredictability of the environment, planning efforts became more emergent and incremental. Top managers were less concerned with prediction and formal analysis, and more concerned with providing an overarching framework, often in the form of financial performance targets, that could accommodate and guide flexible short-term actions. Strategic planning techniques remained popular, but top managers were less involved with them.

As an example, Grant (2003), in an in-depth study of eight of the world's largest oil companies, found that planners in the 1990s were turning away from attempting to make forecasts or even specific strategic decisions. He found that strategic decisions were increasingly being made by line managers in response to threats and opportunities they experienced, rather than by central planners, and the role of top management had to do with coordination, primarily through an increased emphasis on company-wide financial performance goals. As the process shifted from staff to line managers and emphasized meeting the financial targets, planning efforts became more focused on short-term goals. The author also found that the companies became less innovative during this time (ibid., p. 514). Although there seemed to be greater flexibility and freedom to adapt to local conditions, there were few mechanisms in place to foster focused organization-wide innovation.

So at the end of the twentieth century, traditional formal planning mechanisms were still in use, but they were increasingly used by lower-level line managers as a way to manage their slice of the overall organization. This certainly allowed for more adaptive activity at lower levels of the organization. However, given the decreased centralized oversight of this process by top management, it is hardly surprising that Grant found that these decentralized processes were associated with less organization-wide innovation.

Phase 3: seizing fleeting opportunities
There was again considerable discontent with the form of strategizing in the late twentieth century (Mintzberg and Lampel 1999). None of the old models appeared to be working. Bill Ford recently sent an e-mail to all of Ford Motor's employees saying, 'The business model that sustained us for decades is no longer sufficient to sustain profitability' (Taylor 2006, p. 78). It seems that most people today agree that many of the old ways of doing business no longer work, that radical changes are on the horizon, and that they are likely to require new forms of strategizing.

In the face of great uncertainty about how to strategize in today's world, we seem to have opted for letting go at the top, allowing people to figure things out as they go, and letting people 'do their own thing'. Google is held up as a model of this approach (ibid., p. 94). In fact, Eisenhardt and Sull (2001) argued for strategy as 'simple rules'. They contrasted positioning strategies that are concerned with the question 'Where should we be?' and resource-based strategies that are concerned with 'What should we be?', with their recommended simple-rules strategy, concerned with 'How should we proceed?'.

In the strategy-as-simple-rules view, advantage comes from seizing fleeting opportunities. Other than a few simple rules, people are given the freedom to capture opportunities as they arise. The rules that Eisenhardt and Sull described are not broad guiding principles, but rather concrete policies such as Cisco's early acquisitions rule that companies to be acquired had to have no more than 75 employees, 75 percent of whom had to be engineers; or Enron's two simple rules that all trades needed to be balanced with an offsetting trade to minimize unhedged risk, and each trader needed to report a daily profit-and-loss statement. If they followed those two simple rules, Enron's traders were free to pursue whatever opportunities lay before them! Eisenhardt and Sull touted Enron as being a role model of the simple-rules approach to strategizing: 'Few companies have followed the logic of opportunity or the discipline of simple rules as consistently as Enron' (p. 114). While these cases have been held up as positive exemplars of a simple-rules approach, evidence we discuss later calls this into question.

Eisenhardt and Sull recommended a simple-rules approach to strategizing, not only for small start-up organizations, but for large and small, young and old. Others have jumped on the same bandwagon. A high-level executive at Hewlett-Packard recently stated, 'In a big company the reality in your strategy is the way you spend your dollars every day' (Gary 2002, p. 4), thereby confounding what traditionally has been considered a manifestation of strategy (how money is spent) with the strategy itself! And in October of 2006, *Fortune* published an entire issue of its magazine devoted to the topic of 'managing on the edge', a form of strategizing that not only allows, but actually encourages, chaos to rule.

Table 17.1 depicts the three phases of strategizing and our summary of the capacity in each phase for generating a passion for organization-wide innovation and focus. The formal top-down planning processes of Phase 1, with highly formalized and comprehensive plans focused on forecasting and predicting, led to high levels of focus with only

Table 17.1 Passion for innovation and focus in three phases of strategizing

	Passion for innovation	Focus
Phase 1	*Moderate* Focus on forecasting and predicting	*High* Highly formalized and comprehensive plans
Phase 2	*Low* Financial performance targets	*Moderate* Numerous emerging initiatives
Phase 3	*High* Pockets of opportunity seizing	*Low* Pursuit of fleeting opportunities

moderate innovation. The emergent bottom-up processes of Phase 2 generated numerous emerging initiatives from lower levels of organizations, with a decrease in overall organizational innovation. Finally, strategizing in Phase 3 is increasingly about seizing pockets of opportunity, producing pockets of innovation with little focus to hold them together.

What becomes immediately apparent is that as forms of strategizing have allowed for more innovative activity at lower levels of the organization (in Phase 3), they have also produced less focus. Of course, those arguing for the benefits of 'managing on the edge', would likely suggest that this is as it should be. In the 1960s there was greater need for focus; today there is greater need for adaptability and innovativeness. We argue, by contrast, that it has left many of our organizations hollow at the top, with little to no possibility for sustained organization-wide innovation.

Hollow at the top
It is true that focusing on short-term efficiency and adaptability can often placate stakeholders in the short run. The financial numbers receive an artificial bump by minimizing the time and dollar investments to build the foundation required for future success. Initial savings flow to the bottom line and leaders can avoid difficult strategic questions about defining who they are at the core, and building a passionate case for innovation. But without clear answers to these demanding questions, senior leaders have no consistent basis for providing their people with the clarity required to turn a disorganized mob into a passionate and innovative organization. What becomes lost in the shift to more emergent bottom-up strategizing or letting chaos rule is systematic leadership involvement in defining and redefining the organization of the future. What also becomes lost is the focus to harness creative efforts in order to foster organization-wide innovation. Innovativeness without focus may be as suicidal as focus without innovation.

Both Cisco and Enron, held up as exemplars of the effectiveness of the simple-rules approach (Eisenhardt and Sull 2001), actually also serve as exemplars of the potential downsides of this approach. The press after Enron's demise pointed out that Enron's CEOs, Jeff Skilling and Ken Lay, fudged the company's numbers to keep Wall Street happy and to hide Enron's problems. CNN reported that Lay foolishly engaged in public denial, continuing to the end to insist that all was well, and hoping that this would make it so (McLean and Elkind 2006). This is an extreme example of leadership abdication of responsibility, to be sure, but an example not inconsistent with the company's history based on simple rules and a leadership void.

Cisco's operations also spun out of control shortly after being held up as a company successfully following a strategy of simple rules. For a few weeks in the spring of 2000 investors believed CEO Chambers's hype that Cisco was the model for what a Net-based corporation should look like, and for those few weeks they made Cisco the most valuable company on the planet – worth even more than GE, which had six times Cisco's revenues. When Cisco's bubble burst shortly thereafter, Chambers had to axe nearly 10,000 employees, write off $2.5 billion in inventory, and significantly restructure the company (Vogelstein 2002).

And Google, held up as the great example of a company that is 'managing on the edge', supposedly thriving on disorder, disarray, and uncertainty (Lashinsky 2006), has yet to stand the test of time. The company is currently eight years old, and according to analysts, its new products have not made nearly the splash that its original search engine did. Can the company keep from imploding without a guiding compass at the top?

When there is a void at the top, and when strategy making is left to those on the front lines, short-term adaptability and pockets of innovation are certainly likely. For six years running, *Fortune* called Enron the most innovative company in corporate America. But with no focusing energy at the top, such pockets of innovation will almost inevitably spin out of control.

Filling the void

In the process of pushing decision making down to lower levels, many of our organizations have become hollow at the top. Because forecasting and prediction (the early primary functions of strategizing) are close to impossible, many organizational leaders have essentially stepped back to simply allow their people to seize whatever opportunities they perceive amidst the uncertainty and chaos that many of them face.

We do not suggest that filling the void that has resulted should entail going back to traditional roles of formal planning. It cannot. The formal tools for forecasting and predicting the future were never very useful, and would be less so today.

We argue that there should be much less focus on whether or not planning is formal or informal, and much more focus on developing a meaningful guiding frame from the top down, within which those strategic decisions are made. This means that boards and other oversight bodies must ensure that leaders are in place who are willing and capable to make the tough choices about 'who we are' as an organization and 'who we want to be'. Rather than having a reduced role in strategizing due to perceived environmental turbulence, leaders should have a significantly enhanced role.

The following sections delineate some of the ways that leaders can begin to re-fill the void at the top in order to refocus their organizations on sustainable innovation: (i) leaders must engage in the hard work of ensuring that the company's values and vision actually designate the fundamental identity of the organization and the dream it has of its future; (ii) the strategic focus that derives from this set of identity filters must simultaneously harness and unleash organization-wide passion for innovation; and (iii) opportunities (even if fleeting) are evaluated through this same set of identity filters, and accurate situational assessments become secondary to moving toward the articulated dream.

Making the vision and values really mean something

As strategizing became an increasingly emergent and bottom-up process in the late twentieth century, the primary role of top management was seen as the coordination of the flexible short-term actions at lower levels, by providing an overarching framework and the performance criteria that needed to be met (Grant 2003). Not surprisingly, this led to the rise in importance of statements of mission and vision that would provide a guiding framework for the emergent planning processes. Collins and Porras's book, *Built to Last*, published in 1994, was a timely part of that conversation. It argued that many of the best companies adhered to a set of guiding principles, which the authors referred to as 'core values and purpose'. A values fad subsequently swept through the business world. In fact, by the turn of the century, at least 80 percent of the *Fortune 100* companies were touting their values publicly – 'values that too often stand for nothing but a desire to be *au courant* or worse still, politically correct' (Lencioni 2002, p. 114). In our own work with healthcare organizations in the United States, we often see that many of them have meaningless statements to fill in their 'vision boxes'. Typically, these are not able to provide the tangible, specific, sensory descriptions of the way the world will be at a future point in time. For many organizations, then, the new fad provided an easy way for leaders to lay out politically correct value and vision statements and then hide behind them. It is not surprising that most of the organizations' vision and values statements were not at all or, at best, only loosely linked to their strategizing.

When a company's vision and core values mean something, they are integrated into every decision that is made, no matter where in the organization. They serve as an essential compass that guides all actions and can never be compromised. They mark the essential identity of the organization and the dream of what it can become. In a world where more and more of the strategizing is emerging informally in a bottom-up fashion, it is critical that values actually mean something and that a vision of the future guides all of the activities throughout the organization.

Defining the essential nature of an organization by engaging in a serious effort to develop its core values and a vision of the future requires courage and confidence on the part of an organization's leaders. And sticking to them when emerging opportunities appear to conflict with them requires even more courage. So rather than representing a form of leadership evasion or abdication, this leadership task, if taken seriously, may be one of the most important and challenging of any activity of leaders today.

Igniting passion for innovation throughout the organization
In the absence of top-down strategizing, and in the absence of a set of meaningful values and a vision, the glue that is used to hold a company together may be the financial performance targets set by top management, as was the case in the oil companies of Grant's (2003) study. The financial targets can undoubtedly help line managers focus on keeping score of existing advantages and on becoming ever more efficient at the game they are playing. Such targets can also provide a neat and tidy apparent 'recipe for success' that top managers can uphold (hide behind?) even in the face of industry turmoil and uncertainties. Hamel and Prahalad (1989) suggested that attempting to motivate the workforce with financial targets represents a conservatism and caution that reflects a lack of confidence in leadership's own ability to involve the entire organization in revitalization. Instead of heeding Hamel and Prahalad's advice, the trend in business has continued toward top managers hiding behind the numbers that indicate whether the organization is winning in its current game, and at least in some cases, revitalization has suffered (Grant 2003).

Financial metrics such as ROI (return on investment) are clearly essential to the survival of any business. However, their power for motivating innovation throughout the organization is close to zero. In fact, they are most likely to motivate tremendous fear of innovation. If, as a line manager, I am rewarded solely on the basis of my unit's performance against financial targets set by top management, I will focus on improving those financial ratios by reducing investments and cutting costs. Quick adaptation to a downturn, for example, may occur rather effectively under these conditions, but innovation is not a likely outcome of this recipe.

Although small pockets of innovation can certainly emerge as a result of today's 'managing on the edge' approach, true organization-wide revitalization can occur only if top management gets involved in pulling together the efforts of many. Hamel and Prahalad (1989) suggested that this may be accomplished by focusing the organization's attention on the essence of winning, an obsession they termed a 'strategic intent'. Regardless of what the obsession is called, the important point is that it ignites the passion of people to engage in creating something new and deeply meaningful to them, and it does so in a way that supports the organization-wide dream of 'who we can become'. This is the path to true organization-wide innovation.

Maintaining the lifeline between a company's focal strategic intent and its fundamental values and vision for the future in order to harness and focus the organization's innovative activities, while at the same time knowing when and how the intent may need to shift over time, again requires leadership wisdom and courage. Danny Miller (1993) persuasively argued that a seductive trap that faces outstanding companies is that the focus (produced, for example, with a well-defined strategic intent) that was responsible for their success, ultimately also gets them into trouble. He described the analogy of the brave Icarus of Greek mythology, whose father gave him a pair of wax wings. Icarus flew so high and so close to the sun, that his wings melted and he plunged to his death. The same wings that allowed him to soar to unprecedented heights also led to his downfall. In a similar vein, Miller pointed out that in many companies the ultimate cause of their failure is what was once the source of their greatest success. The difference between the simplicity required for unleashing creative passion and the simplicity that leads to failure is often not obvious. Leaders must preserve complexity in their own thinking, even while providing a focused strategic intent for their organization, a challenge we discuss in the following section.

Paying more attention to one's dream than to the accuracy of situational assessments
The inability in today's rapidly changing world to be able to systematically assess the environment and to make accurate predictions is a theme that runs through much of the writing that questions the usefulness of top-down strategizing (Mintzberg 1994; Eisenhardt and Sull 2001). We believe that accuracy of predictions is an overrated concept. In an empirical investigation of the extent to which executives were accurate in noticing particular attributes of their environments, Sutcliffe (1994, p. 1374) found that accurate perceptions actually explained very little of the variance in her study. She conjectured that inaccurate perceptions 'may lead to positive consequences . . . if they enable managers to overcome inertial tendencies and propel them to pursue goals that might look unattainable in environments assessed in utter objectivity'. How true! This is similar to Karl Weick's point that good outcomes can result from a flawed map, because

even a flawed map can get people to move, to learn, and to progress and grow (Quinn 1996). From this perspective, foresight is an evolving process that derives from continuous learning and unlearning.

The same is often true regarding internal assessments of a company's strengths and weaknesses. Porter (1980) provided long lists of generic strengths and weaknesses from which planners can choose in order to build a profile of their firm's strengths and weaknesses. Although it is important to know one's capabilities before attempting to implement a strategy, beginning the strategy-making process with an analysis of a company's strengths and weaknesses is backward looking and will inevitably constrain the process. Almost 20 years ago, Hamel and Prahalad (1989, p. 76) exhorted top managers for 'lacking the courage to commit their companies to heroic goals . . . that lay beyond existing resources'. Their exhortation remains as relevant today as it was then.

It is only with a clear sense of 'who we are' and 'who we can become' that it makes sense to engage in a process of grounding the desired dream of the future in the mindfully assessed realities of the internal and external environment. As early as 1976, Stevenson noted that an appraisal of an organization's capabilities is only valuable in relation to a specific strategic undertaking. Otherwise, most of the data are probably irrelevant and a colossal waste of time. It is little wonder that it is often nearly impossible to get organizational members to agree about their organization's strengths and weaknesses (Marino 1996). Once there is clarity about the organization's focus, agreement about capabilities is much more likely.

Too often external and internal assessments are done in a rote form that relies more on everything that everyone else is doing than on one's own dream and unique requirements. Rather than do the hard work required to assess and courageously act on internal and external realities based on the organization's unique vision of the future, many leaders fall back on tried and trusted recipes as they follow industry fads, assuming that it is a safer way to face the unknown. Is it not actually safer in today's rapidly changing world to allow the strategizing process to be biased by one's own dream, rather than by everyone else's perceptions based on historical data?

We agree with Sutcliffe (1994) that overcoming inertial tendencies when assessing the environment may be more important than accuracy. This relates to the point we made earlier about the need for leaders to preserve the complexity of their own thinking, even while honing the organization's focus. Research has argued that jolts are needed for an organization to overcome strategic inertia, the habitual reliance on a previous organizational recipe for success (Wright 2001). The same is true of the top management team. Henderson et al. (2006), in their interesting longitudinal study of 98 CEOs in the relatively stable branded foods industry and 228 CEOs in the highly dynamic computer industry, found that firm-level performance improved steadily with 10–15-year CEO tenure in the more stable industry. However, in the more dynamic computer industry, firm performance declined steadily after the first year across the CEOs' tenures, presumably as their recipes for success grew obsolete more quickly than they could learn new ones. The implication is that strategists must periodically engage – at the top – in challenging their largely taken-for-granted assumptions about their own organization and the environment in which they operate.

The inclusion of outsiders in the process of assessing both internal and external realities increases the chances that frames of references will be updated more regularly. For example, physicians and administrators in most US hospitals have long been engaged in a battle of wills over appropriate priorities and approaches in running health systems. We found it not at all surprising that a recent study (Goldstein and Ward 2004) found that physician involvement in specifying the hospital's strategy (along with hospital administrators) was positively significantly related to both hospital occupancy rates and market share. Although familiarity with a situation generally leads to greater sensitivity to existing conditions, the lack of familiarity of outsiders can help in sensitizing executives to new and different stimuli. Outsiders' views may thus help executives develop foresight by updating their frames of reference, thereby generating greater openness to seeing new and changing realities.

Discussion

One of the pictures that emerges from our discussion of strategizing over the last several decades, is of an increasingly fearful and retreating leadership that is abdicating responsibilities for the very essence of what it must provide the organization. In the face of great uncertainty, the response too often is to follow the latest fad (as in the case of vision and values developing as mere copy-cat window dressing) and hope that it takes care of the problem. This is tantamount to surrendering the future of the organization to the whims of others, who are typically themselves following someone else's 'good idea'. This is the antithesis of foresight!

Another picture that emerges is one of confusing reactive adaptability with organization-wide innovation. The Merriam-Webster dictionary defines innovation as the 'introduction of something new' and adaptation as 'adjustment to environmental conditions'. The former is proactive; the latter reactive. When strategy making is about identifying changes and adapting to them, it is fundamentally a reactive activity. Adaptation is focused on the past, in that it involves adjusting to something that has already occurred. Although adaptability is likely to result from the emergent bottom-up planning processes as they are now implemented, sustained innovativeness is not a likely outcome. In today's rapidly changing world, can organizations afford to be focused on yesterday?

The fundamental planning dilemma has long been the need for both adaptability and stability (Lorange et al. 1979). Planning tends to emphasize stability over adaptability (Mintzberg 1994, p. 184), which is why less formal emergent strategic decision making is more and more common in a world that requires increasing adaptability. But in the intense debate about stability versus adaptability, organization-wide innovation has been largely overlooked. We have thrown out the baby with the bath water, as they say. In the process of increasing adaptability, we have left a gap that accounts, in part, for the lack of true innovation in many of our organizations.

Mintzberg (1984, p. 176) argued that formal top-down strategic planning has three essential characteristics: (i) it is incremental rather than quantum, (ii) it is generic rather than creative, and (iii) it is oriented to the short term rather than to the long term. In fact, the emergent, bottom-up processes that are guided primarily by financial performance targets share exactly these characteristics! Despite the fact that the emerging bottom-up processes of strategizing that developed in the 1980s and 1990s allowed more freedom for line managers to engage in adaptive activities, and despite the fact that 'managing on the edge' certainly fosters the development of pockets of innovation, in both cases there are few mechanisms for harnessing that energy and focusing it toward overall organizational innovation.

Adaptability makes organizations ever more operationally effective, which allows them to compete better in the current game. Porter (1996) warned that the pursuit of operational effectiveness is seductive because it is concrete and actionable. And given the increased focus on financial performance goals, managers have been under increasing pressure to deliver measurable improvements linked to those goals. In a world where accurate prediction is thought to be essential and at the same time increasingly impossible, it is little wonder that organizations have proliferated programs for operational effectiveness in order to produce the illusion of progress and control. Porter argued that in pursuing this race for operational effectiveness, many managers fail to understand the need to have a strategy. We further suggest that it represents a deplorable abdication of the responsibilities of driving organization-wide innovation, responsibilities that belong fully to a firm's leadership.

Many have argued that a strategy hierarchy tends to disenfranchise most of the organization. Turbulent environments help perpetuate the divide. Employees want to believe that their leaders have the answers. Leaders do not want to admit that they do not. The result is often what Hamel and Prahalad (1989, p. 75) called a 'code of silence', in which the full extent of a company's competitiveness problem is not talked about. The 'code of silence' seems to be operating in the reverse direction today than how Hamel and Prahalad described it in the late 1980s. Given top managers' increasing abdication of direct involvement with identifying 'who we are' and 'who we can be', they increasingly rely on employees as having the answers. The pendulum has swung too far in the other direction. It is time for leadership to (re)claim its essential responsibilities.

Note

1. Though some have argued that today's turbulence is not so different from every other era of the past – the present is always seen as more turbulent than the past (Mintzberg 1994, p. 208).

References

Anderson, P. and M.L. Tushman (1990), 'Technological discontinuities and dominant designs: a cyclical model of technological change', *Administrative Science Quarterly*, **35**, 604–33.
Boyd, B.K. (1991), 'Strategic planning and financial performance: a meta-analysis', *Journal of Management Studies*, **28**, 353–74.
Business Week (1996), 'Strategic planning', 26 August, 45–52.
Collins, J.C. (2001), *Good to Great*, New York: HarperBusiness.
Collins, J.C. and J.I. Porras (1994), *Built to Last: Successful Habits of Visionary Companies*, New York: Harper Business.
Eisenhardt, K.M. and D.N. Sull (2001), 'Strategy as simple rules', *Harvard Business Review*, January, 106–16.
Gary, L. (2002), 'Strategy: separating the essential from the expendable', *Harvard Management Update*, **7**(9).
Goldstein, S.N. and P.T. Ward (2004), 'Performance effects of physicians' involvement in hospital strategic decisions', *Journal of Service Research*, **6**(4), 361–72.
Grant, R. (2003), 'Strategic planning in a turbulent environment: evidence from the oil majors', *Strategic Management Journal*, **24**(6), 491–517.
Hamel, G. (2000), *Leading the Revolution*, Boston, MA: Harvard Business School Press.
Hamel, G. and C.K. Prahalad (1989), 'Strategic intent', *Harvard Business Review*, **67**(3), 63–76.
Henderson, A.D., D. Miller and D.C. Hambrick (2006), 'How quickly do CEOs become obsolete? Industry dynamism, CEO tenure, and company performance', *Strategic Management Journal*, **27**, 447–60.
Hofer, C. (1976), 'Research on strategic planning: a survey of past studies and suggestions for future efforts', *Journal of Economics and Business*, **28**, 261–86.
Huber, G.P. (2004), *The Necessary Nature of Future Firms: Attributes of Survivors in a Changing World*, Thousand Oaks, CA: Sage.
Lashinsky, A. (2006), 'Chaos by design: the inside story of disorder, disarray, and uncertainty at Google. And why it's all part of the plan', *Fortune*, October 2, 86–98.

Lencioni, P.M. (2002), 'Make your values mean something', *Harvard Business Review*, July, 113–17.
Lorange, P., I.S. Gordon and R. Smith (1979), 'The management of adaptation and integration', *Journal of General Management*, Summer, 31–41.
Marino, K.E. (1996), 'Developing consensus on firm competencies and capabilities', *Academy of Management Executive*, **19**(4), 40–51.
McLean, B. and P. Elkind (2006), 'The guiltiest guys in the room', http://money.cnn.com, accessed 6 September 2006.
Mezias, S.J. and M.A. Glynn (1993), 'The three faces of corporate renewal: institution, revolution, and evolution', *Strategic Management Journal*, **14**, 77–101.
Miller, D. (1993), 'The architecture of simplicity', *Academy of Management Review*, **18**(1), 116–38.
Mintzberg, H. (1994), *The Rise and Fall of Strategic Planning*, New York: Free Press.
Mintzberg, H. and J. Lampel (1999), 'Reflecting on the strategy process', *Sloan Management Review*, Spring, 21–30.
Porter, M.E. (1980), *Competitive Strategy: Techniques for Analyzing Industries and Competitors*, New York: Free Press.
Porter, M.E. (1996), 'What is strategy?', *Harvard Business Review*, November–December, 61–78.
Quinn, R.E. (1996), *Deep Change: Discovering the Leader Within*, San Francisco, CA: Jossey-Bass.
Ramanujam, V., N. Ramanujam and J.C. Camillus (1986), 'Multi-objective assessment of effectiveness of strategic planning: a discriminant analysis approach', *Academy of Management Journal*, **29**(2), 347–472.
Rigby, D. (1999), *Management Tools and Techniques*, Boston, MA: Bain.
Starr, M.K. (1971), *Management: A Modern Approach*, New York: Harcourt, Brace, Jovanovich.
Stevenson, H.H. (1976), 'Defining corporate strengths and weaknesses', *Sloan Management Review*, Spring, 51–68.
Sutcliffe, K.M. (1994), 'What executives notice: accurate perceptions in top management teams', *Academy of Management Journal*, **37**(5), 1360–78.
Taylor, A. (2006), 'Managing on the edge', *Fortune*, 2 October, 78–82.
Vogelstein, F. (2002), 'Can Cisco dig out of its hole?', *Fortune*, 9 December, **146**(12), 179–84.
Wright, G. (2001), *Strategic Decision Making*, Chichester: Wiley.

18 Visions and innovation strategy
Jonathan Sapsed

Introduction

The concept of vision has appeared with increasing frequency in management theory and practice. Vision is regularly referred to in everyday popular usage, by business people, journalists, politicians, as well as scholars. Despite this familiarity it is still not clear what vision is, and how its meaning is different from more established terms such as strategy, forecasting or planning. Moreover, the claims about the function and power of visions are not always substantiated through empirical observation. The visions attributed to organizations are not always clearly linked to competences, or to observed strategic decisions and actions. This chapter attempts to consolidate and clarify the idea of vision as it is presented in the management and innovation literatures. It also shows actual instances of visions in use in a variety of different organizational settings. The chapter tries to show what visions are, what they are not, and how they are used.

The chapter is organized as follows: the management literature on visions is reviewed in the second section; it shows how vision is distinguished from terms such as strategy, plan and forecast. The third section reviews the technology and innovation studies literature, which links visions to knowledge bases and strategic actions of organizations. The fourth section describes the method for the case studies. The case studies in sections five to eight illustrate four tactical and strategic uses of vision by firms entering the uncertain area of digital media in the 1990s. The ninth section shows cases where there is 'no vision' and attempts to explain its absence. The tenth section discusses the chapter's findings, and concludes with some thoughts on managerial implications and the scope for future research.

Visions in management

The first question that might be asked of the vision concept is how does it differ from the outputs of traditional strategic planning? In what way is a vision distinguished from a plan? A future-facing statement is central to strategic planning, as observed by Mintzberg: 'Planning is a formalised procedure to produce an articulated result, in the form of an integrated system of decisions' (1994: 12).

For Mintzberg, the compulsion for an explicit statement of intent engages the firm's resources in meaningless and wasteful behaviour. Instead of explicit strategic plans, Mintzberg recommends the adoption of a *visionary* approach. Visions set the broad outlines of a strategy, leaving details to be worked out at a later stage. If the broad vision proves insufficiently robust in the light of unforeseen occurrences, it may be dropped in favour of a learning strategy. According to Mintzberg then, a visionary strategy provides some general direction, but it differs from planning because it is not formal and procedural, it is *informally devised* and flexible. For these reasons it is distinguished from rational strategic planning.

The informal aspect of vision appears to be a key criterion that distinguishes vision from strategic plan, or forecast, or scenario. These last two items are usually produced through formal processes of 'rationalist' strategizing, meaning strategy that is produced through a linear process of appraise–determine–act (Tidd et al., 2001). Under rational strategy making, strategic decision is a prior and distinct phase to strategic action, and is normally performed by different people from those in operations who implement the strategy. It is roughly equivalent to the 'design' school (Mintzberg, 1990) or the 'classical' approach to strategy making (Whittington, 1993). The term 'rational' is used here to signify the traditional logic and reason favoured by this approach, notwithstanding the debates about social rationality and cognitive inference (Reddy, 1996; Chase et al., 1998).

Indeed, the self-interested economic man of rational choice theory in economics is quite at odds with the function of vision as characterized in much of the management literature. Visions are inclusive and involving, they enlist commitment to change (Kanter, 1984). They provide inspirational leadership that the probability calculations and procedure of strategic planning cannot. For an idea to qualify as an organizational vision, it must be communicated with the broader organization, empowering and motivating (Westley and Mintzberg, 1989). This is not simple 'top-down' communication, the vision is constructed through a dialogue where sensegiving and sensemaking roles alternate between the leader and the led (Gioia and Chittipeddi, 1991). Vision effects a collective leap of faith or imagination beyond forecasts and figures.

Oswald et al. (1994, 1997) research the relations between managers' psychological attachment to their organization as a result of involvement in strategy as well as the 'salience' of vision. As regards the relationship between formal planning and vision, the authors argue that strategic planning should support and inform the vision, but in turn planning should be guided by vision. The two processes are mutually dependent but are separate processes. Managers who perceived vision as salient had a strong positive association between involvement in strategy and their organizational commitment. Oswald et al. argue that vision, by virtue of its motivating quality, can make planning work better. In this sense the emergence of the vision concept may be interpreted as an adjunct to the planning process, a reaction to the asserted failure of planning in the 1970s and 1980s (Mintzberg, 1994). It is a strategic device that has emerged as a means to direct the direction.

This view is also seen in Nutt and Backoff (1997: 308) who state that 'visions are used to develop a strategy'. Vision supports strategy development; it is directing, yet compelling, energizing and inspiring, rather than instrumental like mission or strategy. 'Vision taps people's emotion and energy. Properly articulated, a vision creates the enthusiasm that people have for sporting events and other leisure-time activities, bringing this energy and commitment to the workplace. Other means of directing human action seem to lack these qualities' (1997: 309).

The literature then, suggests that visions are not just corporate directives. They require the commitment and enrolment of the employees to be realized and according to Nutt and Backoff, to have a positive impact on organizational performance. Vision for most writers is a good thing, with some qualifications. Harris and Ogbonna (1999) show a 'hangover' effect in family-owned firms, where the founders' vision and strategy locks in subsequent management. Collins and Porras's (1995, 1996) work on 'visionary companies' warns of the importance of sustainable organizational design rather than businesses built around a 'great idea'.

We have seen that the management literature characterizes vision as informally and collectively devised, motivating and compelling. It is different therefore to rational strategizing and planning, but through its energizing qualities may facilitate and support the implementation of plans. However, unless it is made explicit, vision is a difficult phenomenon to research, otherwise how to analyse or even recognize it? And since vision involves large numbers of people, presumably some formality is required in its process of construction? On the first point, there is some empirical work using large datasets of vision statements. For example, Larwood et al.'s (1995) cluster analysis shows variance of the degree of formality and systematic planning involved in visions, as well as a cluster showing executives' visions to be individualistic and less widely accepted throughout their organizations. In another large-scale empirical study, Baum et al. (1998) also found that communication of vision varies, but suggest that there are non-verbal means by which the vision is diffused through the organization. The authors claim that this affects venture growth performance positively. Yet the other possible influences on performance do not figure, for example, supply-side factors such as product or capability, or demand-side factors such as access to major customers or distribution channels. In spite of the empirical work, the vision concept has an intangible and elusive quality in much of management theory. The questions remain how is vision related to the competences and knowledge bases of the firm, and how does it influence strategic decision and action? For insights on these issues we shall turn to the technology and innovation studies literature.

Visions in technology and innovation
Discussion on visions in the technology and innovation studies field relates to competences and challenges the field's orthodoxy of technological path dependence. This holds that technical change proceeds along stable trajectories, and that the firm's technological knowledge bases cannot stray too far, too quickly, from its preceding direction (Dosi, 1982; Pavitt, 1986; Patel and Pavitt, 1997). Some innovation scholars use the vision concept to suggest that managerial agency can relax the constraints of technological path dependency.

Martin Fransman's definition of vision is 'the set of beliefs regarding the firm's circumstances. It is these beliefs (rather than the firm's "objective" circumstances) which shape the leaders' views regarding the activities and knowledge which the firm should have to compete in the future' (1995b: 3). Fransman argues that this enables an *ex ante* analysis of firm competences. Vision construction provides the opportunity for 'competence-creating moments'. These junctures in the evolution of the firm are where decisions are made about competences on which the firm will prospectively compete. This is a contrasting idea to path dependency, where future competences are dependent on the competences of the past.

Strategies and tactics are shaped by the broad outline of the vision. Fransman's vision concurs with the management literature in that it is not an explicit plan derived from rational planning processes. It is based on beliefs of decision makers that are intuitive and influenced by perceptions of the environment and of future developments. For Fransman, such beliefs cannot be rationally processed, because of two complicating conditions: bounded rationality and interpretive ambiguity. Herbert Simon's (1955) bounded rationality notion contends that the decision maker is dealing with a limited information set first, because all relevant information cannot be known, and second because of the constraints on the cognitive processing ability of the decision maker.

Fransman's notion of interpretive ambiguity concerns the *content* of the information set when it is processed, and presents contradictory signals regarding alternative courses of action and their consequences. Inferences are disjunctive and calculations about outcomes are not possible. The world appears 'fuzzy' and rational choice breaks down. Under such circumstances of interpretive ambiguity, Fransman argues, beliefs, rather than information, influence the construction of visions and consequent strategy (Fransman, 1995a, 1999).

Fransman insists that knowledge and belief are in fact synonymous, because both are open-ended and change over time. The know-how and the know-why types of knowledge contained in technological competence are continually being revised. They are no more or less than the beliefs about how to produce a product, and why the effects of certain processes are caused. In this sense, Fransman equates belief with knowledge, beliefs embodied in visions are of the same nature as knowledge embodied in competences (Fransman, 1995b, 1999).

Vision, however, is described as 'bounded' by experience (1992, 1994, 1999); 'vision failure' occurs with an inability of decision makers to break free of prior beliefs and to make leaps of imagination. Fransman's explanation of strategic failure, is therefore rooted in the construction of visions. Beliefs based on past experience are implicated in the strategic errors made. Visions represent the opportunity for breaking free of the constraints of path dependency (1995a, 1999).

By contrast, Swann and Gill's (1993) concept of vision is not so dependent on beliefs. On the contrary, these authors argue that in many cases visions are not believed at all and serve merely as a competitive tactic. For example, Fransman stresses the fact that IBM were aware of the potential of microprocessors and yet continued to focus their business on mainframes. The intransigent belief in the smallness of the microprocessor market resulted in a mistaken vision.

Swann and Gill argue instead that IBM were fully aware of the threat but were seeking to play it down and defend their position: 'For "no need for computers other than large mainframes" read "there is undoubtedly a potential market for small computers, but we desperately hope it doesn't take off"' (1993: 25). While the announced vision was destined to turn out wrong, it was the circumspect statement of strategy for an established mainframe company to declare. Visions for Swann and Gill are strategic and tactical devices for internal organizational purposes or external public relations, for example to attract investors. Table 18.1 shows Swann and Gill's functions of corporate vision.

These uses of visions for what are essentially propaganda purposes are reminiscent of prior work on explicit strategy. Some strategy writers argue that the articulated plan gives coherence and direction to a firm's growth, serving as a steering mechanism (Ansoff, 1984; Kanter, 1984). Mintzberg (1993) argues instead that the primary value of an explicit strategy is often merely public relations. Explicit strategies and plans are required to influence external interests, perhaps to justify investment or reassure stakeholders. For example, 'an organisation that is failing can announce a plan to succeed' (Cohen and March, cited by Mintzberg, 1993: 41).

Empirical work supports this view. Fiol (1995) shows that corporate statements on the future that are targeted externally are typically more positive in their categorizations

Table 18.1   Functions of corporate vision

	Tactical (pre-announcements)	Strategic (long-term visions)
Internal	Commit warring factions to a particular product	Used in reorganizing firm for future technical change
External	User: encourage buyer to wait for new product Rival: signal, or entry deterrent	Encourage user to plan and produce around this vision of future technology

Source: Swann and Gill (1993: 26).

than are internal communications. Similarly Galbraith and Merrill's (1996) study of the political motivations in forecasting exercises finds that senior management frequently intervenes in the forecasting process to adjust revenue, cost or profit projections to a level more favourable to the firm. The integrity and validity of strategic plans, and forecasting statements would appear be open to question, and if the same is true of visions then this perhaps is of no great surprise.

Questions are raised by this brief review of the technology and innovation literature on visions. First, can we find evidence of the tactical and strategic functions of vision as suggested by Swann and Gill, or evidence of the vision based on beliefs in the Fransman sense? Second, to what extent can visions absolve the firm from technological path dependence? Can the firm jump from its historical trajectory of accumulated capability into unfamiliar fields and succeed? The next section describes the method used to research these issues.

Method

The following sections report on exploratory research on the strategies and visions of firms entering the area of new digital media in the 1990s. Each firm was entering from a different segment, such as content, software, service provision, equipment or infrastructure. New digital media encompassed various unproven technologies and markets that were not yet established, and may never be. The entrant firms therefore faced a bundle of opportunities that were characterized by high degrees of uncertainty. The conditions under which firms may construct and deploy visions are less predictable and perilous than in other, more stable industries. The case studies were selected because of these shared conditions of uncertainty.

A second criterion was to have a range of different entry modes represented among the cases. The research shows a variety of firms entering this inchoate area of opportunity from different directions, for example, large firms in established media acquiring a new media company; telecoms operators experimenting with new interactive multimedia technologies through alliances, as well as start-up firms. With this selection of cases the functions of visions can be compared across a variety of entry modes and approaches. The selected cases were drawn from the United States, specifically the Silicon Valley and San Francisco Bay Area and from innovating UK companies. The case studies were focused on the strategic decision making in the firms and the strategic actions that were taken, with a view to analysing the role, if any, of vision.

Primary sources of evidence were 35 semi-structured interviews with senior managers and engineers. To triangulate this data, internal and independent documentation was used, such as internal publicity and communications, technical specifications, annual reports, the trade press, the mainstream press and numerous online industry news sources. Triangulation was also achieved through cross-checking data between respondents from different parts of the same organization, as well as other organizations including competitors. Independent analysts were also consulted to validate the data. Not all cases are discussed in depth here (see Sapsed, 1999 for a full analysis), instead the fifth to eighth sections report on cases that illustrate the strategic and tactical uses of vision as suggested by Swann and Gill in Table 18.1. By contrast, the following section discusses cases where there was 'no vision', and suggests strategic reasons for the absence of vision.

Internal tactical uses of vision: Pearson's move into new media
The first quadrant in the Swann and Gill matrix, internal tactical uses of vision, can be illustrated by the case of Pearson plc, the international media and publishing group. Historically, Pearson had been a highly diverse conglomerate, but by the 1990s focused on its media and publishing assets, which included strong brands in print media such as the Financial Times, The Economist, Penguin Books and Addison Wesley Longman, as well as various television broadcasters, such as Thames and Grundy.

Senior managers within the group observed developments in digital technologies and in the 1980s began to express the need to develop their screen-based media resources. This conclusion was drawn from formal rationalist strategizing exercises, including a SWOT analysis (Strengths, Weaknesses, Opportunities and Threats) in which managers identified gaps in digital technologies within the group portfolio. It was felt that the strong brands and intellectual property in content owned by the various divisions could be exploited through the new media.

However, the rational plan was not sufficient to persuade the managers of the individual divisions. Over a period of around eight years, the Executive Director of Development of the group became an evangelist figure, arguing the case for moving into new technologies. There was some resistance from the newspaper and literary publishers, both of whom saw their role as protecting the interests of the traditional media. The director's arguments and vision were based on the belief that the printed word is an unnatural means of communication: 'when people directly interact there are various sensory communications to do with body language, perspiration, gesticulations as well as words, whereas reading is bloody hard work'.[1] He pointed to the substantial market shares taken by audio-visual media from traditional publishing and argued that the trend would continue in future.[2]

Various figures within the group were persuaded to varying degrees of enthusiasm, as their individual markets were affected to different extents by new media, 'The newspaper people said the newspaper is king in terms of provision of information; the publishers considered themselves the high priests and guardians of English literature, safeguarding the classics . . . ' (author interview). Here we can see the Fransman view of vision in evidence: visions based on beliefs of top management vying against intransigent conservatism. The rational strategy making early on was insufficient to mobilize a decisive strategic action. Eventually in the mid-1990s, the corporate centre took strategic action on the basis of the vision.

The action taken was an acquisition of an apparently 'hot' multimedia start-up from

California, Software Toolworks, later renamed Mindscape, at the extravagant cost of £310 million. The vision was of Mindscape as a strategic 'new technology' division that would exploit the content and brands owned by the group in new media. This vision did not occur, as it turned out that much of the intellectual property was already tied up in deals with third parties, or else the divisions were developing new media themselves.

It also turned out that Mindscape itself was not well-positioned, either in the market or in terms of its own internal processes and capabilities. The division performed badly and was sold four years later at a loss of £212 million. Pearson's senior managers were not familiar with the idiosyncrasies of the digital multimedia industry. For example, Mindscape's apparently strong market position was based on sales of CD-ROM products 'bundled' with new PCs. Mindscape's sales 'off-the-shelf' were much less, which is a better indicator as these reflect consumers' choice directly. One senior manager involved commented: 'The idea was right but it was the wrong company'.[3]

Pearson, typically of a conglomerate, sought to fill gaps in its corporate portfolio with an acquisition, rather than building digital media capability internally. The classical rationalist strategizing exacerbated the problems of the distance from the corporate centre from the divisions. The strategy suffered because of the emphasis on detached reasoning a priori to action, as is prescribed by the rationalist school. The function of vision does appear to concur with what is suggested in the literature: informally derived projections of the future based on beliefs of top management, yet its diffusion throughout the organization was problematic.

The Pearson case illustrates the first quadrant of Swann and Gill's matrix, vision serving for internal advocacy and awareness raising. Its success was not complete; it mobilized the senior management but because of their distance from the divisions they were unaware of the new media activities already ongoing. The vision and strategy were ultimately frustrated. Another important factor was that Pearson was buying into a new and unfamiliar market it did not fully understand. The strategy was therefore path *in*dependent and unsuccessful, in spite of the vision.

External tactical uses of vision: BT and Acorn's interactive TV trial

The second quadrant of the matrix, external tactical uses of vision, can be illustrated from British Telecom (BT) and Acorn Computers' experiments with interactive television in the mid-1990s. At the time, envisioning in the UK's popular media and in politicians' speeches was focused on the potential of interactive services into the home, the 'information superhighway' or 'Infobahn'. The idea was for a broadband infrastructure that would connect businesses, public agencies and institutions such as schools and libraries with homes. A primary uncertainty was who was going to pay for it, as although the government were warming to the theme, it was clearly not a priority for public investment.

Many commentators expected that the provision of interactive entertainment services would provide a sufficient incentive for cable operators to invest in broadband infrastructure. Alternatively, the telecommunications operators might see sufficient opportunity to invest if they were granted the deregulation to broadcast entertainment services. The rationale of this argument was that a 'killer application' was to be video-on-demand: consumers would pay a premium for instant transmission of programming content to their living rooms, thus diverting the revenues of the videocassette rental industry. This would provide the stimulus for further investments in other, perhaps more 'worthy' interactive television services, which would better exploit the capabilities of the new technology.

During this period of the mid- to late 1990s, a large number of experimental trials were announced which were to test the technologies enabling interactive TV, as well as the extent and nature of demand for such services. BT, the UK's dominant telecommunications operator announced a large-scale trial of interactive television to 2000 homes in the region of its central laboratories. This was testing the then unproven technology ADSL (Asymmetric Digital Subscriber Line), a modem-base system that greatly expands the bandwidth of standard twisted pair telephone lines. There was substantial publicity deployed by BT, presenting a vision of consumers dialling up full-length, full motion movies on their telephones, with their choices instantly transmitted via the copperwire line, and played back to VHS quality on their televisions.

More formal strategy making accompanied the vision, as the marketing function devised various scenarios of interactive TV usage in the future. These scenarios set the heuristics that the trial was to test, for example, middle-income households could be expected to pay £5 for a premium movie, or a £4 charge for interactive shopping. These scenarios, however, were for *internal* consumption and were not released externally. Similarly the data that were produced from the experiment were not published, with press releases merely reporting the successful take-up of the services.

At the same time as the BT trial, however, a rival trial was announced and implemented in nearby Cambridge. This was organized by Acorn, one of the first microcomputer manufacturers who were moving into the production of Set-Top Boxes (STBs) for interactive television. This trial, however, was using a CATV[4] cable network operated by Cambridge Cable, and would deploy ATM (Asynchronous Transfer Mode) technology. This was then a leading-edge communications technology that splits digital data into small packets, enabling a fast, stable service with a great potential for interactivity. The Cambridge trial represented the antithetical vision to BT's. Rather than trying to squeeze more bandwidth out of the existing telephone network, this trial was cable TV based and promised more interactivity and a new media experience for consumers.

Many commentators had interpreted BT's trial as a spoiler to the UK's infant cable industry. Cable was not established in the UK and at the time the government was encouraging cable operators – mostly American in origin – to invest in laying infrastructure and to acquire franchises to broadcast. The cable operators were trying to finance this entry into Britain through floating the franchise companies on the stock market. BT's announcement of the ADSL trial was seen as a timely 'spoiler' to the cable operators' attempts to attract investors and consumers to their vision.

The Cambridge trial was one response to BT's tactic, a Cambridge Cable executive of the time commented that the trial was intended 'to tread on their toes a little'.[5] Throughout the parallel trials the two camps issued press releases casting doubts on the viability of the other's technological and market vision. This illustrates the tactical external functions of vision indicated by Swann and Gill. BT and the Cambridge consortium were both signalling to each other as competitors about their intent to engage in a new market, while simultaneously trying to deter consumers from adopting their rival's package. In real terms these packages were no more than visions. Despite the technical successes of the trials, neither service was eventually introduced into the market, as the cost was still prohibitive. Both sides switched strategies: BT to an alliance with BSkyB the satellite TV broadcaster, which led to the Open interactive service, while Acorn switched from STBs to Oracle's Network Computer vision (see below).

The opportunism and frequency of change to the espoused visions suggests that their nature was tactical. If they were based on beliefs then these beliefs were clearly not robust in the light of new opportunities and product fashions. However, in spite of the volatility of the vision, the underlying technological competences deployed within BT and Acorn were consistent and stable. Each new product was an application of accumulated knowledge from prior product and service offerings, albeit with some incremental learning. Unlike the Pearson case, the technological strategies of these cases were path dependent, but like Pearson, the visions did not occur.

Internal strategic use of vision: Oracle's Network Computing Architecture

The third quadrant of Swann and Gill's matrix is on longer-term strategic uses of vision that are targeted internally. This can be illustrated by Oracle Systems' change of strategy to the Network Computing Architecture (NCA) in the late 1990s. Oracle was the world's second largest software company (revenues for 2001, \$7.6 billion[6]) after Microsoft, having grown through its core product and market leading position in relational database management systems. By the later 1990s, its products also included video server and web computing to support e-commerce, applications development, office automation, end-user accounting and manufacturing applications for client–server environments.

Oracle's high-profile CEO Larry Ellison, was renowned for his future-facing statements to the media. His vision at the time was network computing. Ellison's idea was that users would interface with a 'thin client' device. This would have no hard drive for local storage on the desktop, but with the preponderance of processing power and applications at the server end. Ellison's vision was that the device must be cheap and simple to use; running everyday tasks such as email, word-processing, spreadsheets and web browsing. All maintenance and upgrading would be handled at the server end where documents and applications would all be stored. Operating systems would be etched onto ROM memory chips. Users would plug in portable smart cards to any machine and be routed to their allotted storage space via internet connections.

The supporting NCA was a three-tier system, replacing the traditional two-tier architecture of client–server computing. The client-side component of the system was separated into two. This meant that only a very small operating system was needed at the user interface; the 'thin client' or network computer. Applications were to be stored and managed in an applications server, rather than in a hard disk in the client. Essentially the Network Computing (NC) vision was a challenge to the Windows–Intel dominance of computing markets. While Oracle did not compete directly with Microsoft in its existing markets, in the longer-term Microsoft was seen as the firm's chief rival.[7] Network computing was counterpoised to PC architecture.

This new architecture involved all Oracle's organization, as the architectures of all products were adapted to network computing. The new developments of electronic commerce on the Web, and the video server product were incorporated into the NC architecture. The key new development in the new version was the applications server which enabled the 'thin client' to function. Importantly, however, the system continued to support 'fat clients', PCs and workstations.[8] So while Ellison's vision was enabled and indulged by the new generation product, the stable revenues from its customary usage were not endangered. This strategy shows a willingness to enter uncertain areas of opportunity based on an explicit vision, while managing the inherent risks.

Internally, the NCA strategy announced was very much 'top down' in its implementation. However, rather than simply announcing the vision and consequent reorganization, dedicated strategizing was used to explain its implications to all 25,000 employees. The strategy was 'rolled out' throughout the company in a number of seminars. These were half-day off-site strategy retreat meetings. Following this massive strategizing process, all divisions knew where their products and activities fitted into the new strategy.

Interestingly, 18 months previously, a similar scale exercise was implemented to educate employees about the prior strategy, the 'Universal Server' concept. This shows that while strategies are changed and adjusted in reaction to the trends in a turbulent market, every effort is made to ensure that the organization will implement the strategy accordingly. This concurs with the literature on internal uses of visions and explicit strategies (Kanter, 1984; Swann and Gill, 1993). These strategy exercises were in effect closing the internal discussion about technology strategy, while the vision supported its implementation. Although senior management had devised the strategy in an exclusive way, the vision and roll-out exercises effected a reunification around the new direction.

While all Oracle products were made compatible with network computing, an autonomous organization was set up to develop the new products and market, called Network Computing, Inc. The rationale for this independent spin-off, were first, so that other companies would invest in the business.[9] Second, the business could act more rapidly and would be freer from the routines of the Oracle bureaucracy.[10] A third possible reason implied by interviews but not stated, was that should the NC business fail, the ongoing mainstream business of Oracle would not be affected. This shows that Oracle was 'hedging its bets' on the proposed network computing vision.

The entry to the new area of hardware products was discrepant with Oracle's mainstream business and so an autonomous division was the chosen organizational mode of entry. This was an astute choice as in subsequent years network computing was considered unfashionable in the trade press, much as interactive television was previously. Similarly to BT and Acorn, while the underlying technological competences in server software were path dependent, the new products were unsuccessful, in spite of the radical vision. Again, the regular roll-out of new visions and strategies suggests fickleness in any beliefs underlying the visions.

External strategic use of vision: new media start-ups

The fourth quadrant on external strategic uses of vision can be illustrated by several case studies of start-up companies set up to exploit opportunities in new digital media. These cases all used visions in their external publicity. These are briefly described in each case below.

Dimension X

Dimension X was a start-up founded in 1995 in the 'Multimedia Gulch'; a cluster of small firms in the South of Market district of San Francisco. It developed multimedia software tools and content for web applications. The vision of its founder was based first on a belief in the Java language, because of its cross-platform compatibility and rigorous coding requirements. Second, the vision stressed artistic input into web tools development, influenced by the founder's prior experience with mass movie markets. The belief was that the internet would be driven by Java and artistic content to attract 'eyeballs'. Publicity would include statements such as 'It is not the bandwidth of the pipes that matters, it is the bandwidth between the screen and the brain'. Dimension X was acquired by Microsoft in 1997.

First Virtual Corporation

FVC was founded in 1993 by one of the pioneers of the Local Area Network (LAN) industry in his former companies. This start-up was created in the belief that speed is the most important factor in contemporary business. Rather than thinking about technologies and markets, the founder thought about the architecture of the company.

The two core competences for the firm were identified as: (i) engineering capability, and (ii) the ability to build partnerships. FVC was to outsource everything else. The founder started with this virtual organization model and believed that later all companies would outsource to a great extent. He then thought about tools to make possible this type of business and to make it work effectively. He thought about the need to control the requirement for travel in managing external communications, and so focused the company's engineering effort on video networking. The firm was therefore based upon the vision of virtual business organization, in its own structure and practices, as well as in the product markets it targeted.

Strategy making was 'not formal at all';[11] instead, strategy was based on the beliefs of the founder, arising from his experience of the early LAN industry. He explained:

> There is no clear model for the video networking market. You can have very smart people and can think through all these issues and be wrong . . . Every analyst said the video conferencing market would take off, but now you have hundreds of thousands of units not tens of millions. So every analyst was wrong . . . It is no good sitting in rooms projecting what is going to happen. You should work out what *is* happening. Work out what the customer wants, learn how to recognize him, learn how to recognise a VAR [Value Added Reseller] and replicate. That's more important than market research and defining a product.
>
> Nobody asked for a LAN. I employed a market research consultancy in 1979 to interview 100 IT officers. They came back and said there would be zero market for LANs. But I knew there had to be a market. Computers had to talk, it didn't make sense for them to be stand-alone machines. (FVC founder)

Like Dimension X, this conforms to the Fransman vision model: informally derived and based upon the beliefs and experience of the founding manager. The press statements made by its high-profile founder and CEO also support the view of long-term visions signalling to the external world that the firm is directed and attractive to investment. FVC was successful in subsequent rounds of fundraising.

@Home

@Home, a new venture funded by Kleiner Perkins and TCI aggressively publicized and proselytized its vision of fast internet service over cable TV networks during the mid-1990s. This was an attempt to persuade prospective investors that its business model of partnerships with cable providers was superior to the rival broadband internet technologies. At the height of the 'dot.com' boom in Silicon Valley, this public relations campaign was rewarded by an initial stock market valuation of $2 billion, with only 6000 customers and the company expecting only losses for years to come. This supports Swann and Gill's idea of visions serving as tools of public relations and signals to external investors. In the case of start-ups, the use of vision is a powerful device to attract investments and interest from potential partners, often in the absence of a mature product or technical competence.

No vision
The above case studies have all shown evidence of vision, as characterized by Swann and Gill, and Fransman. But is this always the case in new and emerging industries? To answer these questions this section reports that the research has also revealed cases where no recognizable vision was present. The two cases are briefly described.

3Com
3Com is the second largest of the 'big four' giant companies that dominate the data networking industry. They have grown large mainly through a series of acquisitions of other firms, some themselves large, which are later subsumed into the organization. 3Com is quite systematic in its tracking of information regarding potential acquisition targets. Within the corporate centre, a business development group maintains an exhaustive database of small companies who are 'within 3Com's field of interest'.

The database includes information such as each company's management team, the products, the technologies that are in the products or that make them, and financial data such as the firm's profitability. The data are arranged into quadrants of related fields, so that there is information on multiple companies in the same space. In this way, 3Com can monitor rival firms in each product market. When a decision is made to diversify into a new area such as new media, or consolidate an existing one, the company can assess the best company for acquisition in that product space. If the best company is unavailable, 3Com are able to identify alternatives. In all cases 3Com does some research on the best two or three firms to establish the leader in the field.

Although when it was founded 3Com was promoted on a vision of ethernet technology, this envisioning disappeared as the company grew. There is no singular vision or expectation evident in 3Com's publicity or internal communications. Interviews with senior managers revealed a circumspect approach to emerging technologies and markets. While the firm will take stakeholdings and initiate partnerships with various start-ups, these are not seen as a commitment to a particular technological or market vision, but rather an option that may be increased at a later stage when uncertainty has reduced. This is consistent with the strategic management literature on 'real options' (for example, Mitchell, 1990; Mitchell and Hamilton, 1988; Bowman and Hurry, 1993).

New Enterprise Associates
New Enterprise Associates (NEA), as a venture capital fund, copes with uncertainty on an everyday basis. Interviews with NEA revealed formalized thinking to guide the investments that the fund would make in a proactive way. The firm identifies the sectors in which it wants to invest, it then analyses the technological trends that are likely to impact on those sectors, and commits to the strongest areas of opportunity. Similarly to 3Com, the firm has no identifiable singular vision of what will occur in each sector, but 'hedges its bets' by investing in companies with rival technological solutions. The firm recruits partners with technical knowledge to better monitor and understand the various

technological trends. These processes of strategy formation help NEA and its funded companies to cope with the uncertainties of emerging high-tech markets.

3Com and NEA take an incremental and pragmatic approach to committing to new areas of opportunity. Strategy is directed to relatively short time horizons without publicizing the firm's view of the future. The fact that 3Com did have an identifiable vision at the start-up phase suggests that vision may be of less value as a firm matures, perhaps even self-defeating when a level of size and diversity has been achieved.

Discussion and conclusions

In conclusion, the chapter has reviewed and summarized the concept of vision as it is used in the management literature, and in the field of technology and innovation studies. It has also shown four examples of visions in use in observed practice, and cases where vision is not present. The chapter has tried to show what visions are, what they are not, and how they are used.

Vision in the management literature is broadly characterized as an image of how the organization's world will look in the future. This may be an explicit statement but vision is distinguished from plan or scenario as it is informally derived. Vision possesses motivating qualities that are lacking in the more formal procedures of strategic planning. Vision is inspiring because it is inclusive and involving. Much of the literature stresses that envisioning is a process involving top management in negotiation with the broader organization. Through its energizing qualities, vision is argued to support formal strategic planning, it is intended to make planning work better.

The concept of vision in the management literature still has an intangible and elusive nature. The technology and innovation studies literature concurs with the informal characterization of vision but links it more explicitly to the organization's knowledge bases and strategic actions. Fransman argues that visions are based on the beliefs of decision makers; they emerge in circumstances where rational choice breaks down. Visions represent the opportunity for 'competence-creating moments', critical junctures where future trajectories of knowledge accumulation are conceived. This challenges the orthodoxy of technological path dependency, where competences are stable and do not stray too far from the prior direction.

Swann and Gill, by contrast, characterize visions as tactical and strategic devices that serve various corporate objectives. They reflect not so much the beliefs of decision makers but maybe skulduggery or deliberate delusion of competitors. In this characterization, visions follow in an established thread of strategy research on explicit statements as public relations (Mintzberg, 1993; Fiol, 1995; Galbraith and Merrill, 1996).

The empirical case studies serve to illustrate the four functions of vision as suggested by Swann and Gill's two-by-two matrix. These are shown in Table 18.2. The cases therefore provide evidence for Swann and Gill's conception of visions as tactical and strategic devices. Internally, they serve to disseminate ideas and to close debate, while externally they delude and deter competitors or entice investors and customers. The cases where there was no vision showed the value of keeping options open, and not committing to a single vision of the future. Practitioners may observe that while vision can be a powerful tool to the strategy maker, its absence may also be advantageous. A vision is not a 'must-have' business person's accessory. Like handheld devices and executive toys, their usefulness depends on individual circumstances and preference.

Table 18.2   Populating the Swann and Gill matrix: case studies of visions in use

	Tactical (pre-announcements)	Strategic (long-term visions)
Internal	Pearson attempting to close debate on new media within its group of companies	Oracle reorganizing the entire company around the NCA
External	BT and the Cambridge trial consortium, signalling to consumers to wait for their interactive TV services, and to detract from competitors' alternative	New digital media start-ups offering long-term visions that favour their technological solutions, so as to attract investors and publicity

There is some evidence that visions emerge from the informal beliefs of decision makers, as Fransman argues. However, the frequency with which visions are dropped and replaced suggests a fickleness and opportunism rather than devout belief. This ephemeral quality of visions contrasts sharply with the underlying knowledge bases of the firms in the case studies. The technological competencies followed stable, predictable trajectories even while new products and services were developed though their application. Technological path dependency appears still to be a key constraint, despite the presence of a guiding vision, however radical. The Pearson case reminds us of the hazards of leaping too far into the unknown. But as a senior manager of Pearson told this author: 'Hindsight is not a good forecasting tool'. The same might be said of visions.

Notes

1. Author's interview.
2. This is supported by data on media consumption. Shew's (1994) study suggests that the average UK adult spends 40 hours a week consuming media – of which 24 hours are spent watching TV, 11 hours listening to radio, and four hours reading newspapers (cited in Hooper, 1996).
3. Author's interview.
4. Community Antenna Television, popularly known as cable television.
5. Author's interview.
6. For the nine months ended 28 February 2001 (http://biz.yahoo.com/p/o/orcl.html).
7. Author's interviews.
8. Author's interview; 'Ray Lane on Network Computing', *Software Magazine*, January 1997.
9. Author's interviews.
10. Author's interviews.
11. Author's interviews.

References

Ansoff, I.H. (1984), *Implanting Strategic Management*, Englewood Cliffs, NJ: Prentice-Hall.
Baum, J.R., E.A. Locke and S.A. Kirkpatrick (1998), 'A longitudinal study of the relation of vision and vision communication to venture growth in entrepreneurial firms', *Journal of Applied Psychology*, **83** (1), 43–54.
Bowman, E.H. and D. Hurry (1993), 'Strategy through the option lens: an integrated view of resource investments and the incremental-choice process', *Academy of Management Review*, **18** (4), 760–82.
Chase, V.M., R. Hertwig and G. Gigerenzer (1998), 'Visions of rationality', *Trends in Cognitive Sciences*, **2** (6), 206–14.
Collins, J.C. and J.I. Porras (1995), 'Building a visionary company', *California Management Review*, **37** (2), 80–100.
Collins, J.C. and J.I. Porras (1996), 'Building your company's vision', *Harvard Business Review*, September–October, 1–13.
Dosi, G. (1982), 'Technological paradigms and technological trajectories: a suggested interpretation of the determinants and directions of technical change', *Research Policy*, **11**, 147–62.

Fiol, C.M. (1995), 'Corporate communications: comparing executives' private and public statements', *Academy of Management Journal*, **38** (2), 522–36.

Fransman, M. (1992), 'AT&T, BT, and NTT: vision, strategy, corporate competence, path-dependence, and the role of R&D', JETS Paper, No. 8, Institute for Japanese–European Technology Studies, University of Edinburgh.

Fransman, M. (1994), 'Information, knowledge, vision and theories of the firm', *Industrial and Corporate Change*, **3** (3), 713–57.

Fransman, M. (1995a), 'Interpretive ambiguity, theories of the firm, and the evolution of industries', paper presented at the European Management and Organisations in Transition Workshop, 'Technology and the Theory of the Firm: Social and Economic Perspectives', University of Reading, 14–16 May.

Fransman, M. (1995b), 'Theory of the firm and explaining the growth of "real" firms: the case of Japanese information and communications companies', paper presented at the 'Corporate Strategies in Electronics' conference, Centre for Economic Performance, London School of Economics, 25–26 September.

Fransman, M. (1999), *Visions of Innovation: The Firm and Japan*, Oxford and New York: Oxford University Press.

Galbraith, C.S. and G.B. Merrill (1996), 'The politics of forecasting: managing the truth', *California Management Review*, **39** (2), 29–33.

Gioia, D.A. and K. Chittipeddi (1991), 'Sensemaking and sensegiving in strategic change initiation', *Strategic Management Journal*, **12**, 433–48.

Harris, L.C. and E. Ogbonna (1999), 'The strategic legacy of company founders', *Long Range Planning*, **32** (3), 333–42.

Hooper, R. (1996), 'United Kingdom', in *Media Ownership and Control in the Age of Convergence*, Global Report Series, London: International Institute of Communications.

Kanter, R.M. (1984), *The Change Masters: Corporate Entrepreneurs at Work*, London: Unwin.

Larwood, L., C.M. Falbe, M.P. Kriger and P. Miesing (1995), 'Structure and meaning of organisational vision', *Academy of Management Journal*, **38** (3), 740–69.

Mintzberg, H. (1990), 'The design school: reconsidering the basic premises of strategic management', *Strategic Management Journal*, **11**, 171–95.

Mintzberg, H. (1993), 'The pitfalls of strategic planning', *California Management Review*, **36** (1), 32–47.

Mintzberg, H. (1994), *The Rise and Fall of Strategic Planning*, Hemel Hempstead: Prentice-Hall.

Mitchell, G.R. (1990), 'Options for the strategic management of technology', *International Journal of Technology Management*, **3** (3), 253–62.

Mitchell, G.R. and W.F. Hamilton (1988), 'Managing R&D as a strategic option', *Research Technology Management*, **31** (3), 15–22.

Nutt, P.C. and R.W. Backoff (1997), 'Crafting vision', *Journal of Management Inquiry*, **6** (4), 308–28.

Oswald, S.L., K.W. Mossholder and S.G. Harris (1994), 'Vision salience and strategic involvement: implications for psychological attachment to organisation and job', *Strategic Management Journal*, **15**, 477–89.

Oswald, S.L., K.W. Mossholder and S.G. Harris (1997), 'Relations between strategic involvement and managers' perceptions of environment and competitive strengths', *Group and Organisation Management*, **22** (3), 343–65.

Patel, P. and K. Pavitt (1997), 'Technological competencies in the world's largest firms: complex and path-dependent, but not much variety', *Research Policy*, **26**, 141–56.

Pavitt, K. (1986), 'Technology, innovation and strategic management', in J. McGee and H. Thomas (eds), *Strategic Management Research*, Chichester: John Wiley, pp. 171–90.

Reddy, S.G. (1996), 'Claims to expert knowledge and the subversion of democracy: the triumph of risk over uncertainty', *Economy and Society*, **25**, 222–54.

Sapsed, J. (1999), 'Restricted vision: strategizing under uncertainty', unpublished D. Phil dissertation, SPRU, University of Sussex.

Simon, H.A. (1955), 'A behavioural model of rational choice', *Quarterly Journal of Economics*, **69**, 99–118.

Swann, P. and J. Gill (1993), *Corporate Vision and Rapid Technological Change: The Evolution of Market Structure*, London: Routledge.

Tidd, J., K. Pavitt and J. Bessant (2001), *Managing Innovation*, 2nd edn, Chichester: John Wiley.

Westley, F. and H. Mintzberg (1989), 'Visionary leadership and strategic management', *Strategic Management Journal*, **10**, 17–32.

Whittington, R. (1993), *What Is Strategy – and Does It Matter?*, London: Routledge.

19 Innovation through ambidexterity: how to achieve the ambidextrous organization
Constantinos Markides and Wenyi Chu

Introduction

The ability of a firm to exploit its current business while exploring new territory (in terms of new technologies, markets, products or business models) has long been recognized as a critical source of competitive success (Thompson, 1967; Quinn and Cameron, 1988; March, 1991; Tushman and O'Reilly, 1996; Eisenhardt and Martin, 2000). The need to achieve a 'balance' between these two distinct activities has been proposed in a wide range of management areas, including organization theory, managerial economics (for example, Ghemawat and Costa, 1993), international business (for example, Bartlett and Ghoshal, 1989) and strategic management (for example, Winter and Szulanski, 2001).

However, achieving this balance is a 'central paradox of administration' (Thompson, 1967, p. 15). This is because the skills, mindsets, structures and processes required to achieve exploitation of the current business are fundamentally different and often conflict with those required to achieve exploration. For example, in a classic study, Burns and Stalker (1961) proposed that organizations developing new products (that is, exploring) should be organic, whereas organizations engaged in exploiting their existing businesses should be mechanistic. Several other studies have shown that exploration and exploitation require substantially different structures, processes, skills and strategies that appear contradictory and difficult to combine (March, 1991; Levinthal and March, 1993; Tushman and O'Reilly, 1996; Sheremata, 2000; Benner and Tushman, 2003).

Organizations that are capable of achieving the appropriate balance between exploitation and exploration have been labeled 'ambidextrous' organizations (for example, Duncan, 1976; Tushman and O'Reilly, 1996). Recent studies have empirically tested the relationship between organizational performance and the ability to be ambidextrous and have generally found a positive relationship (for example, McDonough and Leifer, 1983; Adler et al., 1999; Ahuja and Lampert, 2001; Benner and Tushman, 2002; Gibson and Birkinshaw, 2004; He and Wong, 2004). But whereas the need for and the beneficial effects of achieving ambidexterity have been recognized, little work has been done on exactly *how* organizations could achieve ambidexterity.

Most authors have viewed the achievement of ambidexterity as a structural issue (for example, Duncan, 1976; Christensen 1997; O'Reilly and Tushman, 2004). For example, Duncan (1976) proposed that organizations achieve ambidexterity by putting in place 'dual structures' so that certain divisions focus on alignment while others focus on adaptation. Similarly, Christensen and Raynor (2003) proposed that established companies could only pursue a disruptive innovation in a separate unit, away from the interference of the parent company. O'Reilly and Tushman (2004) suggested that ambidextrous organizations create separate units to pursue new opportunities but keep the same general manager to manage both the new unit and the parent company.

Recently, attention has begun to shift towards non-structural elements of ambidexterity such as culture and values, incentives, mindsets and strategic foresight (for example, Volberda, 1996; Adler et al., 1999; Eisenhardt and Martin, 2000; Ahuja and Lampert, 2001; Siggelkow and Levinthal, 2003; Costanzo, 2004; Gibson and Birkinshaw, 2004; MacKay and McKiernan, 2004; Siggelkow and Rivkin, 2005). Our chapter builds upon this tradition and proposes several non-structural strategies that firms could pursue in order to achieve ambidexterity. In other words, over and above creating separate units, what else must a firm do to achieve ambidexterity? For the purposes of this research, we take ambidexterity to mean the ability of a firm to simultaneously achieve decentralization and centralized control.

The context of a diversified firm provides a perfect setting to explore this question. This is because the separate units already exist in a diversified firm. Many, though not all, may be pursuing strategies or may be facing external environments that require them to have as much autonomy from the parent as possible (so as to achieve local responsiveness). But these same units may also need to be integrated with the parent or with other divisions within the portfolio so as to exploit synergies with each other. The question then is: 'how could the corporate parent provide autonomy to these divisions while at the same time exercising centralized control over them?'

In this chapter, we utilize questionnaire data from the 100 biggest business groups in Taiwan[1] to explore how these diversified firms achieve this kind of ambidexterity. To collect the necessary data, we administered two questionnaire surveys: one at corporate headquarters (HQ) and one at division level. Because we have been granted access to the divisions of these diversified groups (as well as the CEO of the group at corporate HQ), most of the data that we use in this chapter come from the general managers who actually run the divisions. As a result, we can determine what kind of environment *each* division is facing or what kind of strategy it is pursuing. This in turn will allow us to identify those divisions that are facing situations of strategic ambiguity – a situation that demands ambidextrous behaviors by the corporate parent. In addition, since we have been given data on each division's performance, we are able to assess whether our predictions as to how these divisions should be managed lead to superior performance.

Theory and hypotheses

Organizational ambidexterity has been defined as the ability of a firm to manage demands in its task environment that are in conflict or require trade-offs (for example, Duncan, 1976; Tushman and O'Reilly, 1996; Gibson and Birkinshaw, 2004). The academic literature has identified numerous instances when a firm would be required to reconcile (if not eliminate) difficult trade-offs – for instance, following a differentiation strategy while adopting a low-cost one as well; exploiting the current business while exploring new ones; investing in current versus future projects; managing a mature business as well as a new, emerging business. Within diversified firms, a situation that requires the reconciliation of difficult trade-offs arises when divisions within the portfolio face conflicting strategic imperatives – for example, a division might require autonomy from the parent to pursue its own strategy but at the same time has to integrate with the parent to allow for the efficient exploitation of synergies with other divisions. As we argue below, several such situations may present themselves in a diversified firm and our thesis is that the corporate parent must become ambidextrous if it is to reconcile such conflicting demands.

The need for ambidexterity in diversified firms

Past academic work on diversification has argued that since different divisions within the same multi-business firm often face different levels of volatility in their external environments and often pursue different business-level strategies, then the administrative mechanisms that corporate headquarters use to manage these divisions – such as evaluation and incentive systems – should differ accordingly (for example, Gupta and Govindarajan, 1986; Gupta, 1987; Govindarajan, 1988; Govindarajan and Fisher, 1990; Hill, 1990). Several empirical studies have provided evidence that suggests that such a differentiated approach towards divisions is indeed possible (for example, Gupta and Govindarajan, 1986; Ghoshal and Nohria, 1989; Govindarajan and Fisher, 1990; Lioukas et al., 1993; Chu, 1997).

More specifically, it has been argued and shown empirically that different divisions within the same multi-business firm do indeed receive different degrees of autonomy (from corporate HQ) to take strategic, financial and operational decisions. Several studies have found that the divisions that received the most autonomy were those which: (i) faced a volatile environment; (ii) followed a differentiation strategy; and (iii) did not share resources and were not interdependent with other divisions in the company (for example, Gupta, 1987; Govindarajan, 1988; Chu, 1997). It has been further shown that under these three conditions, divisions that are granted decision-making autonomy perform better than divisions that are not given autonomy (Lioukas et al., 1993; Chu, 1997).

The rationale for the existence of a positive relationship between autonomy and these three contingency factors is well accepted in the literature. A central proposition of organizational theory (for example, Lawrence and Lorsch, 1967; Thompson, 1967) is that there is no one best way to organize and that the different ways of organizing are not equally effective. Building on this principle, the information processing perspective argues that the main purpose of organizational design is to enable each sub-unit to cope with its information processing requirements, which are determined by task uncertainty. Because of variations in environmental uncertainty, different organizations need different arrangements to be able to deal with their information processing requirements (Galbraith, 1973, 1977; Nadler and Tushman, 1988).

Following the classic work of Burns and Stalker (1961), Woodward (1965), and Lawrence and Lorsch (1967), Galbraith (1973) argued that the greater the uncertainty and/or diversity of the task, the greater the amount of information needed to be processed during the decision making and task execution in order to achieve a given level of performance. Therefore, uncertainty is the core concept upon which the organization design frameworks are based. Theoretically, there are at least two sources of uncertainty: uncertainty of the external environment (Burns and Stalker, 1961), and uncertainty of the task (Perrow, 1967). Thus the appropriate design of organizational structure is contingent upon these two contextual variables.

With regard to the uncertainty of the external environment, it has been well established by authors such as Lawrence and Lorsch (1967) and Thompson (1967) that the structures of organizations are and should be differentiated according to the characteristics of the external environments they face. This argument is obviously applicable to multi-business firms: different divisions compete in different industries and thus face different levels of environmental uncertainty. A division that competes in an industry with high environmental complexity needs a more decentralized organization if it is to deal effectively with the high information processing requirement it faces and react quickly and flexibly to environmental changes; conversely, for divisions that compete in industries which are characterized by low levels of complexity, a more centralized control system could be adopted (Govindarajan, 1988).

Furthermore, the competitive strategies adopted by divisions influence the task uncertainty faced by them (Porter, 1985, 1987). As a result, their information processing needs will differ accordingly: a division that follows a differentiation strategy faces a higher level of uncertainty in its task environment because this strategy requires innovation and dynamism to be effective (Porter, 1987). Therefore, such a division would benefit from high degrees of autonomy and decentralization (Govindarajan, 1986; Gupta, 1987). On the other hand, a division that follows a low-cost strategy faces a more stable task environment. Therefore, such a division requires less autonomy so that corporate HQ can monitor divisional operations more closely to ensure that costs are controlled efficiently.

In summary, the information processing perspective suggests two main contingency factors influencing how much autonomy different divisions receive (or should receive) from corporate HQ: the environmental complexity faced by divisions and the competitive strategy adopted by each division. High environmental complexity and a differentiation strategy are argued to be associated with higher divisional autonomy.

A different motivation for structural differentiation within diversified firms has been proposed by authors such as Pfeffer and Salancik (1978), Pfeffer (1981) and Porter (1985). Their position is based on resource sharing and interdependencies among divisions.

Resource sharing refers to the extent to which a focal division shares functional activities (such as marketing, manufacturing, research and development (R&D), and human capital) with other divisions within a firm (Vancil, 1980). Resource sharing among divisions could be a source of value for diversified firms, especially for the related diversified and vertically integrated ones (for instance, Porter, 1987). This is because high resource sharing may yield a synergistic cost advantage in that the divisions can access the shared resource at a lower cost than they would have if they each had to acquire it separately (Porter, 1985; Gupta and Govindarajan, 1986). In addition, resource sharing can enhance differentiation by contributing to the uniqueness of an activity and by lowering its cost (Porter, 1985).

Resource sharing is not cost free. It requires extensive coordination and cooperation among divisions, activities that require the active involvement of corporate HQ (McCann and Fery, 1979). In addition, resource sharing and coordination imply loss of divisional autonomy, constrained flexibility and distorted performance accountability (Gupta and Govindarajan, 1986). Resource sharing has the following implication for how HQ should manage divisions: since different divisions can have different levels of resource sharing with each other, then the administrative mechanisms that the corporate HQ uses to manage these divisions should differ accordingly. When a division's level of resource sharing is high, the need for central coordination is strong and a more centralized control style is suggested. Conversely, when interdivisional resource sharing is low, a decentralized HQ–division relationship is proposed.

Overall, therefore, we would expect that divisions that receive the most autonomy will be those which: (i) face a volatile environment; (ii) follow a differentiation strategy; and (iii) do not share resources and are not interdependent with other division in the company. These predictions have been supported empirically (for example, Gupta, 1987; Govindarajan, 1988; Chu, 1997). It has been further shown that under these three conditions, divisions that are granted decision-making autonomy perform better than divisions that are not given autonomy (Chu, 1997).

While these propositions are well accepted in the diversification literature, they also give rise to an interesting and unexplored conundrum. Namely, what happens in situations where a division faces conflicting strategic imperatives? For example, how should HQ manage a division facing a volatile environment that is also very interdependent with other divisions in the group? Theory suggests that because of the volatility of its environment, this division should be granted autonomy; but because of high interdependence with other divisions, it should be centrally controlled and given little autonomy.

This is an example of what Hamel and Prahalad (1983, p. 341) have called 'situations of strategic ambiguity' – that is, situations where divisions face conflicting demands for integration and responsiveness which makes management of these divisions especially difficult. It is exactly the kind of situation that, as we have argued in this chapter, requires the corporate parent to adopt ambidextrous behaviors. Several such situations may present themselves. For example, a division in a stable (mature) business that is following a differentiation strategy faces a situation of strategic ambiguity. The same is true for a division in a volatile business that has adopted a cost leadership strategy. In fact, given the three contingency variables identified above, we could come up with eight possible scenarios of strategic ambiguity. While we do not want to pretend that these are the only instances when strategic ambiguity may creep in, it appears that such situations happen often enough in practice to warrant further examination.

Situations such as these have been identified and examined in the *multinational* literature. For example, Bartlett and Ghoshal's (1989) examination of the management of the 'transnational' organization tackled exactly this issue. Similar issues have also been explored by Hamel and Prahalad (1983) and by Prahalad and Doz (1987). Our goal here is to use the insights that have emerged from this literature on multinationals to study this phenomenon within a diversified firm.

Given the three contingency variables that we identified above as influencing how much autonomy each division will receive, we can identify eight possible strategic scenarios that a specific division may be facing at any given time. The eight possible scenarios along with their organizational implications are presented in Table 19.1. It should be clear from the table that six of these scenarios (1, 2, 3, 5, 7, 8) represent situations of strategic ambiguity that would require ambidextrous behaviors from the corporate parent.

The discussion so far leads us to propose our first hypothesis. Given the organizational implications outlined in Table 19.1, we would expect that divisions facing scenario (4) – that is, volatile environment, differentiation strategy and low interdependence – will be given the highest level of autonomy; while divisions facing scenario (6) – that is, stable environment, cost strategy and high interdependence – will be given the least amount of autonomy. The other divisions facing any one of the other six scenarios will have intermediate levels of autonomy. Therefore:

Hypothesis 1:   Divisions facing scenario (4) will have statistically significant higher levels of autonomy relative to divisions facing scenarios (1), (2), (3), (5), (7), (8) which in turn will have higher levels of autonomy relative to divisions facing scenario (6).

Table 19.1 *Three contingency variables and eight possible scenarios that a division might face*

Scenario	Environmental conditions	Competitive strategy	Interdependence among divisions	Strategic ambiguity
1	Volatile	Differentiation	High	Yes
2	Volatile	Cost	High	Yes
3	Volatile	Cost	Low	Yes
4	Volatile	Differentiation	Low	No
5	Stable	Cost	Low	Yes
6	Stable	Cost	High	No
7	Stable	Differentiation	High	Yes
8	Stable	Differentiation	Low	Yes

It is important at this point to stress that we do not believe that these eight scenarios are the only possible ones that a division might face. We ended up with eight scenarios because we started out with three contingency variables. It is possible to identify from the literature even more variables that might influence how much autonomy a division gets. Every additional contingency variable will double the possible scenarios facing a division. For example, even the addition of one more contingency variable will give rise to 16 possible scenarios. However, we decided to focus on just the three contingency variables because they are, according to the literature, the most important factors influencing how much autonomy each division gets. In addition, our goal is not to identify every possible scenario that a division might face. Rather, we want to argue that it is possible for a division to face strategically ambiguous scenarios – whether they face one or 10 such scenarios is not important. We further want to examine how such situations are handled. We turn to this topic next.

Managing strategic ambiguity

The management and reconciliation of conflicting demands is not easy. In fact, there has been a lot of discussion in the academic literature as to whether internal organizational tensions, such as those between low cost and differentiation, can ever be effectively reconciled. For example, Porter (1996) has argued that the trade-off between low cost and differentiation strategies is insurmountable.

The primary solution offered to solve this problem is to keep the two strategies physically separate in two distinct organizations. This is the 'innovator's solution' that is primarily associated with Christensen's (1997) work on disruptive innovation but other academics have advocated it as well (for example, Burgelman and Sayles, 1986; Gilbert and Bower, 2002). Even Porter (1996) has come out in favor of this strategy. Despite arguing that most companies that attempt to compete with dual strategies will likely fail, he has also proposed that: 'companies seeking growth through broadening within their industry can best contain the risks to strategy by creating stand-alone units, each with its own brand name and tailored activities' (p. 77).

This structural solution has found some support in the academic literature (for example, Tushman et al., 2004). However, it has also been argued that finding the appropriate structure may be only part of the solution and that we should also look for non-structural elements of ambidexterity (for example, Gibson and Birkinshaw, 2004). Here, we propose that the multinational literature could offer several insights on how situations of strategic ambiguity could be managed within diversified firms. In fact, Ghoshal and Nohria (1993, p. 33) suggest that: 'Our argument [that the complexity of a firm's structure must match the complexity of its environment] can easily be extended . . . to any multidivisional firm'.

The most relevant proposition stemming from this literature is that multinationals which operate in markets where the forces for national responsiveness are as strong as the forces for global integration, will require the 'transnational' form of organization to be effective (see, for example, Bartlett and Ghoshal, 1989; and Ghoshal and Nohria, 1989). This structure allows each subsidiary the freedom to differentiate itself according to local demands but at the same time 'overlays the distinctly structured relationships with a dominant overall integrative mechanism – whether through strong centralization, formalization, or normative integration' (Ghoshal and Nohria, 1993, p. 28).

Therefore, the basic proposition is to find ways to grant the division enough autonomy to make operational decisions suitable for its environment while at the same time making sure that integrative mechanisms are in place to exploit interdependencies. There is no one best way to achieve this, but one possibility may be to follow the suggestions of Williamson (1975) and Hill (1988) and grant the divisions *operational* autonomy while maintaining central control over *strategic* and *financial* matters. This proposition is in the spirit of the 'transnational' solution and allows for a delicate balance to be struck between divisional autonomy on the one hand and central control on the other. Therefore:

Hypothesis 2:   Among divisions facing strategic ambiguity, those that display high operational autonomy but low strategic and financial autonomy will outperform all other divisions.

Another insight that has emerged from the multinational literature is that 'structure may be a relatively ineffective tool for managing strategic responsibility, particularly when the firm faces strategic ambiguity. Management must use other tools at its disposal, including systems, corporate values and culture, and positioning assignment of key people' (Hamel and Prahalad, 1983, p. 347).

This insight suggests two other possible mechanisms for managing strategic ambiguity in diversified firms. The first mechanism is a strong culture or strong shared values. Creating strong shared values and beliefs among the managers of divisions and HQ enables the corporate center to grant autonomy to divisions without fear that the divisions will pursue their own interests at the expense of the group as a whole. As Ouchi (1980, p. 138) noted: 'common values and beliefs provide the harmony of interests that erase the possibility of opportunistic behavior'. Furthermore, as argued by Barnard (1939), shared values enhance the sense of mutual interdependence in the organization and can therefore facilitate the corporate center in its attempts to exploit synergies among divisions, even when these divisions enjoy decision-making autonomy. The useful role of shared values as a mechanism for managing HQ–division relations has been demonstrated in studies by Nohria and Ghoshal (1994) and Chu (1997). Therefore:

Hypothesis 3:   Among divisions facing strategic ambiguity, those that belong to corporations which display high shared values will outperform all others.

The second mechanism for managing strategic ambiguity in diversified firms is the firm's organizational context. For Prahalad and Doz (1981: 5), context means the 'blending of organizational structure, information systems, measurement and reward systems and career planning and a fostering of common organizational culture'. For Hamel and Prahalad (1983: 347) it means: 'sophisticated management of systems, the corporate cultural milieu and people'. The argument is that divisions could be given decision-making autonomy and still be kept integrated within the group through a variety of integrative mechanisms such as high and continuous communication, transfer of managers across functions and divisions, common training of people and the development of a strong culture. Therefore:

Hypothesis 4-1:   Among divisions facing strategic ambiguity, those with high levels of communication will outperform all others.

Hypothesis 4-2:   Among divisions facing strategic ambiguity, those with a high level of transfer of managers will outperform all others.

Hypothesis 4-3:   Among divisions facing strategic ambiguity, those with a high level of training programs will outperform all others.

Data and methodology

The sample
The top 100 business groups in Taiwan were asked to participate in this research. These are the largest and most diversified companies in Taiwan and together account for more than 35 percent of the country's GNP. A total of 34 business groups agreed to participate. We tested for response bias by comparing the size (assets and number of employees) and profitability (return on assets, net profit rate and return on equity) of those business groups that agreed to participate versus those groups that did not want to participate. No response bias was detected for either profitability or size.

The 34 participating groups had a total of 186 divisions. Data were collected via two questionnaires: one was completed in a face-to-face meeting with the CEO of the participating business group; and one was sent to the 186 divisional general managers of these 34 groups. The divisional questionnaire was distributed either by senior staff members at HQ (who helped with contacting divisions, distributing questionnaires and following up); or if HQ did not want to actively participate, the divisional general manager was contacted directly and notified that HQ had already agreed to participate. The draft questionnaires were first tested on two divisional general managers and three senior HQ staff from five business groups, before the final ones were distributed.

Of the 186 divisional general managers who received questionnaires, 148 (80 percent) responded. In total, 136 (73 percent) responses were usable. On average, the responding managers had worked for their business groups for 18.8 years and for their current divisions for 13.4 years.

Table 19.2   Summary statistics and reliability of the autonomy variables

Divisional autonomy	Mean	S.D.	Items	Alpha
STRATEGIC	4.98	1.23	14	0.9175
OPERATE	6.11	1.11	19	0.9573
FINANCIAL	4.83	1.74	5	0.8861
OVERALL	5.31	1.22	38	–*

Note: * The Cronbach alpha of the overall degree of autonomy was not calculated because this variable was simply the arithmetic mean of STRATEGIC, OPERATE, and FINANCIAL.

The variables
Data was collected to calculate the following variables.

Autonomy granted to divisions   Based on instruments developed by Hill (1988), we measured the degree of autonomy given to divisions to take strategic, financial and operational decisions. Using data from the divisional questionnaire, we constructed three composite scales from the responses to 38 questions (see Hill, 1988): OPERATE, STRATEGIC, and FINANCIAL. The scale OPERATE measured head office involvement in the operating decisions of the divisions. It was constructed from the responses to 19 questions. STRATEGIC measured the extent to which strategic controls were centralized. It was constructed from the responses to 14 questions. Similarly, FINANCIAL measured the extent to which the head office exercised centralized financial controls over divisions based upon abstract profit criteria. It was constructed from the responses to five questions.

The three scales ranged in value from 1 to 7. A value of 1 indicated that: 'HQ makes decisions without prior consultation of the divisions' while a value of 7 indicated that: 'Divisions make decisions without prior consultation of the HQ'. High scores indicated a high degree of decentralization of control over strategic, operational and financial decisions. The overall degree of decentralization was measured by averaging the mean scores of these three scales. Summary statistics as well as the results of Cronbach alpha reliability tests are shown in Table 19.2.

Divisional performance   Consistent with the arguments of Gupta and Govindarajan (1984) and Govindarajan (1988), we measured the performance of a division as its actual performance relative to what HQ expected from the division, rather than as an absolute figure. Data was collected at the divisional level on the following performance items: gross profit, profit growth, labor productivity, return on sales, return on investment, development of new products, sales growth, market share, cash flow from operations, capacity utilization, cost control, personnel development, company image, and customer satisfaction. For each of these 14 items, respondents were asked to rate their divisional performance relative to the HQ's expectation on a seven-point scale, ranging from 'not satisfactory at all' ($=1$) to 'outstanding' ($=7$). A straight average of these dimensions was used as the measure. Values ranged from 1.86 to 7.00, with a mean of 4.14 (Cronbach alpha $= 0.9324$).

Since the divisional managers were asked to rate their performance, we expected this answer to be biased upwards (that is, the managers would report that their performance was better than it really was). However, we did not consider this a problem because we did not expect any divisional manager to be systematically *more* biased than others (that is, we expected all to be biased and in the same direction). To make sure of this, we utilized the data collected through the CEO/HQ questionnaire: we first classified the divisions into two groups – one group contained all the divisions which were rated as 'performing very well' by their corporate HQ and one group contained those divisions which were rated as 'not performing well' by their corporate HQ. We then compared the answers (as regards their performance) of divisions that HQ considered as performing well against the answers of divisions whose HQ did not think they were performing well. As expected, the difference in responses between the two types of divisions was not statistically significant.

We tested for bias in another way: from the questionnaire survey conducted with the CEO at corporate HQ, we had objective data on the performance of each business group that participated in this study. Specifically, we had objective data for each group's return on assets (ROA); return on equity (ROE); net profit rate (PR); and sales growth (GS). We therefore compared the responses of divisions that belonged to profitable groups against the responses of divisions that came from unprofitable groups. Again, the difference in responses with respect to the performance variable were not statistically significant.

Independent variables   Data was collected for a number of independent variables. These variables include the three contingency variables (environmental complexity faced by each division, competitive strategy of each division, and resource sharing among divisions), as well as shared values, communication, rotation of managers, and training programs. The independent variables were operationalized using a variety of instruments. Details on how each variable was constructed are presented in Appendix 19A.

Scenarios of strategic ambiguity
In order to test Hypothesis 1, we need to classify divisions into the eight scenarios of Table 19.1. For example, divisions which face a volatile environment, follow a differentiation strategy and are highly interdependent with other divisions should be placed in scenario 1. On the other hand, divisions which face a stable environment, follow a differentiation strategy and have low interdependence with other divisions should be placed in scenario 8.

We carried out this classification as follows: divisions were first ranked according to the complexity of their environment. Those divisions that had a complexity score above the median were placed in the 'volatile environment' group, whereas divisions that had a complexity score below the median were placed in the 'stable environment' group. Next, divisions were ranked according to their competitive strategy scores: those that had scores below the median in the competitive strategy score were placed in the 'low cost' group while those that had scores above the median were placed in the 'differentiation' group. Finally, divisions were ranked according to their resource-sharing scores: those that had scores below the median in the resource-sharing score were placed in the 'low' interdependence group while those that had scores above the median were placed in the 'high' interdependence group.[2] The divisions were then classified into scenarios on the basis of Table 19.1. The results of this classification are summarized in Table 19.3.

Empirical results
Our first hypothesis proposed that divisions facing scenario 4 – that is, volatile environment, differentiation strategy and low interdependence – will be given significantly higher

Table 19.3   Number of divisions in each strategic scenario

Scenarios	Number of divisions	Percentage (%)	Strategic ambiguity
1	23	16.9	Yes
2	15	11.0	Yes
3	18	13.2	Yes
4	19	14.0	No
5	20	14.7	Yes
6	20	14.7	No
7	11	8.1	Yes
8	10	7.4	Yes
Total	136	100	

Table 19.4   Autonomy given to divisions placed in the different scenarios

	Scenarios			One-way ANOVA		Duncan test*
	4	1, 2, 3, 5, 7, 8	6	F value	Sig. F	
	(n = 19)	(n = 97)	(n = 20)			
STRATEGIC mean (s.d.)	5.76 (1.08)	5.02 (1.15)	4.23 (1.18)	8.738	0.000	4 > (1, 2, 3, 5, 7, 8) (1, 2, 3, 5, 7, 8) > 6 4 > 6
OPERATE mean (s.d.)	6.57 (0.74)	6.17 (1.07)	5.61 (1.09)	4.252	0.016	(1, 2, 3, 5, 7, 8) > 6 4 > 6
FINANCIAL mean (s.d.)	5.79 (1.34)	4.84 (1.75)	3.97 (1.62)	5.716	0.004	4 > (1, 2, 3, 5, 7, 8) (1, 2, 3, 5, 7, 8) > 6 4 > 6
OVERALL mean (s.d.)	6.04 (0.96)	5.34 (1.19)	4.60 (1.07)	7.707	0.001	4 > (1, 2, 3, 5, 7, 8) (1, 2, 3, 5, 7, 8) > 6 4 > 6

Note: *Relationships shown here are those with statistical significance at the $p < 0.05$ level.

levels of autonomy than divisions facing scenarios 1, 2, 3, 5, 7 and 8, which in turn will be given higher levels of autonomy than divisions facing scenario 6. One-way ANOVA and Duncan tests were employed to compare the differences in autonomy granted to the different divisions. The results are shown in Table 19.4.

There were 19 divisions facing scenario 4 and their mean levels of strategic, operational and financial autonomy were 5.76, 6.57 and 5.79, respectively. By contrast, there were 97 divisions facing scenarios 1, 2, 3, 5, 7 and 8 and their respective mean levels of autonomy were 5.02, 6.17 and 4.84 – all significantly *lower* than the corresponding values for the divisions in scenario 4 – as proposed by Hypothesis 1. Similarly, there were 20 divisions facing scenario 6 and their mean levels of strategic, operational and financial autonomy were 4.23, 5.61 and 3.97, respectively. Again, these values were significantly lower than the corresponding values for divisions in the other scenarios – exactly what our first hypothesis proposed. Similar results were obtained when the overall autonomy given to divisions was examined. Thus, Hypothesis 1 is strongly supported by the data.

To test the remaining hypotheses, we used only the subsample of divisions which faced strategic ambiguity – that is, the 97 divisions facing scenarios 1, 2, 3, 5, 7 and 8. Our second hypothesis proposed that among divisions facing strategic ambiguity, those that received high operational autonomy but low strategic and financial autonomy should perform better than all other divisions. To empirically test this, we had to classify divisions according to the degree of autonomy that they received from HQ and then determine whether what they received was 'appropriate' or not (as proposed by Hypothesis 2).

We first used the *mean* value of strategic, financial and operational autonomy that each division received as the cut-off point: divisions receiving more autonomy than the mean were classified as receiving high autonomy, whereas divisions receiving less autonomy than the mean were classified as receiving low autonomy. Next, all divisions receiving high operational but low strategic and financial autonomy were classified as receiving appropriate autonomy from HQ (as proposed by our hypothesis). Using this method, we classified 13 divisions as receiving appropriate autonomy. Finally, the performance of those divisions placed in the appropriate group was compared to the performance of all other divisions (84 in total).

To make sure that our results did not depend on the actual cut-off point used, we also utilized three other cut-off points to determine whether a division received high or low autonomy: first, divisions receiving more autonomy than the *median* value of strategic, financial and operational autonomy were classified as receiving high autonomy, whereas divisions receiving less than the median were classified as receiving low autonomy. Second, divisions in the top quartile (of each category of autonomy) were classified as receiving high autonomy, whereas divisions in the bottom quartile were classified as receiving low autonomy. Finally, divisions in the top one-third (of each category of autonomy) were classified as receiving high autonomy, whereas divisions in the bottom one-third were classified as receiving low autonomy. Once the high and low classifications were made, divisions were placed in the appropriate group (as proposed by our hypothesis) in the same manner as before – divisions which had high operational *and* low strategic *and* low financial autonomy were classified in the appropriate group while all others were placed in the inappropriate group. The performance of those divisions placed in the appropriate group was then compared to the performance of those divisions placed in the inappropriate group. According to Hypothesis 2, there should be a statistically significant difference in the performance of the two groups.

Table 19.5 shows the results of this analysis. Row A shows the results when the mean is used as the cut-off point. Row B shows the results when the median is used as the cut-off point. Row C shows the results when divisions are placed in the top one-third and bottom one-third. Row D shows the results when divisions are placed in quartiles. Obviously, the third and fourth methods of classification result in groups that contain too few observations for any meaningful analysis. However, the groups that result from the first two methods contain enough observations for meaningful comparisons to be made. In both cases, the divisions placed in the appropriate autonomy group have a much higher performance (at the 0.1 level) than that of all other divisions. This result provides strong support for our second hypothesis.

We also tested this hypothesis in another way. Our basic proposition is that divisions

Table 19.5   Managing strategic ambiguity: divisional autonomy and performance

Method	Classification[a]	Performance mean (s.d.)	t-values
A	Appropriate autonomy (*n* = 13)	4.59 (0.92)	1.72*
	All others (*n* = 84)	4.18 (0.78)	
B	Appropriate autonomy (*n* = 14)	4.57 (0.89)	1.68*
	All others (*n* = 83)	4.18 (0.78)	
C	Appropriate autonomy (*n* = 3)	4.48 (1.09)	0.52
	All others (*n* = 94)	4.23 (0.80)	
D	Appropriate autonomy (*n* = 0)	–	–
	All others (*n* = 97)		

Notes:
* $p < 0.1$; ** $p < 0.05$; *** $p < 0.01$.
[a] The number of divisions with appropriate autonomy which our four methods produce are quite consistent with probability rules. For method A, the probability for a division to show appropriate autonomy is $0.5 \times 0.5 \times 0.5 = 0.125$ (i.e., low STRATEGIC *and* high OPERATE *and* low FINANCIAL). The same is true for method B. For method C, the probability becomes 0.037 ($0.333 \times 0.333 \times 0.333$), while for method D, the probability is 0.0156 ($0.25 \times 0.25 \times 0.25$).

facing strategic ambiguity should be given high operational but low strategic and financial autonomy. For each division, therefore, we calculated the variable 'structural autonomy' as the product of [STRATEGIC $\times$ FINANCIAL $\times$ (1 $\div$ OPERATE)]. Based on our proposition, we would expect that those divisions facing strategic ambiguity would benefit from having lower levels of structural autonomy. This expectation was supported through simple regression analysis: when divisional performance was regressed against structural autonomy, the beta coefficient of structural autonomy came out as [–0.174] and statistically significant at the 1 percent level. This implied that the lower the structural autonomy to divisions, the higher their performance.

Further tests were carried out by ranking the 97 divisions according to their structural autonomy values. Those placed in the bottom quartile were classified as receiving appropriate structural autonomy, while those placed in the top quartile were classified as receiving inappropriate structural autonomy. For sensitivity analysis purposes, different cut-off points were used as well. As before, the sample median was used as a cut-off point: those divisions with a structural autonomy value below the sample median were classified as receiving appropriate structural autonomy while those above the median were classified as receiving inappropriate structural autonomy. In addition, those divisions in the bottom one-third of structural autonomy values were classified as receiving appropriate autonomy while those in the top one-third were classified as receiving inappropriate autonomy. The performance of the divisions placed in the appropriate group was then compared to that of those divisions placed in the inappropriate group. The results are shown in Table 19.6.

Row A shows the results when the median is used as the cut-off point. Row B shows the results when divisions are placed in the top one-third and bottom one-third. Row C shows the results when divisions are placed in quartiles. In all cases, the performance of divisions placed in the low (that is, appropriate) structural-autonomy group is higher than the performance of divisions placed in the high (that is, inappropriate) structural-

Table 19.6   Structural autonomy to divisions and performance

Method	Classification[a]	Performance mean (s.d.)	t-values
A	Low structural autonomy ($n = 48$)	4.33 (0.73)	1.10
	All others ($n = 49$)	4.15 (0.87)	
B	Low structural autonomy ($n = 32$)	4.42 (0.76)	1.64 *
	All others ($n = 65$)	4.14 (0.82)	
C	Low structural autonomy ($n = 24$)	4.54 (0.81)	2.22 **
	All others ($n = 73$)	4.13 (0.78)	

Notes:
* $p < 0.1$; ** $p < 0.05$; *** $p < 0.01$.
[a]   The number of divisions with low structural autonomy (SF/O) which our three methods produce are also quite consistent with probability rules. For method A, the probability for a division to show low SF/O is 0.5. For method B, the probability becomes 0.333, and for method C, the probability is 0.25.

Table 19.7   Performance comparison between divisions with high shared values and all others

Method	Classification	Performance mean (s.d.)	t-value
A	High shared values ($n = 49$)	4.367 (0.82)	1.67 *
	All others ($n = 48$)	4.099 (0.77)	
B	High shared values ($n = 47$)	4.381 (0.84)	1.76 *
	All others ($n = 50$)	4.098 (0.76)	
C	High shared values ($n = 31$)	4.439 (0.88)	1.73 *
	All others ($n = 66$)	4.139 (0.75)	
D	High shared values ($n = 24$)	4.521 (0.88)	2.04 **
	All others ($n = 73$)	4.141 (0.76)	

Note: * $p < 0.1$; ** $p < 0.05$; *** $p < 0.01$.

autonomy group. In two of the three cases, the difference is statistically significant. Again, these results are in general support of our second hypothesis.

Our third hypothesis proposed that among divisions facing strategic ambiguity, those that belonged to corporations which displayed high shared values will outperform all others. To test for this, we had to sort the 97 divisions into two groups: a group that contained the divisions that had high shared values and a group that had divisions with low shared values. To do this, we employed the same methodology as before: first, all divisions were ranked according to their 'shared values' index; second, they were classified into the two groups using the same four cut-off points as before (mean, median, upper and lower one-third and quartiles). Finally, the performance of divisions placed in the 'high' shared-values group was compared to the performance of divisions placed in the 'low' shared-values group. The results are shown in Table 19.7. No matter which cut-off point is used to separate the divisions, the same result stands out: in situations of strategic ambiguity, divisions displaying high shared values outperform all others. This result provides strong support for Hypothesis 3.

Finally, our fourth hypothesis proposed that divisions with high levels of communication,

Table 19.8   Performance comparison between divisions with low and high levels of communication, transfer of managers and training programs

	Classification	Performance mean (s.d.)	t-value
Communication	High level ($n = 65$)	4.361 (0.72)	2.52**
	All others ($n = 32$)	3.934 (0.89)	
Transfer of managers	High level ($n = 51$)	4.352 (0.75)	1.70 *
	All others ($n = 46$)	4.078 (0.84)	
Training programs	High level ($n = 67$)	4.353 (0.70)	2.49**
	All others ($n = 30$)	3.923 (0.93)	

Note: * $p < 0.1$; ** $p < 0.05$; *** $p < 0.01$.

training and transfer of people will outperform all others. To test this, we used the median value for each one of these variables as our cut-off point to assign divisions into high and low groups. The performance of divisions in the two groups were then compared, as before. The results are shown in Table 19.8. As predicted by Hypothesis 4, divisions with high levels of communication, training and transfer of people tend to outperform all other divisions. The difference in performance is statistically significant and in support of the fourth hypothesis.

Summary and conclusion

In this chapter, we examined the issue of ambidexterity within the context of diversified firms. Specifically, we proposed that ambidexterity is the ability of an organization to pursue two disparate things at the same time. Within a diversified firm, such a situation arises when divisions face conflicting strategic imperatives, forcing the corporate parent to reconcile two disparate demands: granting autonomy to the division while exercising central control. We, therefore, explored how the corporate parent could achieve this kind of ambidexterity.

We proposed a variety of non-structural mechanisms that could be used by corporate HQ to effectively control divisions facing conflicting strategic imperatives. Using insights from the multinational literature (for example, Bartlett and Ghoshal, 1989), we argued that the corporate center should grant these divisions operational autonomy while centralizing strategic and financial decisions so as to achieve coordination and integration within the firm. In addition to this autonomy solution, we proposed a cultural solution (conceptualized as shared values in this chapter) to resolve the strategic ambiguity dilemma. We argued that the existence of strong, shared values within the organization would allow corporate HQ to grant autonomy to divisions without losing control over them. In addition, we proposed that frequent communication, frequent rotation of managers, and corporate-sponsored training programs could all be employed as integrative mechanisms so that on the one hand, divisions could have a lot of decision-making autonomy while on the other, they can remain integrated within the firm.

Our evidence from 136 divisional general managers in 34 Taiwanese business groups suggests that different divisions receive different levels of decision-making autonomy from corporate centers, depending on the strategic scenarios faced by them. In addition, we found that divisions facing scenarios of strategic ambiguity would be better served if they are given operational autonomy but controlled centrally when it comes to strategic or financial issues. We also found evidence that strong, shared values can help in managing strategic ambiguity. Finally, we found that the use of communication, rotation of managers, and training programs can have a positive impact on the performance of divisions facing strategic ambiguity. All these findings contribute to the emerging literature on how to manage internal differentiation within diversified firms.

We believe that our findings are relevant not only for the diversification literature but also for the literature on ambidextrous organizations. Most of the discussion on how to achieve ambidextrous organizations has focused on finding the appropriate structure that would allow the firm to pursue seemingly disparate and conflicting activities (for example, Duncan, 1976; Christensen, 1997; O'Reilly and Tushman, 2004). Yet, organization theory would suggest that structure is only one of the elements of the organizational 'context' that underpin the strategy of a firm (for example, Ghoshal and Bartlett, 1994). Our research has uncovered several non-structural solutions that promote ambidexterity in the firm. Future research should try to explore what other components of a firm's organizational context facilitate the adoption of ambidextrous behaviors by the firm.

Appendix 19A   Measurement of independent variables

Environmental complexity faced by each division
This variable was operationalized as the degree of technical dynamism that each division faced in its industrial environment. Technical dynamism was proposed by Lawrence and Dyer (1983) as an important constituent of environmental information complexity. Respondents were asked to indicate the speed of technical innovation in their main industry, ranging from 'Extremely rapid' (=7) to 'Extremely slow' (=1). The higher the score, the more dynamic the environment they faced. The mean score was 4.62.

Competitive strategy of each division
Each division's competitive strategy (low-cost or differentiation: Porter, 1985) was calculated as follows: using a seven-point response scale ranging from significantly lower (=1) to significantly higher (=7), divisional general managers were asked to position their products relative to their competitors on the following three dimensions: percentage of sales spent on R&D, product quality, and product features. Divisions with higher-than-average combined scores were classified as following the differentiation strategy; divisions with lower scores were identified with the low-cost strategy. Scores ranged from 3.33 to 7.00, with a mean score of 5.07 (Cronbach alpha = 0.7805).

Resource sharing among divisions
Following the measure developed by Gupta and Govindarajan (1986), resource sharing was defined as the importance and extent of resource sharing between a division and other divisions in terms of the following eight functions: manufacturing, marketing/sales, R&D, purchasing, human capital, financing, governance liaison, and other administrative activities. Two questions, both with a seven-point response scale, were asked for each of the functions. The first question collected data on a function's importance in implementing the competitive strategy of a division, ranging from 'not important at all' (=1) to 'extremely important' (=7). The second question collected data on the extent to which a

division shared resources with other divisions in each function, ranging from 'none' (=1) to 'a very great deal' (=7). Using as weights the data on the importance of the various functions on strategic implementation, we then developed a weighted-average measure of a division's degree of resource sharing with other divisions. The higher the weighted-average score, the higher the level of resource sharing that existed. Scores ranged from 0.86 to 5.63, with a mean of 3.57 (Cronbach alpha = 0.8511).

Shared values

This variable was operationalized as the combination of two items: (i) the extent to which corporate HQs emphasized the development and management of organizational value systems, and (ii) the extent to which organizational members recognized the existence of these values. Thirteen questions were developed: 10 items tried to capture the extent to which a firm used functions such as recruitment, selection, socialization processes, rites, ceremonies and rituals to develop and manage its value systems; and three items estimated the degree to which organizational members recognized the existence of organizational values. A seven-point scale was used to ask the respondents to provide information on their degree of agreement on the 13 statements, ranging from 'strongly disagree' (=1) to 'strongly agree' (=7). A mean score for the 13 items was calculated as the measure for 'shared values' in our statistical analysis. The higher the mean score, the higher the degree of shared values within the firm. Scores ranged from 4.19 to 6.19, with a mean of 5.46 (Cronbach alpha = 0.7508).

Communication

Divisional managers were asked how much and how often communication took place between a division and its corporate center. Respondents were asked to answer this on a seven-point scale, ranging from 'never' (=1) to 'very frequently' (=7). The higher the score, the higher the level of communication a division had. Scores ranged from 1 to 7, with a mean of 5.27.

Transfer of managers

A single question asked the respondents to indicate how much and how frequently rotation of managers across divisions within the firm occurred. A seven-point scale was used, ranging from 'it never happens' (=1) to 'it happens very frequently' (=7). The higher the score, the higher the frequency of transfer of managers that the division had. Scores ranged from 1 to 7, with a mean of 4.43.

Training programs

Divisional managers were asked to indicate how frequently they trained their employees by enrolling them in company training programs. A seven-point scale was used, ranging from 'never' (=1) to 'very frequently' (=7). The higher the score, the higher the level of training programs that a division offered. Scores ranged from 1 to 7, with a mean of 4.98.

Notes

1. Our use of Taiwanese firms is opportunistic: as a part of a major research project, we have been granted unprecedented access to divisional-level data in some of the most prestigious business groups in Taiwan.

Thus, unlike most of the previous studies on this subject that gathered their data at the HQ level, we have detailed data for each division.
2. The use of the median as our cut-off point is obviously subjective. Ideally, we would have liked to perform sensitive analysis by using different cut-off points (such as the mean or quartiles). Unfortunately, the use of any cut-off point other than the median results in scenarios with too few divisions in them to make the statistical analysis meaningful. We therefore use only the median out of necessity.

References

Adler, P., Goldoftas, B. and Levine, D. (1999), 'Flexibility versus efficiency? A case study of model changeovers in the Toyota production system', *Organization Science*, **10** (1): 43–68.

Ahuja, G. and Lampert, C.M. (2001), 'Entrepreneurship in the large corporation: a longitudinal study of how established firms create breakthrough inventions', *Strategic Management Journal*, **22**: 521–43.

Barnard, C. (1939), *The Function of the Executive*, Cambridge, MA: Harvard University Press.

Bartlett, C.A. and Ghoshal, S. (1989), *Managing Across Borders*, Boston, MA: Harvard Business School Press.

Benner, M. and Tushman, M. (2002), 'Process management and technological innovation: a longitudinal study of the photography and paint industries', *Administrative Science Quarterly*, **47**: 676–706.

Benner, M. and Tushman, M. (2003), 'Exploitation, exploration and process management: the productivity dilemma revisited', *Academy of Management Review*, **28** (2): 238–56.

Burgelman, R. and Sayles, L. (1986), *Inside Corporate Innovation*, New York: Free Press.

Burns, T. and Stalker, G.M. (1961), *The Management of Innovation*, London: Tavistock.

Christensen, C. (1997), *The Innovator's Dilemma*, Boston, MA: Harvard Business School Press.

Christensen, C. and Raynor, M. (2003), *The Innovator's Solution*, Boston, MA: Harvard Business School Press.

Chu, W. (1997), 'Internal differentiation in diversified companies', paper presented at the Academy of Management Annual Conference, Boston, MA, August.

Costanzo, L.A. (2004), 'Strategic foresight in a high speed environment', Special Issue on Organizational Foresight, Haridimos Tsoukas and Jill Shepherd (eds), *Futures*, **36**: 137–44.

Duncan, R.B. (1976), 'The ambidextrous organization: designing dual structures for innovation', in R.H. Kilmann, L.R. Pondy and D. Slevin (eds), *The Management of Organization*, Vol. 1, Amsterdam and New York: North-Holland, pp. 167–88.

Eisenhardt, K. and Martin, J. (2000), 'Dynamic capabilities: what are they?', *Strategic Management Journal*, **21**: 1105–21.

Galbraith, J. (1973), *Designing Complex Organizations*, Reading, MA: Addison-Wesley.

Galbraith, J. (1977), *Organization Design*, Reading, MA: Addison-Wesley.

Ghemawat, P. and Costa, J. (1993), 'The organizational tension between static and dynamic efficiency', *Strategic Management Journal*, **14**: 59–73.

Ghoshal, S. and Bartlett, C. (1994), 'Linking organizational context and managerial action: the dimensions of quality of management', *Strategic Management Journal*, **15**: 91–112.

Ghoshal, S. and Nohria, N. (1989), 'Internal differentiation within multinational corporations', *Strategic Management Journal*, **10**: 323–37.

Ghoshal, S. and Nohria, N. (1993), 'Horses for courses: organizational forms for multinational organizations', *Sloan Management Review*, **34** (Winter), 23–35.

Gibson, C.B. and Birkinshaw, J. (2004), 'The antecedents, consequences and mediating role of organizational ambidexterity', *Academy of Management Journal*, **47** (2): 209–26.

Gilbert, C. and Bower, J. (2002), 'Disruptive change: when trying harder is part of the problem', *Harvard Business Review*, May: 94–101.

Govindarajan, V. (1986), 'Decentralization, strategy, and effectiveness of strategic business unit in multibusiness organizations', *Academy of Management Review*, **11**: 844–56.

Govindarajan, V. (1988), 'A contingency approach to strategy implementation at business-unit level: integrating administrative mechanism with strategy', *Academy of Management Journal*, **31**: 826–53.

Govindarajan, V. and Fisher, J. (1990), 'Strategy, control system, and resource sharing: effects on business-unit performance', *Academy of Management Journal*, **33**: 259–85.

Gupta, A.K. (1987), 'SBU strategies, corporate–SBU relations, and SBU effectiveness in strategy implementation', *Academy of Management Journal*, **30**: 477–500.

Gupta, A.K. and Govindarajan, V. (1984), 'Business unit strategy, managerial characteristics, and business unit effectiveness', *Academy of Management Journal*, **27**: 25–41.

Gupta, A.K. and Govindarajan, V. (1986), 'Resource sharing among SBUs: strategic antecedents and administrative implications', *Academy of Management Journal*, **29**: 695–714.

Hamel, G. and Prahalad, C.K. (1983), 'Managing strategic responsibility in the MNC', *Strategic Management Journal*, **4**: 341–51.

He, Z. and Wong, P. (2004), 'Exploration vs exploitation: an empirical test of the ambidexterity hypothesis', *Organization Science*, **15** (4): 481–94.

Hill, C.W.L. (1988), 'Corporate control type, strategy, size and financial performance', *Journal of Management Studies*, **25**: 403–17.

Hill, C.W.L. (1990), 'The functions of the headquarters units in multibusiness firms', working paper, University of Washington, Seattle, September.

Lawrence, P.R. and Dyer, D. (1983), *Renewing American Industry*, New York: Free Press.

Lawrence, P.R. and Lorsch, J.W. (1967), *Organization and Environment: Managing Differentiation and Integration*, Boston, MA: Harvard Business School Press.

Levinthal, D.A. and March, J.G. (1993), 'The myopia of learning', *Strategic Management Journal*, **14**: 95–112.

Lioukas, S., Bourantas, D. and Papadakis, V. (1993), 'Decision making autonomy in state-owned enterprises', *Organization Science*, **4**: 135–53.

MacKay, B. and McKiernan, P. (2004), 'Exploring strategy context with foresight', *European Management Review*, special edn, **1**: 69–77.

March, J. (1991), 'Exploration and exploitation in organizational learning', *Organization Science*, **2**: 71–87.

McCann, J.E. and Fery, D.L. (1979), 'An approach for assessing and managing inter-unit interdependency', *Academy of Management Review*, **4**: 113–19.

McDonough, E.F. and Leifer, R. (1983), 'Using simultaneous structures to cope with uncertainty', *Academy of Management Journal*, **26** (4): 727–35.

Nadler, D.A. and Tushman, M.L. (1988), *Strategic Organization Design: Concepts, Tools and Process*, Glenview, IL: Scott, Foresman.

Nohria, N. and Ghoshal, S. (1994), 'Differentiation fit and shared values: alternatives for managing headquarters–subsidiary relations', *Strategic Management Journal*, **15**: 491–502.

O'Reilly III, C.A. and Tushman, M. (2004), 'The ambidextrous organization', *Harvard Business Review*, April, 74–81.

Ouchi, W.G. (1980), 'Markets, bureaucracies, and clan', *Administrative Science Quarterly*, **25**: 129–41.

Perrow, C. (1967), 'A framework for the comparative analysis of organizations', *American Sociological Review*, **32** (2): 194–208.

Pfeffer, J. (1981), *Power in Organizations*, Boston, MA: Pitman.

Pfeffer, J. and Salancik, G.R. (1978), *The External Control of Organizations: A Resource Dependency Perspective*, New York: Harper & Row.

Porter, M.E. (1985), *Competitive Strategy*, New York: Free Press.

Porter, M.E. (1987), 'From competitive advantage to corporate strategy', *Harvard Business Review*, May–June: 43–60.

Porter, M.E. (1996), 'What is strategy?', *Harvard Business Review*, November–December: 61–78.

Prahalad, C.K. and Doz, Y.L. (1981), 'An approach to strategic control in MNCs', *Sloan Management Review*, Summer: 5–19.

Prahalad, C.K. and Doz, Y.L. (1987), *The Multinational Mission: Balancing Local Demands and Global Vision*, New York: Free Press.

Quinn, R. and Cameron, K. (1988), *Paradox and Transformation*, Cambridge, MA: Ballinger.

Sheremata, W.A. (2000), 'Centrifugal and centripetal forces in radical new product development under time pressure', *Academy of Management Review*, **25** (2): 389–408.

Siggelkow, N. and Levinthal, D.A. (2003), 'Temporally divide to conquer: centralized, decentralized and reintegrated organizational approaches to exploration and adaptation', *Organization Science*, **14** (6): 650–69.

Siggelkow, N. and Rivkin, J.W. (2005), 'Speed and search: designing organizations for turbulence and complexity', *Organization Science*, **16** (2): 101–22.

Thompson, J.D. (1967), *Organizations in Action*, New York: McGraw-Hill.

Tushman, M. and O'Reilly III, C.A. (1996), 'The ambidextrous organization: managing evolutionary and revolutionary change', *California Management Review*, **38** (4): 8–30.

Tushman, M., Smith, W., Wood, R., Westerman, G. and O'Reilly, C. (2004), 'Innovation streams and ambidextrous organization designs', working paper, Harvard Business School.

Vancil, R.F. (1980), *Decentralization: Managing Ambiguity by Design*, Homewood, IL: Dow-Jones, Irwin.

Volberda, H.W. (1996), 'Toward the flexible form: how to remain vital in hypercompetitive environments', *Organization Science*, **7** (4): 359–74.

Williamson, O.E. (1975), *Markets and Hierarchies*, London and New York: Macmillan.

Winter, S.G. and Szulanski, G. (2001), 'Replication as strategy', *Organization Science*, **12**: 730–43.

Woodward, J. (1965), *Industrial Organization: Theory and Practice*, London: Oxford University Press.

20 Fast cycle capability: a conceptual integration
V.K. Narayanan*

> *All managers appreciate, at least intuitively, that time is money. . . . Taking time out of a business gets interesting, however, when it represents a systematic change in the way a company accomplishes its work and serves its customers, then saving time can provide sustainable competitive advantage.*
>
> Bower and Hout (1988: 110–11)

Introduction

In recent years, many authors have suggested that speed is a source of competitive advantage for firms. According to Stalk, 'the ways leading companies manage time – in production, in new product development and introduction, in sales and distribution – represent the most powerful new sources of competitive advantage' (1988: 41). Hill and Jones (1998) identify customer responsiveness as a fourth building block of competitive advantage, in addition to quality, efficiency and innovation. They specify customer response time to be a key element of customer responsiveness. Nayyar and Bantel (1994) ascribe central importance to competitive speed in their definition of competitive agility. According to Kevin Rollins, the vice-chairman of Dell Computer Corporation, 'Most of the managerial challenges at Dell Computer have to do with what I call *velocity* – speeding the pace of every element of our business' (1998: 81, italic added). Indeed, time-based management is one of the tools used by Boston Consulting Group to improve the performance of its clients (Micklethwait and Woolridge, 1996).

Thus described, speed represents an organizational capability – often termed 'fast cycle capability' – that should occupy an important place in our discussions of strategic foresight. As argued by the editors in the introduction, strategic foresight is a process involving the deep understanding of complexity rather than an outcome involving prediction and prescription. I propose that in an increasingly hypercompetitive environment, where prediction is hazardous, organizational success may hinge on developing fast response capability: ability to sense and respond to rapidly changing circumstances. This theoretical position is also consistent with currently popular resource-based views that ascribe priority to organizational capability rather than market factors in dynamic environments.

Both external imperatives and internal benefits have been attributed to the importance of speed in building competitive advantage. External imperatives set forth include: (i) advances in communication technology, globalization and the consequent rise in competitive intensity in many industries (Gyllenhammer, 1993); (ii) the advent of advanced manufacturing techniques (AMTs) such as flexible manufacturing systems (FMSs), computer aided design (CAD), computer aided manufacturing (CAM) and robotics, which have made it possible to considerably speed up operations; and (iii) shortened product life cycles and product development times in a variety of industries ranging from automobiles to microprocessors. Internal benefits of faster cycles include a reduction of overall costs due to a decrease in overhead costs per unit produced (Bower and Hout,

1988), first-mover advantages (Lieberman and Montgomery, 1988), and rapid progress down the learning curve (Thomas, 1990).

The theoretical and empirical works related to organizational speed have developed along three hitherto *unrelated* lines. First, research on new product development (Brown and Eisenhardt, 1995), perhaps the most highly developed line of work, has studied ways of speeding up the process. Second, studies of AMTs have sometimes examined the use of these technologies to speed up operations (for example, Kotha, 1995), although the primary thrust of most studies is on flexibility and variety (for example, Parthasarthy and Sethi, 1993; Sanchez and Mahoney, 1996). Finally, a limited number of studies have examined the speed at which strategic decisions are made (for example, Eisenhardt, 1989; Wally and Baum, 1994). These three streams of research have developed relatively independently of each other, despite the underlying recognition of the importance of organizational speed.

The primary objective of this chapter is to articulate an *integrative* model of fast cycle capability (FCC), bringing together streams of research that have hitherto been unrelated. I start with an overview of extant research which relates to FCC but has developed independently. Next, I extend Bower and Hout's (1988) concept of FCC as permeating the entire organization, and identify its key elements to be strategic decision making, new product development and the primary value chain activities. I also develop a model of the concept and relate it to environmental, organizational and technology-related factors. I posit two sets of hypotheses. First, the competitive advantage gained from FCC depends on specific characteristics of the firm's industry environment. Second, organizational (strategic focus, top management team characteristics, organizational structure and project management), and technology-related (the firm's absorptive capacity, network embeddedness and investments in technology) factors impact on the different elements of FCC. While managers of a firm have little control over the characteristics of the environment(s) in which the firm operates, they have more influence over the organizational and technology-related factors that can be used to enable FCC. Finally, I discuss the implications of this chapter for future academic research and for practitioners.

Overview of the literature
Following Bower and Hout (1988), I conceptualize FCC as an organizational capability that management infuses into the firm's operating systems and the attitudes of its employees. As underscored by Bower and Hout, 'the faster information, decisions, and materials can flow through a large organization, the faster it can respond to customer orders or adjust to changes in market demand and competitive conditions' (pp. 110–11). This conceptualization is also consistent with Meyer, who defined fast cycle time as 'the ongoing ability to identify, satisfy, and be paid for meeting customer needs faster than anyone else' (1993: 17). Both Bower and Hout, and Meyer emphasize that FCC is a system-wide capability. In addition, Meyer benchmarks the organization's FCC against that of the competition.

The conceptualization of FCC as an *organizational* capability makes it possible to link it to a firm's value chain. As formulated by Porter (1985), a firm's value chain comprises two interrelated sets of activities: primary (inbound logistics, operations, outbound logistics, marketing and sales, and service) and support (firm infrastructure, technology development, human resource management, and procurement) activities. As a system-wide capability, FCC embraces the speed of conduct of both primary and support activities; in addition, it underscores the linkages among the two sets of activities. For example, technology development may influence the speed of operations, and when resource allocations are involved, both technology development and operations may be influenced by the speed of top management decision making.

Extant empirical research has primarily focused on speed of conduct of three value chain activities: (i) new product development, (ii) manufacturing and (iii) strategic decision making. Within the value chain framework, manufacturing represents a primary value chain activity whereas new product development and strategic decision making represent support activities.

New product development (NPD)

As demonstrated in reviews of research on NPD (for example, Brown and Eisenhardt, 1995; Kessler and Chakrabarti, 1996), the speed of NPD has received a great deal of research attention. NPD speed has been operationalized in a variety of ways: time from product idea to commercialization (Ali et al., 1995), time from receipt of funding for a product to its market introduction (Zirger and Hartley, 1996) and time from the first meeting for a new product until its stabilization (Eisenhardt and Tabrizi, 1995). Some studies have used relative measures such as plotting the actual progress of the project against the planned schedule (McDonough, 1993), speed of the project compared to that of previous projects (Nijssen et al., 1995), and speed of NPD compared to that of the competition (Birnbaum-More, 1993).

In spite of the differences in operationalization, robust findings have emerged regarding the factors that contribute to NPD speed. These include the effect of project team characteristics and senior management support (Rothwell, 1972; Rothwell et al., 1974; Gupta and Wilemon, 1990) on project lead time and productivity. For example, cross-functional teams (Dougherty, 1990) and the presence of gatekeepers, who gather information and communicate it to team members and also facilitate external communication of the team (Katz and Tushman, 1981) increased project performance. Project performance is also related to the importance of communication within the project team (Dougherty, 1992) and political and task-related external communication (Brown and Eisenhardt, 1995). Greater involvement of suppliers in the development process has been found to be associated with faster NPD (Mabert et al., 1992; Eisenhardt and Tabrizi, 1995). In a recent review, Kessler and Chakrabarti (1996) focused on development speed, and hypothesized that in addition to the factors mentioned above, other organizational elements such as goal clarity, an emphasis on speed, and external sourcing contribute to decreased development times.

Extant research has also documented the benefits and costs of increasing NPD speed. Fast NPD can increase market share by introducing products earlier (Urban et al., 1986), decrease development costs (Rosenthal, 1992) and cost of operations (Bower and Hout, 1988). It also helps in establishing first-mover advantages, which include technological leadership, preemption of assets, and creation of switching costs (Lieberman and Montgomery, 1988). However, faster NPD may increase the demand on the firm's resources and could lead to a focus on less risky projects that focus on incremental improvements as opposed to more risky, longer-term projects necessary for breakthrough innovation (Crawford, 1992). Hence improvements in NPD times may not necessarily improve financial performance and can even affect it adversely (Sterman et al., 1997).

Research on NPD has largely been at the project level (Adler, 1989), and has typically not accounted for the strategic decisions that led to the initiation of an NPD. At the organizational level, Firth and Narayanan (1996), using secondary data sources, explored the central tendencies in a firm's product development, and related that to competitive advantage. Nonetheless, the literature that holistically examines the firm's innovation ability is largely practitioner oriented (Kessler and Chakrabarti, 1996). The findings at the project level, on the other hand, have been cumulative and offer a basis for extrapolation to the organizational level.

Primary value chain activities
The predominant focus of studies that have dealt with speed in primary value chain activities has been on the use of AMTs. I shall first review these studies before I summarize research on other primary value chain activities.

Advanced manufacturing technologies   AMTs, FMSs, and flexible automation (FA) are terms used to refer to the use of computers and automation in the manufacturing process (Pennings, 1987). They include CAM, involve computer controlled production scheduling, operations control, handling and transport, using robots, automatic conveyors, or automated guided vehicles (AGVs) (Bessant and Haywood, 1988; Boyer et al., 1997). The basic premise underlying the introduction of AMTs is that efficiency can be achieved without the long production runs typically needed in traditional mass production. Rather than economies of scale, these new techniques realize economies of scope (Pine, 1993).

Empirical literature on AMTs has operationalized speed in many ways. Most researchers conceptualized speed in terms of flexibility – both speed and variety. For example, Upton (1994) defined flexibility as the ability to change or react with little penalty in time, effort, cost or performance. This is similar to the definition of agile manufacturing as the ability to thrive in a competitive environment of continuous and unanticipated change (Herrin, 1994). Suarez et al. (1995) identified three broad types of flexibility: (i) mix flexibility, measured by the number of products produced at any point in time; (ii) new product flexibility, which is the same as speed of NPD; and (iii) volume flexibility, or the ability to vary production with no detrimental effect on efficiency and quality. Ettlie and Penner-Hahn (1994) used several measures of flexibility including average changeover time, which is the time required to switch between two parts, and the ratio of parts to changeover time. All their measures would fall under mix flexibility, using Suarez et al.'s (1995) definition. Some studies have measured the investment in AMTs, rather than the flexibility that resulted from it. For example, Parthasarthy and Sethi (1993) measured the intensity of flexible automation, which is the proportion of the total manufacturing outlay represented by capital outlay in computer automation, including CAD and CAM.

A summary of representative studies on AMTs is presented in Table 20.1. As is evident from the table, extant empirical research suggests that organizational structure and strategy have a significant impact on the extent of benefits realized from AMTs (for example, Hayes and Jaikumar, 1991; Parthasarthy and Sethi, 1993). An organic rather than a mechanistic structure and a clear strategy focus help to increase the potential benefits of AMTs (Small and Yasin, 1997). Research has also documented the key benefits of AMTs:

Table 20.1   Studies on advanced manufacturing technologies

Focus	Findings	Representative studies
Organizational changes required for firm to successfully implement AMTs	Investments in AMTs more likely to improve financial performance if supported by organizational changes such as worker empowerment, emphasis on quality, cross-functional integration and closer relationships with suppliers and customers	Bessant & Haywood (1988), Hayes & Jaikumar (1991), Boyer et al. (1997)
Relationship between strategy and flexibility	Firms with a strategic emphasis on flexibility benefit more from FMS Firms investing in FMS were more concerned with variations in inputs & outputs than firms that did not invest in FMS Flexibility has more to do with organizational factors such as worker and supplier involvement than technology-related factors	Tombak & De Meyer (1988), Ettlie & Penner-Hahn (1994), Suarez et al. (1995)
Relationship of strategy and structure to FA (flexible automation) & AMTs	Following interact positively with FA: strategic focus on quality & flexibility, organic structure & use of teams Low cost strategy & mechanistic organizational structure interact negatively with FA AMTs increase operational efficiency	Parthasarthy & Sethi (1993), Small & Yasin (1997)
Relationship between product variety and manufacturing performance	Lean production plants can handle more variety with less adverse effect on manufacturing performance (productivity and product quality) than traditional mass production plants	Kotha (1995), MacDuffie et al. (1996)
Factors influencing investments in FMS	Diffusion of FMS is lower in the US than in Japan or Western Europe, possibly due to the required rate of return being higher in the US Larger markets and those with more differentiated products lead to more investments in FMS	Mansfield (1993), Roller & Tombak (1993)
Benefits and diffusion of AMTs	AMTs reduce lead times and increase productivity	Voss (1988), Trygg (1993)

increased productivity, decreased production lead times, and flexibility, which is the ability to increase product variety without a significant negative impact on productivity or production lead times (Zammuto and O'Connor, 1992).

Other primary value chain activities   In terms of cycle times or speed, there has been very little research focusing on primary value chain activities other than operations. There were two exceptions. In the first, Daugherty and Pittman (1995) interviewed executives of 10 Fortune 500 firms and found that they were reducing lead time to customers by reducing distribution lead time. Distribution lead time was reduced by three mechanisms: responsiveness, flexibility, and communication. First, responsiveness was increased by: (i) developing performance measures used to monitor service levels and customer feedback; (ii) using information systems and consumer-oriented personnel to ensure that customers were answered immediately ('one call response'); (iii) initiating key account programs providing superior service; and (iv) ensuring that consistent service took precedence over faster but less dependable service. Second, firms reduced distribution lead time through increased flexibility by customizing products at distribution centers rather than during the manufacturing process, and demanding more from transportation carriers and vendors and entering into long-term contracts with them. Finally, firms increased the level of communication and information exchange with the help of quick response programs integrating technologies such as electronic data interchange (EDI) universal product code/bar coding and point-of-sale systems.

The second, Bonaccorsi and Lipparini's (1994) study of an Italian manufacturer, found that the integration of its suppliers into the firm's NPD process allowed the firm to shorten the product development cycle and increase the proportion of successful new product programs. The authors describe the firm as one of the world's leading manufacturers of machines and systems for processing and packaging foods and other products. They suggest that creating conditions favorable for rapid NPD involves paying careful attention to supplier selection and evaluation systems, proximity of the supplier network, a trusting and open relationship with suppliers, and synchronization of the development process among all the firms in the network so as to permit simultaneous rather than sequential development.

In summary, the introduction of AMTs to reduce manufacturing cycle time remains the most widely researched area within primary value chain activities. Unlike the bulk of the literature on NPD, extant research on primary value chain activities has been at the organizational level, and has identified both organizational and technological determinants of cycle time.

Strategic decision making
Overall cycle time should include the time taken to make strategic decisions. In many cases the strategic decision may precede the decision to launch a new product or introduce changes in primary value chain activities. While there has been a substantial amount of research on strategic decision processes (see Rajagopalan et al., 1993, for a review), there have been surprisingly few studies that focus on decision-making speed. Eisenhardt (1989) initiated research in this area, postulating that in high-velocity environments strategic decision-making speed is a determinant of performance. Her study of eight microcomputer companies resulted in several inductive hypotheses, some of which were

subsequently applied to a larger sample by Judge and Miller (1991). They found that the number of alternatives considered simultaneously was positively associated with decision speed. They also found that decision speed was positively associated with the firm's performance in high-velocity environments. Wally and Baum's (1994) study of 151 CEOs found that faster decisions were associated with centralized and formalized decision-making structures and characteristics of the executive such as cognitive ability, use of intuition, risk tolerance and propensity to act.

Integrative studies   Very few studies have simultaneously considered several elements of the value chain, in terms of increasing organizational speed. Choperena (1996) applied the principles of fast cycle time (Meyer, 1993) to a medical equipment manufacturer where he was the head of technology, and found that customer focus, the use of multi-functional teams, empowered individuals and teams and a well-defined roadmap led to valuable innovations in project management and product and process development. Kotha's (1995) case study of the National Bicycle Industry Company (NBIC), Japan's No. 2 bicycle manufacturer, identified the methods used to mass-customize a line of bicycles, which gave the company a significant competitive advantage over its key rival, Bridgestone. Customers of the mass-customized range of bicycles could choose from about 8 million possible variations based on model type, color, frame size, and other features, and receive the bicycle in two weeks. NBIC devoted separate factories to its mass-customized and mass-produced line and rotated top-rated and skilled workers between the factories to transfer knowledge across the different types of operation. Locating the factory close to key suppliers to facilitate frequent and reliable delivery of parts, and direct transfer and processing of the customer order at the factory were other ways used to achieve such remarkable cycle times.

In summary, the empirical literature related to FCC has been evolving along three distinct lines. The bulk of the research has been on NPD. Research on AMTs has been proceeding piecemeal and has reached the stage where a comprehensive conceptual model of its antecedents and consequences is required in order to identify the various facets of the firm and the environment that affect the realization of the benefits of AMTs. While cycle times in technology development and operations have been studied by these two bodies of research, there have been very few studies related to speed or cycle time that focus on other elements of the firm's value chain. Little of the research on strategic decision making has specifically examined the speed at which decisions are made. Finally, there have been relatively few attempts to bring the three streams of research under the umbrella of fast cycle capability.

An integrative framework
The main objective of this chapter is to provide a theoretical integration of several streams of literature focusing on speed or cycle time under the umbrella of the FCC construct first advanced by Bower. Four major ideas constitute the essence of our integration.

1. Our model of FCC is anchored in the *value chain concept*, and focuses on both primary and support activities in the value chain. The model embraces three key constituent elements: speed of strategic decision making, NPD, and operation of primary value chain activities. The first two elements fall under the scope of support activities.

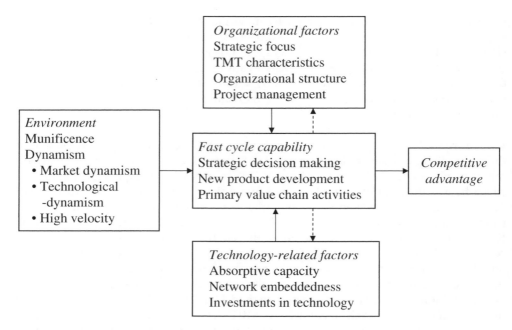

Figure 20.1   Model of fast cycle capability

2. We identify the key *environmental antecedents* of FCC of an organization. I demonstrate that different environmental settings call for different configuration of the three elements of FCC, thus opening the theoretical link to a fine-grained analysis of the relevance of FCC to an organization.
3. We focus on the major *organizational* and *technology-related factors* that enable a firm to achieve high levels of FCC. These enablers provide the action levers for managers to move an organization to higher levels of capability.
4. Finally, I focus on *competitive advantage* as the appropriate outcome for evaluating the relevance of FCC for an organization. This provides the theoretical segue between the concept and strategy analysis.

Our integrative framework is presented in Figure 20.1. I now turn to postulating the linkages between environmental antecedents, organizational and technology-related factors and FCC.

Environmental factors
The environments in which firms operate have been the focus of significant research (for example, Emery and Trist, 1965; Jurkovich, 1974; Starbuck, 1976; Aldrich, 1979; Dess and Beard, 1984) in the field of organization theory. Most conceptualizations of environment have been at the industry level and hence applicable to single-industry firms or strategic business units (SBUs) of diversified firms. I focus on four key factors: environmental munificence, market dynamism, technological dynamism and high-velocity environments.

Environmental munificence   This refers to the extent to which environments support organizational growth and stability (Starbuck, 1976). Munificent environments feature less competition, due to high entry barriers, and allow greater organizational slack for the incumbents (Dess and Beard, 1984). Such industries are characterized by clear differentiation among the few incumbents, and hence FCC is not likely to give a firm any significant competitive advantage. Besides, the investments required to develop FCC might hurt the firm's hitherto successful strategy that was suited to a specific industry environment.

> *Proposition 1: The greater the munificence of the business unit's environment, the less the competitive advantage gained from fast cycle capability.*

Dess and Beard's study on organizational task environments found that environmental dynamism is a multidimensional construct. They labeled the key dimensions of this construct 'market' dynamism and 'technological' dynamism.

Dynamism   Dynamic markets are characterized by unpredictable demand and hence firms which serve such a market need to be able to change production levels at short notice, so as to keep inventory levels manageable while simultaneously fulfilling customers orders in a timely fashion. In such a scenario, FCC in the primary value chain activities would allow the firm to convert inputs into finished products and deliver them to customers faster than the competition. To the extent that the dynamism of the market extends to changes in not only the volume but also the type of products demanded, faster NPD would also result in a competitive advantage.

> *Proposition 2a: The greater the market dynamism of the business unit's environment, the greater the competitive advantage gained from fast cycle capability in the business unit's primary value chain activities, and to a lesser extent, from fast cycle capability in the NPD process.*

Technologically dynamic environments are those in which there is intense technological variation for extended periods of time, prior to the emergence of a dominant design (Anderson and Tushman, 1990). In such an industry, the ability to develop new products rapidly is a key competitive advantage (Lawless and Anderson, 1996). Speed in the primary value chain activities would allow a firm to progress down the learning curve faster than the competition (Thomas, 1990).

> *Proposition 2b: The greater the technological dynamism of the business unit's environment, the greater the competitive advantage gained from fast cycle capability in the NPD process, and to a lesser extent from fast cycle capability in primary value chain activities.*

High-velocity or fast cycle industry environments (Williams, 1994) are characterized by a high level of uncertainty in market demand, technological standards and regulation (Bourgeois and Eisenhardt, 1988). These environments exhibit both market and technological dynamism. Firms operating in this kind of industry need to make fast strategic decisions (Judge and Miller, 1991), develop new products quickly, and execute the primary value chain activities rapidly so as to make the most of a product's short life cycle.

> *Proposition 2c:* In high-velocity environments, the competitive advantage gained from a comprehensive model of fast cycle capability (fast cycle capability in strategic decision making, NPD and primary value chain activities) will be high.

In summary, munificent environments do not support the development of FCC for competitive advantage. In dynamic environments, different constellations of the constituents of FCC contribute to competitive advantage. Speed in primary value chain activities is critical in dynamic markets, whereas speed of NPD is of central importance in environments characterized by technological dynamism. High-velocity environments support the development of a comprehensive model of FCC for competitive advantage.

A second set of factors enables the development and enactment of FCC; these can be grouped into two categories: organizational and technology related.

Organizational factors
As underscored by the extant research on NPD, AMTs and strategic decision-making speed, four organizational factors enable the enactment of FCC: strategic focus, top management characteristics, organizational structure and project management.

Strategic focus Top management's commitment (Ghemawat, 1991) to a particular strategic direction for a sustained period of time demonstrates clarity of vision and enables purposeful implementation. When the firm's overall direction is clear and not changed frequently, the process of making strategic decisions becomes easier and should take less time since the top management would have to spend less time discussing possible changes in the firm's basic strategy.

> *Proposition 3:* The greater the strategic focus of the organization, the higher the strategic decision-making speed.

Top management team (TMT) characteristics Two TMT characteristics may be related to strategic decision-making speed: homogeneity and CEO duality. Cognitive diversity in the TMT leads to a broader discussion of strategic issues and the emergence of several perspectives (Bantel and Jackson, 1989). However, this diversity also impedes communication in heterogeneous TMTs (Miller et al., 1998) and increases the time taken to implement actions and react to competitive moves (Hambrick et al., 1996).

> *Proposition 4a:* A homogeneous TMT will be associated with higher strategic decision-making speed.

'CEO duality' refers to the condition when the CEO is also the chairman of the board of directors (Boyd, 1995). Agency theory (Fama and Jensen, 1983; Lorsch and MacIver, 1989; Millstein, 1992) argues that CEO duality compromises the prime function of the board, which is to oversee and monitor the functioning of the management of the firm. On the other hand, stewardship theory (Donaldson, 1991; Davis et al., 1997), holds that CEO duality facilitates more effective and faster action by CEOs who have the best interests of the firm in mind. While the argument on the relationship between CEO duality and firm performance has not been resolved (Baliga et al., 1996), CEO duality would give greater power to the CEO and hence would facilitate faster decision making.

Proposition 4b: *CEO duality will be associated with higher strategic decision-making speed.*

Organizational structure 'Formalization' refers to the degree to which formal rules and procedures govern organizational activities (Hall, 1996). Organizations that are highly formalized tend to be comprehensive (Frederickson and Mitchell, 1984) decision makers, who encourage very thorough analyses involving extensive data collection, before decisions are made. While consideration of a larger number of alternatives might actually increase the speed of decision making (Eisenhardt, 1989), the time taken to gather the data required in these kinds of organization would considerably impede the speed of the process.

Proposition 5a: *The higher the level of formalization in the organizational structure, the lower the strategic decision-making speed.*

'Centralization' is the degree to which decision-making power is retained at higher managerial levels. When strategic decision making is centralized, it is likely to proceed faster, since there would be less consultation, and top executives would have ready access to more complete information than would managers at lower levels, and hence contribute to their confidence to act (Galbraith, 1977).

Proposition 5b: *The higher the level of centralization of strategic decision making, the higher the strategic decision-making speed.*

There is strong recognition of the importance of communication and coordination between the different functional departments in increasing the speed of NPD (Dougherty, 1990; Song et al., 1997). This recognition has led to an increase in practices such as concurrent engineering (Trygg, 1993), where 'parallel processing' or overlapping activities (Smith and Reinertsen, 1991) leads to better and faster development of new products.

Proposition 5c: *The greater the integration between R&D, manufacturing and marketing, the greater the speed of NPD.*

The 'customer service cycle' (Thomas, 1990: 33) refers to the time taken for the customer to receive the product or service once the order has been received or forecast. This essentially involves the primary activities in the firm's value chain (Porter, 1985), and is a measure of operating efficiency. Achieving superior cycle times here would require a high level of coordination between the departments involved in these activities.

Proposition 5d: *The greater the integration between manufacturing/operations, sales and customer service, the greater the fast cycle capability associated with the primary value chain activities.*

Project management   The support of senior management is critical to the speed and success of an NPD project process (Gupta and Wilemon, 1990), by expediting access to resources and communicating a clear vision of their objectives (Imai et al., 1985).

> *Proposition 6a: The greater the top management support to the project, the greater the speed of NPD.*

A substantial amount of the time taken by an NPD project is consumed by administrative tasks such as obtaining formal approvals (Dumaine, 1989; Blackburn, 1992). Increasing the level of autonomy given to the project team can considerably reduce the time consumed in formal approvals.

> *Proposition 6b: The greater the autonomy given to the project, the greater the speed of NPD.*

When the project team consists of members with different functional backgrounds, there is not only access to more diverse information but also overlapping of development phases, which leads to faster development overall (Imai et al., 1985). Gatekeepers (Allen, 1971) are good performers who communicate with the external world outside the team, and hence not only obtain information and communicate it to team members but also facilitate external communication of the team (Katz and Tushman, 1981). Communication within and outside the team is a key determinant of project speed (Brown and Eisenhardt, 1995).

> *Proposition 6c: Cross-functional teams that include gatekeepers will be associated with faster NPD.*

Leaders of project teams have several roles, which include those of communicator, integrator and planner, and the extent to which each of these roles is important varies depending on the situation (Brown and Karagozoglu, 1993). However, powerful project managers can obtain resources, expedite approvals and perform other enabling activities that require coordinating with other departments and senior management (Clark and Fujmoto, 1991; Eisenhardt and Tabrizi, 1995). Good management skills are essential to increase communication and coordination within the team, while providing an overarching vision.

> *Proposition 6d: A powerful project leader with good management skills will be associated with faster NPD.*

Technology-related factors
Factors related to technology constitute a second set of enablers of FCC. I identify three such factors: absorptive capacity, network embeddedness and investments in technology.

Absorptive capacity   Cohen and Levinthal formulated the concept of 'absorptive capacity' to refer to a 'firm's ability to recognize the value of new external information, assimilate it, and apply it to commercial ends' (1990: 128). Since most new products are based on borrowing information from outside the firm rather than pure invention (March and Simon, 1958), it stands to reason that a firm with superior absorptive capacity will be able to commercialize innovations faster than its competitors. It would also be able to absorb and utilize process innovations in its primary value chain activities.

Proposition 7: *The greater the absorptive capacity of the organization, the greater the fast cycle capability associated with the NPD process and the primary value chain activities.*

Network embeddedness Co-development, which refers to sharing the design process with suppliers, instead of merely giving them the specifications of the part to manufacture, has contributed to increased development speed in the same way that concurrent engineering did (Mabert et al., 1992; Eisenhardt and Tabrizi, 1995). Network embeddedness refers to a closer relationship not only with suppliers and customers but also with competitors. Technological alliances can not only increase efficiency by avoiding 'reinventing the wheel' but also contribute to establishing standards or dominant designs (Anderson and Tushman, 1990) and thus avoid uncertainty in the product development process. The trend towards increased outsourcing has led to 'network' or 'virtual' organizations (Davidow and Malone, 1992) which do only one or a few of the value chain activities and outsource the rest. Outsourcing increases efficiency and speed, since each activity is entrusted to a specialist who would be more of an expert in that particular activity than a traditional firm which does all the activities itself.

Proposition 8: *The greater the network embeddedness of the organization, the greater the fast cycle capability associated with the NPD process and the primary value chain activities.*

Investments in technology Information technology (IT) has become a major tool in increasing the efficiency and speed of financial service operations, from credit card verification to getting cash from automatic teller machines. Walmart's enormous investment in IT is targeted towards logistics management, which enables the retailer to tailor the products in its stores to customer preferences more accurately than the competition, which allows it to turn over its inventory several times faster. Investments in AMTs contribute to increasing production speed (Cordero, 1991) and technologies such as EDI and universal product coding or bar coding systems increase speed of distribution (Daugherty and Pittman, 1995). It would be reasonable to expect that technology-related capital investments which are targeted at the primary value chain activities would contribute to increase the efficiency of these activities and hence their speed.

Proposition 9: *The greater the investment resulting in enhancing the technology used in the primary value chain activities, the greater the fast cycle capability associated with the primary value chain activities.*

Table 20.2 summarizes the hypotheses developed in the chapter. As indicated by the feedback loops in the model (Figure 20.1), developing FCC improves the organization's capacity to learn from the outcomes of the processes it initiated. This, in turn, leads to

Table 20.2   Summary of propositions

	Strategic decision making	New product development	Primary value chain activities
Environment			
Munificence	–	–	–
Dynamism			
Market dynamism		+	+ +
Technological dynamism		+ + .	
High velocity	+ +	+ +	+
Organizational factors			
Strategic focus	+		
TMT characteristics			
Homogeneous TMT	+		
CEO duality	+		
Organizational structure			
Formalization	–		
Integration		+	+
Centralized strategic decision making	+		
Project management			
Top management support		+	
Autonomy		+	
Project team characteristics			
Cross-functional		+	
Presence of gatekeepers		+	
Project leader characteristics			
Powerful		+	
Management skills		+	
Technology-related factors			
Absorptive capacity		+	+
Network embeddedness		+	+
Investments in technology			+ +

Notes:
+: Positive relationship.
+ +: Strongly positive relationship.
–: Negative relationship.
[blank]: No evidence of relationship from extant literature.

a positive spiral which makes cycle time reduction a continuous and ongoing process, as opposed to the one-time gains provided by interventions such as business process re-engineering (Hammer and Champy, 1993).

Implications
The integrative model of FCC presented in this chapter draws upon several lines of extant research on speed that have developed almost independently of each other. It is useful to

summarize three distinct features of this integration to place our ensuing summary of its research and practical implications in context.

First, since the model provides a theoretical basis for the concept of FCC, it can be subject to empirical analyses from distinct theoretical viewpoints. For example, since it is conceptualized as an organization-wide characteristic, FCC may be subject to ecological analyses of the kind prevalent in organization theory. Analyses and evidence pertaining to the survival rates of FCC organizations relative to low cycle times in different environments may be especially useful. Alternatively, since FCC is anchored in the value chain concept, it can be subject to analyses based on strategic management theory. The imitability of FCC practices and the economic rents that may be derived from this capability are illustrative of the kinds of theoretical questions that need exploration.

Second, the integration also highlights the interplay of organizational and technological enablers of FCC. While the literature on NPD speed has studied their relationships to organizational factors such as structure and strategy, there has been comparatively little attention paid to the technology-related factors identified in our integrative framework. On the other hand, technology-related factors have been the focus of theoretical attention in the literatures on AMTs, R&D and management of technology. By bringing the literatures together, I obtain a somewhat broader picture of the factors driving FCC and organizational speed.

Finally, our model of FCC underscores the idea that different models of FCC are appropriate for different environments. As elaborated in our hypotheses, the relative emphasis of the three elements – (i) strategic decision making, (ii) new product development and (iii) primary value chain activities – may vary from industry to industry.

The integrative model of FCC suggests several avenues of fruitful empirical research. On the one hand, ecological analyses of FCC, using archival sources of data, are needed to disconfirm the key hypotheses related to environmental antecedents presented in the chapter. On the other, linking FCC to competitive advantage or explicitly to value creation may be of great usefulness from a strategic management perspective. A key task in both research streams is to introduce measures of speed (NPD, cycle time in value chain and speed of strategic decision making) as significant variables in theoretical and empirical works.

Two practical implications of the model are worthy of elaboration. First, as I have demonstrated, different environments support different models of FCC; in munificent environments, FCC is not particularly useful. From a managerial point of view, therefore, a careful diagnosis is needed before a firm embarks on organizational change efforts to build FCC. Although the increasing turbulence in the macro environment may support the development of FCC in a large number of industries, 'one shoe does not fit all', and firms need to orchestrate a model of FCC suited to its context. Second, both organizational and technology-related factors offer ways to build FCC. These two factors should be viewed as complementary in change efforts; indeed, significant competitive advantage may be gained from the interactions of the two sets of factors.

In other words, I offer a contingent view of strategic foresight. In relatively stable environments, foresight may focus on prediction and prescription; in dynamic and especially hypercompetitive environments, organizational capabilities, especially fast cycle capability, should be an important focus of organizational responses to develop strategic foresight. In this chapter, I have outlined a nuanced view of this capability. FCC itself can be conceptualized as customized to a specific organization as opposed to a standard template that ignores the habitat and history of an organization.

Extant literature which cuts across intra-firm boundaries such as functional and value chain components is almost exclusively practitioner oriented, based on anecdotal evidence, and prescriptive in nature (for example, Stalk and Hout, 1990; Thomas, 1990). While the importance of time in today's competitive environment is something that practitioners understand all too well, academic research on organizational speed or fast cycle capability has been fragmented. The model developed in this chapter provides a framework to stimulate empirical research that takes a *holistic* approach to FCC. In turn, the empirical research may contribute to a greater understanding of this concept, which is highly relevant for the business environment of this age.

Note

* This chapter is based on a paper, earlier drafts of which were presented at the Academy of Management Conference and Strategic Management Society Conference. The chapter has benefited from the comments of reviewers of the conference, and participants in the Management Science and Technology Seminar at the School of Business, University of Kansas. Special thanks are due to Marie Buche, Elaine Hollensbe and Sucheta Nadkarni for detailed comments on an earlier version of this chapter.

References

Adler, P. (1989), 'Technology strategy: a guide to the literature', in R. Rosenblum and R. Burgelman (eds), *Research on Technological Innovation, Management, and Policy*, Vol. 4, Greenwich, CT: JAI Press, pp. 25–151.
Aldrich, H.E. (1979), *Organizations and Environments*, Englewood Cliffs, NJ: Prentice-Hall.
Ali, A., Krapfel, Robert, Jr. and LaBahn, D. (1995), 'Product innovativeness and entry strategy: impact on cycle time and break-even time', *Journal of Product Innovation Management*, 12: 54–69.
Allen, T.J. (1971), 'Communications, technology transfer, and the role of technical gatekeeper', *R&D Management*, 1: 14–21.
Anderson, P. and Tushman, M.L. (1990), 'Technological discontinuities and dominant designs: a cyclical model of technological change', *Administrative Science Quarterly*, 35: 604–33.
Baliga, B.R., Moyer, R.C. and Rao, R.S. (1996), 'CEO duality and firm performance: what's the fuss?', *Strategic Management Journal*, 17: 41–53.
Bantel, K.A. and Jackson, S.E. (1989), 'Top management and innovations in banking: does the composition of the top team make a difference?', *Strategic Management Journal*, 10: 107–12.
Bessant, J. and Haywood, B. (1988), 'Islands, archipelagoes and continents: progress on the road to computer-integrated manufacturing', *Research Policy*, 17: 349–62.
Birnbaum-More, P. H. (1993), *New Product Development Time: A Cross-national Study*, Bethlehem, PA: Center for Innovation Management Studies, Lehigh University.
Blackburn, J.D. (1992), 'Time-based competition: white collar activities', *Business Horizons*, 35(4): 96–101.
Bonaccorsi, A. and Lipparini, A. (1994), 'Strategic partnerships in new product development: an Italian case study', *Journal of Product Innovation Management*, 11: 134–45.
Bourgeois III, L.J. and Eisenhardt, K.M. (1988), 'Strategic decision processes in high velocity environments: four cases in the microcomputer industry', *Management Science*, 34: 816–35.
Bower, J.L. and Hout, T.M. (1988), 'Fast-cycle capability for competitive power', *Harvard Business Review*, November–December: 110–18.
Boyd, B.K. (1995), 'CEO duality and firm performance: a contingency model', *Strategic Management Journal*, 16: 301–12.
Boyer, K.K., Leong, G.K., Ward, P.T. and Krajewski, L.J. (1997), 'Unlocking the potential of advanced manufacturing technologies', *Journal of Operations Management*, 15: 331–47.
Brown, S.L. and Eisenhardt, K.M. (1995), 'Product development: past research, present findings, and future directions', *Academy of Management Review*, 20: 343–78.
Brown, W.B. and Karagozoglu, N. (1993), 'Leading the way to faster new product development', *Academy of Management Executive*, 7: 36–47.
Choperena, A.M. (1996), 'Fast cycle time – driver of innovation and quality', *Research Technology Management*, 39(3): 36–40.

Clark, K.B. and Fujmoto, T. (1991), *Product Development Performance: Strategy, Organization, and Management in the World Auto Industry*, Boston, MA: Harvard Business School Press.

Cohen, W.M. and Levinthal, D.A. (1990), 'Absorptive capacity: a new perspective on learning and innovation', *Administrative Science Quarterly*, **35**: 128–52.

Cordero, R. (1991), 'Managing for speed to avoid product obsolescence: a survey of techniques', *Journal of Product Innovation Management*, **8**: 283–94.

Crawford, C.M. (1992), 'The hidden costs of accelerated product development', *Journal of Product Innovation Management*, **9**: 188–99.

Daugherty, P.J. and Pittman, P.H. (1995), 'Utilization of time-based strategies', *International Journal of Operations and Production Management*, **15**(2): 54–60.

Davidow, W. and Malone, M. (1992), *A Virtual Corporation: Structuring and Revitalizing the Corporation of the 21st Century*, New York: Harper Business.

Davis, J.H., Schoorman, F.D. and Donaldson, L. (1997), 'Towards a stewardship theory of management', *Academy of Management Review*, **22**: 20–47.

Dess, G.G. and Beard, D.W. (1984), 'Dimensions of organizational task environments', *Administrative Science Quarterly*, **29**: 52–73.

Donaldson, L. (1991), 'The ethereal hand: organizational economics and management theory', *Academy of Management Review*, **15**: 369–81.

Dougherty, D. (1990), 'Understanding new markets for new products', *Strategic Management Journal*, **11**: 59–78.

Dougherty, D. (1992), 'Integrative barriers to successful product innovation in large firms', *Organization Science*, **3**: 179–202.

Dumaine, B. (1989), 'How managers can succeed through speed', *Fortune*, February 13: 54–9.

Eisenhardt, K.M. (1989), 'Making fast strategic decisions in high-velocity environments', *Academy of Management Journal*, **32**: 543–76.

Eisenhardt, K.M. and Tabrizi, B.N. (1995), 'Accelerating adaptive processes: product innovation in the global computer industry', *Administrative Science Quarterly*, **40**: 84–110.

Emery, F.E. and Trist, E.L. (1965), 'The causal texture of organizational environments', *Human Relations*, **18**: 21–32.

Ettlie, J.E. and Penner-Hahn, J.D. (1994), 'Flexibility ratios and manufacturing strategy', *Management Science*, **40**: 1445–54.

Fama, E.F. and Jensen, M.C. (1983), 'Separation of ownership and control', *Journal of Law and Economics*, **26**: 301–25.

Firth, R.W. and Narayanan, V.K. (1996), 'New product strategies of large dominant product manufacturing firms: an exploratory analysis', *Journal of Product Innovation Management*, **13**: 334–47.

Frederickson, J.W. and Mitchell, T.R. (1984), 'Strategic decision processes: comprehensiveness and performance in an industry with an unstable environment', *Academy of Management Journal*, **27**: 399–423.

Galbraith, J. (1977), *Organization Design*, Reading, MA: Addison-Wesley.

Ghemawat, P. (1991), *Commitment: The Dynamic of Strategy*, New York: Free Press.

Gupta, A.K. and Wilemon, D.L. (1990), 'Accelerating the development of technology-based new products', *California Management Review*, **32**(2): 24–44.

Gyllenhammer, P. (1993), 'The global economy: who will lead next?', *Journal of Accountancy*, **175**: 61–7.

Hall, R.H. (1996), *Organizations: Structure, Processes and Outcomes*, 6th edn, Englewood Cliffs, NJ: Prentice-Hall.

Hambrick, D.C., Cho, T.S. and Chen, M. (1996), 'The influence of top management team heterogeneity on firms' competitive moves', *Administrative Science Quarterly*, **41**: 659–84.

Hammer, M. and Champy, J. (1993), *Reengineering the Corporation: A Manifesto for Business Revolution*, New York: HarperCollins.

Hayes, R.H. and Jaikumar, R. (1991), 'Requirements for successful implementation of new manufacturing technologies', *Journal of Engineering and Technology Management*, **7**: 169–75.

Herrin, G.E. (1994), 'Agile manufacturing', *Modern Machine Shop*, **67**: 144–6.

Hill, C.W.L. and Jones, G.R. (1998), *Strategic Management: An Integrated Approach*, 4th edn, Boston, MA: Houghton Mifflin.

Imai, K., Ikujiro, N. and Takeuchi, H. (1985), 'Managing the new product development process: how Japanese companies learn and unlearn', in R.H. Hayes, K. Clark and C. Lorenz (eds), *The Uneasy Alliance: Managing the Productivity–Technology Dilemma*, Boston, MA: Harvard Business School Press, pp. 337–75.

Judge, W.Q. and Miller, A. (1991), 'Antecedents and outcomes of decision speed in different environmental contexts', *Academy of Management Journal*, **34**: 449–63.

Jurkovich, R. (1974), 'A core typology of organizational environments', *Administrative Science Quarterly*, **19**: 380–94.

Katz, R. and Tushman, M.L. (1981), 'An investigation into the managerial roles and career paths of gatekeepers and project supervisors in a major R&D facility', *R&D Management*, **11**: 103–10.

Kessler, E.H. and Chakrabarti, A.K. (1996), 'Innovation speed: a conceptual model of context, antecedents, and outcomes', *Academy of Management Review*, **21**(4): 1143–91.

Kotha, S. (1995), 'Mass customization: implementing the emerging paradigm for competitive advantage', *Strategic Management Journal*, **16**: 21–42.

Lawless, M.W. and Anderson, P.C. (1996), 'Generational technological change: effects of innovation and local rivalry on performance', *Academy of Management Journal*, **39**: 1185–217.

Lieberman, M.B. and Montgomery, D.B. (1988), 'First-mover advantages', *Strategic Management Journal*, **9**: 41–58.

Lorsch, J.W. and MacIver, E. (1989), *Pawns or Potentates: The Reality of America's Corporate Boards*, Boston, MA: Harvard Business School Press.

Mabert, V.A., Muth, J.F. and Schmenner, R.W. (1992), 'Collapsing new product development times: six case studies', *Journal of Product Innovation Management*, **9**: 200–212.

MacDuffie, J.P., Sethuraman, K. and Fisher, M.L. (1996), 'Product variety and manufacturing performance: evidence from the international automotive assembly plant study', *Management Science*, **42**: 351–69.

Mansfield, E. (1993), 'The diffusion of flexible manufacturing systems in Japan, Europe and the United States', *Management Science*, **39**: 149–59.

March, J.G. and Simon, H.A. (1958), *Organizations*, New York: Wiley.

McDonough III, E.F. (1993), 'Faster new product development: investigating the effects of technology and characteristics of the project leader and team', *Journal of Product Innovation Management*, **10**: 241–50.

Meyer, C. (1993), *Fast Cycle Time: How to Align Purpose, Strategy, and Structure for Speed*, New York: Free Press.

Micklethwait, J. and Woolridge, A. (1996), *The Witch Doctors*, New York: Times Books.

Miller, C.C., Burke, L.M. and Glick, W.H. (1998), 'Cognitive diversity among upper-echelon executives: implications for strategic decision processes', *Strategic Management Journal*, **19**: 39–58.

Millstein, I. (1992), *The Limits of Corporate Power: Existing Constraints on the Exercise of Corporate Discretion*, New York: Macmillan.

Nayyar, P.R. and Bantel, K.A. (1994), 'Competitive agility: a source of competitive advantage based on speed and variety', in P. Shrivastava, A. Huff and J. Dutton (eds), *Advances in Strategic Management*, Vol. 10A, Greenwich, CT: JAI Press, pp. 193–222.

Nijssen, E.J., Arbouw, A.R.L. and Commandeur, H.R. (1995), 'Accelerating new product development: a preliminary empirical test of a hierarchy of implementation', *Journal of Product Innovation Management*, **12**: 99–109.

Parthasarthy, R. and Sethi, S.P. (1993), 'Relating strategy and structure to flexible automation: a test of fit and performance implications', *Strategic Management Journal*, **14**: 529–49.

Pennings, J.M. (1987), 'Technological innovations in manufacturing', in J.M. Pennings and A. Buitendam (eds), *New Technology as Organizational Innovation*, Cambridge, MA: Ballinger, pp. 197–216.

Pine II, B.J. (1993), *Mass Customization: The New Frontier in Business Competition*, Boston, MA: Harvard Business School Press.

Porter, M.E. (1985), *Competitive Advantage: Creating and Sustaining Superior Performance*, New York: Free Press.

Rajagopalan, N., Rasheed, A.M.A. and Datta, D.K. (1993), 'Strategic decision processes: critical review and future directions', *Journal of Management*, **19**: 349–84.

Roller, L. and Tombak, M.M. (1993), 'Competition and investment in flexible technologies', *Management Science*, **39**: 107–14.

Rollins, K. (1998), 'Using information to speed execution', *Harvard Business Review*, **76**(2): 81.

Rosenthal, S.R. (1992), *Effective Product Design and Development: How to Cut Lead Time and Increase Customer Satisfaction*, Homewood, IL: Business of One Irwin (McGraw-Hill Professional publishing).

Rothwell, R. (1972), *Factors for Success in Industrial Innovations from Project SAPPHO – A Comparative Study of Success and Failure in Industrial Innovation*, Brighton: Science and Technology Policy Research Unit (SPRU).

Rothwell, R., Freeman, C., Horsely, A., Jervis, V.T.P., Robertson, A. and Townsend, J. (1974), 'SAPPHO updated – Project SAPPHO phase II', *Research Policy*, **3**: 258–91.

Sanchez, R. and Mahoney, J.T. (1996), 'Modularity, flexibility, and knowledge management in product and organization design', *Strategic Management Journal*, **17**: 63–76.

Small, M.H. and Yasin, M.M. (1997), 'Advanced manufacturing technology: implementation policy and performance', *Journal of Operations Management*, **15**: 349–70.

Smith, P.G. and Reinertsen, D.G. (1991), *Developing Products in Half the Time*, New York: Van Nostrand Reinhold.

Song, X.M., Montoya-Weiss, M.M. and Schmidt, J.B. (1997), 'Antecedents and consequences of cross-functional cooperation: a comparison of R&D, manufacturing and marketing perspectives', *Journal of Product Innovation Management*, **14**: 35–47.

Stalk, G. (1988), 'Time – the next source of competitive advantage', *Harvard Business Review*, **66**(4): 41–51.

Stalk, G. and Hout, T.M. (1990), *Competing against Time: How Time-based Competition is Reshaping Global Markets*, New York: Free Press.

Starbuck, W.H. (1976), 'Organizations and their environments', in M.D. Dunnette (ed.), *Handbook of Industrial and Organizational Psychology*, Chicago, IL: Rand-McNally, pp. 1069–123.

Sterman, J.D., Repenning, N.P. and Kofman, F. (1997), 'Unanticipated side effects of successful quality programs: exploring a paradox of organizational improvement', *Management Science*, **43**: 503–21.

Suarez, F.F., Cusumano, M.A. and Fine, C.H. (1995), 'An empirical study of flexibility in manufacturing', *Sloan Management Review*, **37**(1): 25–32.

Thomas, P.R. (1990), *Competitiveness through Total Cycle Time*, New York: McGraw-Hill.

Tombak, M. and De Meyer, A. (1988), 'Flexibility and FMS: an empirical analysis', *IEEE Transactions on Engineering Management*, **35**(2): 101–7.

Trygg, L. (1993), 'Concurrent engineering practices in selected Swedish companies: a movement or an activity of the few?', *Journal of Product Innovation Management*, **10**(5): 403–15.

Upton, D.M. (1994), 'The management of manufacturing flexibility', *California Management Review*, Winter: 72–89.

Urban, G.L., Carter, T., Gaskin, S. and Mucha, Z. (1986), 'Market share rewards to pioneering brands: an empirical analysis', *Management Science*, **32**: 645–59.

Voss, C.A. (1988), 'Implementation: a key issue in manufacturing technology: the need for a field of study', *Research Policy*, **17**: 55–63.

Wally, S. and Baum, J.R. (1994), 'Personal and structural determinants of the pace of strategic decision making', *Academy of Management Journal*, **37**: 932–56.

Williams, J. (1994), 'Strategy and the search for rents: the evolution of diversity among firms', in R.P. Rumelt, D.E. Schendel and D.J. Teece (eds), *Fundamental Issues in Strategy*, Boston, MA: Harvard Business School Press, pp. 229–46.

Zammuto, R.F. and O'Connor, E.J. (1992), 'Gaining advanced manufacturing technologies' benefits: the roles of organization design and culture', *Academy of Management Review*, **17**: 701–28.

Zirger, B.J. and Hartley, J.L. (1996), 'The effect of acceleration techniques on product development time', *IEEE Transactions on Engineering Management*, **43**(2): 143–52.

21 Interactions with customers for innovation*
C. Annique Un and Alvaro Cuervo-Cazurra

Introduction

In this chapter we analyze how managers can interact with customers to identify their needs and preferences and create innovations that meet these needs and preferences. The creation of innovations that satisfy customer needs is crucial for the firm's success (Teece, 1986). Despite several decades of research on this topic, it remains challenging for many firms (Hoopes and Postrel, 1999). In some instances, a firm launches a new product that it considers highly innovative but is disappointed by unexpectedly low sales as it missed the market. Despite being a new product with no rival, customers do not appreciate it and avoid it. In other instances, a firm may be surprised when an innovation performs above expectation in the market, but the firm is then unable to meet the unanticipated demand. In both cases, the firm faces a problem. In the first scenario, the innovative efforts of the firm are not rewarded by the market. In the second, the firm is unable to meet demand and may pave the way for competitors.

To avoid both problems, the firm can benefit from interacting with customers. This helps it obtain knowledge needed to innovate the product in a way that improves its success in the marketplace (Flores, 1993; Griffin and Hauser, 1993). This interaction with customers helps the firm better manage the unexpected performance of the innovation by helping to better foresight the needs and preferences of customers. Such foresight goes beyond forecasting future trends. Instead, it involves complex knowledge interactions between the firm and its customers to identify needs and desires, which change as new knowledge is revealed or created. As a result, foresight of customer needs becomes a complex, continuously changing process rather than an outcome of these interactions.

In this chapter we argue that the interaction with customers varies, depending on the type of innovation that the firm is aiming to achieve: product improvement, product versioning, new product development, or new product discovery. Each has distinct knowledge creation challenges in terms of the identification, transfer, and integration of customer knowledge to create innovations that fulfill their needs and preferences. We focus on interactions with customers, and do not address other important aspects of product innovations that are discussed elsewhere in detail (for example, Dougherty, 1990; Clark and Fujimoto, 1991; Ancona and Caldwell, 1992; Brown and Eisenhardt, 1995; for a recent review of the innovation literature see Fagerberg et al., 2005).

This chapter integrates existing but dispersed literature into a comprehensive framework and extends it by providing a new look at interactions with customers as a source of innovation. The separation of customer–innovation relationships into four types helps identify the differences in terms of innovation challenges and their solutions. Thus, researchers can develop better analyses of each type, allowing them to address concerns that are specific to each. At the same time, the framework is useful for managers in providing an explanation of how to use each type of customer relationship to generate different types of innovation. It also provides insights into how managers can solve the difficulties they face in the innovation processes.

The rest of the chapter is organized as follows. In the next section we introduce the key constructs and theoretical background and present the framework that identifies the interactions with customers that occur in four types of innovation. We then analyze each of them in detail. We conclude with a discussion of areas that can be explored in more detail in future research.

Interactions with customers for innovation
Customers hold the key to the present and future of the firm. Most analyses of competitive advantage focus on competitors and how the firm achieves an advantage due to superior resources or a different positioning. However, both resources and positioning are a means to serve customers better than other firms do (Costanzo et al., 2003). Customers are the ultimate source of the present and future advantage of the firm. Finding better ways to serve them enables the firm to develop and maintain its advantage over other firms.

Serving customers better requires greater understanding of their needs and preferences. To achieve this, the firm needs to interact with them and obtain knowledge about their needs and preferences in order to create innovations that meet them. However, this is difficult for two reasons. First, there is the challenge of transferring tacit knowledge from customers to the firm. Customers have deep-seated needs and preferences that may not be apparent even to them, but that are acted upon when they purchase products. The company that wants to create innovations that satisfy these needs and preferences must first identify them. To do so, it must make these needs and preferences explicit so that the products that the firm creates satisfy them. However, converting tacit into explicit knowledge is difficult (Nonaka, 1988), since people know more than they can articulate (Polanyi, 1962). Additionally, in the case of the needs and preferences of customers, these vary depending on their exposure to existing products and to what other customers have.

Second, there is the challenge of transferring tacit knowledge across organizational boundaries. The difficulty in transferring knowledge is one of the explanations for the existence of firms (Kogut and Zander, 1992); a company provides the appropriate incentives and mindsets that enable the transfer of knowledge and its subsequent integration and creation. Despite the incentives and mindsets created in a firm, transferring even explicit knowledge within it is difficult (Szulanski, 1996) because the firm is a distributed knowledge system (Tsoukas, 1996). Transferring tacit knowledge is even more so, especially when transferring it across organizational boundaries (Kogut and Zander, 1992; Nonaka, 1994; Nonaka and Takeuchi, 1995). Customers are not part of the firm. Thus, they do not have an incentive to provide the firm with their knowledge, nor do they have the mindset to interact with people in the firm, and they are not part of an organizational setting that facilitates knowledge transfer and integration. The firm's employees face a similar difficulty: they may lack the incentive to gather customer knowledge, or they may not have the mindset necessary to understand this knowledge.

These two challenges apply to all customer–innovation relationships. However, there are differences in terms of the specific challenges that the manager will face, depending on the type of product that is being innovated and the customers that the firm targets. We thus organize the discussion of customer interactions for innovation around four types of innovation classified by two dimensions: whether the product that the firm innovates is an existing product or a new one,[1] and whether the customers that the firm targets are current or new ones. The result of these two dimensions is a two by two matrix, illustrated in Table 21.1, which also summarizes the innovation processes and the type of customer interactions at each step in these processes. First, product improvement examines how the firm works with customers to innovate existing products to satisfy current customers' needs and preferences. Second, product versioning assesses the firm's interaction with customers to innovate existing products in order to satisfy the needs and preferences of new customers. Third, new product development deals with how the firm works with existing customers to develop new products that meet their needs and preferences. Fourth, new product discovery examines how the company relates to new customers to create new products that satisfy their needs and preferences. Separating the customer–innovation relationships into four types helps organize existing literature and reveal the different types of knowledge identification, transfer, integration, and creation that each type requires.

Product improvement
Product improvement is the innovation of an existing product that is being sold in the marketplace in a way that provides added functionality or value to current users. The objective is to retain current customers and avoid them going to a competitor. An example of product improvement is the changes in the interaction among computer parts to reduce power consumption in a laptop in response to customer complaints about poor battery performance.

Despite constituting the majority of innovations undertaken by companies, product improvement has received comparatively little attention in the literature. Most of the literature on innovation tends to focus on new product development, viewing product improvement as being of little importance. Product improvement tends to be associated with incremental innovation, while new product development tends to be linked with radical innovation. However, product improvement is important for the present and future success of the firm (Banbury and Mitchell, 1995). Even when the firm has introduced a radically new product, failure to address problems with the product and to innovate it to better satisfy the needs of existing customers will result in customers moving to competitors' products, leading to the firm's decline.

Despite the limited attention paid to product improvement, there exists some research on this topic. Previous studies of product improvement have identified the key firm characteristics that relate to product improvement (for example, Quinn, 1992; Banbury and Mitchell, 1995; Martin and Mitchell, 1998; Adler et al., 1999; Un and Cuervo-Cazurra, 2004). However, these studies have not focused on interactions with customers for the purpose of innovation. One exception is Un and Cuervo-Cazurra (2005), who discuss the role of top managers in the product improvement process. They explain some of the challenges of innovation that involve input from customers.

The process of knowledge creation in product improvement comprises three main steps with several substeps, reflecting different knowledge integration and creation objectives, as discussed in Un and Cuervo-Cazurra (2005). First, the top management team initiates the product improvement process. Vice-presidents (VPs) from different functional areas evaluate each product in terms of sales performance and customer satisfaction. They obtain knowledge from external sources such as customer surveys, customer visits, complaints,

Table 21.1   Types of innovations, processes, and interactions with customers

		Customers	
		Existing	New
Product	Existing	Product Improvement	Product Versioning

Product Improvement (Existing):

1. VPs decide to address problems identified by customers and transmitted through the customer service center; VPs delegate problems to middle-level managers
   Interact with existing customers to identify their views of the product and the perceived limitations and problems of the existing product
2. Middle-level manager organizes cross-functional product improvement team to identify root causes of problems and potential solutions to problems
   Interact with existing customers to identify the tacit knowledge, specific problems, and their use of products
3. Product improvement team incorporates solutions and other suggestions to innovate existing product and product is innovated
   Interact with existing customers to make sure that solutions address problems and satisfy needs of customers

Product Versioning (New):

1. VPs decide to serve new customers and delegate the research and development of product version to middle-level managers
   Interact with new customers to identify their market potential and the need to modify the product to cover their needs and preferences
2. Middle-level manager organizes research team to identify how new customers' needs and preferences differ from those of existing customers, and what changes need to be made to the product to address these differences
   Interact with existing and new customers to understand the needs and preferences of each and their differences, identifying reasons for not buying existing product, additional needs and preferences that product must cover, and features of product that do not provide value or create conflict with new customers
3. Product versioning team designs new features and alters existing ones to address the needs and preferences of new customers while keeping existing customers; product is innovated
   Interact with new customers to make sure that the product version addresses their different needs and preferences; interact with existing customers to make sure that the product version does not interfere with their preferences and needs

Table 21.1 (continued)

		Customers	
		Existing	New
Product	New	New Product Development	New Product Discovery

New Product Development

1. Company generates an idea about a new product
   Interact with a limited number of customers to get a sense of value of idea
2. Company translates idea into a potential product that embodies new technologies or new combinations of existing technologies
   Interact with existing customers to further refine the idea and what the product may achieve
3. Company develops a new product that embodies new technologies
   Interact with existing customers to identify their reaction to the new product and areas for improvement
4. Company tests the feasibility of the production and marketing of the new product
   Interact with existing customers to make sure that the product fulfills their needs and preferences
5. Company has a trial test of the product in a limited market
   Interact with trial customers to observe their use of the product in practice
6. Company commercializes the product
   Interact with customers to track performance of new product, and make necessary improvements

New Product Discovery

1. Company generates an idea about a new product for a new market
   Imagine reaction of potential customers to idea
2. Company defines idea into a potential product that embodies new technologies or new combinations of existing technologies
   Identify potential customers for new product
3. Company develops a new product that embodies the new technologies
   Interact with lead users to identify their reaction to the new product and areas for improvement and the features of the new market
4. Company tests the feasibility of the production and marketing of the new product
   Interact with lead users to make sure that the product fulfills their needs and preferences
5. Company has a trial test of the product in a limited market
   Interact with trial customers to observe their use of the product in practice
6. Company commercializes the product
   Interact with customers to track performance of new product, and later need for improvement

For user-innovations, bypass steps 1 and 2 and in step 3 incorporate innovations created by lead users and generate new product

Note: Steps in the innovation process appear in regular font. Interactions with customers appear in *italics*.

comment cards, field service reports, product returns, sales contact reports, trade show intelligence, new product suggestions, and the results of benchmarking. This external knowledge is evaluated and discussed by the VPs. The VPs then identify those products that appear to be underperforming, and select the middle managers to be in charge of improving them. Second, middle-level managers consolidate knowledge about the product selected for improvement in order to determine the root causes of their underperformance. Customer service representatives gather additional knowledge about the product from dealers and retailers, and analyze all return sales and interactions with customers. Middle-level managers select and organize individuals with relevant expertise to help analyze, from their functional perspective, why the products are underperforming in the market. Third, the product improvement team, which is composed of non-management employees, finds and tests causes and solutions to the problems that have been identified. Since product reliability, quality, and design contribute to customer satisfaction and sales performance, engineers from both design and manufacturing are included on the team. The team also includes individuals from customer service and from sales and marketing, who provide knowledge from customers, surveys, and marketing-research companies. The team brainstorms about the root causes of underperformance, generates hypotheses about solutions, and tests them. The successful solutions are then implemented.

In the product improvement process, there are multiple interactions with customers to obtain the knowledge needed to generate innovations that will address their concerns. The requirements in terms of necessary customer knowledge are different at each stage of the product improvement process. In the first step, the knowledge creation objective is to gather customer views about how the existing product is meeting their needs and preferences. The challenge here is to obtain knowledge from customers who do not have an incentive to provide their knowledge to the firm. When the product is not performing well, some customers do not complain to the company but instead switch to a competitor's offer. This is usually the case for products that have low switching costs, perhaps due to low price or because they are consumption goods. The firm needs to provide customers with an incentive to voice their concerns and make suggestions on how to improve the product. This can be done by offering easier access to the firm's customer service department. It can also be done as part of the work of the marketing department, where sales representatives gather knowledge on how well the products are doing and why. Unlike other customer–innovation interactions, communication with the customers can be product specific in terms of how a given product is performing and what customers expect. Since there is an existing product that the customers have purchased and used, they have developed knowledge about how to use it and about the features they want from the product (Habermeier, 1990). This makes gathering knowledge from customers easier, since questions about the product, such as its functionality and its preferred features, can be more easily discussed. In product improvement, the firm can use multiple channels to obtain knowledge about how customers perceive the product, such as directly interacting with customers through the customer service centers or personal visits, or indirectly through distribution channels (Griffin and Hauser, 1993).

In the second phase, the objective changes to obtaining specific tacit knowledge about the customers' perceptions and use of the product. The challenge here is turning customers' tacit knowledge into explicit knowledge that the firm can use to address problems with the product. The customer service department receives and transmits customer complaints to the firm. VPs decide to act upon them and delegate to a middle manager the task of finding a solution to underperformance. However, these complaints are simply perceptions about the product that may or may not be well expressed. The customer may express disappointment with the product, for example, because it is unreliable. The firm then requires additional knowledge about how the product is being used and the conditions of use in order to identify potential problems. In such cases, the firm can visit the customer and observe how the product is being used in order to obtain tacit knowledge from direct observation (Flores, 1993; Nonaka and Takeuchi, 1995). As indicated above, if an existing product is being used by customers, this facilitates such knowledge gathering. Instead of having to rely on focus groups and their perception of how they may use a new product, the company can observe the use of the product in practice and obtain tacit knowledge through direct interactions with customers.

In the final step, once the company has improved the product to address the problems perceived by the customers, it can then go back to the customers with the prototype of the improved product to make sure that the changes address their needs and preferences. This interaction with customers to evaluate an improved product is similar to what is done in other customer–innovation processes. However, in the former case, the customers have experience with the product and can reflect on their previous experiences to let the firm know how the improved product addresses their needs and preferences, and, if necessary, introduce additional changes to the improved product.

In sum, in product improvement the challenge in interacting with customers to innovate products is to obtain their tacit knowledge about the perceived or real shortcomings of the existing product. This knowledge enables the firm to innovate the product in a way that, at a minimum, solves the perceived problems and, ideally, leads to the introduction of additional innovations that help the firm better meet existing customers' additional needs and preferences. Having a current product that is marketed to existing customers facilitates knowledge gathering because customers have created a perception about their preferences for the product, and the firm can observe how customers actually use the product. At the same time, the discussion may be too narrow, focusing only on existing features of the product and limiting the exploration of totally new or unanticipated features of the product, as may happen with completely new products.

Product versioning
Product versioning refers to the introduction of new versions of an existing product to capture customers that the firm is not serving with its current version of the product. Although versions of a product are also created to address problems and concerns with the existing product, as discussed above, here we are focusing on the firm generating a new version of the product to reach new customers. Examples of product versioning are a luggage firm that creates simpler, lower-priced versions of its luxury products to sell to lower-income customers, or a hamburger company that introduces vegetarian and mutton burger patties when it enters India, where it cannot sell beef patties because cows are considered sacred.

Literature on product versioning has focused on the use of product versions to address the needs of new customers (for example, Lee, 1996; Iyer and Soberman, 2000) and its use as a competitive tool (see Lancaster, 1990 for a review). Creating versions of a product to serve different markets has several challenges. The introduction of versions in the product line increases production costs; to reduce these, the firm can use modularity in the production and marketing of multiple versions (for example, Lee, 1996; Sanchez, 1999). More important for our discussion is the negative influence that a version of a product designed to serve new customers may have on existing customers. For example, customers may purchase the new version because it has a lower price, or stop purchasing the product altogether if they feel that it no longer provides exclusivity. To avoid this, the firm must be able not only to introduce versions that address the needs of the new market, but also to maintain a separation between existing and new customers; that is, to avoid competition among product versions (for a review, see Ratchford, 1990; Ahmadi and Yang, 2000).

In the literature, the product versioning process has been discussed primarily in terms of the firm's decision about where in the creation of the actual products it should introduce the changes, be it in the design, parts, assembly, or marketing (for example, Lee, 1996; Sanchez, 1999). Absent from the discussion is the prior analysis of how to innovate the existing product and create a version that addresses the needs of new customers. We build on the analysis of the product improvement process discussed earlier to analyze the product versioning process. The two processes share some commonalities. Both have an existing product that is innovated, and in both cases top management initiates the process. However, the objectives of the innovation differ. Product versioning serves new customers by adapting the existing product to their needs and preferences instead of serving existing customers better by addressing their partially met or unmet needs and preferences. As a result, there are some differences in terms of the steps that are undertaken.

The product versioning process has three phases. It starts with the decision at the level of top managers to serve a new market that the firm is not currently reaching but that could be profitable. This decision requires some preliminary analysis of the potential size of the market and of the reasons why new customers are not purchasing the existing product. Data on the potential size of the new market can be obtained from public sources or consulting companies. If the new market appears to be sufficiently large, top managers may decide to undertake product versioning to reach this new market. Once they reach this decision, they delegate to middle managers the task of analyzing the new market in more detail and coming up with a product to serve it. In the second step, the middle managers organize a research team to identify the exact size of the new market and the reasons why the new customers do not purchase the existing product. In some cases, the existing product may not need to be altered, since the issue may be physical distance rather than differences in needs or preferences. The firm may simply expand the realm of operations, for example, expanding sales from a local to a national level. However, in many cases, there are differences in needs and preferences between existing and new customers. These differences are identified and analyzed while the research team explores the potential size of the market. Once the research team has identified how new customers differ from existing ones, middle managers assemble a cross-functional team that explores how best to incorporate the needs of the new customers into the design, manufacturing, pricing, and marketing of the product, introducing innovations in some or all aspects of the product in order to be able to serve the new customers. The team needs to work with the new customers to identify their needs and preferences with respect to the product in question; this knowledge must then be incorporated into the new version. The tools to gather knowledge from customers are similar to those used in the product improvement process. However, product versioning has two distinct challenges. The new version of the product must incorporate new customers' preferences, but at the same time, existing customers should not be alienated by the new version in a way that would lead them to switch to the competition. To avoid this, in addition to changing the product and creating new versions, the team must decide how to keep the versions separate; for example, they may choose to use different brand names or different distribution channels. The product version is then tested with new customers to determine whether the perceived differences in needs and preferences have been translated into the characteristics of the product version, and whether additional changes should be incorporated before its release.

The firm faces unique customer–innovation relationship challenges in the product versioning process. Similar to the challenges found in the product improvement process, the existing product can be used to elicit specific views of the new customers about its features and what new customers may want from it. However, the firm is unable to observe the actual behaviors of new customers, because these new versions of the product have not been purchased and used. As a result, there is more uncertainty involved in identifying the needs and preferences of new customers and addressing their needs. The main challenge that the firm faces is identifying the new customers to serve and the ways in which their needs and preferences differ from those of existing customers. This can be done using traditional customer intelligence tools such as focus groups or personal interviews (Griffin and Hauser, 1993). Although these tools have limitations because new customers lack actual experience with the product, the firm can use the existing product to elicit specific views on the characteristics of the product and how these may meet their expectations. Having an existing product helps the firm and the new customers more easily identify these needs. The new customers can establish mental models of what the product is like, how to use it, and what features may need to change. The firm can better facilitate the transfer of knowledge by using the product to represent how the firm meets the needs of existing customers (Carlile, 2002). Moreover, since the firm is currently selling the product, it understands how existing customers react to it. It also understands the areas that can be altered to generate the new version without clashing with the preferences and needs of existing customers. This interaction with new customers will help the firm understand why new customers are not buying the product, whether it is simply that they lack knowledge about it, that the price is not right, or whether there are more complex reasons.

Once the firm has identified the new customers and their needs, it alters the existing product to create a version that satisfies potential customers. As in the product improvement process, the prototype is then tested on them to make sure that their needs and preferences are met. At the same time, the firm must also interact with its existing customers to understand their reaction to the new version of the product, in order to avoid creating competition or confusion between versions. The firm can introduce additional changes that would keep existing and new customers separate and avoid competition among versions. For example, when introducing simpler, lower-priced versions of existing products, the firm may want to reduce certain features that are central to existing customers. Alternatively, it can introduce switching costs in the form of necessary complementary products or knowledge, and thus avoid the migration of customers to other products (David, 1985). However, in some instances it may decide to replace the existing product with the new one altogether, if the new version is able to capture the new customers while keeping existing ones satisfied.

In sum, the main customer interaction challenge in product versioning is first to identify the new market potential, and the needs of new customers, introducing them to the product in such a way that the version does not create conflict with the needs of existing customers. The firm benefits from having an existing product that can be used to elicit specific views from new customers with respect to the reasons for not buying it. However, the firm must also evaluate existing customers' view of the product version to ensure that the new version does not conflict with their preferences. Embedded in this tension is the need to keep a consistent product line and benefit from commonalities among products that reduce the cost of development and marketing while benefiting from serving a larger market. The firm can always generate an entirely new product for the new customers; however, this might be more costly than the introduction of a new version of an existing product. The development of new products entails its own set of challenges, as we discuss below.

New product development
New product development is the creation of a new product that is marketed to the existing customers of the firm. Although some authors use this term to refer to any innovation in a product, in this chapter we restrict it to the creation of a new product rather than the change through improvement or variation of an existing product. In the case of product improvement, the product in question has already demonstrated its viability in the marketplace, whereas many new products are not suitable for commercialization (Cooper, 1986). Additionally, we restrict the term to the development of a new product that is marketed to existing customers, and use the term 'new product discovery' when the new product is marketed to new customers. Creating a new product for a new market involves significantly different challenges. An example of new product development is an airplane manufacturer that creates a larger but more fuel-efficient airplane to serve its existing customers. While the introduction of a new product may result in the firm reaching new customers as well, the original objective is to serve existing customers.

There is a large literature on new product development that has discussed in detail the generation of new products and the determinants of their success (for reviews, see Lilien and Yoon, 1989; Montoya-Weiss and Calantone, 1994). Among the multiple factors that influence new product creation, interaction with customers has been identified as beneficial for the success of the product in the marketplace (for a review, see Gruner and Homburg, 2004). However, these studies tend to focus on the quantity of interaction between firm and customer rather than how the type of interaction may vary along the product development process. Here we focus on these qualitative differences.

The new product development process has been discussed by many researchers, albeit with variation in the specific stages presented (for reviews, see Tzokasa et al., 2004; Galanakis, 2006). Effective new product development tends to be middle-up-down rather than the top-middle-down as in product improvement and product versioning processes (Nonaka, 1988; Un and Cuervo-Cazurra, 2005). The initial thrust of the new product comes from middle-level managers, who then convince top-level managers to go ahead with the new product and organize a team of lower-level employees to come up with the prototype for the new product. Cooper (1988) presents 13 steps in the product development process, which are later collapsed into six stages: idea generation and assessment, definition, development, testing, trial, and commercialization. Each stage has an evaluation step or gate to assess the feasibility of continuing with the process.

Specifically, the new product development process starts with the generation of an idea for a new product. The manager, usually middle level, identifies the possibility of developing a new product. This initial idea is then subjected to a technical assessment to make sure that the firm can take it to term, as well as a market assessment to ensure that there is a market for the potential new product. Second, once these assessments are passed, the firm defines the specifications for the new product before committing to its development, undertaking detailed market research and examining feasibility in production, marketing, and financing of the new product. These detailed assessments are coordinated by the middle-level managers, but it is the top managers who decide whether to go ahead with the new product. Third, once this is approved by top managers, middle-level managers organize the new product development team and provide it with the mission, resources, and adequate incentive to succeed in coming up with a new product (for example, Thamhain and Wilemon, 1987; Clark and Wheelwright, 1992; Katz, 1997). Fourth, once the new product has been developed, it is tested with current customers to make sure that the product meets their needs and expectations. The views of the customers are then incorporated into the final design of the product. Fifth, the firm tests the new product, evaluating its ability to manufacture the product according to specifications, and assessing the reaction of customers in a limited market to the new product. Finally, once the new product has met the expectations of customers in the market trial, demonstrating that it can be produced and sold profitably, it is launched.

New product development entails different knowledge creation challenges from product improvement and versioning in terms of the interaction with customers, since there is no existing product that the firm can use to relate to customers. Instead, the firm is aiming to create a new product based on its own knowledge and on the knowledge elicited from customers. However, unlike new product discovery discussed next, the firm has prior knowledge of the characteristics of existing customers, which may guide its product design.

In each of these stages the firm will elicit the views of existing customers to better understand the feasibility of the new product and to introduce features desired by customers. However, not all stages require the same interaction with customers or the same type of knowledge to be transferred to the firm (Zahay et al., 2004). In the first stage, assessment, the firm generates an idea about a product and uses its knowledge of the characteristics of its existing customers to assess the feasibility of this idea as a new product. There is some discussion with key customers and some minimal sampling of customers to determine whether the idea has some merit, and customers may find the new product attractive, but little else in terms of specifying the product's features or the customer needs that it will serve.

In the second stage, definition, there is a high level of involvement with the customers. Customers' stated preferences and needs become key inputs in the definition of the features of the product. However, it is challenging to elicit specific needs and preferences about a product that does not yet exist. The customers will articulate their basic needs about the features of the product, but these will be expressed in terms of preferences about the functionality of the product rather than specific features or technologies (Griffin and Hauser, 1993). The challenge for the firm is to find ways to make these functions a reality in the new product, selecting among the dozens of preferences that take priority over others and can be addressed by the firm and incorporated into the new product. Additionally, since a product has yet to be created, the firm faces the challenge of translating tacit needs and desires that may be currently unmet into explicit preferences that can be used in designing the new product. To facilitate the transfer of tacit needs and preferences of customers, the company can work with its key customers, with whom it has developed a sense of care, trust, and commitment, facilitating the translation of these tacit preferences into explicit ones (Nonaka and Konno, 1998).

In the third stage, development, the new product development team creates a new product that builds on the technological capabilities of the firm and incorporates the preferences of customers. The incorporation of customer preferences may be facilitated by using cross-functional teams or individuals with multifunctional expertise who can take alternative perspectives and better incorporate new features into the product (Takeuchi and Nonaka, 1986). The development phase requires continuous interaction with key customers and with other external parties such as suppliers to use as a sounding board on the progress of the new product and to obtain new ideas that can be incorporated into the product.

In the fourth stage, testing, the new product is evaluated by customers to elicit specific responses on the concept developed and whether the new product does or does not address their needs and preferences. This interaction is similar to those discussed above that occur when the product is improved or a new version is created and then tested with customers. As in these cases, the objective of the interaction with customers is to observe and understand their reactions to the new product and incorporate additional suggestions prior to its launch. Differently from product improvement and versioning, in the case of new product development the product is new and customers may not fully understand how to use the product or some of its features. To address this issue, the firm may have to simplify the interface of the product to facilitate its use by customers with no prior experience.

In the fifth stage, trial, the firm interacts with customers that have actually purchased the product, and can thus observe the use of the product in reality rather than just the reaction to its potential use that was elicited during the previous phases. This observation of use of the new product can give rise to new ideas about the product. These ideas can be introduced before the sixth stage, commercialization, or can be used to improve or vary the product at a later date.

In sum, in new product development interaction with customers becomes a crucial part of the innovation process because their articulated needs and preferences are incorporated into the creation of the new product. The main challenge that the firm faces is to make customers' unmet tacit needs and preferences explicit and then translate these into features of a nonexistent product. Lacking an existing product limits the firm's ability to obtain specific knowledge about customers' preferences and needs, although the interaction can reveal new ideas that can be incorporated as additional features that had not been thought of previously. Since the product is new, there is more room for introducing new concepts and ideas before the firm becomes wedded to a particular product or design. However, at the same time, since the customers used to elicit knowledge are current ones, they may be constrained in their articulation of preferences by their experiences with other products. This type of constraint is not seen in new product discovery.

New product discovery
New product discovery is the identification and transformation of ideas into innovations that the firm then introduces to new customers. We use the term 'new product discovery' to refer to the creation of new products for new customers, distinguishing it from new product development, which is restricted to the development of new products for existing customers. Both involve new products, but in product discovery the firm has to both create a new product and identify a new market for the product; hence the use of the term 'discovery'. New product discovery tends to emerge from technological breakthroughs achieved within the firm that result in a new product, creating a new market. For example, an electronics firm may create a portable cassette player with no recording capabilities, resulting in the creation of a new market segment, portable self-recorded music. However, the initial concept for new product discovery can emerge externally to the company; in this case, the firm faces the task of internalizing the idea and bringing it to fruition. This is the case when customers create solutions to problems they encounter; the firm observes these solutions and appropriates them to create a new product to be marketed to new customers with a similar unmet need. An example is a soft drinks manufacturer who observes athletes mixing water with salt and sugar to stay hydrated, appropriates this idea and launches a new drink that becomes a new market segment, sports drinks.

There is an extensive literature on the creation of new products for new markets. This literature can be separated into two distinct areas: studies of technological discontinuities (for example, Schumpeter, 1950; Abernathy and Utterbach, 1978; Anderson and Tushman, 1990; Christensen, 1997) where a firm introduces a new product that results in the creation of a new market, and studies on lead users (Von Hippel, 1986), where the customer generates the idea and the firm appropriates it to generate an innovation and serve a new market. It is also possible for the individual who generates an idea to create a firm to market the innovation, that is, to become an entrepreneur. For the purpose of this chapter we will not discuss entrepreneurship because the entrepreneur has distinct challenges in terms of creating and managing a new firm that would take our discussion in an altogether different direction (but for a review, see Acs and Audretsch, 2003).

The new product discovery process can be viewed as following similar steps to those followed in the new product development process discussed above: idea generation and assessment, definition, development, testing, trial, and commercialization (Cooper, 1988). In both cases the company balances technological and market forces (Ettlie and Subramaniam, 2004). The difference is in the content of each stage. In particular, new product discovery tends to have a much heavier technological content in the early stages of the process (Veryzer, 1998). This is because, in new product discovery, the firm's ability to interact with customers in order to assess, define, develop, and test the innovation prior to its commercialization is limited, since the firm must identify not only a new product but also a new market for the product. As a result of the lack of a defined market, new product discovery tends to start with technological developments with ill-defined products and markets, or solutions in search of a problem (March and Olsen, 1986). The exploration of multiple unclear paths is transformed in the definition of what the technology or collection of technologies can help achieve, and in thinking about some preliminary ideas that can be converted into products. These ideas are then further developed into products that can provide new utilities to customers, although it may still not be clear who the customers will be. Once a preliminary product is developed and the team has a working prototype, they start moving towards making the innovation a reality in the marketplace, testing the features with potential customers and refining the product before its trial and commercialization.

An alternative to this technology-led new product discovery is the market-led new product discovery that exists in user-led innovations (Von Hippel, 1986). In this process, users are the main driver of the identification of both the innovation and its market potential, and the company only takes part at a later stage (Baldwin et al., 2006). The process begins with one or more users recognizing some new set of possibilities and creating an innovation to solve a particular problem that they face. The solution to the problem is not restricted to one person, but tends to be achieved by several people who form a community of user-innovators, with users exchanging knowledge freely. Once the user-led innovation is created, the first user-purchasers – individuals who face the same problems but who do not want to build the solutions identified by the user-innovators – emerge. As demand from these user-purchasers grows, manufacturers appear. Some of these manufacturers are the user-innovators who create firms to market the product. However, there are also established firms that have been following the development of the innovation and market and that can use their established manufacturing and marketing capabilities to bring the innovation to the market more easily. This is facilitated by the openness of the user-innovators in sharing their knowledge about the solutions they have developed with competing users and manufacturers (Harhoff et al., 2003).

New product discovery faces distinct knowledge creation challenges because of the higher levels of uncertainty. Not only has the new product not been tested in the marketplace, but it is also unclear who the new customers are and which needs the product may satisfy. As a result, interactions with customers differ markedly.

There is much less interaction with the customers at the front-end of the process, where the firm is focused primarily on the identification of a new product that can be developed with the new technology (O'Connor, 1998). The market research done is internal and involves engineers and team members imagining potential applications of the technology and working towards the transformation of these applications into working products. Even in the case of user-generated innovations, the firm does not interact with the customers until the innovation and the potential market have already been identified by user-innovators.

Most of the interaction between firm and customer occurs once the prototype has been developed. Until that point, the firm is preoccupied with generating a new product that takes advantage of technological advances; in many cases a new technology does not find a feasible application until much later. Interaction with customers involves a relatively high degree of exploration, both on the part of the firm in terms of what new customers may want from the product using the new technologies, and on the part of the new customers in terms of the potential uses of the new technology. Once the firm has been able to generate a prototype, it then focuses on identifying the target market for the product in terms of the potential size of the market and needs that the product would have to serve (ibid.). At this stage the firm searches for lead users, users who are at the forefront of the market, and who can provide the firm with some insight into how the product can be used and what other features it may require if it is to serve their needs. These lead users may be current customers of the firm, in which case the firm can elicit a candid response from people it already knows. However, in many instances the lead users are not current customers of the firm. In such cases, the firm may release a working prototype to the market, such as the beta versions that are developed for many software packages, and let lead users find the new product, use it, and identify some of the additional features that a complete version may need. While lead users are identifying areas for improvement, the firm can learn who would be likely to adopt the technology by interacting with lead users and other early adopters of technology. This interaction works in both ways: the firm learns about new customers' needs, while the new customers learn about the characteristics of the product and the underlying technology. Once the firm refines the product and clarifies the characteristics of the new market, it can then start using traditional market evaluation techniques and conduct a full analysis of the likely users and their needs, as is done in the case of the other customer–innovation processes discussed above.

In sum, in new product discovery the interaction with the customer occurs much later than in the other customer–innovation processes. There is a higher level of uncertainty regarding the features of the new product and the characteristics of its potential market. As a result, the firm first focuses on developing the new product, embodying the new technological advances. Only once it has a prototype does it engage in active market research, with limited releases of the product to lead users to obtain a better understanding of who may be interested in the product, benefiting from the knowledge sharing that lead users provide early in development. Alternatively, the firm may keep track of the behavior of the lead users who innovate to solve some of the problems faced by the firm. Only later does it capture the innovation and gain a sense of who the new customers are, taking advantage of the openness of user-innovators to share knowledge, as well as of its established production facilities and distribution channels, to compete against user-entrepreneurs.

Conclusions

We have discussed how the firm can interact with its customers to identify their needs and preferences and develop innovations that satisfy them. Interacting with customers to improve innovations has been discussed in separate literatures as an important element for the success of an innovation. Here we integrate these multiple perspectives into a framework that clarifies the types of challenges that a manager faces when interacting with customers to innovate a product. We highlight how the challenges of interacting with customers in the innovation process differ depending on the type of innovation that the firm is undertaking: product improvement, product versioning, new product development, or new product discovery. Interacting with customers can help the firm reduce uncertainty by gathering knowledge about how the innovation can better serve their needs. As a result, the firm may be able to better foresee current and future trends in customer preferences and develop the innovations that meet these needs, ensuring the profitability of current and future operations. This foresight is a complex process whereby the firm interacts with customers to identify needs and desires and create new knowledge. This, in turn, affects the needs and desires of the customers. As a result, as the firm interacts with the customers and innovates, additional opportunities for new products are generated. Thus, foresight goes beyond traditional forecasting of demand, becoming a process of complex interactions to enable the identification and creation of needs.

The framework provided in this chapter is a first step towards a deeper understanding of innovation and how to better create new products that satisfy the needs of customers. The framework is helpful for managers in identifying the main challenges they face in knowledge creation with customers. It is also useful for researchers in organizing the disparate literature in an integrated framework and providing a better understanding of how the role of customers in innovation varies depending on the type of innovation analyzed.

Future research can extend this framework to analyze other types of innovation and relationships. First, the ways in which customer interactions may vary between products and services and across types of innovation in services should be explored. In the present chapter, we have implicitly focused on products. Product and service innovation share commonalities in terms of the need to interact with customers to better generate innovations that satisfy them, and on the processes used. For example, service firms generate new services internally and later find a market for them, as in the case of telephone banking in the UK, which was developed thanks to technological advances and later marketed to the general public (Costanzo et al., 2003), and service firms benefit from lead users to generate new products, as in the case of open source software (for example, Von Krogh and Von Hippel, 2006). However, in services there are limitations in the firm's ability to separate innovation from delivery of the service (Dougherty, 2004), which may result in different customer relationships across innovation types.

Second, future research can analyze how relationships with other sources of knowledge may vary across types of innovations. We have focused on relationships with customers to generate knowledge for innovation. The firm can use other relationships to generate innovation in the market, such as those with scientific systems, public authorities, and mediating partners (Hauschildt, 1992), relationships that may vary according to the type of innovation.

Notes

* The flip of a coin decided the order of authors. The editors' comments helped improve the chapter. We thank the Center for International Business Education and Research at the University of South Carolina for funding. All errors remain ours.
1. The firm can achieve different types of innovations, such as competence enhancing or competence destroying (Tushman and Anderson, 1986), or incremental, radical, modular, or architectural innovations (Henderson and Clark, 1990), to name a few. Here, we focus on whether the product constitutes an innovation of existing ones, rather than on the type of innovation that the product incorporates.

References

Abernathy, W.J. and J.M. Utterback (1978), 'Patterns of innovation in technology', *Technology Review*, **80** (7), 40–47.
Acs, Z.J. and D.B. Audretsch (2003), *Handbook of Entrepreneurship Research*, Dordrecht: Kluwer Academic.
Adler, P.S., B. Goldoftas and D.I. Levine (1999), 'Flexibility versus efficiency? A case study of model change-overs in the Toyota production system', *Organization Science*, **10**, 43–68.
Ahmadi, R. and B.R. Yang (2000), 'Parallel imports: challenges from unauthorized distribution channels', *Marketing Science*, **19**, 279–94.
Ancona, D.G. and D.F. Caldwell (1992), 'Demography and design: predictors of new product team performance', *Organization Science*, **3**, 321–41.
Anderson, P. and M.L. Tushman (1990), 'Technological discontinuities and dominant designs: a cyclical model of technological change', *Administrative Science Quarterly*, **35**, 604–33.
Baldwin, C., C. Hienerth and E. von Hippel (2006), 'How user innovations become commercial products: a theoretical investigation and case study', *Research Policy*, **35** (9), 1291–313.
Banbury, C.M. and W. Mitchell (1995), 'The effect of introducing important incremental innovations on market share and business survival', *Strategic Management Journal*, **16**, 161–82.

Brown, S.L. and K.M. Eisenhardt (1995), 'Product development: past research, present findings, and future directions', *Academy of Management Review*, **20**, 343–78.
Carlile, P.R. (2002), 'A pragmatic view of knowledge and boundaries: boundary objects in new product development', *Organization Science*, **13**, 442–55.
Christensen, C. (1997), *The Innovator's Dilemma*, Boston, MA: Harvard Business School Press.
Clark, K.B. and T. Fujimoto (1991), *Product Development Performance: Strategy, Organization, and Management in the World Auto Industry*, Boston, MA: Harvard Business School Press.
Clark, K. and S. Wheelwright (1992), 'Organizing and leading "heavyweight" development teams', *California Management Review*, **34**, 9–28.
Cooper, R.G. (1986), *Winning at New Products*, Reading, MA: Addison-Wesley.
Cooper, R.G. (1988), 'The new product process: a decision guide for managers', *Journal of Marketing Management*, **3**, 238–55.
Costanzo, L.A., K. Keasey and H. Short (2003), 'A strategic approach to the study of innovations in the financial services industry: the case of telephone banking', *Journal of Marketing Management*, **19**, 259–81.
David, P.A. (1985), 'Clio and the economics of QWERTY', *American Economic Review*, **75**, 332–7.
Dougherty, D. (1990), 'Understanding new markets for new products', *Strategic Management Journal*, **11** (special issue), 59–78.
Dougherty, D. (2004), 'Organizing practices in services: capturing practice-based knowledge for innovation', *Strategic Organization*, **2**, 35–65.
Ettlie, J.E. and M. Subramaniam (2004), 'Changing strategies and tactics for new product development', *Journal of Product Innovation Management*, **21**, 95–109.
Fagerberg, J., D.C. Mowery and R.R. Nelson (2005), *The Oxford Handbook of Innovation*, New York: Oxford University Press.
Flores, F. (1993), 'Innovation by listening carefully to customers', *Long Range Planning*, **26** (3), 95–102.
Galanakis, K. (2006), 'Innovation process: make sense using systems thinking', *Technovation*, **26** (11), 1222–32.
Griffin, A. and J.R. Hauser (1993), 'The voice of the customer', *Marketing Science*, **12**, 1–27.
Gruner, K.E. and C. Homburg (2004), 'Does customer interaction enhance new product success?', *Journal of Business Research*, **49**, 1–14.
Habermeier, K.F. (1990), 'Product use and product improvement', *Research Policy*, **19**, 271–83.
Harhoff, D., J. Henkel and E. Von Hippel (2003), 'Profiting from voluntary information spillovers: how users benefit by freely revealing their innovations', *Research Policy*, **32**, 1753–69.
Hauschildt, J. (1992), 'External acquisition of knowledge for innovations: a research agenda', *R&D Management*, **22**, 105–10.
Henderson, R. and K. Clark (1990), 'Architectural innovation: the reconfiguration of existing product technologies and the failure of established firms', *Administrative Science Quarterly*, **35**, 9–30.
Hoopes, D.G. and S. Postrel (1999), 'Shared knowledge, "glitches", and product development performance', *Strategic Management Journal*, **20**, 837–65.
Iyer, G. and D. Soberman (2000), 'Markets for product modification information', *Marketing Science*, **19** (3), 203–25.
Katz, R. (1997), 'Managing creative performance in R&D teams', in Katz (ed.), *The Human Side of Managing Technological Innovation: A Collection of Readings*, Oxford: Oxford University Press, pp. 177–86.
Kogut, B. and U. Zander (1992), 'Knowledge of the firm, combinative capabilities and the replication of technology', *Organization Science*, **3**, 383–97.
Lancaster, K. (1990), 'The economics of product variety: a survey', *Marketing Science*, **9**, 189–206.
Lee, H. (1996), 'Effective inventory and service management through product and process redesign', *Operations Research*, **44**, 151–9.
Lilien, G.L. and E. Yoon (1989), 'Determinants of industrial product performance: a strategic reexamination of the empirical literature', *IEEE Transactions on Engineering*, **36**, 3–10.
March, J.G. and J.P. Olsen (1986), 'Garbage can models of decision making in organizations', in J.G. March and R. Weissenger-Baylon (eds), *Ambiguity and Command*, Marshfield, MA: Pitman, pp. 11–36.
Martin, X. and W. Mitchell (1998), 'The influence of local search and performance heuristics on new design introduction in a new product market', *Research Policy*, **26**, 753–71.
Montoya-Weiss, M.M. and R. Calantone (1994), 'Determinants of new product performance: a review and meta-analysis, *Journal of Product Innovation Management*, **11**, 397–417.
Nonaka, I. (1988), 'Toward middle-up-down management: accelerating information creation', *Sloan Management Review*, **29**, 9–18.
Nonaka, I. (1994), 'A dynamic theory of knowledge creation', *Organization Science*, **5**, 14–37.
Nonaka, I. and N. Konno (1998), 'The concept of "Ba": building a foundation for knowledge creation', *California Management Review*, **40** (3), 40–54.

Nonaka, I. and H. Takeuchi (1995), *The Knowledge-creating Company: How Japanese Companies Create the Dynamics of Innovation*, New York: Oxford University Press.

O'Connor, G.C. (1998), 'Market learning and radical innovation: a cross-case comparison of eight radical innovation projects', *Journal of Product Innovation Management*, **15**, 151–66.

Polanyi, M. (1962), *Personal Knowledge*, Chicago, IL: University of Chicago Press.

Quinn, J. (1992), *Intelligent Enterprise: A Knowledge and Service-Based Paradigm for Industry*, New York: Free Press.

Ratchford, B.T. (1990), 'Marketing applications of the economics of product variety', *Marketing Science*, **9**, 207–11.

Sanchez, R. (1999), 'Modular architectures in the marketing process', *Journal of Marketing*, **63**, 92–111.

Schumpeter, J.A. (1950), *Capitalism, Socialism, and Democracy*, 3rd edn, New York: Harper & Row.

Szulanski, G. (1996), 'Exploring internal stickiness: impediments to the transfer of best practice within the firm', *Strategic Management Journal*, **17**, 27–43.

Takeuchi, H, and I. Nonaka (1986), 'The new new product development game', *Harvard Business Review*, **64** (January–February), 136–46.

Teece, D.J. (1986), 'Profiting from technological innovation: implications for integration, collaboration, licensing and public policy', *Research Policy*, **15**, 285–305.

Thamhain, H.J. and D.L. Wilemon (1987), 'Building high performing engineering project teams', *IEEE Transactions on Engineering Management*, **34**, 130–37.

Tsoukas, H. (1996), 'The firm as a distributed knowledge system: a constructionist approach,' *Strategic Management Journal*, **17**, 11–25.

Tushman, M.L. and P. Anderson (1986), 'Technological discontinuities and organizational environments', *Administrative Science Quarterly*, **31**, 439–65.

Tzokasa, N., E.J. Hultinkb and S. Hart (2004), 'Navigating the new product development process', *Industrial Marketing Management*, **33**, 619–26.

Un, C.A. and A. Cuervo-Cazurra (2004), 'Strategies for knowledge creation in firms', *British Journal of Management*, **15** (March), 27–41.

Un, A. and A. Cuervo-Cazurra (2005), 'Top managers and the product improvement process', *Advances in Strategic Management*, **22**, 319–48.

Veryzer, R.W. (1998), 'Discontinuous innovation and the new product development process', *Journal of Product Innovation Management*, **15**, 304–21.

Von Hippel, E. (1986), 'Lead users: a source of novel product concepts', *Management Science*, **32**, 791–805.

Von Krogh, G. and E. Von Hippel (2006), 'The promise of research on open source software', *Management Science*, **52**, 975–83.

Zahay, D., A. Griffin and E. Fredericks (2004), 'Sources, uses, and forms of data in the new product development process', *Industrial Marketing Management*, **33**, 657–66.

22 Organizational innovation of the Toyota Group
Faith Hatani

Introduction
For the past few decades, the global economy has witnessed massive industrial restructuring. Many firms have made dramatic changes by redesigning their organizational structures to improve performance. Making changes in a large interfirm network, however, is a challenging task. This chapter presents a case study of organizational innovation at the network level. In this study, I define organizational innovation of an interfirm network as the creation of new structural, managerial, and relational forms which enhance learning activities and the competitiveness of the network as a whole.

In the light of the adaptively rational model, this chapter suggests that the design of an interfirm network requires flexible, coherent, and progressive coordination through strong leadership from the core firm. This chapter shows that the creation of innovative network formation is achievable by making full use of existing resources through new arrangements and recombinations.

By reporting on the reorganization of the Toyota Group[1] which its core firm, Toyota Motor Corporation, conducted between 1994 and 2004, the case highlights Toyota's orchestration of structural changes and knowledge-sharing processes in its supply network. The case shows that the core firm's large-scale merger and acquisition (M&A) is not the only way to advance the performance of a business network.

The study employed the case study method to provide useful descriptions of variations in organizational structure and the process of change (Simon, 1947) in order to draw the causal relationships of organizational phenomena (Glaser and Strauss, 1967; Yin, 1989). This study is based upon field interviews during two phases of the reorganization. The first phase was in 2003, at which time major changes were taking place, and the second was in 2006, after the reorganization was effected. During the field research, this study carried out more than 50 interviews with chief executives and senior managers in the Toyota Group.

The next section discusses the literature related to interfirm network design. The third section describes the background of organizational innovation within the Toyota Group, and then presents three cases of reform that Toyota carried out. The fourth section analyses the new functions in the network and the change processes. The final section provides implications for network design and presents conclusions.

Organization design and its application to networks
The heart of organization design is the coherence of the bulk of intertwined decision making (Galbraith, 1977). Two major models of organization design have been developed, mainly through analysis of firm-level management. One is the coalition model, which regards organizations as negotiated orders between self-interested actors (March, 1962; Pfeffer and Salancik, 1978). The other is the rational model, which argues that tightly integrated organizations are most effective through the power-holders' direct control of subunits (von Bertalanffy, 1972; Mackenzie, 1986).

Although both models have conceptual rationality, both also have downsides. One of the shortcomings of the coalition model may be the speed of change. According to the coalition model, the power balance is negotiable and subject to resource contributions by the members involved. In this model, responses for adapting to a new form may take time, so it may be insufficiently efficient in rapidly changing business environments. In interfirm networks, however, member firms are neither purely instruments of the central power nor rigidly fixed in a place within a system, as the rational model assumes (Astley and Zajac, 1991, p. 403).

Synthesizing the two models, Astley and Zajac developed an adaptively rational model. They argue that the 'flexible coupling' of subunits in tightly integrated processes is more realistic and relevant to organization design, and that 'process power' – the power to mobilize resources within a decision-making process (p. 408) – does play a central role in creating flexible resource allocation.

Likewise, the core firm of an interfirm network should play a leading role in enhancing and adjusting the network structure by choosing the strategic direction (Gulati et al., 2000). In the global market, multinational enterprises (MNEs) have been redesigning themselves towards more incorporated network-based structures. Network design is associated with deliberately reshaping the structures and business relationships in and around the network (Sydow and Windeler, 1998; Lorenzoni and Lipparini, 1999). It is a process of designing an integrated worldwide strategy through globally distributed but interdependent resources and activities (Hedlund, 1986; Prahalad and Doz, 1987; Bartlett and Ghoshal, 1989). In the light of the adaptively rational model, the important objective in organizational innovation within interfirm networks is to increase the level of subunit interaction rather than to decouple subunit relationships (Astley and Zajac, 1991). Kogut and Zander (1992) also pointed out that firms can develop new skills by recombining their current capabilities.

Moreover, network resources, which include member firms' expertise, aptitudes, and interrelationships in a network, are inherent in the interfirm networks in which firms are embedded (Gulati, 1999). In the automotive industry, for example, the nature of supply networks can be described as being complex portfolios of the resources and capabilities of various supplier firms. Leading carmakers usually manage supply networks under their umbrellas, while being responsible for the quality of final products and their brands. Their business policies tend to determine their respective network structures. In this complex interfirm network system, the leadership of the core firm is particularly important for advancing change processes. The case study described below explores how a well-established large network achieved organizational innovation by exploiting existing resources.

Organizational innovation of the Toyota Group

The following sections report on organizational innovation in the Toyota Group, whose core firm, Toyota Motor Corporation, has been reinforcing its top position as the world's most profitable carmaker. Toyota has 14 Toyota group companies, in the company's official terms, which are organizationally close to Toyota, based on spin-offs or acquisitions during the group's history. Each group company specializes in specific segments or key areas of automotive production (Table 22.1). About 200 first-tier suppliers are organized in Toyota's suppliers' association, Kyohokai, and thick layers of suppliers

Table 22.1   Toyota group companies (before the reorganization)

Company name	Main products/activities	Establishment
Toyota Industries	Manufacture and sales of industrial vehicles, industrial equipment, machinery, and tools	1926
Aichi Steel	Manufacture and sales of speciality steel and forged steel products	1940
Toyoda Koki	Manufacture and sales of machine tools and auto parts	1941
Toyota Auto Body	Manufacture of auto and special vehicle bodies and parts	1945
Toyota Tsusho	Import, export, and trading of raw materials and products	1948
Aisin Seiki	Manufacture and sales of drive-train-related products and brake & chassis-related products	1949
Denso	Manufacture and sales of electronic systems and components for automotives	1949
Toyoda Boshoku	Manufacture and sales of auto parts and fabric products	1950
Towa Real Estate	Real estate development, management, and rental	1953
Toyota Central Research & Development Laboratories	Fundamental technical research for the Toyota Group	1960
Kanto Auto Works	Manufacture of auto bodies and parts and equipment for housing construction	1946
Toyoda Gosei	Manufacture and sales of synthetic resin and rubber products	1949
Hino Motors	Manufacture and sales of trucks and buses	1942
Daihatsu Motor	Manufacture and sales of automobiles	1907

Source: The company descriptions are based on the data of Toyota Motor Company homepage before the restructuring. After a series of organizational changes, there have been several changes in the main activities of the group companies, as well as in some of the company names.

are indirectly attached to Toyota via first-tier suppliers, eventually forming a large, hierarchical network.

The 1990s were a watershed in the global automotive industry. It was a time during which several international M&As took place in the automotive industry, a time often described as 'the merger mania'. In this context, Toyota announced the company's new target, 'the 2005 Vision', in 1996, which designated the beginning of the twenty-first century as the second phase of Toyota's business development. In contrast with its rivals, which have sought external resources to increase competitiveness through mega-alliances with new partners, Toyota has taken a different path.

The Toyota Group has distinctive resources and capabilities in its network, such as strong ties between member firms and their high level of learning capability (Dyer and Nobeoka, 2000). With these assets, the reorganization of the Toyota Group was designed to strengthen group ties to advance further the group companies' capabilities by putting the resources into best practices. Three cases, outlined below, illustrate this.

Case 1: enhancement of a relatively weak group company

Toyota's reorganization of the group began with the reform of Toyoda Boshoku (TB), which was relatively small compared to other group companies. The company was originally Toyota's spinning and weaving department, and was spun off from Toyota in 1950. TB's main business was manufacturing automotive interior parts related to textile products, such as floor carpets and seatbelt webbings. Due to its relatively low-price product segments, harsh cost competition with auto-parts manufacturers from developing countries had a great impact on TB's business. Moreover, as a result of weak domestic-market demand in the early 1990s, TB's revenue dropped by 36 per cent in 1996 from the year before (Toyoda Boshoku, 2001, p. 159).

Strengthening this Achilles' heel of the group was essential for Toyota in order to boost the network's performance as a whole. Taking TB's poor performance seriously, Toyota organized a top management meeting with TB and another group company, Denso, in 1997, and decided on an intra-network business transfer. Shortly after the meeting, Denso began to transfer its cabin-air-filter business, and subsequently its oil-filter business, to TB. This business transfer aimed to increase TB's competitiveness by grafting Denso's technological capacity, and to promote TB's potential skills as a textile manufacturer in filter production.

Toyota also organized other changes to reinforce TB. In 1999, TB was merged with one of Toyota's affiliates, Toyoda Chemical Industry, whose main business was manufacturing automotive floor carpet. In 2004, moreover, another merger was carried out; TB was merged with two of Toyota's subsidiaries, both of which had been working as module suppliers of seat systems for Toyota. This set of intra-group consolidations contributed to scaling up TB and making it a comprehensive interior-systems supplier.[2] Backed by the combined resources of other member firms, TB has enhanced its competence and improved its role in Toyota's supply network.

Case 2: a mechanism of obligatory knowledge sharing

Organizing competitive network members which have substantial businesses outside the network may not be as straightforward as consolidating relatively small firms. The second case, as well as the third case to be described later, involved the establishment of joint ventures among member firms in the Toyota Group (Figure 22.1).

Although advocates of the collaboration-network approach have argued that inter-firm collaboration can provide the benefits of resource sharing and access to knowledge spillovers (Powell et al., 1996; Ahuja, 2000), the process is, of course, not an automatic one. In competitive global markets, key technologies and know-how are usually tightly protected. Dyer and Nobeoka (2000) posited dilemmas in collaborative works, such as network members' unwillingness to share their knowledge, the free-rider problem, and difficulty in knowledge transfer within networks.

Even in the Toyota Group, knowledge sharing does not occur purely voluntarily. In particular, the relationships between Toyota and two of its leading group companies, Denso and Aisin Seiki, are highly complex. Both Denso and Aisin Seiki are internationally competitive in their specialized product segments. Denso is one of the world's leading auto-parts suppliers of electrical and electronic system components, while Aisin Seiki specializes in transmissions and brake systems, and they supply their products to most global car makers.

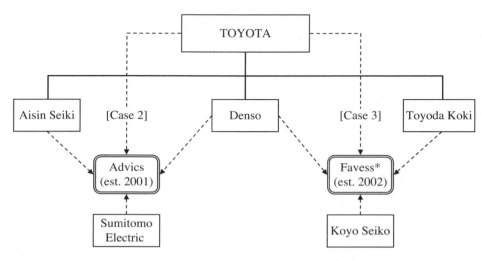

Note: * Favess was dissolved as a result of the merger between Toyoda Koki and Koyo Seiko in 2006. The new company was renamed JTEKT.

Figure 22.1   The creation of intra-network joint ventures in the Toyota Group

When suppliers are highly competitive and less dependent on the core firm for their sales, it is likely to be more difficult for the core firm to devise changes in the interfirm relationships. In fact, the attitudes of the two group companies towards knowledge sharing do not readily support the traditional assumption of collaborative learning, which Japanese *keiretsu* firms are thought to possess. Regarding learning routines in the Toyota Group, Aisin Seiki's project general manager, when interviewed for this study, said: 'We share our knowledge with other Kyohokai members only when we are told to do so by Toyota, or we think demonstration of our expertise is necessary or beneficial for us in order to elevate Toyota's grading of us'.

Denso's general manager also commented in a separate interview: 'We do not need much technical support from Toyota in our specialized areas, although we do need Toyota's business to maintain our position in the global market. Unless it is part of business or otherwise leading to future business, there is little incentive to share our key technology with others'.

In this regard, the creation of learning structures, rather than learning routines, may be more crucial for encouraging competitive network members to partake in a new form of network learning. In order to facilitate knowledge sharing, Toyota established intra-group joint ventures that function as nodes for key suppliers. The establishment of ADVICS Co. Ltd. was an important part of the Toyota Group's organizational innovation.

In 2001, Toyota, Aisin Seiki, Denso, and one of the Kyohokai's member suppliers, Sumitomo Electric, formed ADVICS to develop and manufacture cutting-edge brake systems and components. Prior to establishing the joint venture, Toyota dispatched engineers and purchasing staff to Aisin Seiki, while having gradually concentrated the Toyota Group's procurement of brake-related parts into Aisin Seiki's purchasing department. Accordingly, Aisin Seiki took a lead with a 40 per cent share in ADVICS, while other participants have each held 20 per cent. At ADVICS, the leading suppliers in the Toyota Group have an obligation to share their knowledge and technology. The inclusion of Denso in ADVICS was particularly important for Toyota to be able to achieve a high level of knowledge-sharing activities.

ADVICS was also assigned a clear target to expand its market channels outside the Toyota Group. ADVICS's initial sales target was JP¥250 billion by 2005, but the joint venture came close to the target within a year of its establishment, pushing ADVICS to the position of top manufacturer in the domestic brake market. With the technological competencies of the participants, moreover, ADVICS has rapidly increased its presence in the global market by boosting its production bases abroad, especially in the biggest car market, the United States.

Case 3: adaptation and integration
In the third case, Toyota adopted both the methods used in the previous cases. The main actors in the third case were Toyoda Koki and Koyo Seiko. Toyoda Koki was a Toyota Group company which produces machine tools and steering systems, while Koyo Seiko was a supplier of steering systems, with Toyota its biggest shareholder. Although Koyo Seiki was a Toyota subsidiary and not a Toyota Group company, it was highly competitive in the international steering-parts market, being the world's second-largest supplier of steering systems, while Toyoda Koki was ranked sixth in the product category (*Nihon Keizai Shimbun*, February 4, 2005).

A joint venture, FAVESS, was formed between Toyoda Koki and Koyo Seiko, with the partial participation of Toyota and Denso. In retrospect, Toyoda Koki and Koyo Seiko first formed a basic agreement for the joint development of electric power-steering systems in September 2000. After a two-year preparation period, they established FAVESS in 2002 to produce these systems together.

The equity shares of the participants were Koyo Seiko 45 per cent, Toyoda Koki 35 per cent, Toyota 10 per cent, and Denso 10 per cent. Together with Toyota, Denso played a role as an observer to facilitate learning processes and technological development in FAVESS. Denso's participation had a technical reason, as it had expertise related to electric auto components. It may also suggest that Toyota needed another third party besides itself to promote knowledge sharing between Toyoda Koki and Koyo Seiko, as the existence of common third parties can enforce cooperative behaviour and diminish the risk of opportunism (Gargiulo and Benassi, 2000).

Within two years of the start of sales, however, FAVESS became a temporary entity. In February 2005, Koyo Seiko and Toyoda Koki announced that they would merge in 2006. FAVESS can therefore be seen as an adaptive step towards an intra-group merger. The full integration of the two firms was carried out after the participants had achieved satisfactory results with mutual learning and had confirmed their suitability. This process provided both firms, which had been competing with each other in the same product market, with enough time for the mutual adjustment of their organizational systems and supply chains to the newly incorporated entity.

New functions in the supply network
The three cases indicate that a resource-rich network can achieve organizational innovation based on existing network assets through new organizational arrangements and

by recombining member firms' capabilities. From the cases, two new functions can be identified in Toyota's supply network.

Quasi-core firms

Supply networks in the automotive industry require a great deal of mutual operational adjustment and technological joint works (Fujimoto, 1999; Dyer, 2000). Dyer suggests that the first-tier suppliers in the Toyota Group can be seen as extended enterprises of the core firm because of their organizational closeness and responsiveness to Toyota. In the Toyota Group, most key suppliers organize their own supply networks under the umbrellas that form the substructures of the Toyota Group. They not only proactively respond to Toyota's expectations, but also relay the core firm's strategy to the lower tier of the network. In this regard, the role of those key first-tier suppliers is becoming more than that of extended enterprises. Their role can be regarded as being that of 'quasi-core firms' in the Toyota Group.

An important aspect of Toyota's recent organizational innovation is its arrangements for reinforcing the competitiveness of quasi-core firms in the Group. As the quasi-core firms become more powerful, however, they may develop stronger bargaining power *vis-à-vis* the core firm, and become more prone to pursuing autonomous self-interest. To manage quasi-core firms, Toyota has made them more embedded in the network structure by giving them higher functions and new responsibilities.

One downside of tightly integrated networks may be their rigidity, which hinders firms from responding to technical innovation outside the network and from developing new capabilities (Leonard-Barton 1992; Uzzi 1997). Toyota has avoided such rigidity by encouraging quasi-core supplier firms to diversify their customer base, while tying them to Toyota in the network system. As the quasi-core suppliers, which are internationally competitive while being well linked with Toyota, explore relationships globally by selling their products to other carmakers or by forming joint ventures with local firms in offshore markets, they can learn about different types of customer needs and diverse business settings. This has enabled Toyota to expand its information sources without merging with or acquiring business entities outside the network itself.

Hub joint ventures

Toyota has made full use of various measures, such as managerial ties, operational ties, and, increasingly, financial ties, in its organizational innovations. The two joint ventures established by group members may exemplify how these relational tools can be put into force in order to compel strong suppliers to collaborate. Instead of simply appointing some suppliers as systems suppliers, as other carmakers commonly did, Toyota deputized quasi-core firms to manage and develop the business of key components through the hub joint ventures. The participants of the two hub joint ventures, ADVICS and FAVESS, are key suppliers in Toyota's targeted segments, so they could be reluctant to share their valuable knowledge with others. However, since hub joint ventures are legally established business entities, participants appointed by Toyota have to share their knowledge with their counterparts in order to run them effectively. In other words, these joint ventures are the functional hubs which promote obligatory knowledge sharing among specialist suppliers.

In addition, the establishment of hub joint ventures can facilitate faster development of specific technology and knowledge than network-wide knowledge sharing routines. On

Table 22.2   Three patterns of organizational innovation in the Toyota Group

	Key products	Suppliers' positions in the global market	Main aims	Method of reorganization
Case 1	Fabric and filter parts, seating systems, interior components	Relatively low	Scaling-up, Enhancement of competitiveness and product diversification	Intra-network mergers
Case 2	Brake systems and components	High	Advanced knowledge sharing, Expansion of sales channels	Hub joint venture
Case 3	Electric power steering (EPS) systems	High/medium high	Advanced knowledge sharing, Scaling-up	Hub joint venture and intra-network merger

the one hand, since sufficient learning in highly interactive environments, among many others, can be difficult (Lounamaa and March, 1987; Levinthal and March, 1993), by drawing a clear boundary of knowledge sharing among selected competitive members, the participants of hub joint ventures can exchange their expertise more openly, but with a minimum risk of information leakage outside the loop. On the other hand, hub joint ventures enable Toyota to reduce the problem of the technological black box. By taking part in hub joint ventures as a legal participant, Toyota is able to involve itself in knowledge exchanges of key suppliers' advanced technologies more intimately. At the same time, Toyota can advise them about its needs and strategy for the key product in a focused way.

Processes of organizational innovation
In its group reorganization, Toyota used different processes for the three cases studied, depending on the suppliers' product segments and the purposes of the changes (Table 22.2). The use of different approaches is important, because the firms' capacities for acquiring new knowledge can vary (Cohen and Levinthal, 1990; Lane and Lubatkin, 1998).

In case one, the member firms involved in the change process were relatively small and modestly competitive on the international market, and cost effectiveness was an important factor in their situations. What Toyota sought in the reform of TB was the application of its expertise to a wider range of segments and the creation of a synergy effect between related products to achieve larger economies of scale. Toyota realized this purpose by an intra-network merger of firms which were relatively dependent on the core firm. Intra-network merger was also favourable for the core firm, Toyota, because while the newly established firm diversified its product segments, the size and bargaining power of the new entity has not been a threat to it.

In cases two and three, Toyota used hub joint ventures as the change method. The establishment of hub joint ventures among member firms, which can be seen as strategic quasi-externalization (Sydow, 1992), functions as a forum of knowledge sharing in specific area. ADVICS and FAVESS have functioned for this purpose based on legislative contracts. As Makhija and Genesh (1997) argued, legal contractual arrangements are most appropriate when precise and highly explicit information needs to be transmitted. In the latter case, Toyota promoted further integration by merging Toyoda Koki and Koyo Seiko, aiming to make them the leading specialist supplier for their specific product segments.[3]

As a result of a series of changes in the network structure, member firms in the Toyota Group are now forming an interlocking global strategy, enhancing their performance in their specialized areas. To realize organizational innovation, the core firm needs to coordinate network resources with a dynamic view. The processes are associated with the constant evaluation of member firms' resources and capabilities and a clear understanding of their aptitudes, backed by the competitiveness and competence of the core firm itself.

Conclusion
This study examined how an established interfirm network has achieved organizational innovation by rearranging existing network resources. The reorganization of the Toyota Group may provide a possible approach to organizational innovation, with practical implications. This case study demonstrated that exploring various ties outside the network is not the only option to expand the global reach of a multinational business group.

On the surface, the recent growth of business expansion and competitiveness of group suppliers might appear to indicate that leading Japanese auto-parts suppliers are trying to exit from their *keiretsu* relationships. As far as the Toyota Group is concerned, however, it shows the opposite. While Toyota's key suppliers are expanding business outside the Toyota Group, they are still structurally embedded in the network envisaged by Toyota, and ultimately work for the global strategy of the group as a whole.

This may also imply that if a coherent management network is not feasible, an attempt to increase the variety of external interfirm ties outside the existing network could be somewhat self-destructive, consuming significant time and resources, and could make a network more organizationally vulnerable. The core firm's easy resort to exploring many external ties could also create overlaps and unintended structural holes which do not function to explore useful knowledge. Considering the volume of adaptive processes required in creating new forms, it can be risky for a large network, particularly for a supply network in such a mature industry as the automotive industry, to explore external entities because radical tie-ups with external firms may produce a significant impact on relationships and could jeopardize effective knowledge-sharing activities in its existing supply network. While the positive effects of the exploration of new ties is not ruled out, extensively looking for new opportunities is not the only way to remain innovative.

In the process of organizational innovation of a network, the core firm is likely to need to address a number of tasks to implement changes and thereby enhance network competitiveness. If the core firm neglects to do its utmost to improve its existing network continuously, active searches for alternative resources outside the network may not bear fruit. To create competitive network architecture, the core firm should rigorously re-evaluate network resources and envisage possible ways of making full use of the integrated capabilities that the network already has before jumping to external sources.

Notes

1. The Toyota Group in this study refers to Toyota Motor Corporation and its affiliates and subsidiaries accounted for under equity methods.
2. On this merger, the company name changed from 'Toyoda' Boshoku to 'Toyota' Boshoku.
3. In addition, Denso and Aisin Seiki are significantly larger than Toyoda Koki and Koyo Seiko. Also, Denso and Aisin Seiki already have a range of product segments and established positions in the global auto-parts market.

References

Ahuja, G. (2000), 'Collaboration networks, structural holes, and innovation: a longitudinal study', *Administrative Science Quarterly*, **45**, 425–55.
Astley, W.G. and E.J. Zajac (1991), 'Intraorganizational power and organizational design: reconciling rational and coalition models of organization', *Organization Science*, **2**(4), 399–411.
Bartlett, C. and S. Ghoshal (1989), *Managing across Borders: The Transnational Solution*, Boston, MA: Harvard Business School Press.
Cohen, W.M. and D.A. Levinthal (1990), 'Absorptive capacity: a new perspective on learning and innovation', *Administrative Science Quarterly*, **35**, 128–52.
Dyer, J.H. (2000), *Collaborative Advantage: Winning through Extended Enterprise Supplier Networks*, Oxford: Oxford University Press.
Dyer, J.H. and K. Nobeoka (2000), 'Creating and managing a high-performance knowledge-sharing network: the Toyota case', *Strategic Management Journal*, **21**, 345–67.
Fujimoto, T. (1999), *The Evolution of a Manufacturing System at Toyota*, Oxford and New York: Oxford University Press.
Galbraith, J.R. (1977), *Organization Design*, Reading, MA and London: Addison-Wesley.
Gargiulo, M. and M. Benassi (2000), 'Trapped in your own net? Network cohesion, structural holes, and the adaptation of social capital', *Organization Science*, **11**(2), 183–96.
Glaser, B.G. and A.L. Strauss (1967), *The Discovery of Grounded Theory: Strategies for Qualitative Research*, Chicago, IL: Alpine.
Gulati, R. (1999), 'Network location and learning: the influence of network resources and firm capabilities on alliance formation', *Strategic Management Journal*, **20**, 397–420.
Gulati, R., N. Nohria and A. Zaheer (2000), 'Strategic networks', *Strategic Management Journal*, **21**, 203–15.
Hedlund, G. (1986), 'The hypermodern MNC – a heterarchy?', *Human Resource Management*, **25**(1), 9–35.
Kogut, B. and U. Zander (1992), 'Knowledge of the firm, combinative capabilities, and the replication of technology', *Organization Science*, **3**(3), 383–97.
Lane, P.J. and M. Lubatkin (1998), 'Relative absorptive capacity and interorganizational learning', *Strategic Management Journal*, **19**, 461–77.
Leonard-Barton, D. (1992), 'Core capabilities and core rigidities: a paradox in managing new product development', *Strategic Management Journal*, **13**, 111–25.
Levinthal, D.A. and J.G. March (1993), 'The myopia of learning strategic management', *Management Journal*, **14** (Special Issue, Winter), 95–112.
Lorenzoni, G. and A. Lipparini (1999), 'The leveraging of interfirm relationships as a distinctive organizational capability: a longitudinal study', *Strategic Management Journal*, **20**, 317–38.
Lounamaa, P. and J.G. March (1987), 'Adaptive coordination of a learning team', *Management Science*, **33**, 107–23.
Mackenzie, K.D. (1986), 'Virtual positions and power', *Management Science*, **32**(5), 622–42.
Makhija, M.V. and U. Ganesh (1997), 'The relationship between control and partner learning in learning-related joint ventures', *Organization Science*, **8**(5), 508–27.
March, J.G. (1962), 'The business firm as a political coalition', *Journal of Politics*, **24**, 662–78.
Nihon Keizai Shimbun (2005), 'Toyoda Machine Works, Koyo Seiko Announce April '06 Merger', February 4, web document at http://www.nni.nikkei.co.jp (subscription page).
Pfeffer, J. and G.R. Salancik (1978), *The External Control of Organizations: A Resource Dependence Perspective*, New York: Harper & Row.
Powell, W.W., K.W. Koput and L. Smith-Doerr (1996), 'Interorganizational collaboration and the locus of innovation: networks of learning in biotechnology', *Administrative Science Quarterly*, **41**, 116–45.
Prahalad, C.K. and Y.L. Doz (1987), *The Multinational Mission – Balancing Local Demands*, New York and London: Free Press.
Simon, H.A. (1947), *Administrative Behaviour*, New York: Macmillan.
Sydow, J. (1992), 'On the management of strategic networks', in H. Ernste and V. Meier (eds), *Regional Development and Contemporary Industrial Response*, London: Pinter, pp. 115–31.

Sydow, J. and A. Windeler (1998), 'Organizing and evaluating interfirm networks: a structurationist perspective on network processes and effectiveness', *Organization Science*, **9**(3), 265–84.

Toyoda Boshoku Corporation (2001), *Toyoda Boshoku 50 nen-shi: New TB-21 wo Mezashite – Saikin 5 nen no Ayumi* (Toyoda Boshoku 50-year History: Towards New TB-21 – the Recent Steps), Kariya, Japan: Toyoda Boshoku Corp.

Uzzi, B. (1997), 'The social structure and competition in interfirm networks: the paradox of embeddedness', *Administrative Science Quarterly*, **42**(1), 35–67.

von Bertalanffy, L. (1972), 'The history and status of general systems theory', *Academy of Management Journal*, **15**(4), 407–26.

Yin, R.K. (1989), *Case Study Research: Design and Methods*, Newbury Park, CA: Sage.

PART IV

RESPONDING TO THE FUTURE: INTUITION, INERTIA AND STRATEGIC FLEXIBILITY

23 The role of intuition in strategic decision making*
Marta Sinclair, Eugene Sadler-Smith and Gerard P. Hodgkinson

Introduction

The strategic decisions confronting senior managers and other key stakeholders in modern organizations are complex judgemental problems that demand expertise gained through an amalgam of practical experience and learning for their resolution. At the heart of the strategy formation process is the ability of decision makers to synthesize 'vast arrays of soft information' into new perspectives (Mintzberg et al., 1998: 164) achieved as much by insights which are visioned, imagined and intuited as through a rational analytical process of defining, diagnosing, designing and deciding (see Mintzberg and Westley, 2001: 89). Although many organizations place a premium on analytical skills, analysis is a necessary but insufficient basis for effective strategic decision making (Louis and Sutton, 1991; Simon, 1997; Hodgkinson and Sparrow, 2002; van der Heijden et al., 2002). The situations confronting strategic actors are not so much tightly structured 'puzzles' to be solved as loosely structured problems that require both detailed information processing and holistic interpretation. Adopting the metaphor of photography, the strategy formation process is akin to the use of a 'zoom lens' camera that can be adjusted both in order to view the world narrowly to capture detail and more widely, in order to capture overall patterns and trends.

In this chapter we explore the role that intuition plays in strategic decision making, a process that demands a delicate balance between rational analysis and intuitive judgement. There is a considerable volume of work on intuition in the interrelated fields of cognitive psychology, social cognition and cognitive neuroscience, indicating that reason and affect are served by separate cognitive systems. At this juncture it is opportune to consider the implications of this work for advancing understanding of strategic decision processes in organizations and how these processes might be improved. For the purposes of this chapter, 'intuiting' is defined as a process leading to a recognition or judgement that is arrived at rapidly, without deliberative rational thought, is difficult to articulate verbally, is based on a broad constellation of prior learning and past experiences, is accompanied by a feeling of confidence or certitude, and is affectively charged (Davis and Davis, 2003; Dane and Pratt, 2007). We do not conflate intuition with related concepts such as incubation and insight. Nor do we equate it with creativity, but we do regard it as one of the vital antecedents to the creative process in organizational (and other) contexts (see also Crossan et al. 1999; Runco and Sakamoto, 1999; Raidl and Lubbart, 2001).

We consider intuition, and its counterpart, analysis, from an information processing standpoint, specifically from the perspective of dual-process theory in social cognition (for example, Chaiken and Trope, 1999) and cognitive psychology (for example, Gilovich et al., 2002). We examine critically the notion of a single, overarching intuition-analysis dimension of information processing style, argued by some researchers to underpin managerial and organizational decision making (for example, Hayes and Allinson, 1994), and present a more compelling complex alternative, consonant with recent advances in dual-process theory and research. We begin by offering a critical evaluation of the classical rational choice model of decision making and consider the limits of rationality in the strategic management process. Having set the scene in terms of the limits of rationality, the overarching information processing architecture, dual-process theory and the cognitive, affective and somatic nature of intuition, the chapter specifically examines the role that intuition plays in strategic decision making. The concepts of naturalistic and non-conscious decision making are discussed as a means of understanding how managers use their experience to make decisions in specific contexts. The role of pattern recognition (as a basis for expertise) and the novel combination of stimuli (as a basis for innovation) in decision making in general, and in strategic decision making in particular, are also discussed. In conclusion, we consider the implications of our analysis for fostering intuitive awareness among current and future generations of strategic decision makers, through education and training and development interventions.

Limits of rational choice models in strategic decision making

The model of decision making that many senior managers are taught and expected to employ entails the pursuit of an analytical, linear process in an attempt to optimize decision outcomes. The archetypal rational manager is likely to follow a linear choice process in order to select the 'best' alternative from those with which she or he is faced. Typically, following initial identification of the problem to be addressed, pertinent data are collected and analysed, alternatives are generated, potential solutions are compared against the criteria for success, and a choice is made between competing solutions, based on a (subjective) estimate of the likelihood of each event unfolding (that is, its subjective probability) and its subjective value (or utility) to the decision maker (see Janis and Mann, 1977; Arkes and Hammond, 1986; Miller et al., 1996). The rational choice model has a number of clear advantages; for example, it allows consistency (it is repeatable), serves as a generic decision aid (it can be applied across many different situations), helps novices to learn how to solve problems and make decisions (it is a rigorous training tool) (Klein, 1998), and forces decision makers to make explicit the bases of their actions (Arkes and Hammond, 1986).

However, the rational choice model is predicated upon several assumptions that are highly questionable from a psychological standpoint, given the complex, uncertain and time-pressured environments confronting many organizations, not least the assumption that decision makers have the requisite computational skills and time to go through the sequential optimization process implied by this model (Simon, 1957; see also Hodgkinson and Sparrow, 2002). The assumptions that the required data actually exist in a tangible and, ideally, quantifiable form, and that cause-and-effect relationships are understood sufficiently to enable outcomes to be predicted on the basis of logical and quantitative analyses are also dubious. As observed by Arkes and Hammond (1986: 6): 'likelihoods and utilities are often not easy to assess', and since the effectiveness of the approach is largely based on the accuracy of the likelihoods and utilities used 'every effort should be made to obtain good estimates'. For the most complex problems the decision process is not wholly objective; nor is it devoid of ambiguity and interpretation. Human judgement (however 'expert') is inherently involved in the design and deployment of the 'objectified' decision analysis techniques that flow out of the rational model of decision making.

To reiterate, the effective development and deployment of decision analysis tools are both highly dependent upon the judgement of individuals whose rational analytical capabilities are ultimately fallible. Human input is necessary to build models, and expert judgement is rarely an exclusively rational process (Griffith et al., 2008). For example, in designing expert systems for medical diagnoses it is medical professionals who must decide what criteria to include in the model underpinning the system (such as what to look for in an X-ray image), and how the model should be built, since there is no alternative to a human judge or designer for such a task (Hogarth, 2001).

Modern-day critiques of rational analysis in strategic decision making can be traced back at least as far as the writings of Chester Barnard in the 1930s. Barnard, himself an AT&T executive, drew a distinction between 'logical mental processes' and 'non-logical mental processes' (that is, contrasting modes of cognition). The former encapsulated conscious thinking (that is, reasoning) expressible in words or other symbols. In Barnard's view this type of thinking was a major characteristic of the work of analytical scientists, but was not so much in evidence in high-pressure tasks or in much of the work of 'businessmen [*sic*] or executives' (Barnard, 1938: 302–3). In contrast, he maintained that individuals processed knowledge within the non-logical mode of cognition unconsciously or without conscious effort (in this sense, he anticipated Reber (1989) on the role of implicit learning and knowledge) and by definition, non-conscious processes could not be analysed reliably through self-reflection. Significantly, Barnard argued that the potential harmfulness of logical mental processes lay in their wrongful elevation above their non-logical counterparts, the latter being undervalued and underappreciated as a resource.

However, it was Herbert Simon's notion of 'bounded rationality' (Simon, 1957) that placed psychology centre stage within the field of organization theory. Given the cognitive limitations of decision makers, relative to the complexity of their environments, human behaviour is intendedly rational, but only in so far as this is possible within the bounds of the human information processing system; hence, human beings 'satisfice' rather than maximize in decision making. In marked contrast to the rational model of decision making outlined above, Simon argued that decision makers set a minimally acceptable standard that must be met and search only until the first available alternative is found that meets that threshold criterion (see also March and Simon, 1958; Simon, 1989, 1997).

There is continuity between Simon's and Barnard's work (Barnard wrote the Foreword to the first edition (1947) of Simon's *Administrative Behavior*), but Simon was troubled by Barnard's account because it did not give any clues as to what subconscious processes go on while judgements are being made. Simon turned to work on the psychology of expert judgement and artificial intelligence (AI) in an endeavour to provide a convincing explanation. Simon's position on the role that intuition plays is summarized thus: 'Intuition and judgement – at least good judgement – are simply analyses frozen into habit and the capacity for rapid response through recognition' (Simon, 1987: 63). This perspective, however, was questioned by other researchers who cautioned that such understanding would reduce intuitive information processing to a variant of non-conscious analysis (see Hammond et al., 1987).

Simon's model of intuitive judgement is founded upon the notion of intuition as a manifestation of expertise and as a process of pattern recognition and pattern matching. For example, he estimated that experts, such as the chess players upon which his experiments with co-researcher William Chase were based, are likely to have internalized around 50,000 familiar patterns (Simon, 1997: 134) and have been gained over 10 years or more of intense practice (see also Ericsson and Charness, 1994). According to this view, experts store patterns in long-term memory along with other associated information. Simon (1987) also acknowledged the role of emotion in decision making, but concluded that 'emotion-driven intuition' results in 'irrational decisions'.

Recent research in the field of cognitive neuroscience (Damasio, 1994; Le Doux, 1996) presents a more complex picture. It suggests that the 'other associations' above and below the level of conscious awareness may include the level of danger or opportunity, or the feeling of elation or disappointment that a particular pattern may have induced in past successes or failures. The implications of this work are that memories may be embodied in a resonating emotion as 'somatic markers' that can be re-activated in a context-congruent situation (Damasio, 1994). In other words, the patterns, or at least the judgements that arise from the use of those patterns, may be affect-laden. Mumby and Putnam (1992) go even further, arguing that emotions are present in one form or another in most decisions, a view that is congruent with the notion of the 'affect heuristic', as conceptualized by Finucane et al. (2000) (see also Slovic, 2000, 2002; Slovic et al., 2004). Juxtaposing Simon's satisficing model with these recent advances in cognitive neuroscience, Mumby and Putnam propose that organizational decision making occurs within 'bounded emotionality'.

An important caveat to the critiques of rationality offered here and elsewhere (Hodgkinson and Sparrow, 2002; Sadler-Smith and Shefy, 2004; Sadler-Smith and Sparrow, 2008) is that the value of rational analysis under certain circumstances cannot be denied, nor is it our intention to do so. Research attests, however, to the fact that rational analysis is not the exclusive means by which effective decision making in organizations occurs – intuition has an undoubted role to play (Mintzberg, 1976; Isenberg, 1984; Eisenhardt, 1989; Burke and Miller, 1999; Khatri and Ng, 2000; Hayashi, 2001; Sinclair et al., 2002; Sadler-Smith, 2004). In Simon's theory intuition does not operate in isolation from rational analysis; rather, rational analysis and intuitive judgement are complementary processes:

> [E]very manager needs to be able to analyse problems systematically. Every manager also needs to be able to respond to situations rapidly, a skill that requires the cultivation of intuition and judgement over many years of experience and training. The effective manager does not have the luxury of being able to choose between 'analytic' and 'intuitive' approaches to problems. (Simon, 1997: 139)

In this respect, Simon (ibid.: 131) assumed that conscious and subconscious decision processes are highly similar in the sense that they draw upon 'factual premises and value premises, and operate upon them to form conclusions that become the decisions'.

During the 1980s and 1990s a number of researchers (for example, Taggart and Robey, 1981; Allinson and Hayes, 1996) advanced arguments broadly consistent with Simon's formulation, predicated upon a presumed bipolarity in human information processing (that is, analysis versus intuition). Taggart and others explained this in terms of the brain science of the time (the so-called 'left-brain–right-brain' distinction), manifested most famously perhaps in the widely-cited paper by Mintzberg (1976), entitled: 'Planning on the left; managing on the right'. However, as discussed in the next section of this chapter, the dual-process formulations alluded to earlier have fuelled debates regarding whether or not these two contrasting modes of cognition are in fact served by a common underlying system or, alternatively, by independent cognitive systems, and the nature and extent of their interaction.

The absence of a robust and compelling psychological framework to underpin the models offered by Simon and others resulted in major conceptual problems. Simon, for example, appealed to arguments from the AI research of the time. This offered only weak explanations for the role of affect. In the case of Taggart and his colleagues (for example, Taggart and Robey, 1981), their work was limited by reliance upon oversimplified models of brain lateralization which were popular at that time. Agor (1989) was one of the first researchers to conduct large-scale descriptive studies of intuition among managers for which he used survey research. Unfortunately, however, the instrument he used, the Agor Intuitive Management survey, was predicated upon Jungian notions of psychological type and the aforementioned, ultimately flawed, arguments for the bipolarity of intuitive and thinking styles (see ibid.: 140).

A plausible psychological framework for the analysis of intuition must be capable of accommodating the latest developments in social cognitive neuroscience concerning the limits of rationality and the role of affect in organizational decision making. We maintain that dual-process formulations of cognition present the field of strategic management with such a framework (see also Hodgkinson and Sparrow, 2002; Sinclair et al., 2002; Hodgkinson and Sadler-Smith, 2003a,b; Sinclair and Ashkanasy, 2005; Dane and Pratt, 2007; Hodgkinson and Clarke, 2007; Hodgkinson et al., 2008; Sadler-Smith and Sparrow, 2008).

Dual-process formulations of cognition

In the 1960s and 1970s neurophysiologists and neurosurgeons, spearheaded by the pioneering work of Roger Sperry and Michael Gazzaniga, investigated hemispheric asymmetries in human brain functioning, using various surgical, electroencephalographic (EEG) and experimental techniques. Inferences were drawn by Ornstein (1977) and others regarding differential functions of the brain's two hemispheres, and this notion later became popularized in the concept of 'left-brain–right-brain' differences, more technically known as hemispheric functional asymmetry, underpinned by the lateralization hypothesis (Sperry, 1968; Gazzaniga, 1971). As noted earlier, this idea was adopted by a number of management scholars as a means of explaining several important aspects of behaviour, including interpersonal functioning and decision making. For example, Taggart and Robey (1981) employed the concept of hemispheric functional asymmetry as the basis for their model of management decision strategies, in which a 'left-brain' decision style was characterized as analytic, logical and deductive in nature, while a 'right-brain' style was characterized as synthetic, non-logical and inductive. Their argument was that due to hemispheric dominance, one mode of decision making predominated in most individuals, a hypothesis that was consonant with the then prevalent asymmetric lateralization thesis. Herrmann (1996) expanded this model even further by developing it into a quadrant-based 'brain dominance' thesis, which postulated several finer-grained distinctions that he argued underpinned rational and intuitive processing. In terms of intuition, he differentiated between a form of intuition which he termed 'sensory intuition' and a more abstract type of intuition. He argued that the former was processed in the limbic system, while the latter originated in the more evolved parts of the brain.

Overall, the 'split brain hypothesis' is simple to comprehend, has high face validity and has enjoyed widespread popular appeal. In keeping with this line of reasoning, Hayes and Allinson (1994) reviewed a substantial body of literature and postulated a single, superordinate dimension of individual differences in information processing, which they subsequently labelled 'the intuition–analysis dimension': 'Intuition . . . refers to immediate judgment based on feeling and the adoption of a global perspective. Analysis . . . refers to judgment based on mental reasoning and a focus on detail' (Allinson and Hayes, 1996: 122).

According to this view, intuition and rationality are opposite poles of a common dimension, with the relative contribution of analysis or intuition determined by a combination of dispositional and contextual factors. Allinson and Hayes reported the development and validation of a 38-item self-report inventory, the Cognitive Style Index (CSI), which is designed to locate individuals along a continuum that reflects the unidimensional, bipolar conception of information processing hypothesized by them earlier (Hayes and Allinson, 1994).[1]

Unfortunately the CSI has been found wanting both theoretically and psychometrically. In terms of its construct validity, a series of exploratory and confirmatory factor analyses of large samples in different occupational, educational and national settings consistently fail to uphold the notion of a single unitary dimension of human information processing (Hodgkinson and Sadler-Smith, 2003a,b; Hodgkinson et al., 2006a). Instead what emerges from these construct validation studies is a more complex state of affairs in which analysis and intuition coexist as separate constructs (albeit intercorrelated). Moreover, most researchers would now accept that the notion of a 'split brain', with one hemisphere exclusively processing information 'analytically' and the other processing information 'intuitively', is an oversimplification that is perhaps at best treated as a metaphor for different modes of information processing. In cognitive neuroscience more complex models have emerged in which several systems, not exclusively located in one hemisphere or the other, interact with one another (see, for example, Lieberman et al., 2004). Hence, in theoretical terms the concept of a single processing system, in which individuals exhibit degrees of preference for analysis or intuition, is found wanting in a number of significant respects and must be rejected in favour of an alternative and less-simplified position.

On the basis of the findings reviewed above, a more compelling conceptual position is one in which human information processing is served by a number of independent cognitive systems underlain by separate neural pathways for certain affective and cognitive processes that coexist and interact. Such a conception fits well with the broad range of dual-process theories that have emerged comparatively recently in cognitive psychology and social cognition (see Chaiken and Trope, 1999; Gilovich et al., 2002). This alternative conception of analysis and intuition, predicated on the assumption of two parallel cognitive systems, is supported by both experimental research (Epstein et al., 1996) and empirical evidence from studies in occupational settings (Isenberg, 1984; Burke and Miller, 1999).

One dual-process theory, typical of dual-process conceptions more generally, that provides a particularly convenient framework for advancing our understanding of the complementary roles played by analysis and intuition in strategic foresight and decision making is the Cognitive–Experiential Self-Theory (CEST), developed by Epstein and his colleagues (see Epstein, 1991, 1998, 2000; Denes-Raj and Epstein, 1994; Epstein et al., 1996; Pacini & Epstein, 1999). Epstein et al. (1996: 391) maintain that: 'people process information by two parallel, interactive systems', which interface harmoniously but operate in different ways. The rational system, falling within the realms of conscious control, is analytical in nature, whereas the experiential system operates at a non-conscious level, on the basis of experientially-based intuition. In this model the experiential mode acts as the default, unless the rational processing is consciously activated. More specifically: 'The rational system . . . is conscious, relatively slow, analytical, primarily verbal, and relatively affect free . . . The experiential system . . . is preconscious, rapid, automatic, holistic, primarily nonverbal, intimately associated with affect . . . ' (Pacini and Epstein, 1999: 972).

As with the unidimensional view of cognitive style advanced by Hayes and Allinson (1994) and Allinson and Hayes (1996), Epstein and his colleagues maintain that the extent to which rational–analytical and/or experiential–intuitive processing predominates is an interactive function of dispositional and situational factors. This implies not only a dynamic relationship between both cognitive systems but also a complex structure within each system (for details, see Sinclair et al., 2002). It is also consistent with Forgas's (1994, 1995) conclusion that an information processing strategy is determined by the cumulative effect of problem, decision and personal characteristics. In Forgas's Affect Infusion Model, however, each strategy has a different propensity to be 'infused' by affect, thus resulting in different levels of affect-laden processes or outcomes (Forgas, 1995). This line of reasoning has found support in recent cognitive neuroscience research that has identified separate neural pathways for certain affective and cognitive processes (for further details, see Damasio, 1994, 1999; Le Doux, 1996; Isen, 2000). Additional research has detected activation processes in several specific brain regions that imply a possible connection between affect and intuition that appears to be more complex than previously envisaged connections (Lieberman, 2000; Bechara, 2004).

As noted above, CEST is but one of a family of dual-process theories (for additional representative examples, see Bargh, 1989; Reber, 1989; Epstein, 1994; Evans and Over, 1996; Hammond, 1996; Sloman, 1996; Klein and Kihlstrom, 1998; Adolphs, 1999; Chaiken and Trope, 1999; Smith and DeCoster, 1999; Ochsner and Lieberman, 2001; Lieberman et al., 2004) the respective functions of which may be labelled generically as 'System 1' (including intuitive) and 'System 2' (including analytical) processes, in keeping with the broad System 1/System 2 architecture proposed by Stanovich and West (2000).

System 1 processes are implicit, tacit or automatic self-processes that operate without effort, intention or awareness and with rapid retrieval. Stanovich and West summarized System 1 processes as being associative (Sloman, 1996), heuristic (Evans, 1984, 1989), tacit (Evans and Over, 1996), implicit (Reber, 1989), experiential (Epstein, 1994), quick and inflexible (Pollock, 1991), intuitive (Hammond, 1996), recognition primed (Klein, 1998) and automatic (Shiffrin and Schneider, 1977). System 1 processes lead to judgements based on accumulated experience without the explicit retrieval and evaluation of autobiographical evidence. They are affective, slow to form, slow to change, relatively insensitive to one's thoughts about oneself and behaviour and relatively insensitive to explicit feedback from others. Affect is implicated in System 1 processes to varying degrees, ranging from the affect-free notion of pure heuristics (that is, cognitive 'short cuts' which may or may not be founded upon logically valid assumptions – see Gigerenzer and Todd, 1999; Kahneman and Tversky, 1982) to the notion of experiential processing (Epstein, 1994), in which emotions loom large. In other words, System 1 processes vary with respect to their degree of 'affective charge' (see also Dane and Pratt, 2007).

System 2 processes, in contrast, are effortful and intentional processes that rely on symbolic representations organized into propositions and explicit autobiographical evidence stored in episodic memory. These processes are performed in working memory (Baddeley and Hitch, 1974; Baddeley, 1986). Stanovich and West (2000) summarized System 2 processes as being rule based (Sloman, 1996), analytic (Evans, 1984, 1989), explicit (Evans and Over, 1996; Reber, 1989), rational (Epstein, 1994), intellective (Pollock, 1991), analytical (Hammond, 1996), rational-choice based (Klein, 1998) and controlled (Shiffrin and Schneider, 1977). Unlike System 1 processes, System 2 processes are affect free. System 2 processes are called on to respond flexibly when System 1 processes are ill-equipped to perform the task at hand.

Having offered dual-process formulations as a superordinate conceptual framework and CEST as a theoretical basis for the advancement of better understanding strategic foresight and organizational decision making, we now pause to consider in greater depth the nature of intuition. As shall be seen, this rather complex construct has begun making significant inroads into management theory and management practice.

Exploring intuition in management theory and management practice

In recent years, several management scholars have defined intuition in terms which are relevant and applicable both to management theory (Klein, 1998; Sinclair and Ashkanasy, 2005) and management practice (Klein, 2003; Sadler-Smith and Shefy, 2004). Particular interest in the concept of intuition has arisen in the field of strategic management (see, for example, Hodgkinson and Sparrow, 2002; Hodgkinson and Clarke, 2007). These developments have drawn upon the recent advances in social cognition, cognitive psychology and cognitive neuroscience outlined in the previous section. One possible reason for the interest of strategic management researchers in intuition is because strategic planning and strategic decision making encompass a high degree of uncertainty and ambiguity, both of which are factors that managers attempt to alleviate by employing intuitive judgements (Burke and Miller, 1999; Khatri and Ng, 2000; Klein, 2003). In addition, intuition is employed by strategic decision makers and other key stakeholders as a means to support or engage in creativity, visioning and foresight (see Isenberg, 1984; Mintzberg, 1989; Davis and Davis, 2003; Sadler-Smith and Shefy, 2004; Miller and Ireland, 2005).

The lack of conceptual clarity which dogged intuition research until comparatively recently resulted in a number of disparate definitions of intuition, and presented an additional challenge for the advancement of theory and research. Not only were scholars unable to agree on what intuition is (often conflating it with insight and creativity) but, more importantly, they were unable to agree on what it 'does' (Dane and Pratt, 2007). Nevertheless, a number of researchers (Shirley and Langan-Fox, 1996; Boucouvalas, 1997; Sadler-Smith and Shefy, 2004; Sinclair and Ashkanasy, 2005) have concluded that most conceptualizations of intuition fall into two broad but, we argue, mutually reinforcing categories: (i) intuition as an experience-based phenomenon, drawing on tacit knowledge accumulated through experience and quickly retrieved through pattern recognition (see Behling and Eckel, 1991; Brockman and Anthony, 1998; Crossan et al., 1999) – neatly encapsulated in Herbert Simon's notion of 'analyses frozen into habit' (Simon, 1987); and (ii) intuition as a phenomenon incorporating sensory (sometimes referred to as 'somatic' from the Greek *soma* meaning 'body') and affective elements (see Briggs and Myers, 1976; Agor, 1984; Damasio, 1994; Parikh et al., 1994; Epstein et al., 1996; Petitmengin-Peugeot, 1999). Several additional supplementary observations also emerge from the literature on intuition: first, intuiting occurs below the level of conscious awareness (Reber, 1989); second, intuition involves holistic information processing (Klein, 1998; Davis and Davis, 2003). Based on the above understanding, we view the process of intuition as: a rapid non-sequential information processing mode, which involves cognition *and* affect (including somatic elements), and occurs without deliberative rational thought, while frequently accompanied by a feeling of certitude (compare Simon, 1987; Epstein et al., 1996; Shapiro and Spence, 1997; Sinclair et al., 2002).

Intuitive processing has been linked in strategic management to the fast 'digestion' of complex, ambiguous sources of information that complements (but does not necessarily replace) rational processing (see Mintzberg, 1976; Louis and Sutton, 1991). It involves a non-conscious scanning of internal resources in long-term memory (Reber, 1989) and external cues in the environment (Klein, 1998) in order to identify relevant pieces of information that are fitted into the 'solution picture' (analogous to assembling a jig-saw puzzle). When the assembled pieces begin to cohere they 'start making sense, the "big picture" suddenly appears, frequently announced by a feeling of certitude or relief' (Sinclair and Ashkanasy, 2005: 357). This is not to confuse intuition with insight – although the two are related.

Although insight and intuition are closely interconnected, each is a distinct concept in its own right. At the moment when an insight solution takes place, the problem solver moves rapidly from a position of not knowing to a position of knowing; moreover, the problem solver is able to articulate the problem's solution (hence the process is no longer pre-verbal or below the level of conscious awareness). Insightful experiences may be preceded by 'feelings of knowing' or 'feelings of warmth' (intimations or intuitions that the problem is near to solution) (Reder and Ritter, 1992; Koriat, 1993). Intuition can occur in the process of insight as a precursor to the 'eureka' moment, as in the many anecdotal accounts of insight in the process of scientific discovery (see Gruber, 1995). Eminent creators of scientific and artistic works, for instance, frequently report following a 'tacit understanding' or 'preliminary perception of coherence' when doing their work, which guides them to an explicit representation of it in the form of a 'hunch' or hypothesis (Runco and Sakamoto, 1999: 68).

Wallas (1926), who was one of the first scholars to describe in a systematic way the process of insight via preparation and incubation, referred to the phenomenon of 'intimation' within the incubation process. Hogarth (2001: 255) argued that the term 'insight' is better 'reserved for those *moments* when people suddenly realize that they can see into the structure of problems', which often occur when people are not consciously engaged in seeking the problem solution (our emphasis).

Since intuition concerns judgement (as well as problem solution), not all intuitions manifest themselves as fully formed (insightful) solutions. As noted above, some intuitions remain as judgements which are affectively charged (Dane and Pratt, 2007) to varying degrees. Such intuitive judgement may eventually be empirically verified or refuted, and only at this point is it revealed whether or not the intuitive judgement was accurate. Intuitive judgements (as opposed to insightful solutions) involve rapid and non-conscious pattern recognition and syntheses of past experience and domain expertise where the processing speed is attributed to circumventing relatively slow-paced deliberation (see Bastick, 1982; Isenberg, 1984; Simon, 1987; Myers, 2002). Accurate intuitions rely upon a situational awareness that is grounded in the prior learning and experiences that formed the deep knowledge structures underpinning the intuitive judgement (see Hogarth, 2001). A definition of intuition that encompasses a number of these disparate elements has been offered by Dane and Pratt (2007, p. 40): 'intuitions are affectively charged judgements that arise through rapid and non-conscious holistic associations'.

As we have seen, a distinction may be drawn between the view of intuition offered by Simon (that is, analyses frozen into habit with the capacity for fast recognition and response), in which the issue of affect is overlooked or at least played down, and more recent conceptions (Sadler-Smith and Shefy, 2004; Sinclair and Ashkanasy, 2005; Dane and Pratt, 2007), in which the role played by affect in intuitive judgement is given a greater emphasis. This distinction notwithstanding, it is conceivable that both forms of intuition (affectively charged judgements and analyses frozen into habit) draw upon similar underlying unconscious pattern recognition processes, differentiated merely in terms of the strength of the 'affective tag' associated with the judgement (see also Finucane et al., 2000; Slovic et al., 2004). A continuum can be envisaged in which the non-conscious cognitive processes which support the interpretation of the relevant environmental cues, their matching with an extant pattern or the detection of a mismatch (when the decision maker recognizes that something is 'out of kilter' or simply 'doesn't feel right' – see Klein, 1998) are accompanied to a greater or lesser extent by affect (that is, an affective 'tag' in Finucane et al.'s terminology).

Our proposal for the differential strength of affect in intuitive judgements is in keeping with the argument for the importance of the affect heuristic more generally in human judgement put forward by Finucane, Slovic and their colleagues, who in turn built upon the work of Zajonc (1980). Zajonc not only researched the related area of implicit perception, but also was an early proponent of the importance of affect in decision making (Finucane et al., 2000). Slovic et al. (2004) suggested that we each have our own 'affect pool' which contains positive and negative markers which consciously or unconsciously 'tag' to varying degrees 'all of the images in people's minds' (p. 314). The affect pool is implicated via an involuntary 'sensing' process when people make a wide variety of judgements, including probability judgements (see Slovic, 2000). Following affect as a heuristic can sometimes be quicker and more efficient than laboriously weighing up the 'pros' and 'cons' of a situation (Slovic et al., 2004); it does, however, have potential drawbacks.

This discussion of information processing-based theories of intuition returns us full circle to the question of whether intuition and rational decision making are served by the same basic cognitive systems, notwithstanding the fact that the former process occurs at a much greater speed and without conscious awareness (see Taggart and Robey, 1981; Allinson and Hayes, 1996). On the basis of dual-process formulations outlined in the previous section, we maintain that this is not the case. Intuitions are inherently linked to experiential processing which uses a separate cognitive system that operates without conscious attention or awareness, but does so in concert with the rational system (see also Sinclair and Ashkanasy, 2005; Dane and Pratt, 2007; Hodgkinson et al., 2008). Slovic et al. (2004: 314) summarize the interaction of the two systems thus: 'We now recognise that the experiential mode of thinking and the analytic [that is, rational] mode of thinking are continually active, interacting in what we have characterized as the "dance of affect and reason"'. Strategic foresight and effective organizational decision making, we maintain, are both ultimately the product of analytic and experiential processes (see also Hodgkinson and Clarke, 2007).

Naturalistic decision making: dual-process formulations in action

The view of intuition as 'analyses frozen into habit' is commensurate with the stance taken by those researchers who have explored how experience-based judgements are made in field settings by domain experts, who appear to draw upon non-conscious cognitive processes to arrive at a single course of action (Klein, 1998). This is the perspective of naturalistic decision making (NDM) (Klein, 1997; Zsambok, 1997). Theories and models of NDM (defined as the ways in which people use their experience to make decisions in field settings) posit fast pattern recognition as the means by which experts reach decisions without conscious deliberation: 'in dynamic, uncertain and often fast paced environments' (Zsambok, 1997: 5).

The field of NDM originated in the 1980s in the USA and was the outcome of extensive case study research of decision makers operating in aviation, combat, and other highly pressured work situations including hospital accident and emergency departments and intensive-care units (see, for example, Klein, 1998, 2003). In emphasizing the crucial role of situation awareness in field settings (as opposed to the artificial laboratory settings employed in other areas of decision research) NDM researchers focused upon the ways in which decision makers deploy intuitive processing *in situ*. Experts' knowledge is 'pattern indexed' and it allows the decision maker to immediately retrieve the information needed to focus on solving a problem in a specific situation (Drillings and Serfaty, 1997). Klein and colleagues have analysed the ways in which actors rapidly draw upon the non-conscious elements of the human information processing system (that is, those elements depicted as less effortful within the dual-process formulations discussed in previous sections). NDM adds to our understanding of intuitive judgement in the context of dual-process formulations, but whether or not the switch from the rational to the experiential system or conversely from the experiential system to the rational system is consciously controlled or 'kicks in' automatically is unclear. From our own perspective, it seems most likely that cognitively skilled strategic decision makers learn to recognize when to deploy each of the two systems to best effect and are able to use the two systems in harmony (see also Louis and Sutton, 1991; Epstein et al., 1996; Hodgkinson and Sparrow, 2002; Hodgkinson and Clarke, 2007). Indeed, one of the characteristics that differentiate expert and novice decision makers is the extent to which they are able to recognize when to use intuition and when to fall back on conscious deliberation (Louis and Sutton, 1991). Moreover, experts are able to switch back and forth more readily than their less-expert counterparts and have the capability to engage in a different type of rational processing (Dreyfus and Dreyfus, 1986). Non-experts are more likely to engage in a calculative rationality by applying and improving their concepts, theories and knowledge of procedures. Experts on the other hand engage in a 'deliberative rationality' of detached, contemplative reflection (when time permits), which guards against 'grooved thinking' or 'tunnel vision' and provides an opportunity to challenge intuitions and literally 'recognize' (that is, re-think their assumptions and beliefs; Benner et al., 1996).

The recognition primed decision (RPD) model (one of a number of NDM models) was developed by Klein and his colleagues in order to explain how experienced fire ground commanders used their expertise to identify and carry out a course of action without the need to engage in lengthy, deliberative analyses (the sorts of time-pressured situations in which Klein and his colleagues have undertaken their work preclude such deliberations) (Klein, 1997). In its simplest form RPD consists of two functions, matching the situation to a prior experience to determine a singular course of action ('sizing up' the situation), and evaluating the consequences of the action through a mental simulation to see whether the course of action is likely to run into difficulties ('imagining' the course of action). If the mental simulation suggests potential problems, the decision maker moves on to another singular course of action.

Klein defines intuition as: 'recognizing things without knowing how we do the recognizing' (1998: 33); hence, within RPD the emphasis upon the role played by intuition is at the 'front end' of the process. The 'sizing up' of the situation occurs intuitively on the basis of recognizing prototypes or detecting any deviations from the decision maker's expectations.

The role of affect in intuition-based decision making
At first glance, Klein's RPD model implies a definition of intuition that seems to accord closely with the analysis frozen into habit view of Herbert Simon. However, it is clear from the case studies upon which Klein's RPD model is based that affect is also of vital importance, as for example when an experienced decision maker's situational awareness results in a particular combination of cues not 'feeling' right, but without him or her being able to say why. As noted by Klein (1998), decision makers involved in the sorts of life-or-death situations examined in his NDM research programme are often unable to reflect upon the reasoning mechanisms underpinning their judgements. Indeed, in a number of cases decision makers have misattributed their success to extra-sensory perception (ESP) rather than to their own underlying expertise (see Klein, 1998: 33). This suggests that a more complete account of NDM needs to embrace a wider conception of intuition, in recognition of the fact that decision makers appear to base their judgements not only on what they think about a given problem, but also on what they feel about it. Work on the affect heuristic alluded to above is potentially very helpful in this regard, as might be a more detailed consideration of the work of Damasio (1994, 1999) concerning the role of 'somatic markers' in decision making.

The relationship between intuitive judgement (as opposed to judgements in general) and affect appears to be more complex than is suggested by Finucane et al. (2000). At the onset of the decision-making process, affect may assist or impede access to intuitive processing; for example, negative mood states may predispose an individual to engage in rational analyses to a greater extent (Elsbach and Barr, 1999; Sinclair et al., 2002). Moreover, the experiences and the associated learning under which intuitions are acquired may be affectively encoded, thus making affect an integral element of the mental models and mental simulations (Kahneman and Tversky, 1982; Klein, 1998) upon which intuition draws (Forgas, 1995). This argument is consistent with the notion of affective 'tags' advanced by Slovic and his colleagues, as outlined earlier.

The understanding of the role of affect in intuitive judgements has benefited significantly from recent research in cognitive neuroscience and related fields which has explored the somatic aspects of decision making. For example Bechara et al. (1997) compared the performance on a high-risk gambling task of normal participants and patients with damage to the ventro-medial prefrontal cortex (VMPC) – a brain region implicated in the induction of emotions. Damage to the VMPC region can result in the impoverishment of 'decision-making apparatus to a dramatic degree' (Damasio, 1999: 280 and 302). In an experimental setting, Bechara et al. (1997) observed that normal participants (that is, without damage to the prefrontal cortex) began to choose advantageously before they were consciously aware which strategy worked best; moreover, they generated anticipatory skin conductance responses (SCRs) before they exercised a risky choice and before they became consciously aware of the strategy they were adopting. Patients with prefrontal cortex damage continued to choose disadvantageously, even after they realized the correct strategy; they also failed to demonstrate any anticipatory SCRs.

The amygdala and VMPC are involved in processing that is automatic, fast and involuntary. These structures are implicated not only in the processing of emotionally arousing tasks, but also in several higher-order cognitive activities, such as planning and decision making (Adolphs and Damasio, 2001). Taken as a whole, these findings indicate that the autonomic responses associated with intuitions based upon previous experiences and emotional states guide decision making and outcomes in advance of conscious awareness. Dual-process theorists have speculated that the intuitive system underpinning such processes may have evolved earlier in humans than did the rational system (Epstein, 1994). The pattern of somatic and visceral signals from the body acts as a warning, and the marker signals are adaptive in that they allow the decision maker to anticipate the 'pain' or 'pleasure' of particular outcomes (see also Le Doux, 1996; Shafir and LeBouef, 2002; Bechara, 2004).

In explaining the neuro-anatomical processes which underlie the somatic marker hypothesis, Bechara (2004) proposed a 'body loop' mechanism. According to this view, a somatic state is actually re-enacted and its signal relayed back to cortical and subcortical regions of the brain, impinging in turn upon the neural substrates underpinning conscious and non-conscious decision processes. Previously encountered situations and stored representations also play a key role. When an emotion has been expressed more than once, representations of it are formed in the somato-sensory and insular cortices. The body loop may be bypassed, and a fainter image of the emotional or somatic state created. Hence, bodily feedback is 'imagined' and represented cognitively in working memory and thus influences feelings and decisions. Bechara refers to this mechanism as the 'as-if' loop.

If, as argued by Slovic and his colleagues (Slovic et al., 2004), mental representations are affectively 'tagged', this is likely to be as true of the mental representations that underpin strategic decisions as of those underpinning other forms of decision. The question of which decisions engage the body loop and which engage the as-if loop is the subject of ongoing investigations (Bechara, 2004: 38). Bechara argues that in decision making under certainty, that is, where the outcome is predictable and explicit, it is the as-if loop that is activated, whereas in decision making under uncertainty, that is, where the outcome is unpredictable or unknown and thus cannot be estimated, the body loop proper is activated. Although the detailed programme of scientifically rigorous empirical work to validate this theory has yet to be undertaken, nevertheless, it seems reasonable at this juncture to speculate that the various loop mechanisms postulated by Bechara, the 'body loop' and the fainter 'as-if' loop, might account for variations in the degree of affect accompanying intuitive-based judgements in organizational strategic decision processes.

The development of a more comprehensive account of intuition, incorporating cognitive and affective elements, should hopefully result in a deeper and more complete understanding of strategic foresight and organizational decision making. In this connection, several management researchers have identified different forms of intuition which emphasize the experience/expertise or affective bases of intuition to different extents. For example, Crossan et al. (1999) distinguished between expert and entrepreneurial intuition. Expert intuition entails the use of a pattern recognition process to extrapolate from past situations, in a manner akin to Simon's (1987) notion of analysis frozen into habit or the RPD model of Klein and his colleagues (Zsambok, 1997; Klein, 1998). The nature of entrepreneurial intuition is less clear, but Gaglio (2004) proposes that the cognitive processes of mental simulation and counterfactual reasoning (both of which are key aspects of the simulation heuristic) are mechanisms by which entrepreneurs identify and develop innovative opportunities. These are unlikely to be cognitive processes *per se* and it seems reasonable to hypothesize that they consist of a fusion of cognitive and affective elements that yield decisions that 'feel' appropriate. Many entrepreneurs attest to the role that 'gut feel' plays in their business venturing activities (Hastie and Dawes, 2001) and the popular literature is replete with such accounts.

The multifaceted nature of intuition is apparent in the work of Sauter (1999), who distinguished between an 'operative intuition' that alerts individuals to potential problems and a 'creative (novel) intuition' that serves as a basis for the generation of new ideas or patterns. In this sense, each type of intuition seems to serve a different purpose: a quick recall of expert knowledge versus an innovative outcome in which intuition is an antecedent of the creative process and may draw upon different forms of knowledge that ordinarily lie beyond the realms of conscious awareness. Expert intuition is non-verbal to the extent that it draws upon tacit knowledge (Brockman and Anthony, 1998). It does not require deliberative thinking but the underlying reasoning can be verbalized and analysed if necessary, as borne out by studies using the applied cognitive task analysis (ACTA) methods that have underpinned much RPD research (Crandall et al., 2006). This is consistent with the experience-based view of intuition. Conversely, entrepreneurial intuition mostly precedes verbalization, and thus may play a vital role in foreseeing future without the impediment of 'non-conscious rationalization' (Westley and Mintzberg, 1989). The ways in which intuition, and in particular the role of mental simulation, operates in the business venturing context to foster creativity, innovation and entrepreneurship is an area which requires further research.

Implications for understanding strategic decision making

The ability to imagine a more desirable future and 'invent' ways of achieving it is a critical aspect of strategic decision making and foresight. The dual-process formulations outlined in the previous sections of this chapter not only offer a more viable portrayal of the cognitive processes at work in strategic decision making in field settings, but also contribute a number of practical insights to the attainment of this vital goal.

The term 'strategic planning' has been portrayed by Mintzberg (1994) as an oxymoron, on the grounds that it conflates the fundamentally distinctive cognitive processes of analysis and synthesis. According to Mintzberg, strategy cannot be planned because strategy is about synthesis (a blending of ideas and resources), whereas planning is about analysis (an examination of the parts). The analytic/synthetic distinction is one which was encountered previously in the context of a hypothesized duality in human information processing (see Taggart and Robey, 1981). As noted earlier, Mintzberg (1976) appealed to the prevailing brain science of the time in an attempt to explain this basic distinction (the 'right brain' was postulated to be synthetic and holistic – that is, intuitive in nature – while the 'left brain' was portrayed as analytical in nature). As argued above, recent developments in cognitive psychology, social psychology and cognitive neuroscience (as encapsulated in dual-process theory) point to two different systems that operate in parallel and which are not mutually exclusive (summarized within the overall System 1 and System 2 processing architecture, as outlined by Stanovich and West, 2000).

That dual-process conceptions potentially have much to offer by way of insight into the cognitive processes underpinning strategic decision making, and the attainment of strategic foresight, can be illustrated conveniently in respect of the widely acclaimed practice of scenario planning (for example, Wack, 1985; van der Heijden et al., 2002). The practice of scenario planning does not envisage a single 'right' answer; complex problems are likely to have many possible answers and the ultimate decision is likely to involve a combination of intuitive judgements and creativity as well as rational analysis (see Hodgkinson and Clarke, 2007). In the words of van der Heijden and colleagues:

> There is no suggestion here that analysis is not extremely important, but it cannot do the job entirely on its own. We need to independently define the important questions to analyse. For this reason analysis needs to be complemented by intuition . . . an iterative process in which exploiting intuition and asking the right questions alternates with rational thinking to find answers. (van der Heijden et al., 2002: 235–6)

More generally, Eisenhardt and Zbaracki (1992: 35) have called for: 'a more realistic view of strategic decision making by opening up our conceptions of cognition and conflict to include insight, intuition, emotion, and conflict resolution'. In practice, the balance between intuitive judgement and rational analysis in strategic decision making is determined by a variety of factors, including various characteristics of the decision maker (such as his or her level of domain expertise or personal disposition) and the context in which the decision is being taken (including the degree of 'structured-ness' of the decision problem or the momentary state of the decision maker) (Hodgkinson and Clarke, 2007; Sadler-Smith and Sparrow, 2008).

Shapiro and Spence (1997: 67) drew a distinction between 'well-' (tightly) structured problems (for example, accounts receivable, order entering and inventory control), and 'ill-' (loosely) structured problems (for example, mergers and acquisitions, new product planning and research and development planning). Dane and Pratt (2007) equate well-structured problems to Laughlin's (1980) notion of 'intellective tasks', characterized by objective criteria for success within the definitions, rules, operations and relationships of a particular conceptual system. They equate ill-structured problems to Laughlin's 'judgemental tasks', political, ethical, aesthetic, or behavioural judgements for which there is no objective criterion or demonstrable solution – to which might be added the capability to exercise moral or ethical judgements, both of which are crucial elements of any decision maker's portfolio.

As the problem structure associated with a task becomes tighter and more intellective, the effectiveness of rational decision making is likely to increase; conversely, intuitive judgements are likely to become more effective relative to rational analysis as a problem becomes increasingly unstructured (Khatri and Ng, 2000; Klein, 2003; Dane et al., 2005; Dane and Pratt, 2007; Sadler-Smith and Sparrow, 2008). The situations that favour analytical approaches are characterized by computational complexity, thus requiring optimization, and a need for justification; moreover, in such situations objective criteria for success exist (Laughlin, 1980; Klein, 2003). Conversely, the situations that favour intuitive approaches are characterized by loosely structured decision problems that are judgemental in nature and that cannot be solved by recourse to computational means *per se*. As noted above, such problems are typically characterized by ill-defined goals and require the decision maker to operate under time pressure in dynamic conditions. In these circumstances, experience plays a vital role (Klein, 2003). Time pressure and the need for a speedy decision are the most frequently mentioned triggers of intuitive decision making (Agor, 1986; Wally and Baum, 1994; Klein, 1998, 2003; Burke and Miller, 1999). Although not all intuitive outcomes are reached quickly (see Hogarth, 2001), the extant literature tends to equate intuition with speed of processing (Dane and Pratt, 2007) – indeed this is one aspect of the distinction between intuition and insight; the latter is preceded by a period of 'incubation' of some duration, which ranges from hours to weeks (see Mayer, 1996).

In many instances, when time is short, non-rational processing that circumvents time-consuming deliberation is the only feasible option for decision makers (Schoemaker and Russo, 1993). Research findings suggest, however, that time pressure and associated stress may influence the non-conscious selection of a variety of information processing strategies (Maule and Svenson, 1993; Maule et al., 2003). While time pressure appears to lead to intuitive decision making, it can also elicit stress, which, as a strong emotional response, may act as a block to further processing (Petitmengin-Peugeot, 1999) or precipitate a reversion to processing in the analytical mode (Elsbach and Barr, 1999; Sinclair and Ashkanasy, 2003). A preference for intuition seems to be further influenced by a number of dispositional characteristics, in particular cognitive style (Epstein et al., 1996; Hodgkinson and Clarke, 2007), risk tolerance and emotional awareness (Wally and Baum, 1994; Sinclair et al., 2002; Sadler-Smith and Sparrow, 2008). Risk tolerance assists decision makers in dealing with the ill-structuredness of strategic problems by helping them cope with the inherent ambiguity which lends itself to intuitive processing. This quality, however, relates to a coping ability rather than a propensity to seek out risk (Sitkin and Weingart, 1995).

Much of the earlier research on managerial intuition and decision making centred on executives, and was predicated on the assumption that this group of managers more than others are involved in decision making of a strategic nature (Barnard, 1938; Isenberg, 1984; Hayashi, 2001). More recent large-scale organizational studies conducted by Agor (1984, 1985, 1986, 1989), Parikh et al. (1994), Allinson and Hayes (1996) and Sadler-Smith et al. (2000) have established that senior managers (including senior executives) have a tendency to use intuition more frequently than do their lower-level counterparts. It does not necessarily follow, however, that this is because of a greater involvement in strategic decision making activities, as opposed to decision making more generally (see also Hodgkinson and Sadler-Smith, 2003a).[2]

While research by Parikh and his colleagues focused on canvassing how decision makers perceive intuition, and thus contributed to the development of a better understanding of the construct, Agor's Intuitive Management survey measured the actual predisposition and further development of intuitive ability (although some researchers attempting to replicate Agor's findings encountered difficulties with the reliability of this scale, see Sinclair and Ashkanasy, 2005). More recently, Khatri and Ng (2000) surveyed senior managers across a variety of industrial sectors in the USA. They found not only that intuitive processes are used often in decision making by senior managers, but also that the use of intuitive decision making was positively associated with organizational performance in unstable environments, whereas it was negatively correlated with organizational performance in stable environments. This supports the contingent view of intuitive judgement proposed by Shapiro and Spence (1997), Klein (2003) and Dane et al. (2005). In a replication and extension of Khatri and Ng's work in a UK small business context, Sadler-Smith (2004) observed that there was a positive relationship between intuitive decision style and contemporaneous financial and non-financial performance (however, unlike the Khatri and Ng study, this did not appear to be moderated by environmental instability). In addition, in keeping with the earlier findings of Allinson et al. (2000), Sadler-Smith (2004) observed a statistically significant relationship between intuitive decision style and subsequent financial performance. This finding was taken as prima facie evidence to support the claims of key stakeholders in high-growth enterprises that their success is attributable to the deployment of intuitive judgements. Meanwhile, Dane et al. (2005) have found that analytical decision making works better in highly structured tasks, although intuition is most effective compared to analysis when decision makers are domain experts who are facing tasks that are poorly (loosely) structured. Further work to disentangle the reasons for these inconsistent and somewhat contradictory findings is now urgently needed. Nevertheless, taken as a whole this body of work serves to underscore the fact that analytical and intuitive approaches are required to varying degrees across differing types of organizational decision and organizational decision context. Dual-process conceptions, as outlined earlier in this chapter, provide a potentially fruitful basis for understanding the ways in which decision makers are able to adapt (or not) to the contingencies confronting them.

Sadler-Smith and Sparrow (2008) argued that senior managers and entrepreneurs are often confronted by dynamism, in terms of both the environmental conditions in which the organization operates and the desired business outcomes (as, for example, in a new business venture or the performance of a new hire in a newly created job role). Against this backcloth, the ability to sense changes and detect faint signals, or move beyond statistical models in foresightful ways, can be advantageous. Intuition, since it derives from integrative pattern recognition and holistic judgements accompanied by affect to varying degrees, may be the only avenue open to managers to weigh, aggregate and make sense of intangibles involved in complex judgements.

Wagner (2002: 50) argued that management competence cannot be easily described because it is based more on intuition than on rationality. If asked to explain their actions, managers may *post hoc* rationalize in ways that fit their actions: 'managers are either at a loss for words or will make up an explanation that may be fictitious, perhaps not intentionally, but only in the spirit of trying to satisfy the questioner' (ibid.: 51). However, as argued by Hodgkinson and Sparrow (2002), the fact that the judgemental aspects of senior manager competence are inherently difficult to describe does not mean that they are any less valid than the rational and analytical competencies which are comparatively easy to document and measure.

Entrepreneurs and business executives claim the propensity to be able to recognize faint signals or patterns, but also have the confidence to assume that the missing elements of the pattern will take a shape that they can predict or foresee (Isenberg, 1984; Hayashi, 2001). This anticipatory capability may enable entrepreneurs and managers to keep ahead of potential competition and envisage beyond the present. Anecdotal accounts from managers testify to the faith that some senior executives place in intuitive judgement (Isenberg, 1984; Burke and Miller, 1999; Hayashi, 2001). In many instances, strategic application of intuition is indicated by such words as 'big picture', 'holistic approach' and 'foresight'. Individual differences in the way in which strategic decision makers gather, organize, process and act upon information determine their speed of information decision making and the extent to which they will engage in rational and/or intuitive processing (Hodgkinson and Clarke, 2007). Although recent findings confirm earlier conclusions that intuition is mostly used in conjunction with analysis, both modes can be combined in different ways: (i) some decision makers use analysis to find support for their initial 'gut feeling'; (ii) others conduct an analysis first and then check the results intuitively; (iii) in some instances, the rational and intuitive processes are iteratively applied as a set of formative or interim checks throughout a longer-term process (see Isenberg, 1984; Burke and Miller, 1999).

Intuitive decisions involve making predictions based upon knowledge and past experiences which are woven together and stored tacitly; the processes underpinning such decisions are not always open to introspection or available in conscious awareness. The strategic foresight exercised by chief executives may hinge on their intuitive expertise, as this quote from the multinational cosmetics company L'Oréal reveals:

> L'Oréal's success is due to Owen-Jones' [L'Oréal's Chief Executive Officer (CEO)] acute market intuition. He instinctively knew that the world was ready for L'Oréal to duplicate the enormous success it had in France on a global level, by developing worldwide brands and by choosing the right brands to attack the right markets. Rapidity is also a big part of getting to number one: 'Being fast is sometimes more decisive than verifying every idea and validating every hypothesis', says Owen-Jones. 'The fact that intuition has regained such importance in the world of business is deeply gratifying to me'.[3]

Hayashi (2001: 61) interviewed top business executives (CEOs) in the USA known for their shrewd 'business instincts' to explore how they took decisions that seemed not to involve rational analysis. An executive from Johnson and Johnson who was interviewed in connection with this study is quoted thus:

> 'When someone presents an acquisition proposal to me, the numbers always look terrific: the hurdle rates have been met; the return on investment is wonderful; the growth rate is just terrific. And I get all the reasons why this would be a good acquisition. But it's at that point – when I have a tremendous amount of quantitative information that's already been analyzed by very smart people – that I earn what I get paid. Because I will look at that information and I will know, intuitively, whether it's a good or bad deal.'

Intuition as theorized from a cognitive science and AI perspective by Simon (1947) is relatively affect free and operates to reduce cognitive load through what he referred to as 'analyses frozen into habit'. One way that this might be accomplished is through patterns of activity associated with previously experienced decisions accumulating and which are stored in the form of programmed actions (what in RPD terms would be referred to as 'action scripts') to be drawn upon by the experiential system in subsequent situations that more or less approximate previously encountered scenarios. As was noted earlier with respect to RPD, domain experts, by virtue of the relatively deep knowledge structures that they have developed as a function of their significant experience and learning, are capable of recognizing problems and the solution (usually a singular course of action rather than multiple options) without awareness of the underlying process or a verbalized reason for the decision (for further details, see Klein 1998).

Ultimately, however, cognitively *and* affectively based intuition are *both* required for effective strategic decision making. Affect-based intuition as conceptualized in the affect infusion model of Forgas (1994, 1995), akin to 'gut feel', is the vital spark that stimulates creativity and arguably underpins some aspects of strategic foresight. Less affectively charged and more cognitively based intuition, on the other hand, serves a different role: that of cutting through the detail to extract the bigger picture. In this sense, less affectively charged intuition frees up mental capacity, a vital prerequisite for creative problem solving, lest the decision maker should drown in the detail, the condition popularly referred to as 'paralysis by analysis' (Mintzberg, 1994; Langley, 1995).

Implications and conclusions

The study of intuition, and of the interplay of the systems that underpin reason and affect in strategic decision making, is in its infancy; many conceptual, theoretical and methodological challenges and opportunities present themselves to researchers. What is clear is that managers can and do use intuition in a variety of different ways including sensing a problem, producing an integrated picture, as a check on rational analysis and for bypassing analysis (Isenberg, 1984; Burke and Miller, 1999; Hayashi, 2001). As observed by Hodgkinson and Sparrow (2002), the ability to switch back and forth between the analytic and intuitive modes of cognition, that is, 'switching cognitive gears' (Louis and Sutton, 1991), endows decision makers with a vital competence for effective strategizing (see also Hodgkinson and Clarke, 2007). When this competence is highly developed, decision makers are able to use rational analysis and intuitive judgement in concert. What matters, therefore, is that organizational decision makers are taught to appreciate the nature and significance of the respective roles played by analysis and the two forms of intuition identified and discussed in the earlier sections of this chapter. Although at first glance the implications of this analysis are clear and seemingly straightforward, unfortunately, there are several gaps in the current knowledge base that render this prescription potentially problematic at this critical juncture.

First, psychometric instruments for the assessment of individual differences in a form that would fit this modified dual-process conception are found wanting on reliability and, to some extent, construct validity, grounds (see Hodgkinson and Sadler-Smith, 2003a,b; Hodgkinson et al., 2006a). Second, as observed by Hodgkinson and Clarke (2007), there is the question of how far decision makers are able to adapt their preferred styles of information processing to accommodate the shifting contingencies that come into play in complex strategic decision making of the sort discussed in this chapter. In other words, to what extent is the vital skill of switching cognitive gears attainable through training and development, or to what extent should organizations search for alternative strategies to ensure that decision-making teams are selected with the requisite mix of preferred processing styles for optimal decision making? What exactly is the optimum mix and how would we know? Does the optimum mix vary across different types of organizational decision and decision context or is it fairly constant? These are vital issues that need to be addressed in future work.

Another series of pressing issues concern the potential impact of attempting to blend this range of information processing styles, for previous work on individual differences suggests that task and interpersonal conflict arising from a mismatch of such cognitive styles is likely to be the order of the day (for example, Kirton and McCarthy, 1988). The question of how much latitude is possible in the blending of cognitive styles and the development of leadership strategies for managing the 'cognitive gaps' that might otherwise arise from this line of management practice are further issues equally deserving of urgent scholarly attention (for further discussion of this issue, see Hodgkinson and Clarke, 2007).

Intuition is more likely to be effective when the manager is an expert in the particular domain and rational analysis is not possible or it is inappropriate (Klein, 1998, 2003; Khatri and Ng, 2000; Sadler-Smith, 2000; Hodgkinson and Sparrow, 2002; Sadler-Smith and Sparrow, 2008). Hence, managers may come to rely upon intuition when rationality is at its limits, for example for reasons of underload or overload of information, or because of time pressure. Lengthy analysis is not always possible, and indeed to engage in a rigorous and systematic approach may open up a manager to 'analysis by paralysis' especially in those situations where there is time pressure, forcing him or her to act quickly. The problem with lengthy rational analysis is that a failure to respond in a timely fashion may mean that the problem (or opportunity) could change significantly, disappear altogether or be solved (or capitalized upon) by one's competitors. The way in which intuition is used is likely to depend upon situational factors (for example, the nature of the problem) and individual factors (for example, cognitive style and the level of the manager's expertise in the particular domain) (Hodgkinson and Sparrow, 2002; Hodgkinson and Sadler-Smith, 2003a; Dane and Pratt, 2007; Hodgkinson and Clarke, 2007; Sadler-Smith and Sparrow, 2008).

The question of whether or not managers' intuition can be improved is an open question – the more pressing concern is whether or not managers can be educated in order that they can understand intuition and thus be able to better manage their intuitions in an intelligent fashion. In this regard, management education and training and development programmes should be designed to enable managers to become more aware of the distinctions between insight and intuition and the respective contributions of affect and cognition in decision making, and to equip them with the necessary intra-personal skills to engage in a critically reflective manner upon their learning and decision-making behaviours. To this end, an executive training course in creative intuition has been offered at Stanford Business School since the 1980s, incorporating discussions with individuals who claim to use intuition in their decision making and reflective techniques such as mediation (see Ray and Myers, 1989).

In sum, while the study of intuition is, in many ways, still in its infancy, significant progress has been attained, both in clarifying its nature and in identifying its psychological foundations. Dual-process theories have greatly advanced our understanding of the complementary roles played by intuition and its counterpart, analysis, in strategic foresight and organizational decision making. Furthermore, a considerable volume of theory and research in the field of management and organization studies has begun to suggest a variety of approaches that might enable present and future generations of decision makers to foster greater awareness of these fundamental processes and how they might be harnessed more effectively. Much has been accomplished, but there is still much to be done in advancing scientific understanding and the practical development and skilful deployment of this vital strategic competence.

Notes

* The authors, whose names appear in reverse-alphabetical order, contributed equally to the preparation of this chapter. The financial support of the UK ESRC/EPSRC Advanced Institute of Management Research (AIM) (under grant number RES-331-25-0028, awarded to the third author) is gratefully acknowledged.
1. More recently, Allinson et al. (2000) appealed to Ornstein's research of the 1970s to argue that the analytical or intuitive information processing modes 'reflect what are often referred to as the rational and intuitive *sides* of a person' (p. 34, our emphasis).
2. A recent UK survey of strategy workshops has revealed that participation in these events is largely the preserve of the upper echelons. Moreover, intuition seems to play a dominant role, as evidenced by the fact that participants typically engage in minimal preparation beforehand (Hodgkinson et al., 2005, 2006b).
3. Accessed from L'Oréal's website (http://www.en.loreal.ca/_en/_ca/news/), 14 September 2006.

References

Adolphs, R. (1999), 'Social cognition and the human brain', *Trends in the Cognitive Sciences*, **3**: 469–79.
Adolphs, R. and Damasio, A. (2001), 'The interaction of affect and cognition: a neurobiological perspective', in J. Forgas (ed.), *Handbook of Affect and Social Cognition*, Hillsdale, NJ: Erlbaum, pp. 27–49.
Agor, W.H. (1984), *Intuitive Management: Integrating Left and Right Brain Management Skills*, New York: Prentice-Hall.
Agor, W.H. (1985), 'Managing brain skills to increase productivity', *Public Administration Review*, **45**: 864–8.
Agor, W.H. (1986), *The Logic of Intuitive Decision-making: A Research-based Approach for Top Management*, New York: Quorum Books.
Agor, W.H. (ed.) (1989), *Intuition in Organizations: Leading and Managing Productively*, Newbury Park, CA: Sage.
Allinson, C.W., Chell, E. and Hayes, J. (2000), 'Intuition and entrepreneurial performance', *European Journal of Work and Organizational Psychology*, **9**(1): 31–43.
Allinson, C.W. and Hayes, J. (1996), 'The Cognitive Style Index: a measure of intuition-analysis for organizational research', *Journal of Management Studies*, **33**: 119–35.
Arkes H.R. and Hammond, K.R. (eds) (1986), *Judgement and Decision Making: An Interdisciplinary Reader*, Cambridge: Cambridge University Press.
Baddeley, A.D. (1986), *Working Memory*, Oxford: Oxford University Press.
Baddeley, A.D. and Hitch, G.J. (1974), 'Working memory', in G. Bower (ed.), *Recent Advances in Learning and Motivation*, Vol. 8, New York: Academic Press, pp. 47–89.
Bargh, J.A. (1989), 'Conditional automaticity: varieties of automatic influence in social perception and cognition', in J.S. Uleman and J.A. Bargh (eds), *Unintended Thought*, New York: Guilford Press, pp. 3–51.
Barnard, C.I. (1938), *The Functions of the Executive*, Cambridge, MA: Harvard University Press.
Bastick, T. (1982), *Intuition: How We Think and Act*, New York: John Wiley.
Bechara, A. (2004), 'The role of emotion in decision making: evidence from neurological patients with orbitofrontal damage', *Brain and Cognition*, **55**: 30–40.
Bechara, A., Damasio, H., Tranel, D. and Damasio, A.R. (1997), 'Deciding advantageously before knowing the advantageous strategy', *Science*, **275**: 1293–4.
Behling, O. and Eckel, N.L. (1991), 'Making sense out of intuition', *Academy of Management Executive*, **5**: 46–54.
Benner, P., Tanner, C.A. and Chesla, C.A. (1996), *Expertise in Nursing Practice: Caring, Clinical Judgement and Ethics*, New York: Springer.
Boucouvalas, M. (1997), 'Intuition: the concept and the experience', in R. Davis-Floyd and P.S. Arvidson (eds), *Intuition: The Inside Story*, New York: Routledge, pp. 3–18.

Briggs, K.C. and Myers, I.B. (1976), *Myers–Briggs Type Indicator*, Palo Alto, CA: Consulting Psychologists Press.

Brockman, E.N. and Anthony, W.P. (1998), 'The influence of tacit knowledge and collective mind on strategic planning', *Journal of Managerial Issues*, **10**: 204–19.

Burke, L.A. and Miller, M.K. (1999), 'Taking the mystery out of intuitive decision-making', *Academy of Management Executive*, **13**(4): 91–9.

Chaiken, S. and Trope, Y. (eds) (1999), *Dual-process Theories in Social Psychology*, New York: Guilford Press, pp. 462–82.

Crandall, B., Klein, G. and Hoffman, R.R. (2006), *Working Minds: A Practitioner's Guide to Cognitive Task Analysis*, Cambridge, MA: Bradford Books/MIT Press.

Crossan, M.M., Lane, H.W. and White, R.E. (1999), 'An organizational learning framework: from intuition to institution', *Academy Management Review*, **24**: 522–37.

Damasio, A.R. (1994), *Descartes' Error: Emotion, Reason and the Human Brain*, New York: HarperCollins.

Damasio, A.R. (1999), *The Feeling of What Happens: Body, Emotion and the Making of Consciousness*, London: Vintage.

Dane, E. and Pratt, M.G. (2007), 'Exploring intuition and its role in managerial decision making', *Academy of Management Review*, **32**(1): 33–54.

Dane, E., Rockman, K.W. and Pratt, M.G. (2005), 'Should I trust my gut? The role of task characteristics in intuitive and analytical decision-making', *Academy of Management Annual Meeting, Best Paper Proceedings*, Hawaii, August.

Davis, S.H. and Davis, P.B. (2003), *The Intuitive Dimensions of Administrative Decision-Making*, Lanham, MD: Scarecrow.

Denes-Raj, V. and Epstein, S. (1994), 'Conflict between intuitive and rational processing: when people behave against their better judgment', *Journal of Personality and Social Psychology*, **66**: 819–29.

Dreyfus, H.L. and Dreyfus, S.E. (1986), *Mind over Machine: The Power of Human Intuitive Expertise in the Era of the Computer*, New York: Free Press.

Drillings, M. and Serfaty, D. (1997), 'Naturalistic decision making in command and control', in C.E. Zsambok and G. Klein (eds), *Naturalistic Decision Making*, Mawah, NJ: LEA, pp. 71–80.

Eisenhardt, K.M. (1989), 'Making fast strategic decisions in high-velocity environments', *Academy of Management Journal*, **32**: 543–76.

Eisenhardt, K.M. and Zbaracki, M.J. (1992), 'Strategic decision making', *Strategic Management Journal*, **13**: 17–37.

Elsbach, K.D. and Barr, P.S. (1999), 'The effects of mood on individuals' use of structured decision protocols', *Organization Science*, **10**: 181–98.

Epstein, S. (1991), 'Cognitive–experiential self theory: an integrative theory of personality', in R.C. Curtis (ed.), *The Relational Self: Theoretical Convergences in Psychoanalysis and Social Psychology*, New York: Guilford Press, pp. 111–37.

Epstein, S. (1994), 'Integration of the cognitive and the psychodynamic unconscious', *American Psychologist*, **49**: 709–24.

Epstein, S. (1998), 'Emotions and psychology from the perspective of cognitive–experiential self-theory', in W.F. Flack and J.D. Laird (eds), *Emotions in Psychopathology: Theory and Research, Series in Affective Science*, New York: Oxford University Press, pp. 57–69.

Epstein, S. (2000), 'The rationality debate from the perspective of cognitive–experiential self theory', *Behavioral and Brain Sciences*, **23**: 671.

Epstein, S., Pacini, R., Denes-Raj, V. and Heier, H. (1996), 'Individual differences in intuitive–experiential and analytical–rational thinking styles', *Journal of Personality and Social Psychology*, **71**: 390–405.

Ericsson, K.A. and Charness, N. (1994), 'Expert performance: its structure and acquisition', *American Psychologist*, **49**: 725–47.

Evans, J.St.B.T. (1984), 'Heuristic and analytic processing in reasoning', *British Journal of Psychology*, **75**: 451–68.

Evans, J.St.B.T. (1989), *Bias in Human Reasoning*, Hillsdale, NJ: Erlbaum.

Evans, J.St.B.T. and Over, D.E. (1996), *Rationality and Reasoning*, Hove: Psychology Press.

Finucane, M.L., Alhakami, A., Slovic, P. and Johnson, S.M. (2000), 'The affect heuristic in the judgement of risks and benefits', *Journal of Behavioral Decision Making*, **13**: 1–17.

Forgas, J.P. (1994), 'The role of emotion in social judgements: an introductory review and an affect infusion model (AIM)', *European Journal of Social Psychology*, **24**: 1–24.

Forgas, J.P. (1995), 'Mood and judgement: the affect infusion model (AIM)', *Psychological Bulletin*, **117**: 39–66.

Gaglio, C.M. (2004), 'The role of mental simulations and counter-factual thinking in the opportunity identification process', *Entrepreneurship Theory and Practice*, Winter: 533–52.

Gazzaniga, M.S. (1971), *The Bisected Brain*, New York: Appleton-Century-Crofts.

Gigerenzer, G. and Todd, P.M. (1999), 'Fast and frugal heuristics: the adaptive toolbox', in G. Gigerenzer,

P.M. Todd and the ABC Research Group (eds), *Simple Heuristics That Make Us Smart*, New York: Oxford University Press, pp. 3–34.

Gilovich, T., Griffith, D. and Kahneman, D. (eds) (2002), *Heuristics and Biases: The Psychology of Intuitive Judgment*, Cambridge: Cambridge University Press.

Griffith, T.L., Northcraft, G.B. and Fuller, M.A. (2008), 'Borgs in the Org? Organizational decision making and technology', in G.P. Hodgkinson and W.H. Starbuck (eds), *The Oxford Handbook of Organizational Decision Making*, Oxford: Oxford University Press, pp. 97–115.

Gruber, H.E. (1995), 'Insight and affect. I: the history of science', in R.J. Sternberg and J.E. Davidson (eds), *The Nature of Insight*, Cambridge, MA: MIT Press, pp.397–432.

Hammond, K.R. (1996), *Human Judgement and Social Policy*, Oxford: Oxford University Press.

Hammond, K.R., Hamm, R.M., Grassia, J. and Pearson, T. (1987), 'Direct comparison of the efficacy of intuitive and analytical cognition in expert judgment', *IEEE Transactions on Systems, Man, and Cybernetics*, **17**: 753–70.

Hastie, R. and Dawes, R.M. (2001), *Rational Choice in an Uncertain World: The Psychology of Judgement and Decision Making*, Thousand Oaks, CA: Sage.

Hayashi, A.M. (2001), 'When to trust your gut', *Harvard Business Review*, February: 59–65.

Hayes, J. and Allinson, C.W. (1994), 'The implications of learning styles for training and development: a discussion of the matching hypothesis', *British Journal of Management*, **7**, 63–74.

Herrmann N. (1996), *The Whole Brain Business Book*, New York: McGraw-Hill.

Hodgkinson, G.P. and Clarke, I. (2007), 'Exploring the cognitive significance of organizational strategizing: a dual-process framework and research agenda', *Human Relations*, **60**: 243–55.

Hodgkinson, G.P. and Sadler-Smith, E. (2003a), 'Complex or unitary? A critique and empirical re-assessment of the Allinson–Hayes Cognitive Style Index', *Journal of Occupational and Organizational Psychology*, **76**: 243–68.

Hodgkinson, G.P. and Sadler-Smith, E. (2003b), 'Reflections on reflections ... on the nature of intuition, analysis and the construct validity of the Cognitive Style Index', *Journal of Occupational and Organizational Psychology*, **76**: 279–81.

Hodgkinson, G.P. and Sparrow, P.R. (2002), *The Competent Organization: A Psychological Analysis of the Strategic Management Process*, Buckingham, UK: Open University Press.

Hodgkinson, G.P., Johnson, G., Whittington, R. and Schwarz, M. (2005), *The Role and Importance of Strategy Workshops: Findings of a UK Survey*, London: ESRC/EPSRC (UK), Advanced Institute of Management Research (AIM) and the Chartered Management Institute (CMI).

Hodgkinson, G.P., Langan-Fox, J. and Sadler-Smith, E. (2008), 'Intuition: a fundamental bridging construct in the behavioural sciences', *British Journal of Psychology*, **99**, 1–27.

Hodgkinson, G.P., Sadler-Smith, E. and Sinclair, M. (2006a), 'More than meets the eye? Intuition and analysis revisited', paper presented at the Academy of Management Meeting, Atlanta, GA, 11–16 August.

Hodgkinson, G.P., Whittington, R., Johnson, G. and Schwarz, M. (2006b), 'The role of strategy workshops in strategy development processes: formality, communication, coordination and inclusion', *Long Range Planning*, **39**: 479–96.

Hogarth, R.M. (2001), *Educating Intuition*, Chicago, IL: University of Chicago Press.

Isen, A.M. (2000), 'Positive affect decision-making', in M. Lewis and J.M. Haviland-Jones (eds), *Handbook of Emotions*, New York: Guilford Press, pp. 417–35.

Isenberg, D.J. (1984), 'How senior managers think', *Harvard Business Review*, November/December: 81–90.

Janis, I.L. and Mann, L. (1977), *Decision Making*, New York: Free Press.

Kahneman, D. and Tversky, A. (1982), 'The simulation heuristic', in D. Kahneman, P. Slovic and A. Tversky (eds), *Judgement Under Uncertainty: Heuristics and Biases*, Cambridge: Cambridge University Press, pp. 201–8.

Khatri, N. and Ng, H.A. (2000), 'The role of intuition in strategic decision making', *Human Relations*, **1**: 57–86.

Kirton, M.J. and McCarthy, R.M. (1988), 'Cognitive climate and organizations', *Journal of Occupational Psychology*, **61**: 175–84.

Klein, G. (1997), 'The recognition primed decision (RPD) model: looking back, looking forward', in C.E. Zsambok and G. Klein (eds), *Naturalistic Decision Making*, Mahwah, NJ: Lawrence Erlbaum Associates, pp. 383–97.

Klein, G. (1998), *Sources of Power: How People Make Decisions*, Cambridge, MA: MIT Press.

Klein, G. (2003), *Intuition at Work*, New York: Currency Doubleday.

Klein, S.B. and Kihlstrom, J.F. (1998), 'On bridging the gap between social personality psychology and neuropsychology', *Personality and Social Psychology Review*, **2**: 228–42.

Koriat, A. (1993), 'How do we know that we know? The accessibility model of the feeling of knowing', *Psychological Review*, **100**: 609–39.

Langley, A. (1995), 'Between "paralysis by analysis" and "extinction by instinct"', *Sloan Management Review*, **36**: 63–76.

Laughlin, P. (1980), 'Social combination processes of cooperative problem-solving groups on verbal intellective tasks', in M. Fishbein (ed.), *Progress in Social Psychology*, Vol. 1, Hillsdale, NJ: Lawrence Erlbaum Associates, pp. 127–55.

Le Doux, J.E. (1996), *The Emotional Brain*, New York: Simon & Schuster.

Lieberman, M.D. (2000), 'Intuition: a social cognitive neuroscience approach', *Psychological Bulletin*, **126**(1): 109–37.

Lieberman, M.D., Jarcho, J.M. and Satpute, A.B. (2004), 'Evidence-based and intuition-based self-knowledge: an fMRI study', *Journal of Personality and Social Psychology*, **87**: 421–35.

Louis, M.R. and Sutton, R.I. (1991), 'Switching cognitive gears: from habits of mind to active thinking', *Human Relations*, **44**: 55–76.

March, J. and Simon, H.A. (1958), *Organizations*, New York: Wiley.

Maule, A.J., Hodgkinson, G.P. and Bown, N.J. (2003), 'Cognitive mapping of causal reasoning in strategic decision making', in D. Hardman and L. Macchi (eds), *Thinking: Psychological Perspectives on Reasoning, Judgment and Decision Making*, Chichester: Wiley, pp. 253–72.

Maule, A.J. and Svenson, O. (1993), 'Theoretical and empirical approaches to behavioral decision making and their relation to time constraints', in Svenson and Maule (eds), *Time Pressure and Stress in Human Judgment and Decision Making*, New York: Plenum Press, pp. 3–25.

Mayer, R.E. (1996), 'The search for insight', in R.J. Sternberg and J.E. Davidson (eds), *The Nature of Insight*, Cambridge, MA: MIT Press, pp. 3–32.

Miller, C.C. and Ireland, D.R. (2005), 'Intuition in strategic decision making: friend or foe in the fast-paced 21st century', *Academy of Management Executive*, **19**(1): 19–30.

Miller, S.J., Hickson, D.J. and Wilson, D.C. (1996), 'Decision-making in organizations', in S.R. Clegg, C. Hardy and W.R. Nord (eds), *Handbook of Organizations Studies*, London: Sage, pp. 293–312.

Mintzberg, H. (1976), 'Planning on the left; managing on the right', *Harvard Business Review*, **54**(4): 49–58.

Mintzberg, H. (1989), *Mintzberg on Management: Inside Our Strange World of Organizations*, New York: Free Press.

Mintzberg, H. (1994), *The Rise and Fall of Strategic Planning*, London: Prentice-Hall.

Mintzberg, H., Ahlstrand, B. and Lampel, J. (1998), *Strategy Safari: A Guide through the Wilds of Strategic Management*, London: Prentice-Hall.

Mintzberg, H. and Westley, F. (2001), 'Decision making: it's not what you think', *MIT Sloan Management Review*, Spring: 89–93.

Mumby, D.K. and Putnam, L.A. (1992), 'The politics of emotion: a feminist reading of bounded rationality', *Academy of Management Review*, **17**: 465–86.

Myers, D.G. (2002), *Intuition: Its Powers and Perils*, New Haven, CT: Yale University Press.

Ochsner, K.N. and Lieberman, M.D. (2001), 'The emergence of social cognitive neuroscience', *American Psychologist*, **56**: 717–34.

Ornstein, R. (1977), *The Psychology of Consciousness*, New York: Harcourt Brace Jovanovich.

Pacini, R. and Epstein, S. (1999), 'The relation of rational and experiential information processing styles to personality, basic beliefs, and the ratio-bias phenomenon', *Journal of Personality and Social Psychology*, **76**: 972–87.

Parikh, J., Neubauer, F. and Lank, A.G. (1994), *Intuition: The New Frontier in Management*, Cambridge, MA: Blackwell.

Petitmengin-Peugeot, C. (1999), 'The intuitive experience', *Journal of Consciousness Studies*, **6**: 43–77.

Pollock, J.L. (1991), 'OSCAR: a general theory of rationality', in J. Cummins and J.L. Pollock (eds), *Philosophy and AI: Essays at the Interface*, Cambridge, MA: MIT Press, pp. 189–214.

Raidl, M.-H. and Lubart, T.I. (2001), 'An empirical study of intuition and creativity. Imagination', *Cognition and Personality*, **20**: 217–30.

Ray, M. and Myers, R. (1989), *Creativity in Business*, New York: Doubleday.

Reber, A.S. (1989), 'Implicit learning and tacit knowledge', *Journal of Experimental Psychology: General*, **3**: 219–35.

Reder, L.M. and Ritter, F.E. (1992), 'What determines initial feeling of knowing? Familiarity with question terms, not with the answer', *Journal of Experimental Psychology: Learning, Memory, and Cognition*, **18**: 435–51.

Runco, M.A. and Sakamoto, O. (1999), 'Experimental studies of creativity', in R.J. Sternberg (ed.), *Handbook of Creativity*, Cambridge: Cambridge University Press, pp. 62–92.

Sadler-Smith, E. (2004), 'Cognitive style and the performance of small and medium sized enterprises', *Organization Studies*, **25**: 155–82.

Sadler-Smith, E. and Shefy, E. (2004), 'The intuitive executive: understanding and applying "gut feel" in decision-making', *The Academy of Management Executive*, **18**(4): 76–92.

Sadler-Smith, E. and Sparrow, P.R. (2008), 'Intuition in organizational decision making', in G.P. Hodgkinson

and W.H. Starbuck (eds), *The Oxford Handbook of Organizational Decision Making*, Oxford: Oxford University Press, pp. 305–24.
Sadler-Smith, E., Spicer, D. and Tsang, F. (2000), 'The Cognitive Style Index: a replication and extension', *British Journal of Management*, **11**: 175–81.
Sauter, V.L. (1999), 'Intuitive decision-making', *Communications of the ACM*, **42**(6): 109–15.
Schoemaker, P.J.H. and Russo, E.J. (1993), 'A pyramid of decision approaches', *California Management Review*, **36**: 9–31.
Shafir, E. and LeBouef, A. (2002), 'Rationality', *Annual Review of Psychology*, **53**: 491–517.
Shapiro, S. and Spence, M. (1997), 'Managerial intuition: a conceptual and operational framework', *Business Horizons*, **40**: 63–9.
Shiffrin, R.M. and Schneider, W. (1977), 'Controlled and automatic human information processing: II. Perceptual learning, automatic attending, and a general theory', *Psychological Review*, **84**: 127–90.
Shirley, D.A. and Langan-Fox, J. (1996), 'Review of intuition', *Psychological Reports*, **79**: 563–84.
Simon, H.A. (1947), *Administrative Behavior*, New York: Free Press.
Simon, H.A. (1957), *Models of Man: Social and Rational*, New York: Wiley.
Simon, H.A. (1987), 'Making management decisions: the role of intuition and emotion', *Academy of Management Executive*, February: 57–64.
Simon, H.A. (1989), 'Theories of bounded rationality', in Simon (ed.), *Models of Bounded Rationality: Behavioral Economics and Business Organization*, Vol. 2, Cambridge, MA: MIT Press, pp. 408–23.
Simon, H.A. (1997), *Administrative Behavior*, 4th edn, New York: Free Press.
Sinclair, M. and Ashkanasy, N.M. (2005), 'Intuition: myth or a decision-making tool?', *Management Learning*, **36**(3): 353–70.
Sinclair, M., Ashkanasy, N.M., Chattopadhyay, P. and Boyle, M.V. (2002), 'Determinants of intuitive decision-making in management: the moderating role of affect', in N.M. Ashkanasy, W.J. Zerbe and C.E.J. Härtel (eds), *Managing Emotions in the Workplace*, Armonk, NY: M.E. Sharpe, pp. 143–63.
Sitkin, S.B. and Weingart, L.R. (1995), 'Determinants of risky decision-making behavior: a test of the mediating role of risk perceptions and propensity', *Academy of Management Journal*, **38**: 1573–92.
Sloman, S.A. (1996), 'The empirical case for two systems of reasoning', *Psychological Bulletin*, **199**: 3–22.
Slovic, P. (2000), *The Perception of Risk*, Sterling, VA: Earthscan.
Slovic, P. (2002), 'Rational actors or rational fools: implications of the affect heuristic for behavioral economics', paper presented as part of the lecture series commemorating the 10th anniversary of the Centre for the Study of Rationality, Hebrew University, Jerusalem, Israel, June.
Slovic, P., Finucane, M.L., Peters, E. and MacGregor, D.G. (2004), 'Risk as analysis and risk as feelings: some thoughts about affect, reason, risk and rationality', *Risk Analysis*, **24**: 311–22.
Smith, E.R. and DeCoster, J. (1999), 'Associative and rule based processing', in S. Chaiken and Y. Trope (eds), *Dual-Process Theories in Social Psychology*, New York: Guilford Press, pp. 323–36.
Sperry, R.W. (1968), 'Hemisphere disconnection and unity in conscious awareness', *American Psychologist*, **23**: 723–33.
Stanovich, K.E. and West, R.F. (2000), 'Individual differences in reasoning: implications for the rationality debate?', *Behavioral and Brain Sciences*, **23**: 645–65.
Taggart, W. and Robey, D. (1981), 'Minds and managers: on the dual nature of human information processing and management', *Academy of Management Review*, **6**: 187–95.
van der Heijden, K., Bradfield, R., Burt, G., Cairns G. and Wright, G. (2002), *The Sixth Sense: Accelerating Organisational Learning with Scenarios*, Chichester: John Wiley.
Wack, P. (1985), 'Scenarios: uncharted waters ahead', *Harvard Business Review*, **63**(5): 73–89.
Wagner, R.K. (2002), 'Smart people doing dumb things: the case of managerial incompetence', in R.J. Sternberg (ed.), *Why Smart People Can Be So Stupid*, New Haven, CT: Yale University Press, pp. 42–85.
Wallas, G. (1926), *The Art of Thought*, New York: Franklin Watts.
Wally, S. and Baum, R.J. (1994), 'Personal and structural determinants of the pace of strategic decision making', *Academy of Management Journal*, **37**: 932–56.
Westley, F. and Mintzberg, H. (1989), 'Visionary leadership and strategic management', *Strategic Management Journal*, **10**: 17–32.
Zajonc, R.B. (1980), 'Feeling and thinking: preferences need no inferences', *American Psychologist*, **35**: 151–75.
Zsambok, C.E. (1997), 'Naturalistic decision making: where are we now?', in C.E. Zsambok and G. Klein (eds), *Naturalistic Decision Making*, Mahwah, NJ: Lawrence Erlbaum Associates, pp. 3–16.

24 (Un) great expectations: effects of underestimations and self-perception on performance
Rodolphe Durand

Introduction

While foresight permeates everyday strategic activity, it remains quite ignored by strategy research. More than 10 years ago, Starbuck and Mezias pleaded diligently for further research on the relationships between firms' estimation accuracy and performance:

> To find out whether [perceptions are accurate or not], researchers need to investigate the larger or smaller errors and different biases. Nevertheless, surprisingly little research focuses on the accuracies of perceptions. Studies comparing subjective with objective data may be rare because it is so difficult to design good questionnaires, to obtain good 'objective' data and to obtain enough suitable respondents. (1996: 115).

Since then, some studies have assessed the reasons and strategic consequences of an absence of foresight, through the study of the relationships between overconfidence (optimistic errors) and strategic actions (Hayward and Hambrick, 1997; Coff, 1999; Simon and Houghton, 2003). However, scholars know little about how underestimations relate to performance. Underestimations are pessimistic estimates of an actual event, like, for instance, a negative forecast on success odds or a below-average estimated development of a favorable environmental trend. Therefore, this chapter aims at refining our understanding of the impact of underestimations as another manifestation of a lack of organizational foresight.

Just as overestimations are associated with overconfidence, underestimations can be associated with underconfidence. Underconfidence results from an excessive value attribution to negative diagnostic cues. A simple assumption is that the higher the level of underconfidence, the lower the resulting performance. However, underestimations may also be associated with other factors, such as prudence. Conscious and voluntary pessimism may lead to a welcome surprise: in a sense, understating favorable future trends through prudent judgment might represent a better chance of meeting objectives. Thus, the resulting relationship between underestimations and performance might not be linear and needs further exploration.

Moreover, inaccurate estimates of environmental evolutions must be distinguished from biases in self-perception. In one of the rare research articles devoted to underconfidence, Kirchler and Maciejovsky (2002: 80) stress the disjunction between the raters' increased objective accuracy in repeated estimations and the absence of an equivalent change in the raters' subjective certainty about their estimates. This subjective certainty about one's capacities characterizes self-perception. Biases in self-perception are the most common sources of strategic mistakes, flawed foresight, and impaired performance (Schwenk, 1986; Hayward and Hambrick, 1997; Das and Teng, 1999). Notably, exaggerated self-perception characterizes illusion of control and leads to risky behavior (Sitkin and Pablo, 1992; Hayward and Hambrick, 1997; Coff, 1999). Organizational self-perception is the perception of organizational strengths relative to rivals. Previous studies have shown how organizational settings influence risk assessments (McNamara and Bromiley, 1997; Sutcliffe and Huber, 1998) and how a high organizational self-perception increases forecast errors (Durand, 2003). It is likely that an inflated self-perception moderates positively the impact of underestimations on performance. By contrast, a depressed organizational self-perception would reinforce the negative relationship between underestimations and performance.

Therefore, this chapter is a response to – among others – Starbuck and Mezias's concerns about the often ignored perspective of underestimations. In particular, the chapter examines the effect of underestimations on firm performance. It includes not only a direct approach of this effect but also tests its interaction with the levels of organizational self-perception. We use a representative sample of 343 manufacturing firms to explore these relationships. Our findings confirm the presence of a curvilinear relationship between underestimations and performance, revealing the distinct impacts of underconfidence and prudence. The results show the moderating impact of self-perception, and especially the worsening combination of underconfidence and depressed self-perception on performance. Implications concern the definition of forecasting ability and the importance of considering both organizational capabilities and organizational dispositions.

The structure of the chapter is classical. We first present our hypotheses, then the methods, and results. In the final section, we discuss our findings.

Hypotheses

Underestimations and performance
In this chapter, we focus on the underestimation of the probability or the level reached by a supposedly beneficial environmental change. For instance, the underestimation of future industry growth can characterize underconfidence for manufacturing companies, while an excessively upbeat forecast would characterize overconfidence. Estimating accurately short-term industry evolutions is an important capability for manufacturing companies. Underestimations lead to mis-estimations of market potentials in terms of undercapacity leading to below-industry-average sales and returns. Also, the strategic value of resources depends on the flows of investments (Dierickx and Cool, 1989) and underestimation of market potential may reduce such flows, thereby potentially damaging the future competitiveness of the firm.

Minimal forecasting errors help strategic management authors to make sound decisions in terms of production and resource investments. Accurate forecasts enable the organizations to (i) adjust the size of their operations, (ii) invest adequately in resources, and (iii) identify undervalued assets and appropriate their rent potential (Barney, 1986). Therefore, the expected performance should decline with the magnitude of underestimations.

Although based on different groundings, organizational behavior literature converges with that assessment. For instance, goal-setting theory suggests that it is better for performance to slightly overestimate variations (Locke and Latham, 1990; Mosakowski, 1998). Organizational behavior is affected by the available information, and challenging and specific objectives tempt individuals to attain higher levels of performance on average (Smith et al., 1990). Managers and employees are not indifferent to the nature of corporate information, attributions, and prescriptions (Salancik and Meindl, 1984). Goal-setting theory assumes (over pure rational behavior based on accuracy or a 'fix-your-own-objectives' type of motivational technique) that the value generated by a moderated optimistic scenario differs favorably from the value generated from a scenario with perfect accuracy (Locke and Latham, 1990). At least there would exist a general 'rule for *chances* of riches' (Mosakowski, 1998: 1170, original italic), that is, the fact that slightly positive errors would increase the odds of improving performance relative to an accurate scenario (Salancik and Meindl, 1984). This implies in turn that for the same level and book value of resources, the performance effect of an underestimated forecast would not be mean preserving relative to the performance associated with an accurate forecast. For instance, the exploitation of rent-generating resource-tied services would be worsened when the future looks less promising for the company than for its competitors and when there are no challenging objectives. Therefore, underestimations, as an expression of underconfidence, would reduce performance.

However, one of the key problems posed by underconfidence as expressed by actual underestimation comes from its distinction *vis-à-vis* prudence. Prudence stems from a particular attention to *ex post* negative consequences. While underconfidence is an understatement of an organizational capacity to face the anticipated negative consequences, prudence is rather an exaggeration of the negative consequences, resulting in underestimations. Hence, while underconfidence manifests itself by perceived or actual below-average capacities, prudence does not. Therefore, while underconfidence is negatively associated with performance, prudence is not.

When producing estimates, human beings tend naturally to underestimate positive information and overestimate negative information, and therefore cap their estimates to avoid disappointment (Schweitzer and Cachon, 2000). In an organizational context, underestimations may reflect not only underconfidence but also prudence. Notably, larger underestimations could manifest a propensity to preserve the odds of obtaining good results. The unconscious cognitive bias of avoiding unwelcome surprises as well as the conscious tactic implemented to reserve some turnaround, leads to the same conclusion: larger understated expectations are likely to be prudent estimates. As such, they could even be linked to positive outcomes, and therefore a greater underestimation would be associated with a higher performance.

Overall, we argue that as the level of underestimation grows, performance declines because underestimation is equated with underconfidence. But, the greater the level of understatements, the more prudence is likely to predominate over underconfidence. Thus, after an inflection point, greater understatements are more likely related to higher performance. Hence:

Hypothesis 1: There is a curvilinear relationship between underestimates and performance.

The moderating role of self-perception
For more than two decades, self-perception has been recognized as a critical factor influencing strategy making and performance (Barnes, 1984; Kahneman and Tversky, 1984; Salancik and Meindl, 1984; Clapham and Schwenk, 1991; Coff, 1999; Simon et al., 2000).

The self-perception argument states that the higher the perception of one's abilities in a particular situation relative to others' abilities, the higher the likelihood of underestimating the risks associated with a situation. For instance, if managers have an exaggerated perception of the control they exert over their resources, they will overvalue the success ratio for a task (Matute, 1996). At the organizational level, a company that claims to have disproportionate advantages over its rivals in the key activities of its industry, that is, which exhibits a high self-perception, is likely to have non-optimal returns (Powell, 1992; Hayward and Hambrick, 1997).

While sustaining enthusiasm and a good working climate, inflated self-perception may pervert managers' decision abilities. They may succumb to hubris and put the organizational existence in jeopardy (Coff, 1999). Arguably, a depressed self-perception leads to a disheartened management, a below-average opportunity recognition and a lack of reactivity. All these factors lead to a below-average performance for the firm. In this research, we anticipate that the underestimation–performance relationship will be influenced by the degree of self-perception.

A reasonable extension of the above arguments is that the relation between underestimations and performance should be lower for a company with a depressed self-perception than for a company with an unbiased self-perception. A depressed self-perception indicates that the organization perceives itself unfavorably on key industrial success factors, ill-positioned in its environment relative to rivals, or deprived of strategic ambitious vision. A depressed self-perception characterizes an organization's lack of adaptability and a damaged ability to bounce back. Therefore, we posit that the curvilinear underestimation–performance relationship should reach lower levels of performance when associated with a depressed self-perception (than with an unbiased self-perception).

However, a further analysis indicates that prudent estimates differ from underconfident estimates. Prudence as a protective behavior may suggest an organization's concealed resource potential whereas underconfidence is very likely to manifest an effective organizational malaise *vis-à-vis* external evolutions perceived as unfavorable. Hence, the cross-effect of self-perception with underestimations on performance will be greater when associated with prudent forecasts than with underconfident forecasts. Indeed, the lack of adaptability potential relative to rivals, manifested by a depressed self-perception, reinforces the negative association between underestimation and performance. By contrast, this lack of adaptability potential reflected in a depressed self-perception could be compensated de facto by understated existing stocks of resources and capabilities in the case of prudent estimates. Indeed, in the case of prudent estimates (as opposed to underconfident), a depressed self-perception would likely delay the rebound rather than impair it entirely. Likewise, an inflated self-perception should overvalue the rapidity of reaction. On the contrary, the association of a depressed self-perception with underconfident forecasts would cumulate both an assessment of an organizational disadvantage relative to competitors and an estimation of a specific inadequacy of the organization to face anticipated unfavorable environmental evolutions. Therefore, we posit that the association of underconfident estimates with depressed self-perception corresponds to the worst cross-effect on performance:

Hypothesis 2a: The curvilinear effect of underestimates on performance will be lower for firms with a lower degree of self-perception.

Hypothesis 2b: The interaction effect between underestimations and self-perception will be lowest for companies exhibiting underconfidence and a depressed self-perception.

Methods

Data

The Banque de France, the French central bank, provided the initial data. Every two years, econometricians from the bank constitute a representative sample of firms operating in manufacturing industries. The questionnaire is administrated by the Banque de France's trained agents who electronically collect the responses from firms' CEOs during face-to-face interviews. In conformity with the characteristics of the French economic landscape, the great majority of firms in the survey are small to medium sized. In 1996, the year of the survey used in this research, 90 percent of the 2,145 surveyed firms had 30 to 1,500 employees. The database represents a very reliable sample of French manufacturing industries and has been used in previous empirical studies (Cool and Henderson, 1998; Durand, 2003). We complemented the 'Sesame' data with financial information from the official source that gathers the accounting data (balance sheets and profit and loss accounts) of French companies, called 'Fiben', over the 1993–98 period.

Sample selection

In the sample for this study, we selected only four-digit NACE-code industries for which there were at least 15 firms (using the European classification of industries, NACE, comparable to the American SIC codes). This selection procedure has been widely used, and particularly in earlier studies using the Banque de France dataset in order to minimize the presence of outliers and compare a firm's situation relative to a statistically valid industry average (Cool and Henderson, 1998; Wiggins and Ruefli, 2002; Durand, 2003). Some 1,750 firms representing 84 industries remained after this first selection.

Prior to testing our hypotheses, it was necessary to check the presence of intra-industry commonality of firms' perceptions. It is recognized that cross-sectional studies carry the risk of including in industry categories, firms which share SIC codes but do not really belong to the same industry clusters (Lubatkin et al., 2001). If firms are part of the same industry code while not being competitors, they will diverge in their estimates due to reasons of sample construction. As a consequence, the evaluation of a firm's forecasting ability would be biased and the comparison across firms of their forecasts erroneous. Therefore, to reduce this risk, we selected industries for which firms were likely to be competitors by controlling their agreement on the nature of their industry structure. For each of these 84 industries, we calculated kappa-statistics on interfirm agreements when assessing industry variables: bargaining power of suppliers, bargaining power of customers, barriers to entry, industry rivalry, and threat of substitutes. If the firms agreed on these structural characteristics, they were likely to belong to the same industry clusters. By selecting industries for which firms agree about the industry structure, we reduced the risk that their divergences in estimates proceeded from problems of industry classification.

The 'kappa-statistics measure of agreement' is a coefficient scaled to zero when the amount of agreement is what would be expected to be observed by chance and one when there is perfect agreement among evaluators. It is a widely used and recognized inter-rater agreement (Cohen, 1968; Larsson, 1993). Landis and Koch (1977) suggest that above

0.20, kappa-statistics represent a fair level of agreement among observers. Therefore, we disregarded industries for which 'kappas' based on firm estimations were less than 0.20. The sample consisted of 36 industries and 785 firms. Due to the severe reduction of the sample size (from 1,750 to 785 firms), we tested whether we introduced selection biases. No significant differences appeared on sample descriptive statistics, before and after the application of the kappa procedure. Finally, we selected firms that underestimated their future industry growth (*Underestimation* variable, see below), and the final sample consists of 343 firms.

Variables

- *Performance*   We chose two widely-used performance indicators: gross margins (*GrossMargin*) and return on assets (*ROA*) as our dependent variables. *GrossMargin* is a performance indicator that deals with the firm's economic exchanges, and as such it is less liable to be modified by extraneous financial and exceptional operations than *ROA* or stock-based indicators, for instance. Both have been calculated as a three-year average (1996–98) from the Fiben source, and have been standardized at the industry level.

- *Underestimation*   We calculated the difference between a firm's 1997 industry growth forecast and the actual industry growth rates that occurred in 1997 for the industries of the sample (from national statistics). We standardized the differences to avoid inter-industry disparities concerning the level of industry growth. We kept in our sample only the absolute values of the negative standardized differences, corresponding to the *Underestimation* variable. We chose future industry growth as the factor to be forecast by organizations because it is a non-ambiguous variable, important for a firm's decision, available for each respondent, and not likely to be influenced by the respondents' personal judgments.[1] According to Eurostat, 1997 was a year when the real GDP growth rate in France was 1.9 (after 1.1 in 1996 and before 3.4 in 1998). It was therefore not a particularly depressed year – which could have explained pessimistic estimates.

- *SelfPerception*   For self-perception, we used the sum of a firm's perceived strengths on factors identified by the firm as key success factors (out of seven available) weighted relatively to the other firms' assessments of the seven key success factors within the industry.

$$SelfPerception_{i,j} = \Sigma n[Strength_i \times (KSF_i/\Sigma(KSF_j/j)]$$

where *i* stands for a firm, and *j* for the number of different firms in an industry, and *n* for the seven industry factors listed below.

- *Strength* is the answer to the following questions: among the following factors, indicate your relative strength *vis-à-vis* your competition on (five-point scale): 1: cost/price; 2: quality; 3: technical performance; 4: reputation; 5: delays, responsiveness; 6: services; 7: proximity.

- *KSF* is the answer to the question: among the following variables (same items as for *Strength*), indicate those which are the most valued in your industry (multiple binary answers). $KSF_i/\Sigma(KSF_j/j)$ indicates that we weight the perceived *KSF* of a firm by the interfirm (and intra-industry) average acknowledgment of the factor as a key success factor.

- The *SelfPerception* variable contains characteristics common to formerly used metrics. First, industry key success factors are similar to previous studies on top management teams (Beyer et al., 1997; Chattopadhyay et al., 1999). Second, the method used to calculate this item consists of a sum of the respondents' grade, controlled for variability (for example, see Knight et al.'s (1999) study on consensus or, in the same logic while applied to a different construct, the weighted average of the individual-level complexity measures used in McNamara et al. (2002)). Unlike Durand's (2003) self-perception construct, we controlled for interfirm agreement on industry key success factors rather than indexing the values by dividing the numerator by the maximum value of each factor (that is, 5). Smaller values of *SelfPerception* characterize a depressed self-perception (that is, the firm under-estimates industry key success factors relative to its competitors or declares itself to be weak relative to its competitors on the identified factors) while larger values show an inflated self-perception (that is, the firm overestimates industry key success factors relative to its competitors and pretends to be strong).

Data analysis and control variables

Table 24.1 presents the descriptive statistics and correlation matrix of the variables used in the models. No variable exhibits distribution or correlation problems. We detail below the procedure that leads us to retain the variables present in Table 24.1.

We used the RSREG procedure in SAS.8.2 to perform a test of polynomiality (because Hypothesis 1 assumes a curvilinear relationship) and to select control variables to be included in the final model. The RSREG procedure tests the significance of linear, quadratic, and cross-product effects of independent variables on performance indicators. It also provides an evaluation of the lack of fit of the model and gives the characteristics of a surface model. In particular, it provides a canonical analysis of the response surface and the characteristics of the stationary point.

From the analysis reported in Table 24.2, we draw several conclusions. First, there is some evidence of a quadratic relationship between underestimation and performance (both performance indicators), of a linear relationship between *SelfPerception* and performance (quadratic term not significant) and of a significant interaction effect.

Second, the 'lack of fit' test shows that additional variable should be included at least in the *GrossMargin* model. Finally, the canonical analysis indicates that the shape of the surface model differs. For *GrossMargin*, it is a saddle point while for *ROA* it happens to be a minimum. Looking at the corresponding value of the axes for the *ROA* model (0.12, 7.17), it appears that the minimum performance (−0.22) would correspond to an under-confident estimate and a depressed self-perception, giving some preliminary support to Hypothesis 2b. For *GrossMargin*, we do not have an indication of the minimum value but of the saddle point.

The RSREG models gave a first assessment of the effect of potential covariates on performance indicators. The stepwise covariate selection method (Proc REG) enabled us to complete that first analysis and select among all the available potential influential factors on performance. For the sake of brevity, we kept in the presented tables (Tables 24.1 and 24.3) only the control variables that exhibited significant coefficients for one of

Table 24.1   Correlation matrix

	Mean (s.d.)	1 Gross Margin	2 ROA	3	4	5	6	7	8	9	10	11	12	13	14
1 GrossMargin	0.12														
	0.92														
2 ROA	0.08	0.34													
	0.46	0.00													
3 Concentration	57.74	-0.14	0.07												
	30.06	0.01	0.19												
4 Rivalry	2.11	-0.09	0.03	0.01											
	1.30	0.11	0.60	0.86											
5 Customer Power	4.38	-0.21	-0.22	0.02	-0.09										
	1.05	0.00	0.00	0.66	0.09										
6 IND22	0.26	0.03	-0.13	-0.35	-0.02	-0.18									
	0.44	0.60	0.01	0.00	0.76	0.00									
7 IND28	0.19	-0.03	0.09	-0.12	0.00	0.07	-0.29								
	0.39	0.65	0.12	0.02	0.95	0.23	0.00								
8 IND29	0.11	-0.05	0.07	0.11	-0.01	0.04	-0.21	-0.17							
	0.31	0.37	0.20	0.05	0.86	0.45	0.00	0.00							
9 IND34	0.16	0.04	0.10	0.33	0.04	0.11	-0.26	-0.21	-0.16						
	0.36	0.45	0.07	0.00	0.44	0.04	0.00	0.00	0.01						
10 Marketing	0.08	0.10	0.09	-0.09	0.03	0.04	0.01	-0.04	0.02	0.02					
	4.47	0.07	0.09	0.09	0.58	0.56	0.91	0.46	0.77	0.79					
11 Size	4.53	-0.21	-0.01	0.16	0.00	0.13	-0.23	-0.12	0.02	0.22	0.08				
	0.86	0.00	0.82	0.00	0.96	0.00	0.00	0.03	0.75	0.00	0.14				
12 Coordination	3.23	0.06	0.05	0.00	-0.03	0.07	-0.13	0.03	0.09	0.03	0.05	0.13			
	1.60	0.27	0.34	0.99	0.62	0.19	0.02	0.60	0.12	0.54	0.34	0.02			
13 SelfPerception	12.00	0.11	0.13	-0.06	0.05	0.04	0.04	0.16	0.24	-0.06	0.09	-0.16	0.05		
	1.77	0.05	0.02	0.32	0.42	0.51	0.45	0.00	0.00	0.27	0.12	0.00	0.33		
14 Under estimation	0.81	0.03	0.02	0.14	0.04	-0.09	-0.13	-0.09	-0.13	-0.08	0.01	0.08	-0.01	-0.07	
	0.68	0.63	0.13	0.01	0.45	0.09	0.02	0.12	0.02	0.16	0.91	0.15	0.89	0.19	
15 Under estimation²	1.12	0.33	0.00	-0.02	-0.06	-0.14	-0.34	0.17	-0.12	-0.20	-0.07	-0.11	0.04	-0.09	0.16
	1.79	0.00	0.98	0.73	0.27	0.01	0.00	0.00	0.03	0.00	0.21	0.04	0.50	0.10	0.00

Table 24.2   Polynomial analysis

	GrossMargin	ROA
Analysis of Variance	*F*-stat (Pr > *F*)	
Linear	2.22 ($^+$)	6.19 (***)
Quadratic	12.08 (***)	4.80 (**)
Cross-product	5.15 (*)	3.40 (*)
Parameter	Unstandardized coefficient (*T*-value)	
Underestimation	0.16 (0.30)	0.23 (0.84)
SelfPerception	0.46* (1.99)	−0.08 (−0.66)
Underestimation^2	0.37*** (4.17)	0.12** (2.65)
Underestimation × *SelfPerception*	−0.09* (−2.27)	−0.04* (−1.84)
SelfPerception^2	−0.01 (−1.37)	0.00 (1.16)
R^2	9.11%	6.57%
Lack of fit (*F*-value, and Pr > *F*)	5.23*** (0.00)	0.73 (0.81)
Canonical analysis		
Underestimation	1.31	0.12
SelfPerception	12.92	7.17
Predicted value at stationary point (optimum)	−0.07	−0.22
Stationary point is a . . .	Saddle point	Minimum

Note: + *p* < 0.1; * *p* < 0.05; ** *p* < 0.01; *** *p* < 0.001.

the two dependent variables. The control variables selected out are: assessment of the bargaining power of the supplier, a measure of the barriers to entry, a proxy for the threat of substitutes, the relative expenditures in research and development (R&D), the relative expenditures in education and training, a measure of the firm's internal variability (that is, the standard deviation of the 1994–96 sales divided by the 1994–96 average sales), the degree of diversification, the firm's structure type (functional or not), the increase in production over the last two years, and the ease of forecasting industry growth (portion of industry growth not explained as a function of the past industry growth rate).

Ten covariates have remained in the equations. At the industry level, *Concentration* represents the cumulated market share of the four industry leaders. *Rivalry* is the answer to the following question: 'Do companies in your industry modify their offering frequently? (every two years)' using a five-point Likert scale from 'strongly disagree' to 'strongly agree'. *CustomerPower* is the answer using the same Likert scale to the question: 'Do your customers have a high bargaining power that enables them to negotiate contracts?'. Finally, four industry dummies (at the three-digit NACE-code level) remained in the model.

At the firm level, *Marketing* measures the difference between a firm's marketing expenditures (in percent of sales) and the average percentage of marketing expenditures at the 4-digit industry level. *Size* is the logged three-year average number of employees in the company. *Coordination* corresponds to the answer to the following question: 'Does there exist a financial accounting service that diffuses efficient reporting and budgeting services to top executives?' (five-point Likert scale from 'strongly disagree' to 'strongly agree').

Results

Final models consist of ordinary least squares interactive regressions as expressed by equation (24.1):

$$\text{Perf} = b_0 + b_1\,Underestimation + b_2\,Underestimation^2 + b_3\,SelfPerception$$
$$+ b_4\,Underestimation \cdot SelfPerception + b_i Controls + e \qquad (24.1)$$

Table 24.3 shows the results. Model 1 presents the *GrossMargin* model and model 2 the *ROA* model. As we proceeded through a preliminary RSREG stage, we present the full interactive model (that is, with direct, quadratic, and cross-product). While not presented, the R^2 of control models are significantly below the full models. Model 1 improves significantly the R^2 (+ 6.87%) as well as model 2 (+5.83%) relatively to the control models.

Concerning the effects of control variables, in model 1, industry *Concentration, Rivalry, CustomerPower* and firm *Size* tend to significantly reduce *GrossMargin*, while *Coordination* favors it. In model 2, *CustomerPower* significantly reduces ROA but *Marketing* expenditures marginally improve it.

Hypothesis 1 postulates a curvilinear relationship between underestimates and performance. The impact of a variable that comprises a multiplicative term (*Underestimation*) is conditioned by the value of the other value in that term (*SelfPerception*).

Equation (24.1) can be rewritten as:

$$\text{Perf} = b_0 + (b_1 + b_4 \cdot SelfPerception)\,Underestimation$$
$$+ b_2\,Underestimation^2 + b_3\,SelfPerception + b_i Controls + e,$$

Table 24.3   *Result of regression analysis for gross margin and ROA (standardized parameters)*

	Variables	GrossMargin	ROA
	Intercept	0.79 (1.19)	−0.33 (−0.96)
b_1	Underestimation	0.11 (0.29)	0.42 (1.06)
b_2	Underestimation²	0.69*** (3.90)	0.43* (2.37)
b_3	SelfPerception	0.28*** (3.26)	0.21** (2.49)
b_4	Underestimation × SelfPerception	−0.75* (−2.24)	−0.67* (−1.96)
	Concentration	−0.11* (−1.91)	0.05 (0.90)
	Rivalry	−0.12** (−2.39)	−0.02 (−0.46)
	CustomerPower	−0.22*** (−4.31)	−0.26*** (−4.82)
	ind22	−0.07 (−1.07)	−0.01 (−0.00)
	ind28	−0.09 (−1.45)	0.15* (2.24)
	ind29	−0.10⁺ (−1.65)	0.10 (1.58)
	ind34	0.16* (2.02)	0.18** (2.89)
	Marketing	0.07 (1.38)	0.07⁺ (1.60)
	Size	−0.21*** (−3.80)	−0.03 (−0.50)
	Coordination	0.09⁺ (1.79)	0.05 (0.89)
	F	6.38***	4.66***
	R^2	22.04%	17.13%

Note: $+\ p < 0.1$; $*\ p < 0.05$; $**\ p < 0.01$; $***\ p < 0.001$.

where $(b_1 + b_4 \cdot SelfPerception)$ corresponds to the conditional linear effect of *Under-estimation*. From models 1 and 2, b_1 appears to be non-significant while b_4 is negative and significant. For the purpose of conducting tests of significance for interactions, we can construct standard errors for the combination of coefficients (Friedrich, 1982). For example, the standard error for b_1 and b_4 for the average *SelfPerception* value of 12.0 is given by:

$$\text{Standard error}_{(b_1 + b_4 \cdot SelfPerception) \ Underestimation} = [\text{var}(b_1) + (12)^2 \text{var}(b_4)$$
$$+ (12)2\text{cov}(b_1, b_4)]^{1/2} = [0.27 + 144 \cdot 0.002 + 24 \cdot (-0.017)]^{1/2} = 0.38.$$

Therefore, at the average value for *SelfPerception*, and using the unstandardized parameters, the *t*-statistics for model 1 equal:

$$(b_1 + b_4 \cdot SelfPerception)/\text{Standard error}$$
$$= (0.15 - 0.085 \cdot 12)/0.38 = -0.87/0.38 = -2.29.$$

With the same procedure, we calculate the *t*-statistics for model 2 (*ROA*) as:

$$(b_1 + b_4 \cdot SelfPerception)/\text{Standard error}$$
$$= (0.29 - 0.039 \cdot 12)/0.083 = -0.178/0.083 = -2.14.$$

For both models, the linear effect coefficient of *Underestimation* at the average value of *SelfPerception* is negative and significant at $p < 0.05$. This holds true over the range of observed *SelfPerception* values (min: 7 to max: 19). We know from Table 24.2 that the partial fit statistics of a second-order model is required and from Table 24.3 that the quadratic effect coefficients for *Underestimation* in both models are positive and significant. Therefore, the relationship between *Underestimation* and both performance indicators is of the following form: $Y = aX + bX^2$, with a being negative and significant and b being positive and significant. This equation corresponds to a curvilinear relationship between *Underestimation* and performance indicators (*GrossMargin* and *ROA*) and Hypothesis 1 is supported.

However, that relationship varies according to the *SelfPerception* variable for which the linear effect is positive and significant (at least at $p < 0.01$) and the cross-product coefficient with *Underestimation* is negative and significant at $p < 0.05$ in both models. At first sight, it seems that lower levels of self-perception reduce performance (linear effect coefficients are positive and significant), giving some support to Hypothesis 2a. However, the cross-product effect mitigates that effect. In order to visualize the relationship, we used the G3grid and G3 procedures to represent the response surface models.

Figure 24.1 shows that (i) the curvilinear effect of underestimates on *GrossMargin* is lower for lower degrees of self-perception, notably when underestimations are small, that is, when they likely manifest underconfidence; (ii) for larger estimations, the moderating impact of self-perception is less clear; (iii) the minimum value for performance coincides with a small underestimation and a low self-perception.

Figure 24.2 emphasizes these results. The curvilinear underestimation–performance relationship is obvious for higher degrees of self-perception but for lower levels of self-perception the relationship becomes almost linear. For larger underestimations, the

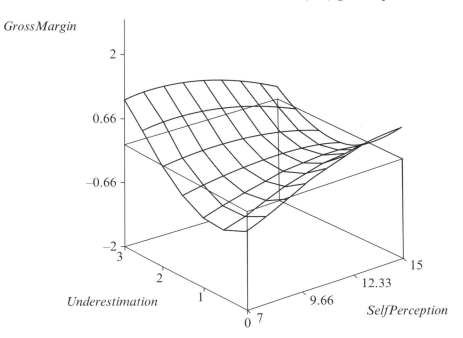

Figure 24.1   Response surface for gross margin

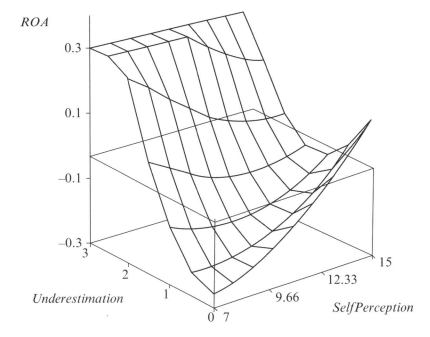

Figure 24.2   Response surface for ROA

moderating influence of self-perception disappears. As formerly revealed by the RSREG model (Table 24.2), the minimum performance results from the association of a depressed self-perception and a small underestimation.

From these analyses, the findings give support to Hypotheses 2a and 2b. The curvilinear effect of underestimates on performance is greater for firms with a higher degree of self-perception. The interaction effect between underestimations and self-perception is least for companies with a relatively small underestimation (characterizing underconfidence) and a depressed self-perception.

Discussion

Tested on two performance variables (gross margin and return on assets), our key findings can be summed up in three points:

1. Small to moderate underestimations of industry growth have a negative effect on performance.
2. As a result of the interaction effect, the lower the level of self-perception, the lower the U-curve effect between underestimations and performance.
3. The lowest observed performance results from the cross-effect of small underestimation and a depressed self-perception.

These findings open three interesting discussion points. First, in addition to having paid attention to an understudied phenomenon, namely underestimations *vis-à-vis* overestimations, a twofold distinction is proposed in this research that has implications for future research. A distinction concerns what underestimations manifest, that is, either underconfidence or prudence. As a primary approximation, we posited that lower underestimations contain more underconfidence than prudence, and as the magnitude of underestimations grows, the proportion of prudence grows accordingly. Although this approximation has to be examined more precisely in future studies, it contributes to the theoretical elaboration of the debate relating inaccuracies and performance (Starbuck and Mezias, 1996).

From our empirical setting, small to moderate underestimations correspond to firms having undervalued industry growth by a 1.5 standardized difference or less (Figures 24.1 and 24.2). Larger underestimations (from 1.5 to 3 standardized difference) show a change in the slope function and have an increasing effect on performance. Our range of observations did not contain extreme underestimations (beyond 3 standardized difference), and it is difficult to generalize our results to these situations. Several questions emerge from our findings: is 1.5 standardized difference an acceptable value to define a threshold? Can we extrapolate a continuously growing effect on large errors on performance beyond another threshold (3 standardized difference) or should we assume that beyond, underestimations are again negatively associated with performance? Finally, what further tests can help to dissociate underconfidence from prudence more objectively than we could in the present study?

Another distinction of interest concerns the differences between what underestimations manifest and self-perception. Underestimations are the expression of an organizational forecasting ability and result from an excessive value attribution to negative diagnostic cues. Underestimations reflect underconfidence (when the negative cues are correlated with understated organizational capabilities to face the challenge) or prudence (when there is no specific correlation between the external negative cues and the internal organizational capabilities). Self-perception is an organizational disposition that characterizes an organizational context *vis-à-vis* competitors. It influences organizational behavior and strategy, and as such can moderate, among other things, the relations between capabilities and performance. In this chapter, we studied one particular interaction and its effects on performance. These distinctions shed light on the internal determinants that affect firm performance, and help disentangle complex relationships between too often confused concepts.

Second, underestimations are an interesting object of analysis for two other reasons:

1. They deal with the measurement problem that is faced by the resource-based view of the firm (Porter, 1991; Priem and Butler, 2001). Indeed, as explained elsewhere, a firm's resource endowment and capability reservoir matter for creating rents, appropriating growth opportunities, and fostering performance (Dierickx and Cool, 1989; Barney, 1991). Organizational forecasting ability is an observable organizational ability (through the magnitude of the forecasting error) whose consequences on performance can be measured (Barney, 1991, 2001).

2. Underestimations are a complex object as underestimations may be due to underconfidence or prudence. Our findings show that there are two situations that favorably impact on a firm's performance: accuracy in estimating future industry growth and prudent estimates. Forecasting ability posited as an organizational capability is a valuable competence: it is positively related to performance. However, under certain circumstances, inaccurate estimates can be the expression of protective attitudes such as prudence, and also lead to a similar effect. Alternatively, organizational dispositions such as a depressed self-perception interact with that underestimation–performance relationship. As a matter of fact, an unfavorably oriented disposition may ruin the potential benefits of an organizational capability such as forecasting ability.

   Hence, not looking competent in forecasts might not equate with being incompetent. Furthermore, being competent may not correspond with the performance peak but rather with a below-average performance when associated with an incapacitating disposition. Therefore, what is the real strategic value of an organizational ability? Are there other capabilities that require organizational dispositions to positively impact on performance? It seems that an ability is a competence depending on the organizational context in which the ability operates (in our case because of the moderating effect of self-perception). Being excellent in one task or domain needs a complementary set of conditions (an organizational context) to deliver rents and imply performance.

Third, organizational self-perception moderates the effect of pessimistic estimations on performance. This result indicates that strategic scholars need to focus more on organizational self-judgment, identity, and representations when we consider whether or not an organizational ability entails above-average returns (Daft and Weick, 1984; Wood and Bandura, 1989; Park et al., 2002). These representations constitute the cognitive context that impacts on how a firm perceives its own organizational abilities (resource-based view) and managerial practices (goal-setting arguments).

Empirically, this study tries to overcome some of the measurement difficulties underlined by Starbuck and Mezias (1996) through (i) carefully selecting the sample to reduce *ex ante* sample heterogeneity at the industry-code level, (ii) cautious introduction of polynomial and interactive effects, (iii) controlling for direct effects of a firm's idiosyncratic traits and industry structure on firm performance, and (iv) testing the relationships on two performance variables.

However, this study presents some limitations. We used secondary data to test our hypotheses. As the Banque de France has increased the reliability of its survey over the years, using well-trained interviewers and specialists in econometrics to ensure the quality of the data, we are rather confident that our results can be generalized (see earlier studies by Cool and Henderson, 1998; Durand, 2003). However, we regret the absence of additional questions that could have enabled us to test the external validity of our constructs. We controlled the respondents' biases from the inside of the organization (via marketing expenditures and *Size*, which remained in the final models) and from the outside (through the kappa procedure). However, it was not possible to have either an internal cross-evaluation of the organizational perceptions or a complementary evaluation of industry forces – which is a regrettable but intrinsic limitation of studies using secondary data. Also, due to the limited access to the data and its inherent limitations (resampling procedures over the years), we were not able to repeat the tests on further years using paired samples and to provide better proxies for the used concepts (notably underconfidence and prudence).

Despite the acknowledged limitations of our study, we might consider some further extensions. First, it would be interesting to study the impact on firm performance of forecasting errors about not just industry evolutions but also resources available in the market. Second, previous studies have shown that national culture can impact on how individuals and organizations respond to strategic issues (Schneider and de Meyer (1991) studied deregulation, for instance). A replication of this study in different national contexts or in a multicultural context will help to shed more light on the organizational and cultural interactions *vis-à-vis* underconfidence, prudence, and self-perception. Third, it would be interesting to deepen the analysis in order to uncover the chain of causes and effects from resource endowment, organizational capabilities, organizational dispositions, and performance (King and Zeithaml, 2001). Notably, organizational attention appears to be an important trait that enables firms to focus (or not) on relevant signals (Ocasio, 1997). Organizational attention and other factors (such as structure or compensation characteristics) could therefore be added to the future models.

As far as management is concerned, this study shows that top managers must be attentive to the influence of the organization's dispositions to which they belong when they have to deliver estimates and build scenarios for decision making. Foresight is a contextual capacity of organization, which entails strategic consequences. From our results, we recommend that decision makers be aware of the short-term complex relationships among the organizational context, the propensity to underestimate future trends, and performance; in the long term, potential (predictable while not tested here) negative outcomes may result from a lasting depressed self-perception. Moreover, beyond the technical recommendations drawn from the forecasting and foresight literature, many actions may improve a firm's estimation ability and corollary decisions. These management actions presumably deal with organizational balance (in terms of the teams in charge of forecasts and estimates), organizational diversity (in terms of education, background, culture within and across teams), and organizational governance (in terms of vested interests, opportunism, and agency relationships). Together, these factors may help a firm better estimate its environmental conditions, realize the reality of its own resourcefulness, and improve its foresight and performance.

Note

1. One may argue that CEOs gave the estimates, and not the organization *per se*. However, the survey does not ask for a personal estimate but a firm's estimate, since the question belongs to a section of the questionnaire that concerns the firm's industry characteristics. Also, the question in itself does not raise any issue that would tempt the CEO to dissociate his/her personal judgment from his/her role as the head of a firm – as ethical questions, opinions, or advice could imply. Therefore, the use of subjective data is as valuable in this study as it is for the evaluation of strategic issues (Hambrick, 1981; Salancik and Meindl, 1984; Starbuck and Mezias, 1996).

References

Barnes, J.H. (1984), 'Cognitive biases and their impact on strategic planning', *Strategic Management Journal*, **5**, 129–37.

Barney, J.B. (1986), 'Strategic factor markets: expectations, luck, and business strategy', *Management Science*, **42**, 1231–41.

Barney, J.B. (1991), 'Firm resources and sustained competitive advantage', *Journal of Management*, **17**, 99–120.

Barney, J.B. (2001), 'Is the resource-based "view" a useful perspective for strategic management research? Yes', *Academy of Management Review*, **26**, 41–56.

Beyer, J., P. Chattopadhyay, E. George, W.H. Glick and D. Pugliese (1997), 'The selective perception of managers revisited', *Academy of Management Journal*, **40**, 716–37.

Chattopadhyay, P., W.H. Glick, C.C. Miller and G.P. Huber (1999), 'Determinants of executive beliefs: comparing functional conditioning and social influence', *Strategic Management Journal*, **20**, 763–89.

Clapham, S.E. and C.R. Schwenk (1991), 'Self-serving attributions, managerial cognition, and company performance', *Strategic Management Journal*, **12**, 219–29.

Coff, R.W. (1999), 'How buyers cope with uncertainty when acquiring firms in knowledge-intensive industries: caveat emptor', *Organization Science*, **10**, 144–61.

Cohen, J. (1968), 'Weighted kappa: nominal scale agreement with provision for scaled disagreement or partial credit', *Psychology Bulletin*, **70**, 213–20.

Cool, K. and J. Henderson (1998), 'Power and firm profitability in supply chains: French manufacturing industry in 1993', *Strategic Management Journal*, **19**, 909–26.

Daft, R. and K. Weick (1984), 'Toward a model of organizations as interpretation systems', *Academy of Management Review*, **9**, 284–95.

Das, T.K. and B.S. Teng (1999), 'Cognitive biases and strategic decision processes: an integrative perspective', *Journal of Management Studies*, **36**, 757–78.

Dierickx, I. and K. Cool (1989), 'Asset stock accumulation and sustainability of competitive advantage', *Management Science*, **35**, 1504–11.

Durand, R. (2003), 'Predicting a firm's forecasting ability – the role of organizational illusion of control and organizational attention', *Strategic Management Journal*, **24**, 821–38.

Friedrich R.J. (1982), 'In defense of multiplicative terms in multiple regression equations', *American Journal of Political Science*, **26**, 797–833.

Hambrick, D.C. (1981), 'Strategic awareness within top management teams', *Strategic Management Journal*, **2**, 153–73.

Hayward, M.L. and D.C. Hambrick (1997), 'Explaining premium paid for large acquisitions: evidence of CEO hubris', *Administrative Science Quarterly*, **42**, 103–27.

Kahneman, D. and A. Tversky (1984), 'Choice, values, and frames', *American Psychologist*, **39**, 341–50.

King, A.W. and C.P. Zeithaml (2001), 'Competencies and firm performance: examining the causal ambiguity paradox', *Strategic Management Journal*, **22**, 75–99.

Kirchler, E. and B. Maciejovsky (2002) 'Simultaneous over- and underconfidence: evidence from experimental asset markets', *Journal of Risk and Uncertainty*, **25**, 65–85.

Knight, D., C.L. Pearce, K.G. Smith, J.D. Olian, H.P. Sims, K.A. Smith and P. Flood (1999), 'Top management team diversity, group process, and strategic consensus', *Strategic Management Journal*, **20**, 445–65.

Landis R.J. and G.G. Koch (1977), 'The measurement of observer agreement for categorical data', *Biometrics*, **33**, 159–74.

Larsson, R. (1993), 'Case survey methodology: quantitative analysis of patterns across case studies', *Academy of Management Journal*, **36**, 1515–46.

Locke, E.A. and G.P. Latham (1990), *A Theory of Goal Setting and Task Performance*, Englewood Cliffs, NJ: Prentice Hall.

Lubatkin, M., W. Schulze, A. Mainkar and R.W. Cotterill (2001), 'Ecological investigation of firm-effect in horizontal mergers', *Strategic Management Journal*, **22**, 335–57.

Matute, H. (1996), 'Illusion of control; detecting response-outcome independence in analytic but not in naturalistic conditions', *Psychological Science*, **7**, 289–99.

McNamara, G. and P. Bromiley (1997), 'Decision making in an organizational setting; cognitive and organizational influences on risk assessment in commercial lending', *Academy of Management Journal*, **40**, 1063–88.

McNamara, G., R.A. Luce and G.H. Tompson (2002), 'Examining the effect of complexity in strategic group knowledge on firm performance', *Strategic Management Journal*, **23**, 153–70.

Mosakowski, E. (1998), 'Managerial prescriptions under the resource-based view of strategy: the example of motivational techniques', *Strategic Management Journal*, **19**, 1169–82.

Ocasio, W. (1997), 'Towards an attention-based view of the firm', *Strategic Management Journal*, **18**, 187–206.

Park, S., R. Chen and S. Gallagher (2002), 'Firm resources as moderators of the relationship between market growth and strategic alliances in semi-conductor start-ups', *Academy of Management Journal*, **45**, 527–45.

Porter, M.E. (1991), 'Towards a dynamics theory of strategy', *Strategic Management Journal*, **12**, 95–117.

Powell, T.P. (1992), 'Organizational alignment as competitive advantage', *Strategic Management Journal*, **13**, 119–34.

Priem, R.L. and J.E. Butler (2001), 'Tautology in the resource-based view and the implications of externally determined resource value: further comments', *Academy of Management Review*, **26**, 57–66.

Salancik, G.R. and J.R. Meindl (1984), 'Corporate attributions as strategic illusions of management control', *Administrative Science Quarterly*, **29**, 238–54.

Schneider, S.C. and A. de Meyer (1991), 'Interpreting and responding to strategic issues: the impact of national culture', *Strategic Management Journal*, **12**, 307–20.

Schweitzer, M. and G. Cachon (2000), 'Decision bias in the newsvendor problem with a known demand distribution: experimental evidence', *Management Science*, **46**, 404–20.

Schwenk, C.R. (1986), 'Information, cognitive biases, and commitment to a course of action', *Academy of Management Review*, **11**, 298–310.

Simon, M. and S.M. Houghton (2003), 'The relationship between overconfidence and the introduction of risky products: evidence from a field study', *Academy of Management Journal*, **46**, 139–50.

Simon, M., S.M. Houghton and K. Aquino (2000), 'Cognitive biases, risk perception, and venture formation: how individuals decide to start companies', *Journal of Business Venturing*, **15**, 113–34.

Sitkin, S.B. and A.M. Pablo (1992), 'Reconceptualizing the determinants of risk behaviour', *Academy of Management Journal*, **17**, 9–38.

Smith, K.G., E.A. Locke and D. Barry (1990), 'Goal setting, planning, and organizational performance: an experimental simulation', *Organization Behavior Human Decision Processes*, **46**, 118–34.

Starbuck, W.H. and J. Mezias (1996), 'Opening Pandora's box: studying the accuracy of managers' perceptions', *Journal of Organizational Behavior*, **17**, 99–117.

Sutcliffe, K.M. and G.P. Huber (1998), 'Firm and industry as determinants of executive perceptions of the environment', *Strategic Management Journal*, **19**, 793–807.

Wiggins, R.R. and T.W. Ruefli (2002), 'Sustained competitive advantage: temporal dynamics and persistence of superior economic performance', *Organization Science*, **13**, 82–105.

Wood, R.E. and B. Bandura (1989), 'Social cognitive theory of organizational management', *Academy of Management Review*, **14**, 361–84.

25 Strategic foresight and the role of organizational memory within a punctuated equilibrium framework*

Stelios C. Zyglidopoulos and Stephanie W.J.C. Schreven

Worlds on worlds are rolling ever
From creation to decay
Like the bubbles on a river
Sparkling, bursting, borne away.

(Shelley, in Whitehead, *Modes of Thought*, 1938: 45)

Introduction

According to Whitehead (1938), strategic foresight is the capacity for establishing appropriate generalities and anticipating future developments. Therefore, he continues, strategic foresight is *the* crucial feature of a competent business mind, and, we might add, functions as a valuable and decisive characteristic of an organization's ability to successfully deal with the future. However, despite the importance of the matter in terms of understanding the conditions under which strategic foresight enables organizations to successfully navigate uncertainties and capitalize on changing future conditions, it has not received adequate attention within the strategic management and organization theory literatures. In this chapter, drawing on the appropriate literatures, we develop a conceptual model that addresses the role that organizational memory plays in a firm's capability for strategic foresight, within a punctuated equilibrium framework.

Strategic foresight, as an organizational capability, refers to an organization's ability to conceptualize novel developments and anticipate them (Whitehead 1938; Slaughter 1998; Tsoukas and Shepherd 2004). In other words, an organization's capability to engage in strategic foresight has two aspects to it. The first refers to an organization's ability to conceptualize novel developments, which depends on its understanding of the situation, and its ability to engage in speculative imagination, whereas the second refers to the organization's ability to take the appropriate actions in anticipation of novel developments, which is facilitated by a critical level of flexibility and information availability. It is reasonable to expect that organizational memory (Walsh and Ungson 1991) influences foresight on both aspects, but this influence is not adequately understood, and might even be thought of as contradictory at first. For example, if we assume that foresight presupposes and originates in an understanding of the present, which, partly retrieved from the past and pieced together from the organization's memory, is brought to bear on current decision making and planning, the following opposing arguments could be made. One could argue that organizational memory has a positive impact on the organization's ability for strategic foresight in terms of it 'facilitating problem definition, alternative generation and evaluation and choice' (ibid.). But, on the other hand, given that strategic foresight refers to an organization's ability to conceptualize and anticipate novelty, organizational memory can be seen as a hindrance, because the memory of 'how things used to work' might prevent organizations from conceptualizing 'how things will work'; in other words, organizational memory can be a major source of myopia (Levitt 2004) and inertia (Hannan and Freeman 1977). Accordingly, one could argue that the greater the organization's ability to forget the greater its capacity for strategic foresight. Of course, it is more likely that organizational memory impacts on an organization's ability for strategic foresight in both positive and negative ways, which brings us to an interesting research issue: the identification of the conditions under which organizational memory would have a predominantly positive or negative effect on strategic foresight.

In this chapter, we propose a conceptual model that addresses the relationship between memory and foresight, against the background of a world changing in accordance with a punctuated equilibrium perspective (Gersick 1991; Romanelli and Tushman 1994). Two cognitive factors (deep structure understanding, and speculative imagination) and two structural factors (information availability, and organizational flexibility) that link organizational memory to strategic foresight are identified. Our model suggests that developing strategic foresight is assisted or hindered by organizational memory depending on the period (convergence, or punctuation) in which the organization is temporally located and the period within or onto which it is trying to generate or project strategic foresight. Moreover, different characteristics of organizational memory assist or hinder the organization's capacity for foresight within and between different kinds of periods. Foresight implies something different and places different demands on the organization depending on where the organization finds itself temporally located in relation to convergence and punctuation periods.

In brief, the contribution of our work here is twofold. First, we contribute to the long-running debate on how constrained organizations *are* in their ability to change, by explaining how organizational memory influences the ability of organizations to conceptualize their *future* and act on it. Second, we contribute to the developing literature of strategic foresight by clarifying that different kinds of foresight are required depending on the time period within which an organization operates – a contingency-type approach. In broader terms, our contribution consists of better understanding the ways in which the past can help us prepare for the future, given the frequent dissimilarity of the two (Weick 2005).

To achieve our goals, the remainder of this chapter proceeds as follows. First, the notions of strategic foresight, punctuated equilibrium, and organizational memory are briefly presented and discussed. Second, we present an overview of the theoretical model proposed and discuss the four dimensions along which organizational memory interacts with foresight. Third, we use this model to examine, at a conceptual level, the impact that organizational memory has on strategic foresight within periods of convergence and across periods of convergence, and punctuation. The chapter concludes with a discussion of its contributions, implications, and limitations.

Major concepts

Strategic foresight

The notion of strategic foresight has two main aspects, namely, understanding, and anticipating the future (Whitehead 1931; Slaughter 1998). The first, understanding of the future, can be illustrated with the help of the following example that points out the difference between someone engaged in forecasting versus someone engaged in foresight. A person engaged in forecasting simply extends the line put together by past measurements into the future and argues that the sales of product x will continue to increase (or decrease) by so much for the next year(s). Whereas, on the other hand, if someone faced with the same data can conclude that after a certain point in time the sales will drop, this person bases his or her predictions on foresight. The difference between forecasting and foresight lies in an actual understanding of the past and present in relation to the future. In the case of forecasting, the past through some techniques of proven usefulness indicates the future. No understanding is necessary. As Toulmin (1961) illustrated, in many sciences, forecasting has often predated understanding.[1] But for foresight to be possible, an understanding of the underlying dynamics, laws, factors or structures that manifest in observable phenomena is required. Based on these, one can conclude beforehand which way the sales will go, irrespective and independent of the forecasting technique indications, or the degree to which one can quantify these future predictions. In the example of forecasting, the past is 'dwelled upon for its own sake', which is to make the mistake of substituting 'the reminiscence of old-age for effective intelligence' (Dewey in Stuhr 1999: 449). Or, as Whitehead observes, as we read him, in forecasting 'the sense of advance is lost in the certainty of completed knowledge' (Whitehead 1938: 58). The second aspect of foresight is anticipation of the future. This anticipation could take the form of a passive/ reactive or proactive preparation. In both cases, taking action is involved, but while in a passive/reactive preparation an organization sees itself preparing to take advantage of an 'inevitable' future, in a proactive preparation the organization finds itself actually trying to influence and determine its future. Both kinds of actions can be understood as part of what Whitehead (1931) meant when he stated that anticipating future developments separates successful from unsuccessful business organizations.

In short, if we are to metaphorically expand on the logic of map making in relation to probing the future it seems that organizations, by means of their managers, are trying to map out the territory onto which to project their decision making and strategic planning. The coordinates of the map represent and capture future requirements with which the organization will be faced. An organization that succeeds in approximating the coordinates of the territory well enough creates a strategic position, the reward of which will be reflected in its performance.

But the rate and kind of change that organizations have to deal with is not always the same. Therefore, if we are to investigate the impact that organizational memory has on strategic foresight, we must clarify what kind of change the organization is up against. In the following subsection we present the punctuated equilibrium theory (Tushman and Romanelli 1985; Gersick 1991), which acts as a background in our discussion of the impact that organizational memory has on strategic foresight.

Punctuated equilibrium theory
Punctuated equilibrium theory claims that organizations evolve through a succession of relatively long periods of stability, where only incremental changes take place, and short periods of upheaval, where major discontinuous, dramatic changes occur (Tushman and Romanelli 1985; Gersick 1991). The notion of punctuated equilibrium was imported into organization theory, mainly, but not exclusively, from evolutionary biology, where the theory was introduced by natural historians Eldredge and Gould (1972), who reconciled

in their punctuated equilibrium theory notions of slow, evolutionary (Darwinian) change and rapid, revolutionary change.[2]

Punctuated equilibrium theory is quite similar to the empirically derived theory of quantum change by Miller and Friesen (1984: 1), who found that organizations are entities whose elements 'have a natural tendency to coalesce into quantum states or "configurations" which reflect integral interdependencies among [them]'. Miller and Friesen also found that organizations tend to spend relatively long periods within the same configuration and relatively short periods transforming themselves from one configuration to the next. In addition, punctuated equilibrium resembles Kuhn's (1970) scientific revolution theory within the history of science field. According to Kuhn, science evolves through the succession of periods of normal science, where a dominant paradigm prevails in the field, and scientific revolutions, where the dominant paradigm is overthrown and a new one is developed.

Drawing on numerous domains where punctuated equilibrium has been used, Gersick (1991) identifies three key components of the punctuated equilibrium 'paradigm'. These components are deep structure, equilibrium or convergence periods, and revolutionary or punctuation periods.

According to Gersick (1991), 'deep structure is the set of fundamental "choices" a system has made of (1) the basic parts into which its units will be organized and (2) the basic activity patterns that will maintain its existence' (p. 14). Tushman and Romanelli (1985) identified the following five kinds of activities that make up an organization's deep structure: '(1) core beliefs and values regarding the organization, its employees and its environment; (2) products, markets, technology and competitive timing; (3) the distribution of power; (4) the organisation's structure; and (5) the nature, type and pervasiveness of control systems' (p. 176). In a similar manner, Miller and Friesen (1984) found that configurations of different organizational aspects tend to be orchestrated around a central 'theme', which defines the configuration and the fit between its various elements. In other words, deep structure[3] refers to the underlying structure, or pattern, of the different organizational elements, that either coalesces around a central theme, or links some critical parts together. What is important to notice about deep structure is that once it locks into place and is determined, it conditions the remainder of the organizational (or system) elements, which cannot but follow suit and can exist/make sense only in a particular way, relative to the overall order. Thus, deep structure compels a high level of internal consistency. However, the deep structure of an organization, during a period of convergence, could vary with respect to the interdependence it imposes on the parts of the organization. A deep structure could be 'tight', in the sense that the interdependence (Thompson 1967) between its different elements is high, or it could be 'loose', allowing for a level of autonomy between different organizational elements. Tight configurations because of their high level of interdependency allow little room for organizational slack (Cyert and March 1963), whereas the opposite is true for loose ones.

The second aspect of punctuated equilibrium theory refers to convergence periods. These periods are characterized by relative stability, where organizational elements change, but only gradually, as their capacity for change is restricted and kept in check by the underlying deep structure, which stays the same. In a sense, these periods are equilibrium periods, where Darwinian evolution prevails. As Gersick (1991: 16) proposes:

If deep structure may be thought of as the design of the playing field and the rules of the game, then equilibrium periods might be compared loosely to a game in play. The stable integrity of the field and the rules and, thus, of the game itself does not mean that play is uninteresting, that every match is the same, or that scores and performances are static.

According to Tushman and Romanelli (1985), during periods of convergence barriers in cognition, motivation, and obligation prevent radical change. For instance, because of cognitive barriers, certain phenomena that signal and eventually require radical change are often not perceived, because as anomalies they fit outside the box (Kuhn 1970). In addition, even if the system perceives these changes and starts to change in ways inconsistent with its underlying deep structure, these changes are not allowed to proceed very far, as they are 'pulled back' into place (Miller and Friesen 1984) by the system's dominant deep structure. In other words, the organization's deep structure allows only for some types of changes to take place, namely those that do not threaten its existence and that reinforce rather than challenge the existing order.

The third element of a punctuated equilibrium perspective is made up by the notion of revolutionary or punctuation periods. During these periods, the deep structure of the organization 'breaks down', and out of this discontinuity a new type of equilibrium emerges around a new deep structure. An underlying assertion of the punctuated equilibrium framework is that drastically new deep structures cannot emerge out of gradual changes, and that these periods of discontinuity, where the old deep structure breaks down, are necessary before a new deep structure can emerge (Gersick 1991). This breakdown of the old deep structure could be triggered through internal or environmental changes (ibid.). For example, an organization might grow to a certain critical size, where its old structures and practices become clearly unsuitable and new, radically different structures and practices might be needed (Tushman and Romanelli 1985). Or, organizations, in trying to secure their access to the external resources they need, might have to change a part of their deep structure beyond a certain point, in which case the whole structure gets dismantled because of the interconnectedness of its elements (Miller and Friesen 1984).

At this point, having discussed the notions of strategic foresight and punctuated equilibrium, we proceed to the third major concept of our model, organizational memory, where the accumulated knowledge of the organization resides, as this concept has been developed by Walsh and Ungson (1991).

Organizational memory

Under the assumption that 'as information-processing systems, organizations exhibit memory that is similar in function to the memory of individuals' (1991: 60), Walsh and Ungson argue that 'organizational memory is both an individual- and organizational-level construct' (p. 61). Memory as such is referred to as 'stored information about a decision stimulus and response, that, when retrieved, comes to bear on a present decision' (p. 61). Memory consists of 'interpretations of the past,' or lessons learned based on 'information about decisions made and problems solved' (p. 62).

Walsh and Ungson, in synthesizing a broad array of related literature, conceptualize organizational memory as being composed of four elements: the structure of its retention facility, the processes of information acquisition, the process of information retrieval, and the information contained in it (p. 61). Thus, they distinguish between those mechanisms through which memory works (retention, acquisition and retrieval), and the actual content of organizational memory. These four elements are discussed in the following paragraphs, and the dimensions relevant to the purposes of this chapter are identified. The mechanisms through which organizational memory functions and its content on the one hand, and interdependency, internal consistency and resistance to change characteristic of deep structure and equilibrium on the other, mutually reinforce each other's workings. If taken into consideration together, not only does organizational memory function the way it does because of the demands placed on it by the need for tightness of fit and internal consistency, but slack within the deep structure is reduced because of the way in which organizational memory functions. Also, to the extent that memory functions as a barrier to change, and deep structure develops resistance to such barriers, organizational memory and deep structure enhance each other's potential resistance to change even further.

First, with respect to the structure of an organization's retention facility, Walsh and Ungson identify six storage bins: five internal to the organization and one external to it. These storage bins are made up by individuals, culture, transformations, structures, ecology (meaning the physical structure of the workplace), and external archives. These storage bins do not exist in one location but are distributed throughout the organization (Simon 1976; Walsh and Ungson 1991). For the purposes of this chapter in relation to punctuated equilibrium theory, the distribution of storage bins in terms of their autonomy and relative independence from one another is of interest. More specifically, what is of interest is the extent to which there is such autonomy and independence among storage bins. Organizations could be characterized by either highly autonomous or highly coordinated retention structures. In highly autonomous retention structures different storage bins, or different parts of a storage bin, function independently, whereas in highly coordinated retention structures this is not the case. The result is that in relatively autonomous structures, information diversity could be high at the cost of duplication and inefficiencies, whereas in relatively coordinated retention structures, the diversity of information would tend to be low, with a low level of duplication or inefficiency. In relation to punctuated equilibrium theory, it could be argued that organizations configured around tight, deep structures would tend to have highly coordinated retention structures, whereas organizations configured around loose ones would tend to have more autonomous retention structures. Thus, the interdependency among storage bins is indicative of the amount of slack or lack thereof, within deep structures.

The second element of organizational memory is the process of information acquisition. This process, according to Walsh and Ungson (1991: 62), depends on numerous individual- or organizational-level schemata[4] (Bartlett 1932; Shrivastava and Schneider 1984; Schwenk 1989), which 'may block, obscure, simplify, or misrepresent' the information to be acquired. This bias, selective perception, or even censorship imposed on the information acquisition process can be seen again as a direct consequence of the configuration's tightness, and constitutive of a further tightening of the deep structure. In other words, organizations with tight, deep structures would tend to impose high levels of control and a great demand for internal consistency – and therefore cognitive bias – on their information acquisition process, whereas the reverse, for loose structures, should also be the case. The overall effect of the interaction between information acquisition and deep structure is a reduction of the amount of informational slack within the system.

According to Walsh and Ungson, a third mechanism through which organizational memory functions is the process of information retrieval, which varies in its level of passivity based on a continuum that ranges from automatic to controlled retrieval (Kahneman 1973; Langer 1983; Walsh and Ungson 1991). As Walsh and Ungson describe, automatic retrieval refers to situations where information is retrieved 'effortlessly and intuitively, partly as a function of the execution of some well-established or habitual sequences of action' (p. 69), whereas controlled retrieval is an effort that is purposively and consciously accomplished. Because of the way in which retrieval is engaged with, either habitually or 'intelligently', the content of that which is retrieved is affected likewise, which has repercussions for dealing with change. Passive or automatic information retrieval, which functions as mechanical routine, stands in the way of appreciating and experiencing novelty, developing creativity and exercising flexibility, all of which make up the gateway to effectively dealing with the future and the change it brings. Active or controlled information retrieval involves thought invention and initiative in applying existing 'lessons learned' to new aims. As such, controlled information retrieval, through its varied and 'elastic' use, allows organizations to draw on their memory in such a way that change is facilitated. In linking this notion of automatic/controlled information retrieval with punctuated equilibrium theory, it is reasonable to expect that automatic information retrieval would tend to be more in line with the way in which an organization's deep structure functions than a controlled one. To the extent that controlled retrieval signals a level of activity that might open up room to challenge the existing order, and thus functions as means through which to overcome barriers to change, the system, through its resistance to change, would be more geared towards a method that reduces the potential for disturbance and that effectuates reinforcement, resulting in continuity, rather than questioning, resulting in discontinuity.

Finally, we identify and relate two dimensions of organizational memory in terms of its content to punctuated equilibrium theory: a broad/narrow dimension and a long-/short-term one. The broad/narrow dimension of organizational memory refers to the extent to which the content of the stored information, that is, 'the interpretation of the past', is restricted to domains, problems, and solutions determined by the firm's deep structure. A broad memory would include a wealth of unsolved problems, uncertainties and inconsistencies, which came up but were ignored and put aside because they could not be solved or dealt with within that particular convergence framework, and because the need to solve or address them was not that great. In other words, broad memories would include what Kuhn (1970) refers to as 'anomalies' within normal science periods. Narrow memories on the other hand would tend to forget, lose, not record, or distort such information. In addition to the broad/narrow memory distinction, we conceptualize a long-/short-term memory distinction against the background of punctuated equilibrium theory. Long-term memories would extend to issues and events beyond the last convergence period that the organization has experienced. Organizations with long-term memories would tend to remember more than one convergence, or punctuation periods, whereas organizations with short-term memories would have forgotten most of what happened in their history beyond their last period of convergence. In relation to the defining width (broad/narrow) and depth (long term/short term) of organizational memory, what is of primary importance is the potential for creating organizational slack. Remembering what is not currently necessary is a form of maintaining excess resources, which, from a punctuated equilibrium point of view, creates the openings through which to question the limits of the existing order and prepare for change. 'Forgetful' organizations, in terms of their memory lacking width or depth, experience a tighter deep structure, might be more efficient, but are thus less able to envisage, and are less prepared for, major change.

In this section, we have presented and discussed those three main elements, strategic foresight, punctuated equilibrium, and organizational memory, on which we draw to build our model, presented in the following section.

Model development
As mentioned in the introduction, this chapter develops a theoretical model that addresses how organizational memory impacts on the predisposition for organizational foresight within a punctuated equilibrium framework. As can be identified from an overview of the model, provided in Figure 25.1, organizational memory interacts with strategic foresight along four dimensions, which, in the context of this chapter, are seen as defining the organization's understanding and anticipation of the future. These four dimensions are deep understanding, speculative imagination, information availability, and organizational flexibility. The results of these interactions can be seen as the conditions under which organizations, in relation to memory and depending on the period of convergence or punctuation, are actually enabled to develop a capacity for strategic foresight. In short, memory through its interaction with either deep structure or revolutionary change determines a positive or negative predisposition towards foresight.

Within a framework of punctuated equilibrium, foresight takes on a different form and places different demands on the organization and its memory depending on the period in which the organization finds itself and the period towards which foresight is projected. The four different types of foresight within a punctuated equilibrium framework and in terms of the demands made on the organization (and their interaction with organizational memory) are: remembering (scenario 1), forgetting (scenario 2), change (scenario 3) and integration (scenario 4).

As indicated previously, the notion of strategic foresight consists in an understanding as well as an anticipation of the future. In addition, we broke down 'understanding' into

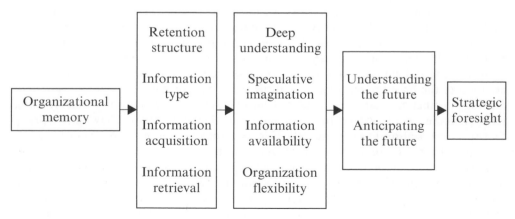

Figure 25.1   From organizational memory to strategic foresight

'deep understanding' and 'speculative imagination', and 'anticipation' into 'information availability' and 'organizational flexibility', in order to develop distinctly different scenarios for strategic foresight. However, before we address the scenarios for strategic foresight, we first discuss what encompasses deep understanding, speculative imagination, information availability and organizational flexibility.

Within a punctuated equilibrium framework, an understanding of the future is made up of an understanding of the deep structure of the upcoming period (or the lack thereof, in the case of an upcoming punctuation period). In the context of this chapter, this kind of understanding is referred to as 'deep understanding'. Deep understanding within the same period of convergence means an understanding of the prevailing and defining deep structure, whereas deep understanding from convergence to punctuation means understanding that the deep structure is or will be 'breaking down' and why this is the case. From a period of punctuation to a period of convergence, deep understanding implies 'seeing' through the current upheaval the outline and parameters of the pattern of the upcoming configuration. It requires sensemaking not only in the sense of rationally putting the pieces together (deductive thinking), but, as the term indicates, also as a function of sensing the way in which the parts fit, or will fit, together (inductive thinking). The latter type of sensemaking is 'had', not 'known' (Shustermann in Haskins and Seiple 1999), and insufficient as evidence to advance specific knowledge claims. However, immediate experience like this is invoked not to justify particular truth claims, but to ground the coherence of any type of thinking for which such claims emerge. In other words, in a period of upheaval, deep understanding makes coherent thought possible. Finally, deep understanding across convergence periods demands its own denial or annihilation even. That is, to be able from within a period of convergence to project foresight onto a new period of convergence is only possible through significant memory loss.

The second dimension to strategic foresight as understanding is speculative imagination, which refers to an organization's ability to conceptualize different possible future scenarios. We identify two kinds of speculative imagination, namely a 'first-order' type and a 'second-order' type. In the first-order type, speculative imagination refers to an organization's ability to conceptualize, visualize, and conceive of the possibility of different outcomes given the current rules of the game, which are determined by the deep structure of the period. In other words, if we use Gersick's (1991) metaphor of deep structure as the rules of the game, and convergence periods as the game at play, then first-order speculative imagination refers to the organization's ability to conceive the full variance of the possible outcomes of the game, given the current rules. The second-order type of speculative imagination refers to an organization's ability to conceptualize and conceive that the current game is 'constructed' in the sense that its order or coherence bears no necessity beyond its orderliness, and that alternative sets of rules (deep structures) are also possible in the future. In other words, this second-order type speculative imagination, as 'a new vision of the great Beyond' (Whitehead 1938: 57), would allow organizations to 'see', either intuitively or rationally, beyond the 'taken for grantedness' of the current rules of the game into alternative games and different futures. Whereas a first-order type speculative imagination focuses attention on 'detail within assigned patterns' and signals 'transition within the dominant order', a second-order type of speculative imagination 'with its emphasis on novel detail' discovers 'novel pattern' and thus signals 'transition to new forms of dominant order' (ibid.: 57, 87). Whitehead labels the latter transition as 'a frustration of the prevalent dominance' that 'elicits the excitement of life', and argues: 'The essence of life is to be found in the frustrations of established order. The Universe refuses the deadening influence of complete conformity' (pp. 87–8).

The next antecedent component to developing a capacity for foresight refers to strategic foresight as anticipation and is identified as information availability. The underlying assumption is that for an organization to be able to anticipate the future, it must have information about it. However, the information available concerns the present and the past. Information about the future is derivative information, that is, derived from the present and the past, and varies with respect to its levels of certainty. Therefore, one could easily argue that the greater the wealth of information available to an organization, both in depth and width, the greater the possibility that relevant information about the future can be derived. An understanding of the present and past, if retrieved in a controlled as opposed to habitual way, favorably and imaginatively interacts with the anticipation of the future in that it allows organizations to fully grasp the dynamics and possibilities that help them shape the future. As Dewey (1922; in Garrison 1995: 53) implores concerning the importance of the present specifically:

> Is there any intelligent way of modifying the future except to attend to the full possibilities of the present? Scamping the present in behalf of the future leads only to rendering the future less manageable. It increases the probability of molestation by future events.

Fourth, organizational flexibility in strategic foresight as anticipation refers to an organization's adaptability to changing conditions. Flexibility facilitates adaptability, which facilitates foresight in that if an organization cannot change it cannot be prepared for the future ahead, and it cannot actually 'exercise' foresight. While organizational flexibility can be defined as the opposite of organizational inertia (Hannan and Freeman 1977), within a punctuated equilibrium framework organizational flexibility can be conceptualized in two ways. First, within a convergence period, organizational flexibility can be conceptualized as an organization's ability to adapt to environmental changes without dismantling its dominant configuration. Second, within punctuation periods, organizational flexibility would refer to an organization's ability to 're-invent' itself and achieve a new kind of viable configuration.

We now turn to a discussion of the four different types of strategic foresight (remembering, forgetting, change, integration) as defined by the four different scenarios of organizational memory within a punctuated equilibrium framework. As Figure 25.2 indicates, the four possible scenarios are: (1) foresight within the same convergence period – remembering, (2) foresight across different convergence periods – forgetting, (3) foresight from a period of convergence to a punctuation period – change, and (4) foresight from a period of punctuation to a period of convergence – integration. Thus, each scenario creates different conditions for, and, in interaction with organizational memory, places different demands on organizations that together determine the extent to which organizations can be said to have a positive or negative predisposition towards strategic foresight.

Foresight within the same convergence period: remembering
Strategic foresight within the same convergence period (scenario 1 in Figure 25.2) is the easiest to achieve out of the four possible scenarios, because the future is qualitatively the same as the present and the past. Thus more than anything else it seems that foresight is

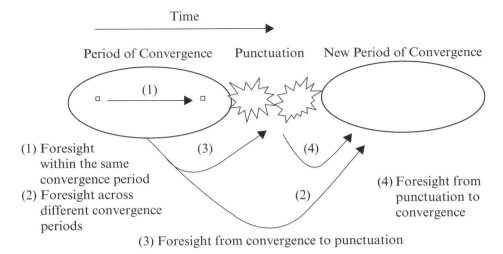

Figure 25.2   Different foresight scenarios within a punctuated equilibrium framework

determined by the organization's ability to remember the past. Strategic foresight in such a case does not require the understanding or conception of the possibility of radically different futures, nor does it require that the organization stretches its structure beyond a breaking point. In such a scenario, organizational memory, which through its interaction with deep structure contributes to an overall tightness of the configuration, would tend to play a positive role in an organization's ability to engage in strategic foresight for the following reasons.

First, the organization's ability to have a deep understanding of its situation and its environment depends on the 'lessons' it has learned while functioning in its current configuration. In other words, deep understanding depends on the acquisition and retention of, and ability to retrieve the lessons that the organization has learned in its current configuration. As we have discussed in one of the previous sections, memory and deep structure in a period of convergence mutually reinforce each other in such a way that the lessons that are learned can easily find their way back into the present. And while only individuals have the cognitive capacity to understand the 'why' behind certain situations (Wong and Weiner 1981; Walsh and Ungson 1991), these 'lessons' from past experiences can be stored in organizational routines (transformations), in the organization's culture, structure, and even ecology, which are available to the organizations as such. Thus, in this scenario, deep understanding of the future equates, to a great extent, to remembering the past.

Second, for achieving foresight within the same convergence period only first-order speculative imagination is required. In other words, to use Gersick's (1991) metaphor of a convergence period as a game at play, the firm has to imagine future scenarios from within and projected onto the continuation of the ongoing game. Although the variance could be extreme and possibly challenge a firm's ability for speculative imagination, this variance lies within the horizon of established meanings made up by past experience. In such a setting, organizational memory has a positive impact on the firm's ability for speculative imagination for two reasons. First, because managers by remembering prior similar experiences (problems and solutions) have honed their judgment skills and thus their speculative imagination abilities within this convergence period. In addition, the capacity for speculative imagination is influenced by information availability, and given the similarity of the past, and the influence of the period's deep structure on information acquisition, retention, and retrieval, it is reasonable to expect that the right kind of information will be available to managers. The rationale is that this kind of information was needed in the past and the organization (guided by its deep structure) has developed the mechanisms to store and retrieve this kind of information and acquire complementary, matching information.

Third, organizational memory should also have a positive impact on the firm's flexibility in anticipating and taking advantage of upcoming developments, mainly because the problems encountered will not be very different from the ones that the firm has encountered in the past, and similar solutions can be implemented. Therefore, the extent to which a firm's memory has stored and can effectively retrieve these routines affects how easily the firm can show the required flexibility, which given the overall sense of continuity is relatively low to begin with. But, since a firm's configuration within a particular convergence period can be seen as the result of selective environmental forces that allow only functional forms to survive (Miller and Friesen 1984), this must be the case.

Since organizational memory in this scenario has a positive impact on all four antecedent to strategic foresight, proposition 1 follows.

Proposition 1: Organizational memory will play a positive role in the organization's strategic foresight capability within a given convergence period.

Foresight across different convergence periods: forgetting

If foresight within the same convergence period is the easiest of the four possible scenarios to achieve, then foresight across convergence periods (scenario 2 in Figure 25.2) is the hardest, if not next to impossible, to achieve. The future is radically different: a new game with new rules. In this scenario, organizational memory plays a negative role in developing an ability to exercise foresight. For similar reasons as to why basketball players in the middle of a game do not have the time or the inclination to imagine how a tennis match might be played, organizations cannot conceive the next convergence period while they are in the present one. The role that memory, among others, plays in such a scenario determines and explains this inability to a large extent for the following reasons.

First, as our basketball player must keep in her mind what she knows about basketball in order to play the game, the organization must keep retrieving from its various memory bins the information needed to compete within its present period. Such a retrieval and use of information commits the organization to the present and is aimed at continuity, keeping the game in play, and preferably winning. The same applies to business organizations competing within a particular convergence period. They have to constantly remember how things work in this configuration, and this not only occupies resources but also gets rewarded by the environment, as the firm plays the game more effectively. The main obstacles to foresight across convergence periods are not only the result of lack of adequate speculative imagination, and deep understanding, but also of information unavailability and organizational inflexibility. Information unavailability is a direct consequence of the fact that the firm most likely will not have in place the information-gathering mechanisms it needs for a convergence period it cannot yet imagine. Organizational inflexibility is a result of specialization. A firm that would be so flexible as to be able to function under a new convergence period is most probably not specialized enough to survive in its current one. Through specialization the world 'contracts': 'it presupposes a strictly defined environment' (Whitehead 1938: 54), the effect of which is that foresight across periods of convergence is made even more unlikely. In sum, Proposition 2 follows.

Proposition 2: Organizational memory will play a negative role in the organization's strategic foresight capability across different periods of convergence.

Foresight from convergence to punctuation: change

Foresight from convergence to punctuation is defined in terms of the ability to conceive of, understand and adapt to change from within a convergence period. In this scenario (scenario 3 in Figure 25.2), organizational memory could inhibit the organization from strategic foresight, or it could assist it, which depends on the tightness of the deep structure in relation to the amount of slack within the system. If the deep structure is tight, there is no slack to stretch beyond the current configuration, neither conceptually nor 'physically' in terms of flexibility. Thus, the potential for change is a function of the amount of slack, which in turn depends on the tightness of the configuration. As discussed earlier, leverage within the system is brought about by the mechanisms through which memory works and on the width (broad/narrow) and depth (long term/short term) of the content of organizational memory.

Compared to the above two scenarios, this scenario is less difficult than achieving foresight between different convergence periods, but more difficult than achieving foresight within the same period of convergence. Within the overall framework of the level of tightness of deep structure, whether memory helps or hinders foresight hinges on the 'width' of organizational memory. We argue that a broader type of organizational memory will increase the likelihood of strategic foresight, whereas a narrower type of memory will decrease this likelihood. The main reasons for this statement follow.

A broader type of memory will tend to be less restricted by the period's deep structure, whose 'looseness' allows for a critical amount of leverage in relation to memory and its acquisition, retention, and retrieval functions. This means that the information that the organization would acquire and retain would not all be directly necessary, given the current needs of the organization. There is a diversity and excess of resources. More specifically, unresolved problems, or unnecessary solutions that came up at one point or another in the firm's history might get recorded, retained and remain retrievable, even if they do not fit in the current configuration. In other words, information regarding events similar to Kuhn's (1970) anomalies of normal science would have a higher likelihood of getting stored within a broader type of memory than within a narrow one. Thus, although less efficient, because it allocates resources to record and retain information not immediately relevant, a broader type of memory records some of the 'problem areas' of the current organizational configuration within a given period of convergence. And, since it is these problem areas that hold the seeds of the next punctuation, an organization that records anomalies in its memory would have a greater likelihood of opening up the current configuration to change and understanding what drives the upcoming punctuation, compared to an organization that has not recorded these anomalies. Together with controlled retrieval, as opposed to automatic retrieval, retention, and acquisition of anomalies creates the potential for change and drives the kind of deep understanding necessary for foresight from a period of convergence to a period of punctuation. Moreover, taking into account anomalies allows the organization to stretch beyond its current configuration, thus enhancing flexibility, which, as we argued, is a critical component of foresight. Furthermore, working off from anomalies fuels the kind of speculative imagination of the 'second order' that is needed to question and see beyond the 'taken-for-grantedness' brought about by the current rules of the game. Proposition 3 follows.

> *Proposition 3: A broad type of organizational memory will increase the chances of an organization in convergence to foresee the nature of the upcoming punctuation period.*

Foresight from punctuation to convergence: integration
Foresight from within a period of punctuation is aimed towards that point on the horizon when, given the current lack of deep structure, the world starts to make sense again in the form of a new configuration or convergence period. Foresight then is geared towards and promises integration, sensemaking and the enactment of order. In this case, viewing the organization from an organizational becoming perspective where change is considered ontologically prior to the organization makes more sense (Tsoukas and Chia, 2002: 570). Foresight in such cases, we argue, is facilitated by long-term memory and the act of memory retrieval as follows.

Long-term memory familiarizes organizations with and sensitizes them to the rhythm of punctuated equilibrium, that is, the rhythm of change, or, 'the pattern of being and becoming' (Bunge 1979: 332). In a period of punctuation, the guiding principle towards order is derived from this overall rhythm, that is, the organization is geared towards finding a pattern or overall theme among the pieces. Or, as Tsoukas and Chia (2002: 570) put it, 'organization is an attempt to order the intrinsic flux of human action, to channel it towards certain ends, to give it a particular shape, through generalizing and institutionalizing particular meanings and rules'. Moreover, to the extent that retrieving memory consists of the act of piecing together different parts of information, the organization when active, that is in the case of controlled retrieval, is used to making a whole out of parts, the overall need for which is pressing in a situation that can best be described by lack of order. However, the mere expectation of finding the existence of a pattern or theme leaves unexplained what defines patterns of understanding in a period of punctuation in such a way that we can develop the ability to perceive them.

Understanding, to Whitehead, always involves the notion of composition out of which the 'self-evidence of pattern' arises that rests in the mere connectivity of things: 'In the full concrete connection of things, the characters of the thing connected enter into the character of the connectivity which joins them' (1938: 58).

Connectivity, as self-evident, applies beyond logic: 'the aesthetic experience is another mode of the enjoyment of self-evidence' (ibid.: 60). Thus, in understanding, there is a construction of an aesthetic composition and the enjoyment of that composition when grasped. The enjoyment lies in the 'vivid grasp of interdependence' which signals self-evidence, or 'brute' connectivity. If logic enacts order by starting at the parts, which are worked into a whole, 'the characters of the many are understood as permitting that unity of construction' (ibid.: 61). However, in a period of punctuation characterized by an over-whelming amount of uncertainty and possible worlds, logic does not seem to apply, as it would imply building too many different configurations in the search for the most likely one. The shortcomings of logic in a period of punctuation lie in the nature of information processing, as explained through, for instance, the notion of bounded rationality (Simon 1956). In aesthetic composition on the other hand, 'the whole precedes the details' and we then 'pass to discrimination'. In an instant, we grasp the unity in variety, characteristic of the experience of the beautiful. This brings along a 'feeling of enjoyment' of sheer connectivity, which is 'had' not 'known' and insufficient as evidence to advance specific knowledge claims (Shustermann, in Haskins and Seiple 1999). That is, this felt sense of unity that re-establishes fluent activity out of disorder cannot be taken for 'a reason that justifies knowledge, a reason that seems evident and irrefutable by its brute immediacy' (ibid.: 209). However, immediate experience like this is invoked not to justify particular truth claims, but to ground the coherence of any type of thinking for which such claims emerge. As such, it is 'the antecedent cause for knowing something' (ibid.: 209), or 'the opening of awareness of a situation's latent possibilities for meaning' (Garrison 1995: 54). Moreover, aesthetic composition, as a Gestalt through which order is enacted and sense is made, functions, contrasted with logic, as a short cut in information processing. In short, in a period of upheaval, deep understanding by means of aesthetic composition makes coherent thought and meaning possible, which is, given the level of disorder and wealth of possible worlds, the most that foresight can promise. Proposition 4 follows.

Proposition 4: A long-term organizational memory will increase the chances of an organization in a punctuation period foreseeing the nature of the next convergence period.

In this section we have developed four propositions dealing with the role that organizational memory plays in facilitating or hindering strategic foresight in different time periods within a punctuated equilibrium background. However, from discussing about and arguing for these propositions, the contributions of our model and its implications for management practice and research are not immediately obvious, something which we correct in the following section.

Discussion
The purpose of this chapter is to develop a conceptual model that addresses the role that organizational memory plays in a firm's capability for strategic foresight, within a punctuated equilibrium framework. Such a model is of interest to at least two areas of organizational theory. First, it is of interest to the debate on the extent that organizational inertia (Hannan and Freeman 1977) influences the firm's ability to change. Second, it is of interest to the developing area of strategic foresight, because it identifies some of the conditions under which organizational memory helps or hinders a firm in developing a strategic foresight capability.

In addition, the model developed in this chapter and its application on the four foresight scenarios suggested from punctuated equilibrium theory has a number of implications for research and management practice. Starting with the implications of our model for research, one could argue that in addition to the four types of foresight settings identified in this chapter, using and drawing from different theoretical frameworks, different types of foresight typologies could be developed. However, even if we just stick to these four scenarios discussed here, different operationalizations might be needed if we are to measure foresight in the different settings identified here. Furthermore, while this chapter discussed the four foresight scenarios with relation to the firm's organizational memory at a conceptual level, further research could examine these scenarios through historical, in-depth case studies. Such research could lead into inductively developing more detailed theories about the factors and conditions that affect the firm's capacity for foresight in different settings.

Coming now to the managerial implications of our model, there are a few implications that seem to follow. We could argue, for example, that each scenario resembles the setting of a different kind of industry, and that achieving foresight useful for a particular industrial setting would require different tools to facilitate the appropriate kind of understanding and anticipation. For example, for a firm operating in an emerging industry, or an industry that has recently undergone a significant punctuation and has multiple uncertainties coexisting, achieving foresight means being able to determine as accurately as possible the next certainty, the next dominant design, or industrial standard. In such cases, remembering how things worked under the previous regime is quite useless, if not counterproductive, as we have seen with Kodak, where its experience with chemical technology did in fact hinder it in visualizing the digital future and preparing for it (Munir 2006). According to what we have argued here, Kodak might have had a better chance in achieving some level of strategic foresight if its management had used their very long-term organizational memory to see how it was that Kodak was able to get its unassailable position early last century by providing its customers with a simple solution to what was at the time a very messy technological process. Realizing this might have led them in a different and possibly more insightful direction.

Similar examples can of course be developed for other kinds of mature, declining, or growing industries, the point being that our model indicates that managers have to use what they have in their organizational memory in different ways if they are to increase their chances of achieving foresight, depending on the setting in which they find themselves. Such an approach will not only enable managers to optimize the use of their organizational memory, but might also provide indications for those different kinds of retrieval strategies required in different settings.

Conclusions
In conclusion, this chapter drawing on the literature of punctuated equilibrium develops a conceptual model which addresses the impact that organizational memory has in four different foresight scenarios, suggested by punctuated equilibrium theory. In each scenario the role of organizational memory is addressed and propositions concerning its role are developed and argued for. In short it is argued that while organizational memory assists the firm in its capability for strategic foresight within the same period of convergence, it hinders it from achieving foresight across different convergence periods. Furthermore, a broad type of organizational memory assists the firm's foresight capability from a period of convergence to a punctuation period, whereas a long-term type of memory assists the firm in achieving foresight from a punctuation to a convergence period. This model is relevant for both managerial research and practice in that it enables researchers to narrow down the specific conditions under which organizations have to

refer to strategic foresight, and it enables managers to better utilize their organizational memory in different settings.

Notes

* An earlier version of this chapter was presented at the International Conference at the University of Strathclyde, Glasgow, UK, titled: 'Probing the future: developing organizational foresight in the knowledge economy', 11–13 July 2002.

1. 'The Babylonians acquired great forecasting-power, but they conspicuously lacked understanding. To discover that events of a certain kind are predictable – even to develop effective techniques for forecasting them – is evidently quite different from having an adequate theory about them, through which they can be understood' (Toulmin, 1961: 30).

2. Gould (1980: 185) captures the underlying notion of punctuated equilibrium by saying that evolution consists of 'long periods of boredom and short periods of terror'.

3. Gersick (1991) borrows the term 'deep structure' from linguistics (Chomsky 1966), where the term is used to refer to the underlying stable structure of language, which is common for many (if not all) languages, despite their surface structure differences.

4. The term 'schema' is borrowed from cognitive psychology, first defined by Bartlett (1932: 21) as 'an active organization of past reactions or past experiences'.

References

Bartlett, F.C. (1932), *Remembering: A Study in Experimental and Social Psychology*, London: Cambridge University Press.

Bunge, M. (1979), *Causality and Modern Science*, New York: Dover Publications.

Chomsky, N. (1966), *Cartesian Linguistics: A Chapter in the History of Rationalist Thought*, New York: Harper & Row.

Cyert, M.R. and J.G. March (1963), *A Behavioral Theory of the Firm*, 2nd edn 1992, Cambridge: Blackwell.

Eldredge, N. and S.J. Gould (1972), 'Punctuated equilibria: an alternative to phyletic gradualism', in T.J.M. Schopf (ed.), *Models in Paleobiology*, San Francisco: Freeman, Cooper & Co., pp. 82–115.

Garrison, J. (ed.) (1995), *The New Scholarship on Dewey*, Dordrecht: Kluwer Academic.

Gersick, C.J.G. (1991), 'Revolutionary change theories: a multilevel exploration of the punctuated equilibrium paradigm', *Academy of Management Review*, **16** (1), 10–36.

Gould, S.J. (1980), 'The episodic nature of evolutionary change', in *The Panda's Thumb: Reflections in Natural History*, New York: W.W. Norton & Company.

Hannan, M.T. and J. Freeman (1977), 'The population ecology of organizations', *American Journal of Sociology*, **82**, 929–64.

Haskins, C. and D.I. Seiple (eds) (1999), *Dewey Reconfigured: Essays on Deweyan Pragmatism*, Albany, NY: State University of New York Press.

Kahneman, D. (1973), *Attention and Effort*, Englewood Cliffs, NJ: Prentice-Hall.

Kuhn, T. (1970), *The Structure of Scientific Revolutions*, Chicago, IL: University of Chicago Press.

Langer, E.J. (1983), *The Psychology of Control*, Beverly Hills, CA: Sage.

Levitt, T. (2004), 'Marketing myopia', *Harvard Business Review*, **82** (7/8), 138–51.

Miller, D. and P. Friesen (1984), *Organizations: A Quantum View*, Englewood Cliffs, NJ: Prentice-Hall.

Munir, K. (2006), 'Cut ties to sentimental images of the past', *The Financial Times*, 5 December.

Romanelli, E. and M.L. Tushman (1994), 'Organizational transformation as punctuated equilibrium: an empirical test', *Academy of Management Journal*, **37** (5), 1141–66.

Schwenk, C. (1989), 'Linking cognitive, organizational and political factors in explaining strategic change', *Journal of Management Studies*, **26** (2), 177–85.

Shrivastava, P. and S. Schneider (1984), 'Organizational frames of reference', *Human Relations*, **37**, 795–807.

Simon, H.A. (1956), 'Rational choice and the structure of the environment', *Psychological Review*, **63**, 129–38.

Simon, H.A. (1976), *Administrative Behavior*, New York: Free Press.

Slaughter, R.A. (1998), 'Futures studies as an intellectual and applied discipline', *American Behavioral Scientist*, **42** (3), 372–85.

Stuhr, J. (ed.) (1999), *Pragmatism and Classical American Philosophy: Essential Readings and Interpretative Essays*, Oxford: Oxford University Press.

Thompson, J.D. (1967), *Organizations in Action*, New York: McGraw-Hill.

Toulmin, S. (1961), *Forecasting and Understanding*, New York: Harper.

Tsoukas, H. and R. Chia (2002), 'On organizational becoming: rethinking organizational change', *Organization Science*, **13** (5), 567–99.

Tsoukas, H. and J. Shepherd (2004), *Managing the Future: Strategic Foresight in the Knowledge Economy*, Oxford: Blackwell.

Tushman, M.L. and E. Romanelli (1985), 'Organizational evolution: a metamorphosis model of convergence and reorientation', in L.L. Cummings and B.M. Straw (eds), *Research in Organizational Behavior*, vol. 7, Greenwich, CT: JAI Press, pp. 171–222.

Walsh, J.P. and G.R. Ungson (1991), 'Organizational memory', *Academy of Management Review*, **16** (1), 57–91.

Weick, E.K. (2005), 'Review of "Managing the future: foresight in the knowledge economy" edited by Haridimos Tsoukas', *Academy of Management Review*, **30** (4), 871.

Whitehead, A.N. (1931), 'Introduction. On foresight', in W.B. Donham (ed.), *Business Adrift*, New York: Whittlesey House, pp. xi–xxix.

Whitehead, A.N. (1938), *Modes of Thought*, New York: Free Press.

Wong, P.T.P. and B. Weiner (1981), 'When people ask "why" questions, and the heuristics of attributional search', *Journal of Personality and Social Psychology*, **40**, 650–63.

26 Adaptation, inertia and the flexible organization: a study of the determinants of organizational flexibility in an emerging economy*
Andrés Hatum and Andrew M. Pettigrew

Introduction

The business literature on organizational change is replete with prescriptions regarding the management and design that organizations require to confront highly competitive and changeable environments (Miles and Snow, 1986; Pettigrew and Fenton, 2000). But in spite of all the business literature offering these signposts for flexibility, there is little theory on the determinants of organizational flexibility as a way of adapting under environmental turmoil.

In particular, we shall focus our attention on the determinants of organizational flexibility that made it possible for some firms to adapt rapidly in uncertain contexts. Argentina was the selected country due to the competitive environment prevailing there in the 1990s. We shall study the transformation process in four firms – two of which are considered flexible and two less flexible in two different industries: pharmaceuticals and edible oils. Our analysis draws upon longitudinal data collected from the firms by means of interviews, archive material and statistical data. Using an innovative analysis, we combine coding analysis from interview transcripts, statistical analysis and the use of original display charts, to show the determinants of organizational flexibility as a set of organizational capabilities that enabled some firms to adapt rapidly in the changing and highly competitive business environment that prevailed in Argentina in the 1990s.

By means of our analysis we were able to identify a set of five determinants of organizational flexibility: heterogeneity of the dominant coalition, centralization and formalization of decision making, low macroculture embeddedness, environmental scanning and strong organizational identity.

Our findings contribute empirical evidence to the importance of viewing adaptation as a dynamic concept which includes both the managerial choice and the pressures imposed by the internal and external environments in which firms operate. In this context, flexibility is a set of organizational capabilities allowing the firms to adapt rapidly in conditions of environmental turmoil. Organizational flexibility is, in effect, an alternative to strategic foresight.

This chapter is divided as follows. First, we explore the concepts surrounding adaptation and inertia in organizations. Second, we examine in greater depth the literature on determinants of organizational flexibility. Third, we describe the research design: sample selection, data collection and data analysis. Fourth, we discuss and interpret the main findings of this research: the determinants of organizational flexibility. Finally, we provide a summary of the chapter and some concluding remarks.

Review of adaptation and inertial theory

Many writers have characterized today's business environment as 'hypercompetitive' (D'Aveni, 1994; Volberda, 1996, 1999), 'high velocity' (Brown and Eisenhardt, 1997), or shaped by 'jolts' (Meyer et al., 1990). In emerging economies, such as the Argentinian one, these environmental features have been exacerbated by a sudden opening up of the markets to free competition. In these circumstances, rapid adaptive organizational processes are essential to a firm's survival and success (D'Aveni, 1994; Volberda, 1999).

From a social science point of view, organizational adaptation is 'the ability of an organisation to change itself, or the way in which it behaves, in order to survive in the face of external changes which were not predicted in any precise way when the organisation was designed' (Tomlinson, 1976: 533). This definition confirms March's assertion that adaptation is essential to survival: those companies that do not adapt 'seem destined to expire' (March, 1995).

However, in an attempt to distinguish between the different debates within organizational theories, adaptation views of organization development have been contested. Astley and Van de Ven (1983) argue that one of these debates is about the adaptation–selection dichotomy. Even though the adaptation approach is widely accepted in strategy and organization theory (Lewin and Volberda, 1999), some theories emphasize the idea of selection, retention, or inertia (Hannan and Freeman, 1977, 1984; DiMaggio and Powell, 1983).

Those favouring the inertia approach – such as the ecological perspective – stress environmental selection rather than 'selection of the environment' (Child, 1997: 45). For them, organizations are swept along by environmental pressures. These approaches highlight tensions between the possibilities an organization has for adaptation and change, preservation and inertia.

So what makes it possible for organizations to adapt rapidly to environmental changes? How can organizations learn to adapt to volatile conditions? Concepts such as the flexible firm (Volberda, 1999), the innovative firm (Pettigrew et al., 2003), the adaptive firm (Haeckel, 1999), the 'chaordic' learning organization (Eijnatten and Putnik, 2004) or the agile firm (Goldman et al., 1995) were coined as a way of explaining the organizational capabilities needed in organizations to allow them to adjust to the ever-changing environment.

This study draws heavily on the concept of organizational flexibility for two reasons: first, because of its appropriateness to understanding unpredictable and uncertain contexts such as the Argentinian one (D'Aveni, 1994; Dreyer and Gronhang, 2004); second, the concept of organizational flexibility also sheds light on the enhanced capabilities that organizations under environmental turmoil develop to enable them to adapt quickly and undertake great transformations (Bahrami, 1992; Volberda, 1999).

So, why and how can organizations adapt? In particular, what are the contextual, managerial, and organizational challenges that organizations have to meet so that they can adapt? What role do environmental forces play in a firm's adaptation? And does the organization and its top management have an active or reactive role in the adaptation process? By asking two final questions we aim to understand those factors that are preventing firms from adapting: why are organizations inert? And, do inertial forces stem from environmental forces or from within the organization? In our analysis of the adaptation and inertia approaches, we focus on three main issues (that is, role of outer context, organization and top management team) that will help us to determine why and how adaptation is possible and identify the forces that may prevent organizations from adapting.

We therefore use key organizational frameworks to understand the possibilities that organizations have for adaptation and the inertial forces that might prevent them from doing so. Following traditional studies in the field of organizational adaptation and inertia (Lewin et al., 1999; Lewin and Koza, 2001; Lewin and Volberda, 1999) we note four organizational perspectives in which the role of the context, organization and management feature as key elements in understanding a firm's adaptation process. These perspectives are: contingency theory, strategic choice theory, population ecology theory and elements of strategic management theory. In the following pages we briefly describe key organizational frameworks and the dominant themes of these frameworks as they relate to adaptation or inertia.

Organizational adaptation

How can firms adapt? And what is the role of organizational flexibility in a firm's adaptation? The answer is highly dependent on one's conceptions of the environment and perspective on the organization–environment relationship. In this section, two theories dealing with the organization–environment relation are considered: contingency theory and strategic choice theory. These theories may clarify the extent to which the environment affects the possibilities that a firm has of adapting and being flexible.

The old contingency approach was based on the assumption that organizations adjust their aims and shape in order to suit themselves to market and other environmental characteristics (Astley and Van de Ven, 1983; Singh et al., 1986). Burns and Stalker (1961: 21) pointed out: 'Very often, the environment of the person or organisation is itself changing, so that even to maintain the same degree of fitness for survival, people and institutions may have to change their ways'. The consequence of the contingency approach for a firm's adaptation is that the firm should achieve a fit with the changing and competitive environment through 'appropriate organisational form' (Lewin and Volberda, 1999: 522).

On the basis of their qualitative research, Burns and Stalker (1961) identified organizational forms which they characterized as 'mechanistic' and 'organic'. They postulated that the more variable and unpredictable the environment is, the more flexible the organizational structure and process must be to enable the firm to adapt rapidly. According to this perspective, organizational flexibility is considered to be the reactive capacity of organizations to confront turbulent environments (Volberda, 1999).

Burns and Stalker (1961) and Woodward (1965) also emphasize that an organization's successful adaptation to the environment depends on the ability of top management to interpret the conditions facing the firm in an appropriate manner and to adopt relevant courses of action. The role of the top team then is to be reactive and their most important task is to be in tune with the environment (Singh et al., 1986).

Contingency theory is useful in identifying the importance of environmental pressure in organizational life and in balancing out more subjective approaches towards organizational adaptation. In emerging markets in which environmental turmoil is frequent (Hoskisson et al., 2000), it is essential to appreciate the role exerted by the environment in triggering internal changes.

The strategic choice perspective, on the other hand, suggests that proactive adaptability and loose coupling between organizations and environments allows structural variation and renders organizations less vulnerable to homogenizing forces exerted by the environment. Child and several others (Khandwalla, 1977; Hrebiniak and Joyce, 1985) have argued that organizations are not always passive recipients of environmental influence but also have the power to reshape the environment. Organizational flexibility is thus necessary to enable a firm to make rapid and viable choices (Child, 1997) and to enact environments (Weick, 1979). Organizational flexibility will not, however, be a reactive capacity (as it is in contingency theory) but a proactive one (Volberda, 1999).

The strategic choice approach then drew attention to the active role of those who have the power to make decisions. However, new approaches within the theory (Child, 1997; Hrebiniak and Joyce, 1985) argue that organizational adaptation is the result of the interdependence of and interaction between strategic choice and environment. Both agency and environment are necessary for a satisfactory explanation of organizational adaptation.

In this research we view the adaptation process as a dynamic one in which, for any given organization, elements or variables related to managerial choice and environmental influence coexist. But what are the factors that may hinder an organization's ability to adapt? Do those factors stem mainly from the firm's outer context or can inertia be found in the inner context of the organization? Organizational inertia is offered as an explanation as to how and why firms are prevented from adapting.

Organizational inertia
Many authors have argued that organizations are fundamentally inert and therefore constrained in their ability to respond to environmental change (Hannan and Freeman, 1977; Miller and Friesen, 1980). In other words, organizations may be limited in their ability to recognize and act upon opportunities despite the fact that those opportunities are present in their industry.

Early organizational theory researchers recognized some of the negative consequences of bureaucracy (Blau, 1956; March and Simon, 1958). Stinchcombe (1965) suggested that firms tend to become institutionalized and that the basic structure of organizations remains relatively stable over time. More recently, organization theorists have argued that major stimuli are required for organizations to undergo periods of revolution, and therefore organizations are, by nature, sluggish in their ability to respond to environmental change (Miller and Friesen, 1980).

However, population ecology writers have taken a more extreme stance on the subject of organizational inertia. Organizational ecology has developed in response to the reactive adaptation bias generated by contingency theory. It considers the dynamic processes affecting the development of organizational populations over time and, in contrast to the prevailing adaptive perspective, focuses on selection as the main mechanism of adaptation and change. According to this perspective, adaptation and change is severely constrained and most organizations flounder helplessly in the grip of environmental forces (Carroll, 1988).

Hannan and Freeman (1984) argue that inertial properties in organizations are so strong that timely adaptation to environmental change is impossible. When levels of inertia are high, adaptive behaviour is more difficult and the environment selects out those organizations that do not fit (Delacroix and Swaminathan, 1991). For the population ecology approach, environmental selection replaces internal adaptation (Astley and Van de Ven, 1983). As the environment is relentlessly efficient in weeding out any organization that does not fit, the role of managers is therefore insignificant (Hannan and Freeman, 1977, 1984).

In population ecology theory, there is no place for flexibility; rather, population ecology emphasizes the anti-flexibility of organizations and their slowness in responding to changing environmental opportunities and threats. In this view, organizations are rarely able to engage in transformations (Hannan and Freeman, 1984; Carroll, 1988).

Latterly some population ecology theorists, however, have admitted structural change of units. In his study of strategic business exit in Intel Corporation, Burgelman (1994) argued that it was not corporate strategy but the internal selection environment that caused a shift from memory chips to the more profitable microprocessor business. Burgelman found that the context set by top management had strong selective effects on the strategic actions of the firm. Similarly, Noda and Bower (1996) try to explain how selection processes operate within organizations. They reveal how the initial internal constraints in two different companies – BellSouth and US West – shaped the firms' very different strategies in cellular telephony over the 1984–90 period.

While some researchers in the field of population ecology have thus admitted structural change, the general fatalistic tendency of population ecology exposes it to more fundamental criticism. Its underlying theories represent a view of individual–organization interactions that are grounded in the assumption that the human role in organizations is essentially passive (Hannan and Freeman, 1984).

The early ecologist approach also failed to explain several relational and organizational aspects. This approach could not explain situations in which the environment had been altered (that is, regulated environments such as the pharmaceutical industry in this research). Moreover, while theories of structural inertia can explain variation in change across large populations of organizations, they provide less insight into variation in change within organizations. Their tendency to take inertial forces for granted has led population ecologists to overlook the process by which individual firms adapt to environmental changes by renewing their organizations to confront different contextual realities in a competitive way. Nor could it explain how radical change and innovation can occur.

While the population ecology perspective has emphasized the ruthless role of the environment as a key factor in understanding inertia in organizations, elements of the *strategic management* literature have placed considerable importance on internal sources of inertia.

Miller and Chen (1994) point out that competitive inertia reflects the number of market changes a company makes to attract customers and overcome competitors' practices. Inertia would be high when, compared with competitors, firms make few changes in competitive practices. In their analysis of 32 US domestic airlines, Miller and Chen found the sources of competitive inertia in the managers' willingness to act. Like Miller and Chen, Sull (1999a,b) tries to determine what the internal sources of inertia in organizations are. Studying the process of adaptation in Firestone and Laura Ashley, Sull (1999a,b) mentions four factors that may cause companies to fail to adapt appropriately in the event of environmental shifts: strategic frames; processes; relationships; and values. Each of these factors can restrict adaptation. Strategic frames or mental models can act as blinkers and make it difficult to assess competitors, customers and business strategies. Processes may become routines, thus impeding effective responses (that is, as in the case of Firestone and radial technology). Relationships (that is, with customers and suppliers) may fetter the company, thereby limiting flexibility. Finally, the company's set of beliefs may harden into dogma, thereby precluding other business possibilities. Elements of the strategic management literature thus widen our understanding of the problems that the less flexible firms may have when they try to adapt.

Concluding remarks
The review of adaptation and inertial theories has stressed different challenges that organizations have to meet to be able to adapt and those factors that may deter them from doing so. Some perspectives (population ecology, contingency theory) emphasize the constraining influence of contextual forces; others (strategic choice) recognize the opportunities for human agency. Each of these perspectives helps to understand a particular aspect of how organizations develop 'fitness' within a given context, but they do not explain how organizations survive in endogenously dynamic environments and how they cope with unknown future states. In the perspectives analysed, nothing is said about what organizational capabilities are needed to adapt and avoid inertial traps. What are the enhanced capabilities that organizations need to cope with higher levels of disorder? Is it possible for some organizations to learn to adapt to more volatile conditions?

By 'organizational capabilities' we mean the 'unique internal management processes and intangible resources, which are less visible and less easily copied [and which] have come to be seen as potential sustainable sources of advantage' (Galbraith, 1994: 2). Capabilities are developed by organizations as they grow in size and scope (Galbraith, 1994).

Firms that are careful about the capabilities they develop relative to the environment in which they operate can transform and adapt quickly to very dynamic markets (Helfat, 1997, 2000; Eisenhardt and Martin, 2000; Raff, 2000; Huygens et al., 2001). However, under extreme competitive pressure, very persistent or long-standing core capabilities that do not incorporate new competences and skills may evolve into core rigidities (Leonard-Barton, 1992; Rosenbloom, 2000), thereby impeding organizational adaptation. Organizational flexibility is the concept we use in this research to refer to those capabilities that allow organizations to adapt rapidly under conditions of environmental turmoil.

But what determines whether an organization is more or less flexible? In the following section we deal in particular with the literature on organizational flexibility.

Research on determinants of organizational flexibility
'What is organisational flexibility? What does being a flexible firm imply? How do we know if we are in the presence of a flexible organisation?' (Bahrami, 1992: 34). Bahrami indicates that organizational flexibility varies according to the situational context, and attributes this variation to the polymorphous nature of the concept of flexibility. Thus,

the precise meaning of flexibility is dependent on the focus of the research, making it possible to talk about manufacturing flexibility (Adler, 1988; Heijltjes, 2000), numerical flexibility, functional flexibility (Atkinson and Meager, 1986), flexible information systems (Boynton and Victor, 1991; Golden and Powell, 2000), flexible automation (Adler, 1988) and a flexible workforce (Dastmalchian, 2001).

The polymorphous nature of the concept of flexibility indicated by Bahrami (1992) led us to expect difficulties in finding an accurate definition. However, there have been some attempts to bring conceptual clarity into the field of organizational flexibility.

The most relevant work on organizational flexibility has been done by Volberda (1999: 100). In his book he defines organizational flexibility as 'the degree to which an organization has a variety of managerial capabilities and the speed at which they can be activated, to increase the control capacity of management and improve the controllability of the organization'. Through this definition, Volberda articulates one of his core arguments: the flexible organization needs to balance the conflicting demands of stability (namely, control) and dynamism. While many organizational scholars present flexibility and stability as opposite ends of a continuum (Adler, 1988; Boynton and Victor, 1991), Volberda argues that flexibility and stability are two sides of the same coin, in that flexibility without stability results in organizational chaos.

A more comprehensive definition of organizational flexibility is given by Teece et al. (1997). American literature has tended to use the concept of dynamic capabilities to refer to flexibility (ibid.; Rosenbloom, 2000; Tushman and Smith, 2001). In their theoretical framework, which is based on dynamic capabilities as enablers of adaptation and change in a rapidly changing environment, Teece et al. (1997: 516) define dynamic capabilities as 'the firm's ability to integrate, build, and reconfigure internal and external competences to address rapidly changing environments'. More concretely, Teece et al. indicate that dynamic capabilities should be able to enhance technological, organizational, and managerial processes inside the firm to enable it to organize more effectively. Teece et al. (p. 521) also state that firms that have honed and perfected these capabilities are referred to as 'high-flex'.

Daniel and Wilson (2003) pointed out that dynamic capabilities are necessary for business transformation. Others, such as Hatum (2007), have shown that under dynamic and changing environments, organizations have to be flexible and to adapt to continuous change.

In this chapter we use the concept of organizational flexibility in a way similar to that proposed by Teece et al. (1997), considering organizational flexibility as a repertoire of organizational and managerial capabilities that allow organizations to adapt quickly under conditions of environmental change. We must now consider the organizational and managerial capabilities mentioned in the literature that allow organizations to be flexible.

Organizational flexibility as an organizational task
For many authors, the ability of an organization to achieve organizational flexibility depends on the design adequacy of organizational variables, such as technology, structure and culture (Zammuto and O'Connor, 1992; Volberda, 1999). Organizational structure, however, is the main focus of the organizational flexibility writers (Volberda, 1999). The design of the organizational structure encompasses not only the actual distribution

of responsibilities in an organization, but also the planning and control systems set up in the companies, the process of decision making and coordination (Zammuto and O'Connor, 1992; Volberda, 1999).

The theoretical literature on organizational flexibility stresses the importance of multidimensional design (that is, units that can be easily added and subtracted) (Ackoff, 1977), lateral organization (that is, in terms of coordination across functions and businesses) (Galbraith, 1994), innovative structure (that is, a structure that allows the rapid shift of product composition and decentralization of decision making) (Krijnen, 1979), and an organizational design aligned with market needs, the nature of competitors, and the industry (Overholt, 1997).

From an empirical point of view, many other writers have suggested networking forms of organizing (in Liebeskind et al.'s (1996) study of two biotechnology firms), flat structures (in Rosenbloom's (2000) analysis of the process of transformation in NCR), and collaboration partnerships (in Bahrami (1992) and Bahrami and Evans's (1995) study of organizational flexibility in the hi-tech sector in the Silicon Valley). These empirical studies provide evidence of how a flexible design allows companies to become front-line organizations that deal with problems rapidly by reducing the lag between strategy and operation.

One of the problems associated with the foregoing research is that it does not examine how the suggested designs can be implemented in organizations. The authors do not attempt to clarify whether 'a flexible design' is suitable for every company or whether it should apply to those organizations competing in industries with fast product cycles (that is, information technology). This chapter undertakes an examination of the changes in the organizational design of the firms under study from an empirical point of view, and thereby complements the existent theoretical studies.

Besides organizational design, other organizational factors are also mentioned as influencing organizational flexibility. For example, Volberda (1999) considers that culture plays an important role in promoting flexibility. He distinguishes between conservative and innovative culture: an innovative culture (the culture required to encourage flexibility) will be heterogeneous, with a delegative leadership style and managers with an attitude that favours improvisation rather than routine. It will also tolerate ambiguity and autonomy.

Delegation and autonomy are not new ideas in the literature, however (Krijnen, 1979; Overholt, 1997). Overholt examines the organizational archetypes needed under conditions of environmental change and severe competition. He points out that flexibility may be achieved through highly autonomous and decentralized organizations. These firms are process based with fewer layers and high levels of permeability of boundaries.

In flexible organizations, not only are levels of centralization of decision making low, but there is also a low number of formalization processes (Volberda, 1996). Again, Volberda (1996, 1999) indicates that organizations with the potential to be highly flexible have low levels of standardization (that is, specification of the contents and result of the work), and low levels of formalization (that is, job descriptions, work instructions and general rules). (See also Ng and Dastmalchian, 2001.)

Such flexible organizational factors – decentralization and formalization of decision making – will provide great leeway for managers to assume more responsibilities in the firms and to move quickly, thereby achieving fast responsive capacity. The managerial role in achieving organizational flexibility will be the subject of the analysis of the following subsection.

Organizational flexibility as a managerial task

In this subsection we concentrate on two main questions: what are the managerial features of flexible firms? And what kind of flexible capabilities are needed to respond and adapt to sudden environmental shifts?

From a manufacturing perspective, Adler (1988) states that technological flexibility requires managerial flexibility. He highlights the new content of these managerial capabilities as attitudinal, that is taking responsibility for the whole process; cognitive, meaning the process of identifying and solving problems; and, last, systemic interdependence, which is reflected in interfunctional cooperation and teamwork.

Volberda (1999) asserts the importance of a broad knowledge base and a variety of managerial expertise in devising appropriate responses. The heterogeneity of backgrounds and experiences needed in a flexible firm is related to the need to face competitive environments. Boynton and Victor (1991) show how a company such as Corning, which had managers with a broad knowledge base deriving from a variety of expertise, was able to develop capabilities in order to introduce new products and seize market opportunities.

Diverse managerial expertise may encourage the organization to recognize the need for change (Volberda, 1999; Rosenbloom, 2000). Heterogeneity and broad managerial mindsets foster the ability to create and support ideas. Bahrami (1992) points out how the cosmopolitan mindset at Apple Computers has led to different cultural assumptions and premises being incorporated. Volberda (1999) indicates that management must have the ability to identify, experiment and explore new fields and ideas rather than exploiting existing routines.

The literature on organizational flexibility makes a number of predictions about the factors determining the flexibility of an organization. Each company's flexibility will be determined by a variety of organizational and individual factors. At the organizational level, an adequate 'flexible' organizational design and low levels of centralization and formalization of decision making were mentioned. In addition, the literature has suggested that at the top management level, heterogeneity of the managerial team and a broad knowledge base are required to build a flexible organization.

From our analysis three other determinants of organization flexibility emerged inductively: environmental scanning, organizational identity and macrocultural embeddedness. It will be necessary to examine the empirical result of this research in order to understand the extent to which the last three determinants are significant in explaining organizational flexibility.

In summary, this research is guided by three broad questions as follows. Do some firms display more flexibility than others in similar competitive circumstances? Why are some firms able to do so? And last but not least, how do they do it?

Research design

Understanding the determinants of organizational flexibility is an important task to tackle in this research. Therefore, we needed to be both reflective and convincing about the methods used to highlight and analyse the determinants of organizational flexibility. Three main aspects are discussed in this section: sample selection, data collection and data analysis.

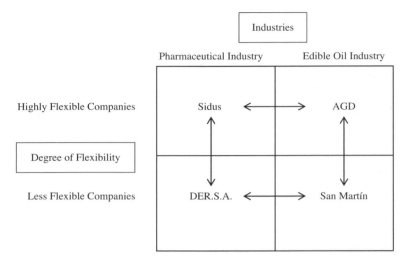

*Figure 26.1   Highly flexible and less flexible companies in the pharmaceutical and edible
             oil industries*

Sample selection
The analysis focuses on four case studies from a population of large indigenous family-
owned businesses in two industries: pharmaceuticals and edible oils. The case studies –
two in each sector – are polar types: one highly flexible firm and another less flexible firm
(see Figure 26.1).

Both the pharmaceutical and edible oil industries were chosen as sites of this research
into organizational flexibility primarily as a result of the strong competitive pressures
these industries underwent during the 1990s. The level of competition they faced during
this period is indicated by the general level of foreign direct investment (FDI).

Argentina was the second largest recipient of FDI in Latin America – after Mexico
– over the 1990–97 period (Toulán and Guillén, 1997). The substantial levels of foreign
investments changed the internal dynamic of the sectors in terms of levels of competition
and efficiency (Dunning, 1993). The food and pharmaceutical sectors are among those
that received most foreign investment.

A list of the first 20 companies in the pharmaceutical and edible oil industries were
compiled and ranked so as to reflect their organizational flexibility according to four
indicators of organizational flexibility deriving from the literature on organizational
flexibility and innovativeness. These indicators are: product innovation, collaboration
and partnerships, and internationalization and diversification. These indicators were
measured as high, medium and low and the companies were ranked accordingly.

Due to the limited number of cases it makes sense to choose polar types as case studies
as they reflect opposite extremes of the phenomena to be studied (Eisenhardt 1989;
Pettigrew 1990). In the ranking, Sidus and DER.S.A. emerged as the most flexible and
least flexible firms, respectively, in the pharmaceutical industry. Similarly, AGD and San
Martín emerged as the most and least flexible firms in the edible oil industry. Table 26.1
shows the company profiles.

Table 26.1   *Company profiles*

Company	Industry	Related businesses	Employees (1999)	Turnover (1999) in US$m
Sidus	Pharmaceuticals	Biotechnology Pharmaceutical products Retail (pharmacies) Intermediary companies Distribution	950	232
DER.S.A.	Pharmaceuticals	Pharmaceutical products (mainly dermatological products)	342	48.2
AGD	Edible oils	Farming Crushing Transport (railways/port) Branding Distribution	1,500	1,042
San Martín	Edible oils	Crushing Port Branding Cotton ginning	350	578.7

Source: Company data.

Data collection

Longitudinal data about the transformation process in the four companies was collected, covering the firms' activities over the 1989–99 period. While 1991 represents the opening up of the Argentinian economy and the starting-point of the market liberalization, 1989 is a critical year for the whole economy – the peak of the 1980s economic crisis. Understanding how organizations transform their core activities can help to shed light on the determinants of organizational flexibility (Djelic and Ainamo 1999; Volberda 1999). The sources of data in the companies were threefold: in-depth interviews; documentary and archival material; and quantitative and statistical data. The quality of the data collection has been the outcome of high-quality access negotiated with the companies.

Fifteen semi-structured interviews were held in each company. People affected by the transformation process – managers and employees, family and non-family members – and those initiators of strategic initiatives that entailed a shift in the core activities of the company were interviewed. A pro-forma interview was used to provide a set of trigger questions to guide the process (Table 26.2).

Data analysis

The data were first stored using a database designed specifically for the task, to avoid what Pettigrew (1990: 281) calls 'death through data asphyxiation'. Writing down analytical chronologies, as suggested by Pettigrew (1990), was the way chosen to display the data and to start shaping possible determinants of organizational flexibility.

To analyse the determinants of organizational flexibility, different methods of analysis were selected based on the empirical tradition in the bodies of literature used in this

Table 26.2   Interviews in the different companies analysed

Company	Board of directors	Top manage-ment	Middle manage-ment	Consultants Others	Total interviews	Family members	Non-family members
AGD	4	6	4	1	15	5	10
Sidus	2	6	5	2	15	6	9
DER.S.A.	3	6	6	0	15	3	12
San Martín	6	3*	8	0	14	7	7

Note: *These are also part of the Board of Directors.

research. This is the case of the following methods used in analysing determinants of organizational flexibility: demographic analysis (for heterogeneity of the dominant coalition); coding analysis (for centralization and formalization of decision making, low macroculture embeddedness, a strong organizational identity and environmental scanning); and significance test (for heterogeneity of the dominant coalition and centralization and formalization of decision making).

Determinants of organizational flexibility
How did the firms in this study build up the flexible capabilities needed to adapt under environmental pressure? Why were some firms able to achieve flexibility while others could not? The analysis of the determinants of organizational flexibility will seek to answer these questions.

The structure of the analysis is similar for the five determinants analysed: first we explain how the determinants are operationalized; second, we analyse and compare the highly flexible and less flexible firms in each industry. Finally, we present some patterns common to the flexible and the less flexible firms.

Characteristics of the dominant coalition
To avoid confusion, it is important to clarify what is understood by dominant coalition. This study uses a broad definition of the dominant coalition as the individuals responsible for determining a firm's direction (Wieserma and Bantel (1992); see also Cyert and March (1963) for organizational coalition). This means that directors of the companies and the top management team are included in the definition of dominant coalition used in this research.

The study of this determinant is operationalized through the demographic studies tradition that analyses demographic variables to understand the characteristics of the management team (Hambrick and Mason 1984; Wieserma and Bantel 1992 among others). To attain a holistic view of the features of the dominant coalition, this chapter uses different variables such as age, tenure in the company, tenure in the role, experience in the industry, experience in the industry and other related industries, and finally, experience in other industries (see Tables 26.3a and b, 26.4a and b and the evolution of the different variables throughout different periods of time[1]). The quantitative

Table 26.3a Demographics of top management team at Sidus and DER.S.A. (mean)

Mean (average)	Companies	Average	1989	1996	1999
Age	Sidus	46.3	48.4	45.6	45.0
	DER.S.A.	54.2	54.0	58.9	49.8
Tenure in company	Sidus	15.0	19.0	13.4	12.6
	DER.S.A.	14.3	16.1	17.8	8.9
Tenure in present role	Sidus	7.9	13.0	5.4	5.2
	DER.S.A.	10.7	11.2	14.3	6.7
Experience in industry	Sidus	18.4	21.6	17.3	16.2
(pharmaceuticals)	DER.S.A.	19.7	19.1	23.1	16.8
Experience in industry	Sidus	19.7	23.8	18.1	17.3
and related industries[1]	DER.S.A.	23.4	23.8	28.1	18.7
Experience in other	Sidus	5.2	0.8	7.0	7.8
industries[2]	DER.S.A.	2.9	2.4	3.2	3.0

Notes:
1. Experience in industry and related industries refers to the number of years working in a traditional pharmaceutical industry and related industries such as health and biochemistry.
2. Experience in other industries refers to the number of years working in industries other than pharmaceuticals.

Table 26.3b Demographics of top management team at Sidus and DER.S.A. (standard deviation)

Standard deviation	Company	1989	1996	1999
Age	Sidus	13.3	9.1	10.3
	DER.S.A.	10.0	11.0	9.0
Tenure in company	Sidus	5.0	10.4	11.0
	DER.S.A.	9.0	8.5	5.6
Tenure in present role	Sidus	3.6	4.2	3.7
	DER.S.A.	5.0	6.4	6.8
Experience in industry	Sidus	4.5	10.3	11.1
	DER.S.A.	9.1	10.7	10.7
Experience in industry	Sidus	3.9	9.9	10.3
and related industries	DER.S.A.	11.1	12.6	12.6
Experience in other	Sidus	1.3	11.1	11.2
industries	DER.S.A.	1.7	2.1	2.1

results of the demographic analysis are combined with qualitative data drawn from the interviews.

Our analysis of the demographics of the top management team and our interviews in the different companies revealed significant differences between highly flexible and less flexible firms (as stated in Tables 26.3a,b and 26.4a,b in the analysis of demographics of the top team of the four companies). While in the highly flexible firms more heterogeneity prevailed among the top team (that is, less years of experience in the industry or related industries, more experience in unrelated industries as shown in Tables 26.3a

Table 26.4a   Demographics of the dominant coalition team at AGD and San Martín (mean)

Mean (average)	Companies	Average	1989	1996	1999
Age	AGD	42.1	43.0	42.6	40.8
	San Martín	53.9	60.5	51.0	50.2
Tenure in company	AGD	11.6	12.3	11.8	10.6
	San Martín	21.1	27.0	17.1	19.1
Tenure in present role	AGD	7.8	10.8	7.1	5.4
	San Martín	12.7	15.5	9.9	12.7
Experience in industry	AGD	13.6	15.9	13.9	10.9
(pharmaceuticals)	San Martín	22.6	30.0	18.1	19.8
Experience in industry	AGD	14.6	18.7	14.2	10.9
and related industries[1]	San Martín	23.3	31.0	18.7	20.2
Experience in other	AGD	4.7	1.3	5.9	6.8
industries[2]	San Martín	1.0	1.25	0.9	0.8

Notes:
1. Experience in the industry and related industry refers to the number of years working in a traditional edible oil industry and related industries such as agrifood industries.
2. Experience in other industries refers to the number of years working in industries other than edible oils.

Table 26.4b   Demographics of the dominant coalition team at AGD and San Martín (standard deviation)

Standard deviation	Company	1989	1996	1999
Age	AGD	10.5	6.0	6.4
	San Martín	10.8	5.4	7.6
Tenure in company	AGD	11.7	8.4	8.8
	San Martín	6.1	6.4	6.9
Tenure in present role	AGD	11	7.9	7.3
	San Martín	1.3	7.6	7.8
Experience in industry	AGD	10.3	7.2	8.7
	San Martín	9.0	5.9	7.1
Experience in industry	AGD	13.5	7.0	8.9
and related industries	San Martín	9.8	6.5	7.6
Experience in other	AGD	1.7	3.4	3.7
industries	San Martín	1.5	1.5	1.2

and 26.4a), the less flexible firms presented a more compact and homogeneous managerial elite (that is, similar average age, experience and background, in Tables 26.3a,b and 26.4a,b).

AGD and Sidus are more heterogeneous than DER.S.A. and San Martín. AGD and Sidus appointed managers from outside the firm before changes in the Argentinian economy had begun. AGD started to appoint executives from outside the firm earlier in the 1980s when the company made its first logistic investments. Sidus, on the other hand, did the same when early in the 1980s it forged a strategic alliance with Merk (the multinational pharmaceutical firm). In addition, the inflow of managers with non-traditional backgrounds in edible oils (that is, in AGD) and pharmaceuticals (that is, in Sidus) reduced the degree to which the company was influenced by institutional pressures. As a manager at AGD stated: 'The variety of experience and backgrounds of our top team allowed us to leapfrog the competition because we were better prepared with more skills than them' (Interview with HR Manager, AGD).

These appointments, together with internal promotion of young executives with different backgrounds and great potential, increased the diversity of views and cognitive mindsets among the top management team. That diversity of mental models generated a variety of interpretations of the firm and its environment. As Eisenhardt and Schoonhoven (1990) argue, the presence of divergent cognitive frameworks is essential in a turbulent environment. It granted AGD and Sidus a deeper understanding of the patterns of change that were occurring and allowed them to decide on the most appropriate actions to take or develop (that is, in both companies the different strategic initiatives). So, in the hypercompetitive environment in which the pharmaceutical and edible oil industries operated in the 1990s, Sidus and AGD were better able to understand the new environment and act more quickly than the less flexible firms.

In contrast, in the less flexible firms the flow of outsiders into senior positions started either late in the 1990s (that is, in the case of DER.S.A., after 1997) or it did not start at all (that is, the case of San Martín in which the managerial positions were all occupied by family members). As a result, in both companies the top team in the 1990s was highly homogeneous as regards both its background and the way they saw the company and its environment. This homogeneity increased the degree to which the company was embedded in the industry macroculture. The lack of cognitive diversity that stemmed from the prevailing homogeneity in DER.S.A. and San Martín's top team also made it difficult for the firms to interpret the signals from the environment and be proactive.

Centralization and formalization of decision making

From our review of the literature on organizational flexibility (Volberda, 1999; Englehardt and Simmons 2002) we would expect that the more formalized and centralized decision making is, the less flexible an organization will be.

Formalization reflects the emphasis on rules, procedures and control when carrying out organizational activities. Formalization is frequently measured by the presence of manuals, job descriptions, procedures and mechanisms of control (Corwin, 1975; Damanpour, 1991).

Centralization, on the other hand, reflects the extent to which decision-making autonomy is dispersed or concentrated. It is generally measured by the degree of participation of organizational members in decision making (Aiken and Hage, 1971; Damanpour, 1991).

To avoid misinterpretation, the interviewees were consistently informed how these concepts of centralization and formalization of decision making were applied in this research. In the light of these definitions, the interviewees were questioned about their perception of the levels of strategic and operational centralization and formalization in Sidus and DER.S.A. throughout the 1989–99 period. For example, were strategic decisions formalized? Were strategic decisions made mainly by the CEO or the board?

The interviewees were also asked to assess the questions according to degree: low, medium–low, medium, medium–high and high. The answers were coded on an ordinal scale starting from 1 (low) to 5 (high). An independent intercoder reliability check gave a score of 87.5 per cent. The reliability score was calculated by the independent recoding of four interviews in each company of the set of questions related to the centralization and formalization process in the four companies. The recoding was then compared with the original coding and the percentage score calculated.

In the flexible firms we found three common patterns in the way they have managed centralization and formalization processes: first, both AGD and Sidus had centralized strategic decision making while the operation of the business was delegated to the managers; second, both firms underwent deep structural reforms; and finally, the formalization levels had increased over time in both firms.

Our analysis of the centralization process at AGD and Sidus highlighted the high level of strategic centralization and low level of operative centralization of decision making (see Figures 26.2 and 26.3, in which the levels of centralization are compared between 1989 and 1999). In both firms, the board delegated the operation of the business to the managers while the board itself concentrated on strategic issues. The reduction of operational centralization increased the autonomy of business managers and with it their freedom to act and be flexible. In so doing, the firms believed that new strategic initiatives would be encouraged and implemented quickly.

The interviewees also stressed the importance of the structural changes throughout the 1990s. For the boards of both AGD and Sidus, changes in the structure of the firms were essential in helping them to delegate and dedicate their premium time to strategic issues.

The changes in the structure helped AGD and Sidus mitigate the possible harmful consequences of the upsurge of formalization (see Figures 26.2 and 26.3, in which the levels of formalization in the late 1990s were similar to 1989 or rose over time). The business units at AGD and the new companies or divisions at Sidus had fewer layers, thus facilitating communication and fast responsiveness. In AGD they claimed: 'We built a flatter structure which was an advantage we had over our competitors. Our flat structure gave the managers more autonomy, and we were very flexible and adapted quickly' (Interview with HR Manager, AGD).

Regarding the less flexible firms – San Martín and DER.S.A. – the main similarities lay in the high levels of centralization and formalization of decision making over time.

Levels of strategic and operative centralization were higher in DER.S.A. and San Martín than in their fellow flexible firms (see Figures 26.2 and 26.3, in which it is clear how the levels of centralization rose over the period analysed). However, it is important to note that in DER.S.A., operative centralization has tended to decrease while in San Martín it has increased. This different tendency over time may be explained by the internal changes that the new CEO in DER.S.A. was trying to implement (in terms of more delegation of the operation to the new top team) after the reshuffle of the top management team in 1997.

The high level of centralization in both San Martín and DER.S.A., as Fredrickson (1986: 284) highlights, increases the probability that cognitive limitations of the top management will constrain the 'comprehensiveness of the strategic process'. Our interviewees have been clear about the lack of fresh ideas or lack of strategic orientation in both San Martín and DER.S.A.

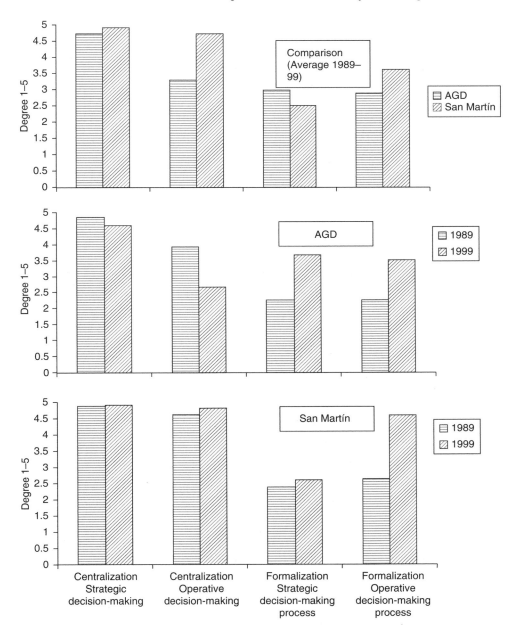

Figure 26.2   Centralization and formalization at AGD and San Martín, 1989 and 1999

Formalization, on the other hand, also presents its differences. Formalization at the operation level was higher in both DER.S.A. and San Martín than in the highly flexible companies, and was increasing over time (Figures 26.2 and 26.3). In San Martín, one inter- viewee indicated: 'The level of bureaucracy in this company stifles our decision-making

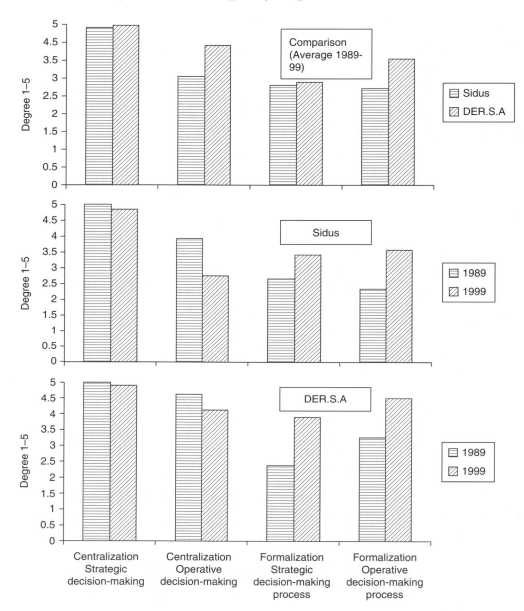

Figure 26.3   Centralization and formalization at Sidus and DER.S.A., 1989 and 1999

process. We suppressed any incentive our managers might have had to innovate' (Interview with Commercial Manager and fourth-generation family member, San Martín).

Conversely, the formalization of the strategic decision-making process varied in both companies: San Martín showed low levels of formalization (even lower than AGD, Figure 26.2) and DER.S.A. saw this level soar over the 1989–99 period (Figure 26.3).

The differences between the companies stem from the ways strategy is formulated and implemented. DER.S.A.'s high level of strategic formalization was the outcome of the implementation of strategic planning and control. San Martín's low level, on the other hand, was the result of informality and lack of strategic planning.

We have seen then how the flexible firms balanced out the effects of different levels of centralization and formalization. The less flexible firms were not able to balance the levels of centralization and formalization needed over different periods. The overlaying of more centralization and formalization in DER.S.A. and San Martín in the 1990s increased the negative influence on organizational flexibility (with the exception of strategic formalization in San Martín, see Figure 26.3).

Macroculture embeddedness
Another factor identified by this study as a determinant of organizational flexibility is the extent to which the companies are embedded in their macroculture. This factor reflects the institutional pressures exerted upon the organization and the speed with which it can adopt new strategies (Abrahamson and Fombrun, 1994; Webb and Pettigrew, 1999),

From our inductive analysis, two factors emerged that indicated the degree of embeddedness of the companies analysed in their macroculture: their perceived similarity and dissimilarity to other firms in the industry; and their degree of connectedness to other firms in the industry.

Institutional theory describes how these factors influence the degree of embeddedness within the industry macroculture. The higher the perceived similarity to others in the industry, the more likely it is that firms will accept the prevailing norms and become more institutionalized in that industry (Greenwood and Hinings, 1996). On the other hand, the degree of connectedness refers to interpersonal contacts between executives in the same industry (Di Maggio and Powell, 1983; Webb and Pettigrew, 1999).

To shed light on the two factors mentioned as influencing the low level of embeddedness within the industry macroculture – perceived similarity and degree of connectedness – the interviewees were asked to answer a set of questions. To understand the perceived similarity/dissimilarity in their macroculture, interviewees were asked about which company or companies were used for benchmarking. Similarly, to understand the level of connectedness, the interviewees were asked whether their company supported any professional association in the industry and, if so, which professional association they supported. Questions were asked regarding the two years, 1989 and 1999.

Answers to each question were displayed in a table and different percentage scores calculated as shown in Tables 26.5–12. An intercoder reliability check gave a reliability score between 85 and 90 per cent. The reliability score was calculated using Huberman

Table 26.5   Level of similarity/dissimilarity within the industry: benchmarking at AGD

With whom is the company benchmarking?	1989 (%)	1999 (%)
Benchmarking with indigenous edible oil companies	61	7
Benchmarking with multinational edible oil companies	44	27
Benchmarking with food-processing companies	0	67

Table 26.6   Level of similarity/dissimilarity within the industry: benchmarking at San Martín

With whom is the company benchmarking?	1989 (%)	1999 (%)
Benchmarking with indigenous edible oil companies	73	87
Benchmarking with multinational edible oil companies	33	33
Benchmarking with food-processing companies	7	0

Table 26.7   Degree of connectedness in the industry: AGD's support for participation in professional associations

Support for participation in professional associations	1989 (%)	1999 (%)
YES. Participation in professional associations is actively supported by the company	80	47
NO. Participation in professional associations is not actively supported by the company	20	53

Table 26.8   Degree of connectedness in the industry: San Martín's support for participation in professional associations

Support for participation in professional associations	1989 (%)	1999 (%)
YES. Participation in professional associations is actively supported by the company	64	79
NO. Participation in professional associations is not actively supported by the company	36	21

Table 26.9   Level of similarity/dissimilarity within the industry: benchmarking at Sidus

With whom is the company benchmarking?	1989 (%)	1999 (%)
Benchmarking with indigenous pharmaceutical companies	87	9
Benchmarking with multinational pharmaceutical companies	20	39
Benchmarking with biotechnology or health companies	7	52

and Miles's (1994) formula: reliability = number of agreements/(total number of agreements + disagreements) over a sample of six interviews, three from each company.

The differences between highly flexible and less flexible firms were self-evident: AGD and Sidus – both highly flexible companies – demonstrate a degree of 'disembeddedness', that is, a low degree of embeddedness (Dacin et al., 1999: 341). On the contrary, the less flexible firms illustrate a higher level of embeddedness in the industry macroculture.

This notion of low embeddedness, or 'disembeddedness', relies on intentional action

Table 26.10   Level of similarity/dissimilarity within the industry: benchmarking at DER.S.A.

With whom is the company benchmarking?	1989 (%)	1999 (%)
Benchmarking with indigenous pharmaceutical companies	91	63
Benchmarking with multinational pharmaceutical companies	18	37
Benchmarking with biotechnology or health companies	0	9

Table 26.11   Degree of connectedness in the industry: Sidus's support for participation in professional associations

Support for participation in professional associations	1989 (%)	1999 (%)
YES. Participation in professional associations is actively supported by the company	40	27
NO. Participation in professional associations is not actively supported by the company	60	73

Table 26.12   Degree of connectedness in the industry: DER.S.A.'s support for participation in professional associations

Support for participation in professional associations	1989 (%)	1999 (%)
YES. Participation in professional associations is actively supported by the company	53	73
NO. Participation in professional associations is not actively supported by the company	47	27

by AGD and Sidus to step back from institutional frameworks of cognition, culture and the social structure of inter-actor relations. This was indicated by the perceived high levels of dissimilarity and low levels of connectedness in both companies (see Tables 26.5, 26.7, 26.9 and 26.11 in which the percentages show the differences of connectedness and similarity over time). San Martín and DER.S.A., on the other hand, demonstrated high levels of perceived similarity and connectedness over time (see Tables 26.6, 26.8, 26.10 and 26.12).

The flexible companies in this study adapted by exploring new competitive advantages but moving rapidly from one advantage to another, from one series of short-lived actions to another, thereby disrupting the marketplace (March, 1995; Lewin et al., 1999; Lewin and Volberda, 1999). The most flexible companies in this study showed what Tushman and Anderson (1986) and Anderson and Tushman (1990) called 'competence-destroying discontinuities' instead of 'competence-enhancing discontinuities' (that is, AGD through strengthening its logistic chain and through launching its branding strategy; Sidus through its biotechnological initiative and through its retail strategy).

DER.S.A. and San Martín, on the other hand, did not show any of the patterns evidenced by AGD and Sidus. On the contrary, their strategic initiatives were isomorphic with the predominant strategies in the sector (DiMaggio and Powell, 1983). The institutional pressures these firms had to conform to and the high level of similarity to other companies in their sector meant that it was very difficult for them to achieve non-isomorphic behaviour such as that found in AGD and Sidus.

The study of the cognitive mechanisms of the organization is concerned with the way the frameworks of meaning affect individual and corporate actors as they interpret and make sense of their world (Dutton and Dukerich, 1991). With a more heterogeneous management team, the flexible firms had the possibility of a broader cognitive range that helped them to act fast and take risks (that is, such as the strategic initiatives undertaken by the flexible firms). The less flexible firms, however, with a more compacted and homogeneous top team with background experiences mainly in the edible oil and pharmaceutical industries, were constrained by institutional pressures and thus their strategies were isomorphic with the rest of the industry.

Environmental scanning
Organizations must be able to cope with the instability and turmoil of the environment in which they function. To compete successfully, policy makers have to obtain superior information about the environment in which their company is participating (Duncan, 1972). Environmental scanning is the means by which managers can perceive and cope with external events and trends (Pettigrew and Whipp, 1991).

So, why is it important for a flexible company to be aware of the mechanism of scanning the environment? Thomas et al. (1993) argue that when managers implement mechanisms to increase information use by scanning the environment, they increase the likelihood of interpreting issues quickly and sensing the controllability of the process. This last idea of fast responsiveness capacity is reinforced by Pettigrew and Whipp (1991) and Garg et al. (2003), who emphasize that companies that can absorb signals and mobilize resources from the environment will be more proactive and able to complete successful changes. Thus, scanning may represent a 'dynamic capability' for the firm (Eisenhardt and Martin, 2000).

From the inductive analysis, two indicators emerged as factors illustrating the importance of environmental scanning in the companies analysed. First, under severe competition the firms sought new sources of information over the 1989–99 period and second, formal structures as well as informal mechanisms to scan the environment were set up.

Pettigrew and Whipp (1991), recognize that environmental scanning happens across the organization. They also point out that assuming that a single specialist can by him/herself achieve an adequate interpretation of the outer context is highly dangerous. Therefore, formal structures for scanning the environment are not only not enough, but also dangerous as they can lead the organization to inadequate interpretations. More informal ways of scanning are also necessary.

What are the similarities and differences between the scanning behaviour of the flexible and less flexible firms? And what has influenced that behaviour?

In the flexible companies we found three common patterns in the way they scanned the environment: first, both AGD and Sidus created formal and informal structures of scanning; second, both companies attempted to create an external openness and orientation;

and, finally, the scanning behaviour of both companies was boosted by the new mental models that prevailed during the 1990s.

Regarding the first aspect, AGD and Sidus tried to limit the ambiguity of the environment by setting up information processing structures (Thomas et al., 1993) and informal mechanisms of scanning (Pettigrew and Whipp, 1991). AGD set up the Economic Analysis Unit and Sidus convened three units to keep the company abreast of the macroeconomic situation, the sector, and legal and regulatory changes.

The second aspect – external openness and orientation – was also seen as a common factor in both AGD and Sidus. Externally oriented companies are more able to sense competitors' moves (Thomas et al., 1993) and perceive themselves as more capable of implementing competitive responses than internally focused firms. Managers in these firms are also more confident at creating a fit between the organization and the environment by using environmental scanning (Smith et al., 1991; Barr and Huff, 1997).

It was essential for AGD and Sidus to scan the environment to become externally oriented:

> From the foundation of the company, the founders were aware of the importance of understanding what was going on outside the company. We were never a self-absorbed company. We were always aware of the importance of being externally oriented . . . Every employee is aware of the importance of having an open mind and catching all they can from the sector, competitors and customers. This is our constant message to them. (Interview with Director, AGD)

> Watching what was going on outside the company, and observing the trends and changes in the competition was the only way of succeeding, we found. This [external orientation] helped us to seize the opportunity while others [competitors] were more concerned with domestic problems. (Interview with family member and Executive Director of Retail Businesses, Sidus)

The third common aspect we found in AGD and Sidus was the influence of the new mental models on their scanning behaviour. While analysing the heterogeneity of the dominant coalition as a determinant of organizational flexibility, we flagged the importance of the cognitive diversity or diversity of mental models in the dominant coalition. These new mental models helped managers to sense signals from the outer context and it also helped them to make sense of those signals (Pettigrew and Whipp, 1991: 117).

> The fact that we have changed the profile of our management over the last 10 years to suit the requirements of the Argentinian environment, also swayed our decision-making process. Managers are fully aware of what is happening in the external context through our department of economic studies and their own information, reports and contacts. We have internal meetings or workshops – a word that is trendy now – to clarify and share information and make decisions accordingly. (Interview with Director, AGD)

> Before, we [the Board] made decisions by relying on common sense. Today things are different. The new professionals come better prepared and are very quick off the draw. That is better because it accelerates our response. (Interview with President and CEO, Sidus)

Regarding the less flexible firms – San Martín and DER.S.A. – the main similarities lay in the lack of a formal structure for scanning and the importance of scanning the general environment instead of the task environment during the 1980s.

Neither San Martín nor DER.S.A. have formal structures for scanning. There are different reasons for this lack of formal structure. In San Martín they claimed that there was no formal structure because there was no need or because the main scanning activity fell to the board of directors. In DER.S.A., on the other hand, they are more hesitant regarding the usefulness of such a structure: 'We are not a big enough company to afford an area fully dedicated to assessing the context. We found, however, that companies in the sector are setting up these structures. We have still not made up our mind about the best route to follow' (interview with CEO, DER.S.A.).

In the 1980s, both companies also highlighted the importance of scanning the general environment. This attitude has changed since 1990 and the focus of the scanning behaviour has been placed firmly on the task environment. The lack of support in the 1980s for task scanning in the companies had harmful consequences for business, as can be seen in the opinion of the interviewees:

> The problems we have are the result of not caring much about our customers' taste and our competitors' moves. Now there is an awareness that the customer is the king and our competitors are there to watch them and care about what they are doing. (Interview with Promotion and Sales Manager, DER.S.A.)

> We were a closed company. The result in San Martín was clear: crisis, low profitability and a low level of professionalism in the company. (Interview with Commercial Manager, San Martín).

The highly flexible firms in this research sought new sources of information much more actively and applied a rich array of formal and informal mechanisms for scanning the environment. The less flexible firms had a less well organized approach to environmental scanning. The outcome of the scanning behaviour was self-evident: flexible firms anticipated changes in the sector and seized opportunities while the less flexible firms simply could not.

Organizational identity
Why does the concept of organizational identity emerge as an important one in understanding how flexible firms adapt? And what are the main features of this concept of organizational identity?

Albert and Whetten (1985) characterize organizational identity as a concept with three dimensions: first, what is considered central to the organization; second, what makes the organization distinctive; and finally, what is perceived by its members to be an enduring or continuing feature linking the present of the organization with its past.

At the heart of this definition are core values that make organizations act or react in a particular way and are the lenses through which managers interpret organization-level issues (Dutton and Penner, 1993; Gioia and Thomas, 1996; Collins and Porras, 2000).

Therefore, how can a firm's identity enhance or harm organizational flexibility? How can identity and change become a constructive tension? Some writers on organizational identity emphasize that because organizational identity is composed of values that are enduring and deeply ingrained, it is likely to provide a natural inertial force (Reger et al., 1994; Stimpert et al., 1998) and cause resistance to change (Dutton and Dukerich, 1991).

The questions that emerge are: what type of organizational identity do the flexible and less flexible firms have? And how were the companies' organizational identity – through their set of core values – enablers or constrainers of their organizational flexibility?

In order to understand how the identity of the company was forged and how values evolved during the tenures of successive generations of family members (AGD and Sidus is in its second-generation tenure and San Martín and DER.S.A. in its third) quotations that best illustrated the sharing of a particular value throughout the generations of family owners or the incorporation of new values into the companies were selected and coded. An intercoder reliability check from three speeches from each company with an independent coder gave a score of 78 per cent This score is the result of applying Huberman and Miles's (1994) formula: reliability = number of agreements/(total number of agreements + disagreements).

The main difference between highly flexible and less flexible firms is in the way their identity – through their organizational values – helped them to change or trapped them in inertial forces.

However deeply rooted, the strong identities of both AGD and Sidus did not trap them in the rigidity of inertial forces. On the contrary, both companies were able to change quickly and smoothly without affecting their organizational core values. So how were AGD and Sidus able to cope with the relationship between strong identity and change? And why did San Martín and DER.S.A. fail over time to undertake substantial transformations?

Both AGD and Sidus incorporated values related to innovation and change (in AGD values such as agile decision making and innovation; in Sidus values such as innovation and risk taking). The incorporation of these values enabled them to undertake major transformations without damaging their core identities and yet avoiding resistance to change (Barney et al., 1998).

San Martín and DER.S.A., on the other hand, rejected those values from a previous generation that emphasized change or transformation. San Martín, for example, rejected the value of innovativeness. DER.S.A., conversely, dismissed the value of risk taking that had been emphasized by previous generations.

The strong sense of identity gave the most flexible companies the organizational anchor they needed to be able to move forward and change (Gustafson and Reger, 1995; Calori et al., 2000). By maintaining core values but changing their strategies, products and processes, AGD and Sidus managed to transform themselves without creating internal turmoil. The interviews are revealing in this respect:

> Over the 1990s the company has changed a lot. However, if you ask an employee whether they have felt the changes, they would say that they had not noticed internal turmoil. They did not feel threatened by the changes. I do not know how or why this has happened. However, if you compared our business now and ten years ago, you would think we were a different company. (Interview with Director, AGD)

> One amazing aspect of this company is that over the last decade or over the last thirteen years, Sidus has shifted its strategy completely but we still have the spirit of the old times, even similar traditions and stories. We did not lose the thread that links us with our past, although we look to the future – a wise combination that was fostered by the founders and their children. (Interview with HR Manager, Sidus)

We have therefore underlined the critical role of identity in the process of change. Both AGD and Sidus were conservative about their core values but dynamic at the same time. This dynamism is represented by organizational values that were enablers of change and

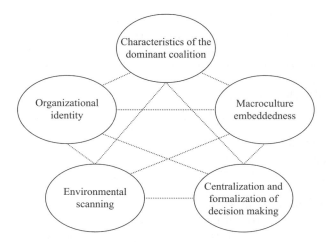

Figure 26.4   Interconnection of determinants of organizational flexibility

transformation. The strong identity found at Sidus and AGD did not imply, as some writers in the field of organizational identity state, an inertial force impeding change and transformation. On the contrary, their strong organizational identity enhanced their organizational flexibility by providing the anchor they needed to change, try new things and take risks.

Interconnection of determinants of organizational flexibility
The results of the analysis of determinants of organizational flexibility are revealing in several aspects. First, they give an insight into the process of adaptation in emerging countries; second, they clarify the process of organizational flexibility in family-owned businesses. Finally, they reveal some of the characteristics of the content and process of being flexible.

So far, we have considered the different determinants of flexibility individually, and have not addressed the linkages between them. The evidence provided suggests that there is an interconnection between the five determinants of organizational flexibility, which facilitated the rapid adaptation in the flexible firms analysed.

The analysis of the determinants of organizational flexibility highlights first the way that companies in emerging countries and under environmental turmoil adapt. What stands out in this analysis is the way the five determinants we have analysed individually in previous pages form an interconnected model that enhances our understanding of the way flexible firms have successfully adapted in conditions of environmental turmoil. This model (see Figure 26.4) is not a prescriptive one. On the contrary, it has emerged from the interplay of the initial theoretical framework and the empirical research undertaken in the four companies as shown throughout this chapter.

Figure 26.4 illustrates the existent interrelation between different determinants of organizational flexibility as revealed by the evidence provided in this chapter. This relationship is shown through dotted lines. The lines represent a qualitative interpretation and do not imply a quantitative relationship.

The inflow of new managers with diverse experience background in the 1980s and early

1990s helped both AGD and Sidus to reduce the influence of institutional pressures. The heterogeneous top team had different cognitive frameworks that also both helped the firms to sense the signals from the environment and broadened their capacity for interpretation. As a result, both AGD and Sidus explored new strategic initiatives and became either early adopters or first movers of strategies (that is, Sidus in biotechnology and retail in the pharmaceutical industry; AGD in branding and logistics in the edible oil industry).

The importance of the low level of macroculture embeddedness of AGD and Sidus (that is, through the low level of connectedness and similarity in their industries) has been demonstrated by the fact that both firms were able to move rapidly and anticipate other competitors' moves. The 'disembeddedness' of AGD and Sidus from their macroculture was facilitated first, by mechanism of scanning (that is, formal and informal mechanisms as previously analysed) and second, by managers who came from industries other than those in which the firms participated.

The low levels of centralization and formalization demonstrated by the flexible firms, on the other hand, increased the possibilities the top team had for interacting more (that is, the constructive conflict we have analysed in this chapter), participating in decision making (that is, through the process of delegation started by the boards of both Sidus and AGD in the 1990s), and speeding up the responses of both firms when needed (that is, the strategic initiatives of the flexible firms).

Scanning the environment in the flexible firms not only became a critical factor for anticipating competitors' actions (that is, through the firms' formal and informal mechanism) but also influenced other determinants of organizational flexibility. Similarly, scanning has also been important in the firms' decisions to rearrange their structure and initiate a delegation process to allow greater participation of the business managers in operative decisions and allow the boards of AGD and Sidus to perform a strategic role in the firms.

Finally, the strong organizational identity of AGD and Sidus represented by their set of core values impacted on the rest of the determinants. By supporting values related to change and innovation (such as a risk-taking attitude and innovation in Sidus, and agile decision making and innovation in AGD), the firms were able to avoid isomorphic behaviour in their industries. The same set of values enabled the firms to achieve external openness in an attempt to find new opportunities and maintain the competitive advantages that made them successful at adapting quickly. AGD's and Sidus's set of beliefs also made it necessary for managers to realize those values. Finally, the values also necessitated organizational arrangements to enact those values. The changes in structure and delegation process implemented in AGD and Sidus were the fruit of the companies' values of innovation and change.

The five determinants of organizational flexibility interconnected and complemented each other in a way that allowed the flexible firms to adapt rapidly under environmental turmoil, to move fast and first in their industries (that is, through their strategic initiatives) and to cope with political and economic changes (that is, changes in regulations and government policies).

Conclusion

Throughout this chapter we have further developed the term 'organizational flexibility' to refer to the repertoire of organizational and managerial capabilities that allow organizations to adapt quickly under conditions of environmental change. The term 'organizational flexibility' has previously been used to refer to the means firms have for limiting the impact of environmental change on the organization (Ansoff, 1988). In Ansoff's words, the aim of organizational flexibility is to provide the firm with a buffer to protect the organization from disturbances so that uncertainty will be reduced. However, the passive connotation of the idea of organizational flexibility as used by Ansoff does not result in fundamental changes to the organization.

Nevertheless, we have demonstrated the significance of a much more active interpretation of organizational flexibility than that offered by Ansoff. The active interpretation includes factors that made the flexible firms analysed highly responsive to environmental change, allowing them to adjust their strategy and organization quickly to exploit changes in their environments. Flexible firms were able to respond successfully to sudden environmental changes and able to build up new organizational capabilities (that is, flexible capabilities) if required.

Flexible organizations do not just respond quickly to change in the environment, they also proactively influence that environment and force others to match their moves. AGD's and Sidus's strategic initiatives have changed the map of competition in their industries as they became first movers or early adopters of strategies, while other companies attempted to imitate the strategies adopted by Sidus and AGD in their respective industries.

In the case of the flexible firms analysed in this chapter, organizational flexibility also involved adaptation to environmental turmoil across the organization and at different levels within the organization, namely the strategic, organizational and managerial levels. Both AGD and Sidus have simultaneously changed their strategic orientation (that is, both firms invested backwards and forwards in the chain of value of their respective industries), while transforming their organizations (that is, introducing new managerial skills, and working on new organizational practices such as enhancing the delegation process, developing more professional management and a structure that stresses operational autonomy).

In emerging countries, shaped by jolts and turbulence, organizational flexibility might be a way not only of adapting quickly under conditions of environmental change, but also of surviving when others are succumbing under the threats of deep transformations of the outer context. Given the quickly changing nature of organizational environments, developing organizational flexibility is in effect an act of strategic foresight boosting the capacity of firms to strategize and organize under conditions of environmental turmoil and high levels of competition.

Notes

* The empirical results of this chapter have previously been published in the *British Journal of Management*, **17** (2), 115–37 (2006).
1. The three periods of time in the analysis were decided according to the following criteria: 1989 represents the starting-point of the analysis and shows the companies before the opening up of the markets for competition. The year 1996 is a date after a period or five years of far-reaching changes up to the Mexican crisis (1995). During the 1990–95 period, the companies under analysis underwent important changes in terms of the renewal of their top managerial team. Finally, 1999 represents the end of a period of a turnaround for the less flexible companies due to strategic changes these companies underwent, thus impacting on the formation of the top team. For the most flexible firms this year represents a consolidation of their strategies (the consolidation process was done between 1996 and 1999).

References

Abrahamson, E. and Fombrun, C.J. (1994), 'Macrocultures: determinants and consequences', *Academy of Management Review*, **19**(4), 728–55.

Ackoff, R.L. (1977), 'Towards flexible organizations: a multidimensional design', *OMEGA*, **5**(6), 649–62.

Adler, P.S. (1988), 'Managing flexible automation', *California Management Review*, **30**(3), 34–56.

Aiken, M. and Hage, J. (1971), 'The organic organization and innovation', *Sociology*, **5**, 63–93.

Albert, S. and Whetten, D.A. (1985), 'Organizational identity', in L.L. Cummings and B.M. Staw, *Research in Organizational Behaviour*, Vol. 7, Greenwich, CT: JAI Press, pp. 263–95.

Anderson, P. and Tushman, M.L. (1990), 'Technological discontinuities and dominant designs: a cyclical model of technological change', *Administrative Science Quarterly*, **35**, 604–33.

Ansoff, I.H. (1988), *Corporate Strategy*, London: Penguin Books, rev. edn.

Astley, G.W. and Van de Ven, A. (1983), 'Central perspectives and debates in organization theory', *Administrative Science Quarterly*, **28**, 245–73.

Atkinson, J. and Meager, N. (1986), 'Is flexibility just a flash in the pan?', *Personnel Management*, **18**(9), 26–9.

Bahrami, H. (1992), 'The emerging flexible organization: perspectives from Silicon Valley', *California Management Review*, **34**(4), 33–52.

Bahrami, H. and Evans, S. (1995), 'Flexible re-cycling and high-technology entrepreneurship', *California Management Review*, **37**(3), 62–89.

Barney, J.B., Bunderson, J.S., Foreman, P., Gustafson, L.T., Huff, A.S., Martins, L.L., Reger, R.K., Sarason, Y. and Stimpert, J.L. (1998), 'A strategy conversation on the topic of organization identity', in D.A. Whetten and P.C. Godfrey (eds), *Identity in Organizations*, Newbury Park, CA: Sage, pp. 99–168.

Barr, P.S. and Huff, A.S. (1997), 'Seeing isn't believing: understanding diversity in the timing of strategic response', *Journal of Management Studies*, **34**(3), 337–70.

Blau, P.M. (1956), *Bureaucracy in Modern Society*, New York: Random House.

Boynton, A.C. and Victor, B. (1991), 'Beyond flexibility: building and managing the dynamically stable organization', *California Management Review*, **34**(1), 53–66.

Brown, S.L. and Eisenhardt, K.M. (1997), 'The art of continuous change: linking complexity theory and time-paced evolution in relentlessly shifting organizations', *Administrative Science Quarterly*, **42**, 1–34.

Burgelman, R.A. (1994), 'Fading memories: a process theory of strategic business exit in dynamic environments', *Administrative Science Quarterly*, **39**, 24–56.

Burns, T. and Stalker, G.M. (1961), *The Management of Innovation*, London: Tavistock.

Calori, R., Baden-Fuller, C. and Hunt, B. (2000), 'Managing change at Novotel: back to the future', *Long Range Planning*, **33**, 779–804.

Carroll, G.R. (1988), 'Organizational ecology in theoretical perspective', in Carroll (ed.), *Ecological Models of Organizations*, Cambridge, MA: Ballinger, pp. 1–6.

Child, J. (1997), 'Strategic choice in the analysis of action, structure, organizations and environment: retrospect and prospect', *Organization Studies*, **18**(1), 43–76.

Collins, J.C. and Porras, J.I. (2000), *Built to Last*, London: Random House Business Books.

Corwin, R.G. (1975), 'Innovation in organizations: the case of schools', *Sociology of Education*, **48**, 1–37.

Cyert, R.M. and March, J.G. (1963), *A Behavioral Theory of the Firm*, Englewood Cliffs, NJ: Prentice-Hall.

D'Aveni, R.A. (1994), *Hyper-Competition*, New York: Free Press.

Dacin, T.M., Ventresca, M.J. and Beal, B.D. (1999), 'The embeddedness of organizations: dialogue and directions', *Journal of Management*, **25**(3), 317–56.

Damanpour, F. (1991), 'Organizational innovation: a meta-analysis of effects of determinants and moderators', *Academy of Management Journal*, **34**(3), 555–90.

Daniel, E.M. and Wilson, H.N. (2003), 'The role of dynamic capabilities in e-business transformation', *European Journal of Information Systems*, **12**(4), 282–96.

Dastmalchian, A. (2001), 'Workplace flexibility and the changing nature of work: an introduction', *Revue Canadienne de Sciences de l'Administration*, **18**(1), 1–4.

Delacroix, J. and Swaminathan, A. (1991), 'Cosmetic, speculative, and adaptive organizational change in the wine industry: a longitudinal study', *Administrative Science Quarterly*, **36**, 631–61.

DiMaggio, P.J. and Powell, W.W. (1983), 'The iron cage revisited: Institutional isomorphism and collective rationality in organizational fields', *American Sociological Review*, **48**(April), 147–60.

Djelic, M.-L. and Ainamo, A. (1999), 'The coevolution of new organizational forms in the fashion industry: a historical and comparative study of France, Italy and the United States', *Organization Science*, **10**(5), 622–37.

Dreyer, G. and Gronhang, D. (2004), 'The phenomenon of organizational evolution', *Leadership and Organization Development Journal*, **23**(3–4), 200–215.

Duncan, R.B. (1972), 'Characteristics of organizational environments and perceived environmental uncertainty', *Administrative Science Quarterly*, **3**, 313–27.

Dunning, J.H. (1993), *Multinational Enterprises and the Global Economy*, Reading, MA: Addison-Wesley.
Dutton, J.E., and Dukerich, J.M. (1991), 'Keeping an eye on the mirror: image and identity in organizational adaptation', *Academy of Management Journal*, **34**(3), 517–54.
Dutton, J.E. and Penner, W.J. (1993), *The Importance of Organizational Identity for Strategic Agenda Building*, Chichester: John Wiley.
Eijnatten, F.M. and Putnik, G.D. (2004), 'Enterprise: structural change', *American Sociological Review*, **49**(2), 100–150.
Eisenhardt, K.M. (1989), 'Building theories from case study research', *Academy of Management Review*, **14**(4), 532–50.
Eisenhardt, K.M. and Martin, J.A. (2000), 'Dynamic capabilities: what are they?', *Strategic Management Journal*, **21** (Special Issue), 1105–21.
Eisenhardt, K.M. and Schoonhoven, C.B. (1990), 'Organizational growth: linking founding team, strategy, environment, and growth among U.S. semiconductor ventures, 1978–1988', *Administrative Science Quarterly*, **35**, 504–29.
Englehardt, C.S. and Simmons, P.S. (2002), 'Organizational flexibility for a changing world', *Leadership Development Journal*, **23**(3) May, 113–21.
Fredrickson, J.W. (1986), 'The strategic decision process and organizational structure', *Academy of Management Review*, **11**(2), 280–97.
Galbraith, J.R. (1994), *Competing with Flexible Lateral Organizations*, Reading, MA: Addison-Wesley.
Garg, V.K., Walters, B.A. and Priem, R.L. (2003), 'Chief executive scanning emphases, environmental dynamism, and manufacturing firm performance', *Strategic Management Journal*, **24**, 725–44.
Gioia, D.A. and Thomas, J.B. (1996), 'Identity, image, and issue interpretation: sensemaking during strategic change in academia', *Administrative Science Quarterly*, **41**, 370–403.
Golden, W. and Powell, P. (2000), 'Towards a definition of flexibility: in search of the Holy Grail?', *OMEGA*, **28**, 373–84.
Goldman, S.L., Nagel, R.N. and Preiss, K. (1995), *Agile Competitors and Virtual Organizations*, New York: Van Nostrand Reinhold.
Greenwood, R. and Hinings, C.R. (1996), 'Understanding radical organizational change: bringing together the old and the new institutionalism', *Academy of Management Review*, **21**(October), 1022–54.
Gustafson, L.T. and Reger, R.K. (1995), 'Using organizational identity to achieve stability and change in high velocity environments', *Best Papers Proceedings Academy of Management Journal*, 464–8.
Haeckel, S.H. (1999), *Adaptive Enterprise*, Boston, MA: Harvard Business School Press.
Hambrick, D.C. and Mason, P.A. (1984), 'Upper echelons: the organization as a reflection of its top managers', *Academy of Management Review*, **9**(2), 193–206.
Hannan, M.T. and Freeman, J. (1977), 'The population ecology of organizations', *American Journal of Sociology*, **82**(5), 929–64.
Hannan, M.T. and Freeman, J. (1984), 'Structural inertia and organizational change', *American Sociological Review*, **49**(April), 149–64.
Hatum, A. (2007), *Adaptation of Expiration in Family Firms: Organizational Flexibility in Emerging Economies*, Cheltenham, UK and Northampton, MA, USA: Edward Elgar.
Heijltjes, M.G. (2000), 'Advanced manufacturing technologies and HRM policies. Findings from chemical and food and drink companies in the Netherlands and Great Britain', *Organization Studies*, **21**(4), 775–805.
Helfat, C.E. (1997), 'Know-how and asset complementarity and dynamic capability accumulation: the case of R&D', *Strategic Management Journal*, **18**(5), 339–60.
Helfat, C.E. (2000), 'The evolution of firm capabilities', *Strategic Management Journal*, **21** (Special Issue), 955–9.
Hoskisson, R.E., Eden, L., Lau, C.M. and Wright, M. (2000), 'Strategy in emerging economies', *Academy of Management Journal*, **43**(3), 249–67.
Hrebiniak, L.G. and Joyce, W.F. (1985), 'Organizational adaptation: strategic choice and environmental determinism', *Administrative Science Quarterly*, **30**, 336–49.
Huberman, A.M. and Miles, M.B. (1994), 'Data management and analysis methods', in K.N. Denzin and S.Y. Lincoln (eds), *Handbook of Qualitative Research*, Thousand Oaks, CA: Sage, pp. 428–44.
Huygens, M., Baden-Fuller, C., van den Bosch, F.A.J. and Volberda, H.W. (2001), 'Co-evolution of firm capabilities and industry competition: investigating the music industry, 1977–1997', *Organization Studies*, Special Issue: *Multilevel Analysis and Co-evolution*, **6**, 971–1011.
Khandwalla, P.N. (1977), *The Design of Organizations*, New York: Harcourt Brace Jovanovich.
Krijnen, H.C. (1979), 'The flexible firm', *Long Range Planning*, **12**, 63–75.
Leonard-Barton, D. (1992), 'Core capabilities and core rigidities: a paradox in managing new product development', *Strategic Management Journal*, **13**, 111–25.
Lewin, A.Y. and Koza, M.P. (2001), 'Empirical research in co-evolutionary processes of strategic adaptation

and change: the promise and the challenge', *Organization Studies*, Special Issue: *Multi-level Analysis and Co-evolution*, **6**, v–xi.

Lewin, A.Y., Long, C.P. and Carrol, T.N. (1999), 'The coevolution of new organizational forms', *Organization Science*, **10**(5), 535–50.

Lewin, A.Y. and Volberda, H.W. (1999), 'Prolegomena on coevolution: a framework for research on strategy and new organizational forms', *Organization Science*, **10**(5), 519–34.

Liebeskind, J.P., Oliver, A.L., Zucker, L.G. and Brewer, M. (1996), 'Social networks, learning, and flexibility: sourcing scientific knowledge in new biotechnology firms', *Organization Science*, **7**(4), 428–43.

March, J.G. (1995), 'The future, disposable organizations and the rigidities of imagination', *Organization*, **2**(3/4), 427–40.

March, J.G. and Simon, H.A. (1958), *Organizations*, New York, London: Wiley.

Meyer, A.D., Brooks, G. and Goes, J.B. (1990), 'Environmental jolts and industry revolutions: organizational responses to discontinuous change', *Strategic Management Journal*, **11**, 93–110.

Miles, M.B. and Snow, C.C. (1986), 'Network organizations: new concepts for new forms', *California Management Review*, **28**, 62–73.

Miller, D. and Chen, M.-J. (1994), 'Sources and consequences of competitive inertia: a study of the U.S. airline industry', *Administrative Science Quarterly*, **39**, 1–23.

Miller, D. and Friesen, P.H. (1980), 'Momentum and revolution in organizational adaptation', *Academy of Management Journal*, **23**(4), 591–614.

Ng, I. and Dastmalchian, A. (2001), 'Organizational flexibility in Western and Asian firms: an examination of control and safeguard rules in five countries', *Revue Canadienne de Sciences de l'Administration*, **18**(1), 17–24.

Noda, T. and Bower, J.L. (1996), 'Strategy making as iterated process of resource allocation', *Strategic Management Journal*, **17** (Special Issue), 159–92.

Overholt, M.H. (1997), 'Flexible organizations: using organizational design as a competitive advantage', *Human Resources Planning*, **20**(1), 22–32.

Pettigrew, A.M. (1990), 'Longitudinal field research on change: theory and practice', *Organization Science*, **1**(3), 267–92.

Pettigrew, A.M. and Fenton, E.M. (2000), *The Innovating Organization*, London: Sage.

Pettigrew, A.M. and Whipp, R. (1991), *Managing Change for Competitive Success*, Oxford: Blackwell.

Pettigrew, A., Whittington, R., Melin, L., Sanchez-Rundes, C., Ruigrok, W. and Van den Bosch, F. (2003), *Innovative Forms of Organising: International Perspectives*, London: Sage.

Porter, M. (1990), *The Competitive Advantage of Nations*, London: Macmillan.

Raff, D.M.G. (2000), 'Superstores and the evolution of firm capabilities in American bookselling', *Strategic Management Journal*, **21** (Special Issue), 1043–59.

Reger, R.K., Gustafson, L.T., Demaried, S.M. and Mullane, J.V. (1994), 'Reframing the organization: why implementing total quality is easier said than done?', *Academy of Management Review*, **19**(3), 565–84.

Rosenbloom, R.S. (2000), 'Leadership, capabilities, and technological change: the transformation of NCR in the electronic era', *Strategic Management Journal*, **21** (Special Issue), 1083–103.

Singh, J.V., House, R.J. and Tucker, D.J. (1986), 'Organizational change and organizational mortality', *Administrative Science Quarterly*, **31**, 587–611.

Smith, K.G., Grimm, C.M., Gannon, M.J. and Chen, M.-J. (1991), 'Organizational information processing, competitive responses and performance in the U.S. domestic airline industry', *Academy of Management Journal*, **34**(1), 60–85.

Stimpert, J.L., Gustafson, L.T. and Sarason, Y. (1998), 'Organizational identity within the strategic management conversation', in D.A. Whetten and P.C. Godfrey (eds), *Identity in Organizations*, Thousand Oaks, CA: Sage, pp. 83–98.

Stinchcombe, A.L. (1965), 'Social structure and organizations', in J.G. March (ed.), *Handbook of Organizations*, Chicago, IL: Rand-McNally, pp. 142–93.

Sull, D.N. (1999a), 'Why good companies go bad', *Harvard Business Review*, July–August, 42–52.

Sull, D.N. (1999b), 'The dynamics of standing still: Firestone Tire and Rubber and the radial revolution', *Business History Review*, **73**, 430–64.

Teece, D.J., Pisano, G. and Shuen, A. (1997), 'Dynamic capabilities and strategic management', *Strategic Management Journal*, **18**(7), 509–33.

Thomas, J.B., Clark, S.M. and Gioia, D.A. (1993), 'Strategic sensemaking and organizational performance: linkages among scanning, interpretation, action, and outcomes', *Academy of Management Journal*, **36**(2), 239–70.

Tomlinson, R.C. (1976), 'OR, Organisational design and adaptivity', *OMEGA*, **4**(5), 527–37.

Toulán, O.N. and Guillén, M.F. (1997), 'Beneath the surface: the impact of radical economic reforms on the outward orientation of Argentine and Mendozan firms, 1989–1995', *Journal of Latin American Studies*, **29**, 395–418.

Tushman, M.L. and Anderson, P. (1986), 'Technological discontinuities and organizational environments', *Administrative Science Quarterly*, **31**, 439–65.

Tushman, M.L. and Smith, W. (2001), 'Technological change, ambidextrous organizations and organizational evolution', in J.A.C. Baum (ed.), *Companion to Organizations*, Malden, MA: Blackwell.

Volberda, H.W. (1996), 'Toward the flexible form: how to remain vital in hypercompetitve environments', *Organization Science*, **7**(4), 359–74.

Volberda, H.W. (1999), *Building the Flexible Firm*, Oxford: Oxford University Press.

Webb, D.L. and Pettigrew, A.M. (1999), 'The temporal development of strategy: patterns in the U.K. insurance industry', *Organization Science*, **10**(5), 601–21.

Weick, K.E. (1979), *The Social Psychology of Organizations*, 2nd edn, Reading, MA: Addison-Wesley.

Wieserma, M.F. and Bantel, K.A. (1992), 'Top management team demography and corporate strategic change', *Academy of Management Journal*, **35**(1), 91–121.

Woodward, J. (1965), *Industrial Organization: Theory and Practice*, London: Oxford University Press.

Zammuto, R.F. and O'Connor, E.J. (1992), 'Gaining advanced manufacturing technologies' benefits: the role of organization design and culture', *Academy of Management Review*, **14**(4), 701–28.

27 Addressing path dependency in the capabilities approach: historicism and foresight meet on the 'road less travelled'

Swapnesh K. Masrani and Peter McKiernan

Introduction

This chapter challenges the commonly held notion in the capabilities approach, arising out of an overemphasis on path dependency, that capability development follows a single path-dependent route, which is determined positively by interrelatedness among existing technologies. It queries the fascination especially within the empirical literature with examining a single, successful choice. The chapter argues, like Penrose (1959) and Hamel and Prahalad (1994), that a firm seldom considers only one strategic capability development route. Often, a route is chosen from a bounded option set, anchored by the 'do-nothing' default. This is supported by empirical case evidence, which also suggests that, in some instances, technological interrelatedness is not a major factor influencing the development of capabilities from the available options.

The chapter is structured as follows. First, we review key literature in the capabilities approach (that is, Barney 1991; Teece et al. 1997) and describe how, in an attempt to 'engage' with history, path dependency has played a central role in its theoretical construct. We then argue that an attempt by strategy researchers to equate 'serious' engagement with history by using only the notion of path dependency is highly erroneous. In particular, three issues of concern are identified, namely, a myopia in strategic choice, causal bias and efficiency assumption.

Second, we review how historians have addressed these problems, with a view to incorporating these suggestions into an empirical study. A key historicist technique is to examine the multiple options that were available before a particular alternative was decided upon and to identify reasons why the others were not pursued. The resulting implications for the capabilities approach are twofold: there is a need, first, to acknowledge the presence of various capability options available to the firm; and second, to also examine why a capability option (that is, the 'road less travelled') was 'not' pursued (here the emphasis is on juxtaposing alternatives and inductively identifying historical events and factors that led to the selection of one option over the others) as opposed to a sole focus upon why an option 'was' pursued (here the emphasis is solely on the justification of path dependency and its underlying features, for example, technological interrelatedness, increasing returns, dominant logic and so on, associated with the successful choice).

Third, we use this theoretical suggestion to examine capability development in the Dundee jute industry (DJI). The section addresses the three major concerns with path dependency, illustrating them from the archival-based case studies of firms in the DJI between 1880 and 1970. This phase is divided into three: period 1 (1880s–1890s), period 2 (1919–39), and period 3 (1945–70). During the first period, firms in the industry began to formulate capability development alternatives, whereas during the second and third periods the different options were employed. The section then reflects on the strategic response of the DJI to the growing competition from the Indian industry since the late nineteenth century and the industry's decline in general.

Fourth, we underline the major findings of the research and emphasize their importance for theoretical development in the capabilities literature. The role of path dependency has also been acknowledged in influencing organizational foresight. Hence, this section outlines key implications arising out of the empirical case for research on organizational foresight.

The final section concludes.

Path dependency and application of history in the capabilities approach

Path dependency and strategic capabilities
The significance of path dependency in resource commitment was established by David (1985) and Arthur (1989). David argued that in order to understand the 'logic or illogic world around us'; it is necessary to understand 'how it got that way' (p. 332). He examined the case of the continued preference of the 'QWERTY' over the 'DSK' format for setting keys on typewriters and computers, when it was demonstrated that the latter form was more efficient than the former. He argued that the combination of three conditions led to this preference: first, the technical interrelatedness of system components, such as typists and keyboards; second, increasing returns, as in the greater value of keyboard systems with larger market shares; and third, quasi-irreversibility of investment, as in the costs of switching from one keyboard system to another owing to 'learning and habituation' (p. 336). Building on this framework, Arthur emphasized the importance of increasing returns of scale that developed over time and suggested that these can be derived from both the demand and supply sides. On the supply side, it is the result of learning effects (learning by doing or learning by using), which lower the cost or improve the quality of a product. On the demand side, increasing returns can occur owing to positive network externalities, which raise the value of a product or technique for each user as the total number of users increases.

The notion of path dependency has played an important role in building the theoretical pillars of the resource-based view (RBV), the intellectual root of the capabilities approach. However, the primary aim has been to incorporate history within its framework. Distinguishing the RBV approach from that of the industrial organization (IO) perspectives, Barney (1991) pointed out that the proponents of the latter approach examined a firm's performance independent of its history (p. 107). In contrast to this, the RBV framework gave due importance to the role of history in its analysis. In particular, it played an important role in ensuring the 'imperfect inimitability' of resources through 'path dependency':

> [T]his approach asserts that not only are firms intrinsically historical and social entities, but their ability to acquire and exploit some resources depends upon their place in time and space. Once this particular unique time in history passes, firms that do not have space- and time-dependent resources cannot obtain them, and thus these resources are imperfectly imitable. (pp. 107–8)

Hence, the role of contextual history in creating path dependency has been important for researchers examining firm capabilities. As Teece et al. (1997) noted, 'the notion of path-dependency recognizes that history matters' (p. 522). Path dependency plays an important role in determining the nature of the capabilities that a firm is able to develop, thus limiting what it can do and where it can go in the future. As Teece et al. argued, a firm's 'previous investments and repertoire of routines (its history) constrain its future behavior' (p. 523).

Consequently, the focus in empirical studies, when historical analysis is conducted, has been upon the examination of causes that lead to the path-dependent nature of capabilities at both the industry and firm levels. For example, Klepper and Simons (2000) studied the American television receiver industry from 1945 to 1989 using a statistically sophisticated model of industry evolution. They found that greater experience in the radio industry acted positively on firm entry and the sustaining of competitive advantage in the television industry, thus indicating that existing capabilities help determine successful entry to new related markets. Similarly, Langlois and Steinmueller (2000) studied the history of the American semiconductor industry from 1980 to 1995. They examined the industry's general response to the Japanese challenge during this period and found that, although some new capabilities were developed, firms relied heavily on the capabilities that had been developed in the earlier periods, thereby emphasizing the importance of existing technology in determining the nature of capability evolution in the face of international competition.

Studies at firm level gave relatively greater emphasis to the examination of the historical context, especially within the firm. Nonetheless, their primary aim was to establish path dependency. For example, Tripsas and Gavetti (2000) examined the company history of Polaroid from its inception in 1937 to 1990, with particular attention to the 1980–90 period, in order to study the relationship among capabilities, cognition and leadership. They found that investment in developing a particular capability was closely related to the dominant belief pattern of its leadership. With the change in leadership came a change in the leader's cognitive beliefs, which in turn led the direction for developing a particular capability. Similarly, Holbrook et al. (2000) used a case-study approach to examine the company histories of four firms within the American semiconductor industry. They found that each individual firm's commitment to technology and the ability to integrate research and manufacturing were the two major aspects in determining heterogeneity of capabilities and developing unique path dependency. Consequently, the latter played an instrumental role in the way capabilities were developed in these firms. However, as will be discussed in the next subsection, this approach to history in the capabilities literature has been questioned by scholars who have called for a greater attention to history in the strategy literature.

Concerns with path dependency
Researchers have argued that an overemphasis on path dependency has been the result of a 'narrow perspective' of history in the strategic management literature (Booth 2003: 99; Clark and Rowlinson 2004). Although path dependency has made a valuable contribution in terms of fortifying the theoretical underpinnings of the capability approach, it has also led to concerns among researchers resulting from its treatment of history. Booth (2003) and Clark and Rowlinson (2004) have identified three major areas of concern relating especially to the capabilities literature.

First, a major implication of path dependency in terms of capability development is the 'lock-in' effect. As current capabilities are considered a result of past investments and future capability developments are a result of current investments, the focus has been on examining factors that lead to the 'lock-in' (a form of determinism), such as technological interrelatedness, dominant logic and so on, which determine the development of the existing capabilities. Path dependency often underplays the significance of *alternatives* available in history, in the present, and in the future. On the other hand, a distinct theoretical contribution of resource/capabilities approach has been to recognize and underline the importance of management's ability to leverage their existing resource/capabilities into multiple strategic possibilities (Penrose 1959; Hamel and Prahalad 1994). This is also reflected in practice, where managers often consider more than one option before committing to any particular strategy. Therefore, by giving greater attention to path-dependency-related issues, empirical studies have often underplayed the importance attributed to strategic options within the theoretical framework. Second, path dependency gives particular emphasis to specific decisions, turning-points and events in history that led to the development of current capabilities. Consequently, the 'flux, continual crisis, and dilemma' within history are often underplayed in the empirical studies. Third, in economics, where it was originally applied, the notion of path dependency recognizes the inefficiencies in strategic choices as a result of lock-in effects of technological interrelatedness. In strategy, some researchers have made an attempt to theoretically examine this aspect, especially through notions such as 'core rigidities' (Leonard-Barton 1992) and 'strategic liabilities' (Arend 2004). Yet, within the empirical literature, researchers have to a large extent assumed that the capabilities that are developed as a result of technological interrelatedness are efficient strategy formulations.

To summarize, the notion of path dependency has been an integral part of the theoretical construct of the capabilities approach. Researchers have it mainly to assert the importance of history. In particular, it has helped to underline the uniqueness of a resource/capability, which is specific to a particular firm, thus helping it to maintain its distinctive advantage over competitors. As a result, empirical studies have devoted their efforts to establishing the path dependency of a capability by examining the role of determining factors such as technological interrelatedness in selection of the successful choice. However, an overemphasis on this aspect has led researchers, especially in empirical studies, to underplay an original tenet of the capabilities approach, that is, the management's ability to craft multiple strategic options from existing resource/capabilities. This has resulted in an exclusive analysis of critical turning events and an unqualified assumption that the capability developed as a result of interrelatedness is an efficient strategy. The next section examines how these issues can be overcome through greater engagement with the history literature.

Historicist approach to countering path dependency
One way to counter the problems of path dependency as discussed above is to give greater attention to the historical context and highlight the multiplicity of choices that were available before a particular course of action had been decided. Usually, firms consider more than one strategic capability development option before they choose a specific one. Therefore, attention should be given to identifying the options that were under consideration and underline why certain options were not pursued. Historians (for example, Carr 1964; Elton 1967) have pointed out the importance of this aspect.

For Elton (1967), history is an examination of events in the past that have left deposits in the present. It deals with the happenings, changes and particulars of the events that occurred in the past (p. 24). Hence, the study of history amounts to a 'search for truth' concerning these incidents (p. 70). In this endeavour, a 'professional' historian's aim is to get closer to the past and understand the characters 'until one knows what they are going to say next' (p. 30). While recreating this past, the determinist tendencies, which arise from a researcher's aim to justify a researcher's preconceived theories, must be avoided (pp. 64–5). Elton argued that although some form of 'pattern making' may be necessary to put forward an explanation, the aim should be to highlight the 'multifarious and particular' nature of events (p. 128).

On the other hand, for Carr (1964), the essence of history is in the interpretation of the past as opposed to the pursuit of truth. Carr questioned the overdependence on documents as a source through which to give accurate accounts of historical events. He argued that the content recorded in documents often depended on what the recorder thought had happened, or what he wanted others to think had happened (p. 13). As a result, the interpretation that the historian derives from the records carries greater weight. In order to arrive at a plausible interpretation, the historian is required to gain 'contact with the mind of those about whom he is writing' (p. 19). Carr also suggested that history is about the general as opposed to the particular (p. 62), arguing that history is concerned with the 'relation' between the unique and the general, rather then the precedence of one over the other (p. 65). He acknowledged that in the quest for generalization, the historian might be faced with the charge of being deterministic (p. 85). However, he questioned the notion that there were limitless possibilities at one's disposal (p. 87). Every human action is both free and determined to a certain extent (p. 89). Carr quelled the charge of determinism by suggesting that researchers sometimes use rhetorical language to label an event as inevitable when they want to underline the point that a set of factors would make the likelihood of its occurrence 'overwhelmingly strong' (p. 90). Yet, he acknowledged that in practice, historians are aware of fluxes created by the alternative course of actions that were being considered by the actors:

> In practice, historians do not assume that events are inevitable before they have taken place. They frequently discuss alternative courses available to the actors in the story on the assumption that the option was open, though they go on quite correctly to explain why one course was eventually chosen over the other. (p. 90)

Notably, Carr did not consider it a high priority to further explore the range of options that were under consideration. He left this job to 'poets and metaphysicians' (p. 90). Nevertheless, it is clear that historians from both 'traditional' and 'post-modern' schools have recognized the presence of multiple options prior to the selection of a course of action. Indeed, the examination of multiple options has received greater attention by historians practising counterfactual analysis. In underlining the need to examine the various alternatives that were available, Trevor-Roper (1981) argued: 'At any given moment in history there are real alternatives . . . How can we *explain* what happened and *why* if we only look at what happened and never consider the alternatives, the total pattern of forces whose pressure created the event?' (p. 363, original italics).

But not all historians have been receptive to the idea of counterfactual analysis. For instance, Carr (1964) termed the method as being akin to a 'parlor game' (p. 91). A major objection has been that counterfactual analysis relies on 'facts, which concededly never existed' (Ferguson 1997: 86). In order to counter this, Ferguson suggested that researchers should consider plausible options as 'those alternatives, which can be shown on the basis of contemporary evidence that contemporaries actually considered' (p. 86).

Arguably, the use of history to establish path dependency only as an element within its theoretical construct would leave it short of fulfilling the potential that researchers have expected from its use. For example, when Helfat (2000: 955) cautioned strategy researchers by citing the American philosopher George Santayana who remarked 'those who cannot remember the past are condemned to repeat it', and Teece et al. (1997) argued that 'history matters', there was an implicit call for greater attention to the prevailing historical context and the available alternatives. Theoretically, in order to avoid repeating history (assuming that events and lessons indicate issues that are not worth repeating), the first step would be a closer examination of various alternatives that were available during the historical context, so as to be able to make a judgement on exactly what to avoid.

This study examines the strategic options as a means of addressing the three major problems associated with path dependency identified in the earlier section. It does not aim to conduct a detailed counterfactual analysis of strategy options. Its focus is on the identification of the various strategic capability development options available to firms within a specified and localized industry and to examine why they were not pursued. Of course, it is possible that a capability developed by a firm may reflect path dependency. However, initial identification of the option set allows an examination of why a particular capability was developed over the others and highlights the problems or barriers faced in pursuing the rejected options. In addition, by taking this approach, a greater understanding of the historical context is created and a better assessment of the influence of path dependency is possible.

Using this framework, the following sections describe the development of technological capabilities in the DJI between the late nineteenth century and 1970, in order to counter the growing international competition. In particular, it identifies the strategic options available to firms and the capabilities that were actually developed by four firms[1] – Buist Spinning, Jute Industries (JI), Scott & Fyfe (S&F) and Craiks – between periods 2 and 3. It also identifies factors which led to the selection of one capability development option over the other.

The Dundee jute industry

Like cotton, jute is a natural fibre. It is grown primarily in the Indian subcontinent, especially in the eastern Indian state of Bengal and Bangladesh. To this day, this region supplies the majority of the world's demand for raw jute. Its cultivation is confined to this region owing to the climatic conditions that are particularly suitable for growing this crop. Although jute was spun and woven by handlooms in India for over two thousand years, it was in Dundee, Scotland, where modern production techniques were first introduced that enabled the industry to achieve its worldwide reputation.

Historically, textile firms in Dundee had used Russian flax as their primary fibre. Jute was introduced in Dundee in the 1820s and 1830s. Initially, the flax manufacturers were not keen to use jute because it was considered an inferior option to flax (Woodhouse and Brand 1934). However, the sudden cessation in the supply of flax from Russia during the Crimean War (1854–56) left little room for this resistance. Jute provided a cheaper option

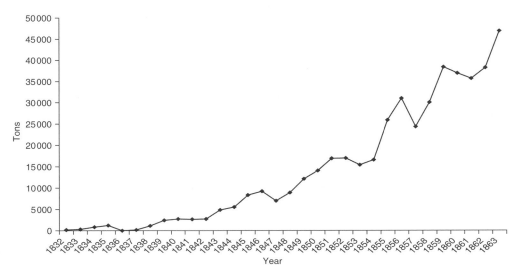

Source: Howe (1982).

Figure 27.1   Raw jute import into the UK, 1832–63

Table 27.1   Number of spindles, looms and employed, 1870 and 1890

	Spindles	Looms	Employed
1870	94,520	3,774	14,911
1890	268,165	14,107	43,366

Source: Board of Trade (1948).

to flax and the customers also accepted it. Thus, using modern production techniques, the DJI was born. With little international competition, it soon emerged as the leading global supplier of jute goods. The industry continued its growth over the second part of the nineteenth century due to both its global monopoly on supply and a large demand for sand bags during the American Civil War (1861–65) (Carrie 1953). The quantity of imported raw jute gives an indication of the rapid growth of the industry during this period (see Figure 27.1). Correspondingly, the number of spindles, looms and people employed in the industry expanded significantly (see Table 27.1).

The rise of Indian competition and contraction of the Dundee jute industry
Like the UK cotton industry, the jute industry witnessed a dramatic decline from the end of the nineteenth century. By 1944, raw jute imports into the UK had collapsed to less than 25 per cent of their 1896 levels (see Figure 27.2) and the sector's size ranking had fallen to third in the world.

The major challenge facing the jute industry up to the late nineteenth century was the closing of traditional markets in Europe due to the imposition of import tariffs and, more

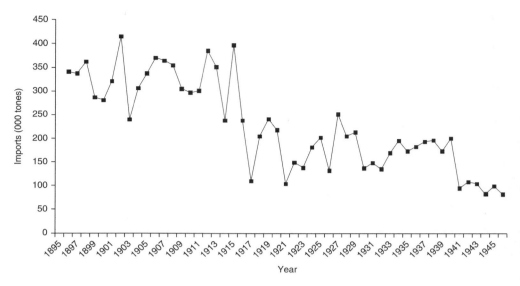

Source: Board of Trade (1948).

Figure 27.2   Raw jute imports into the UK

importantly, the rise of competition from the Indian industry. As with the case of continental European countries, tariffs were also imposed by India on the import of jute goods. By 1869, this duty was 7.5 per cent.[2] There was a feeling within the Dundee industry that this was less to do with collection of revenue for the state government and more to do with protecting the growing industry in India.[3] As a result, attempts were made to repeal the tariffs by making representations to the Indian government directly[4] and later to the Select Committee of the House of Commons on Indian Finances.[5] The industry's petition appeared to have been heard as the tariffs were soon removed.[6] Nonetheless, by the 1890s, the Indian industry had expanded rapidly. By 1882, it had 21 mills, with a total of 5,655 looms and 91,000 spindles. And by 1892, the number of mills had increased to 26, with 8,101 looms and 162,000 spindles.[7] Hence, growth of competition from the Indian industry was very rapid.

The dramatic growth of the Indian industry was due to the cost advantage that it enjoyed over the Dundee industry. This advantage was a result of three major aspects: (i) the Indian industry enjoyed a lower cost of raw material as it was closer to the jute growing region. This closeness eliminated the shipping cost that Dundee had to incur to import jute; (ii) the Indian industry also enjoyed the benefit of longer working hours. The extended working hours meant increased production and reduced cost of production owing to economies of scale. While average working time in Dundee was 56 hours per week, the Indian industry clocked up to 84 hours a week, with an average of 72 hours a week;[8] (iii) the third major advantage stemmed from the lower exchange rate. The monetary instability in the world markets resulting from the demonetization of silver had devalued the Indian currency significantly. For example, an estimate by the Secretary of the Dundee Chamber of Commerce in 1894 indicated that 'with the Rupee at 16d, a Calcutta mill could earn a profit of 20 Rupees per ton where a Dundee mill would simply

Table 27.2   Yarn and cloth categories

Yarn	Pounds	Cloth	Inches
Fine	Up to 6	Narrow	Up to 56
Medium	7–16	Medium	57–68
Heavy	16–48	Wide	69 and above
Rove	46–1000		

Table 27.3   Major yarn and cloth: type, product and markets

	Pounds	Width (inches)	Weight (ounces)
Yarn			
Fine	1.75–3	–	–
Carpet warp	3.5–6	–	–
Hessian warp	7–9	–	–
Sacking warp	8–10	–	–
Hessian weft	7–12	–	–
Carpet weft	14–24	–	–
Cloth			
Sacking	–	22–30	11–24
Tarpaulin and canvas	–	36–45	14–20
Hessian	–	22–80	5–14
Scrim	–	28–80	5–20
Linoleum backing	–	72–84	5–9
Carpet backing	–	150–210	5–9
Wall covering	–	40–145	8–10.5

pay expenses, and with the rupee at 12d the profit to the Indian mill would increase to about 53 Rupees, or some 50 per cent'.[9]

By the mid-1870s, the industry in Dundee found itself squeezed between two sides. First, the growth in the Indian industry challenged the DJI in major international markets such as the United States, South America, Asia and Australia and second, high continental European tariffs made it difficult to access major local markets and also gave rise to the growth of industries within these countries. The consequent capacity increase led directly to an excess of global supply with concomitant effects on price. The DJI had to develop a strategic response or face collapse. Its extant capabilities formed the basis for its reaction. The next subsection describes key capabilities in jute manufacturing.

Capabilities in jute manufacturing
Like any textile industry using natural fibre, there are three major phases in jute manufacturing: preparation (assorting of raw jute), spinning (making yarn) and weaving (making cloth). Similarly, like any textile industry, jute manufacturing had two major products, yarn and cloth.

In weaving, capabilities can be categorized as the ability to make different widths, lengths, and weights of cloth. Tables 27.2 and 27.3 illustrate the different combination of

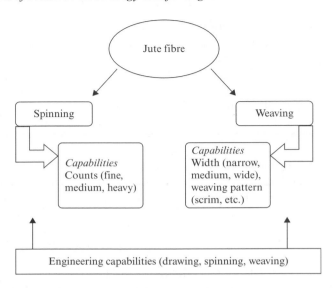

Figure 27.3   Jute manufacturing capabilities

widths and weights required to manufacture a certain type of yarn and cloth. For example, narrower-width and relatively heavier cloth was suitable for the traditional sacking and bagging. On the other hand, lighter-weight and narrow-width cloth was suitable for scrim cloth, which can be used in the building industry. However, a wider-width and lightweight cloth is required for linoleum, wall coverings and carpet backing. In yarn, the weight was the major determinant. While the heavier counts went into making sacks and bags, the lighter ones were required for woven carpet yarns. Therefore, the variation in the width and weights in cloth and yarns also helped a firm's entry into new markets.

However, manufacturing cloth of wider widths and yarn of finer qualities required a slightly different process and skills from those required for traditional narrow-width cloth and heavy yarns. The traditional looms suitable for making sack and bag cloth were of narrow widths. They could be customized to produce wider-width and long-length cloth using internal engineering knowledge on existing machines. Traditionally, the machineries for jute manufacturing, including the drawing machine, spinning frames, looms and ancillary parts, were provided by specialized engineering firms. Internal engineering knowledge enables textile firms to make alterations on their own in order to make yarn and cloth of a particular weight and width. These engineering skills also acted as an important supporting capability in developing capability in the wide widths, long lengths and the introduction of new fibre, especially polypropylene. Hence, although a purpose-built machine can be bought at market prices from a specialized engineering firm, if a textile firm possesses internal engineering skills, it can carry out modifications to existing machines to enable new fibre adoption faster than rivals and so develop new product, or adapt existing product, at much lower cost. In spinning, the capability takes the form of 'counts', which are broadly categorized into fine, medium and heavy. Figure 27.3 illustrates capabilities in the spinning and weaving section of the jute industry.

The following two subsections describe how firms within the industry used these capabilities to reposition themselves against the growing international competition between the late nineteenth century and 1970.

Dundee's strategic repositioning and capability options during the late nineteenth century
In order to meet the challenge of growing international competition, the DJI tried to reposition itself strategically in the late nineteenth century. The industry's efforts were guided by the idea of competing in areas where the Indian manufacturers would not be able to challenge them. In order to do so, two major strategic capability development options were being considered within the industry.

First, there was a move to develop capabilities where the Indian industry could not compete. The basis of this argument was that workers in Dundee possessed superior skills in the spinning of yarn and the manufacturing of cloth, which the Indian workers were thought to be not capable of developing. By leveraging their skills, the Dundee manufacturers could develop specialized and higher-class goods, which would fetch them better margins. Particular attention was given to the development of products for the linoleum and carpet industries. In addition, it was also felt that closer contacts with the customers were needed in order to develop 'speciality' products. These fine and speciality products soon provided advantages to Dundee firms. For instance, although the trade was bad during 1892, the speciality products recorded a particularly good turnover over normal types.

The efforts to focus on developing specialized products culminated in the establishment of a technical school in 1888. It was hoped that besides teaching essential engineering skills for operating spinning and weaving machines, the institute would help in developing valuable skills in textile designs. The suggestion for a technical institute appears to have first emerged in the mid-1880s. When a question was asked by the Royal Commission about Dundee's efforts to deal with growing international competition, the Dundee Chamber of Commerce could offer no suggestions except point towards the fact that a 'great deal of money was invested in machinery in Dundee, and that it was difficult to alter it' (DCC Minute Book, 31st March 1886). A suggestion was made to diversify from jute by providing the example of how the ribbon industry in Coventry went into making bicycles after the tariff on French ribbons was repealed in 1860. However, not all firms were prepared to make a 'jump of that sort'. A technical institute, on the other hand, would help the industry to cultivate specialized skills in jute that were necessary to develop capabilities to meet the growing competition.

Although there was a general consensus within the industry that it was important to develop capabilities in areas where the Indian industry could not compete, there was always a lingering threat that the Indian manufacturers would soon catch up with Dundee in whatever superior capabilities it developed. This was due to the relative technological simplicity in jute manufacturing.

Second, attempts were made to develop capabilities in new fibres. This was driven by the realization that any development within jute would soon be adopted by the Indian industry. By the 1890s, the DJI had become proactive in their search for alternative fibres. In his address to the industry, the local MP, Sir John Leng, acknowledged that if manufacturers 'develop the utmost finer class of goods, and aim at supplying the specialties which the markets of the world continually require', they could meet the challenge of international competition. He also urged them to be on a constant search for 'new varieties and new combination of materials, patterns, and finish'. Commenting on the possibility of exploring Rhea, a fibre that he had come across on his visit to Asia, he had the following suggestion for the industry:

> [We should investigate] the manipulation of Rhea, which has great possibilities, and which, I believe within a few years will occupy a great position in the world of commerce and manufactures. Where I went in the East I found it was engaging the attention of the most intelligent and far-seeing men, and I saw and heard so much that if I were the head of a great manufacturing firm I would at once set aside 50,000 to 100,000 yards to thoroughly test the capabilities both of the Eastern production and British manufacture of their most promising fibre.[10]

Strategic repositioning and capabilities between 1919–39 and 1945–70
The examination of selected case studies suggests that firms responded to the growing international competition during 1919–39 (period 2) and 1945–70 (period 3) by repositioning themselves strategically through the development of two broad sets of capabilities, within jute and with new fibre.

During period 2, the competition from the Indian industry was limited to the 'standard' sack and bag market and narrow-width cloth. The examination of Buist and JI during this period indicates that these firms had consciously decided to move away from the areas where Indian competition was getting intense. The case of JI indicated that, in weaving, firms built capabilities in wide-width, lighter-weight and long rolls of cloth. These were used mainly as backing cloth for linoleum. On the other hand, the case of Buist suggested that, in spinning, this corresponded to capability in medium and fine qualities of yarn for carpets and yarns for lighter weight jute cloth that were being developed by weaving firms. Therefore, during this period, the repositioning was limited to entering new markets by developing further capabilities in jute. But this strategy was limited to only a few firms, while others stuck to their capability in narrow-width cloth and continued to operate in the traditional markets.

However, during period 3, a two-pronged repositioning strategy and capability development strategy was followed in both jute and new fibre. Up to the 1950s, a large part of the industry that had continued to operate in the traditional sack and bag market during period 2, began to specialize and enter new markets. For example, S&F, after operating in the traditional narrow-width sack and bag market during this time, began to build its capability in the 1950s in wide widths and long lengths. On the other hand, firms that had already specialized during period 2, found new product applications. For example, JI was one of the few firms that had already built a substantial capability in wide-width cloth that was used as a backing cloth for linoleum (a floor covering) by the end of period 2. During the 1950s, JI leveraged its capability in wide width to develop carpet backing cloth. Besides specialization in jute, firms also began to introduce new fibres during period 3. For example, Craiks introduced cotton immediately after the end of the Second World War and, by the 1950s, half of its production was in cotton and synthetics. JI also made such strategic forays, with the establishment of paper sacks and bags manufacture. However, until the second-half of the 1960s, the new fibres were not adopted widely within the industry, though usage increased dramatically thereafter.

The general strategy of repositioning into new markets and the importance of capability in wider widths and finer yarns is also supported by Whately (1992), in his company history of the firm Don Brother Buist Ltd. Whately found that during period 2, owing to growing competition from the Indian industry in the 'standard goods' (that is, sacks and bags), Dons were 'very much in the forefront of the search for markets for non-standard goods' (p. 179). The majority of the firm's looms at this time were in narrow widths that were found to be 'too narrow for the contemporary market' (p. 181). In their effort to enter into specialized markets, Dons went on to build their capability in medium and wide widths up to 80 inches by the mid-1930s (p. 181). During period 3, Dons were able to leverage these capabilities further (p. 196). However, as illustrated in the next subsection, the development of new capabilities in jute and new fibres was constrained by certain critical barriers.

Barriers to strategic repositioning and capability development
A major aspect of this research is to identify factors that played a part in a particular capability option that was not adopted. The jute industry faced options in developing capability within jute and for new fibres. The importance of these options was prominent during two key phases, periods 1 and 3. An exploration of the factors that led the industry to develop its capability within jute, rather than new fibre, in periods 1 and 2, and vice versa in period 3, will help to illustrate the contextual barriers that firms faced.

Periods 1 and 2 (1880s–1945)   This is the first period when strategic capability options were created in order to counter growing international competition. Between the two alternatives, jute and new fibre, firms concentrated their efforts on developing capabilities in the former until 1945.

Trials conducted with new fibres, especially with Ramie, between the 1880s and 1890s highlight two major factors that acted as barriers in building capability in this area. The first was the unsuitability of new fibres to existing jute machineries and thus the requirement for new machinery and processing techniques. However, with some modifications to the machines, the fibre could be manufactured to a satisfactory quality.

Second, it transpired that the cost of manufacturing this fibre was higher than that of jute. Between the two, the second issue had a greater implication than the first one. It is important to appreciate the industry's concern for price sensitivity when introducing new fibres. The cheapness of jute was one of the major factors in its substitution of flax. Therefore, the matter of cost would be a major issue if a new fibre were to replace jute. Furthermore, jute had been able to maintain its dominance in the world markets due to its cheapness.

During period 2, the industry was unable to find a cheaper fibre than jute. For example, when a sample was sent to JI in 1928, its director described the fibre as being 'too good' for them. As a result, firms continued to build their capability in jute as part of the strategic response. But the potential of capabilities in jute to counter international competition declined dramatically during period 3, leading to the importance of developing capabilities in new fibre, as discussed in the following subsection.

Period 3 (1945–1970)   The second period when the strategic capability options became important within the DJI was after 1945. Various forces determined the future pathway, as discussed below.

Limitations with the attributes of jute   During period 3, developing further capabilities in jute beyond the recent innovations in wide widths and long lengths proved to be a major challenge. The coarse nature of the fibre and cheapness in price were the two most important features that had enabled jute to replace flax in Dundee during the Crimean War in the 1850s. But these physical properties meant that jute was not accepted widely beyond its traditional markets. For example, in an effort to promote the awareness of jute and its uses, the DJI had marketed jute as a versatile fibre, having around 101 applications. However, almost all these applications were in the industrial market. In these markets, jute had very little competition from other fibres due to its durability and cost. However, its coarseness was a major constraint in entering consumer markets, where finer and softer fabrics were needed, for example, wall coverings. Recalling the problems faced in carrying out further innovations in jute between 1945 and 1970, Mr McKay, the Head of the Research Department at Jute Industries and a Research Committee member of the British Jute Trade Research Association (BJTRA),[11] observed:

> Unfortunately, the mere nature of the fibre limited the scope. I mean if it was exposed to sunlight it would rot away, so from that point of view its durability. But on the other side, the fibre itself limited the extent you could produce lighter yarns, because beyond a certain point it is not possible because of the coarseness of the fibre – unlike cotton – so you were faced with, relatively speaking, bulky yarns because you could not get it down to anything really fine. And even had you succeeded in doing that, the applications were fairly limited. There is a certain restriction on development because of the nature of the fibre itself.[12]

However, these limitations were not just prevalent during the 1950s and 1960s, but persist even to this day. Mr Atkinson's reflection on the outcome of major research institutes (including Dundee, India and Bangladesh) gives a startling insight into the developments in machinery, processing and the application of jute since the 1950s:

> [Y]ou had the jute research institute working from about 1950 till 1974 or whenever it folded up; 20 years. And nothing came out of it. You've got the Indian research institute, which has been working longer. Nothing of significance has come out. You've got the Bangladesh institute working from 1960s into the present being. Nothing has come out of it. Yes alright, minor things here and minor things there, little bits and pieces. But there has been no wholesale redevelopment of the process. The process today is exactly the same as it was in the 1890s. Fundamentally it's the same. The machines have changed slightly; they are going a little bit faster now. But it's been fundamentally the same. There has been no significant change there. And equally there has been no market of any size developed, despite about 150 research years. It's rather sad but I think it just means that jute is ideal for sacks and bags. Finish. Full stop.[13]

By 1939, it seemed that jute had reached the limit of its technological development and stood at the top of its S-curve. Physical properties restricted progress severely. With the dismantling of protection under the Monopolies Act during the early 1960s, international competition again posed a serious challenge. In this context, the importance of a new fibre became paramount to the industry's survival.

Significance of new fibre   While attempts were made to find a new fibre after 1945, these had begun as far back as the 1880s–1890s. Surprisingly, by the end of the 1950s, no new fibres were adopted widely within the industry. The Pilmott Committee Report in 1959 on the 'Future of the Jute Industry' found that only a handful of firms had begun using new alternatives. As Table 27.4 indicates, of the total 57 firms surveyed, 38 were wholly dependent on jute. Of the remaining, only nine were using synthetic fibres to some extent

Table 27.4   Number of firms in jute and other fibres

	Wholly on jute	Mainly on jute	Jute and other products	Formerly on jute
Number of firms	38	8	11	1

Source: Pilmott Committee Report, 1959; Scottish Records Office: SEP 4/823.

(largely rayon, with two also using nylon), two were using wool, one was making paper and felt, one had diversified partly into engineering, three were engaged in carpet and brattice cloth, and one in flax. Only one firm had completely changed over from jute to rayon.

Among the firms that were using new fibres, the majority of them had introduced rayon. Rayon is a fine fibre and has a feel and texture akin to that of cotton, silk linen and wool. Owing to its fineness, rayon is widely called an 'artificial silk'. Therefore, it was more suitable for the markets where fineness of yarn/cloth was of paramount importance. On the cloth side, it was more suited for the apparel and furnishing markets. It was not particularly suitable for the traditional jute markets of sacks, bags and backing cloths where the emphasis was on the coarseness of the fibre. With properties similar to that of cotton, it could also be processed on looms such as the Northrop, which was primarily made for weaving cotton. The rayon yarn was more suitable for pile yarns,[14] which were required to have a softer feel. Jute, on the other hand, was used as a weft yarn,[15] which was required to be tougher. Consequently, rayon could not be used to replace jute as a weft yarn. Therefore, rayon was more suitable for firms that had moved away from the traditional industrial markets of jute into the apparel and furnishing industry. This could explain why, during period 3, Craiks, which had entered into the furnishing market with the introduction of cotton, laid greater emphasis on rayon than S&F, who continued to operate in the industrial market.

However, it was not until the introduction of polypropylene in the mid-1960s that any serious replacement for jute was found. This replacement was used in traditional jute markets and proved economically viable. Comparing this new fibre with other fibres, the industry had tried previously, Dr Stout, Director of Research at Scottish Textiles Research Association (formerly BJTRA) noted:

> What is the future? Polypropylene tape is the first synthetic material to challenge jute both on technical merit and price. It is likely to be the first of many challenges. So research work must keep well ahead of commercial development.[16]

Polypropylene had three major technical advantages over jute in traditional products. First, jute was prone to rotting if used in damp conditions. Second, because jute is a bio-degradable fibre, it tended to lose its colour and texture if it was exposed to sunlight for an extended period. Because polypropylene is a synthetic fibre, it was able to overcome these two limitations of jute. Third, in the process of making tufted carpets – a primary market for jute – the jute primary backing cloth was highly prone to breaking needles that were inserted in it. When needles were punched though it, they tended to get brushed aside. On the other hand, polypropylene fabric was an 'acceptor' of needles. As the needle was

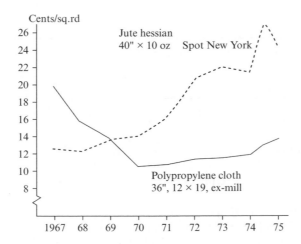

Source: McDowell and Draper (1978).

Figure 27.4   *Polypropylene resin, jute hessian and polypropylene cloth equivalent prices: 1964–74 (actual), 1975 (estimated)*

punched down, the fabric would spread around it. As a result, the pile was placed much closer to where it was intended to be. On the other hand, the fibrous nature of jute provided a better 'bond' than polypropylene for the backing of tufted carpet (McKay 1973). However, in order to overcome this, latexing was introduced to achieve better bonding between the polypropylene backing and the carpet pile. Other aspects such as less waste in production and relative stability in raw material supply and prices also combined to make polypropylene an attractive option to jute.

Besides being technically superior, polypropylene was also cheaper than jute, at least during the late 1960s. The fluctuation in the price of raw jute in the late 1960s had led to a significant price increase in jute goods, making polypropylene cheaper than jute. Figure 27.4 shows the dramatic increase in the price of jute cloth on the one hand and a fall of polypropylene cloth on the other. The relative cheapness of polypropylene played a major role in this new fibre being adopted widely by the industry.

As discussed, there were limitations associated with the physical characteristics of jute. Therefore, initiating further development work was very difficult, if not impossible during period 3. The 'latest' development, that is, backing cloths for tufted carpets, was also under threat from Indian competition, once protection was lifted in the 1960s. The industry therefore faced a 'squeeze' whereby at one end, low-cost-based competition was looming and at the other end, the limiting properties of jute imposed further capability development constraints.

Under these circumstances, the introduction of a new fibre was viewed within the industry as a possible strategic option. If a new fibre could have been applied in the existing industrial market, it would have given the industry a chance to move away from the Indian industry's jute-based competition. Therefore, the replacement of jute by a new fibre should not be viewed as a 'threat' or 'death knell' for the 'jute' industry, but a necessity through which the Dundee 'textile' industry could continue to survive. Gauldie

(1987) supports this notion and has drawn a parallel between the introduction of jute and polypropylene and suggested that 'the coming of jute was as inevitable as the replacement by Polypropylene' (p. 125).

Why did it take the industry until the 1960s to introduce it? An initial analysis points to both physical and cognitive 'lock-in' effects. The physical properties of the fibre and its relative cost advantage restricted its use to industrial markets in the main. The characteristics of jute limited further developments within jute, which meant that it was difficult to apply it to other more lucrative global markets, for example, consumer goods. In addition, the relative cheapness of jute meant that it was tough to find another fibre to match the commercial and technological qualities of jute to replace it in the traditional markets. The second explanation is cognitive. MacKay et al. (2006) have argued that a 'jute' mentality dominated thinking within the sector. Its intensity and symbolism were reflected and reinforced in local committees, institutes, supply chains, press and research papers. For instance, since the introduction of jute in the 1850s, the industry was widely known by its supply-side raw material, as the 'Dundee Jute Industry', rather than by demand-side customers it served in the industrial markets, for example, the packaging industry. As a result, the innovations, both products and process, were mainly within jute (pp. 935–6). Had the industry perceived itself as a 'packaging' industry, it could have avoided locking itself into jute-only innovations and could have been more vigorous in its search for new fibres (p. 936). These two explanations are not necessarily mutually exclusive. In fact, it is also possible that the cheapness of jute and the inability to find any other fibre to replace it could have led to the belief within the industry that 'jute is king' and is irreplaceable.

Conclusion

This study has made an attempt to address the three major problems associated with path dependency in the capabilities literature: (i) it examined the strategic options and reasons why some options were selected over others; (ii) it gave emphasis to the ongoing flux and crisis in selecting the capability alternatives; and (iii) it queried the predominant belief that the capabilities actually developed formed the most efficient strategy.

Clearly, the pattern of capability development in the DJI during periods 2 and 3 that was generated to counter growing international competition can be explained by the traditional path-dependency-related aspects such as technological interrelatedness. For example, firms developed capabilities in jute wide-width cloth and jute finer yarns by making use of their existing capabilities in jute. But assuming that, because of technological relatedness, the further development of capabilities within jute was the only option considered by the firms within the industry would be incorrect. As this study has found, the firms also considered the possibility of developing capability in a new fibre (the road less travelled) as early as the 1880s and again after the end of the Second World War. Nonetheless, the inability to find a fibre with technological and commercial viability to replace jute in its traditional markets played a major role in selecting the jute capability development option over the new fibre option. But when firms were able to develop capability in a new fibre, as with polypropylene, the significance of developing capability in jute declined dramatically. This study made an attempt not to limit the examination to a single event or turning-point as a dominant factor in influencing capability development. As a result, the findings of the study have been able to illuminate the constant flux and dilemmas pertaining to the selection of strategic capability options. Yet, it is evident from the case study that, in the long term, the further development of capabilities within jute was not the most efficient option in order to counter growing international competition. Although it offered some support in the medium term, this became tough to sustain and the DJI collapsed finally during the 1980s.

This chapter has argued that the attribution of the development of a particular capability only to path dependency and its determinant factors such as technological inter-relatedness does not lead to a full understanding of the historical context within which the capabilities are developed. Such myopia robs the analysis of knowledge of the range of options available to a firm and an opportunity to gain deeper understanding as to why a particular capability was pursued over others. This can be addressed by following a two-pronged strategy: first, through the identification of strategic capability development options that were being considered by the firm before committing to a particular capability and second, through the juxtaposition of alternatives and the examination of the reasons why certain alternatives were discarded. In particular, an investigation of the role of factors other than those traditionally related to path dependency would shed fresh light on the issue. In this context, the role of agency in influencing the rejection, or selection, of particular capability development option offers a possible avenue for future research. The capabilities literature should make, and note, a greater concentrated attempt to engage with history. This chapter made a concerted attempt to engage with history within the strategy literature illustrating that there is great scope for the use of historicist methodology to gain a better understanding of firm strategies.

The findings of this study have several implications for research on foresight. First, sectors exhibit a patterning throughout history whose signatures are repeated in the present. These case studies illustrate that 'not much is new' in strategic terms in modern industries that was not replicated at some stage in past sectors. For example, the events and crises in the DJI have a parallel in the history of the UK cotton industry (for example, see Rose 1990; Singleton 1991) and can also be witnessed in any study of UK car production from 1945 to 1985. Hence, a methodical study of firm and industry histories can help to put the present and future into context. Second, firms can confuse a path-dependent option with a best way forward. Cognitive freezing coupled with asset specificity can cause 'lock-in' and an ignorance of other options in the set which may have more sustainable future pathways. In practice, these might be left underexplored and thus presented as 'straw' options in comparison to the 'locked' version. Consequently, due diligence is damaged and foresight restricted. Finally, as this study has indicated, components of strategy, which may appear to be less suitable in the present, could very well become an integral part of the future. The fuller exploration of capability options can benefit from techniques of scenario modelling. This will assist in the systematic appraisal of their future planning and may lead to a more informed choice.

Notes

1. The primary criterion that governed the selection of cases was the availability of relevant archival data. The case studies represent the cross-section of the industry during this period, in terms of size (small and large), and focus (specialized and generalized). Buist: small and specializing in spinning. Craiks: small and specializing in weaving. S&F: small and specializing in weaving. JI: large and generalized.
2. Dundee Chamber of Commerce (DCC) Minute Book, 31 March 1869.
3. Ibid.

4. DCC Minute Book, 30 March 1870.
5. DCC Minute Book, 29 March 1871.
6. DCC Minute Book, 3 September 1874.
7. Dundee Year Book (DYB), 1892, p. 87.
8. DYB 1894, p. 96.
9. DCC Minute Book, 27 September 1894.
10. *Dundee Advertiser*, 8 April 1896.
11. The BJTRA was established in 1947 with the aim of fostering research within the DJI. It was jointly funded by the government and the industry.
12. Interview with Mr Sandy McKay, 26 September, 2006.
13. Interview with Mr R.R. Atkinson, 15 April, 2006.
14. Pile yarn: this yarn, cut or looped, is projected from the substrate and acts as the use-surface.
15. Weft yarn: this yarn is laid out horizontally to hold together the entire construction of the carpet.
16. 'Adding another string to the textile bow', *Glasgow Herald*, 25 August 1969.

References

Arend, R. (2004), 'The definition of strategic liabilities and their impact on firm performance', *Journal of Management Studies*, **41** (6), 1003–27.

Arthur, B. (1989), 'Competing technologies, increasing returns, and lock-in by historical events', *Economic Journal*, **99** (394), 116–31.

Barney, J. (1991), 'Firm resources and sustained competitive advantage', *Journal of Management*, **17**, 99–120.

Board of Trade (1948), 'Report of Jute Working Party', London: HMSO.

Booth, C. (2003), 'Does history matter in strategy? The possibilities and problems of counterfactual analysis', *Management Decision*, **41** (1), 96–104.

Carr, E. (1964), *What is History?*, Harmondsworth: Penguin.

Carrie, C. (1953), *Dundee and the American Civil War 1861–65*, Abertay Historical Society.

Clark, P. and Rowlinson, M. (2004), 'The treatment of history in organisation studies: towards a "historic turn"?', *Business History*, **46** (3), 331–52.

David, P. (1985), 'Clio and the economics of QWERTY', *American Economic Review*, **75** (2), 332–7.

Elton, G.R. (1967), *The Practice of History*, London: Fontana.

Ferguson, N. (1997), 'Virtual history: towards a chaotic theory of the past', in Ferguson (ed.), *Virtual History: Alternatives and Counterfactuals*, London: Picador, pp. 1–90.

Gauldie, E. (1987), 'The Dundee jute industry', in Butt, J. and Ponting, K. (eds), *Scottish Textile History*, Aberdeen: Aberdeen University Press, pp. 112–25.

Hamel, G. and Prahalad, C.K. (1994), *Competing for the Future*, Cambridge, MA: Harvard Business School Press.

Helfat, C.E. (2000), 'Guest Editor's Introduction to the Special Issue: The Evolution of Firm Capabilities', *Strategic Management Journal*, **21**, 955–60.

Holbrook, D., Cohen, W., Hounshell, D. and Klepper, S. (2000), 'The nature, sources and consequences of firm differences in the early history of the semiconductor industry', *Strategic Management Journal*, **21**, 1017–41.

Howe, S. (1982), *The Dundee Textile Industry, 1960–1977*, Aberdeen: Aberdeen University Press.

Klepper, S. and Simons, K. (2000), 'Dominance by birthright: entry of prior radio producers and competitive ramifications in the US television receiver industry', *Strategic Management Journal*, **21**, 997–1016.

Langlois, R. and Steinmueller, E. (2000), 'Strategy and circumstance: the response of American firms to Japanese competition in semiconductors, 1980–1995', *Strategic Management Journal*, **21**, 1163–73.

Leonard-Barton, D. (1992), 'Core capabilities and core rigidities: a paradox in managing new product development', *Strategic Management Journal*, **13**, 111–25.

MacKay, B., Masrani, S. and McKiernan, P. (2006), 'Strategy options and cognitive freezing: the case of the Dundee jute industry in Scotland', *Futures*, **38**, 925–41.

McDowell, S. and Draper, P. (1978), *Trade Adjustments and the British Jute Industry: A Case Study*, Fraser of Allander Institute.

McKay, A.D. (1973), 'Primary and secondary backings – woven', *Textile Trade Press*, 21–30.

Penrose, E. (1959), *The Theory of the Growth of the Firm*, Oxford: Basil Blackwell.

Rose, M. (1990), *International Competition and Strategic Response in the Textile Industries Since 1870*, London: Routledge.

Singleton, J. (1991), *Lancashire on the Scrapheap: The Cotton Industry, 1945–1970*, Oxford: Oxford University Press.

Teece, D., Pisano, G. and Shuen, A. (1997), 'Dynamic capabilities and strategic management', *Strategic Management Journal*, **18** (7), 509–33.

Trevor-Roper, H. (1981), 'History and imagination', in Worden, B. and Lloyd-Jones, H. (eds), *History and Imagination: Essays in Honour of H.R. Trevor-Roper*, London: Duckworth, pp. 356–69.
Tripsas, M. and Gavetti, G. (2000), 'Capabilities, cognition and inertia: evidence from digital imaging', *Strategic Management Journal*, **21**, 1147–61.
Whately, C. (1992), *Onwards from Osnaburgs: The Rise and Progress of a Scottish Textile Company*, Edinburgh: Mainstream Publishing.
Woodhouse, T. and Brand, A. (1934), *A Century's Progress of Jute Manufacture*, Dundee: David Winter.

28 Dynamic knowledge creation
Taman H. Powell and Howard Thomas

Introduction

In the dynamic environments faced by many of today's firms, market positioning can become rapidly obsolete due to new innovations, process improvements and hypercompetitive environments. To successfully compete in these markets, it is argued that firms need to continually create new sources of competitive advantage – but how?

Much research in the field has focused on competitive strategy and competitive advantage (Porter, 1980, 1985; McGee and Thomas, 1986) and at the firm level on the characteristics of resources that are of importance to achieve sustainable rents (Barney, 1991; Peteraf, 1993), or how to determine what resources will be crucial to compete in the future (Hamel and Prahalad, 1994). However, this research focuses on the knowledge creation process itself and links the knowledge-based view of the firm to the literatures on the resource-based view and competitive strategy. It illustrates the theoretical arguments with examples from the consulting industry.

By focusing on facilitating the knowledge creation process, rather than fortifying current resources, or predicting future strategic resources, this chapter also adopts a somewhat evolutionary approach (Nelson and Winter, 1982) to the development of a knowledge-based view of the firm.

If strategy is defined as occupying a unique strategic position, or a 'viable who–what–how combination' (Markides, 1999, p. 58), dynamic strategy in firms involves both competing in a current position and also:

> [searching] continuously for new strategic positions. After identifying another viable strategic position in its industry, the company then must attempt to manage both simultaneously . . . As the old position matures and declines, the company must slowly make a transition to the new. (Ibid., p. 63)

However, in today's environment, some would argue that the transition needs to be anything but slow.

Dynamic strategy and the resource creation process

In this section the major literature influences on dynamic strategy and the knowledge creation process are briefly reviewed. Figure 28.1 provides a context in which the five forces model of industry analysis (Porter, 1980), the resource-based view (Wernerfelt, 1984) and the dynamic capabilities approach (Teece et al., 1997) can be structured and examined.

The resource-based view

Moving on from the long dominant market view of strategy (Porter, 1980) that treated the behaviour of firms as a 'black box', the quality and quantity of distinctive firm resources are increasingly being seen as a key component of competitive strategy (Wernerfelt,

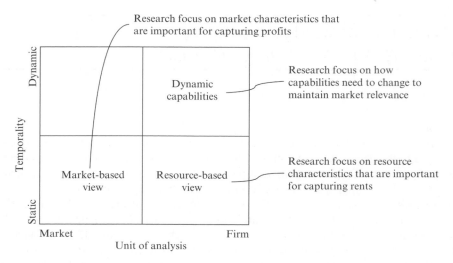

Figure 28.1   Strategic model overview

1984). In fact, resource heterogeneity is now viewed as a defining characteristic of firms (Penrose, 1959; Nelson and Winter, 1982; Wernerfelt, 1984).

For firm resources to deliver sustained competitive advantage, Barney (1991) has argued that the resources need to be valuable, rare, inimitable, and non-substitutable. Similarly, Peteraf (1993) has claimed that there needs to be resource heterogeneity, imperfect mobility, and *ex ante* and *ex post* limits to competition. Rumelt (1984) added the concept of 'isolating mechanisms', effectively barriers to entry at the resource level that enable firm resources to generate sustained rents.

While it is undoubtedly beneficial for a firm to have unique resources that deliver rents, the characteristics highlighted above by Barney, Peteraf and Rumelt effectively identify how a particular firm can protect unique resources. What this analysis does not explain is how these resources need to change over time to ensure their continued market relevance for the firm.

Dynamic markets and dynamic capabilities
The dynamic capability approach aims to address the concerns over the static nature of the previous models. The dynamic capability approach argues that for firms to maintain their unique competitive positioning, the resources that comprise them need to change and evolve over time. This has been argued by Hamel and Prahalad (1994) and Teece et al. (1997) among others. They claim that predicting and developing new resources that are relevant for the future should be the key objective of top management. It is worth noting, however, that not all futures will be available to all firms. A firm's past, and indeed its present, constrain the future possibilities for that firm (Nelson and Winter, 1982).

While all markets change, firms operating in dynamic markets – defined by Eisenhardt (1989) as where change becomes nonlinear and less predictable, market boundaries are blurred, successful business models are unclear, and market players are ambiguous and shifting – face the most significant challenge (this is also argued in D'Aveni's (1999) 'hypercompetitive markets' model). In the context of these dynamic markets, it has been argued that the sustained competitive advantage targeted by resource fortification (such as that described by Barney, Peteraf, and Rumelt above) is simply not possible due to the rapid changes in the market – effectively making today's advantage, tomorrow's disadvantage. What is key in these markets is continued creation of temporary advantage via new relevant resources, processes, capabilities and products.

Influencing resource development
There are a number of streams of research that address how resources are acquired or developed. In terms of acquisition, resources can come from 'strategic factor markets' (Barney, 1986), or in cases of market failure, by mergers and acquisitions (Capron et al., 1998). It is generally argued, however, that acquiring resources will not deliver value to the acquirer as they will be forced to pay the present value of the rents for the resource, the vendor thereby capturing the value and the acquirer only breaking even (Barney, 1986). Additionally, Dierickx and Cool (1989) comment that 'deployment of such assets does not entail a sustainable competitive advantage, precisely because they are freely tradeable' (p. 1506).

It is therefore claimed that, in terms of strategic advantage, accumulated resources are superior to tradable ones. Resource accumulation can be the result of evolutionary processes (Nelson and Winter, 1982), accumulation processes (Dierickx and Cool, 1989), top management foresight and fiat (Hamel and Prahalad, 1994), or from 'productive opportunity' (Penrose, 1959; Moran and Ghoshal, 1999; Ghoshal et al., 2000).

Penrose (1959, p. 32) defines an organization's 'productive opportunity' as those possibilities for deploying resources that an organization's employees can see and which they are willing and able to act on. This opportunity is highly dependent upon the resource variety in the firm. As Kogut and Zander (1992) note, 'firms learn new skills by recombining their current capabilities' (p. 383) so, '[t]he more [diverse] resources a firm controls, the more new possibilities it has for growing in new directions' (Ghoshal et al., 2000, p. 152). This is both from a computational sense, and a willingness sense: 'The likelihood that a particular combination will be of value to someone also will increase with the number of people and the variety of their interests' (Moran and Ghoshal, 1999, p. 394).

This diversity, and hence potential for new resource creation (illustrated in Figure 28.2), is particularly important for firms operating in dynamic environments. This is also noted by Morgan (1986, p. 54): 'organizations operating in uncertain and turbulent environments need to achieve a higher degree of internal differentiation, e.g., between departments, than those in environments that are less complex and more stable'. This variety is generally seen as being internal to the firm, it can also be enhanced via external linkages to other firms (Powell and Koput, 1996).

Figure 28.2   Diversity leads to resource creation

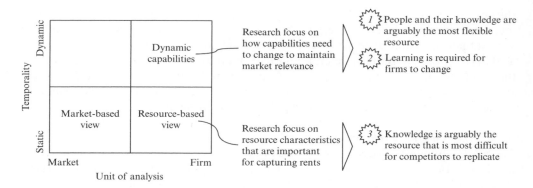

Figure 28.3   Capability-level research focus

While defining new resource creation as being dependent upon the level of diversity among the resource base has decidedly evolutionary overtones, it is possible to influence this evolutionary pattern through firm-level processes. In fact, '[i]t is . . . an organization's unique ability to influence and leverage "the interaction of institutional forms and entrepreneurial activity, the 'shaping' influence of the former and the 'bursting' influence of the latter" (Schumpeter, 1947, p. 153), that gives firms the ability to continue to create value' (Ghoshal, et al., 2000, p. 148). Indeed, a number of the available levers for the firm are discussed under the title of 'guided evolution' by Lovas and Ghoshal (2000).

Knowledge as a resource
Knowledge is increasingly being recognized as a key resource and one of the major influences for the firm to shape its future. The perspectives on knowledge as a resource are evident from current literature. First, tacit knowledge is hard to copy and therefore provides a good source of sustainable competitive advantage (Nonaka, 1994).

Second, people and knowledge are more flexible than other types of resources (Miller and Shamsie, 1996). This therefore provides firms with valuable flexibility which is vital in the dynamic markets that we are discussing.

Third, knowledge is a key reason for the existence of firms: '[W]hat firms do better than markets is the sharing and transfer of the knowledge of individuals and groups within an organization' (Kogut and Zander, 1992, p. 383). This view is in complete contrast to the more traditional economics-based perspectives which view the firm as an option 'of last resort, to be employed when all else fails' (Williamson, 1991, p. 95). This traditional argument is advanced despite the 'ubiquity of organizations' (Simon, 1991a, p. 27), which prompted Simon (p. 28) to ask '[w]ouldn't "organizational economy" be the more appropriate term?'.

In summary, from Figure 28.3 it is clear that knowledge in its various forms is important, but what exactly is knowledge? Knowledge is a somewhat enigmatic entity, so much so that McGee and Thomas (2007) define knowledge from four viewpoints to help highlight its nuances: knowledge as an asset, knowledge embedded in organizational routines, knowledge as learning, and knowledge as innovation.

Knowledge as an asset

The resource-based view highlights the importance of the sticky, embedded, tacit, and path-dependent characteristics of knowledge as a differentiating characteristic. Although there are many entities that could be described as knowledge assets, the most strategically relevant is often the knowledge embedded in individual employees, as it has many of the characteristics just listed.

From an organizational standpoint, it would be ideal to isolate the knowledge from the individuals who own it and share it with others in the firm (Morris and Empson, 1998, p. 615). This would enable the knowledge to be leveraged to less knowledgeable (within this particular knowledge area) employees, therefore increasing the firm's capacity to utilize this knowledge. It would also reduce the power of the employees that own this knowledge, therefore increasing the ability of the firm to capture the rents created by the delivery of this knowledge.

The issue is that this knowledge is bespoke, highly tacit, and in the case of dynamic markets often has a very short useful life. This means that the knowledge created for one context may not be relevant to any other context (Brown and Duguid, 1998, p. 101), and even if it is relevant, it may not be possible to articulate this knowledge to easily share it (Szulanski, 2003). Further, even if it were possible to make this tacit knowledge explicit (Nonaka, 1994), given the time and effort required to do this, it may either have become obsolete, or simply not justify the cost required to undertake this explicit translation activity.

While it may not be possible to leverage knowledge as an asset in a deliberate way, even the more modest goal of knowing what knowledge the firm's employees possess is extremely challenging in itself. As Lew Platt, former chairman of Hewlett-Packard, noted: 'If only HP knew what HP knows, we could be three times more productive!' (quoted in Prusak, 1997, p. xii).

Polanyi (1966, p. 4) famously said 'we know more than we can tell', making the production of a company directory or library of knowledge and individual experts quite problematic. Achievement of such a directory would, however, facilitate a more strategic selection of resources for different tasks, and would lower costs associated with searching for knowledge in the firm.

As a consequence, it is evident that at an individual and a firm level, we do not know what knowledge we have and are equally unable to articulate it in order to share with others in the firm. But we believe that aspects of this rich information library are key for the competitive advantage of the firm.

Knowledge as routines

When looking at knowledge in terms of a firm, it is useful to look also at knowledge as routines. Routines are the shared beliefs within a firm as to the way things are done. While routines can be partially articulated in the form of procedures or process models, it is the more tacit elements of routines that are of interest. In a sense, routines are the knowledge as an asset at the firm level, or the genetics of the organization.

Knowledge as routines has a significant benefit for a firm in that the routines are effectively tacit knowledge that the firm 'owns'. This claim is valid in the sense that an organizational routine will not be destroyed if an employee participating in the routine leaves, and in fact, is reinforced when a new participant fills this vacancy, and learns from the others about how the routine operates. As Hedberg (1981, p. 6) notes,

> [A]lthough organizational learning occurs through individuals, it would be a mistake to conclude that organizational learning is nothing but the cumulative result of their members' learning. Members come and go, and leadership changes, but organizations' memories preserve certain behaviours, mental maps, norms and values over time.

Knowledge as routines has the same sticky, embedded, tacit, and path-dependent characteristics at the routine level as knowledge as an asset does at the individual level. Members of a routine can be equally unaware of why routines occur as they do, as they are of why they know what they know. And while it has been argued that the knowledge as assets logic adds little to the resource-based view (Eisenhardt and Santos, 2002), the same could be claimed of knowledge as routines, except for the fact that routines are typically viewed in conjunction with the knowledge as learning perspective.

Knowledge as learning
Knowledge as an asset and knowledge as routines are effectively static concepts in that they are embedded in the organization and define the knowledge base at the current point of time. So while these concepts of knowledge may be effective in the present, as they are static, they are unlikely to prove as effective when confronting a dynamic market. To compete in such environments, the concept of knowledge as learning is extremely important.

Knowledge as learning brings a dynamic perspective to both the knowledge as assets (Teece et al., 1997) and knowledge as routines perspective (Nelson and Winter, 1982). Knowledge as learning is often coupled with knowledge as routines under the evolutionary economics banner. In this conceptualization, learning occurs at the organizational level via routines changing over time and the best routines surviving.

For this evolution in routines to occur, there needs to be diversity in the way these routines operate, and there needs to be a selection mechanism that identifies the 'best' routines (Cohendet et al., 2000). This process is often described as 'survival of the fittest', but could more accurately be described as 'survival of the fitter', as it is generally a case of the weakest dying out. Or given that performance is inextricably linked to the environment that the routine operates in, a more correct description could be 'survival of the fitting' as noted by Kenneth Boulding (1981).

This form of evolution can occur at the individual, routine or firm level. What is important to note is that selection mechanisms can only identify whether a bundle of items is better than another bundle of items, not what element within the bundle is providing the advantage (Cohendet et al., 2000). For example, with regard to organizations, the selection mechanism can identify that a firm is a strong performer versus other firms in the market. What the selection mechanism cannot do is identify which routines in the firm are good and which are poor. Potentially, there are a number of poor-performing routines in the organization that are being supported by some particularly strong routines.

In summary, however, it is critical to recognize that learning is about cognitive diffusion of knowledge, not the creation of new knowledge. Given the huge base of knowledge in firms, diffusion of this knowledge to different firm members is extremely valuable. This process is different from the concept of knowledge as innovation and the creation of new knowledge, product forms and so on.

Knowledge as innovation

While knowledge as learning could be described as knowledge diffusion from one individual to another, or at an organizational level, via the propagation of strong routines and the death of poor ones, knowledge as innovation centres on the creation of new knowledge. This is, in fact, the critical difference between the Penrosian (1959) and Schumpeterian (1934) conceptualizations of growth. At the firm level, the former is about leveraging what you have, while the latter is about creating something new.

Defining how innovation occurs is clearly highly problematic. Building on the Moran and Ghoshal (1999) model discussed previously, innovation is more likely to occur through the interaction of diversity. So in the case of knowledge creation, this would be when people with diverse knowledge bases interact.

As noted by Cohendet et al. (2000), in organizations there is always a trade-off between commonality and diversity of knowledge. This trade-off is effectively one of exploitation and exploration (March, 1991); both exploitation and exploration are necessary for the survival of an organization. Without the exploration of new possibilities, the organization would find itself trapped in suboptimal states and would eventually become maladapted to changing environmental conditions. But organizations that devote all their resources to the exploration of new possibilities will face too high a degree of risk, and even in the case of successful discoveries they will often fail to exploit the knowledge they acquire and will systematically perform worse than fast followers and imitators.

This exploration/exploitation balance will be different for different industries. Firms competing in dynamic markets, where there is a greater need for continued innovation, would be expected to place a relatively greater emphasis on exploration activities than would be the case for firms competing in more stable industries.

To summarize the four lenses of knowledge in an approximate manner, we can say that knowledge as an asset and knowledge as a routine are largely static concepts and embedded in the current knowledge base, while knowledge as learning has to do with organizational diffusion (at the cognitive level) and knowledge as innovation is related to new knowledge creation.

Influencing knowledge development

If we apply to knowledge the Moran and Ghoshal conceptual model that was stated above, we arrive with the idea that the more diverse knowledge a firm controls, the more new possibilities it has for developing new knowledge. Conversely, if all employees have exactly the same knowledge (unlikely as this may be) it would be impossible for new knowledge to be created from their interaction.

Acting counter to this relationship, however, is the value in knowledge redundancy or common knowledge in a team context. This is because it is this common knowledge that enables communication between the team members. As noted by Bechky (2003), different language reflecting different work practices and knowledge can create significant communication problems between communities.

Combining these two factors, we would anticipate knowledge creation to increase with an increasing level of knowledge diversity until the communication problems stemming from this high-level knowledge diversity (and therefore low levels of common knowledge) offset the benefits. At this level of knowledge diversity, knowledge creation would be expected to decrease. This would result in a relationship as depicted in Figure 28.4.

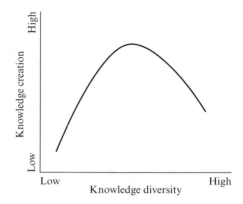

Figure 28.4   Knowledge diversity impact on knowledge creation

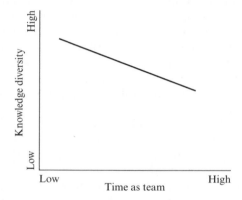

Figure 28.5   Impact of time on knowledge diversity

There is also a temporal impact that would be expected to influence these factors (Figure 28.5). As a team work together for a period of time, the level of knowledge commonality would be expected to increase. This is simply from the act of working together on a common problem.

If we agree with Simon (1991b) and his statement that '[a]ll learning takes place inside individual human heads; an organization learns in only two ways: (a) by the learning of its members, or (b) by ingesting new members who have knowledge the organization didn't previously have' (p. 125), we can say that having diverse knowledge within an organization will not foster the development of new knowledge, unless the people possessing the knowledge come into contact with one another to share their knowledge.

So while the firm can be conceptualized as a 'bundle of assets' (Dierickx and Cool, 1989), structure, in the Chandlerian (Chandler, 1962) sense of the term, and process will impact how and which resources interact. This influence on interaction will impact on the level of diverse knowledge that comes together, and this in turn affects the level of knowledge creation. Therefore organizational structure and process, in that it impacts on resource interaction, would be expected to directly influence the level of new knowledge creation.

It is worth noting that in addition to the new knowledge creation (that is, knowledge as innovation), the interaction of people with diverse knowledge bases working together is likely to also result in knowledge as learning as each person learns from the knowledge base of the other. Both of these outcomes will influence the stocks of knowledge in terms of knowledge as an asset and knowledge as routines. This chapter, however, focuses on knowledge as innovation in the form of knowledge development.

Management consulting
To illustrate this theory in a less conceptual way, we examine the business of management consulting. Management consulting, and 'the professional service firm represents the confluence of two major trends . . . the growing importance of the service sector, and the increasing numbers of "knowledge workers"' (Maister, 1985, p. 3).

Management consulting provides a strong context to examine the impact of the above theories, as it is an industry whose key resources are in the form of its employees and their knowledge. It therefore provides a relatively pure view of a firm that can be conceptualized as a bundle of knowledge assets. Additionally, the competitive capability of a management consulting company depends heavily on its ability to mobilize and synthesize these professionalized bodies of expertise in order to create knowledge that satisfies client demands (Løwendahl, 1997). Essentially, though, we are sure some would debate this, consulting companies are generally tasked with knowledge creation. As such, from both a resource-based view and knowledge standpoint, management consulting provides a suitable context.

Business model
A consulting firm can be conceptualized as having a pool of heterogeneous resources (for example, consultants, computers, databases) that they bring together in a project team to address a problem for a client organization. Each consultant on the team will have a different skill base. In the case of Accenture, for example, consultants are categorized by their seniority, industry, competency (for example, strategy, change management, process, technology), and geographic knowledge.

The challenge for a consulting company is to balance utilization of these expensive resources while also ensuring that their skill bases maintain their future market relevance. The consulting firm also needs to capture some of the value from these resources, while providing enough value to the individuals possessing the knowledge resources to maintain their services within the firm.

Project-level knowledge development
Consulting project teams are tasked with delivering new knowledge to address a client problem. Therefore, using the model described previously (depicted in Figure 28.4), we would expect that the more diverse the knowledge base of the project team, the greater the chance of creating new knowledge for the client. The consulting firm's structure and processes will have a direct impact on how the project team is composed and therefore on the level of knowledge development on the project.

To provide a simple example, if we have a consulting company that is primarily

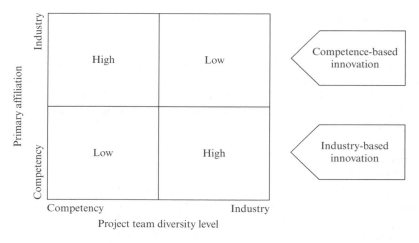

Figure 28.6   Innovation base

structured by competency and secondarily by industry, consultants will tend to be assigned primarily to projects that relate to their competency and that secondarily relate to their industry background. Therefore project team composition will tend to reflect consistency in terms of competency knowledge and diversity in terms of industry knowledge. (There will generally be diversity on the secondary dimension as consulting firms are not able to support many specialists at the intersection of both structural elements.)

The outcome of this project team membership is that it would be more likely to achieve a less innovative competency approach (as team members have relatively similar knowledge on this dimension), and a more innovative industry approach (as team members have a relatively diverse knowledge base on this dimension).

In contrast, if the consulting company is structured primarily by industry and secondarily by competency, consultants will tend to be assigned to projects that relate to their industry expertise and secondarily to their competency. Therefore projects will tend to reflect consistency in terms of industry knowledge and diversity in terms of competency knowledge. In contrast to the previous example, the expected result would be greater innovation in terms of competency area than industry area.

Figure 28.6 is a highly simplistic two by two category matrix in our effort to illustrate theoretical concepts. This shows that structure and process do impact on diversity. This is significant given our theoretical viewpoint that diversity is believed to have a positive impact on knowledge creation.

Firm-level knowledge development
Moving the unit of analysis one level higher, from the project team to the consulting firm, we can begin to see a different impact of project team composition. At the same time that consultants are working on a project team to solve a client problem, they are also learning. This learning affects the knowledge bases of the consultants who then return to the firm at the completion of the project.

The project team logic does not translate entirely to the firm level. At the project level the challenge is to create a team with a diverse knowledge base to enhance the chances

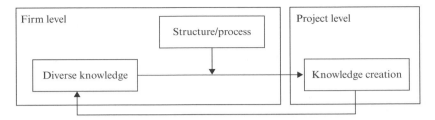

Figure 28.7   Project-level knowledge-base feedback

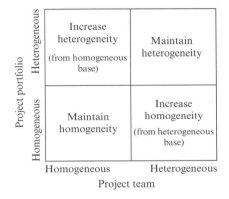

Figure 28.8   Heterogeneity of consulting firm knowledge base

of knowledge creation occurring (Figure 28.7). At the firm level, the challenge translates to having a diverse project base. The diverse project base, however, is not to create new knowledge at the firm level, as these projects do not interact. Instead, the project diversity is required to maintain the knowledge diversity of the firm, and hence the firm's capacity to deliver diversity on future projects.

If projects are not diverse, with the learning that occurs at the project level, there will be a gradual decline in the level of diversity of employees at the firm. In turn this will reduce the capacity of the firm to deliver diversity and also knowledge creation at the project level. Combining the project team and project portfolio level effects together, we can see a relationship similar to that depicted in Figure 28.8.

Conclusion

In looking at the strategic requirement of continued innovation for survival in dynamic markets, this chapter has posed the question: what role does diversity play in knowledge creation? The investigation has built on the resource-based view, the knowledge-based view, and theories on diversity and resource creation.

While not simple, the propositions in this chapter are researchable. To conduct this research, we would propose a multimethod approach structured in three phases. The first phase would focus on the industry level. This would investigate the industry structures and firm characteristics with the aim of understanding the level of diversity at the industry level.

The second phase of the research would consist of a number of case studies that would investigate in detail a cross-section of the firms identified in the first phase. These case studies should provide a deeper understanding of the impact of knowledge diversity on new knowledge creation and also the impact of firm structure and process on resource interaction, and therefore on knowledge creation.

The final phase of the research would be a broad-based survey to investigate whether the findings from the case studies in the second phase apply more broadly to the industry as a whole.

The main challenge for this research involves the difficulties around defining and measuring knowledge. As noted by Nachum (1999, p. 926), '[i]n addition to the conceptual problems, there are also technical difficulties of measurement. The factors at work are intangible, abstract constructs which cannot be measured directly'. Nonetheless, '[i]ntangibility makes measurement difficult, but is seldom a reason to avoid measurement even if proxies must be used' (McLaughlin and Coffey, 1990, p. 47).

References

Barney, J.B. (1986), 'Strategic factor markets: expectations, luck, and business strategy', *Management Science*, **32**(10), 1231–42.
Barney, J.B. (1991), 'Firm resources and sustained competitive advantage', *Journal of Management*, **17**(1), 99–121.
Bechky, B.A. (2003), 'Sharing meaning across occupational communities: the transformation of understanding on a production floor', *Organization Science*, **14**(3), 312–30.
Boulding, K.E. (1981), *Evolutionary Economics*, Beverly Hills, CA: Sage.
Brown, J.S. and Duguid, P. (1998), 'Organizing knowledge', *California Management Review*, **40**(3), 90–111.
Capron, L., Dussauge, P. and Mitchell, W. (1998), 'Resource redeployment following horizontal acquisitions in Europe and North America, 1988–1992', *Strategic Management Journal*, **19**(7), 631–62.
Chandler, A. (1962), *Strategy and Structure: Chapters in the History of the Industrial Enterprise*, Cambridge, MA: MIT Press.
Cohendet, P., Llerena, P. and Marengo, L. (2000), 'Is there a pilot in the evolutionary firm?', in N. Foss and V. Mahnke (eds), *Competence, Governance and Entrepreneurship*, Oxford: Oxford University Press, pp. 95–115.
D'Aveni, R.A. (1999), 'Strategic supremacy through disruption and dominance', *Sloan Management Review*, **40**(3), 127–36.
Dierickx, I. and Cool, K. (1989), 'Asset stock accumulation and sustainability of competitive advantage', *Management Science*, **35**(12), 1504–12.
Eisenhardt, K.M. (1989), 'Making fast strategic decisions in high-velocity environments', *Academy of Management Journal*, **32**(3), 543–76.
Eisenhardt, K.M. and Santos, F.M. (2002), 'Knowledge-based view: a new theory of strategy?', in A. Pettigrew, H. Thomas and R. Whittington (eds), *Handbook of Strategy and Management*, London: Sage, pp. 139–64.
Ghoshal, S., Hahn, M. and Moran, P. (2000), 'Organizing for firm growth: the interaction between resource-accumulating and organizing processes', in N.J. Foss and V. Mahnke (eds), *Competence, Governance and Entrepreneurship*, Oxford: Oxford University Press, pp. 146–68.
Hamel, G. and Prahalad, C.K. (1994), 'Competing for the future', *Harvard Business Review*, **72**(4), 122–9.
Hedberg, G.P. (1981), 'How organizations learn and unlearn', in P.C. Nystrom and W.H. Starbuck (eds), *Handbook of Organizational Design*, New York: Oxford University Press, pp. 3–27.
Kogut, B. and Zander, U. (1992), 'Knowledge of the firm, combinative capabilities, and the replication of technology', *Organization Science*, **3**(3), 383–98.
Lovas, B. and Ghoshal, S. (2000), 'Strategy as guided evolution', *Strategic Management Journal*, **21**(9), 875–96.
Løwendahl, B.R. (1997), *Strategic Management of Professional Service Firms*, Copenhagen: Copenhagen Business School Press.
Maister, D.H. (1985), 'The one-firm firm: what makes it successful', *Sloan Management Review*, **27**(1), 3–13.
March, J.G. (1991), 'Exploration and exploitation in organizational learning', *Organization Science*, **2**(1), 71–87.
Markides, C.C. (1999), 'A dynamic view of strategy', *Sloan Management Review*, **40**(3), 55–63.

McGee, J. and Thomas, H. (1986), 'Strategic groups: theory, research and taxonomy', *Strategic Management Journal*, **7**(2), 141–60.

McGee, J. and Thomas, H. (2007), 'Knowledge as a lens on the jigsaw puzzle of strategy: reflections and conjectures on the contribution of a knowledge-based view to analytic models of strategic management', *Management Decision*, **45**(3), 539–63.

McLaughlin, C.P. and Coffey, S. (1990), 'Measuring productivity in services', *International Journal of Service Industry*, **1**(1), 46–64.

Miller, D. and Shamsie, J. (1996), 'The resource-based view of the firm in two environments: the Hollywood film studios from 1936 to 1965', *Academy of Management Journal*, **39**(3), 519–44.

Moran, P. and Ghoshal, S. (1999), 'Markets, firms, and the process of economic development', *Academy of Management Review*, **24**(3), 390–413.

Morgan, G. (1986), *Images of Organization*, London: Sage.

Morris, T. and Empson, L. (1998), 'Organisation and expertise: an exploration of knowledge bases and the management of accounting and consulting firms', *Accounting Organizations and Society*, **23**(5–6), 609–24.

Nachum, L. (1999), 'Measurement of productivity of professional services – an illustration on Swedish management consulting firms', *International Journal of Operations and Production Management*, **19**(9–10), 922–49.

Nelson, R.R. and Winter, S.G. (1982), *An Evolutionary Theory of Economic Change*, Cambridge, MA, and London: Harvard University Press.

Nonaka, I. (1994), 'A dynamic theory of organizational knowledge creation', *Organization Science*, **5**(1), 14–37.

Penrose, E.T. (1959), *The Theory of the Growth of the Firm*, New York: Wiley.

Peteraf, M.A. (1993), 'The cornerstones of competitive advantage: a resource-based view', *Strategic Management Journal*, **14**(3), 179–91.

Polanyi, M. (1966), *The Tacit Dimension*, New York: Doubleday.

Porter, M.E. (1980), *Competitive Strategy*, New York: Free Press.

Porter, M.E. (1985), *Competitive Advantage*, New York: Free Press.

Powell, W.W. and Koput, K.W. (1996), 'Interorganizational collaboration and the locus of innovation: networks of learning in biotechnology', *Administrative Science Quarterly*, **41**(1), 116–45.

Prusak, L. (1997), *Knowledge in Organizations*, London Butterworth-Heinemann.

Rumelt, R.P. (1984), 'Towards a strategic theory of the firm', in N.J. Foss (ed.), *Resources, Firms, and Strategies*, New York: Oxford University Press, pp. 131–45.

Schumpeter, J.A. (1934), *The Theory of Economic Development*, Cambridge, MA: Harvard University Press.

Schumpeter, J.A. (1947), 'The creative response in economic history', *Journal of Economic History*, **7**(2), 149–59.

Simon, H.A. (1991a), 'Organizations and markets', *Journal of Economic Perspectives*, **5**(2), 25–45.

Simon, H.A. (1991b), 'Bounded rationality and organizational learning', *Organization Science*, **2**(1), 125–34.

Szulanski, G. (2003), *Sticky Knowledge*, London: Sage.

Teece, D.J., Pisano, G. and Shuen, A. (1997), 'Dynamic capabilities and strategic management', *Strategic Management Journal*, **18**(7), 509–34.

Wernerfelt, B. (1984), 'A resource-based view of the firm', *Strategic Management Journal*, **5**(2), 171–80.

Williamson, O.E. (1991), 'Strategizing, economizing, and economic organization', *Strategic Management Journal*, **12**(8), 75–95.

29 Foreseeing the problem of conformity in strategy teaching, research and practice
Gregory B. Vit*

Forecasting conformity

The central idea of this chapter is to shed light upon a paradox in the teaching and research of strategy and foresight. While some academics and practitioners appear to be involved in cutting-edge approaches to strategy and foresight; significant time, effort and print continues to be spent upon building legitimacy for arcane dominant strategic management models (Fayol 1916; Andrews 1987; Hitt and Ireland 2006) that often simply do not work. Their persistence may be due to non-economic social reasons that contribute to conformist approaches to strategy and foresight. This chapter will begin with a review of the dominant 'strategic management model' as it appears in many business school strategy texts. It will then highlight implicit and questionable assumptions behind this model. Last, the chapter will suggest alternative lines of thinking about strategy and foresight that should be addressed in courses aimed at teaching and practice.

The all-pervasive conformist and prescriptive strategy model

Arguably most texts that endeavour to teach strategy at the undergraduate or MBA level still rely heavily upon a prescriptive and unproven strategy analysis–formulation–implementation approach as illustrated in Figure 29.1.

This dominant strategy model has been institutionalized within many business schools (Mintzberg 2004) and manifests itself in the discourse that surrounds 'strategic managing'. One way of illustrating the pervasiveness of this model is to look at how strategy is treated in most business school textbooks. The conventional strategy text that is used by many business schools is generic. The reader may determine how close the following observations are to his or her personal experience of basic strategy texts. My impression of dominant conventional texts looks something like this.

Chapters 1 to 3 deal with analysis. As illustrated in Figure 29.1, Chapter 1 introduces the entire model which includes strategy formulation using SWOT analysis (strengths, weaknesses, opportunities, threats), and then strategy implementation (Fayol 1916; Andrews 1987). Chapter 2 is often entitled 'external analysis' and exhorts neophytes and experienced managers alike to predict unpredictable trends (Gimpl and Dakin 1984; Galbraith 2004) related to externalities beyond the boundaries of the organization. This is sometimes called PESTEL (political, economic, social, technological, ecological and

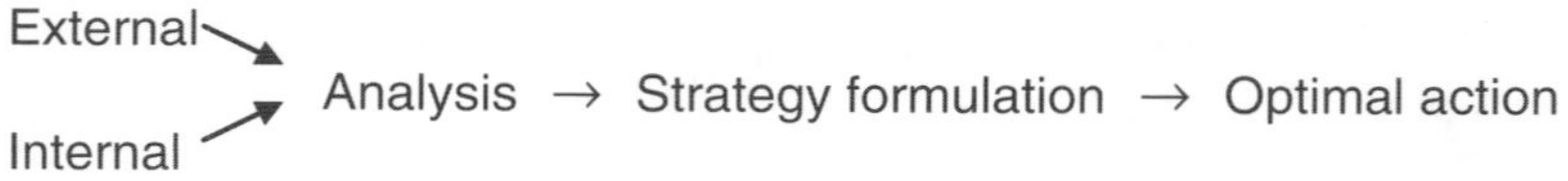

External ↘
         Analysis → Strategy formulation → Optimal action
Internal ↗

Figure 29.1 The dominant prescriptive strategic management model

legal) analysis. Two other Porterian (Porter 1985, 1990) levels of analysis are also often introduced. Porter's (1985) five forces model (threat of new entrants, substitute products, buyer and supplier power, intensity of rivalry) is proposed as a method of gauging industry attractiveness. A higher level of analysis may involve using Porter's (1990) competitive national diamond (factors of production, demand conditions, related and supporting industries, and intensity of industry rivalry) framework to determine location-based national or regional cluster advantages or disadvantages. Chapter 3 usually involves some form of internal analysis. Strengths and weaknesses are analysed across functional areas and for the organization across business units and as a whole (Ansoff 1965; Andrews 1987). More recently, a resource-based view (Wernerfelt 1984; Barney 1991) of the firm has emerged that includes an analysis of organizational tangible and intangible resources and their combination into capabilities. Invincible capabilities, called 'core competencies', must be rare, valuable, non-substitutable and imperfectly imitable. These are said to add value and create many years of sustainable growing cashflows and wealth. Incompetency is outsourced. Other less perfect market contexts such as market manias and bubbles, family-controlled businesses, visible and invisible cartels and market failures are ignored.

Chapters 4 to 8 or so, are dedicated to strategy formulation at different levels of analysis. Chapter 4 might deal with lower-order 'business-level' strategies. Again, Porter (1980) provides a menu of generic strategies that allow a firm to successfully compete by being generically different (?) or by being the lowest-cost producer, or possibly both, for all or part of a business and market. The value chain analysis (ibid.) is often introduced to track where value is added from the input of factors of production through process through output in primary and related firm activities. If at any point, value is not being created in the minds of consumers due to differentiation or in the pockets of consumers due to cost leadership, the activity can be outsourced to somewhere else (possibly offshore) if feasible. Chapter 5 might offer a higher level of analysis and explore overall corporate-level strategies. In-house degrees of diversification and types of related or unrelated diversification are usually discussed. This leads to Chapter 6 which looks at acquisition strategies and the rationale for horizontal and vertical acquisitions and their degree of relatedness to the firm. Chapter 7 often looks at overall corporate big-picture strategy from an international perspective. This will include the pros and cons of different modes of foreign entry/degrees of international involvement section (exporting, licensing, strategic alliances, acquisitions, joint ventures, and wholly owned subsidiaries). Also common is a 2 × 2 matrix that addresses need for local responsiveness versus need for global integration and then prescribes international (low/low), global (low/high), transnational (high/high) or multidomestic (high/low) strategies as means of dealing with the dialogue between these two forces. Discussion of international financial and political risk and the benefits of international diversification and reduced risk due to negative covariance of returns is sometimes added. Chapter 8 may deal with restructuring (downsizing, leveraged financing by fix and flip private equity firms, or its opposite, de-leveraging, and spinoffs) and workouts that may ensue if Chapters 1 to 7 have failed to create shareholder value and wealth. Chapter 9 might focus on a topical subject such as corporate governance, sustainability and ethics. It has some discussion of who should control an organization and may use agency versus stewardship theory and a hierarchy of economic, legal (Friedman 1970) and other criteria (Carrol 1999) for effective governance. The role of the board of directors, its composition and its involvement with management is examined. Chapters 10 to 12 or so, focus upon implementation and control. Chapter 10 might be about organizational structure and usually deals with the classical progression of entrepreneur/one-person show to functional structure, to multidivisional form and variations thereof such as matrix and possibly networks, together with the pros and cons of these different organizational forms. This is often accompanied by many uniform boxes connected by lines called organizational charts. Chapter 11 invariably looks at how controls can be put in place that will ensure that Chapters 1 to 10 are successful. These involve MBO (management by objective) metrics that are based upon behavioural and financial controls (Taylor 1911; Ford 1926), and more recent questionable 'modern' management techniques (Staw and Epstein 2000). These are sometimes compared to untested 'best practices' and benchmarks. Chapter 12 concludes the text with a filler or nebulous topical subject such as leadership and the CEO. It endeavours to explain how vision and a good CEO can make a difference.

Thus, the strategy student is exposed to reductionist frameworks, checklists and generic recipes without questioning their underlying taken-for-grantedness. Many implicit assumptions exist behind this dominant model that could be made explicit.

Implicit assumptions
First, the above model and accompanying texts are highly prescriptive. It is assumed that if managers use the above framework, they will be more competitive and achieve greater shareholder wealth creation than those that do not. Evidence is mixed in this regard. For example, Vit's (1993) preliminary study of Canadian bank CEOs found that the bank that had the least formalized strategy process had the best returns over a decade. Staw and Epstein (2000) noted that trendy modern management techniques did not improve US firm performance but improved reputation and legitimacy and increased CEO compensation.

Second, this dominant model also assumes that the organization is considered to be a subject, that can act upon the world and 'make' the 'right' optimal rational strategic choices. As discussed above, most strategy texts are structured following the Cartesian lines of: analysis formulation and optimized action (Clegg et al. 2004). Others argue that strategies often unfold due to intended and unintended actions that cause other strategies to form (Merton 1936; Mintzberg and Waters 1985), and are then understood. The process of *ex post* reconstruction is sometimes called 'sensemaking' (Weick 1979). Often, successful random events are coupled with unrelated actors or causes (Gimpl and Dakin 1984). Thus, successful strategies may be attributed to unrelated and vague activities such as 'managing strategically' and 'CEO leadership'. This attributive model of strategy is outlined in Figure 29.2, below.

Third, hard data and analysis are relied upon, cognition is used to recognize patterns, and strategies are codified and communicated. Others have argued that soft data and intuition are equally important (Nonaka 1991); however, this is largely neglected by the model. Also, the strategic management model is assumed to be a top-down activity reserved for senior management. Many organizations do just the opposite (Pascale 1996). They create loose boundaries, avoid orthodox patterns and use junior managers to create new visions of their futures (Hamel 2000; Quinn et al. 1996).

Fourth, the model is temperal-centric, and USA-centric. Temperal-centric means that

a) Attributive model
   action → sensemaking

b) Evolutionary model
   chance
                  suboptimal adaptation
   incumbency

c) Institutional model
   social structure → action or inaction

d) Appreciative model
   fact selection → fact valuation → action

e) Configurational model
   organizational forces ↔ organizational forms

Figure 29.2   Alternative strategy models

the model, and its recent incremental variations, assumes that it is the most advanced and contemporary way of dealing with strategy, even though its antecedents are dated (Fayol 1916; Andrews 1987). Observers have also noted (March 2006) that this model and its texts became nested and sedimented within business schools. The business school, with its quantitative and analytic functional silos emerged as the dominant design in management education in the USA. Although there is scant academic evidence to suggest that the dominant model is successful, or used in the manner prescribed, business schools outside the USA engaged in the mimetic perpetuation of the dominant model in order to further teaching at all levels and facilitate consultancy and research. Other descriptive schools have emerged and continue to compete with the traditional prescriptive view of strategy for share of mind of managers and academics (Mintzberg 1979).

Fifth, old ideas are modified incrementally due to this process. As in academe, stasis is maintained in many large organizations by the above 'strategic management process' and it simply reaffirms muddling through (Lindblom 1958) until crisis causes change to happen in quantum leaps (Miller and Friesen, 1984).

An alternative approach
Most MBAs and undergraduate students are exposed to the above body of knowledge in numerous courses, which is often complemented by intensive case analysis and number crunching. Decisive answers are produced from available case facts and figures garnered from self-contained case data and convenient case appendices.

An alternative strategy course would comprise small classes and would include a text of conceptual readings that would comprise two sections, de-freezing and re-freezing. This would be complemented where possible by experiential learning activities such as in-depth student-as-scholar field projects and internships. Mintzberg (2004) has noted that students are overequipped with the tools and techniques of truncated analysis such as the dominant strategic management model discussed above, and other reflective, collaborative, wordly, and action mindsets are essential for managerial effectiveness.

Exposure to alternative descriptive strategy models is one way for students of strategy to step away from the rule of the tool that is the dominant strategy model. Although by no means exhaustive, an alternative text would have students reading and thinking in new directions and might resemble the following.

De-freezing: describing prescription
Chapters 1 to 6 would highlight that strategy means different things to different people for different reasons. The dominant strategy model outlined above would be addressed immediately, along with its implicit assumptions and limitations. The first chapter would underline the fact that the dominant model is also useful for ceremonial purposes as it creates an illusion of control (Gimpl and Dakin 1984), yet may provide little foresight due to its inherent biases (Clegg et al. 2004).

Re-freezing: prescribing description
Competing views of strategy would also be introduced in subsequent chapters that challenge the conventional model. I have highlighted five interesting and different approaches to strategy formation in Figure 29.2.

As discussed above, the first framework presented in Figure 29.2, the attributive model, assigns causality and creates sense from observed action (Weick 1979; Shapira and Berndt 1997).

A further variation of this theme is illustrated in the second, evolutionary model of strategy, of Figure 29.2. This evolutionary model of strategy would suggest that an organization could be viewed as being the object of random variation within a population. Suboptimal strategies are selected, retained and infused with meaning by chance events and the deeply entrenched orthodoxies, identifications and discourses of societies, organizations, groups and managers (Morison 1966; Gould 1987; Philips et al. 2004). Wesley et al. (2006) call less predictable complex processes 'getting to maybe'.

As represented by the third institutional model of strategy shown in Figure 29.2, the power and structure of the environment may override attempts at foresight by organizational planners. For example, Vit and Graham (1997) have noted that the top five Canadian banks enjoyed 85 per cent of market share 100 years ago and continued to do so today, even though laws have been changed to permit foreign bank entry. Vit (1996) has called the powerful pressures of conformity sedimented within industry and organizational structures 'conformist strategy' and 'mismanagement'. Thompson's (1967) open system view of inputs–process–output may be applied to undergraduate and graduate programmes and the teaching of strategy and foresight. Due to the structure of a demanding selection process, excellent student input with strong cognitive ability is preselected by many leading business schools. The strategy teaching process could be negligible (that is, texts and constructs that are dated or ineffectual) since the resultant output will continue to be excellent.

An understanding of the dynamics of the first three models presented in Figure 29.2 may improve our understanding of strategy and foresight since they describe how strategies form. Nevertheless, common appreciative systems resist change, and new appreciative systems create new frame-breaking ideas that continue to destroy the competencies of veteran firms (Strebel 1992). This raises another question. Where does new radical strategy come from?

The appreciative model of strategy presented in Figure 29.2 attempts to map out a route to strategy and action using cognition and pattern recognition. Simon (1945) has noted that facts are selected, valued and acted upon differently and often suboptimally based upon predispositions that exist in the mind of the manager. Vickers calls this 'an appreciative system' (1965). The text would also examine how and why common and different predispositions emerge. It would further discuss the nature of intuition and seek to gain insight into what strategists actually do, and how they might approach strategy creation and foresight. How is it that some individuals make connections between seemingly unconnected facts that allow them to create new paradigms and strategies (Bronowski 1958; Kuhn 1970; Drucker 1999)? We do not know enough about where new disruptive strategies come from and how they are induced within complex systems. Wesley et al. (2006) note that C.S. Holling explores transformational learning via scaleable breakthroughs. The development and management of intellect requires an understanding of instrumental know-how and know-what, but it also increasingly means that we must also help managers ask more difficult questions infused with collective and individual values: to know why and care why (Quinn et al., 1996).

The last entry in Figure 29.2, the configurational model of strategy, would be dealt with in a separate chapter. This chapter would step back and view strategy at an organizational level of analysis as a subset of institutional theory. Configuration theory would be introduced to explain that different forces act upon organizations and produce different organizational forms that morph over time. Among others (Miller 1987,1996; Greenwood and Hinings 1996), Thompson (1967) and Mintzberg (1991) have noted that the behaviour of organizations can be understood by examining different underlying processes that exist to standardize behaviour. For example, the standardization of work processes and outputs will lead to conformity within the context of a machine organization such as a bank machine bureaucracy. The standardization of norms can lead to predictable behaviour by organizations (Zald and Denton 1963) and sadly may provide insight into more extreme forms of ideologically driven action such as terrorism (Allison 2005). The standardization of expert skills may lead to proficiency and cognition being codified in expert systems such as those related to medical diagnosis that also have high predictive power (Simon 1987). Thus, standardizing and non-standardizing forces and forms interact and create configurations. This is represented in the last entry in Figure 29.2 as the configurational model of strategy.

Another chapter might return to institutional theory and use it to explain how large organizations behave within a broader context including business schools. As outlined by the constructs described above, institutional theory provides a powerful non-economic explanation of conformity (Meyer and Rowan 1977; DiMaggio and Powell 1983; Scott 1995). A higher level of analysis is also useful as it includes organizations that are interdependent within an organizational field (Holm 1995). For example, Vit (2006) has argued that large banks may de-couple from economic rationality for years and continue to build legitimacy for questionable actions by relying upon socially nested routines and beliefs. The body of knowledge that is institutional theory may explain the question and paradox of 'individualistic herding' by strategy students and business schools underlined by the discussion above. It may help in answering the question of why large businesses are full of very clever and rational individuals, who often teach common recipes that do not work. It might also consider contrarian anomalous organizations, business schools and individuals who intendedly or unintendedly successfully deviate from the pack (Vit 2007).

A further chapter may explore ideas related to power, social structure and change. Pfeffer (1992) has noted that most students of organizations are encouraged to work as individuals throughout their undergraduate and graduate careers yet organizational life requires an understanding of interdependencies that inhibit and accelerate action. Thus, universities are recruiting and producing students that are very good at getting high grades by memorizing and applying handy analytic models that may be detrimental to the synthesis involved in independent critical thought (Vit 2006). Rather than ignoring these invisible forces, an understanding of resource dependencies and power and politics may lead to more effective forethought, action, change and afterthought.

Yet another chapter could be devoted to extending this notion of configurations across time and space by examining business history and particularly panics, manias and crashes. While financial theorists may argue that each moment is the confluence of unique forces, expectations and events (Brealey 1985), others have argued that broad patterns over time can be identified (MacKay 1914). For example, building upon Minsky's (1972) work on the economics of disaster, Kindleberger (1978) has suggested that most manias occur due to a displacement that creates three phases: boom–euphoria, mania–bubble, and revulsion–crash. Although bubbles are easy to spot *ex post*, the decoupling of economic rationality and its override by social forces that build legitimacy is worthy of attention a priori, at a meta level of analysis. Due to their dramatic economic and social impact, strategy students should be exposed to accounts of the social construction of various recent and not so recent financial market bubbles and crises in the same way that students of geology study earthquakes. Purely economic explanations of foresight are ineffectual. For example, Galbraith (2004) notes that an entire financial forecasting industry exists to predict the unpredictable timing and direction of markets.

Conformity and contrarianism

Later chapters could be devoted to contrarian strategy and foresight. The first chapters dealt with the problem of conformity. Chapter one suggested that the dominant model used to teach strategy has many hidden underlying assumptions that build conformity. It is also ethically empty, as the instrumentality of a plan can be used for good or evil purposes. Thus, the analysis–formulation–implementation model may or may not work. If we agree with the preceding discussion that it does not appreciably improve strategy or foresight, what are we left with? The chapters of the new text outlined thus far would suggest that the problem of conformity is reinforced at many levels of analysis. Some individuals do not conform despite formidable pressures to do so (Merton 1938). Our understanding of patterns in conformist managerial behaviour is not complete, nor is unorthodox or contrarian managerial behaviour fully understood. Morison (1966) has observed that the limited identification of individuals to both in- and out-groups may help explain both.

Tremendous pressure to conform also exists within organizations; new and old, small and large. Strong organizational ideologies create common values that may override atomistic value-maximizing economic behaviour. Social forces, orthodoxies, and embedded organizational algorithms may create taken-for-granted cognitive routines that may not require critical questioning or deviant behaviour. Finally, underlying economic relationships may drive herding behaviour in the medium term, and we do not understand how this may result in manias, panics and crashes at macro levels of analysis. Vit (2006) calls these multiple logics 'ideo-logics', 'socio-logics' and 'eco-logics', respectively.

Although we may not understand or be able to fully foresee the impact of displacements on managers, organizations, organizational fields and economic booms and busts, an understanding of the dynamics of conformity at these levels of analysis allows us to be aware of pressures that close down independent thought and action. Contrarianism begins with this understanding. In order to understand how being different can be advantageous or disadvantageous, it is necessary to understand the dynamics of conformity.

Relevance and big ideas
The final chapters of the text would endeavour to open up other philosophical problems, and deal with topics that have major managerial and human relevence. A chapter would be devoted to contrarian organizations such as non-owned organizations and their role in our world. Many organizations such as universities and non-governmental organizations are not accountable to shareholders. Social purpose and social innovation may eclipse the maximization of free cash flow (Wesley et al. 2006). Beyond factory-type organizations that may lend themselves to bureaucracy and strategic managing, other organizational forms such as networks, cooperatives, and micro-credit lending agencies represent interesting forms of alternative action. Strategies related to managing these organizations could also be examined (Quinn et al. 1996; Mintzberg 2004). Observers (Christensen et al. 2001) have noted that business teaching and research applications cater to the top billion human beings within developed nations. 'Bottom of the pyramid' approaches to strategy and foresight that address the other four billion inhabitants of this planet represent another promising contrarian contribution to strategy. This could be integrated with other broader issues related to sustainability, such as global food, water and energy demand, supply and alternative solutions.

As noted, SWOT analyses together with strategy formulation and implementation are instrumental and sterile. They do not deal with ethical issues and social questions such as the dangers of technological advancement that may have a major impact upon managers and society. For example, Joy (2000) has noted that nuclear, biological and chemical weapons of mass destruction (WMD) were largely controlled by governments, yet new self-replicating technologies such as genomics, nano-technology and robotics are potentially open to abuse by many individuals and groups. In the race for material gain, growth and commercialization, wilful or accidental mass replication could have serious negative consequences. The alternative text would highlight these risks and seek to engage students to think about personal moral dilemmas and risk (Srinivas 1999). While significant attention is given to governance at a top management and board level using reductionist checklists and strategic plans, effective thought, understanding and responsibility for potentially revolutionary change must occur at an individual level.

For example, Bird and Shirwin (2005) have noted that the intended and unintended consequences of the creation of the nuclear bomb was not foreseen by J. Robert Oppenheimer and his colleagues. Few policy researchers write about big problems and risks. An exception is Allison (2005), who ends on a cautiously optimistic note regarding the threat and prevention of nuclear terrorism.

Conclusion
This brief chapter has argued that a well-worn dominant strategy model is still pervasive and present in texts and the teaching of strategy and foresight. We may foresee with some

certainty that this model will continue to contribute to the problem of conformity in management education and research. This chapter has also suggested several promising alternative views of strategy and lines of thinking. A first step to improving our understanding of foresight and strategy is to continue to prescribe description. This may open our minds to alternative ways of viewing strategy that could have a much greater impact upon managers and society.

Note

* McGill University, Canada.

References

Allison, G. (2005), *Nuclear Terrorism: The Ultimate Preventable Catastrophe*, New York: Henry Holt.
Andrews, K.R. (1987), *The Concept of Corporate Strategy*, Dow Jones-Irwin.
Ansoff, H.I. (1965), *Corporate Strategy*, New York: McGraw-Hill.
Barney, J.B. (1991), 'Firm resources and sustained competitive advantage', *Journal of Management*, **17**, 99–120.
Bird, K. and M.J. Shirwin (2005), *American Prometheus: The Triumph and Tragedy of J. Robert Oppenheimer*, New York: Random House.
Brealey, R. (1985), *An Introduction to Risk and Return*, London: Blackwell.
Bronowski, J. (1958), 'The creative process', *Scientific American*, September, 59–65.
Caroll, A.B. (1999), 'Corporate social responsibility: evolution of a definitional construct', *Business & Society*, **38**(3), 268–95.
Christensen, C., T. Craig and S. Hart (2001), 'The great disruption', *Foreign Affairs*, **80** (2), 80–95.
Clegg, S., C. Carter and M. Kornberger (2004), 'Get up, I feel like being a strategy machine', *European Management Review*, **1**, 21–8.
DiMaggio, P. and W.W. Powell (1983), 'The iron cage revisited: institutional isomorphism and collective rationality in organizational fields', *American Sociological Review*, **48**, 147–60.
Drucker, P. (1999), 'Beyond the information revolution', *Atlantic Monthly*, October, 47–57.
Fayol, H. (1916), *General and Industrial Management*, New York: Pitman.
Ford, H. (1926), *Today and Tomorrow*, New York: Doubleday.
Friedman, M. (1970), 'The social responsibility of business is to increase its profits', *The New York Times Magazine*, 13 September.
Galbraith, J.K. (2004), *The Economics of Innocent Fraud: Truth for Our Times*, Boston, MA: Houghton Mifflin.
Gimpl, M.L. and S.R. Dakin (1984) 'Management and magic', *California Management Review*, **27** (1), 125–36.
Gould, S.J. (1987), 'The panda's thumb of technology', *Natural History*, **96** (1), 16–23.
Greenwood, R. and C.R. Hinings (1996), 'Understanding radical organizational change: bringing together the old and the new institutionalism', *Academy of Management Review*, **21** (4), 1022–54.
Hamel, G. (2000), *Leading the Revolution*, Cambridge, MA: Harvard Business School Press.
Hitt, M.A., R.D. Ireland and R.E. Hoskisson (2006), *Strategic Management: Competitiveness and Globalization*, New York: Thomson South-Western.
Holm, P. (1995) 'The dynamics of institutionalization: transformation processes in Norwegian fisheries', *Administrative Science Quarterly*, **40** (3), 398–422.
Joy, W. (2000), 'Why the future doesn't need us', *Wired*, 8 April, 1–12.
Kindleberger, C. (1978), *Manias, Panics and Crashes*, New York: Basic Books.
Kuhn, T.S. (1970), *The Structure of Scientific Revolutions*, Chicago: Chicago University Press.
Lindblom, C. (1958), 'The science of "muddling through"', *Public Administration Review*, **19**, 79–88.
MacKay, C. (1914), *Memoirs of Extraordinary Delusions and the Madness of Crowds*, reprinted 1932, Boston, MA: L.C. Page Co.
March, J.G. (2006), 'The study of organizations and organizing since 1945', Keynote address to the European Group of Organizational Studies, Bergen, Norway, 6 July.
Merton, R.K. (1936), 'The unanticipated consequences of purposive social action', *American Sociological Review*, **1** (6), December, 894–904.
Merton, R.K. (1938), 'Social structure and anomie', *American Sociological Review*, **3** (5), October, 672–82.
Meyer, J.W. and B. Rowan (1977), 'Institutionalized organizations: formal structures as myth and ceremony', *American Journal of Sociology*, **83**, 340–63.

Miller, D. (1987), 'The genesis of configuration', *Academy of Management Review*, **12** (4), October, 686–701.
Miller, D. (1996), 'Configurations revisited', *Strategic Management Journal*, **17** (7), July, 505–12.
Miller, D. and P. Friesen (1984), *Organizations: A Quantum View*, Englewood Cliffs, NJ: Prentice Hall.
Minsky, H.P. (1972), 'Financial stability revisited: the economics of disaster', in *Board of Governors of the Federal Reserve System, Reappraisal of the Federal Reserve Discount Mechanism*, **3**, 95–136.
Mintzberg, H. (1979), *The Structuring of Organizations: A Synthesis of the Research*, Englewood Cliffs, NJ: Prentice-Hall.
Mintzberg, H. (1991), 'The effective organization: forces and forms', *Sloan Management Review*, **32** (2), 57–67.
Mintzberg, H. (2004), *Managers, Not MBAs: A Hard Look at the Soft Practice of Managing and Management Development*, San Francisco, CA: Berrett-Koehler Publishers.
Mintzberg, H. and J. Waters (1985), 'Of strategies, deliberate and emergent', *Strategic Management Journal*, **6**, 257–72.
Morison, E. (1966), 'Gunfire at sea: a case study of innovation,' in E.E. Morison (ed.), *Men, Machines and Modern Times*, Cambridge, MA: MIT Press, pp. 17–44.
Nonaka, T. (1991), 'The knowledge creating company', *Harvard Business Review*, **69**, November–December, 96–104.
Pascale, R.T. (1996), 'The Honda effect', *California Management Review*, **38**, 80–94.
Pfeffer, J. (1992), 'Understanding power in organizations', *California Management Review*, **34** (2), 29–50.
Phillips, N., T.B. Lawrence and C. Hardy (2004), 'Discourse and institutions', *Academy of Management Review*, **29**, 635–52
Porter, M.E. (1980), *Competitive Strategy: Techniques for Analyzing Industries and Competitors*, New York: Free Press.
Porter, M.E. (1985), *The Competitive Advantage: Creating and Sustaining Superior Performance*, New York: Free Press.
Porter, M.E. (1990), *The Competitive Advantage of Nations*, New York: Free Press.
Quinn, J.B., P. Anderson and S. Finkelstein (1996), 'Managing professional intellect', *Harvard Business Review*, **74**, 72–80.
Scott, W.R. (1995), *Institutions and Organizations*, Thousand Oaks, CA: Sage.
Shapira, Z. and D.J. Berndt (1997), 'Managing grand scale construction projects: a risk-taking perspective', *Research in Organizational Behaviour*, **14**, 303–60.
Simon, H.A. (1945), *Adminstrative Behaviour*, New York: Macmillan.
Simon, H. (1987), 'Making management decisions: the role of intuition and emotion', *Academy of Management Executive*, February.
Srinivas, N. (1999), 'Managers as androids: reading moral agency in Philip Dick', *Organization*, **6** (4), 609–24.
Staw, B.M. and L.D. Epstein (2000), 'What bandwagons bring: effects of popular management techniques on corporate performance, reputation, and CEO pay', *Administrative Science Quarterly*, **45** (3), 523–56.
Strebel, P. (1992), *Breakpoints: How Managers Exploit Radical Business Change*, Boston, MA: Harvard Business School Press.
Taylor, F. W. (1911), *The Principles of Scientific Management*, New York: Harper Bros.
Thompson, J.D. (1967), *Organizations in Action*, New York: McGraw-Hill.
Vickers, G. (1965), *The Art of Judgement: A Study of Policy Making*, New York: Basic Books.
Vit, G. (1993), 'Canadian bank strategy: the CEO's perspective', *Cahier de Recherche CETAI 93-18*, École des Hautes Études Commerciales, Montreal, Canada, pp. 1–15.
Vit, G.B. (1996), 'Financial services industry mismanagement', *International Journal of Service Industry Management*, **7** (3), 6–16.
Vit, G. (2006), 'Organizational conformity and contrarianism: regular irregular trading at National Australia Bank', *Corporate Governance*, **6** (2), 203–14.
Vit, G.B (2007), 'The multiple logics of conformity and contrarianism: the problem with investment banks and bankers', *Journal of Management Inquiry*, **16** (3), 217–26.
Vit, G. and J. Graham (1997), 'Canada changes foreign bank laws', *Butterworth's Journal of International Banking & Financial Law*, September, 363–68.
Weick, K.E. (1979), *The Social Psychology of Organizing*, 2nd edn, Reading, MA: Addison-Wesley.
Wernerfelt, B. (1984), 'A resource-based view of the firm', *Strategic Management Journal*, **5**, 171–80.
Wesley, F., B. Zimmerman and M. Patton (2006), *Getting to Maybe: How the World is Changed*, Toronto: Random House.
Zald, M.N. and P. Denton (1963), 'From evangelism to general service: the transformation of the YMCA', *Administrative Science Quarterly*, **8** (2), 214–34.

Index

a-contextual change agents 251–2
Aaken, Dominik van 6
abnormal events 102
absorptive capacity 350, 354–5, 356
abstract conceptualization (AC) 279–80
Academy of Management (AOM) 5
Accenture 513
accessibility 122
Acker, J. 255
Acorn Computers 315–17, 318, 322
acquisitions 507
action 68–75, 98, 185–6
active experimentation (AE) 279–80
actor network theory 171
actors 208–12, 213–14, 219–20, 251–2, 262–3, 264
adaptability 193, 306–7
adaptation 306, 385, 453, 454–6, 458, 480
adaptive learning 279
adaptive systems 30–39
adaptive tension 28–9
adaptively rational model 381
Adler, P.S. 461
advanced manufacturing techniques (AMTs) 343, 344, 346–8, 355, 357
ADVICS Co. 384–5, 386
AES 239, 246
aesthetic composition 448–9
aesthetic of imperfection 194
affect, and intuition 399–400, 402, 404–6
AGD 462–78, 479, 480
agency 8, 219, 232–3, 249–50, 270
    see also change agency
Agocs, C. 254
Agor, W.H. 397, 408, 409
Ahuja, G. 1
Aichi Steel 382
air transport 139–40
Aisin Seiki 382, 383, 384
Albert, S. 476
alethic modality 114–15, 124
Allen, P.M. 21, 30
Allinson, C.W. 398, 399, 408, 409
alternative histories 117, 119, 124
aluminium plant (empirical example) 240–43, 247
Alvesson, M. 172
ambidextrous organizations
    achievement of 9, 324–5

definition 325, 338
exploration and exploitation 182, 183–4, 278
management mechanisms 325–40
American Civil War 117
analyser 156
analysis
    dual-process theories of cognition 397–400, 402–3
    and intuition 393, 406–13
    naturalistic decision making (NDM) 403–4
analytic managers 290, 291, 292–3
Anderson, P. 473
Andrews, K. 106
anomalies 441
Ansoff, H.I. 48, 49, 95, 154, 155, 298, 480
antenarrative 100
anti-positivism 145
anticipating critique 53–5, 61, 63
Antonacopoulou, Elena P. 7, 173, 176
Apple Computers 280–81, 461
appreciative model 521, 522–3
Archer, M. 219–20
ARESE 260, 266, 269
Argentina 453, 454, 462–78, 479, 480
Argyris, C. 41, 279
Arkes, H.R. 394
artefacts 188, 189–90
Arthur, W.B. 20, 33, 67, 486
artificial intelligence (AI) 31, 395, 397
as-if loop 405
Ashby, W.R. 21, 24
Asllani, A. 288
asset, knowledge as 509
assignments of blame 101
Astley, W.G. 381, 454
asymmetric lateralization 397
AT&T 395
@Home 319–20
attitudes 253
attractors 33–6, 38–9
attributive model 521, 522
automotive industry 9, 37, 76, 94, 300, 380, 381–8, 502
autonomy
    ambidextrous organizations 325–40
    change agents 250–51
    fast cycle capability (FCC) 354, 356

and organizational flexibility 460, 467–71, 478
    organizational memory 440
autopoiesis
    case studies 224–30
    middle managers 222–4
    organizational systems 220–23
    transformation criteria 230–34
awe and wonder 78–9
axiological modality 115, 124

Backoff, R.W. 310
backstage 242–7, 253
Bahrami, H. 458, 459, 461
Bak, P. 33
Bakken, T. 220, 221
Balogun, J. 98
Bangladesh 490, 498
banking 94, 173, 422, 432, 520, 523
Banque de France 422, 432
Bantel, K.A. 343
Barings Bank 94
Barnard, Chester 1, 68, 330, 395
Barney, J. 1, 486, 506
Barr, P. 94
Bartlett, C.A. 328
Bass, B.M. 251
Battilana, Julie 8
Baum, J.R. 311, 349
Bazerman, M. 2
Beard, D.W. 351
Bechara, A. 405
Bechky, B.A. 511
Beck, U. 91
Beer, S. 220
behaviour 101, 156
beliefs
    ambidextrous organizations 330–31, 333, 337, 338–9, 340
    change agency 253
    doxastic-axiological counterfactuals 116, 124
    and knowledge 312
    and organizational flexibility 458, 477
Belkin, A. 116
BellSouth 457
Bennis, W.G. 20, 38, 39–40, 42
Berdrow, I. 282
Berger, Gaston 128
Berkhout, F. 256
Bérnard, H. 15
Bessant, J. 347
better-than-experienced worlds 103
Bettis, R.A. 277, 282, 283, 284
Bhaskar, Roy 17, 18–19, 42, 219

Bilmes, Linda 93
Bird, K. 525
Birkinshaw, J. 202
Black Swans 93
blue ocean strategies 66–7
Boddy, D. 253
bodily action 70–73
body loop 405
Bohler, D. 70
Bohm, D. 146
Boisot, Max 5, 23, 31, 42
Boje, D. 100
Boland, R.J. 285
Bonaccorsi, A. 348
Booth, Charles 6, 115, 116, 119, 120, 123, 487
Boston Consulting Group 343
Boston Red Sox 94
bottom-up strategizing 297, 299–300, 301, 303, 306
Boulding, K.E. 33, 510
boundary spanners 288–9, 292
bounded rationality 90, 311–12, 395–6, 448
Bourdieu, P. 170, 173, 219, 254
Bourgeois, L.J. 155
Bower, J.L. 9, 343, 344, 349, 457
boy with the knife, autopoiesis case study 226–7
Boyer, K.K. 347
Boynton, A.C. 461
Braun, Armand 128
breakout strategies 67
British Academy of Management (BAM) 5
British Telecom (BT) 315–17, 318, 322
Brown, S.L. 37, 152, 278
Bruner, J. 62
Bryman, A. 40
BSkyB 316
Buchanan, D. 253
budget games 204
Buist Spinning 490, 496
bureaucracies 223
Burgelman, R.A. 457
Burns, Tom 200, 324, 326, 455
Burrell, G. 145, 147
Burt, George 7, 153
business schools 136–9, 412, 521, 523
    see also MBA (Master of Business Administration) programmes
business wargaming 83
Business Week 299

C&NW (Chicago and North Western Transportation Company) 94
Cairns, G. 153
Caldwell, R. 251

California 135
capabilities
    core competencies 519
    development 172–3
    dynamic capability 172–3, 459, 474, 506–7, 508
    historical analysis 488–90
    jute manufacturing 493–502
    organizational 305, 458
    and path dependency 10, 485, 486–8, 501–2
car industry 9, 37, 76, 94, 300, 380, 381–8, 502
career ambitions 204, 209–12
Carlile, P.R. 285
Carr, E. 489
case studies
    autopoiesis 224–30
    capabilities and path dependency 490–502
    foresight 134–42
    organizational becoming 240–43
    organizational flexibility 461–79
    organizational innovation 381–8
    research design 158–61
    self-perception 422–30
    subsidiary mandate change 205, 210–12
    vision in digital media companies 313–22
causal ascriptions 101
causally potent antecedent action 103–4
centralization 353, 356, 460, 467–71, 478, 479
CEOs (Chief Executive Officers)
    duality 352–3, 356
    organizational learning 283
    role of 37, 38–9, 42
    sensemaking 97–8
    strategic management 520
    see also senior executives; top management
Chakrabarti, A.K. 345
Chambers, John T. 302
Chandler, A.D. 27, 512
change
    and changing 238–47, 251
    continuous 235, 245, 250–51, 253
    and foresight 94–5
    improvisational bricolage 184–92
    institutional change 265–9
    ontology of 234–5
    and organizational memory 442, 444, 445, 447–8
    and stability 235–8
change agency
    a-contextual change agents 251–2
    in change management literature 250–53, 254–6
    definition 249–50
    foresight in 249, 253–4, 256–8
    organizational learning 288

change management literature 249, 250–56
changing (change in organization) 238–47
charismatic leadership 32, 39–41, 251
Chase, W. 396
Chen, M.-J. 457
Chermack, T.J. 124
Chia, R. 1, 67, 84, 92, 234, 235, 236, 237, 238, 239, 244, 246, 448
Child, J. 149, 456
China 135
Chittipeddi, K. 97, 153
choices 488–90
Choperena, A.M. 349
Christensen, C. 66, 324, 329
Chu, Wenyi 9, 330
Cisco 300, 301–2
Clark, E. 203
Clark, Peter 6, 116, 117, 487
Clarke, I. 411
Clegg, Stewart R. 7, 284
climate change 93
closed systems 222–3, 232
coalition model 380–81
code of silence 307
cognition 397–400
cognitive estrangement 123
Cognitive–Experiential Self-Theory (CEST) 399
cognitive linguistic categories 51–3, 59–64
cognitive styles 57–63, 398
Cohen, W.M. 354
Cohendet, P. 511
Cold War 118
Colgan, F. 256
collaborative learning 382, 383–5
Collins, J.C. 16, 298, 299, 303, 310
Coltrane, John 185
Colville, Ian 8
common knowledge 511
communication
    ambidextrous organizations 331, 333, 337–9, 340
    authenticity 62–3
    fast cycle capability (FCC) 348, 354
    foresight, role of 84, 87–8
    knowledge development 511
    new product development (NPD) 345
    organizational learning 283
    product improvement 367
communicative linguistic categories 51–3, 59–64
competences 311, 519
competition 368–9, 474–6, 478, 479, 480
competitive advantage 11, 343–4, 350, 473
competitive dynamics 192

competitive intelligence 82
competitive strategy 327, 333, 339
competitiveness 179, 315–17
complex adaptive systems 30–39, 220–23
complexity, of environments 188, 326–7, 333, 339
complexity theory
    and Ashby's Law 21–2
    attractors 33–6, 38–9
    farsight 19–20, 22–30, 41–2
    fastsight 20, 30–39
    foresight 41–2
    types of complexity 34
    use of 16
computer aided design (CAD) 343
computer aided manufacturing (CAM) 343, 346
computer industry 305, 348
concrete experience (CE) 279–80
Conde, C. 257
configurational model 521, 523
conformity 11, 524–5
conservative critique 54–5
constraints 21, 148
context 25, 97, 155, 208, 331
contingency 114, 121, 124
contingency planning 3, 92
contingency theory 251, 455
continuous change 235, 245, 250–51, 253
contrarianism 525
convergence periods 438–9
conversation 144, 148
Cool, K. 507
Cooper, R.G. 371
coordination 440
Corley, K. 99
Corning 3, 461
corporate failure 94–5
cosmology episode 97
Costanzo, Laura A. 8
cotton 496, 502
counterfactual analysis 101–4, 107, 115–17, 119, 124, 489–90
counterfactual processes, in sensemaking 91, 101–4, 105
Courtney, H. 5
Craiks 490, 499
Cramer, F. 33, 34
creative destruction 188
creativity 188
crisis 97
critical incidents 224–30, 232
criticism (critique) 53–5, 61, 63
Cromby, J. 146
cross-functional teams 284–7, 288, 345, 354, 356, 365, 369

Crossan, M.M. 280, 282, 291, 406
Crozier, M. 204, 205
Cuervo-Cazurra, Alvaro 9, 364
culture
    and change 240–43
    macroculture embeddedness 471–4, 478, 479
    and organizational flexibility 460
    strategic ambiguity 330–31, 333, 337, 338–9, 340
Cunha, João Vieira Da 7
Cunha, Miguel Pina e 7, 93
customer interactions
    customer responsiveness 343
    customer service 353
    and innovation 9, 362–4, 376–7
    new product development (NPD) 366, 371–3
    new product discovery 366, 371, 374–6
    and organizational flexibility 458
    product improvement 364–8, 371
    product versioning 365, 368–71
Cyert, R.M. 148

Dahrendorf, R. 222
Daihatsu Motor 382
DaimlerChrysler 94
Dallis, Bob 76
Damasio, A.R. 404
Dane, E. 402, 407, 409
Daniel, E.M. 459
Dansereau, F. 39
data collection 159–60
Daugherty, P.J. 348
D'Aveni, R. 66
David, P. 486
Day, D.S. 83
De Certeau, M. 170
de la Ville, I. 132
De Meyer, A. 347
decentralization 460
deep structure 438–9, 440–41, 443, 447
deep understanding 442, 443, 445, 446
defender 156
Delahaye-Dado, Agnés 6
delegation 460
Dell Computer Corporation 343
Delors, Jacques 265
Delphi method 83, 142
demand-side management (DSM) 134–6
Dening, G. 119
Denmark 135, 214
Denso 382, 383, 384, 385
deontic modality 115, 124
DER.S.A. 462–77
Dess, G.G. 351

determinism 156, 204, 489
deviations 194
Dewey, John 69
dialogue 144, 148–9
Dibella, A.J. 283
Dierickx, I. 507
differentiation strategy 327, 333, 339
diffusion 194–5, 258, 267–9
digital media case studies 313–22
DiMaggio, P.J. 211, 269, 271
Dimension X 318–19
discontinuities
    anticipation of 188–9, 192–4, 299
    and competitive advantage 473
    and foresight 17–18, 24, 48, 83
    technological 374
discrepancy, and sensemaking 96–7
disembodied actors 251–2
disruptive innovation 66, 329
distributed information processing systems 96
distributed knowledge systems 96
distributed seeing 20, 24, 30–41
diversity 29–30, 176, 325–40, 507–8, 511–16
Dodge, Wagner 97
Doležel, L. 114–15, 122, 124
domain definition 155–6
domain navigation 155–6
dominant coalition 285, 464–7, 475, 478–9
dominant logic 282
Don Brothers, Buist & Co Ltd 496–7
Dopson, S. 286
Dorado, S. 268
Dörrenbächer, Christoph 7
doxastic-axiological counterfactuals 116, 124
Doz, Y.L. 328, 331
Drisse, L. 132
Drucker, P. 2
dual-process theories of cognition 396–400,
    403–4, 406–13
dual structuring 132, 141, 324, 329–30
Dubin, R. 39
Duncan, R.B. 154–5, 324
Dundee jute industry (DJI) 485, 490–502
Durand, Rodolphe 10
Durand, Thomas 7, 130, 424
Dyer, J.H. 383, 386
dynamic capability 172–3, 459, 474, 506–7,
    508
dynamic knowledge
    development 511–13
    in management consulting 513–16
    as resource 508–11
dynamic markets 506–7
dynamic strategy 505–8
dynamism 350, 351–2, 356, 409

early adopters 479, 480
Easterby-Smith, M. 157, 173
ecology theory 456–7
edible oils 453, 462–78, 479, 480
Edwards, T. 202
Eisenhardt, K.M. 15, 37, 152, 155, 158, 159,
    160, 278, 300, 348, 407, 467, 506
Eldredge, N. 22, 437
Electricité de France (EdF) 134–6
Eliot, T.S. 246
Ellison, Larry 317
Elton, G.R. 489
embeddedness
    agency 270
    institutional embeddedness 261–2, 264
    macroculture embeddedness 471–4, 478, 479
    networks 350, 355, 356
    social embeddedness 270
Emery, F.E. 148, 154
Emirbayer, M. 250
emotions 101, 176, 396
employees 193–4, 195, 206–7, 318, 349
enactment 98, 147
Encyclopedia Britannica 94
endogenous forces 144, 174, 262
endogenous learning 172–3
Enron 300, 301–2
entertainment industry 27
entrepreneurship 8, 23, 210, 374, 406, 409–10
    see also institutional entrepreneurship
environment
    complexity of 188, 326–7, 333, 339
    endogenous 144
    exogenous 144
    fast cycle capability (FCC) 350–52, 356
    managers and 148–9, 150–153
    and organizational flexibility 455
    types 154–5
    see also organization–environment
        relationship
environmental determinism 148–9, 150–53
environmental scanning 474–6, 478, 479
environmental selection 454
episodic change 235, 244, 245, 250–51, 253
epistemic modality 115, 124
epistemological organization–environment
    relationship 145–53, 157–61
Epstein, L.D. 520
Epstein, S. 399
equilibrium 19–20, 22, 192, 437–9, 442–51
errors 186, 194
ethnography 239–43
Ettlie, J.E. 346, 347
Europe 136–9, 493
European Union (EU) 128, 137, 265

Everett, H. 123
evolution
  evolutionary model 521, 522
  improvisational bricolage 191–2
  of language 51
  punctuated equilibrium 437–9
  resource creation 508
  routines 510
  sub-forces 19
  supra-forces 19, 22–30
ex-tensions 175
existential experience 75–6
exogenous forces 144, 174, 262
exogenous learning 172–3
expatriates 209
expectations 102
experiential learning 176, 279–80
experimental learning 279–80
expert intuition 406
explicit knowledge 287–8, 293
exploitation
  exploitative exploration 187–9
  and exploration 182, 183–4, 278, 281–4,
    290–91, 324, 511
  and foresight 192–4, 293
  improvisational bricolage 195
exploration
  and exploitation 182, 183–4, 278, 281–4,
    290–91, 324, 511
  exploitative exploration 187–9
  and foresight 192–4, 292
  improvisational bricolage 184–6, 195
external goods 174
externalization of knowledge 287–8, 289

Fabbri, T. 99
failure myopia 277, 281–2
Fairclough, N. 254
farsight
  complexity theory 19–20, 22–30, 41–2
  definition 16, 22
  and fastsight 6, 16, 20–21, 23
fast cycle capability (FCC)
  and competitive advantage 343–4, 350
  integrative framework 9, 349–58
  and strategic foresight 343
  in value chain activities 344–9
fastsight
  complexity theory 20, 30–39
  definition 16, 22
  and farsight 6, 16, 20–21, 23
FAVESS 384, 385, 386
Fayol, Henri 1, 92
feed-forward 282–3, 291
feedback 282–3, 291

Ferguson, N. 490
Férone, Geneviève 266, 269
Feyerabend, Paul 6, 53–5, 57–9, 63
field, and practice 173
financial markets 260, 266, 269
financial oversight 330, 332, 335–7, 338–9
financial performance 213–14, 303–4, 409
Fink, A. 257
Finkelstein, S. 94–5
Finucane, M.L. 396, 402, 404
Fiol, C. Marlene 8, 312
fire disaster 97
Firestone 94, 457
first-mover advantages 345, 479, 480
First Virtual Corporation 319
Firth, R.W. 346
Fischoff, B. 257
fleeting opportunities 297, 300–301, 304, 306
flexibility *see* organizational flexibility
flexible automation (FA) 346, 347
flexible manufacturing systems (FMSs) 343,
    346, 347
Fligstein, N. 265, 268, 269
flow 176–8, 179
Floyd, S.W. 287
food industry 305
Ford, Bill 300
Ford, Henry 20
Ford, J.D. 150
Ford Motors 300
forecasting
  and foresight 129, 130, 437
  underestimations 418–19, 431
  unreliability of 2
  and vision 309–11, 321
foreign direct investment (FDI) 462
Foren Project (Foresight for Regional
    Development) 128
foresight
  case studies 134–41
  and change 94–5
  in change agency 249, 253–4, 256–8
  and communication 84, 87–8
  complexity theory 41–2
  definition 2, 16–17, 67, 82–3
  and discontinuities 17–18, 24, 48, 83
  exercises 140, 142
  existential experience 75–6
  exploitation 192–4, 293
  exploration 192–4, 292
  and forecasting 129, 130, 437
  improvisational bricolage 192–4, 195
  and innovation 362, 376
  and intuition 410
  and knowledge 129

and learning 85, 87–8, 277–8, 291–3
limits of 83–4
manager's role 66–7
mapping 141
meaning of 91–2, 130, 277
nature of 79
objectives 130
organizational 113–14
and organizational learning 277–81, 291–3
participation 140–41, 142
philosophical capability 76–9
process 83, 86–7
role of 7, 84–5
semantics 141, 142
and sensemaking 106–7, 443
as strategic learning 178
and strategic planning 92–3
strategic representations 133–4, 141–2
and strategy 141–2
syncretic model 257
transcendental foresight 16–22
underestimations 432–3
variants 17–18
and vision 277
see also strategic foresight
Forgas, J.P. 399, 411
forgetting 442, 444, 445, 446–7
formalization 353, 356, 460, 467–71, 478, 479
Forsgren, M. 202
Forster, E.M. 99
Fortune 300, 302, 303
Foundation for Management Education and
   Research (FNEGE) 136
4I framework of learning 280–81, 291
framing 265–6, 458
France
   foresight case studies 134–41
   future studies 128, 130
   socially responsible investment (SRI) 260,
      266, 269
   subsidiary mandate change case study 205,
      210–12
   underestimations 422
Fransman, Martin 311–12, 313, 314, 320, 321,
   322
Fredrickson, J.W. 468
free will 148
freedom, degrees of 25–6
Freeman, J. 456
Freeman, L.C. 269
Freire, P. 257
Friedberg, E. 204, 205
Friesen, P.H. 151, 438
frontstage 242–7
Fruit of the Loom 94

Fuller, T. 113
further research areas
   dynamic knowledge 515–16
   fast cycle capability (FCC) 357–8
   foresight 142
   innovation and customer interaction 377
   institutional entrepreneurship 270–71
   intuition 411–12
   modal narratives 124
   organization–environment relationship 162
   organizational memory 449–50
   reasoning, modes of 64
   sensemaking 105, 106
   strategic capabilities 502
   underestimations 432
future, concepts of 49–52
future-oriented psychotherapy 85–6
future perfect 91, 98–100, 106
future studies 82, 83, 113–14, 128, 130
   see also foresight
futuribles 128, 129, 130
Futuribles (journal) 128
futuristic foresight 254, 256–7
futurology *see* foresight

Galbraith, C.S. 313
Galbraith, J.K. 524
Galbraith, J.R. 38, 326
Galer, G. 148
games 203–5
Garg, V.K. 474
Garrick, J. 284
gatekeepers of knowledge 288–9, 292, 345,
   354, 356
Gates, Bill 67, 78, 122
Gauldie, E. 500–501
Gavanski, I. 102–3
Gavetti, G. 487
Gazzaniga, Michael 397
GE (General Electric) 3, 36
Gell-Mann, M. 25, 26
general environment 155
Genesh, U. 388
George, G. 172, 288
Geppert, Mike 7, 203
Germany 205, 210–12, 213
Gersick, C.J.G. 438, 443, 445
gestures 74
Ghoshal, S. 285, 328, 330, 508, 511
Giddens, A. 91, 131, 132, 220–21, 254
Gill, J. 312, 313, 314, 315, 316, 320, 321–2
Gioia, D. 97, 99, 100, 153
Gleick, J. 32, 33, 35
GM (General Motors) 37, 39
goals 68–70

Godet, Michel 128, 134, 142
Goffman, E. 132, 242, 243, 244
gold chain, autopoiesis case study 227–30
Google 302
Gould, S.J. 22, 437
Govindarajan, V. 332
Graham, J. 522
Grant, R.M. 84, 299, 303
Gravenhorst, K.M.B. 253
Greenwood, R. 266, 267, 271
Greenwood, Wilf 8
Grimshaw, D.J. 223
Grinyer, P.H. 152
Gros, André 128
group narratives 100
Grove, Andy 66
Gunter, R. 66
Gupta, A.K. 332

Habermas, J. 62
Haken, H. 20, 25, 26
Hamel, G. 1, 15, 19, 24, 37, 38, 92, 277, 297,
   303, 304, 305, 307, 328, 331, 485, 506
Hammond, K.R. 394
Handy, C. 83
Hannan, M.T. 456
hard sciences 90, 105
Harris, L.C. 310
Hart–Rudman Commission 3
Hatani, Faith 9
Hatum, Andrés 10, 459
Hayashi, A.M. 410
Hayes, J. 398, 399, 408
Hayes, R.H. 347
Haywood, B. 347
headquarters–subsidiary relationships
   202–3
healthcare organizations 303, 306
Heaney, Seamus 234
Heckscher, C. 286
Hedberg, G.P. 509
Hedlund, G. 202
Heidegger, M. 73, 76, 78–9, 106
Helfat, C.E. 490
hemispheric functional asymmetry 397
Henderson, A.D. 305
Hendry, C. 235
Heraclitus 77–8, 236, 237
hermeneutic methodology 147
Hernes, T. 220, 221
Herrmann, N. 397
Hertin, J. 256
Heskett, J.L. 40
heterarchies 202
Hewlett-Packard 300, 509

high-velocity environments 15, 155, 350,
   351–2, 356
Hill, C.W.L. 330, 332, 343
Hinings, C.R. 271
Hino Motors 382
historical-foresight 92, 106, 256–7
history 107, 486–90, 502
Hodgkinson, Gerard P. 9, 409, 411
Hofer, C. 298
Hogarth, R.M. 401
Holbrook, D. 487
Holland, J.H. 20, 32, 33
home-country nationals 209
Homes, D. 284
homogeneity of management 352, 356, 464–7,
   475, 478–9
host-country nationals 209
House, R.J. 39, 40
Hout, T.M. 9, 343, 344
Hu, Y.-S. 201
hub joint ventures 386–7
Huber, G.P. 297–8
Huberman, A.M. 160, 471, 477
human capital 30–39
Hungary 210–212
Hunt, J.G. 39
Huy, Q.N. 250, 252, 287
HydroQuébec (HQ) 134–6
hypercompetition 15, 66, 155, 467, 507
hypotactic styles 57–63
hypothesis construction 160–61

IBM 3
ICI 151
identity 188, 476–8, 479
idiographic counterfactuals 116
imagination 6, 435, 436, 442, 443–4, 445–6
impossibility 114, 120, 121, 124
improvisational bricolage
   definition 182
   and foresight 192–4, 195
   institutionalization of 194–5
   and strategy 184–92
India 490, 492–3, 495, 496, 498, 500
individual learning 283–4
individuality 250–51
industrial organization 486
inertia 436, 454–5, 456–8
information 15–16, 435, 436, 440–41, 442, 444,
   446–8
information technology (IT) 355
Ingvar, D.H. 85
inner conversation 219–20, 232
innovation
   vs adaptation 306

and customer interactions 9, 362–4, 376–7
definition 297
disruptive innovation 66, 329
and foresight 362, 376
free will 148
improvisational bricolage 184–92
knowledge as 511, 513
and leadership 8–9, 297–8, 301–7
new product development (NPD) 366, 371–3
new product discovery 366, 371, 374–6
organizational innovation 380, 381–8
product improvement 364–8, 371
product versioning 365, 368–71
strategizing phases 298–301
studies 311–13, 321
user-lead innovation 374, 375
inpatriates 209
insecurity zone 205
insight 401–2
Institute for Prospective Technological Studies (IPTS) 128
institutional change 265–9
institutional compliance 263–4
institutional embeddedness 261–2, 264
institutional entrepreneurship 8, 260, 261, 262–3, 264–72
institutional model 521, 522, 523
institutional strategies 261
institutional theory 201, 270, 471
institutionalization 194–5, 280–81, 291, 471
integration
    fast cycle capability (FCC) 353, 356
    4I framework of learning 280–81, 291
    and organizational memory 442, 444, 445, 448–9
    Toyota Group 385
Intel 66, 457
intentional action 68–70, 71
inter-connectivity of learning 176
interfirm networks
    organizational innovation 380, 388
    and organizational structure 380–81
    Toyota Group 9, 381–8
internal goods 174
internalization of knowledge 287–8, 289
internationalization strategies
    further research areas 213–14
    micro-political strategies 203–5
    multinational corporations (MNCs) 201–3
    subsidiary mandate change 205–12
interpersonal relations 254–5
interpretation 132, 141, 280–81, 291, 312
intersubjectivity 147

intuition
    and affect 399–400, 402, 404–6
    definitions 393, 395, 402, 404
    dual-process theories of cognition 397–400
    4I framework of learning 280–81, 291
    further research areas 411–12
    and insight 401–2
    middle managers 290, 291, 292–3
    naturalistic decision making (NDM) 403–4
    and rationality 398
    and strategic decision making 9–10, 400–403, 406–13
investment 350, 355, 356
Iraq War 93

Jaikumar, R. 347
James, William 113, 236
Janczak, S. 290, 292
Japan 347, 349
Java computing platform 268, 318–19
jazz 184–6
Joas, H. 68
Jobs, Steve 281
Johanson, J. 202
Johnson and Johnson 410
Johnson, G. 152
Johnson, J. 98
Johnson, N.L. 30
joint ventures 386–7
jolts 156, 305
Jones, G.R. 343
Jones, O. 288
Jouvenel, Bertrand de 128
Joy, W. 525
Judge, W.Q. 349
judgement 395, 401–2
Jute Industries (JI) 490, 496, 497
jute industry 485, 490–502

Kahn, Herman 3
Kahneman, D. 102, 103
Kambartel, Friedrich 51, 63
Kanto Auto Works 382
Kauffman, S. 20
Keats, John 91
Kenton, Stan 185
Kessler, E.H. 345
Khatri, N. 409
Kindleberger, C. 524
Kirchler, E. 418
Kirkland, J. 5
Klein, G. 403–4, 409
Klein, K.J. 39, 40
Klepper, S. 487
knitwear industry 98

knowledge
    barriers to knowledge sharing 284–6
    and beliefs 312
    blocks 133
    boundaries 285, 292
    development 11, 511–13
    of employees 193–4
    and foresight 129
    internalization of 287–8, 289
    in management consulting 513–15
    middle managers 222, 286–91
    multinational corporations (MNCs) 202–3
    product improvement 364–8
    provinces of meaning 247
    representations of 132–4, 141–2
    as resource 508–11
    seekers 288, 292
    sharing 383–5, 386–7
    speed of distribution 15–16
    and strategic foresight 129
    and strategy 130–131, 169
    tacit 287–8, 293, 363, 367–8, 373, 400–401,
        508
    see also learning
Koch, G.G. 422
Kodak 450
Kogut, B. 381, 507
Kolb, D.A. 279
kosoryoku 79
Kotha, S. 347, 349
Kotter, J.P. 40
Koyo Seiko 384, 385
Kripke, S.A. 120
Kristensen, P.H. 212, 213, 214
Kuhn, T. 91, 438, 441, 447
Kyohokai 381, 384

La Prospective (Berger) 128, 130
Landis, R.J. 422
Lane, D. 185
Langlois, R. 487
language 50–53, 59–64, 74, 141, 142, 285
Larwood, L. 311
Laughlin, P. 407
Laura Ashley 457
Lave, J. 189, 279
Lawrence, P.R. 326
Lawrence, T.B. 261, 263
Lay, Ken 301
lead times 348
leadership
    CEO role 37, 38–9, 42
    and change agency 250–54
    charismatic leadership 32, 39–41, 251
    and innovation 8–9, 297–8, 301–7

    and path dependency 487
    and strategizing 8–9, 297–8, 301–7
    vision 302–3, 317–19
    void in 301–2
learning
    boundaries 285, 292
    collaborative learning 382, 383–5
    connecting 176–8
    dialogue 148–9
    endogenous learning 172–3
    exogenous learning 172–3
    experiential learning 176, 279–80
    experimental learning 279–80
    and foresight 85, 87–8, 277–8, 291–3
    4I framework of learning 280–81, 291
    improvisational bricolage 189–91
    jute manufacturing 495
    knowledge as 510, 513
    learning-as-practice 171
    learning-in-practise 177
    myopia 277, 281–2, 284, 292
    and practising 172–9
    representations of 132–4
    role of 7
    social process of 278, 279, 287–9
    and strategizing 170–72
    and strategy 130–31, 169
    theories of 278–81
    see also knowledge; organizational learning
leaves, of knowledge 133
LeBaron, B. 30
Leca, Bernard 8
Ledwith, S. 256
Lee, K. 269
left-brain–right-brain differences 396, 397
legitimacy 267
Leibniz, Gottfried Wilhelm 120
Leng, John 495–6
Leonard-Barton, D. 288
Lesourne, Jacques 128
Levi Strauss 94
Levinthal, D.A. 277, 281, 354
Levy, D.L. 172
Lewin, K. 234, 235, 238, 244, 247, 250
Lewis, D.K. 120, 121, 123
line managers 297, 299–300
    see also managers; middle managers
linguistic systems 50–53, 59–64
linguistic turn 50
Lipparini, A. 348
Livian, Y.-F. 286
Loasby, B. 4, 92
lock-in 488, 501, 502
logical mental processes 395
London bombings 23

L'Oréal 410
Lorenz, E.N. 33
Lorsch, J.W. 326
Louis, M. 97
Lovas, B. 508
Luhmann, N. 219, 220, 221, 222
Luthans, F. 288

MacDuffie, J.P. 347
Maciejovsky, B. 418
MacKay, Robert Bradley 6, 118, 152, 501
Mackey, A. 38, 42
macro practices 173–6, 178
macro theories 219
macroculture embeddedness 471–4, 478, 479
Mactor method 134, 137, 142
Madrid bombings 23
Maguire, S. 269
Mainzer, K. 25
Makhija, M.V. 388
Makridakis, S. 83
management
    ambidextrous organizations 325–39, 340
    dominant coalition 285, 464–7, 475, 478–9
    education 521
    homogeneity 352, 356, 464–7, 475, 478–9
    intuition 400–403
    sensemaking 94, 97–8, 107
    see also leadership; top management
management consulting 513–15
managers
    and environment 148–9, 150–53
    improvisational bricolage 194–5
    line managers 297, 299–300
    and organizational flexibility 461, 467–71, 478
    practice-based approach 7, 75–6
    role 66–7
    subsidiary mandate change 206–7, 208–12, 213–14
    see also middle managers; top management
managing on the edge 297, 300–301, 304, 306
Mann Gulch fire disaster 97
Mansfield, E. 347
manufacturing 346–8
many worlds 123–4
mapping 141
Mara-Drita, I. 265
March, J.G. 68, 148, 200, 277, 281, 454
market-based view 506
market dynamism 188–9, 350, 351, 356
market experiments 192
Markides, Constantinos 9
Marks and Spencer 30, 94
Marsh, Craig 8

Martin, J. 40, 240, 241
Maruyama, M. 33
Marx, Karl 183
Masrani, Swapnesh K. 10
Matsushita, Konosuke 67
Maturana, H.R. 220, 221
Maxfield, R. 185
May, E. 107
May, R. 69
MBA (Master of Business Administration)
    programmes 35, 36, 66, 75–6, 518, 521
    see also business schools
McGee, J. 508
McHugh, A. 185
McKelvey, Bill 5, 23, 28, 31, 33, 42
McKiernan, Peter 10, 118
McNeill, David 74–5
Mead, George Herbert 72–5
meaning 74
media 314–15
medical equipment industry 349
Mélèse, J. 32
memory *see* organizational memory
mergers 383, 385, 387, 507
Merk 466
Merleau-Ponty, M. 71
Mermet, L. 113
Merrill, G.B. 313
meta-knowledge 129
Meyer, A.D. 152
Meyer, C. 344
Meyer, J.W. 268
Meyerson, D.E. 253, 255, 256
Mezias, J. 10, 419, 432
micro-political strategies
    further research areas 213–14
    multinational corporations (MNCs)
        200–201, 203–5
    strategizing in 203–5
    subsidiary mandate change 7, 205–12
    theory of 201–3
micro practices 173–6, 178
micro theories 219
Microsoft 268, 317, 319
middle managers
    autopoiesis 222–4
    case studies 224–30
    inner conversation 232
    intuition 290, 291, 292–3
    knowledge 222, 286–91
    new product development (NPD) 371, 372
    organizational DNA 222–4
    organizational learning role 8, 278, 286–91, 292
    product improvement 365, 367, 368

product versioning 365, 369
  sensemaking 97–8
  see also managers
Miles, M.B. 160, 472, 477
Miles, R.E. 156
Mill, John Stuart 55
Miller, A. 349
Miller, D. 104, 151, 152, 192, 304, 438, 457
Miller, T. 102, 103
Milliken, F. 94
Mindscape 315
Minsky, H.P. 524
Mintzberg, H. 3, 75–6, 95, 106, 152, 185, 204,
    299, 306, 309, 312, 396, 406–7, 521, 523
Mische, A. 250
mistakes 186
modal actualists 121
modal narratives
  many worlds 123–4
  nature of 114, 115–19
  possible worlds 120–23
  strategic foresight 113–14, 124–5
  temporal branching 119–20
modal realists 121–2
modality 114–19
model narratives 7
Moore, F. 213
Moran, P. 511
Morgan, G. 38, 145, 147, 203, 212, 214, 507
Morison, E. 524
motivation 303–4, 321
Motorola 94
Muir, C. 252
multinational corporations (MNCs)
  further research areas 213–14
  internationalization strategies 201–3,
    330
  micro-political strategies 200–201, 203–5
  subsidiary mandate change 205–12
multinational enterprises (MNEs) 381
multinational studies 328
Mumby, D.K. 396
Munduate, L. 253
munificence 350, 351, 352, 356
mutation 231
myopia 277, 281–2, 284, 292, 436

Nachum, L. 516
Nadler, D.A. 251
Nanus, B. 40
Narayanan, V.K. 9, 346
narratives 7, 100, 115–19
  see also modal narratives
National Bicycle Industry Company (NBIC)
  349

naturalistic decision making (NDM) 403–4
Nayak, Ajit 6
Nayyar, P.R. 343
Neale, C. 284
necessity 114, 120, 121, 124
negative capability 91
Netherlands 135
Network Computing Architecture (NCA)
    317–18, 322
networks
  diversity 29–30
  embeddedness 350, 355, 356
  fastsight 30–39
  institutional entrepreneurship 269
  organizational innovation 380, 388
  organizational structure 380–81
  social 16, 30–39, 171
  supply networks 345, 385–8
  Toyota Group 381–8
Neustadt, R. 107
New Enterprise Associates 320–21
new product development (NPD) 345–6,
    349–58, 366, 371–3
new product discovery 366, 371, 374–6
new visions 133
Newby-Clark, I. 99
Ng, H.A. 409
Nicolis, G. 33
Nightingale, D.J. 146
9/11 2001 terrorist attacks 22, 23, 24, 48, 93
Nobeoka, K. 383
Noda, T. 457
Nohria, N. 330
nomothetic counterfactuals 116
non-logical mental processes 395
Nonaka, I. 287
norms 101–2
Norway 240–243, 247
Nutt, P.C. 310
Nystrom, P. 107

objectivism 145
observational learning 279
occasional reason 53–9, 61–2, 63
O'Connor, Edward J. 8
Ogbonna, E. 310
oil market 48, 154, 268, 299, 303
Oliver, C. 261
Olson, J.M. 103, 115
ontological organization–environment
    relationship 145–53, 157–61
open source software 377
open systems 222–3, 232
opera singer 174–5
operational autonomy *see* autonomy

opportunities
  fleeting 297, 300–301, 304, 306
  opportunistic environment 156
  opportunity trap 182, 183, 184
Oracle Systems 317–18, 322
order, and change 237
O'Reilly III, C.A. 16, 278, 324
organization–environment relationship
  alternative perspectives 150–53, 161–2
  approaches 144–5
  literature 153–7, 158, 161
  nature of 145–50
  research design 157–61
organization theory 221
organizational adaptation 306, 385, 453,
    454–6, 458, 480
organizational attention 432
organizational becoming
  change and changing 238–47
  meaning of 234
  and organizational memory 448
  and stability 235–8
organizational behaviour 155–6, 419–20
organizational capabilities 305, 458
organizational change *see* change
organizational culture *see* culture
organizational development 250–51
organizational DNA
  case studies 224–30
  middle managers 222–4
  transformation criteria 8, 230–34
organizational ecology 456–7
organizational flexibility
  and adaptation 453, 454–6, 458
  definition 459
  determinants 453, 464–79
  empirical analysis 461–4
  employees 193
  fast cycle capability (FCC) 346, 347
  and inertia 10, 454–5
  knowledge 508
  literature 458–61
  organizational memory 435, 436, 442, 444,
    446–7, 448
  and strategic foresight 479–80
organizational foresight *see* foresight
organizational identity 476–8, 479
organizational inertia 454–5, 456–8
organizational innovation 380, 381–8
  see also innovation
organizational knowledge *see* knowledge
organizational learning
  barriers to knowledge sharing 284–6
  exploration and exploitation 281–4
  and foresight 277–8, 291–3

middle managers' role 8, 278, 286–91, 292
  practice-based learning 170–71
  routines 510
  strategic loop 130–31
  theories of 278–81
  see also learning
organizational memory
  improvisational bricolage 191–2
  meaning of 439–42
  memories of the future 6, 85, 88
  memorizing 132
  and strategic foresight 10, 435–6, 442–51
organizational performance 98
organizational resources *see* resources
organizational self-perception
  empirical analysis 422–30
  and underestimations 10, 418–19, 420–22,
    430–33
organizational structure 202, 350, 353, 356,
    380–81, 459–60
organizational symbolism 82, 85–8
organizations
  advanced manufacturing techniques (AMTs)
    347
  autopoiesis 220–23
  fast cycle capability (FCC) 350, 352–4, 356,
    357
  foresight, role of 84–5
  future, concepts of 49–52
  institutional compliance 263–4
  institutional entrepreneurship 264–5
  mental state 86
  reasoning, modes of 59–64
  sensemaking in 95–6, 98, 100
  tacit knowledge of customers 363
Ormerod, P. 33
Ornstein, R. 397
Ortmann, G. 204
Oswald, S.L. 310
O'Toole, J. 39, 42
Ouchi, W.G. 330
Overholt, M.H. 460
Owen-Jones, Lindsay 410
Özbilgin, Mustafa F. 8

paradoxical way 77–8
paratactic styles 57–63
Parikh, J. 408
Parker, Charlie 184
Parthasarthy, R. 346, 347
path dependency 10, 315–17, 485, 486–90,
    501–2
pattern recognition 22–30, 395–6, 403, 406,
    411
Pearson plc 314–15, 322

Peat, F.D. 124
Penner-Hahn, J.D. 346, 347
Penrose, E. 485, 511
performance
    divisional 332–3
    empirical analysis 422–30
    and underestimations 418–20, 421, 430–33
peripheral vision 67, 92
pessimism *see* underestimations
PEST (political, economic, socio-cultural and technological) analysis 122, 155
PESTEL (political, economic, socio-cultural, technological, ecological, and legal) analysis 518
Peteraf, M.A. 506
Peterson, R.B. 209
Pettigrew, Andrew M. 10, 151, 234, 237, 246, 463, 474
Pfeffer, J. 16, 327, 524
phantom organs 71–2
pharmaceuticals 453, 462–78, 479, 480
Phillips, N. 268, 269
philosophical capability 76–9, 113, 114–19
Pidgeon, N. 242
Pitsis, T. 100
Pittman, P.H. 348
planning *see* strategic planning
Platonic fold 93
Platt, Lew 509
plausibility 122
Plessner, H. 71
Polanyi, M. 509
police sergeants 224–30, 232
politics 173, 177, 254–5
polypropylene 494, 499–501
Poole, M. 235, 236
Popper, Karl 53, 56
population ecology theory 456–7
Porac, J. 98
Porras, J.I. 16, 303, 310
Porter, M.E. 1, 15, 17, 19, 22, 305, 307, 327, 329, 344, 519
positivism 145
possibility 114, 120, 121, 124
possible worlds 120–23, 124
Powell, Taman H. 11
Powell, W.W. 211, 269
power dynamics 252–3, 268
practice
    and field 173
    strategizing and learning 170–72
    strategizing as practising 172–9
practice-based approach 7, 75–6, 170–71, 176, 184–92
practices 173–4

practising 172–9
pragmatic managers 290–91, 292–3
Prahalad, C.K. 1, 15, 19, 24, 37, 38, 92, 277, 282, 283, 284, 303, 304, 305, 307, 328, 331, 485, 506
Pratt, M.G. 402, 407
praxis 173–4
precognition 67
prediction 2, 304
prefactual mental simulations 104
preparation 2, 103–4
prescience *see* foresight
presentational styles 58–9
presented realities 146, 150
Pries, L. 203
Prigogine, I. 26, 33
primary value chain activities 346–8, 349–58
principle-based reason 56–7
proactive environment 156
proactive learning 279
probes 192
problem structure 407–8
process
    change and changing 238–47, 251
    and organizational flexibility 458
    and stability 235–8
Procter, Stephen 7
product development 344
product improvement 364–8, 371
product variety 347
product versioning 365, 368–71
project management 350, 354, 356
project myopia 284, 292
projective capacity 260
prospecting 91, 104–5, 106
prospective analysis *see* foresight
Prospective (journal) 128
prospective processes 91
prospective sensemaking 6, 99, 101–4, 105
prospector 156
provinces of meaning 242–6, 247
prudence 420, 421, 430–31
Prusak, L. 15
psychological techniques 101–4
psychotherapy 85–6
publishing 94, 314–15
punctuated equilibrium 22, 192, 437–9, 442–51
Putnam, L.A. 396

quasi-core firms 386
Quinn, J.B. 152
Quinn, R. 235, 236, 250

radical change 235, 244, 245, 250–51, 253
radically open future 6, 49–50, 63

railways 94, 139–40
ramie (rhea fibre) 496, 497
RAND Institute 3, 118
Rao, H. 264
Rappaport, H. 85
rational choice 201, 394–7
rational model of organization structure
    380–81
rationalist strategizing 310, 315
rationality
    assumptions of rational action 68–75
    change agents 250–51
    contextual rationality 97
    and intuition 398
    linear strategic rationality 97
    naturalistic decision making (NDM)
        403–4
    occasional reason 56–7, 61–2, 63
Raynor, M. 324
rayon 499
reactor 156
Reading, A. 85
realism 145–8
reason
    occasional reason 53–9
    and strategic foresight 48–52, 59–64
Reason, J.T. 242
Reckwitz, A. 173
recognition primed decision (RPD) 404, 406,
    411
reflective observation (RO) 279–80
reflexivity 219–20, 254, 256–7
reinforcement 132
relationality of action 73–5
relationships 458
relativism 145–8
remembering 442, 444–6
repertory grid 159
representations
    case studies 134–41
    meaning of 129, 131
    and scenarios 132–4, 141–2
    represented realities 146
research design 157–61
    see also further research areas
resource-based view 1, 431, 486, 505–6,
    513–15, 519
resource dependency theory 149
resources
    creation of 505–8
    definition 263
    improvisational bricolage 189
    and institutional compliance 263–4
    and institutional entrepreneurship 261,
        264–72

knowledge as 508–11
    resource sharing 327, 333, 339
    Toyota Group 382
retention 147, 440
retrospective sensemaking 6, 90–91, 101–4,
    106
revolutionary periods 439
rhea fibre (ramie) 496, 497
risk tolerance 408
road transport 94, 139–40, 381–8, 502
Rock Island 94
Rockefeller, John D. 268
Roese, N.J. 103, 115
Roller, L. 347
Rollins, Kevin 343
Romanelli, E. 438, 439
Ronen, R. 115
Roos, J. 221
Ropo, A. 39
Rosenfeld, G. 117
Ross, M. 99
routines, knowledge as 509–10
routinization 132, 141, 191–2
Rowan, B. 268
Rowlinson, Michael 7, 487
Royal Dutch/Shell 2, 3, 84, 95, 117
Ruigrok, W. 201
Rumelt, R.P. 506
Russia 490
Ryan, M.-L. 120, 124

Saatchi and Saatchi 94
Sadler-Smith, Eugene 9, 408, 409
safety in aluminium plant (empirical example)
    240–43, 247
Salancik, G.R. 327
Sally, R. 201
Salthe, S.N. 19, 41, 42
San Martín 462–77
Sanna, L. 104
Santayana, George 490
Sapsed, Jonathan 9
Sauter, V.L. 406
Scandinavia 135
scanning, environmental 474–6, 478, 479
Scarbrough, H. 285
scenario planning
    in the foresight process 3, 28, 82, 83, 84, 92,
        107
    future studies 113–14
    and intuition 407
    memories of the future 85
    modal narratives 115–16, 117–19
    prefactual mental simulations 104
    temporal branching 119

scenarios
  case studies 134–41
  and knowledge 130–31
  managerial choice 148–9
  meaning of 130
  strategic representations 132–4, 141–2
  and vision 309–11, 321
Schatzki, T.R. 170, 174
Schoemaker, P.J.H. 83
Schön, D. 279
Schoonhoven, C.B. 467
Schreven, Stephanie W.J.C. 10
Schumpeter, J.A. 511
Schur, D. 77, 78
Schütz, A. 99, 237
Schwarz, Jan Oliver 6, 85
Scotland 98, 485, 490–502
Scott & Fyfe (S&F) 490, 496, 499
Sculley, John 281
Scully, M.A. 253, 256
Seidl, David 6
selection 147
self-organization of learning 176–8
self-perception
  empirical analysis 422–30
  and underestimations 10, 418–19, 420–22,
    430–33
semantics 141, 142, 285
semiconductors 487
semifactuals 117
senior executives 97–8, 345, 408–10
  see also CEOs (Chief Executive Officers);
    top management
sensemaking
  change and changing 238–47, 251
  counterfactual processes 91, 101–4, 105
  criticisms 100, 520
  future perfect 98–100
  management 94, 97–8, 107
  meaning of 90, 95, 100
  in organizations 95–6, 100
  prefactual mental simulations 104
  prospective sensemaking 6, 99, 101–4, 105
  relativism 147
  as retrospective process 90–91, 105
  and stability 235–8
  and strategic foresight 106–7, 443
  and surprise 96–7
September 11 2001 terrorist attacks 22, 23, 24,
    48, 93
service 348, 377
Sethi, D. 286
Sethi, S.P. 346, 347
Shapiro, S. 407, 409
Sharpe, D. 213

Shell 2, 3, 84, 95, 117
Shelley, Percy Bysshe 435
Shepp, Archie 185
Sheppard, J. 67
Sherer, P.D. 269
Shirwin, M.J. 525
Sidus 462–78, 479, 480
Simon, Herbert A. 23, 68, 90, 311, 395–6, 401,
    404, 406, 410, 508, 512, 523
Simons, K. 487
simplicity trap 183, 184
Sinclair, Marta 9
Sivakumar, K. 264
Skilling, Jeff 301
Slater, R. 38
Slovic, P. 402, 404
Slywotsky, A. 15, 23
Small, M.H. 347
Smircich, L. 106, 156
Smith, Roger 37, 39
SNCF 139–40
Snow, C.C. 156
social capital 269
social construction 156, 193, 203, 204
social embeddedness 270
social interactions 132, 141
social networks 16, 30–39, 171
social perceptions 101
social processes
  environment 144
  improvisational bricolage 189–91
  of learning 278, 279, 287–9
  organizational sensemaking 95–6, 98, 100
  reflexivity 219–20
  and sensemaking 105
socially responsible investment (SRI) 260, 266,
    269
soft sciences 90, 105
Software Toolworks 315
Sölvell. O. 202
somatic markers 404–5
Sony 66, 94
Sorensen, J.B. 40
Sowunmi, A. 222–3
Spanish Armada 117
Sparrow, P.R. 409, 411
spatial myopia 277, 281–2
Spear, S.J. 76
speculative imagination 435, 436, 442, 443–4,
    445–6
speed
  and competitive advantage 343–4
  improvisational bricolage 187
  integrative framework 349–58
  and intuition 408, 410

of linguistic change 52
and strategic foresight 15–16, 31–9
in value chain activities 344–9
Spence, M. 407, 409
Sperry, Roger 397
Spies, P.H. 84
Spinner, Helmut 6, 56–9, 63
spiral model of organizational learning 287–8
stability
   vs adaptability 306
   and change 8, 235–8
   change and changing 238–47
   ontology of 234–5
   and organizational flexibility 459
Stalk, G. 343
Stalker, G.M. 324, 326, 455
standardization 460, 523
Stanford Business School 412
Stanovich K.E. 399, 400
Starbuck, W.H. 10, 94, 107, 419, 432
start-ups 318–21, 322
Staw, B.M. 520
Steinmueller, E. 487
Stern, Nicholas 93
Stevenson, H.H. 305
Stevenson, W.B. 244
Stiglitz, Joseph 93
Stinchcombe, A.L. 456
Stone, Andrew 30
strategic ambiguity 328–39, 340
strategic capabilities
   historical analysis 488–90
   jute manufacturing 493–502
   and path dependency 486–8, 501–2
strategic change initiations 100
strategic choice 113–14, 148–9, 456
strategic conversations 84, 105–6
strategic decision making
   and affect 404–6
   dual-process theories of cognition 397–400
   fast cycle capability (FCC) 344, 348–9
   and intuition 9–10, 400–403, 406–13
   naturalistic decision making (NDM) 403–4
   rational choice in 394–7
strategic drift 156
strategic early warning systems 82
strategic focus 350, 352, 356
strategic foresight
   cognitive limitations 48–9
   existential experience 75–6
   failures of 93–5, 107
   and fast cycle capability (FCC) 343
   and intuition 410
   and knowledge 129

manager's role 66–7
meaning of 2–4, 79, 91–2, 435, 436–7
modal narratives 113–14, 124–5
and organizational flexibility 479–80
and organizational memory 10, 435–6, 442–51
philosophical capability 76–9
and reason 48–52, 59–64
role of 1–2, 4–5, 82
and scenario planning 107
and sensemaking 106–7, 443
and speed 15–16, 31–9
and strategic planning 95
types of 442, 444–9
see also foresight
strategic frames 458
strategic intent 37, 304
strategic issue management 82
strategic learning
   connecting 176–8
   nature of 169–70
   and practising 172–6, 178–9
strategic loop 130–31, 142
strategic management 90, 92–3, 170–71, 270, 457–8, 518–26
strategic planning
   characteristics 3, 306
   in dynamic environments 185–6, 187
   and foresight 92–3
   and intuition 406–7
   and strategic foresight 95
   and vision 9, 309–11, 321–2
strategic representations
   case studies 134–41
   meaning of 129, 131
   and scenarios 132–4, 141–2
strategizing
   and leadership 8–9, 297–8, 301–7
   and learning 170–72
   as lived experience 105–6
   micro-political strategies 203–5
   phases 298–301
   as practising 172–9
   subsidiary mandate change 205–12
   terminology 169
strategy
   advanced manufacturing techniques (AMTs) 347
   ambidextrous organizations 330, 332, 335–7, 338–9
   dynamic strategy 505–8
   and foresight 141–2
   and improvisational bricolage 184–92
   institutional strategies 261
   and knowledge 130–31, 169

and learning 130–31, 169
  meaning of 68–9, 130
  strategy-as-practice 169, 171
  strategy-finding processes 5–6
  and vision 313–22
stress 408
structural understanding *see* deep
    understanding
structuration 171, 188–9, 207
structure 219, 232–3, 339
  see also deep structure; organizational
    structure
Stubbart, C. 106, 156
Suarez, F.F. 346, 347
sub-forces, in evolution 19
sub-prime mortgage crisis 93
subjectivism 145, 418–19
subjunctive reasoning 6
subsidiaries 202–5
subsidiary mandate change 205–12, 213–14
Sull, D.N. 300, 457
Sumitomo Electric 384
Sun Microsystems 268
superfactuals 117
supply networks 345, 385–8
support activities 345–6, 348–9
supra-forces, in evolution 19, 22–30
surprise 96–7, 177, 224, 257
surprise machines 116, 124
Sutcliffe, K.M. 304, 305
Suvin, D. 123
Swann, P. 312, 313, 314, 315, 316, 320, 321–2
SWOT (strengths, weaknesses, opportunities,
    threats) analysis 518, 525
symbolism, organizational 82, 85–8
syncretic model of foresight 257
synthetic fibre 496, 498–501
System 1 processes of cognition 399–400
System 2 processes of cognition 400
system readiness approach 252

tacit knowledge 287–8, 293, 363, 367–8, 373,
    400–401, 508
Taggart, W. 396, 397
Taiwan 325, 331–8
Takeuchi, H. 287
Taleb, N. 93
task environment 155
Tatli, Ahu 8
Taylor, B. 104
teaching of strategic management 518–26
teams
  cross-functional teams 284–7, 288, 345, 354,
    356, 365, 369
  fast cycle capability (FCC) 345, 356

knowledge sharing 284–6
  middle managers' role 286–91, 292
  role of 284
technology
  fast cycle capability (FCC) 350, 354–5, 356,
    357
  studies 128, 311–13, 321
  technological discontinuities 374
  technological dynamism 350, 351–2, 356
  technological innovation 148
Teece, D.J. 459, 486, 490, 506
telecoms industry 27, 377, 457
television 315–17, 319–20, 487
tempered radicals 255–6
temporal branching 119–20, 124
temporal myopia 277, 281–2
Tenkasi, R.V. 285
tensions 171, 175, 178
terrorism 22, 23, 24, 48, 93, 523
Tetlock, P.E. 116
TGV 139
Thatcher, Margaret 135
The Economist 24, 30, 39, 42, 314
theorization 266
third-country nationals 209
Thomas, C. 29
Thomas, Howard 11, 508
Thomas, J.B. 98, 99, 100, 474
Thompson, J.D. 32, 326, 522, 523
threats 186
3Com 320, 321
Tichy, N.M. 255
time 30, 79, 343
  see also fast cycle capability (FCC); speed
Tombak, M. 347
top-down strategizing 297, 298–9, 300–301,
    304, 306
top management
  fast cycle capability (FCC) 350, 352–4, 356
  new product development (NPD) 371, 372
  and organizational flexibility 464–7, 478–9
  organizational learning 277–8, 283
  product improvement 364–7
  product versioning 369
  sensemaking 94, 97–8, 107
  strategizing 8–9, 297–8, 302–7
  vision 315, 318, 321
  see also CEOs (Chief Executive Officers);
    senior executives
Toulmin, S. 3, 437
Towa Real Estate 382
Toyoda Boshoku 382, 383
Toyoda Chemical Industry 383
Toyoda Gosei 382
Toyoda Koki 382, 384, 385, 388

Toyota Auto Body 382
Toyota Central Research & Development
    Laboratories 382
Toyota Group 9, 37, 76, 380, 381–8
Toyota Industries 382
Toyota Tsusho 382
training 331, 333, 338–9, 340, 412
transactional environment 155
transactional leadership 251
transcendental foresight 16–22
transformational leadership 251
transnational solution 209
transport 139–40
Trevor-Roper, H. 489
Tripsas, M. 487
Trist, E.L. 154
Trygg, L. 347
Tsai, W. 285
Tsoukas, H. 67, 234, 235, 236, 237, 238, 239,
    244, 246, 448
Tulder, R. van 201
turbulence 154–5
Turley, K. 104
Turner, B. 4, 93
Turner, S. 170, 174
Tushman, M.L. 251, 278, 324, 438, 439, 473
Tyco 94
Tzoumpa, Vicky 8

Un, C. Annique 9, 364
uncertainty 188, 326
underconfidence 430–31
underestimations
    empirical analysis 422–30
    and performance 418–20, 421, 430–33
    and self-perception 10, 418–19, 420–22,
        430–33
understanding 435, 436, 442, 443, 445, 446
unexpected 257
Ungson, G.R. 439
United Kingdom (UK) 135, 213, 214, 377,
    491
United States (US) 135, 268, 303, 347, 385,
    493, 521
Upton, D.M. 346
US West 457
user-lead innovation 374, 375

value chain activities
    integrative framework 349–58
    speed 344–9
values
    ambidextrous organizations 330–31, 333,
        337, 338–9, 340
    change agency 253

doxastic-axiological counterfactuals 116,
    124
    leadership responsibilities 302–3
    and organizational flexibility 458, 477
Van de Ven, A. 235, 236, 454
Van der Heijden, K. 84, 85, 118, 148, 407
van der Merwe, L. 124
van Krogh, G. 221
Van Maanen, J. 246
van Notten, P.W.F. 118
vantage points 29–30
Varela, F.J. 220, 221
variety, Ashby's Law 21
verbalism 257
vicarious learning 279
Vickers, G. 523
Victor, B. 461
Viguerie, P. 5
vision
    definition 311
    digital media case studies 313–22
    and foresight 277
    of knowledge 133
    and leadership 302–3, 317–19
    peripheral vision 67, 92
    and strategic planning 9, 309–11, 321–2
    technology and innovation studies 311–13,
        321
    uses of 321–2
Vit, Gregory 11, 520, 522, 523, 524
Volberda, H.W. 459, 460, 461
volunteerism 204
Voss, C.A. 347

Wack, P. 66, 95, 133
Wagner, R.K. 409
Wai-Kwong, F.Y. 286
Waldman, D.A. 40
Wallas, G. 401
Wally, S. 349
Walmart 355
Walsh, J.P. 439
Wang Labs 94
war 154
Warde, A. 173
wargaming 83
Waters, J.A. 106, 152
Watkins, M. 2
Watzlawick, P. 238
weak signals 48, 49, 82, 83, 95, 107, 192
Weber, Max 56
Weick, Karl 90–91, 96, 97, 98–9, 106, 147, 156,
    161, 186, 187, 194, 221, 234, 235, 236, 245,
    250, 304
Weir, David 8

Welch, Jack 36, 37, 38, 39, 78
Wells, G. 102–3
Wenger, E. 189, 279
Wesley, F. 522, 523
West, R.F. 399, 400
Whately, C. 496–7
Whetten, D.A. 476
Whipp, R. 474
Whitehead, Alfred North 1, 16, 67, 83, 91, 106, 435, 437, 443, 448
Whitley, R. 201
Whittington, R. 174, 175
Whorf, B.L. 50, 238
Wilensky, H. 93
Williamson, O.E. 27, 330
Willmott, H. 40
Wilson, H.N. 459
winner's curse 182
Winter, S.G. 172
Wittgenstein, L. 51
women 256
wonder and awe 78–9

Woodward, J. 326, 455
Wooldridge, B. 287
world, meaning of 69
World War II 117
World Wide Web 50–51, 63
worse-than-experienced worlds 103

Yammarino, F.J. 39, 40
Yannow, D. 247
Yasin, M.M. 347

Zahra, S.A. 172, 288
Zajac, E.J. 381
Zajonc, R.B. 402
Zander, I. 202
Zander, U. 381, 507
Zbaracki, M.J. 407
Zeitlin, J. 213
Zohar, D. 30
Zollo, M. 172
Zucker, L. 262
Zyglidopoulos, Stelios C. 10